THE EAST MOOR EXPERIENCE

1942 - 1946

This book is dedicated to all who served at East Moor

ISBN 1 900604 01 9

Published by Compaid Graphics

Little Ash, Street Lane
Lower Whitley
Warrington
Cheshire
WA4 4EN

100705.3155@Compuserve.com

THE EAST MOOR EXPERIENCE

1942 - 1946

158 Squadron Royal Air Force

429 Squadron Royal Canadian Air Force

1679 Heavy Conversion Flight Royal Canadian Air Force

432 Squadron Royal Canadian Air Force

415 Squadron Royal Canadian Air Force

54 Operational Training Unit Royal Air Force

288 Squadron Royal Air Force

compiled by

Brian Shields

Contents

ACKNOWLEDGEMENTS

My sincere thanks to the following for information, recollections, photographs, copies of Flying Log Books and many incidental notes,

415 Squadron
Sam Bell, Sam Chiles, Bert Dennis, John Harpin, Jim Northrup, Fred Rackley, Doug Sample.

429 Squadron
Marc Blais, Doug Chard, Roy Goatham, Ron Kettell, Glenys Kennea, Eric Lapham, Lewis Heushaw, Jean Murga-troyd, Jim Rollinson, Charles Schofield, Stan Watkins, Bill Willshire, Bill Palmer.

432 Squadron
Johnny Banks, Morris Carson, Bill Chubb, Ewan Cooper, John Cooper, Bob Day, David Darnell, Frank Germaney, Joe Gonda, Geoff Goom, Cliff Haining, Russ King, Bill Miller, Ivan Mulley, Morgan Pryce, George Rogers, Tony Yaunish.

1679 HCF
Alan A Avant.

54 OTU
Harold Martin, Peter Montgomery, Jack Sharp.

East Moor
Helen Goodrow, Marion Weller, Len Greenham, Alan Bryson, Marion Latham, Gerald Inns, David Thompson, Ian Winduss, Jim Freer, Bill Rust.

MOD (RAF)
Personnel management.

My special thanks to Doug Sample and Ivan Mulley fro providing me with invaluable material, and to Derek Reed for pointing me in the right direction. Also to Keith Hall for his valued assistance with proof reading.

I am most grateful to Mr W. R. Chorley for the kind permission to extarct information from 'In Brave Company' (158 Squadron History) by W.R. Chorley and the late R.N. Benwell.

Sources of information
Public Records Office, Kew
RAF Museum, Hendon
Air 27 Squadron Operational Record Books
Air 28 Station Operational Record Books
Air 29 Miscellanious Units Record Books
AM Forms   78 Aircraft Loss and Movement Cards
AM Forms   1180 Aircaft Accident cards

My personal records which include notes and observations made at East Moor during WW II.

AUTHOR'S PREFACE

As a lifelong East moor enthusiast and amateur historian this work has truly been a labour of love and represents my humble efforts at research and an attempt to document a part of our history.

I hope that the result will evoke memories for the veterans of east Moor and provide an opportunity for other readers to appreciate the contribution and sacrifice made by the men and woman who served there. Their gallantry, indomitable spirit and achievement are truly worthy of a wider appreciation and I hope that this diary will go some way towards achieving that end.

Researching for the diary has for me proved to be a most rewarding experience, and the associated correspondence has led to many lasting friendships with veterans of the base both in the United Kingdom and in Canada.

Have tried to produce an accurate account of events as they unfolded at east Moor, and in the interests of the realists, enthusiasts and model makers I have wherever possible included aircraft serial numbers and code letters. Each order of battle is simply listed on a daily and nightly basis giving the aircraft details and names of the pilots. Complete crews are listed at the end of each section. The exeption is in the case of 158 squadron where it has been necessary to show each crew separately in the order of battle as the records show that there was a lack of consistency in the composition of the crews.

My royalties from the sale of this book will be donated to the Yorkshire Air Museum's 'Halifax Rebuild' project.

To the best of my knowledge no copyright has been infringed. Should the contrary be the case, pardon is sought, apology made and future reprints of the book will be amended.

Brian Shields

INTRODUCTION

In an attempt to keep alive the memory of the hastily constructed World War II airfield at East Moor, a number of years have been spent in collecting information, photographs and general data and compiling the following narrative. Presented in the form of a diary-cum-scrapbook, it contains many memories that are deep rooted in East Moor Station and the drama that it supported for almost four years, at a time when the fate of the whole free world hung in the balance. It is also an attempt to record the contribution made by so many men and women who were based at the airfield, and in particular those who paid the ultimate price for their effort.

Much of the recorded activity was viewed from outside the stations barbed wire from where it was quite difficult to imagine how the aircrews came to terms with a situation which could suddenly wrench them from the calm and beauty of a Yorkshire evening amongst the birds,flowers and trees of East Moor, and dispatch them on snarling engines into hell and destruction of the target area. It must have been equally grim and stressful for those who were left behind and who could be seen waving them off, and who would anxiously count them down again, no doubt wondering if they had been seperated forever from comrades and loved ones.

The often unsung heroes, men and women of the groundstaff cannot go unmentioned,as it was through their untiring efforts, at times in the most trying conditions, that the raids over enemy occupied countries were made possible.

It is still possible to stand around the airfield boundary and, with a little imagination , see and hear the bombers as they thundered along the runway at half minute intervals before lifting over the hedgerows in full throttle, their bomb bays pregnant with high explosives as they carried the war to Nazi Germany and its occupied areas.

It is most unlikely that scenes the likes of which were seen at East Moor between 1942 and 1946 will ever be seen again, and it is hoped that memories will be evoked and that much of interest will be found by readers of this diary. During its short, action packed operational life span, East Moor was the base for five squadrons and two training units, had no fewer than fourteen Station Commanders and mounted over two hundred and thirty operations against enemy targets. More than one hundred of the bases aircraft were lost on operations, in crashes or in other accidents, and several hundred aircrew were killed, missing or became prisoners of war.

The information contained in the following pages has been culled from a variety of sources and includes personal observations noted at the time, extracts from the flying log books of East Moor veterans, personal recollections of air and ground crews, copies of squadron operational records and from private collections and researches. Thanks must go out to the following people who have made a most valuable contribution to the diary with material, information and in some cases with the photographs which have been used to compliment the researches.

Now that the airfield and its numerous dispersed sites have almost disappeared and its once throbbing squadrons long since gone, it is probably the time to record as much of the history as possible before memories fade and the personal records disappear too.

The area known as East Moor is situated in the Vale of York and lies in a triangle between the villages of Strensall, Sutton on Forest and Wigginton. York is the nearest large town and is approximately nine miles to the South. During the airfields existence Strensall was the nearest wayside railway facility and from where much of the equipment and supplies vital to East Moors operational capability was received.

BACKGROUND

The airfield was a hastily constructed wartime base carved out of former agricultural land and had map headings - Latitude 5404 North and Longitude 0105 west and the whole area constituted approximately 328 hectares or 820 acres.

Before the airfield was developed in 1941, the woodland and hedgerows were much more extensive, the former covered an area of 51.8 hectares as opposed to 30 in 1942 and the latter constituted approximately 15.5 miles which were ultimately reduced to 3 miles. High Carr Wood is by far the largest of the two surviving ones and its 28 hectares (78 acres) consists mainly of Silver Birch together with Willow, Beech, Oak and Scottish Pine. Low Nursery Wood which lies on the South west boundary covers a mere 2 hectares.

As can be expected the whole area is fairly flat and being situated some 65 feet above sea level, only varies a maximum of 3 feet.

The great upheaval that occurred with the advent of World War II brought more changes to the countryside around East Moor than any other event in the previous one thousand years. Farms and land acquired by the Air Ministry under compulsory purchase orders were vacated by their occupants and two of the former, East Moor and Brotherton Cottage, were demolished. Murton Lane which had been the access road to White Carr Barn was swallowed up together with North Plantation and Shepherds Moor through which it ran. White Carr Barn and High Carr House survived until well after the war the latter being used by the Motor Transport Sections.

As the many trees and hedgerows were torn out by the roots and numerous ditches filled in, uneven ground was levelled by huge blade graders and bulldozers, a vast drainage scheme was undertaken , water and power supplies were installed and gradually an A class base emerged.

Much of the perimeter track and many of the dispersal pads were installed ahead of the runway construction, presumably to allow the heavy machinery and the many vehicles to be moved more easily in what had become a mass of churned up soil and mud. Runways and hangers soon followed along with many of the essential buildings such as bomb stores and fuel facilities.

The runways were cut like huge scars across the landscape almost forming a triangle. Constructed of concrete they were fifty yards wide and six inches in depth. The longest one of the three was approximately 5,160 feet, ran from north to south and was somewhat higher at its northern end. The others intersected it from east to west, 4,620 feet long and north east to south west 4,290 feet. The latter one ran from the eastern end of the east/west one through the mid point of the north/south one and was hump backed and proved inadequate for the operation of fully laden bombers and as a consequence it was only used on rare occasions.

The ever present danger of a bombing attack by the enemy necessitated the dispersal of East Moor based aircraft around the airfield perimeter and to this end some 36 concrete frying pan shaped pads were installed. These were 125 feet in diameter and connected to the perimeter tracks by taxi ways, and secured to the centre of each was a large metal picketing ring.

The many ancillary sites were spread around the outside of the airfield boundary but mostly within a thousand yards of it. Many were of the standard nissen type together with those of Maycrete construction, and served as living quarters and technical buildings, all were very plain but functional. Within the confines of High Carr Wood there was a well hidden bomb store and a rifle range together with underground shelters for use by the personnel in the event of an air raid. The living and messing facilities numbered around 20 and included dining rooms, institutes, Officers and Sergeants messes, bath and shower facilities and collectively catered for up to 2,000 personnel.

Nearby Sutton Hall was requisitioned and served as an Officers Mess and some other ranks were billeted with families in the villages.

Other functional sites contained sewerage works, aviation fuel stores where high octane was held in 72,000 gallon tanks, a range for testing turret guns and reaching skywards were numerous water tanks mounted on steel legs.

Buildings of the flying complex surrounded the control tower or watch office and all were situated just west of the mid point of the north/south runway and adjacent to the western perimeter track. The tower afforded an extensive view over the airfield with an uninterrupted one of 340 degrees, nevertheless in its latter days it had a green house added to its roof presumably to allow the air traffic controllers an even better view. Close by was the Squadron Commanders offices and the garages for the emergency vehicles along with huts for their crews. In front of the tower was the signals square which displayed the large EM identification letters and any landing instructions and directions that were in force.

Station Headquarters occupied approximately one third of the western boundary of the airfield and covered a total of fifteen acres in area. Standing out from the countryside were three ugly black hangers of the T2 type erected by Teeside Bridge & Engineering Works. Provision was made for a fourth one of these buildings which were two hundred and forty feet long and one hundred and fifteen feet wide with doors at each end. These were twenty five feet in height and had an opening span of one hundred and five feet.

The bleak windswept and wet winters from which East Moor suffered led to many unspecified erections appearing around the dispersal points as the ground crews sought refuge from the elements in crude huts made from wooden crates and packing cases.

The station remained in Bomber Command throughout its wartime operation, firstly within No. 4 Group and later with No.6 (Canadian) Group and its Wellingtons, Lancaster's and Halifax bombers rose from the runways night after night and latterly by day,for almost four years. They pounded factories, railways, oil supplies, submarine pens, troop concentrations and almost every other type of target in Germany and the occupied territories.

At the end of hostilities in Europe, Bomber Command relinquished control of East Moor and the station then took on a new role in the guise of an Operational Training Unit. During the last month of operations an anti aircraft co-operation squadron moved in. In 1946 the station was handed over to Care & Maintenance and the airfield slowly returned to agriculture, whilst some of the dispersed sites became home to a number of so called Displaced Persons. These refugees from enemy occupied Europe had amongst their numbers a large amount of Polish nationals.

The air space over East Moor continued to be used for some time after its closure when the aforementioned inhabitants were treated to regular beat ups of their quarters by a Polish compatriot who was at the time a Topcliffe based pilot. As late as 1948/49 aircraft from nearby Leeming could be seen almost daily making low level passes over the rapidly deteriorating runway which by this time had huge white crosses painted on the surface of each approach.

Probably the last aircraft to use the runway at East Moor was a Gloster Meteor jet which put down in an emergency in the 1950s. After bouncing over the rough grass logged seams of runway 16 the pilot was seen to walk to Low Carr Farm to summon assistance. A visit by an RAF mobile unit preceded a most spectacular take off and a low level pass as the pilot set course in a southerly direction.

As each year passes there are less and less reminders of East Moor as a wartime environment. Gone are the hangers and many of the other buildings, much of the runway area has been dug up along with most of the dispersal's. Only memories are left of the days when the air was filled with the snarling of up to 160 Hercules engines as the bombers took off and set course for the East coast and beyond.

AIR MINISTRY PROPERTY

LOITERING STRICTLY

PROHIBITED

So read the signs on the approach roads to East Moor, but it was possible to acquire the viewpoint of a personal eye witness and watch, stage by stage the days events unfold, providing of course, that one kept an eye open for Police Constable Simpson. The village 'Bobby' from Sutton on Forest made regular patrols of the airfields perimeter on his bicycle in an attempt to enforce the signs.

Not knowing what might come into ones view next, gave rise to one of the most exciting aspects of snooping around East Moor (other than running the gauntlet of the local Constabulary). The wide variety of vehicles and aircraft seen were eagerly recorded in our notebooks, and their activities made lasting impressions on our memories.

Some of the earliest recollections are of the exchange of chocolate and chewing gum with members of 158 Squadron, for apples and pears scrumped by us from some poor unfortunates orchard. As the war progressed, a more relaxed atmosphere prevailed and we were allowed to attend the station cinema and sports events. A never to be forgotten sight was the first close up view of the four engined bomber. This was a Halifax II and coded NP-W trundling along the airfields northern perimeter track towards St.Johns Well where after a sudden burst of power. from each engine the four white tipped propellers windmilled to a stop.

Memory recalls a whole range of motor vehicles at the base, numerous examples of the Ford War Office Type 1 (WOT1) four and six wheeled versions and fitted with a variety of bodies, together with a similar range bearing the Crossley badge. Coles cranes on Thorneycroft and Bedford chassis, Hillman cars, PUs and Standard 5 cwt vans were always much in evidence, and in latter times so too were Canadian Ford and Dodge specialist vehicles. Tractors were a familiar sight and usually of the Fordson or David Brown type, and it seemed as though every airman/woman had a service issue bicycle.

It was most noticeable that the majority of the aircrew were very little older than our teenage brotherhood when they were supporting and flying nightly, the huge and fascinating machines against the heavily defended heart of the enemies homeland. They were noted in tears as they tumbled from bomb laden aircraft that were over-running the airfield perimeter unable to lift off, and laughing and singing on wobbling bicycles when leaving the village public houses.

My home village, Strensall, boasted two pubs, the Half Moon and the Ship Inn and both were regular targets for squadrons of East Moor cyclists. Here they were able to wash away their operational fears of running the gauntlet of enemy fighters and anti aircraft fire (flak), on missions that often entailed being airborne between six and eight hours. The geographical position of East Moor resulted in its crews often being in the air for much longer periods than their colleagues based in the more southerly counties as the distance to the targets was greater. The local population came to understand that it was natural that those highly spirited airmen should feel the need to let their hair down if they were lucky enough to return to friendly soil. In general, the blunt locals soon accepted the airmen and women of the RAF and of the Dominion Air Forces and came to share their homes and traditional Yorkshire hospitality during leave and leisure periods,,and as a result many romances flourished.

The airfield and its numerous dispersed sites provided employment for large numbers of the local populace throughout the wars duration where they were engaged in the development, maintenance, supply and the every day running of the establishment, which included Sutton Hall taken over as an Officers Mess.

No matter how early one arrived at the airfield the scene always seemed to be one of great activity. If preliminary orders for operations had been received the fuelling and bombing up crews would begin, and an early morning walk in the fields adjacent to High Carr Wood provided a glimpse of the handling crews at work in the bomb dump. The long trains of special trolleys would be loaded with high explosives, flares and incendiary devices, a task which often lasted all morning, and after which they could be seen trundling along behind the tractors to the widely dispersed aircraft.

Whilst all this was going on other sections could be seen equally hard at it. Armament crews feeding belts containing thousands of rounds of cartridges into the aircraft's guns, fuelling staff handling petrol bowsers of 2,500 gallons capacity and oil tenders containing 450 gallons shuttling between storage tanks and aircraft, specialist staff checking every part of the bombers, all trying to accomplish their tasks and rectify any known faults before the take off time which would already have been set for the operation.

Where it was possible to get close to the dispersal points, one was able to see the bombs being winched up into the huge open bellies of the bombers, and despite the rigid adherence to safety procedures being followed, accidents did occur. Memory recalls occasions when men and machines were destroyed in explosions during the activities at East Moor.

It was possible to get within seeing distance of the inside of the hanger that was located in Nursery Wood, where aircraft could be seen in various states of repair and maintenance. Sometimes it was an engine change or maybe a new fin and rudder or even a new wing section being fitted by the skilful hands of the fitters and riggers.

Everywhere, men and women were to be seen working feverishly to beat the deadline set for take off. An engine fitters daily inspection required at least three hours, and entailed working many feet above ground and exposed to the elements on the open dispersal also If there were any known faults, they would have to be rectified in time for a test flight to be carried out.

Behind the scenes and well out of sight of us enthusiasts, the aircrews would be absorbing a complexity of information concerning the chosen target, and the pilots and navigators planned their routes to and from it. Catering staff had to provide sandwiches, flasks of tea and coffee, biscuits and sweets, to help refresh and sustain the crews during their long, cold and often stressful ops.

As take off time approached, crew buses and other vehicles used for the same purpose appeared on the scene, ferrying the flying crews to the dispersal's where, before climbing aboard the bombers they were seen enjoying a smoke, answering a call of nature (sometimes in line abreast) or carrying out traditional rites.

A visit to East Moor airfield just before dusk gave the observer a never to be forgotten experience. One by one the bombers engines were started and within a a short time the air was filled with the reverberating sound of up to 160 aero engines. Soon there was a constant stream of heavily laden aircraft being taxied towards the duty runway, each one stopping momentarily before turning on to it. As each one lined up against the wind,there was a deafening crescendo of noise as the engines were brought to full power against the brakes, then a sudden lurch forward indicated that the latter had been released. In what seemed to the observer to be a never ending, swinging and lurching take off run, the huge bombers would thrust their crews into the sky at one minute intervals, until the sky was filled with their snarling and straining engines. After circling in an anti clockwise manoeuvre while slowly gaining height, the entire aerial armada gradually disappeared over the Yorkshire Wolds towards the North Sea and beyond, leaving a comparatively tranquil environment behind them.

By getting away before dusk it was possible for the long journey outwards from East Moor to Nazi Germany to be completed before the moon rose, and with any luck, to recover to the base before the dreaded fog of the early morning manifested itself. Nevertheless, the crews had to be diverted to other landing grounds on many occasions, returning home later in the day. This was known to make it most difficult at times for the station to meet further operational commitments until all men and machines were back on the field.

A shift system was employed by the groundstaff at East Moor, and when operations were on it was not until the last aircraft had risen from the runway that,the by now , thoroughly tired personnel were able to stretch their aching limbs and enjoy the stations plain but functional canteen and messing facilities. A few precious hours in bed and up for an early start the next morning was often the routine at East Moor station.

As soon as the aircraft landed on their return from a sortie, the night staff covered the engines and turrets with special yellow canvas sheets. At daylight the riggers and fitters went over the machines, carefully checking for any damage. Fuel and oil consuption had to be checked against any notes made by the Flight Engineers and the testing of spark plugs, electics, bomb release gear, flying controls and tyres carried out.

It was the duty of the ground crews to keep the aircraft serviceable which made their importance and responsibility very great indeed. Success of the operations and the lives of the aircrew depended to some degree on the skill and efforts of them. Conditions at East Moor during winter months could be extremely difficult for the many groundstaff, and the ones experienced in 1942/43 were no exception. The heavy snowfalls, severe frosts and the consequent mud and water made even walking a formidable task. Many were seen battling against the elements, pushing their cycles which the conditions had made impossible to ride. Sometimes, unable to work for very long periods on the exteriors of the aircraft, a refuge was sought in the hastily erected shelters which were constructed out of packing crate materials. Nevertheless, the East Moor men and women were not found lacking and their efforts to carry the war to the enemy soon gathered momentum.

Returning to the base after experiencing perilous attacks on enemy targets, the aircrews often found themselves having to endure further danger while running the gauntlet of flak and fighters and consequently a number were unable to reach base, coming down in the North Sea or on English soil. Of those that did arrive back at East Moor, many were in battle damaged aircraft and were unable to make safe landings. It was not uncommon to find several bombers lying in the most undignified positions across the Strensall Road or in the fields adjacent to Low Carr Farm, having suffered brake or hydraulic failure. No less than thirteen aircraft lost their undercarriages in the deep boundary ditch at the end of runway 16 before the Air Ministry Works and Bricks department were called in to pipe and fill it in.

From mid 1944, when daylight operations became more frequent, it was possible to for the observer to witness more of the operational returns than previously, and memory recalls the most spectacular incidents created by badly shot up aircraft passing within a few yards of where one was standing, churning up the soil and hedgerows in the process. Today, almost fifty years on, one cannot pass the old airfield site without stopping to reflect on those far off days and the memories associated with the base. The occasion in the summer of 1944 when, during an operational take off one bomber crashed and burnt on the field, whilst the others took off over it only to see it explode in the most spectacular manner as the last one cleared the runway. The occasion in 1945 when a number of diverted American Flying Fortresses, short of fuel, attempted to land on several runways simultaneously until clusters of red flares were fired in an attempt to discourage the process. The giant ball of fire which followed a deafening explosion of a Halifax and its bombs on the airfield, and the ensuing pall of dense black smoke rising hundreds of feet into the air. Memories that will remain in our minds forever.

Gone now are the heroes who flew the Wellingtons, Lancaster's and Halifax bombers, along with their post war counterparts and their Mosquitos, Hurricanes and Martinet trainers. Gone too, are all those unsung heroes in the ground trades together with the WAAF and WD girls who cooked, nursed and supported them all. The only inhabitants of what is once again an area given over to agriculture,are the birds and the bees, and the only sounds are of cattle lowing and of tractors working the land as peace and tranquillity once more prevails over this piece of Yorkshire countryside.

Today, fifty years later, many veterans make an annual pilgrimage to the East Moor Memorial at nearby Sutton on Forest. Not surprisingly some of them experience great difficulty in locating their old haunts around the base and the associated sites in which they lived and worked during those far off days. Very few buildings remain and most are in a state of decay, only three dispersal pads are to be found and the runways and perimeter tracks are rapidly disappearing. While Bettys Bar and its famous mirror are permanent reminders and have become legendary, the passage of time has seen the disappearance of several other favourite watering holes, the Black Swan at Sutton on Forest and the Half Moon in Blake Street, York to name but two.

The men and women of East Moor fought long and bravely,and for many the base was the last place upon which they saw the sun rise and set or felt mother earth under their feet. At the going down of the sun...............

STATION COMMANDERS AT EAST MOOR

7.6.42-31.3.43		Group Captain	J.R Whitley	(Linton on Ouse)
1.4.43-4.6.43	33066	Wing Comander	J.A.P Owen	
4. 6.43-18. 6.43	C1664	Wing Comander	J.C Savard DFC	
18. 6.43-10. 2.44	C148	Group Captain	H.M Carscallen DFC	
10. 2.44-29. 5.44	C1399	Group Captain	J.E FauquierDSO, 2 Bars, DFC	
29. 5.44-12. 4.44	37220	Group Captain	G.L Wurtele	
12. 4.44-15.10.44	C149	Group Captain	G.C Rutledge OBE	
14.10.44- 1. 6.45	C1637	Group Captain	R.A McLernon DFC	
1. 6.45-28. 7.45	C841	Wing Commander	F.W Ball	
28. 7.45- 3. 9.45	C8412	Wing Commander	W.F McKinnon DFC	
3. 9.45-31.10.45	J15175	Wing Commander	J.F Clark DFC	
1.11.45-28. 3.46		Group Captain	F.B Bristow	
28. 3.46-29. 5.46		Group Captain	F.M Donaldson DSO, AFC	
29. 5.46-28. 6.46		Group Captain	R.S Ryan	

The Station was handed over to Care & Maintenance on 5 June 1946 leaving Flight Lieutenant R.S Wilson as Camp Commandant.

EAST MOOR

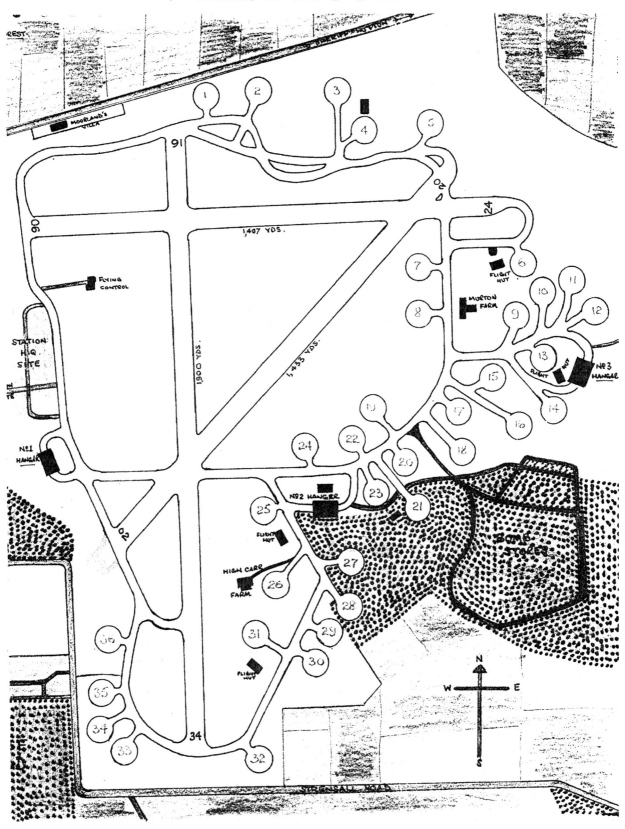

Fig 1 Eastmoor 1942

1942
THE EASTMOOR RELAUNCH

May 1942

During the latter part of the month and before East Moor station had a resident squadron, local agricultural workers and construction projects were still much in evidence on the airfield and several sightings were made of aircraft including Oxford, R6241 and Lysander V9606. A low level pass by a Wellington, W5424 was also noted. Presumably these were unofficial/training visits to the airfield.

1 June 1942

Believed to be the date upon which East Moor was handed over by the Ministry of Works to the RAF, and opened as a satellite to RAF Linton on Ouse.

4 June 1942

The advance party of 158 Squadron arrived at East Moor from RAF Station Driffield and the first RAF motor vehicles were seen there. These in the form of personnel carriers and displaying B/4 identification insignia had been noted routing through the village of Strensall.

5 June 1942

Further sections of 158 Squadron continued to arrive at East Moor and these included 'A' flight under the command of Squadron Leader M.R. Skeet and B with Squadron Leader F.P. Hewitt. No squadron aircraft seen to date.

6 June 1942

The main body of 158 Squadron under the command of Wing Commander P. Stevens, DFC arrived at East Moor. Some of the aircrew were converting to the Halifax bomber with 1652 HCU at Marston Moor while ground crew were gaining experience of the type with 35 Squadron at Linton on Ouse.

7 June 1942

No.158 Squadron now established at East Moor and a Conversion Flight formed, under Squadron Leader Wilkerson, DFC. Pilot Officer C.W. Martin appointed Engineering Officer. Two uncoded Halifax IIs were seen at the northern end of the airfield and both being towed by tractors. These were W1157 and R9373.

8 June 1942

No.158 Conversion Flight commenced training under Squadron Leader Wilkerson, DFC, and had Wing Commander Stevens, DFC, Squadron Leader Hewitt and Flight Lieutenant Porter as their first pilots under training. In the evening two more Halifaxs were seen at East Moor, W7745 and W1190, the latter was displaying a greyish white single letter 'T' aft of the roundel.

9 June 1942

Further Halifax IIs were seen parked on the loop between dispersals No.2 and No.4 at the northern end of the airfield, W1108, W1162 and W1003 which had faintly discernible ZA codes.

16 June 1942

Squadron Leader S.L. Ennis, DSO, DFC, appointed 'A' Flight Commander vice Squadron Leader M.R. Skeet

17 June 1942

The squadron reached an advanced state of training with the first night flying training exercises from East Moor.

20 June 1942

Further night flying training exercises carried out.

23/24 June 1942

Almost all the squadrons aircraft were engaged in air to air firing exercises with the Whitley and Lysanders of 1484 Target Towing Flight based at Driffield. A demonstration of Halifax Dinghy Drill was carried out on the second day.

25 June 1942

158 Squadron dispatched the following eleven crews to form part of the Thousand bomber raid on Bremen. Some of the Conversion Flight aircraft were used. Wing Commander Stevens, DFC, lifted W7745 off East Moors runway at 23.36 hrs and was thus the first operational sortie from the base.

'K' W7745			'E' W1108			'A' W1157	
W/C. Stevens	Pilot		S/L. Ennis	Pilot		P/O. Agutter	Pilot
Sgt. Beckman	2/Plt		W/O. Williamson	2/P		Sgt. Hughes	2/Plt
F/O. Fairburn	A/O		F/S. Powell	A/O		P/O. Serpell	A/O
Sgt. Pierre	A/B		F/S. Beck	A/B		Sgt. Oliver	A/B
Sgt. Evershed	WOP		P/O. Slide	WOP		Sgt. Holmes	WOP
Sgt. Perrett	M/U		Sgt. Hotson	M/U		Sgt. Cantillon	M/U
Sgt. Palm	R/G		P/O. Marshal	R/G		Sgt. Martin	R/G
Sgt. Hop	F/E		Sgt. Lewis	F/E		Sgt. Galloway	F/E

'F' W7751			'M' W7750			'P' W7753	
Sgt. Hardy	Pilot		F/L. Haydon	Pilot		Sgt. Chambers	Pilot
F/L. Porter	2/Plt					P/O. Withy	2/Plt
P/O. Archer	A/O		P/O. Tudor/Jones	A/O		Sgt. Thomas	A/O
Sgt. Irwin	A/B					Sgt. Godfrey	A/B
Sgt. Hall	WOP		Sgt. Shearer	WOP		Sgt. Seymour	WOP
Sgt. Paton	M/U		Sgt. Greenfield	M/u		Sgt. Bailey	M/U
F/S. Bayfield	R/G		Sgt. Leakey	R/G		Sgt. Pedler	R/G
Sgt. Godwin	F/E		Sgt. Fox	F/E		Sgt. Smith	F/E

'L' W1166			'N' DG225			'Y' R9388	
Sgt. White	Pilot		P/O. Bradbury	Pilot		Sgt. Dillon	Pilot
S/L. Hewitt	2/Plt		Sgt. Froming	A/O		P/O. Pears	A/O
P/O. Johnstone	A/O		Sgt. Smart	A/B		Sgt. Daubon	A/B
Sgt. Mogg	A/B		Sgt. Walton	WOP		Sgt. Davis	WOP
Sgt. Stewart	WOP		Sgt. Brindley	M/U		Sgt. Hooper	M/U
F/S. Blott	R/G		P/O. Petherbridge	R/G		Sgt. Davies	R/G
Sgt. Wright	F/E		Sgt. Edlington	F/E		Sgt. Sharp	F/E

'W' R9373			'X' W1014	
P/O Skelly	Pilot		S/L. Wilkerson	Pilot
Sgt. Patterson	A/O		W/O. Mylrae	2/Plt
Sgt. Hall	A/B		Sgte Pridden	A/B
F/S. Meagher	WOP		Sgt. Thorp	WOP
Sgt. Linklater	M/U		Sgt. Cains	M/U
Sgt. Willan	R/G		Sgt. Lowe	R/G
Sgt. Gissing	F/E		Sgt. Rogers	F/E

26 June 1942

At 05.30 hrs on the return flight from Bremen, Pilot Officer Bradbury was forced to put DG225 down in the North Sea when it ran out of fuel. The crew survived and travelled the half mile to Scarborough on a fishing vessel leaving NP-N to become the first aircraft lost from East Moor and the squadrons first Halifax loss. It was DG225s first operation.

Sgt.White returned with W1166 badly shot up by an enemy aircraft. W/C.Stevens returned with his bomb load intact, flak damage prevented their release.

28/29 June 1942

Air to Air firing with 1484 Target Towing Flight over Filey Bay Range. Training and cross country flights carried out by day and night.

30 June 1942

158 Squadron carried out circuits and bumps exercises. Squadron Leader Hewitt assumed command while W/C.Stevens DFC, took leave.

1 to 7 July 1942

Weather was unfit for flying for much of the week with rain and thunderstorms prevalent. W/C.Stevens, DFC, resumed command of 158 sqd on the 2nd. A full day of ground training lectures given by S/L.Wilkerson and F/L.Lawson on the 4th. On the 5th seven aircraft engaged on navigation training and formation air firing and six on night cross countries. After early rain on the 6th the last official Conversion training was concluded.

8 July 1942

158 Squadron dispatched the following eight crews to Wilhelmshaven to attack the docks area.

'A' W1157			'F' W7751			'D' W1162	
P/O. Agutter	Pilot		S/L. Ennis	Pilot		P/O. Phillips	Pilot
Sgt. Quinlan	2/Plt		W/O.Williamson	2/Plt		P/O. Yeo	2/Plt
P/O.Serpell	A/O		F/S.Powell	A/O		P/O. Harvey	A/O
Sgt. Oliver	A/B		Sgt. Simkins	A/B			
P/O. Slide	WOP		Sgt.Hotson	WOP		Sgt. Thompson	WOP
Sgt. Cantillon	M/U		Sgt.Silverman	M/U		Sgt. Byrne	M/U
Sgt. Martin	R/G		F/L Watkins	R/G		P/O. Curtis	R/G
Sgt. Galloway	F/E		Sgt. Lewis	F/E		Sgt. Furness	F/E

'P' W7753			'N' W1038			'M' W7745	
P/O.Chambers	Pilot		P/O.Bradbury	Pilot		Sgt.Dillon	Pilot
P/O.Withy	2/Plt					Sgt.Roberts	2/Plt
Sgt.Thomas	A/O		Sgt.Fromimgs	A/O		Sgt.Watkins	A/O
Sgt.Lister	A/B		Sgt.Smart	A/O			
Sgt Stewart	WOP		Sgt Davis	Wop		Sgt.Seymour	WOP
Sgt Leakey	M/U		Sgt.Brindley	M/U		Sgt.Stait	M/U
P/O.Marshall	R/G		P/O.Petherbridge	R/G		Sgt.Davies	R/G
Sgt Smith	F/E		Sgt.Roy	F/E		Sgt.Rogers	F/E

'K' W7745			'S' W1179	
W/C.Stevens	Pilot		P/O.Skelly	Pilot
Sgt.Beckman	2/Plt			
F/O.Fairburn	A/O		Sgt.Smith	A/O
Sgt.Perrett	WOP		Sgt.Walton	WOP
Sgt.Campbell	M/U		Sgt.Pat	M/U
Sgt.Palm	R/G		Sgt.North	R/G
Sgt.Hope	F/E		Sgt.Dunn	F/E

The following crew was dispatched to Amiens (Nickels)

'B' W1164	
Sgt. Bond	Pilot
Sgt. Surridge	A/O
Sgt. Evershed	WOP
Sgt. Cams	M/U
Sgt. Forgie	R/G
Sgt. Marshall	F/E

The following two crews were dispatched to Rouen (Nickels)

'Q' DG227			'G' W1040	
F/S.Robb	Pilot		S/L.Hewitt	Pilot

Sgt.Fewtrell	A/O	F/L. Somerville	A/O
Sgt.Cantell	WOP	Sgt.Hooper	WOP
Sgt.Craft	M/U	Sgt.Beber	M/U
Sgt.Harkness	R/G	Sgt.Davison	R/G
Sgt.Dodd	F/E	Sgt Sharp	F/E

All aircraft returned safely, despite heavy flak and presence of night fighters.

9 to 12.July 1942

Some local flying, Air firing and Navigation training carried out. F/L. Porter and P/O. Sparke completed their conversion course on the 11th.

13 July 1942

158 Squadron dispatched the following seven crews to Duisburg.

	'B' W1164				**'H' W7766**				**'S' W1179**	
Sgt.	Dale	Pilot	Sgt.	Bond	Pilot	P/O.	Skelley	Pilot		
P/O.	Yeo	2/Plt								
F/O.	Davies	A/O	Sgt.	Surridge	A/O	Sgt.	Smith	A/O		
Sgt.	Sproston	A/B	Sgt.	Pridden	A/B	Sgt.	Pierre	A/B		
Sgt.	Bailey	WOP	Sgt.	Evershed	WOP	Sgt.	Paton	WOP		
Sgt.	Greenfield	M/U	Sgt.	Cains	M/U	Sgt.	Murphy	M/U		
Sgt.	Davison	R/G	Sgt.	Forgie	R/G	Sgt.	McLachlan	R/G		
Sgt.	Edlington	F/E	Sgt.	Narshall	F/E	Sgt.	Jillings	F/E		

	'Q' DG227			**'K' W7745**			**'D' W1162**		
F/S.	Robb	Pilot	S/L.	Hewitt	Pilot	Sgt.	Dillon	Pilot	
Sgt.	Fewtrell	A/O	F/L.	Somerville	A/O	Sgt.	Watkins	A/O	
Sgt.	Maas	A/B	Sgt.	Simkins	A/B				
Sgt.	Cantell	WOP	Sgt.	Hooper	WOP	Sgt.	Seymour	WOP	
Sgt.	Craft	M/U	Sgt.	Stewart	M/U	Sgt.	Stait	M/U	
Sgt.	Harkness	R/G	Sgt.	Gray	R/G	Sgt.	Davies	R/G	
Sgt	Dodd	F/E	Sgt.	Sharp	F/E	Sgt.	Pogers	F/E	

	'P' W7753	
P/O.	Bradbury	Pilot
Sgt.	Kendall	2/Plt
Sgt.	Fromings	A/O
Sgt.	Smart	A/B
Sgt.	Walton	WOP
Sgt.	Brindley	M/U
P/O.	Petherbridge	R/G
Sgt.	Poy	F/E

Two aircraft failed to return, Flight Sergeant Robb and crew together with Pilot Officer Bradbury and his crew became the first East Moor casualties on operations and the squadrons first Halifax crews lost. Nothing was heard from these crews after take off from East Moor and sadly all were killed. Squadron Leader Hewitt returned early with the rear turret u/s and jettisoned his bombs off Bridlington. Sgt.Bonds a/c iced up causing an early return.

14 July 1942

No flying - inclement weather.

15 July 1942

The body of Sgt.Craft the mid upper gunner in DG227 was washed up at Great Yarmouth. Despite rain and heavy cloud local flying and air firing exercises were carried out.

16 July 1942

At 11.35 hrs, Halifax II, BB203 a 158 Squadron Conversion Flight aircraft crashed at Comborough Farm Sheriff Hutton with the loss of Pilot Officer Craig the instructor together with two pilots under training, Pilot Officer Withy and Warrant Officer Williamson also two Flight Engineers, Sergeant Place and Sergeant Dunn. The aircraft was recovering to East Moor when it stalled and was subsequently burnt out.

17 & 18.July 1942

Continuous heavy rain made conditions unfit for flying at East Moor

19 July 1942

158 Squadron dispatched the following six crews to attack the U-Boat yards and town at Vegesack.

'E' W1108			'A' WII57			'K' W7745		
S/L.	Ennis	Pilot	P/O.	Agutter	Pilot	S/L.	Hewitt	Pilot
F/S.	Powell	A/O	P/O.	Serpell	A/O	F/O.	Fairburn	A/O
F/S.	Beck	B/A	F/S.	Meagher	B/A	Sgt.	Pierre	B/A
Sgt.	Hotson	WOP	Sgt.	Evershed	WOP	Sgt.	Perrett	WOP
Sgt.	Silverman	M/U	Sgt.	Cantillon	M/U	Sgt.	Campbell	M/U
F/L.	Watkins	R/G	Sgt.	Martin	R/G	Sgt.	Palm	
Sgt	Lewis	F/E	Sgt.	Galloway	F/E	Sgt.	Hope	F/E

'S' W1179			'D' W1162			'B' W1164		
P/O.	Skelley	Pilot	Sgt.	Dillon	Pilot	P/O.	Hardy	Pilot
Sgt.	Smith	A/O	Sgt.	Watkins	A/O	P/O.	Archer	A/O
Sg.	Simkins	A/B	Sgt.	Redler	A/B	Sgte	Urwin	A/B
Sgt.	Paton	WOP	Sgt.	Seymour	WOP	Sgt.	Bailey	WOP
Sgt.	Rennie	M/U	Sgt.	Godfrey	M/U	Sgt.	Greenfield	M/U
F/S.	McLachlan	R/G	Sgt.	Fergie	R/G	Sgt.	Wilson	R/G
Sgt.	Jillings	F/E	Sgt.	Rogers	F/E	Sgt.	Godwin	F/E

The target was cloud covered, the bombing was scattered and East Moor lost its 5th and 6th aircraft when W1162 was presumed lost in the North Sea and W1179 was shot down by an Me 110 near Tersehellinge All crew members lost their lives and the bodies of Sgts Dillon, Godfrey and Rogers were washed up near Borkum and buried in the Lutheran Cemetery. F/Sgt McLachlan washed up on later date.

20 July 1942

Sea searches for Sgt. Dillon and crew were carried out by aircraft of 16 Group.
Newton on Ouse was the scene of funeral services for Pilot Officer Withy and Warrant Officer Williamson killed in BB203s crash. Almost all squadron members attended and full service honours were awarded and a tea followed at Aldwark Manor.

21 July 1942

Further sea searches for Sgt.Dillon and crew were made, Flight Lieutenant Porter flew one of over four hours, and 16 Group continued their search.

158 Squadron dispatched the following five crews to Duisburg in a 291 aircraft attack.

'C' W1215			'H' W7766			'G' W1040		
P/O.	Phillips	Pilot	Sgt.	Bond	Pilot	P/O.	Hardy	Pilot
P/O.	Tudor-Jones	A/O	Sgt.	Surridge	A/O	P/O.	Archer	A/O
			F/S.	Neaghers	A/B	Sgt.	Urwin	A/B
Sgt.	Thompson	WOP	Sgt.	Evershed	Wap	Sgt.	Hall	WOP
Sgt.	Byrne	M/U	Sgt.	Campbell	M/U	Sgt.	Greenfield	M/U

P/O.	Curtis	R/G	Sgt.	Davison	R/G	Sgt.	Wilson	R/G
Sgt.	Furness	F/E	Sgt.	Marshall	F/E	Sgt.	Godwin	F/E
						P/O	.Yeo	2/Plt

	'M' W7750			'K' W7745	
F/L.	Haydon	Pilot	P/O.	White	Pilot
F/O.	Davies	A/O	P/O.	Johnstone	A/O
Sgt.	Hudless	A/B	Sgt.	Nogg	A/B
Sgt.	Shearer	WOP	Sgt.	Holmes	WOP
Sgt.	Beber	M/U	Sgt.	Bridgewater	M/U
Sgt.	Palm	R/G	F/S.	Blott	R/G
Sgt.	Fox	F/E	Sgt.	Wright	F/E
			Sgt.	Quinlan	2/Plt

The seventh East Moor based aircraft was lost when Pilot Officer Hardy and crew were shot down in WI040 by a night fighter near Utrecht. Nothing was heard from this crew after take off., and the aircraft crashed in Holland.,(Schoonrewoerd) Two crews were dispatched on Nickel raids, both returned safely.

	J W1211 to Angers			V BB208 to Nantes	
F/L.	Porter	Pilot	P/O.	Sparke	Pilot
Sgt.	Patterson	A/O	P/O.	Aris	A/O
Sgt.	Hall	A/B	Sgt.	Watson	A/B
Sgt.	Linklater	WOP	Sgt.	Middleton	WOP
Sgt.	Collins	M/U	Sgt.	Silverman	M/U
Sgt.	Wilman	R/G	P/O.	Marshall	R/G
Sgt.	Gissing	F/E	Sgt.	Alcock	F/E

22 July 1942

The weather prevented any flying, overcast and rain all day.

23 July 1942

One crew carried out a searchlight co-operation exercise (Leeds) of one and three quarter hours duration and recorded as unsuccessful. (Sgt.Caplan) 158 Squadron dispatched the following four crews to Duisburg,

	'K' W7745			'A' W1157			'E' W1108	
W/C.	Stevens	Pilot	S/L.	Hewitt	Pilot	P/O.	Phillips	Pilot
F/O.	Fairburn	A/O	P/O.	Tudor-Jones	A/O	P/O.	Harvey	A/O
Sgt.	Pierre	A/B	Sgt.	Sproston	A/B	Sgt.	Price	A/B
Sgt.	Perrett	WOP	Sgt.	Hooper	WOP	Sgt.	Thompson	WOP
Sgt.	Campbell	M/U	Sgt.	Stewart	M/U	Sgt.	Byrne	M/U
Sgt.	Palm	R/G	Sgt.	Clark	R/G	P/O.	Curtis	R/G
Sgt.	Hope	F/E	Sgt.	Sharp	F/E	Sgt.	Furness	F/E
Sgt.	Beckman	2/Plt						

	'P' W7753	
P/O.	Chambers	Pilot
Sgt.	Thomas	A/O
Sgt.	Lister	A/B
Sgt.	Davis	WOP
Sgt.	Beber	M/U
Sgt.	Davies	R/G
5gt.	Smith	F/E
Sgt.	Quinlan	2/Plt

All four crews returned safely.

24/25 July 1942

On a cloudy and showery day some early navigation exercises were Flown and eight 158 Squadron aircraft were prepared for operations, and the following six crews were dispatched to Duisburg the first taking off at OO.11hrs

	'J' W1211				'K' W7745				'P' W7753	
F/L.	Porter	Pilot	S/L.	Hewitt	Pilot	P/O.	Chambers	Pilot
Sgt.	Patterson	A/O	P/O.	Tudor-Jones	A/O	Sgt.	Thomas	A/O
Sgt.	Hall	B/A	Sgt.	Sproston	A/B	Sgt.	Lister	A/B
Sgt.	Linklater	W/O	Sgt.	Hooper	W/O	Sgt.	Davis	W/0
Sgt.	Collins	M/U	Sgt.	Stewart	M/U	Sgt.	Dyer	M/U
Sgt.	Wilman	R/G	Sgt.	Clark	R/G	Sgt.	Davies	R/G
Sgt.	Gissing	F/E	Sgt.	Sharp	F/E	Sgt.	Smith	F/E

	'B' W1164				'V' BB208				'C' W1215	
P/O.	White	Pilot	P/O.	Sparke	Pilot	P/O.	Phillips	Pilot
P/O.	Johnstone	A/O	P/O.	Aris	A/O	P/O.	Harvey	A/O
Sgt.	Mogg	A/B	Sgt.	Watson	A/B	Sgt.	Price	A/B
Sgt.	Holmes	W/O	Sgt.	Middleton	W/O	Sgt.	Thompson	W/O
Sgt.	Bridgewate	M/U	Sgt.	Dawson	M/U	Sgt.	Byrne	M/U
F/S.	Blott	R/G	Sgt.	Collyer	R/G	P/O.	Curtis	R/G
Sgt.	Wright	F/E	Sgt.	Edlington	F/E	Sgt.	Furness	F/E
Sgt.	Hughes	2/Plt						

One crew was dispatched on a Nickel operation to Chartres,

	'T' W1190	
Sgt.	Caplan	Pilot
Sgt.	Fleet	A/O
Sgt.	Harcourt	W/O
Sgt.	Stait	M/U
Sgt.	Daubon	R/G
Sgt.	Frederick	F/E

At 02.43 hrs a signal was received from Flight Lieutenant Porters crew to say that they were under attack by fighters . The aircraft was abandoned and East Moor lost its eighth aircraft in W1211. Sgt. Collins was killed the remainder of the crew became POWs.

Squadron Leader Hewitt turned back at 01.20 hrs with a u/s rear turret. Pilot Officer Phillips turned back with a u/s rear turret and jettisoned the bomb load in the sea 60 miles off the Dutch coast.

The eighth detailed Halifax was H W7766 - was u/s before take off.

26 July 1942

158 Squadron dispatched the following ten crews to Hamburg,

	'E' W1108				'A' W1157				'C' W1215	
S/L.	Ennis	Pilot	P/O.	Agutter	Pilot	P/O.	Phillips	Pilot
P/O.	Powell	A/O	P/O.	Serpell	A/O	P/O.	Harvey	A/O
F/S.	Neagher	A/B	Sgt.	Oliver	A/B	Sgt.	Price	A/B
Sgt.	Hotson	W/O	P/O.	Slide	W/O	Sgt.	Thompson	W/O
Sgte	Silverman	M/U	Sgt.	Cantillon	M/U	Sgt.	Byrne	M/U
P/O.	Hanson	R/G	Sgt.	Martin	R/G	P/O.	Curtis	R/G
Sgt.	Lewis	F/E	Sgt.	Galloway	F/E	Sgt.	Furness	F/E

	'T' W1190				'H' W7766				'P' BB.208	
S/L.	Hewitt	Pilot	F/Le	Haydon	Pilot	P/O.	Chambers	Pilot
P/O.	Tudor-Jones	A/O	F/O	Davies	A/O	Sgt.	Thomas	A/O
Sgt.	Sproston	A/B	Sgt.	Hudless	A/B	Sgt.	Lister	A/B
Sgt.	Hooper	W/O	Sgt.	Shearer	W/O	Sgt.	Davis	W/O
Sgt.	Stewart	M/U	Sgt.	Beber	M/U	Sgt.	Dyer	M/U

Sgt.	Clark	R/G	F/L.	Watkins	R/G	Sgt.	Davies	R/G
Sgt.	Sharp	F/E	Sgt.	Fox	F/E	Sgt.	Smith	F/E

	'B' W1164			'V' W7777			'D' W1214	
P/O.	White	Pilot	P/O	Sparke	Pilot	Sgt.	Caplan	Pilot
P/O.	Johnstone	A/O	P/O.	Aris	A/O	Sgt.	Fleet	A/O
Sgt.	Mogg	A/B	Sgt.	Watson	A/B			
Sgt.	Holmes	W/O	Sgt.	Niddleton	W/O	Sgt.	Harcourt	W/O
Sgt.	Bridgewater	M/U	Sgt.	Dawson	M/U	Sgt.	Stait	M/U
F/S.	Blott	R/G	Sgt.	Collyer	R/G	Sgt.	Daubon	
Sgt.	Bright	F/E	Sgt.	Edlington	F/E	Sgt.	Frederick	F/E

	'K' W7745	
W/C.	Stevens	Pilot
F/O.	Fairburn	A/O
Sgt.	Pierre	A/B
Sgt.	Perrett	W/O
Sgt.	Campbell	M/U
Sgt.	Palm	R/G
Sgt.	Hope	F/E

27 July 1942

On the return flight W1164 was attacked by a night fighter and as a result of the damage inflicted upon it, Pilot Officer White set it down on the North Sea when he and W/Op. Sergeant Holmes together with Sergeants Mogg and Bright were lost. After many hours in the water Pilot Officer Johnston, flight sergeant Blott and Sergeant Bridgewater became POWs. Their tour completed - were doing an extra op. At 02.05 hrs Pilot Officer Phillips lost power on the port outer engine and the rear turret became u/s resulting in his turning W1215 back to base which he reached at 04.12 hrs.

Flight Lieutenant Haydon was unable to open the bomb doors on W7766 over the target and after a determined effort by sergeant Fox he was able to jettison the load 30 miles west of the target.
Pilot Officer Chambers made the return flight with only three of BB2O8s engines functioning, the port outer having failed over the target.

28 July 1942

The day started with East Moor shrouded in dense fog. No flying was carried out and an operational call for 11 aircraft was later cancelled. The station was was visited by representatives of the Australian Press.

29 July 1942

Some Fighter Affilliation exercises carried out by W7766 and BB209. 158 Squadron dispatched the following six crews to attack Saabrucken,

	'A' W1157			'D' W1214			'N' W1038	
P/O	Agutter	Pilot	Sgt.	Caplan	Pilot	P/O.	Chambers	Pilot
P/O	Serpelle	A/O	Sgt.	Fleet	A/O	Sgt.	Thomas	A/O
Sgt.	Oliver	A/B	P/O.	Domaille	A/B	Sgt.	Lister	A/B
P/O.	Slide	W/O	Sgt.	Harcourt	W/O	Sgt.	Davis	W/O
Sgt.	Cantillon	M/U	Sgt.	Stait	M/U	Sgt.	Dyer	M/U
Sgt.	Martin	R/G	Sgt.	Daubon	R/G	Sgt.	Davies	R/G
Sgt.	Galloway	F/E	Sgt.	Frederick	F/E	Sgt.	Smith	F/E
Sgt.	Winch	2/Plt				Sgt.	Beckman	2/Plt

	'M' W7750				'H' W7766				'V' W7777	
F/L.	Haydon	Pilot	P/O.	Phillips	Pilot		P/O.	Sparke	Pilot
F/O.	Davies	A/O	P/O.	Harvey	A/O		P/O.	Aris	A/O
Sgt.	Hudless	A/B	Sgt.	Price	A/B		Sgt.	Walton	A/B
Sgt.	Shearer	W/O	Sgt.	Thompson	W/0		Sgt.	Niddleton	W/O
Sgt.	Beber	M/U	Sgt.	Byrne	M/U		Sgt.	Dawson	M/U
Sgt.	Gray	R/G	P/O.	Marshall	R/G		Sgt.	Collyer	R/G
Sgt.	Fox	F/E	Sgt.	Furness	F/E		Sgt.	Edlington	F/E
Sgt.	Beasley	2/Plt	Sgt.	Hughes	2/Plt				

Flight Lieutenant Haydon and crew were the only ones to bomb, the remainder were unable to identify the target,Sergeant Caplan and PilotOfficer Chambers jettisoned, Pilot Officer Agutter jettisoned some east of Goole when his starboard outer cut and Pilot Officer Phillips and Pilot Officer Sparke brought all bombs back to base.

30 July 1942

Nothing recorded on this date

31 July 1942

158 Squadron dispatched ten crews to form part of a force of 630 aircraft to attack Dusseldorf,

	'S' W1222			'V' W7777				'W' R9373	
W/C.	Stevens	Pilot	P/O.	Sparks	Pilot		P/O.	Chambers	Pilot
F/O.	Fairburn	A/O	P/O.	Aris	A/O		Sgt.	Thomas	A/O
Sgt.	Pierre	A/B	Sgt.	Watson	A/B		Sgt.	Lister	A/B
Sgt.	Perrett	W/O	Sgt.	Middleton	W/O		Sgt.	Davis	W/O
Sgt.	Campbell	M/U	Sgt.	Dawson	M/U		Sgt.	Dyer	M/U
Sgt.	Palm	R/G	Sgt.	Collyer	R/G		Sgt.	Davies	R/G
Sgt.	Hope	F/E	Sgt.	Edlington	F/E		Sgt.	Smith	F/E

	'M' W7750			'Z' BB193				'E' W1108	
F/L.	Haydon	Pilot	S/L.	Holden	Pilot		S/L.	Ennis	Pilot
F/O.	Davies	A/O	F/O.	Walker	A/O		P/O.	Powell	A/O
Sgt.	Hudless	A/B	Sgt.	Bailey	W/O		F/S.	Meagher	A/B
Sgt.	Shearer	W/O	Sgt.	Murray	M/U		Sgt.	Hotson	W/O
Sgt.	Beber	M/U	Sgt.	Leakey	R/G		Sgt.	Silverman	M/U
Sgt.	Gray	R/G	Sgt.	Nunday	F/E		P/O.	Hanson	R/G
Sgt.	Fox	F/E	Sgt.	Winch	2/Plt		Sgt.	Lewis	F/E

	'T' W1190			'D' W1214				'H' W7766	
S/L.	Hewitt	Pilot	Sgt.	Caplan	Pilot		P/O.	Phillips	Pilot
F/L.	Somerville	A/O	Sgt.	Fleet	A/O		P/O.	Harvey	A/O
Sgt.	Sproston	A/B	P/O.	Domaille	A/B		Sgt.	Price	A/B
Sgt.	Evershed	W/O	Sgt.	Harcourt	W/O		Sgt.	Thompson	W/O
Sgt.	Stewart	M/U	Sgt.	Stait	M/U		Sgt.	Byrne	M/U
Sgt.	Clark	R/G	Sgt.	North	R/G		P/O.	Marshall	R/G
Sgt.	Sharp	F/E	Sgt.	Marshall	F/E		Sgt.	Furness	F/E

	'X' W1014	
F/O.	Cresswell	Pilot
W/O.	Nylrae	A/O
Sgt.	Murphy	W/O
Sgt.	Walton	M/U
Sgt.	Lowe	R/G
Sgt.	Alcock	F/E
Sgt.	Hughes	2/Plt

A signal was received at 02.39 hours by Sergeant Perrett the wireless operator in Wing Commander Stevens crew that Squadron Leader Hewitt and crew were under attack by a night fighter, W1190 became the tenth East Moor based aircraft to be lost. The B Flight Commander and his crew became POWs.
After bombing, Pilot 0fficer Sparkes aircraft was on the receiving end of some flak blast which blew it into a loop, followed by a rapid descent which reached a speed of 330 mph before recovery was attained.

Pilot Officer Phillips aircraft returned with some flak damage to the tail unit. Aircraft D, E, and H landed at Ayr while X landed at Bourn.

General:

During August 1942 the East Moor crews together with No.4 Group Halifax crews in general, received a well earned rest from operations whilst modifications to certain design faults were carried out on the type.
During this period, extra training programmes were followed.

L/2/3/4 August 1942

Fog, heavy rain and cloud dominated the East Moor scene for these four days, and the only flying was in the form of ten air tests. Operations were called for daily but were later scrubbed on each occassion. Squadron Leader P.B.Robinson appointed B Flight Commander vice Squadron Leader Hewitt.

5 August 1942

158 Squadron dispatched four crews from East Moor, two to Bochum and two on Nickel raids to   Paris,

	'C' W1215			'R' W1221	
P/O.	Phillips	Pilot	P/O.	Chambers	Pilot
P/O.	Harvey	A/O	Sgt.	Thomas	A/O
Sgt.	Price	A/B	Sgt.	Lister	A/B
Sgt.	Thompson	W/O	Sgt.	Davis	W/O
Sgt.	Byrne	M/U	Sgt.	Dyer	M/U
P/O.	Marshall	R/G	Sgt.	Davies	R/G
Sgt.	Furness	F/E	Sgt.	Smith	F/E

Pilot Officer Chambers bombed Bochum, nothing was heard from Pilot Officer Phillips after take off. Shot down by a night fighter W1215 Pilot Officer Phillips and Pilot Officer Marshall lost their lives, Sergeant Price evaded capture and returned to the U.K, the remainder of the crew became POWs.

Pilot Officer Chambers aircraft received flak damage to fuselage, wings and both the inner engines.

	'V' W7777			'K' W7745	
P/O.	Sparke	Pilot	Sgt.	Caplan	Pilot
P/O.	Aris	A/O	Sgt.	Fleet	A/O
Sgt.	Watson	A/B	P/O.	Damaille	A/B
Sgt.	Middleton	W/O	Sgt.	Hand	W/O
Sgt.	Dawson	M/U	Sgt.	Hardy	M/U
Sgt.	Collyer	R/G	Sgt.	Gray	R/G
Sgt.	Billington	F/E	Sgt.	Jenkins	F/E

Pilot Officer Sparke and crew Nickelled as ordered, and Sergeant Caplans rear turret became u/s and he landed 24 minutes after take off.

6 August 1942

158 Squadron dispatched six crews on a raid against Duisburg, the first on left East Moor at 00.22 hrs,

	'G' BB209			'S' W1222			'M'W7750	
F/S.	Dale	Pilot	P/O.	Sparke	Pilot	F/L.	Haydon	Pilot
Sgt.	Kay	A/O	P/O.	Aris	A/O	P/O.	Davies	A/O
F/S.	Sanderson-		Sgt.	Watson	A/B	Sgt.	Hudless	A/B
	Miller	A/B	Sgt.	Middleton	W/O	Sgt.	Shearer	W./O
Sgt.	Stait	W/O	Sgt.	Dawson	M/U	Sgt.	Beber	M/U
Sgt.	Anstruther	M/U	Sgt.	Collyer	R/G	Sgt.	Gray	R/G
Sgt.	Martin	R/G	Sgt.	Billington	F/E	Sgt.	Fox	F/E
Sgt.	Anderson	F/E						

	'E' WII08			'D' W1214				'K' W7745	
S/L.	Ennis	Pilot	P/O.	Chambers	Pilot		Sgt.	Caplan	Pilot
P/O.	Powell	A/O	P/O.	Jeffrey	A/O		F/O.	Walker	A/O
F/S.	Beck	A/B	Sgt.	Lister	A/B		P/O.	Domaille	A/B
Sgt.	Hotson	W/O	Sgt.	Davies	W/O		Sgt.	Hand	W/O
Sgt.	Silverman	M/U	Sgt.	Byrne	M/U		Sgt.	Culley	M/U
P/O.	Hanson	R/G	Sgt.	Davies	R/G		Sgt.	Murray	R/G
Sgt.	Lewis	F/E	Sgt.	Smith	F/E		Sgt.	Jenkins	F/E

Shot down ten miles before reaching the target W7750 became the 12th East Moor based aircraft to be lost. Flight Lieutenant Haydon, Flying Officer Davies (both Australians) and Sergeants Beber and Fox evaded capture. Sergeant Huddless lost his life and Sgts Shearer and Gray became POWs.

7/8 August 1942

No flying was recorded on these two dates and visibility at East Moor was very poor with overcast and heavy rain on both. Aircraft were stood by on both days but operations did not take place.

9 August 1942

A stand by of three aircraft for a daylight operation was cancelled at 16.50 hrs and 158 Squadron dispatched two crews to attack Osnabruck,

	'F' W7751				'K' W7745	
P/O.	Chambers	Pilot		Sgt.	Caplan	Pilot
Sgt.	Thomas	A/O		Sgt.	Fleet	A/O
Sgt.	Lister	A/B		P/O.	Domaille	A/B
Sgt.	Davies	W/O		Sgt.	Stait	W/O
Sgt.	Byrne	M/U		Sgt.	Hardy	M/U
Sgt.	Davis	R/G		Sgt.	Daubon	R/G
Sgt.	Smith	F/E		Sgt.	Jenkins	F/E

10 August 1942

Weather was again cloudy with heavy rain and only one short air test carried out. Three aircraft were stood down at 17.00 hrs.

11 August 1942

Two air tests and a gunnery flight carried out.
One 158 Squadron crew dispatched to Nainz, and a second one to Le Havre.

	'K' W7745				'D' W1214	
P/O.	Sparke	Pilot		Sgt.	Hughes	Pilot
P/O.	Aris	A/O		Sgt.	Clarke	A/O
Sgt.	Kennedy	A/B		Sgt.	Bradley	A/B
Sgt.	Middleton	W/O		Sgt.	Harcourt	
Sgt.	Dawson	M/U		Sgt.	Smith	M/U
Sgt.	Collyer	R/G		Sgt.	Leakey	R/G
Sgt.	Mundy	F/E		Sgt.	Anderson	F/E
P/O.	Cole	2/Plt				

Five Halifax bombers from 102 Squadron - Pocklington were diverted to East Moor arriving between 04.27 and 05.50 hrs, DY-B, DY-T, DY-N, DY-J, and DY-P.

12 to 21 August 1942

The weather was genarally cloudy and showery, 158 Squadron carried out a programme of cross country, fighter af-filliation, bombing practice and air to air firing exercises together with routine air tests.

Due to heavy losses, morale fell to an extreme low amongst the crews of Halifax squadrons and all 4 Group operations were suspended for almost one month. It was during this period that the Pathfinders came into being. Major operations resumed late in the month,

22 August 1942

158 Squadron dispatched three crews on Nickel operation to Paris.

	'M' W1253			'T' W1251			'J' W7783	
Sgt.	Quinlan	Pilot	Sgt.	Beckman	Pilot	Sgt.	Roberts	Pilot
F/S.	Sanderson-		F/S.	Cooper	A/B	Sgt.	Pridden	A/B
	Miller	A/O	P/O.	Smyth	A/O	Sgt.	Kay	A/O
F/O.	Walker	A/B	F/S.	Miller	W/O	Sgt.	Hand	W/O
F/S.	Murphy	W/O	Sgt.	Hanks	M/U	Sgt.	Culley	M/U
Sgt.	Hirshbein	M/U	Sgt.	Byrne	R/G	Sgt.	North	R/G
Sgt.	Green	R/G	Sgt.	Brogden	F/E	Sgt.	Jenkins	F/E
Sgt.	Halse	F/E						

Despite the firing of their recognition cartridge and displaying of I.F.F. signals Sgt. Beckmans crew were treated to a frightening barrage of friendly ack ack over Hendon on their return flight.
All three aircraft were diverted to Pocklington but W1251 landed at Topcliffe,
Bad weather prevented their recovering to East Moor.

23/24/25/26/27 August 1942

W1253, W1251 and W7783 returned to East Moor during the early afternoon of the 23rd. Only approximately twenty hours flying during the five days, mainly formation flying, beam approach and cross country exercises. Early thick fog with considerable rain and severe thunderstorms later was the general pattern.

28 August 1942

158 Squadron dispatched the following three crews to Saarbrucken, Bourges and
Paris respectively. The two latter ones were Nickel operations.

	'F' W7751			'O' W7777			'K' W7745	
Sgt.	Hughes. C.	Pilot	P/O.	Sparke. C.	Pilot	Sgt.	Caplan. M.	Pilot
Sgt.	Clarke. L.D	A/B	P/O.	Jeffrey. J.B	Nav	Sgt.	Fleet. A.G	Nav
Sgt.	Bradley. J.	Nav	Sgt.	Watson. P.	A/B	Sgt.	Stait. J	W/O
P/O.	Browne. O.L	W/O	Sgt.	Niddleton. H.	W/O	Sgt.	Bowley. K.	M/U
Sgt.	Anstruther. J	M/U	P/O.	Martin. T.	R/G	Sgt.	Daubon. A.N	R/G
Sgt.	Leakey. K.W	R/G	Sgt.	Dawson. C.G	M/U	Sgt.	Frederick. A.	F/E
Sgt.	Anderson. A	F/E	Sgt.	Edlington. R	F/E			
Sgt.	Benford. S	W	2/Plt					

During the night the weather closed in on East Moor and on their return all crews were diverted, Sgt.Hughes to Oakington, P/O. Sparke to Waterbeach and Sgt.Caplan to Catfoss.

1 September 1942

158 Squadron dispatched the following four crews in a force of 231 aircraft which set out to attack Saarbrucken but due to a marking error most of the bombs fell on Saarlouis north west of the target.

	'D' W1214			'E' W1108			'O' W7777	
Sgt.	Hughes. G	Pilot	S/L.	Robinson. C	Pilot	Sg.	Caplan. N.	Pilot
Sgt.	Surridge, A	Nav	P/O.	Powell. R	Nav	Sgt.	Fleet. A.G	Nav
Sgt.	Bradley. J	A/B	F/S.	Beck. H	A/B	Sgt.	Laws. J	A/B
P/O.	Browne. O	W/O	Sgt.	Hotson. J	W/O	Sgt.	Stait. J	W/O
Sgt.	Anstruther.	M/U	Sgt.	Silverman. P	M/U	Sgt.	Bowley. K	M/U
P/O.	Martin. T	R/G	P/O.	Hanson. A	R/G	Sgt.	Daubon. A	R/G
Sgt.	Anderson. A	F/E	Sgt.	Lewis. P	F/E	Sgt.	Frederick. A	F/E
Sgt.	Benford. S	2/Plt	Sgt.	Wiley.J	2/Plt	Sgt.	White. S	2/Plt

	'F' W7751		
F/L.	Agutter. V	Pilot	
P/O.	Serpell. V.G	Nav	
Sgt.	Oliver. T.E	A/B	
P/O.	Slide. G.V	W/O	(4 Group Halifaxs now back on major ops)

Sgt.	Hutchinson.J	M/U
F/S.	Martin. J	R/G
Sgt.	Galloway.	F/E
Sgt.	McAlpine.W	2/Plt

Sergeant Hughes turned W1214 back after approximately one hours flight with the mid upper turret u/s and the intercom not working. The bombs were jettisoned safely into the north sea.

2 September 1942

On a showery day a six aircraft operational detail was called for, and news was received from International Red Cross that Pilot Officer Skelley and Sergeant Rennie were dead on the 20th July 1942. 158 Squadrons strength was so reduced that again only the four following crews could be mustered to join 4 Groups first Halifax main force participation for some time, the target, Karlsruhe.

	'K' W7745			'S' W1222				'D' W1214	
W/C.	Stevens. C	Pilot	S/L.	Robinson. P.B	Pilot		Sgt.	Hughes. G	Pilot
F/O.	Fairburn. L	Nav	P/O.	Jeffrey. F	Nav		Sgt.	Surridge	Nav
Sgt.	Perrett. N.G	W/O	Sgt.	Ellsworth. G	A/B		Sgt.	Bradley. J	A/B
Sgt.	Campbell. T	M/U	Sgt.	Hooper. L	W/O		P/O.	Browne.O	W/O
F/L.	Watkins. K	R/G	Sgt.	Hardy. H	M/U		Sgt.	Anstruther.J	M/U
Sgt.	Hope. V	F/E	Sgt.	Dawson. C	R/G		P/O.	Martin. T	R/G
Sgt.	Wylie. J	2/Plt	Sgt.	Greensrnith. P	F/E		Sgt.	Anderson.A	F/E
			Sgt.	McAlpine.W	2/Plt		Sgt.	Benford. S	2/Plt

	'O' W7777	
P/O.	Chambers. I	Pilot
Sgt.	Thomas.W	Nav
Sgt.	Kennedy. J	A/B
Sgt.	Davis. J	W/O
Sgt.	Corpe. A	M/U
Sgt.	Palm. C	R/G
Sgt.	Smith. C	F/E
Sgt.	White. S	2/Plt

The attack on Karisruhe was regarded as a very successful one. Wing Commander Stevens aircraft was approached by two enemy aircraft the first of which had a nose light showing. A burst from Flight Lieutenant Watkins guns at approx 400 yds and it was extinguished. Sergeant Campbell and F/L.Watkins fired several bursts at the second one which then broke away.

3 September 1942

Only Navigation Flying Training exercises carried out.

4 September 1942

Message received at Eastmoor via Air Ministry that Pilot Officer Yeo was killed on 22nd July 1942.

158 Squadron dispatched six crews in a force of 250 aircraft on an operation to Bremen.

	'A' W1157			'D' W1214				'F' W7751	
F/L.	Agutter. V	Pilot	Sgt.	Hughes. C	Pilot		S/L.	Robinson. C.G	Pilot
P/O.	Serpell. D	Nav	Sgt.	Surridge. A	Nav		P/O.	Powell. P	Nav
P/O.	Slide. G.V	W/O	P/O.	Browne. O	W/O		Sgt.	Hotson. J	W/O
Sgt.	Hutchinson. J	M/U	Sgt.	Anstruther.J	M/U		Sgt.	Silverman.P	M/U
Sgt.	Davison. F.N	R/G	P/O.	Martin. T.J	R/G		P/O.	Hanson. A	R/G
Sgt.	Oliver. T	A/B	Sgt.	McLennon.C	A/B		F/S.	Beck. H	A/B
Sgt.	Galloway.	F/E	Sgt.	Anderson. A	F/E		Sgt.	Lewis. P	F/E
F/S.	Owen.O	2/Plt	Sgt.	Benford. S	2/Plt		Sgt.	Wylie. J	2/Plt

	'L' W1166			'P' BB208				'O' W7777	
Sgt.	Caplan. N	Pilot	P/O.	Chambers.I	Pilot		S/L.	Pobinson.P.B	Pilot
Sgt.	Fleet. A	Nav	Sgt.	Thomas. W	Nav		P/O.	Jeffrey. F.C	Nav
Sgt.	Stait. J	W/O	Sgt.	Davis. J	W/O		Sgt.	Cooper. L.B	W/O
Sgt.	Bowley. K	M/U	Sgt.	Corpe. K	M/U		Sgt.	Hardy. H	M/U
Sgt.	Daubon. A	R/G	Sgt.	Palm. C	R/G		Sgt.	Murray. J	R/G

Sgt.	Laws. J	A/B	P/O.	Gatis. E	A/B	Sgt.	Ellsworth. G	A/B
Sgt.	Frederick.A	F/E	Sgt.	Smith. C	F/E	Sgt.	Greensmith.P	F/E
Sgt.	Davidson.A	2/Plt	P/O.	Jowett. F	2/Plt	Sgt.	McAlpine. W	2/Plt

All six aircraft were diverted to Newmarket on their return where after stalling, W1214 broke its back in two places and burnt, becoming the 13th East Moor based aircraft to be lost. Crew safe. Raid successful.

5 September 1942

The only flying recorded was the return of WII57, W7751, W1166, BB208 and W7777 to East Moor from Newmarket.

6 September 1942

Seven 158 Sqd crews carried out NFTs and three crews were dispatched to attack Duisburg and a further one to Nickel Paris.

	'F' W7751			'M' W1253			'T' W1251	
F/L.	Agutter. V.G	Pilot	Sgt.	Quinlan. B.P.	Pilot	S/L.	Robinson.P.B	Pilot
P/O.	Serpell. D.J	Nav	F/O	Walker. F.A	Nav	Sgt.	Thomas. W.A	Nav
Sgt.	Oliver. T.E	A/B	P/O.	Domaille. W	A/B	Sgt.	Ellsworth. G	A/B
P/O.	Slide. G.V	W/O	Sgt.	Murphy. J.W	W/O	Sgt.	Davis. J	W/O
Sgt.	Hutchinson. J	M/U	Sgt.	Hirshbein. I	M/U	Sgt.	Murray. J	M/U
F/S.	Martin. J	R/G	Sgt,	Green.	R/G	Sgt.	Palm. C.P	R/G
Sgt.	Galloway.	F/E	Sgt.	Halse. J	F/E	Sgt.	Smith. C.H	F/E
P/O.	Jowitt. F	2/Plt	Sgt.	Ensor. F.W	2/Plt	G/Cpt.	Whitley	2/Plt

All three aircraft returned safely from this operation. The Nickelling crew was,

	'B' BB205	
Sgt.	Caidwell. A	Pilot
Sgt.	Hunt. O.A	Nav
Sgt.	Reid. J.J	A/B
Sgt.	Readman. D.F	W/O
Sgt.	Bailey.	M/U
Sgt.	Soper. L.J	R/G
Sgt.	Bren. P	F/E

This crew had an extremely uneventful trip, no flak or searchlights encountered.

7 September 1942

Wing Commander Stevens in W7745 NP-K, Pilot Officer Sparke in W1253 NP-M and Sergeant Caplan in W1166 NP-L had their operation scrubbed as they took off for Warnemunde.
Air Ministry message received at East Moor that Flight Lieutenant Porter and Sergeants Hall and Gissing had become POWs, together with Pilot Officer Johnstone an Sergeant Blott. The two latter ones having been rescued by lifeboat.

8 September 1942

Two crews carried out cross country exercises and a further three on N.F.T's.
158 Squadron dispatched the following five crews to Frankfurt,

	A W1157			'O' W7777			'K'W7745	
F/L.	Agutter. V	Pilot	P/O.	Sparke. C.L	Pilot	S/L.	Pobinson.P.B.	Pilot
P/O.	Serpell. D	Nav	P/O.	Aris. J.B	Nav	Sgt.	Thomas. W. A	Nav
Sgt.	Oliver. T.E	A/B	Sgt.	Watson. P	A/B	Sgt.	Ellsworth. G	A/B
P/O.	Slide. G.V	W/O	Sgt.	Middleton.H	W/O	Sgt.	Davis. J	W/O
Sgt.	Hutchinson J	M/U	Sgt.	Lewis. J.D	M/U	Sgt.	Campbell. T	M/U
F/S.	Martin.	R/G	Sgt.	Dawson. C.G	P/O	Sgt.	Palm. C.P	R/G
Sgt.	Galloway.	F/E	Sgt.	Edlington. P	F/E	Sgt.	Smith. C.H	F/E
Sgt.	Bartlett. J	2/Plt	Sgt.	Davidson. J.F	2/Plt	F/S.	Owen. O.P	2/Plt

	'L' W1166			'M' W1253	
Sgt.	Caplan. N	Pilot	Sgt.	Quinlan. B.P	Pilot
Sgt.	Fleet. A.G	Nav	F/O.	Walker. A.L	Nav
Sgt.	Laws. J.P	A/B	P/O.	Domaille. W	A/B
Sgt.	Stait. J	W/O	Sgt.	Murphy.	W/O
Sgt.	Corpe. A	M/U	Sgt.	Hirshbein. I	M/U
Sgt.	Daubon A.M	R/G	Sgt.	Green. D.E	R/G
Sgt.	Frederick. A	F/E	Sgt.	Halse. J	F/E
P/O.	Thomas. W	2/Plt	Sgt.	Ensor. F.W	2/Plt

The bombing was reported as scattered!

9 September 1942

Eight crews involved in night cross countries and N.F.T's.

10 September 1942

158 Squadron dispatched the following six crews in a 479 aircraft force to Dusseldorf,

	'T' W1251			'B' BB205			'K' W7745	
P/O.	Sparke C.L	Pilot	Sgt.	Caldwell. F	Pilot	S/L.	RobinsoneP.B.	Pilot
P/O.	Aris. J.B	Nav	Sgt.	Hunt. C.A	Nav	Sgt.	Thomas. W	Nav
Sgt.	Watson. P	A/B	Sgt.	Reid. J	A/B	Sgt.	Ellsworth. G	A/B
Sgt.	Middleton.	W/O	Sgt.	Harcourt. D	W/O	Sgt.	Davis. J	W/O
Sgt.	Lewis. P	M/U	Sgt.	Harrison. P.N	M/U	Sgt.	Silverman. P	M/U
Sgt.	Dawson. C	R/G	Sgt.	Soper. L.J	R/G	P/O.	Hanson. A.H	R/G
Sgt.	Edlington. P.	F/E	Sgt.	Bren. P	F/E	Sgt.	Smith. C.li.	F/E
						Sgt.	Sutton. A.J	2/Plt

	'L' W1166			'M' W1253			'F' W7751	
Sgt.	Caplan. N	Pilot	Sgt.	Quinlan .D.R	Pilot	F/L.	Agutter. V.G	Pilot
Sgt.	Surridge. A	Nav	F/O.	Walker. A	Nav	P/O.	Serpell. D.J	Nav
Sgt.	Laws. J.P	A/B	P/O.	Domaille. W	A/B	F/S.	Beck. H.J	A/B
Sgt.	Staite J	W/O	Sgt.	Murphy. J.W	W/O	P/O.	Slide. G.V	W/O
Sgt.	Corpe. A	M/U	Sgt.	Hirshbein. I	M/U	Sgt.	Hutchinson. J	M/U
Sgt.	Daubon. A	R/G	Sgt.	Green. D.B	R/G	F/S.	Martin. J	R/G
Sgt.	Frederick. A	F/E	Sgt.	Halse. J	F/E	Sgt.	Galloway. D	F/E
P/O.	Thomas. W	2/ Plt	Sgt.	Ensor. F.W	2/Plt	Sgt.	Bartlett. J	2/Plt

Squadron Leader P.B.Robinson and crew were shot down near Harlingen by an Me 109 and W7745 fell into the Waddensea with the loss of all on board, the fourteenth East Moor based aircraft to be lost.

In Halifax W1253 Pilot Officer Domaille was killed a flak wound in his chest as he was about to release the bombs which were immediatley released by the pilot. Sergeant Edlington was wounded in the shoulder in W1251. W7751 was also hit and damaged by flak.

11 September 1942

Squadron Leader C.G. Robinson appointed B Flight Commander vice Squadron Leader P.B. Robinson, 158 Squadron.
Message received at East Moor - Pilot Officer Harvey, Sergeants Thompson, Byrne and Furness had become POWs. Further Air Ministry signal to say that Pilot Officers Marshall and Phillips both dead. Repeat signal to confirm death of Sergeants Holmes, Mogg and Wright all dead also Pilot Officer White.

12 September 1942

After early fog had cleared three aircraft were stood by for operations but cancelled later. Air Ministry signal received stating that Sergeant Huddless was dead and that Flight Sergeant McLachlans body had been washed up on 3rd August 1942.

13 September 1942

158 Squadron provided four crews towards Bomber Commands 446 dispatched to attack Bremen, two took off just before midnight and two just after,

	'T' W1251				P' BB208				'B' BB205		
P/O.	Sparkee C.L	Pilot	F/L.	Agutter. V.G	Pilot	Sgt.		Caidwell. F	Pilot		
P/O.	Aris. J.D	Nav	P/O.	Serpell. D.J	Nav	Sgt.		Hunt. C.A	Nav		
P/O.	Gatis. E	A/B	Sgt.	Lewis. J.P	A/B	Sgt.		Reid. J.J	A/B		
Sgt.	Niddleton. H	W/O	P/O.	Slide. G.V	W/O	Sgt.		Cantillon	W/O		
Sgt.	Furness. J.W	M/U	Sgt.	Hutchinson. J	M/U	Sgt.		Readman. D.E	M/U		
Sgt.	Dawson. C.G	R/G	Sgt.	Galloway. D	F/E	Sgt.		Soper. L.J	R/G		
Sgt.	Steadman. D	F/E	F/S.	Owen. C.R	2/Plt	Sgt.		Bren. P	F/E		
Sgt.	Wade. E	2/Plt									

	'J' W7783	
S/L.	Robinson.C.G	Pilot
Sgt.	Pay	Nav
F/S.	Beck F	A/B
Sgt.	Hotson. J	W/O
Sgt.	Booker. D.N	M/U
Sgt.	Davison. F	R/G
Sgt.	Lewis. P	F/E
Sgt.	Davidson. J.F	2/Plt

East Moor lost its fifteenth aircraft in BB205 of which nothing was heard after take off, believed to have been ditched on the return flight.

Flight Lieutenant Agutters mission was aborted with the rear turret u/s and the bombs were jettisoned off Hornsea.

Pilot Officer Sparke and Squadron Leader Robinson were diverted to West-Raynham & Massingham on their return.

East Moor had been host to six Halifaxs of 10 Squadron from Melbourne & ten of 102 Squadron from Pocklington.

14 September 1942

W7783 and W1251 returned to East Moor, the former calling at Pocklington en route.

Message received from Air Ministry saying that Squadron Leader Hewitt, Flight Lieutenant Somerville and Sergeants Stewart, Sharp, Evershed, Sproston and Clarke were all POWs.

158 Squadron dispatched two crews to Wilhelmshaven,

	'S' W1222			'J' W7783	
Sgt.	Caplan. N.	Pilot	F/L.	Agutter. V.G	Pilot
Sgt.	Surridge. A	Nav	P/O.	Serpell. D.J	Nav
Sgt.	George. A	A/B	Sgt.	Lewis. J.P	A/B
Sgt.	Stait. J	W/O	P/O.	Slide. G.V	W/O
Sgt.	Corpe. A	M/U	Sgt.	Hutchinson. J	M/U
Sgt.	Daubon. A	R/G	P/O.	Martin. T.J	R/G
Sgt.	Frederick. A	F/E	SLt.	Galloway. D.C	F/E
P/O.	Thomas. W	2/Plt	F/S.	Owen. O.P	2/Plt

15 September 1942

Sergeant NcAlpine carried out a cross country exercise in BB208. Sergeant White carried out a three hour sea search for Sergeant Caidwell and crew using W1038. Sergeant Wyllie carried out a night cross country in BB208.

W1157 and W1246 proceeded to Mildenhall in readiness for a special operation but both were found to be u/s, the former had a starboard outer glycol leak and a burst hydraulic pipe while the rear and mid upper turrets were faulty on the latter.

Air Ministry signal received to say that Sergeants Wilman, Patterson and Linklater were all POW's and that Sergeant Collins was dead.

16 September 1942

Four 158 Squadron crews left East Moor for an attack on Essen forming part of a 370 aircraft force, which inflicted considerable damage to the Krupps works,

	'P' BB208			'S' W1222			'L' W1166	
P/O.	Sparke. C.L	Pilot	Sgt.	Beckman. L.J	Pilot	Sgt.	Caplan N	Pilot
P/O.	Aris. J	Nav	P/O.	Smythe. J.S	Nav	Sgt.	Fleet. A.G	Nav
F/S.	Bullen. H.G	A/B	F/S.	Cooper. S	A/B	Sgt.	Laws. J.P	A/B
Sgt.	Niddleton. H	W/O	Sgt.	Murphy. J.W	W/O	Sgt.	Stait. J	W/O
Sgt.	FurnessJ.W	M/U	Sgt.	Walton.	M/U	Sgt.	Corpe. A	M/U
Sgt.	Dawson. C	R/G	Sgt.	Byrne. L	R/G	Sgt.	DaubonA.N	R/G
Sgt.	Reynolds G	F/E	Sgt.	Brogden. F.W	F/E	Sgt.	Frederick.A	F/E

	'J' W7783	
S/L.	Robinson.C.G	Pilot
Sgt.	Pay. H	Nav
F/S.	Beck. H.J	A/B
P/O.	Browne	W/O
Sgt.	Booker. D.N	M/U
Sgt.	Davison. F.M	R/G
Sgt.	Marshall. W	F/E

The sixteenth East Moor aircraft lost was W1222 and nothing was heard from Sergeant Beckman and crew after take off the Halifax crashed at Ossum,Bosinghofen Germany.

17 September 1942

Signal received at East Moor to say that the body of Sergeant Paton had been washed up on 8th August 1942.

Two 158 Squadron crews proceeded to Tempsford for a special operation but only one carried out the detail as ordered, Sergeant Benfords Halifax W7766 was found to have a u/s engine, the Nickel raid special Lyons and St.Etienne was carried out by,

	'O' W7777	
P/O.	Jowitt.	Pilot
Sgt.	Stansfield.K.	Nav
P/O.	Gatis. E	A/B
Sgt.	Williams. D	W/O
Sgt.	Bailey. W.E	M/U
Sgt.	Palm. C.R	R/G
Sgt.	Steadman. D	F/E

18 Setember 1942

Pilot Officer Cole in W1108 and Pilot Officer Beasley in W7777 carried out cross country details and Sergeant Wadd a night exercise in W7783. Signal received at East Moor saying that Sergeant Shearer was a POW. W7859 seen as NP-K presumably replacing the lost W7745.

19 September 1942

Night cross country details by Pilot Officer Beasley in W1166 and Pilot Officer Cole in W1246.
Two 158 Squadron crews were dispatched to Saarbrucken,

	'C' W1246			'O' W7777	
Sgt.	Wyllie. J.N	Pilot	P/O.	Jowitt. F	Pilot
Sgt.	Stamp. P.E	Nav	Sgt.	Stansfield.K	Nav
Sgt.	Warr. B.J	A/B	P/O.	Gatis. E	A/B
Sgt.	Skinner. P.s	M/U	Sgt.	Williams. D	W/O
Sgt.	Watts. L.G	R/G	Sgt.	Hale J.E	M/U
Sgt.	Gowing. P	F/E	Sgt.	Palm. C.P	R/G
			Sgt.	Steadman. D	F/E

Nothing was heard subsequent to take off of Pilot Officer Jowitt and crew and W7777 beacme East Moors 17th aircraft loss. Sergeant Palm became a POW the fate of the remainder is unknown.

20/21/22/23/24/25 September 1942

With rainy conditions almost daily the only flying recorded was on aircraft with two pilots to Tempsford to collect W7766 on the 21st, three N.F.T's on 22nd, gunnery testing over Filey Bay and night cross countries by Sergeant McAlpine in W7783 and Sergeant White in W1221 on the 23rd and four aircraft on formation flying exercise plus BB208 on night flying on the 24th.

158 Conversion Flight left East Moor and moved to Rufforth.

26 September 1942

158 Squadron dispatched five crews to join twenty three other Halifax crews of 4 Group to attack the shipyards at Flensburg, the total force was recalled but one East Moor crew did not receive the message and continued the operation,

	'C' W1246				'J' W7783				'M' W1253	
Sgt.	Hughes. G	Pilot	S/L	Robinson.G.S	Pilot		F/S.	Quinlan. B	Pilot
Sgt.	Clarke. L.D	Nav	Sgt.	Kay. H	Nav		F/O.	Walker. L.K	Nav
Sgt.	Anderson. J	B/A	F/S.	Beck. N.J	B/A		Sgt.	Pridden W.E	B/A
Sgt.	Hand. H.F	W/O	Sgt.	Hotson. J	W/O		Sgt.	Hooper. L.V	W/O
Sgt.	Anstruther J	M/U	Sgt.	Bowsfield.J.H	M/U		Sgt.	Hirshbein. J	M/U
Sgt.	North. A	R/G	P/O.	Fagan. L.W	R/G		Sgt.	Green. W	R/G
Sgt.	Anderson. A	F/E	Sgt.	Lewis. P	F/E		Sgt.	Greensmith P	F/E

	'F' W7751			'L' W1166	
F/L.	Agutter. V	Pilot	F/L.	Sparke. C.L	Pilot
P/O.	Serpell. D.J	Nav	P/O.	Aris. J.D	Nav
Sgt.	Pierre. N	B/A	F/S.	Bullen. H	B/A
P/O.	Slide. V.G	W/O	Sgt.	Middleton. H	W/O
Sgt.	Gibson. N.A	M/U	Sgt.	Dawson. C	M/U
F/S.	Martin. J	R/G	Sgt.	Collyer. D.P	R/G
Sgt.	Galloway. D	F/E	Sgt.	Edlington. P	F/E

Sergeant Hughes report says that as he was almost over the target he decided to carry on and return as routed, W1246 received damage to tailfins and petrol tanks from an attack by enemy aircraft using cannon and machine gun fire. Sergeant North returned fire and the enemy aircraft was believed to be damaged. Flight Lieutenant Agutter brought his bombs back to East Moor the remainder of the recalled crews jettisoned their loads into the sea.

27/28/29/30 September 1942

Fighter affiliation exercises, gun testing over Filey Bay,daylight cross country and N.F.Ts during the latter three days. Night Fighter lectures given on the 28th by Flight Lieutenant Bowden from Wittering. On the 30th news was received at East Moor that Flight Lieutenant Haydon, Flying Officer Davies and Sergeants Fox and Beber had all evaded capture.

1 October 1942

Day cross countries and air firing over Filey Bay.

2 October 1942

158 Squadron dispatched three crews to Krefeld,

	'F' W7751			'M' W1253			'B' W1221	
Sgt.	Hughes. G	Pilot	Sgt.	Benford. S	Pilot	Sgt.	White. S.H	Pilot
Sgt.	Clarke. A	Nav	Sgt.	Ledger. P	Nav	Sgt.	Hammond. K.C	Nav
Sgt.	Pridden. W.E	B/A	Sgt.	Smith. E.E	B/A	P/O.	Woods. P	B/A
Sgt.	Hand. H.F	W/O	Sgt.	Rees. N	W/O	Sgt.	Smith. A.T	W/O
Sgt.	Anstruther.J	M/U	Sgt.	Gibson. M.A	M/U	Sgt.	Gray. T.L	M/U
Sgt.	North. J	R/G	Sgt.	Griffin J.P	R/G	Sgt.	Moorshead. N	R/G
Sgt.	Anderson. A	F/E	Sgt.	Hewetson. E	F/E	Sgt.	Pringle. N	F/E
P/O.	Herbert. G	2/Plt						

Sergeant Hughes Halifax was coned by searchlights for five minutes and was damaged by flak, pilots escape hatch was blown out, mid upper turret holed and tailplane too.
Sergeant Whites starboard outer was rendered u/s by flak just before bombing and two S.B.Cs hung up and returned to East Moor.

3/4 October 1942

Three day cross country exercises and fuel test flights and two Q.G.H details on the first day, no flying on the 4th.

5 October 1942

Eight air tests carried out, one aircraft set out on a night cross country but aborted due to engine failure.

158 Squadron dispatched the following five crews to Aachen where the marking was off target due to bad weather,

	'G' BB209			'H' W7766			'J' W7783	
Sgt.	Hughes. G	Pilot	Sgt.	McAlpine.J	Pilot	Sgt.	Wyllie. J.N	Pilot
Sgt.	Clarke. L.D	Nav	Sgt.	White. JeD	Nav	P/O.	Garrett. E	Nav
Sgt.	Pridden. W.E	B/A	Sgt.	Anderson. J.S	B/A	F/S.	Bullen. H.G	B/A
Sgt.	Hand. H.F	W/O	Sgt.	Campbell. C	W/O	P/O.	Winship. T	W/O
Sgt.	Anstruther.A	M/U	Sgt.	Bradley. E	M/U	Sgt.	Hannan. V.P	M/U
Sgt.	North. A.J	R/G	F/S.	Lewis. A.D	R/G	P/O.	Nartin.T.J	R/G
Sgt.	Anderson. A	F/E	Sgt.	Ellerby. H.D	F/E	Sgt.	Martin. H.P	F/E
P/O.	Cole. D	2/Plt				Sgt.	ONeill. J.P	2/Plt

	'T' W1251			'L' W1166	
Sgt.	Benford. S	Pilot	P/O.	Beesley.P.L	Pilot
Sgt.	Ledger. P	Nav	Sgt.	Brindle. F	Nav
Sgt.	Smith. E.E	B/A	Sgt.	Bygrave. L	B/A
Sgt.	Pees. N	W/O	Sgt.	Carr. F.G	W/O
Sgt.	Gibson. M.R	M/U	Sgt.	Bowley. K	M/U
Sgt.	Griffin. J.R	R/G	Sgt.	Cowper. E.F	R/G
Sgt.	Hewetson. E	F/E	Sgt.	Jackson. E	F/E
P/O.	Herbert. G	2/Plt			

Much of the bombing was scattered. Sergeant Benford had to land at Manston where the undercarriage of W1251 collapsed. The aircraft had both flak and bullet holes damage and a thunderstorm just north of the Thames rendered the compass u/s. No tracer had been seen and the crew not aware of an attack by aircraft.

6 October 1942

East Moor received signal to say that Sergeant Hallows was found dead near Rostock on 19 May 1942.

Information received through Intrnational Red Cross that Sergeant Watkins body was washed ashore 24th July 1942. Wing Commander Stevens DFC posted to 10 OTU.

Squadron Leader C.G.S.R. Robinson appointed Squadron Commander 158 Squadron.

Four 158 Squadron crews dispatched to Osnabruck,

	'F' W7751			'H' W7766			'K' W7859	
Sgt.	Hughes. G	Pilot	Sgt.	McAlpine.J	Pilot	Sgt.	Wyllie.J.N	Pilot
Sgt.	Clarke. L	Nav	Sgt.	White. J.D	Nav	P/O.	Garrett. E.A	Nav
Sgt.	Bridden. W.	B/A	Sgt.	Anderson. J	B/A	F/S.	Bullen. H.G	B/A
Sgt.	Hand. H.F	W/O	Sgt.	Campbell. C	W/O	P/O.	Winship. T	W/O
Sgt.	Anstruther.J	M/U	Sgt.	Bradley. E	M/U	Sgt.	Hannan. V.P	M/U
Sgt.	Anderson. A	R/G	Sgt.	Ellerby. H.D	R/G	P/O.	Martin. T.J	R/G
Sgt.	North. A.J	F/E	F/S.	Lewis. D	F/E	Sgt.	Martin. H.P	F/E
P/O.	Cole. J.D	2/Plt	P/O.	Beveridge.	2/Plt	Sgt.	ONeill. J.P	2/Plt

	'P' BB208	
P/O.	Beesley.P	Pilot
Sgt.	Brindle. E	Nav
Sgt.	Bygrave. L	B/A

Sgt.	Carr. F.G	W/O
Sgt.	Bowley. K	M/U
Sgt.	Jackson. E	R/G
Sgt.	Cowper. E.F	F/E

Sergeant McAlpine was diverted to Acklington on his return. The operation was regarded as successful

7 October 1942

No Flying recorded

Squadron Leader W. Fletcher, DFC, DFM appointed 'B' Flight Commander, 158 Sqd. vice Squadron Leader C.G.S.P. Robinson.

8/9/10 October 1942

Flying restricted to local, N.F.T's, cross countries and circuits and landing exercises on the 9th.

Air Ministry signal received that Sergeants Ellsworth and Thomas bodies had been recovered from the sea on 11th September 1942 also that Sergeant Gray was dead. Further signal stated (10th) Sergeant Cantillon was POW.

11/12 October 1942

Four day cross country, three air tests, five night cross country, and one Bulls eye exercises carried out on the former date, No flying recorded on the 12th.

13 October 1942

In their best effort since July, 158 Squadron dispatched the following nine crews to a total force of 288 aircraft on an operation to Kiel, when 50% of the bombing was said to have fallen away from the target,

'V' W7863

F/L.	Sparke. C.G	Pilot
P/O.	Aris. J.D	Nav
Sgt.	Watson. P	B/A
Sgt.	Middleton.H	W/O
Sgt.	Furness J.W	M/U
Sgt.	Davison. F.M	R/G
Sgt.	Edlington. P	F/E
P/O.	Herbert. G	2/Plt

'D' W1862

Sgt.	Hughes. G	Pilot
Sgt.	Clarke. L	Nav
Sgt.	Oliver. T.E	B/A
P/O.	Browne. G	W/O
Sgt.	Anstruther.J	M/U
Sgt.	Murray. J	R/G
Sgt.	Anderson. A	F/E
Sgt.	Scafford. H	2/Plt

'O' DT521

Sgt.	Caplan. N	Pilot
Sgt.	Fleet. A.G	Nav
Sgt.	Laws. J.R	B/A
Sgt.	Stait. J	W/O
Sgt.	Corpe. J	M/U
Sgt.	Dauban. A	R/G
Sgt.	Frederick.A	F/E
P/O.	Beveridge.D	2/Plt

'F' W7751

Sgt.	Wyllie. J.M	Pilot
P/O.	Garrett. E.A	Nav
Sgt.	Kennedy. P.J	B/A
Sgt.	Bailey. W.E	W/O
Sgt.	Hannan. V.P	M/U
Sgt.	Wheatcroft.G	R/G
Sgt.	Martin. N.R	F/E
Sgt.	Steer. J.T	2/Plt

'K' W7859

Sgt.	White. S.H	Pilot
Sgt.	Hammond. K	Nav
P/O.	Woods. P	B/A
Sgt.	Smith. A.T	W/O
Sgt.	Gray. F.L	M/U
Sgt.	Noorshead. L	R/G
Sgt.	Pringle. N	F/E
Sgt.	Bartlett. J	2/Plt

'H' W7766

Sgt.	McAlpine.W	Pilot
Sgt.	Surridge. A	Nav
Sgt.	Anderson. J	B/A
Sgt.	Campbell. C	W/O
Sgt.	Bradley. E	M/U
Sgt.	Lewis. A.D	R/G
Sgt.	Ellerby. H.D	F/E

'C' W1246

Sgt.	Benford. S	Pilot
Sgt.	Ledger. P	Nav
Sgt.	Smith. N	B/A
Sgt.	Rees. N	W/O
Sgt.	Gibson. M.A	M/U
Sgt.	Griffen. J.P	R/G

'M' W1253

P/O.	Beesley. L	.Pilot
Sgt.	Brindle. E	Nav
Sgt.	Bygrave. L	B/A
Sgt.	Carr. F.G	W/O
Sgt.	Bowley. K	M/U
Sgt.	Cowper.E.F.	R/G

'J' W7783

F/S.	Roberts. P	Pilot
Sgt.	Langeland.A	Nav
Sgt.	Pridden. W.E	B/A
Sgt.	Hand. H.F	W/O
Sgt.	Culley. E.J	M/U
Sgt.	North. A.J	R/G

| Sgt. | Greensmith. P | F/E | Sgt. | Jackson. E | F/E | | Sgt. | Marshall. W. | F/E |
| Sgt. | Smith. N | 2/Plt | | | | | | | |

Flight Lieutenant Sparke had to abort when the elevator controls of W7863 failed and he was unable to control the ascent or descent of the aircraft.

Pilot Officer Beesley turned back in W1253 with all the gun turrets suffering stoppages.

A taxiing accident resulted in W1014 being damaged by R9370 a 35 CF aircraft.

14 October 1942

The eighteenth East Moor based aircraft was lost at 00.50 hrs when W7766 stalled and crashed before burning on its approach to the airfield. It was returning from Kiel and had been struck by flak rendering the port inner u/s. The bombs were jettisoned on approach to the target. Sergeant Anderson died of injuries in the York Military HosPltal at Fulford, where four other crew members were admitted.

15 October 1942

For the second time in 48 hours, 158 Squadron were able to mount a ten aircraft force and dispatched the following crews to Cologne,

'V' W7863

				'E' W1108				**'A' WII57**	
F/L.	Fletcher. W	Pilot	Sgt.	Ensor. W.F	Pilot	P/O.	Cole. J.D	Pilot
Sgt.	Kay. H	Nav	Sgt.	Fernie. P.B	Nav	Sgt.	Steep. P.C	Nav
Sgt.	Pierre. M.A	B/A	Sgt.	Bell. A.E	B/A	Sgt.	Warr. B.J	B/A
F/S.	Miller. G.H	W/O	Sgt.	Jones. P	W/O	Sgt.	Ward. A.	W/O
Sgt.	Bousfield. J.H	M/U	Sgt.	Warre. W.C	M/U	Sgt.	Harrison. P	M/U
Sgt.	Davison. F.N	R/G	Sgt.	Jenner. S.G	R/G	Sgt.	Watts. L.G	R/G
Sgt.	Lewis. P	F/E	Sgt.	Edwards. R.G	F/E	Sgt.	Gowing. P	F/E

'O' DT521

				'M' W1253				**'D' W7862**	
Sgt.	White. S.H	Pilot	F/S.	Quinlan. B	Pilot	Sgt.	Hughes. G	Pilot
Sgt.	Hammond.K.C	Nav	F/O.	Walker. A.L	Nav	Sgt.	Clarke. L.D	Nav
P/O	Woods. R.T	B/A	F/S.	Bullen. H.G	B/A	Sgt.	Oliver. T.E	B/A
Sgt.	Smith. A.T	W/O	Sgt.	Cooper. L.V	W/O	P/O.	Browne.O.L	W/O
Sgt.	Gray. T.L	M/U	Sgt.	Hirshbein. I	M/U	Sgt.	Anstruther. J	M/U
Sgt.	Moorshead. N	R/G	Sgt.	Green. W	R/G	Sgt.	Murray. J	R/G
Sgt.	Pringle. N	F/E	Sgt.	Galloway. D.C	F/E	Sgt.	Anderson. A	F/E
P/O.	Ayscough. P.L	2/Plt	Sgt.	Steer. A.	2/Plt	P/O.	Herbert. G	2/Plt

'J' W7783

				'F' W7751				**'P' BB208**	
F/S.	Roberts. P	Pilot	Sgt.	Wyllie. J.M	Pilot	P/O.	Beesley. P	Pilot
F/S.	Langeland.A.B	Nav	P/O.	Garrett. E	Nav	Sgt.	Brindle. E	Nav
Sgt.	Pridden W.E	B/A	Sgt.	Kennedy. E.G	B/A	Sgt.	Bygrave. R.L	B/A
Sgt.	Hand. H.F	W/O	F/S.	Bailey. W.E	W/O	Sgt.	Carr. G	W/O
Sgt.	Culley. E.J	M/U	Sgt.	Hannan. E.P	M/U	Sgt.	Bowley. K	M/U
Sgt.	North. A.J	R/G	Sgt.	Wheatcroft.G	R/G	Sgt.	Cowper. E.F	R/G
Sgt.	Marshall. W.H	F/E	Sgt.	Martin. N.R	F/E	Sgt.	Jackson. E	F/E
			Sgt.	Smith. P	2/Plt			

'K' W7859

Sgt.	Caplan. N	Pilot
Sgt.	Fleet. A.G	Nav
Sgt.	Laws. J.P	B/A
Sgt.	Stait. J	W/O
Sgt.	Corpe. A	M/U
Sgt.	Dauban. A.N	R/G
Sgt	Frederick.	F/E

Nothing was heard from Sergeant Ensor and crew subsequent to take off from East Moor on what was their first operation. Their Conversion Flight Halifax W1108 was shot down and crashed at Hellendoorn, Holland becoming the nineteenth aircraft lost from the airfield. Sergeant Fernie became a POW the remainder lost their lives.
Sergeant White and crew had to abort their mission when the Pitot head and the intercom iced up. Bombs jettisoned into sea.

Sergeant Caplans W7859 was the victim of flak damage and just after leaving the target his port engine became u/s, a safe landing was made on three.

16 October 1942

East Moor lost its twentieth aircraft when W1038 a Conversion Flight Halifax crashed and burnt at Wigginton

22 October 1942

Information via International Red Cross received at East Moor to the effect that the bodies of Sergeants Dillon, Rogers and Godfrey had been washed up at Borkum and buried in the Lutheran Cemetery there.

23 October 1942

Three Flying Fortresss and their American crews were diverted to East Moor in the early afternoon arriving in a vic of three from an easterly direction.

Arrangements had been made for nine 158 Squadron aircraft to take off from an advanced base for the long flight to Genoa and the ground crews were en route when it was decided to dispatch the following crews from East Moor,

	'E' W7880				'K' W7859				'V' W7863	
W/C.	Pobinson. C.G	Pilot	F/L.	Fletcher. W	Pilot	F/L.	Sparke. C.L	Pilot
F/O.	Fairburn. L.J	Nav	Sgt.	Kay. H	Nav	P/O.	Aris J.B	Nav
P/O.	Beck. H.J	B/A	Sgt.	Pierre. M.A	B/A	Sgt.	Watson. P	B/A
F/S.	Hotson. J.D	W/O	F/S.	Miller. G.H	W/O	Sgt.	Middleton. H	W/0
Sgt.	Hutchinson. J	M/U	Sgt.	Bousfield. J.	M/U	Sgt.	Furness. J.W	M/U
P/O.	Dean. W.T	R/G	Sgt.	Davison. F.M	R/G	Sgt.	Murray L	R/G
Sgt.	Hope. E.J	F/E	Sgt.	Lewis. P	F/E	Sgt.	Edlington. P	F/E
Sgt.	Bartlett. J	2/Plt	F/L.	Viney. J.M	2/Plt	P/O.	Beueridge.	2/Plt

	'P' DT544				'J' W7783				'D' W7862	
F/S.	Quinlan. B.	Pilot	F/S.	Roberts. P	Pilot	Sgt.	Hughes. G	Pilot
F/O.	Walker. A.L	Nav	Sgt.	Langeland.	A.	Nav	Sgt. Clarke. L.D	Nav
F/S.	Bullen. H	B/A	Sgt.	Pridden. W.E	B/A	Sgt.	Oliver: T	B/A
Sgt.	Kooper. L.N	W/O	Sgt.	Hand. H.F	W/O	F/S.	Perrett. N.G	W/O
Sgt.	Hirshbein. I	M/U	Sgt.	Culley. E.J	M/U	Sgt.	Hardy. H	M/U
Sgt.	Green. W	R/G	Sgt.	North. A.J	R/G	P/O.	Leakey. K.W	R/G
Sgt.	Galloway. D.C	F/E	Sgt.	Marshall. W	F/E	Sgt.	Anderson. A	F/E
P/O.	Herbert. J.B	2/Plt	Sgt.	Wade. E	2/Plt	P/O.	Thomas. W.H	2/Plt

	'F' W7751				'O' DT521				'A' W7865	
Sgt.	Wyllie. J.N	Pilot	Sgt.	Caplan. N	Pilot	Sgt.	Benford. S	Pilot
P/O.	Garrett. E.A	Nav	Sgt.	Fleet. A.G	Nav	Sgt.	Ledger P	Nav
Sgt.	Kennedy. E.J	B/A	Sgt.	Laws. J.R	L/A	Sgt	Smith. N	B/A
P/O.	Winship. T	W/O	Sgt.	Stait. J	W/O	Sgt.	Pees. N	W/O
Sgt.	Hannan. V.H	M/U	Sgt.	Corpe. A	M/U	Sgt.	Robinson. W	M/U
P/O.	Martin. T	R/G	Sgt.	Daubon. N	R/G	Sgt.	Griffin. J.P	R/G
Sgt.	Martin. N.P	F/E	Sgt.	Frederick. A	F/E	Sgt.	Greensmith. P	F/E
Sgt.	O'Neill. J.P	2/Plt	Sgt.	White. S.J	2/Plt	Sgt.	Smith. N	2/Plt

Sergeant Hughes and crew failed to return frot this operation in W7862,.nothing was heard from them after take off and their Halifax became the twenty first East Moor aircraft to be lost, together with the entire crew.

On returning Flight Sergeant Quinlan landed at Castle Camps, Sergeant Wyllie at Stradishall and Sergeant Benford at Duxford.

Sergeant Caplans Halifax was attacked by two unidentified aircraft using cannon fire. Flight Lieutenant Fletcher also landed at Castle Camps while Flight Lieut. Sparke touched down at Coleby Grange.

24 October 1942

The three American Flying Fortresss departed and were seen to set a south easterly course from East Moor.

25 October 1942

Five aircraft and crews together with fourteen groundstaff of 158 Squadron left

East Moor and flew to Beaulieu for detached duty with Coastal Command.

26/27/28/29/30/October 1942

Apart from a number of air tests, six cross countries on the 27th and air firing over Filey Bay on the 30th is the only flying recorded at East Moor.

31 October 1942

Five night cross countries carried out. Information received from International

Red Cross that Sergeant Palm was POW and in Stalag 8B.

1 November 1942

Instructions were receiued by 158 Squadron to prepare to move from East Moor to nearby Rufforth.

3 November 1942

158 Squadron advance party left East Moor by road for Rufforth.

4/5/6/7 November 1942

158 Squadrons departure continued by road and air and was completed by the latter date. The depleted number of aircraft on strength were flown out on the 6th.

Halifax II based at East Moor with 158 Squadron

R9367	*NP-W 2	ops		transferred to HCU	
R9388	*NP-Y 1	op		" " "	
R9434	*NP-W				
W1003	*NP-U				
W1014	*NP-X 2	ops		transferred to HCU	
W1038	*NP-N 2	ops		crashed and burnt at Wigginton	16/10/42
W1040	*NP-G 2	ops	FTR	- Duisburg - crashed in Holland	22/7/42
W1108	*NP-E 8	ops	FTR	- Cologne - crashed in Holland	16/10/42
W1157	NP-A 9	ops			
W1162	NP-D 3	ops	FTR	- Vegesack	20/7/42
W1164	NP-B 5	ops	FTR	- Hamburg - ditched	27/7/42
W1165	*NP-R				
W1166	* NP-L 8	ops			
W1179	*NP-S 5	ops	FTR	- Vegesack - crashed in Holland	20/7/42

W1190	NP-T	3	ops	FTR	- Dusseldorf	31/7/42
W1211	NP-J	2	ops	FTR	- Duisburg	26/7/42
W1214	NP-D	8	ops		crashed at Newmarket - ex Bremen	4/9/42
W1215	NP-C	4	ops	FTR	- Bochum - crashed in Holland	5/8/42
W1217	NP-S					
W1221	NP-R	2	ops			
W1222	NP-S	6	ops	FTR	- Essen - crashed in Germany	17/9/42
W1246	NP-C	4	ops			
W1251	NP-T	5	ops		crashed at Manston - ex Aachen	6/10/42
W1253	NP-M	8	ops			
W7668	NP-N					
W7745	NP-K	16	ops	FTR	- Dusseldorf - crashed in Holland	11/9/42
W7750	NP-M	7	ops	FTR	- Duisburg - crashed in target area	7/8/42
W7751	NP-F	16	ops			
W7753	NP-P	5	ops	FTR	- Duisburg	14/7/42
W7766	NP-H	8	ops		undershot East Moor - crashed and burnt - ex Keil	14/10/42
W7777	NP-V	10	ops	FTR	- Saarbrucken when coded 0	20/9/42
W7783	NP-J	9	ops			
W7859	NP-K	4	ops			
W7862	NP-D	3	ops	FTR	- Genoa	24/10/42
W7863	NP-V	3	ops			
W7865	NP-A	1	op			
W7880	NP-E	1	op			
W7884	NP-H					
BB189	NP-E					
BB193*	NP-Z	1	op			
BB203*	NP-U				crashed at Comborough, Sheriff Hutton	16/7/42
BB205	NP-B	3	ops	FTR	- Bremen - ditched	14/9/42
BB207	NP-N					
BB208	NP-V	8	ops			
BB209	NP-G	2	ops			
DG223	NP-Q					
DG225	NP-N	1	op		ditched off Scarborough - ex Bremen	26/6/42
DG227	NP-Q	2	ops	FTR	- Duisburg	14/7/42
DT492*	NP-C					
DT521	NP-O	5	ops			
DT524	NP-T					
DT544	NP-R					
DT558	NP-H					

*Denotes Conversion Flight aircraft. Where there is no transfer or ultimate fate recorded it is presumed that the aircraft moved with 158 Squadron to Rufforth in November 1942.

ROLL OF HONOUR - 158 SQUADRON

EAST MOOR

F/S J.S	Anderson	N	17/10/42 RCAF	F/S W.N McLachlan	AG	20/7/42 RCAF
Sgt A	Anderson	FE	24/10/42	Sgt W.J Maas	B	14/7/42
Sgt L.J	Beckman	P	17/9/42	Sgt D.G Mogg	B	27/7/42
Sgt A.E	Bell	B	16/10/42	P/O J.E Marshall	AG	6/8/42
Sgt R.W	Brindley	AG	14/7/42 RAAF	Sgt J.W Murphy	WO	17/9/42 RNZAF
P/O L.E	Bradbury	P	14/7/42	Sgt T.E Oliver	B	24/10/42 RCAF
Sgt F.W	Brogden	FE	17/9/42	Sgt J.K Paton	WO	20/7/42
Sgt L	Byrne	AG	17/9/42	P/O R.A Petheridge	AG	14/7/42
Sgt N.W	Cantell	WO	14/7/42	F/S N.G Perrett	WO	24/10/42
Sgt L.D	Clark	N	24/10/42 RNZAF	P/O C.H Phillips	P	6/8/42
F/S S	Cooper	B	17/9/42	Sgt E Place	FE	16/7/42
Sgt B.0	Collins	AG	26/7/42	Sgt D.A Pedler	B	20/7/42
P/O J.W	Craig	P	16/7/42	Sgt J.R Rennie	AG	20/7/42
Sgt C	Craft	AG	14/7/42	F/S G.S Robb	P	14/7/42 RCAF
Sgt J.G	Davis	WO	11/9/42	S/L P.B Robinson	P	11/9/42 (DFC)
Sgt P.J	Dillon	P	20/7/42	Sgt W.H Rogers	FE	20/7/42
Sgt E.G	Dodd	FE	14/7/42	Sgt P Roy	FE	14/7/42

Sgt W.E Domaille	B	11/9/42		Sgt R.H Seymour	WO	20/7/42	
Sgt A Dunn	FE	16/7/42		Sgt P Silverman	AG	11/9/42	
Sgt E.G Edwards	FE	16/10/42		Sgt F.H Simkins	B	20/7/42	
Sgt G.L Ellsworth	B	11/9/42 RCAF		Sgt H.J Skelley	P	20/7/42	
Sgt W.F Ensor	P	16/10/42 RNZAF		Sgt J.A Smith	N	20/7/42 RCAF	
Sgt R.G Fewtrell	N	14/7/42		Sgt G.A Smith	FE	11/9/42	
Sgt R Forgie	AG	20/7/42		F/S W.J Smart	WO	14/7/42 RCAF	
Sgt A.J Fromings	N	14/7/42		P/O J.S Smyth	N	17/9/42	
P/O E Gatis	B	20/9/42		Sgt K.R Stansfield	N	20/9/42	
Sgt H.E Godfrey	AG	20/7/42 RNZAF		Sgt G Steadman	FE	20/9/42 RCAF	
Sgt W.J Gray	AG	7/8/42 RNZAF		Sgt A.J Sutton	P	11/9/42	
Sgt A.M Greenfield	AG	22/7/42 RAAF		P/O W.H Thomas	N	11/9/42	
Sgt J.E Hale	AG	20/9/42		Sgt W.C Warne	AG	16/10/42	
Sgt A.H Hanson	AG	11/9/42 (DFC)		Sgt S.G Walton	AG	17/9/42	
Sgt A Harkness	AG	14/7/42		Sgt W Walton	WO	14/7/42	
Sgt H Hardy	AG	24/10/42		Sgt A.E Watkins	N	20/7/42	
Sgt F.W Holmes	WO	27/7/42		P/O F.S White	P	27/7/42	
Sgt H Hudless	B	7/8/42		Sgt J Wilson	AG	22/7/42	
Sgt G.S Hughes	P	24/10/42		P/O J.F Withy	P	16/7/42	
Sgt S.G Jenner	AG	16/10/42		W/O H.W Williamson	P	16/7/42 RCAF	
SGt D.G Jillings	FE	20/7/42		Sgt F.N Wright	FE	27/7/42	
LAC J.A Johnston		17/9/42		P/O A.T Yeo	P	22/7/42	
Sgt P Jones	WO	16/10/42		P/O W.A Thomas	P	24/10/42 RCAF	
Sgt E.G Kendall	P	14/7/42					
P/O K.W Leakey	AG	24/10/42					

General:

The first East Moor delivered bombs were released from Flight Lieutenant Haydons Halifax, W7750 over Bremen at 02.03 hrs on 26 June 1942.

No.158 Squadron carried out a total of thirty three operations from East Moor on forty five targets. During their period at the base, twenty one Halifaxes were lost, sixteen on operations, three crashed in the United Kingdom as a result of operational flying and two on local training flights. Seventy three aircrew were lost, ten crews in the first six weeks at East Moor (over half of their total strength) and a further six before the squadrons departure to Rufforth approximately nine weeks later.

7 November 1942

No.429 Squadron Royal Canadian Air Force was formed at East Moore a medium Bomber Unit and known as the Bison squadron, it was the tenth Canadian squadron to be formed overseas and contained a mixture of Royal Air Force and Commonwealth personnel. Formed under the aegis of No. 4 Group Bomber Command it was commanded by Wing Commander J.A.P Owen (RAF) who had in his opening up crew, Flight Lieut T.G Sheriff (RAF) Adjutant, Flight Lieutenant J. Feller (RCAF) Medical Officer and sixteen other ranks.

11 November 1942

The squadron numbers increased daily and time was spent organising its routines. Flight Lieutenant J.C Cairns, DFC assumed command of B Flight on his arrival from Wellesbourne, Pilot Officer C.S Campbell, DFC, (RCAF)assumed duties of the Squadron Navigation Officer.

12 November 1942

It was arranged that 429 Squadron aircrew should operate with the Halifax crews of 76 and 78 Squadrons, and accompany them on raids.

18 November 1942

Fig 2. Some of the 'Unsung Heroes', members of 429 Squadron ground staff after a foray into Goose Wood collecting fuel with which to supplement their coal and coke ration. Winter 42/43. Photo S. Watkins

Sergeants Lancaster and De Bussac flew as second pilots with the Linton on Ouse crews in full sorties lasting almost nine hours when the target was Turin.

20 November 1942

The squadron strength had reached 150 Officers and men of which around one half were Canadians.

Squadron Leader F.R Holmes, DFC, (RAF) was posted in to East Moor and assumed command of 'A' Flight, 429 Squadron,

22 November 1942

Pilot Officer Fox and Sergeant Ellison flew as second pilots on a full sortie to Stuttgart with the Linton on Ouse squadrons, and were in the air around nine and a half hours.

23 November 1942

429 Squadron strength had reached approximately two hundred personnel.

25 November 1942

429 Squadron received its first four Wellington IIIs (ex 466 Squadron)

Squadron Leader J.C Cairns, DFC collected BJ799 from Driffield and with three other crews in BJ798, BJ908 and DF625 flew them over the Yorkshire Wolds and into East Moor where they were seen parked in the area adjacent to Murton Farm. Flying Officer Chipling flew as second pilot in a Halifax crew from Linton on Ouse on a mining operation to the Fresian Islands.
Warrant Officer S. Whitehead arrived at East Moor and assumed duties as 429 Sqd Warrant Officer.

28 November1942

A Commanding Officers Parade was held at East Moor on the occasion of the hoisting of the RCAF Ensign for the first time on the station. The Parade Commander was Wing Commander J.A.P Owen and Flight Lieutenant Sheriff and Warrant Officer Whitehead were Parade Adjutant and Warrant Officer respectively. Sergeants Bruce and Rodgers flew as second pilots from Linton on Ouse with 76 and 78 Squadron crews and were in the air between nine and ten hours on an operation to the Northern Italy target, Turin.

30 November 1942

Considerable difficulties were experienced by 429 Squadron due to the cancellation of numerous postings in to East Moor. Nevertheless, Flying Officer E.G Burton did arrive as Squadron Engineering Officer as did Flight Lieutenant H.F Lowery the Protestant Padre.

General:

During this period and the first week in December, fourteen day and ten night training sorties were carried out from East Moor by 429 Squadron. The total flying time being 18.35 and 22.45 hours respectively, and included cross country exercises and circuits and bumps etc.

3 December 1942

Sergeant R.F Conroy and crew arrived at East Moor from the OTU at Wellsbourne.

An Australian, Stan Norris took over as YMCA representative vice the most popular Don MacDonald who was posted to Leeds on promotion.

4 December 1942

Posted in to East Moor and 429 Squadron were, Sergeant D.E Crockatt (pilot),

Sergeant S.Sleeth (Air Bomber), Sergeant J. Marriott (Navigator), Sergeant W. Davis (Air Gunner) and Flight Sergeant OHare (Wireless Operator) all from 1659 HCU.

6 December 1942

Further 429 Squadron aircrew took part in operations with 76 and 78 Squadrons crews from Linton on Ouse when the target was Mannheim. Flying as second pilots in the Halifaxes were Sergeant Burini, Flight Sergeant Beckett, Pilot Officer Johnson, Pilot Officer Fox and Pilot Officer Knott who was a Navigator.

Four operational training flights were mounted from East Moor during the day.

7 December 1942

King George VI decorated Flight Lieutenant C.S Campbell with the DFC at Buckingham Palace.

8 December 1942

New arrivals at East Moor and 429 Squadron were Sergeant S. Hanan (Pilot),Sergeant J.K Wood (B/A), Sergeant F.S Lane (A/G), Sergeant N. Brown (Nav),Sergeant Litchfield (WOP/OG) all from 16 OTU.

Four operational training flights were carried out by 429 Squadron.

9 December 1942

The Northern Italy target, Turin,was the target for Linton on Ouse crews and again they were accompanied by personnel from East Moor viz, Sergeant Conroy, Sergeant Lancaster, Sergeant Rodgers and Sergeant Hanan all flew as second pilots.

Three day and one night training training flights carried out by 429 Squadron from East Moor.

10 December 1942

Four day and two night training flights took place at East Moor by 429 Squadron.

Fig 3. East Moor , December 1942. 429 Squadron crew.
Harry Jones (RAF) from London and Stan Watkins (RCAF) Winnipeg.
Photo S. Watkin.

12 December 1942

As of this date 429 Squadron had on strength at East Moor, seventeen aircraft, sixteen Wellington IIIs and one Mk.X. The latter and several of the former were unserviceable due to shortage of spares

Flying Officer A.O Appleby was posted in to the squadron for Adjutant duties, having previously been with 402 Squadron, RCAF.

13 December 1942

Inclement weather and shortage of spares, very little flying recorded, ground training continued.

15 December 1942

The station messing arrangements improved when the Senior NCOs returned to their own facility, having shared the Airmens Mess hitherto. The consequent overcrowding in the latter had been brought about by alterations to the Sergeants Mess and kitchens and shortage of staff to cater for them. The recreational site on the WAAFs Goose Lane area having been used as a theatre, was returned to its designated role and the theatre facility moved to part of the Airmens Mess,

16 December 1942

429 Squadron postings in to East Moor included, Sergeant J.H Black (Pilot), Pilot Officer F.N Bartlett (WOP/AG), Sergeant P.G Rothera (A/G), Sergeant A.Napier (Nay) and Sergeant P.G Moore (A/G) all from 29 OTU.

17 December 1942

429 Squadron continued with night training exercises.

19 December 1942

Flying Officer A.O Appleby assumed duty as Squadron Adjutant, vice Flight Lieutenant T.G Sheriff who left East Moor for Marston Moor.

The A.O.C visited 429 Squadron for the Officers Mess inaugral dance.

Sergeant W.A Jamieson and crew arrived at East Moor from 26 OTU and swelled the numbers of 429 Squadron.

21 December 1942

429 Squadron had only eight aircraft serviceable and this number was reduced to seven when it experienced its first crash at 21.50 hours. DF624 was on a training flight when it crashed two and a half miles SSE of Stokesley and was a total loss, after being abandoned by the crew: Sergeant J.H Black (Pilot), Sergeant A. Napier (Nav), Sergeant P.G Rothera (B/A), Pilot Officer d. Bastion (WOP/AG), Sergeant P.G Moore (A/G) and second WOP/AG Sergeant J.A West, Sergeant Moore was admitted to hospital with serious back injuries. East Moor station took all proper steps on receipt of the news of the crash, transport was dispatched to collect the crew, W/T staff to destroy the secret equipment and a guard was mounted at the scene. This was the twenty second aircraft lost by East Moor station and 429s first.

Seven day,and four night training flights were carried out from the base.

25 December 1942

Flight Lieutenant Lowery the Protestant Chaplain distributed Christmas boxes for Canadian War Services.

26 December 1942

Boxing Day saw No.4 Groups Engineering Officer, Squadron Leader G. Wass on a visit to East Moor station.

27 December 1942

Sergeant D.N Smith (Pilot), Sergeant D.P Nelson (B/A), Sergeant W.G Nicholl (WOP) .Sergeant R.F Crimins (A/G), and Sergeant H. Tennis (Nav) were posted in to 429 Sqd.

28 December 1942

Flying Officer G.A Lunn was appointed Squadron Gunnery Leader, 429 Squadron, having been posted from 75 Squadron.

Five day training flights were carried out from East Moor.

29 December 1942

Four day, and five night training flights were mounted by 429 Squadron.

30 December 1942

During the night a fire broke out in Wellington III, BK430. The flames were soon extinguished, and a Court of Inquiry was set up to investigate the incident which occured in a hanger during maintenance.

31 December 1942

Seven day, and six night training flights were carried out by 429 Squadron.

General:

December was a bad month for flying at East Moor. Inclement weather prevented flying on many occasions, as thick fog and rain prevailed around the base. Nevertheless, ground training went ahead apace and included lectures and training films and generally working up the personnel of 429 Squadron to operational readiness. Throughout the month the squadron was still dogged by a shortage of spare parts for the aircraft

1943

1 January 1943

A further two pilots were added to the strength of 429 Squadron with the arrival at East Moor of Flying Officer G. Pentony and Pilot Officer J.G Messenger from 26 OTU.

3 January 1943

No flying was recorded at East Moor other than circuits and landing practice by 429 Squadron.

Flying Officer A. Norris and Sergeant A.W Jamieson left East Moor for a course at No.1 ECDU

4 January 1943

Halifax II, W7910 DY-D of 102 Squadron Pocklington, crashed in Folly Wood while approaching East Moor on a training exercise.

7 January 1943

A further eight aircrew personnel arrived at the base to swell the ranks of 429 Squadron, Pilots Sergeants Holbech and Kilburn, Navigator Sergeant R.Parry, WOP/OGs Sergeants Heydon and Craig, Bomb Aimers Pilot Officer Cartwright and Sergeant Nesbitt together with Air Gunner Sergeant Tremblay. All were straight from OTUs.

9 January 1943

429 Squadron promotions included,

Squadron Adjutant	F/O A.C Appleby	to Acting Flight Lieutenant
Squadron Bombing Leader	P/O C.M Awad	to Acting Flight Lieutenant
Air Gunner	P/O D.P Wiley	to Temporary Flying Officer

10 to 12 January 1943

Five aircrew personnel arrived to join 429 Squadron and twenty four WOP/AG's completed their wireless operator Grade.l courses.

17 January 1943

Several 429 Squadron aircrew personnel left East Moor for RAF Station Driffield to attend Aircrew Refresher courses.

Flying Officer Pentony returned and was promoted Flight Lieutenant.

18 January 1943

Flying Officer H.A Davis of 1658 HCU, Riccall, suffered engine failure in Halifax W1227 during take off from East Moor. It was on a training exercise when it struck a tree and crashed at 15.00 hours.

21 January 1943

429 Squadron dispatched the following six aircraft on a Sea Search for lost aircrew,
BK163 Sgt G De Bussac
HE172 Sgt P Ellison
BJ908 FS.P. Conroy
BJ799 Sgt S. Bruce
DF625 Sgt S. Hanan
Z1696 P/O B Rawson

Sergeant Ellison and Sergeant Hanan made early returns, both landing within a few minutes of take off. The remainder searched without result.

Within an hour of their return to East Moor a further operation was mounted involving three aircraft and crews on a Gardening mission to Terchelling in the Frisian Islands, BK499 Sgt S Hanan BK432 F/O I Johnson BK162 F/O G Pentony
Sergeant Hanans Wellington was attacked by a flak ship and after a second unsuccessful attempt to find the target he returned to East Moor with his mines.

Sadly Flying Officer Johnson and crew failed to return. It was later learnt that BK432 had been shot down by ack ack fire north of Harlingen and the wreckage was found twenty years later when part of the Zuider Zee was drained. At the time it was recorded as having crashed at Papenzy.

Fig 4. HE593, AL-M

23 January 1943

The City of Bradford in West Yorkshire, formerly adopted 429 Squadron at a Lord Mayors luncheon, which was attended by Wing Commander J.A.P Owen, Flight Lieutenant H. Lowery the Padre and the RCAF Press Liasion Officer, Flight Lieutenant Field. The event received much publicity and resulted in many friendships between Yorkshire and Canadian families.

26 January 1943

Ten crews were dispatched from East Moor by 429 Squadron on a bombing raid to L'Orient, all becoming airborne in six minutes forty four seconds.

Z1670	Sgt	D Smith	BK540	Sgt	J Lancaster	BJ799	Sgt	S Bruce
BK162	F/L	G Pentony	HE172	Sgt	P Ellison	BK163	Sgt	L Rodgers
BJ715	Sgt	G De Bussac	DF625	Sgt	S Hanan	Z1696	P/O	B Rawson
BJ908	F/S	P Conroy						

Sergeant Bruce made an early return due to a u/s rear turret, and Sergeant De Bussac with a u/s Intercommunication System.
Four aircraft landed away from the station, one each to Boscombe Down, Lindholme, Middle Wallop and Harwell

429 Squadron experienced its first losses from bombing operations when nothing was heard from Sergeant Rodgers and crew after they left East Moor. They were believed to have been lost at sea.

Fig 5. BK162,AL-F Photo W. Willsher

General:

This proved to be the last operation carried out from the station during the month of January, and it was not until the third week in February that further ones were mounted.

Throughout January flying training was greatly hampered by a combination of inclement weather conditions and unserviceability of aircraft.

1 February 1943

Squadron Engineering Officer, Flying Officer G.E Burton was posted to Linton on Ouse and was replaced by Flying Officer S.P Warren from Pershore.

5 February 1943

Wing Commander Owen the Officer Commanding 429 Squadron, was the conducting officer during the official inspection of Air Vice Marshal C.arr the Air Officer Commanding No.4 Group.

Fig 6. BK162, AL-F Photo W Willsher

6 to 15 February 1943

During this period flying training took place whenever possible and included fighter affiliation exercises with Spitfires on the 7th and Mustangs on the 11th, beam approaches, circuits and landings and some local flying.

A number of pilots were attached to No.1 E.C.D.U where Engine Handling Courses were being held.

16 February 1943

Eight crews from 429 Squadron set out from East Moor for another attack on Lorient the first was airborne at 18.26 hours, all returned safely, the last one landing at 00.59 hours.

Z1670	Sgt	D Smith	BK162	Sgt	J Lancaster
HE172	Sgt	G De Bussac	HE414	Sgt	S Bruce
DF622	Sgt	S Hannan	Z1696	F/O	B Rawson
X3399	S/L	J Cairns	BJ908	F/S	T Hayes

One crew landed at Middle Wallop, and Sergeant Holbeck returned early with a u/s oxygen system.

19 February 1943

Wilhelmshaven was the target for the following East Moor crews who took off at around 18.00 hours and all were safely down again before midnight having completed their mission. All were airborne within 3½ minutes.

Z1670	Sgt	D Smith	BK540	Sgt	G De Bussac	BKl62	Sgt	J Lancaster
HEl72	F/S	T Hayes	HE414	Sgt	S Bruce	BK429	F/L	A Chipling
BK499	F/O	B Rawson	X3399	Sgt	H Carty			

This operation was regarded as not too successful.

20 to 24 February 1943

No operations from East Moor. Flying training included air to air firing exercises and cross countries.

On the latter date Wellington BJ798 overshot the landing ground at Henley the crew having mistaken it for White Waitham.

25 February 1943

Gardening again, this time to the Nectarine 2 fields. Unsettled weather at East Moor had delayed the planned take off time further adverse conditions, including fog, resulted in four of the six crews dispatched to return with their mines intact,

Z1670	Sgt	S Willey	HE172	Sgt	K Holbeck	HZ260	Sgt	G De Bussac
BK429	F/L	A Chipling	HE160	F/O	B Rawson	DF625	Sgt	S Hanan

26 February 1943

More than 400 aircraft set out to attack Cologne when the following twelve East Moor based Wellingtons formed part of the total force,

Z1670	Sgt	J Black	BK540	Sgt	J Lancaster	HE172	F/S	T Hayes
HZ260	Sgt	G De Bussac	HE160	F/L	A Chipling	Z1696	F/O	B Rawson
BK162	S/L	F Holmes	HE414	Sgt	S Bruce	BK499	Sgt	A Jameson
X3399	Sgt	H Carty	DF622	Sgt	S Hanan	BJ908	Sgt	K Holbeck

Squadron Leader Holmes made an early return with electrical trouble, Flight Lieutenant Chipling with a u/s constant speed unit and Sergeant Carty due to arriving at the concentration point too late.

Sergeant Holbeck landed at East Wretham.

27 February 1943

A very successful night operation to lay mines in the Nectarine fields off Terschelling got under way at 18.30 hours, the five 429 Squadron crews were all safely back at East Moor by 22.10 hours,

BK162	Sgt	E Willey	HZ26O	Sgt	J Black	BK499	Sgt	A Jameson
Z1696	Sgt	G Kennedy	BK429	Sgt	H Carty			

28 February 1943

The fourth consecutive night of operations for 429 Squadron and the following ten crews took off from East Moor on another very successful mission, this time the target was the U-Boat pens at St.Nazaire,

DF622	Sgt	H Carty	BK162	Sgt	J Lancaster	BK429	F/L	A Chipling
Z1696	Sgt	S Hanan	HZ260	Sgt	G De Bussac	BK499	F/S	R Conroy
BK540	Sgt	E Willey	HE414	Sgt	S Bruce	BJ755	Sgt	K Holbeck
BJ908	Sgt	G Kennedy						

Sergeant Willey made an early return and landed at Abingdon after a fire in the bomb bay had rendered the electrics u/s. Eight of the remaining aircraft were diverted on their return, DF622 to Middle Wallop, BK429 to Hurn, Z1696 to High -Ercall, HZ260 to Hemswell, BK499 to Chivenor, HE414 to Exeter and BJ755 to Pershore

2 March 1943

The following six crews took off in three minutes for a night Gardening mission to the Nectarine fields,

BK162 S/L	F Holmes	HZ260 Sgt	J Black	X3399 Sgt	G Kennedy
BK429 Sgt	A Jameson	BJ755 Sgt	K Holbech	BK499 F/S	R Conroy

Sergeant Black and crew failed to return and believed to have come down in the sea. Sergeant Jameson was unable to find the target and brought his mines back.

3 March 1943

Hamburg was the target for East Moor crews and seven of 429 Squadron set out at around 18.30 hours,

BK499 Sgt	E Willey	BJ755 Sgt	S Hanan	X3399 Sgt	H Carty
HE414 Sgt	S Bruce	BK429 F/O	B Rawson	HE172 Sgt	G De Bussac
HE636 Sgt	J Lancaster				

Sergeant Carty and crew made an early return for a reason not recorded. The remainder attacked and returned safely.

4 March 1943

A sea search was mounted by five crews from East Moor but sadly the results were negative. The following four were in the air shortly after midday and returned around 15.45 hours,

HE160 W/O	D Jeffries	BJ755 F/S	K Mills	Z1670 Sgt	K Burini
BK162 F/L	G Pentony				

The fifth crew skippered by Sergeant S. Bruce in HE172 set out a few minutes before the return of the above returning around 18.22 hours.

5 March 1943

No.4251 Flight of the RAF Regiment airfield defence force moved from East Moor. Sergeant Rothera the bomb aimer in Sergeant Blacks crew, was picked up in a dinghy along with the body of his skipper who had died from exposure only a few hours previously. His report indicated that Flight Sergeant Billington DFC, was killed in action and that Flight Lieutenant C. Campbell DFC, and Pilot Officer Bartlett went down with the aircraft. Sergeant Blacks body was returned to East Moor.

Seven 429 Squadron crews set off along East Moors runway destined to bomb Essen at the outset of the Battle of the Rhur. At 19.21 hours the sixth in order of take off crashed on the airfield killing the navigator, Sergeant E.M Bell and injuring other members of the crew in BJ755 which was skippered by Flight Sergeant R.F Conroy. The following crews made a safe return,

BK540 Sgt	E Willey	BK162 Sgt	J Lancaster	HE172 Sgt	G De Bussac
HE160 F/O	B Rawson	X3399 Sgt	S Hanan	HE414 Sgt	S Bruce

The latter made an early return due to engine failure. The Krupps factories were said to have been severely damaged and crews reported that fires could still be seen an hour after leaving the target.

6 March 1943

Seems to have been a quiet day at East Moor.

7 March 1943

Another Gardening operation saw six 429 Squadron crews set out from the station to lay their mines in the Nectarine fields off the Friesian Islands before returning safely to East Moor,

Z1670 Sgt	K Burini	BK540 F/O	G Fox	HE172 F/L	G Pentony
HEl60 Sgt	H Carty	X3399 Sgt	G Kennedy	BK429 Sgt	W Jameson

Sergeant Carty and crew made an early return unable to find the target in fog.

8 March 1943

The village church All Hallows, at Sutton on Forest was the scene for the funeral services of Sergeant J.H Black and Sergeant E.H Bell. 429 Squadron provided an escort and the Squadron Padre, Flight Lieutenant H.G Lowrey conducted the service assisted by Reverend Canon Coombs the parish priest. At midday the bodies were interred at the local cemetary in Huby Road with full military honours.

9 March 1943

Gardening sorties were the order of the day again at East Moor when six crews from 429 Squadron took off for the 'Carrots' fields,

Z1670 Sgt	E Willey	BK162 Sgt	S Bruce	HE172 F/S	T Heyes
HE160 Sgt	S Hanan	X3399 Sgt	G Kennedy	BK429 Sgt	K Holbech

Sergeant Willey made an early return with a u/s compass.

Sadly, Sergeant Holbech and crew failed to return from this mission, believed to have been lost at sea.

10 March 1943

A sea search for Sergeant Holbech and crew was carried out by two 429 Squadron aircraft in the late morning when both were airborne around three hours and without results,

X3399 W/O	D Jefferies	HE414 Sgt	G Kilburn

11 March 1943

No operations were called for but a flying training programme was followed including night flying.

12 March 1943

The giant Krupps works were severely damaged in a bombing raid carried out by more than 400 aircraft on Essen with nine East Moor crews amongst them,

HE635 Sgt	J Lancaster	MS487 Sgt	G De Bussac	HE414 Sgt	S Bruce
HE172 F/S	T Heyes	BK162 F/O	G Fox	HEl60 F/L	A Chipling
X3399 Sgt	G Kennedy	BK499 Sgt	A Jameson	DF622 Sgt	S Hanan

All returned safely with Sergeant Jameson landing at East Wretham after displaying great skill and courage when the aircraft was damaged in a collision with another, leaving gunner Flying Officer D. Wiley in a jammed rear turret.

Fig 7. Sergeant Pilot Dennis Carty RAF Sergeant H.D. Carty and crew left East Moor on the night of 29/30 March 1943 as part of a force which set out to attack Bochum in the Rhur. Sadley Dennis lost his life after he had to ditch his 429 Sqd. Wellington. BK540 in the North Sea on their return flight. Photo G. Kennea

14 March 1943

Just before 20.00 hours the first of four Wellingtons of 429 Squadron rose from the station for a Gardening mission to the Nectarine 1 fields and after planting the Vegetables all were safely down again by seven minutes past midnight,

Z1670 F/O	G Fox	BK162 Sgt	K Burini
HE635 Sgt	G Kilburn		
HE430 W/O	D Jeffries		

15 March 1943

No operations were scheduled, the squadron was engaged in flying training during both day and night. Numerous air tests were carried out.

The Discipline Warrant Officer, W02 S. Whitehead was posted out to Middle Wallop and was replaced by Flight Sergeant J. Tumilty.

16 March 1943

Squadron Leader F.A Holmes DFC, was appointed acting Squadron Commander of 429 Squadron.

17 & 18 March 1943

There were no operations from East Moor on either day.

19 March 1943

A group of 429 Squadron personnel paid a visit to the City of Bradford in West Yorkshire as guests of the citizens who had previously adopted them. Traditional Yorkshire hospitality was enjoyed by all.

22 March 1943

Vegetables were planted in the Trefoil fields as detailed by six crews from 429 Squadron and take off commenced just before 19.00 hours. All returned safely,

Z1670 F/O	G Fox	BK540 Sgt	K Burini	HE635 Sgt	J Lancaster
BK162 Sgt	R Ellison	HE172 F/L	G Pentony	HE414 F/S	T Heyes

25 March 1943

Wing Commander J.A.P Owen resumed command of 429 Squadron.

Seventy RAF ground tradesmen were posted out of East Moor.

26 March 1943

East Moor crews returned to the Battle of the Rhur when eleven of them set out between 19.29 and 19.38 hours for a concentrated attack on Duisburg,

BJ929	Sgt	G Kilburn	HE172	Sgt	R Ellison	HE414	Sgt	K Burini
HE593	F/S	R Conroy	HE430	S/L	J Cairns	BK540	Sgt	A Jameson
MS487	F/O	G Fox	BK162	F/S	T Heyes	DF625	Sgt	G Kennedy
HE636	F/L	A Chipling	HE635	F/O	B Rawson			

Nothing was heard from Flying Officer Fox and crew after take off who were thought to have come down in the sea.

Flying Officer Rawson landed at Coltishall with oil leaking from his starboard engine.

Unable to release their bomb load, Sergeant Kilburns crew managed to jettison it on the return flight.

27 March 1943

Sixty one ground tradesmen arrived at East Moor from Canada via the 3. PRC at Bournemouth.

28 March 1943

A sea search was carried out by two 429 Squadron crews in a vain attempt to locate Flying Officer Fox and crew. It was later established that MS487 had crashed in the Utrecht Leiden area,

HE172	S/L	A Holmes	HE414	Sgt	S Bruce

Both aircraft set out around 10.00 hours and returned four hours later. At 11.43 hours a 429 Squadron Wellington, 'V' is believed to have crashed on take off at East Moor.
St.Nazaire was the target for 429 Squadron when twelve crews bombed successfully in a night raid, four returned to East Moor the remainder were diverted,

Z1670	Sgt	D Smith	BK540	Sgt	K Burini	HE635	F/L	G Pentony
BJ920	F/S	T Heyes	HE414	Sgt	G De Bussac	HE382	Sgt	A Jameson
HE593	F/S	R Conroy	HE636	F/L	A Chipling	HE429	P/O	B Geale
DF622	F/O	B Rawson	DF625	Sgt	G Kennedy	X3704	F/S	G Kilburn

Flying Officer Rawson landed at Stanton Harcourt, Sergeant Jameson at MiddleWallop, Flight Sergeant Conroy also,

29 March 1943

East Moor lost two 429 squadron Wellington bombers on a night raid to Bochum when Bomber Command lost twelve of the type. The attack was not thought to have been a success, the night was cloudy, take off commenced at 19.45 hours and the seven Bison aircraft were airborne within four minutes in the following order,

HE635	Sgt	S Bruce	BK540	Sgt	H Carty	HE172	Sgt	R Ellison
BJ920	Sgt	K Burini	HE636	S/L	J Cairns	DF625	Sgt	S Hanan
Z1670	Sgt	D Smith						

Sadly, Sergeant Carty lost his life when his Wellington was ditched in the North Sea during the return journey.

Sergeant Burini and his entire crew were lost when their aircraft crashed north east of Duisburg.

Severe icing caused Sergeants Smith and Bruce to make early returns.

30 March 1943

At 00.58 hours, Sergeant Ellison and crew had a lucky escape when their aircraft crashed at Linton on Ouse on return from Bochum. All were uninjured in the Cat.E accident.

No operations were scheduled for the East Moor crews.

This was East Moors last day as a satellite of RAF Linton on Ouse, a status held since its opening in June 1942, and the last day within No.4 Group. The aircraft strength of 429 Squadron was on average 17 Wellingtons, ten of which were Mk.IIIs and the remainder Mk.X.

The station personnel were by now able to enjoy film shows twice weekly, on Tuesdays by courtesy of Y.M.C.A (Canada) and Friday through ENSA.

1 April 1943

East Moor attained STATION status and together with No.429 Squadron RCAF entered No.6 Group RCAF, whose Headquarters were at Allerton Park. RCAF Station East Moor and its units became a part of No.62 Beaver Base with RCAF Station Tholthorpe and RCAF Station Linton on Ouse.

The Air Officer Commanding No.4 Group, Air Vice

Fig 8. Flying Officer E.F. Lapham. (RAF)

Navigator- 429 Sqd.

1st April. 1943-22 June 1943. Shot down in Holland- became POW. (Target Krefeld). Photo E. Lapham.

Marshal Carr and Wing Commander Owen exchanged pleasantries by signal and the latter assumed duties as Station Commander East Moor.

429 Squadron was the seventh to join No.6 Group Bomber Command.

No less than fifty two operations had been carried out from East Moor during its connection with No.4 Group Bomber Command.

As of this date the following list of Officers assumed their respective duties at East Moor Station,

Wing Commander	J.A.P Owen	Station Commander
Squadron Leader	N.F Foster	Station Medical Officer
Squadron Leader	R.G Bradbury	Station Admin Officer
Flight Lieutenant	G Gurney	Operations Officer
Flight Lieutenant	D.B Davies	Station Intelligence Officer
Flight Lieutenant	A.G Fenn	Station FCO
Flight Lieutenant	H.P McCurry	Station Equipment Officer
Flight Lieutenant	B.V Smith	SSO
Flying Officer	H Midgely	Station Meteorological Officer
Pilot Officer	T.H Parry	Meteorological Officer
Pilot Officer	A.W Hall	Armaments Officer
Pilot Officer	J.C Thurston	Catering Officer
Pilot Officer	H Pltwood	FCO
Pilot Officer	H.J Owens	FCO

Squadron Leader Bradbury was appointed to supervise the M.T Section in the ab.scence of an M.T Officer.

Squadron Officer C.H Maxfield was attached as WAAF General Duties Officer and Pilot Officer L.H Fourte was attached from No. 6 Group for Armament duties.

Flying Officer J. Loomis arrived and assumed Engineering duties with 429 Squadron.

3 April 1943

Wellington III, Z1670 of 429 Squadron was completely destroyed during an air test. At 15.30 hours it crashed at Broad Farm, South Kilvington after hitting high tension cables. On board were Sergeant D.M Smith,(pilot) Flight Sergeant D. Nelson, (Nav/B) Flight Sergeant W.J Nicholl,(WOP) Sergeant R.T Crimmins,(A/G) and passengers Corporal J.L Maddox,(Nursing Orderly) Corporal T.C Lane (Fitter) and Corporal H. Butler, (Fitter). All escaped lightly except the Wireless Operater who fractured both of his legs. Flight Lieutenant A Chipling immediately convened a Court of Inquiry to look into the accident.

4 April 1943

The first operation to be mounted from the station under the aegis of No.6

Group was in an attack on Kiel when the following twelve crews were dispatched between 20.35 and 20.46 hours,

HE635	Sgt	J Lancaster	HZ312	S/L	F Holmes	HE414	Sgt	S Bruce
HE429	F/L	A Chipling	DF622	Sgt	G De Bussac	HE430	F/O	B Rawson
HE593	F/S	R Conroy	BJ799	W/O	D Jeffris	HE382	Sgt	S Hanan
MS474	F/L	G Pentony	X3704	Sgt	G Kennedy	DF625	F/S	T Heyes

Engine trouble and the loss of the rear turret door led to an early return after three hours in the air for Flight Sergeant Conroy and crew. Their bombs were jettisoned.

This operation was the Canadian Groups greatest Wimpy effort with 168 of the type being involved.

5 April 1943

No operations were called for and crews were engaged in flying training.

No.4251 Airfield Defence Flight of the RAF Regiment moved out of East Moor to Littlehampton and were replaced by No.4313 from RAF Station Pershore.

8 April 1943

It was to the Rhur and Duisburg the target for 429 Squadron crews, when seven set out three of which were forced to make early returns due to severe icing

HZ312	Sgt	J Lancaster	HE414	Sgt	S Bruce	HE430	F/O	B Rawson
HE382	W/O	D Jeffries	HE593	F/L	A Chipling	X3704	Sgt	A Jameson
HZ303	Sgt	R Ellison						

Sergeant Lancasters aircraft had a faulty engine adding to the icing problems which caused his early return along with Warrant Officer Jefferies and Sergeant Jameson. Sergeant Ellison's mount received damage to port side from flak.
Flying Officer Rawson landed at Downham Market on his return.

10 April 1943

RAF Station Pocklington's soccer team were the visitors when East Moor lost the match by seven goals to one.

429 Squadron dispatched eleven Wellingtons in a night bombing raid on Frankfurt that involved more than 500 aircraft and it was said that the results were poor,

HE635	Sgt	J Lancaster	HZ363	F/S	T Heyes	HZ303	Sgt	R Ellison
HZ312	Sgt	S Bruce	HE572	Sgt	G De Bussac	BK162	F/S	G Kilburn
HE429	F/O	B Rawson	HE636	W/O	D Jefferies	HE160	F/S	K Mills
X3704	Sgt	G Kennedy	HE593	Sgt	A Jameson			

Nothing was heard from Warrant Officer Jefferis and crew after take off. Sergeant Kennedy's aircraft was fired upon over the southern coast of England.

11,12 & 13 April 1943

Three days without any operational commitments at East Moor.

The Operations Officer Flight Lieutenant Gurney took on the role of Station Entertainments Officer replacing Flight Lieutenant Leach.

14 April 1943

Tragedy struck 429 Squadron when for the second time in eleven days another of their Wellingtons was lost during an air test.

Take off was at 15.10 hours and Flying Officer G.W Gray and his crew headed first to the north before turning over the White Horse above Kilburn. Soon after their change of course the aircraft entered a left hand spin before losing power on both engines at 1,000 feet and consequently stalling. The ensuing crash demolished two houses in Huntington Village killing two civilians and the five crew members. The aircraft was HZ303 a Mk.X, and an immediate investigation was ordered. Squadron Officer M.E Langley was posted in to East Moor and assumed duties of Operations Officer.

Stuttgart was the target for another night bombing mission and eight 429 Squadron crews climbed into their Wimpies shortly before 21.00 hours. All returned to Coltishall except the two early ones, which landed at East Moor,

HE572	Sgt	G De Bussac	HE635	Sgt	J Lancaster	HZ312	S/L	F Holmes
HE414	Sgt	S Bruce	HE429	F/S	R Conroy	HE160	F/S	K Mills
HE382	Sgt	S Hanan	HZ363	Sgt	A Jameson			

Squadron Leader Holmes port engine failed and Sergeant Jamesons aircraft was unable to climb due to severe icing leading to both returning early.

15 April 1943

Flight Lieutenant A.R.H Riley assumed the duties of Station Adjutant East Moor.

Routine air tests and flying training exercises were carried out but no operations were detailed at the station.

16 April 1943

The York Coroner held an inquest and was told that HZ303 was so destroyed in the crash at Huntington that its cause was impossible to determine.

Flight Lieutenant J.Ridley was posted from East Moor to RAF Station Bottesford. A night bombing raid to Mannheim was ordered and East Moor put up thirteen Wellingtons the first of which left the ground at 21.15 hours and all were away by 21.27 hours,

BK162	S/L	F Holmes	HZ354	Sgt	R Ellison	HE635	Sgt	J Lancaster
HZ363	F/S	T Heyes	HE414	Sgt	S Bruce	HE572	Sgt	G De Bussac
HE913	F/S	G Kilburn	HE429	S/L	J Cairns	HE912	F/O	B Rawson
HEl60	Sgt	A Jameson	HE915	F/S	K Mills	HE914	Sgt	J Pendleton
HE593	F/S	R Conroy						

Squadron Leader Holmes and crew failed to return from this operation and nothing was heard from them after leaving base. The aircraft crashed at Soissons.

Also on board was second pilot Sergeant J.R Milne an Aberdonian. Sergeant Ellison returned early and landed at Cottesmore with a u/s starboard engine, while Sergeant Kilburn had similar trouble and returned to East Moor. Sergeant De Bussac and crew were fired on by a Halifax gunner while over the target and were forced to take evasive action. They landed at Manston safely. Flying Officer Rawson landed at Wattisham where he was severely shaken after overshooting the airfield. The aircraft was damaged but the crew were unhurt. Sergeant Pendleton landed at Colerne, and Flight Sergeant Conroy at Manston.

17 April 1943

Sergeant R.E Clark the only Canadian in the crew of the ill fated HZ303 was buried with full military homours at Sutton on Forest in the afternoon. The funeral service was conducted by Flight Lieutenant H.G Lowrey the 429 Squadron Padre and was assisted by Canon Coombs the village Rector. The RAF Regiment provided an escort and six fellow air gunners bore his coffin to the grave. Flight Lieutenant A.P Chipling resumed duty as Flight Commander with 429 Sqd, and Flight Lieutenant A.O Appleby the squadron adjutant was posted out. Work was started on in the stables at Sutton Hall to provide a temporary dark room for the photographic section. A permanent building was under construction on one of the technical sites.

18 April 1943

No operations for the second day. Amongst the numerous postings in were Flight

Lieutenant F.W Ballance-Stewart as S.I.O. and Flight Lieutenant W.L Collins as Station Accounts Officer.

19 April 1943

Another op free day at East Moor.

A new Squadron Gunnery Officer arrived for 429 Squadron in the form of Pilot Officer J.C Garton, and the HF/DF station was opened.

20 April 1943

Sergeant A Jameson and crew were posted out to 142 Squadron, North Africa. Squadron Officer Delius the station Cypher Officer received the latest Type X machine.

429 Squadron returned to Gardening and six crews set out for the Jellyfish fields,

| HE635 F/L | G Pentony | HE414 Sgt | R Ellison | HE572 F/S | G Kilburn |
| HE429 F/S | G Kennedy | HE382 Sgt | S Hanan | HE593 F/S | R Conroy |

After searching unsuccessfully for the target Flight Sergeant Conroy returned to base with all his mines intact.

21 April 1943

On the return flight Sergeant Ellisons Wellington was struck by flak when over the French coast resulting in a crash landing at Exeter. The aircraft was burnt but the crew escaped.The time was 02.55 hours.

No operations were carried out from East Moor.

22 to 25 April 1943

No operations were scheduled for the stations crews.

On the latter date Flight Lieutenant N₉ Carrie was posted in to become Station Adjutant and Flight Lieutenant A.R Riley moved to RCAF Leeming,

26 April 1943

A five day lull in operations came to an end when 429 Squadrons crews formed part of an attacking force of more than 560 dispatched to attack Duisburg in the early hours.

HE912	F/S	G Kilburn	HZ354	F/S	T Heyes	HE572	Sgt	G De Bussac
HZ312	F/L	G Pentony	LN438	Sgt	S Bruce	HE589	Sgt	J Pendleton
MS474	P/O	B Geale	HE382	Sgt	S Hanan	HE737	S/L	J Cairns
HE593	F/S	G Conroy						

Two crews failed to return from this operation, when Squadron Leader Cairns DFC, Flying Officer Pozer and Flight Sergeant Lang survived to become POWs.

The entire crew including second pilot G.K Thompson in Sergeant Hanans were casualties.

27 April 1943

At 01.35 hours the following 429 Squadron crews commenced take off for another Gardening operation and after successfully planting their mines all safely returned to East Moor. The Trefoil fields being their target,

HE312	F/L	G Pentony	HZ363	F/S	T Heyss	HE572	Sgt	De Bussac
HE913	Sgt	S Bruce	HE684	S/L	A Chipling	HE593	F/S	R Conroy

At 11.43 hours AL-V believed to be DF625 crashed on take off at East Moor resulting in a category A accident. The East Moor soccer team were defeated by Cooks of York 10 goals to 3.

A 429 Squadron rigger recalls :

I'd have to say the Padre was a genius to try and compile a record of casualties and also of aircrew personnel who survived 429 Squadrons Wellington period. Quite often he did not get the co-operation of all aircrew members, re-photoraphs and next of kins addresses. I realize that some were not with us long enough to do much more than hoist one pint of ale. After getting some very beat up Wimpies which should have been on the scrap heap, we began to get regularly Wellingtons that had that fresh factory odour, so too often it was a case of losing a brand new aircraft along with its brand new crew of mostly Sergeants. Some of the unfortunates probably hadn't had time to say more than hello to anyone, let alone to dig down into the kit bag for photos usually reserved for the popsies and mature ladies they happened to meet:

On 16 April 1943, the Squadron Leader and his crew left my dispersal for Mannheim. While waiting for take off I stood at the rear of the aircraft. The rear gunner smoked a cigarette, flipping the butt away, he said to me Give me a leg up. I cupped my hands, he put one foot into them and swung up into the rear turret and that was the last time anyone did that for him. He was taking the place of the regular rear gunner, an American, who was lost later with another 429 Squadron crew.

1679 Heavy Conversion Flight

"I was a Canadian pilot flying bombers in World War II, and flew Wellingtons with 115 Squadron from September 1942 - then converted to Stirlings - then to the Lancaster II. I finished my tour of operations in late May 1943 and was immediately posted to Eastmoor in 6 Group to help form 1679 HCF and to instruct on the Lancaster II with which several squadrons in 6 Group were being re-equipped. The Lanc II had the radial Hercules engines.

Our conversion flight was very small - just four Lancs - we were given a few dispersal buttons in one corner of the field - a hut for administration with space for a few offices and lecture rooms - and a few groundcrew under an RAF Flight Sergeant to maintain our aircraft. I and my Flight Engineer were the flying nucleus. Our officer commanding had just finished his second tour of ops with 426 Squadron and the other instructor and his crew had just finished a tour on Wellingtons. Fortunately the Lancaster was simple to fly, no vices, the Hercules engines were the same as in the Wellington and the radio, navigation, gun turrets, bomb sight and so on were also pretty much the same - so the conversion part of our job was mostly familiarisation and getting to know the aircraft.

Looking at my log book I see that most of the entries are circuits and 2 & 3 engine flying including overshoots both day and night. The duration of each flight exercise was 1 hour 10 minutes to 1 hour 30 minutes, as I recall this enabled us to do about four or five landings after which the brakes became too hot for further taxying.
I taught the other two pilots to fly the Lanc - then we shared the instruction of pilots from 408 Squadron and from 426 Squadron. Once the pilots had done a few hours with us and were comfortable with the aircraft, they returned to their home base Linton on Ouse, and finished their further conversion (cross country flights, bombing, air to air, fighter affiliation, night flying) on their own squadron aircraft. I recall giving the first few lectures to navigators, wireless ops, bomb aimers, gunners, imparting such knowledge as I had about the aircraft as it applied to their trade. Thereafter one of the other instructors and his crew took on this chore.

During the period June 3rd to December 13th 1943, I see from my log book that I gave dual instruction to fifty three pilots plus several flights which read Engineers instruction. I have put quotes on the dual because the aircraft did not have dual controls) rather I demonstrated from the left hand seat, then sat in the F/Es jump seat and talked the pilot under instruction around the take off and landing sequence. I see that the CO left in July and I was promoted S/L and put in charge of the flight. In August we went from four to six aircraft.

On December 13th we moved to Wombleton and became C Flight in 1666 HGU) the other flights were Halifaxes.

As this is a brief sketch of the Lancaster II Conversion Flights activity at Eastmoor in the summer of 1943, its history would not be complete without reference to this units short existence there.

In the main flying went well with no major incidents. Our biggest headaches were hot brakes - wearing out the pads as the pilots werc all from twin engined aircraft and had to adjust to the outboard engines. We also struggled with low visibility for night flying as the industrial smoke from the Vale of York edged our way".

28 April 1943

429 Squadron dispatched four crews on a further mining operation this time to the Eglantine fields, take off was around 21.00 hours,

HZ363 S/L   A Chipling
HE635 P/O J Lancaster
HE915 P/O B Geale
HE589 Sgt J Pendleton

Three completed the mission as ordered.

29 April 1943

Pilot Officer Lancaster was unable to locate the target on the above operation and returned to East Moor where at 01.49 hours he overshot the airfield and on to the roadway. The crew were unhurt and the mines were safely removed.

30 April 1943

Flight Lieutenant E.J Strathdee assumed the duties of Squadron Adjutant vice Flight Lieutenant N. Carrie, who had become Station Adjutant East Moor.

Four 429 Squadron officers were promoted to acting ranks, F/L Chipling to Squadron Leader and B.F Rawson, J. Dilworth and F.A Reynolds became Flight Lieutenants.

General:

Station strength - 50 Officers, 153 NCOs, 938 other ranks, total 1,141. Regular training programmes including ground and training flights were carried out from East Moor throughout the month of April. organized parties from 429 Sqd were visiting Bradford on a regular fortnightly basis in pursuiance of the hospitality scheme resulting from the former's adoption by the city.

1 May 1943

Pilot Officer A.W Hill was posted from Linton on Ouse for Armaments duties.

Pilot Officer L.H Fourtie posted from Linton on Ouse for Armaments duties.

Section Officer C.H Maxfield posted from Linton on Ouse as WAAF GD Officer.

Flight Lieutenant A.G Fenn together with Pilot Officers J.J Owens and Pltwood were posted from Linton on Ouse as Flying Control Officers.

3 May 1943

Squadron Leader J.L Savard was posted in to join 429 Squadron from 425 Squadron.

The Station Commander, Wing Commander J.A.P Owen was admitted to hospital.

4 May 1943

Dortmund was the target for the stations crews and 429 Squadron dispatched the following eleven on a night raid involving almost 600 aircraft,

HZ354	F/L	G Pentony	HZ355	Sgt	R Ellison	HE572	Sgt	G De Bussac
HE595	P/O	J Lancaster	HE915	F/S	T Heyes	HE913	F/S	G Kilburn
HE430	F/L	B Rawson	HE429	F/S	G Kennedy	HE593	F/S	R Conroy
HE589	Sgt	J Pendleton	HE423	P/O	B Geale			

Pilot Officer Geale and crew made an early return due to engine trouble after being airborne around 45 minutes. The remainder returned safely after a successful attack.

5 May 1943

A sea search carried out by two 429 Squadron crews proved negative,

HE595	Sgt	G De Bussac	HE915	S/L	A Chipling

6 to 11 May 1943

No operations were scheduled from East Moor.

Flight Lieutenant W.L Marshall was posted in for Admin duties on the 7th. Pilot Officer H.H Woodhead arrived on detached duty from 6 Group for Signals duties on the 8th.
At 07.30 hours on the 10th,the steel framework of the T2 type hanger which was being erected near High Carr Wood, collapsed making the steel useless.

12 May 1943

The Station Commander resumed duty on discharge from hospital.

429 Squadrons largest effort to date, fifteen crews,set out for the Rhur and Duisburg,the first being airborne just before midnight. The centre and the port facilities were severely damaged,

HZ363	F/S	T Heyes	HE865	S/L	A Chipling	HZ354	P/O	J Lancaster
HZ312	F/L	G Pentony	HZ355	Sgt	R Ellison	HE595	Sgt	S Bruce
HE572	Sgt	J Pendleton	HE913	Sgt	A Halstead	HE423	P/O	B Geale
HE429	F/S	G Kennedy	HE430	F/L	B Rawson	HZ470	Sgt	E Eames

MS474 Sgt	L Southwood	HE593 F/S	R Conroy	HE915 F/S	K Mills

Flight Sergeant Mills and Sergeant Southwood made early returns while Pilot Officer Geale and Sergeant Haleteads aircraft were not heard from after leaving East Moor. The latter crew paid the ultimate price and their aircraft crashed at Asten in the Netherlands.

Sergeant Crimmings the air gunner in Pilot Officer Geales crew was killed.

13 May 1943

429 Squadron dispatched twelve Wellingtons in a night raid on Bochum, two of which did not reach the target,

HZ3l2	F/L	G Pentony	HZ363	F/S	T Heyes	HZ354	P/O	J Lancaster
HZ355	Sgt	R Ellison	HE595	Sgt	S Bruce	HE430	F/L	B Rawson
HE915	F/S	K Mills	HE593	F/S	R Conroy	HE684	F/S	G Kennedy
HZ470	Sgt	L Southwood	MS474	Sgt	E Eames	LN439	Sgt	F Windibank

Sergeant Eames made an early return due to intercom failure.

Sergeant Windibank and crew were not heard from after leaving East Moor, their aircraft crashed in the Rhur Valley at Munchen Gladbach killing all except the WOP Sergeant McKinley who was taken prisoner.

14 & 15 May 1943

No operations were called for on either day.

Accounts Officer Flying Officer P.H Morris was posted in from Whitchurch Heath. on the second day.

16 May 1943

Five crews from 429 Squadron set out to lay mines on Nectarine 1 fields, all five were aiborne between 01.25 and

01.29 hours. Sergeant A Floren was down again by 03.24 with port engine trouble and a u/s rear turret.

HZ354	Sgt	G Clark
HZ355	Sgt	R Murray
HE915	Sgt	H Floren
HE684	P/O	J Lown
HE593	Sgt	R McIntyre

A satisfactory operation.

17 May 1943

The Station Adjutant Flight Lieutenant N. Carrie was posted to RCAF Station

Linton on Ouse and in the abscence of a replacement the duties were carried out by Flight Lieutenant W.L Marshall and Warrant Officer A. Brown.

Fig 9. Flying Officer Peter Dunger(RAF) Navigator 429 Sqd. FTR. From his first operation, May 13th. 1943 (target Duisburg). Photo E. Lapham.

East Moor was still without any operational commitments.

Pilot Officer Pltwood arrived for Flying Control duties and Pilot Officer J. Garton was promoted to Flight Lieutenant.

21 May 1943

A nucleus of personnel arrived at East Moor from Dishforth to form No.1679 HCF

Heavy Conversion Flight. The Officer in charge was Flight Lieutenant A Avant DFC, who had just completed his tour of operations with 115 Squadron.

Another visit to the Nectarine 1 fields by seven crews from 429 Squadron. Only two managed to penetrate the adverse weather conditions in the target area, the rest returned their mines to East Moor.

HZ354	Sgt	G Clark	HZ312	Sgt	R Murray	HZ355	Sgt	W Trofenenko
HE684	P/O	J Lown	HE915	Sgt	H Floren	HF515	P/O	R Davies
HE429	Sgt	H Wilton						

22 May 1943

A Wellington X, HE177 and coded NA-G overshot East Moor crossed the Strensall Road, losing the starboard undercarriage in the process, and ended at right angles to the runway in the fields of Low Carr Farm. Based at RCAF Station Dalton the 428 Squadron crew were returning from a minelaying operation in the Frisian Islands Nectarine fields on the 21st.
No operations were carried out from East Moor.

No.1679 HCF was formed at East Moor to provide crew conversion to Lancaster IIs.

23 May 1943

Just after 05.40 hours three 429 Squadron crews set out on a sea search from which they returned after four hours without any results.

HE593	Sgt	H Wilton	HZ470	Sgt	E Starr	HZ355	Sgt	D Smalley

At 22.55 hours the first of fourteen 429 Squadron Wellingtons rose from the East Moor runway as part of a total force of more than 820 aircraft to attack Dortmund,

HE865	Sgt	R Murray	HZ354	Sgt	G Clark	HZ363	F/S	T Heyes
HZ312	F/S	K Mills	HZ355	Sgt	R Ellison	HE595	Sgt	E Eames
HF514	Sgt	G De Bussac	HZ471	P/O	E Richmond	HE429	F/S	G Kennedy
HE430	F/L	B Rawson	HE684	P/O	J Lown	HZ470	Sgt	J Pendleton
HF515	Sgt	L Southwood	HE593	Sgt	H Floren			

Sergeants Pendleton and Southwood returned early with engine trouble,the remainder had a successful operation and large areas of Dortmund were devastated.

24 May 1943

A further sea search was carried out by three crews from 429 Squadron who returned safely but without result,

HE429	P/O	J Lancaster	HE595	Sgt	S Bruce	HE915	P/O	H Elliot

Take off was around 12.40 hours all landing around three hours later.

25 May 1943

Dusseldorf was the target for fourteen crews from 429 Squadron and take off from East Moor commenced at 23.23 hours. From a total force of more than 750 aircraft that took part in the operation all fourteen returned safely to East Moor,

HE865	S/L	A Chipling	HZ354	Sgt	G Clark	HZ363	Sgt	W Trofanenki
HZ312	F/S	R Ellison	HE865	Sgt	R Murray	HF514	Sgt	D Smalley
HF541	F/O	E Richmond	HE429	P/O	R Davies	HE430	F/L	B Raweon
HE684	P/O	J Lown	HE915	Sgt	H Floren	HZ470	Sgt	E Eames
lHF542	Sgt	L Southwood	HE593	Sgt	R McIntyre		

Sergeant Murrays aircraft was hit by flak which damaged the starboard engine nacelle and burst the tyre resulting in a one wheel landing on return. Not a particularly successful operation, the crews reported much of the bombing as scattered.

26 May 1943

Seems to have been a quiet day at East Moor with no operations and very little else recorded.

27 May 1943

Further numbers of personnel arrived at East Moor from Dishforth to join the ranks of 1679 Heavy Conversion Flight. Initially the flight received four Lancaster IIs and these were allocated dispersals at the northern end of the airfield, and an administration hut and lecture room. The small ground crew was under the command of an RAF NCO while the flying nucleous consisted of Flight Lieutenant A Avant DFC and his Flight Engineer, Sergeant Hargreaves.

429 Squadron took part in a night attack on Essen when only five of the seven aircraft dispatched from East Moor reached the target,

HE865	P/O	J Lancaster	HZ312	Sgt	S Bruce	HZ355	F/S	R Ellison
HF542	Sgt	J Pendleton	HZ363	F/S	G Kennedy	HE992	Sgt	L Southwood
HE915	F/S	K Mills					

Early returns were made by Sergeant Pendleton with control problems and a spinning gyro and Flight Sergeant Kennedy was unable to catch up after a late take off. The remainder returned safely from the operation.

28 May 1943

A successful Gardening operation was carried out by six crews from 429 Sqd who planted their vegetables in the Jellyfish fields at night before returning safely to East Moor,

HZ363	S/L	A Chipling	HZ312	Sgt	R Murray	HZ354	Sgt	G De Bussac
HE429	F/S	G Kennedy	HE593	Sgt	J Pendleton	HE684	Sgt	E Eames

29 May 1943

While Bomber Command considered an attack by more than 700 aircraft against Wuppertal in the Rhur a successful one, 429 Squadron was not so fortunate. Of the eleven crews dispatched from East Moor one failed to return and three aborted the mission,

HE430	F/L	G Pentony	HE993	Sgt	D Smalley	HZ354	F/S	T Heyss
HZ355	F/S	E Champion	HZ471	F/O	E Richmond	HE684	Sgt	E Star
HF542	P/O	R Davies	HE992	Sgt	H Floren	HE915	F/S	K Mills
HE914	Sgt	H Wilton	HE595	Sgt	L Southwood		

Fig 10. Corporal Marc Blais. 429 Sqd. Equipment section. Photo M. Blais

Sadly, Flying Officer Richmond and crew were not heard from after leaving the station and were believed to be lost at sea.

Pilot Officer Davies returned early with oxygen trouble and Flight Sergeant Mills with starboard engine problem.

Sergeant Smalley was unable to maintain height and aborted the operation.

30 May 1943

Flight Lieutenant A.F Avant, DFC and Flight Sergeant J Hargreaves assumed duties as the only instructors to date with 1679 HCF. The former officer took command of the Flight pending the arrival of Squadron Leader S.W Parker.

1 June 1943

The Station Commander Wing Commander J.A.P Owen, was officially posted to 3A.F.U station and relinquished command of 429 Squadron. He was succeeded in the latter post by Wing Commander J.L Savard the ex 425 Squadron Leader.

Intelligence Officer Flying Officer J. Provost posted in from Bournemouth.

2 June 1943

The third consecutive day without operations at East Moor.
Squadron Leader Parker, DFC arrived at East Moor and assumed command of 1679 Heavy Conversion Flight having completed two tours.

From 426 Squadron the HCF received instructors Flying Officer V. Rolfe, DFC, Pilot Officer J.J MeGavock, Pilot Officer G. Kerr and Pilot Officer T. Newman, as Pilot, Navigator, Signals Leader and Gunnery Leader respectively.

3 June 1943

No.1679 HCF commenced flying training with Flight Lieutenant Avant converting Squadron Leader Parker and Flying Officer McGavock to the Lancaster II.
Four crews from 429 Squadron successfully completed a mining operation on the Jellyfish fields before returning safely to East Moor,

| HE430 | Sgt | E Eames | HE595 | F/S | R Conroy | HZ355 | F/S | P Ellison |
| HE865 | Sgt | S Bruce | | | | | | |

Flight Sergeant Ellison encountered considerable flak and experienced some navigation problems.The four were airborne before 22.30 hours returning around 04.30   hours on the 4 th.

4 June 1943

Wing Commander J.C Savard assumed command of RCAF Station East Moor, vice Wing Commander J.A.P Owen who was posted out to No.3 AFU at Bobbington.

Pilot Officer H.H Woodhead the Signals Officer was posted out to RCAF Station Linton on Ouse.

No operations were scheduled at East Moor.

1679 HCFs training was going ahead and the first pupils for conversion to the Lancaster II were drawn from 408 and 426 Squadrons at nearby Linton on Ouse.

5 to 10 June 1943

A break of seven days without any operations from the station.

Flying training programmes were carried out by 429 Squadron and 1679 heavy Conversion Flight, the latter being largely involved in circuits and bumps, and two and three engined flying together with overshoots.

Flying Officer G.F Ruddock joined 1679 HCF and assumed the duties of Bombing Leader. The ex 426 Squadron officer had completed his tour.

11 June 1943

Operations were resumed from the station with 429 Squadron participating in a heavy and successful attack on Dusseldorf by more than 780 aircraft,

HE865	F/L	G Pentony	HE993	Sgt	D Smalley	HZ354	P/O	J Lancaster
HZ363	P/O	H Elliott	HZ312	W/C	J Savard	HZ355	F/S	P Ellison
HF541	Sgt	S Bruce	HF514	F/L	P Brinton	HE429	F/S	G Kennedy
HF542	P/O	P Davies	HE430	F/L	B Rawson	HE992	Sgt	D Smith
HE915	W/O	K Mills	HE470	Sgt	E Eames	MS494	Sgt	H Wilton
HF515	Sgt	L Southwood	HE593	F/S	P Conroy	HE981	Sgt	E Willey

This was the squadrons record number of aircraft put up on an operation to date and three were lost on a night when command lost ten Wellingtons.

Nothing was heard from Pilot Officer Davies or Flight Sergeants Conroy and Ellison after take off.

P/O Davies and crew crashed at Wisch, Flight Sergeant Ellison South West of Ophoven. Those killed included all F/S Conroys crew except himself who evaded, F/S Ellison, Pilot Officer Davies and his gunner Sgt,A. McLachlan. Sergeant Bruce got as far as the Dutch coast when his starboard engine stopped forcing an early return and a landing at Great Ashford after jettisoning the bomb load.

12 June 1943

Engineering Officer Flight Lieutenant A.S Summers of No. 6 Group was attached to RCAF Station East Moor.

Four crews from 429 Squadron set out shortly before midnight to lay mines on the Nectarine fields. Only one was successful but all returned safely,

HZ312	F/L	G Pentony	HE915	F/S	K Mills	HE865	P/O	J Lancaster
HZ363	F/S	T Heyes						

Flight Sergeant Mills and crew planted their mines as ordered, the remainder were returned to station.

Flight Lieutenant Pentony found the Gee equipment u/s and after circling East Moor for ten minutes he landed to have it repaired. By that time it was considered too late to allow him to take off again.

13 June 1943

And yet another sea mining operation for the Wellingtons of 429 Squadron. Six aircraft were dispatched at approximately one minute intervals commencing at 22.15   hours and set course for the Jellyfish fields off Brest,

HE865	Sgt	E Willey	HZ363	F/S	T Heyes	HZ312	F/L	C Pentony
HF515	Sgt	E Eames	HE992	Sgt	H Floren	HE429	F/S	C Kennedy

All planted their vegetables as ordered before returning safely to station.

14 June 1943

Just after midday five crews from 429 Squadron carried out a fruitless sea search,

HZ519 Sgt	D Murray	HZ354 F/S	L O'Leary	HF514 Sgt	D Smith
HF9O1 Sgt	F Hingston	HE993 Sgt	D Smalley		

15 June 1943

Flight Lieutenant G. Carton the 429 Squadron Gunnery Leader was posted to 434 Squadron and Squadron Leader D.T French was posted in from 426 Squadron for Flying duties.

16 June 1943

Another day without any operations from the station.
A 429 Squadron navigator recalls .

"On 21 June 1943, the day we were to bomb Krefeld, the previous week had been a Bombs for Britain National Savings Week, when the villagers had been persuaded to buy stamps, and, ideally, sacrifice them by sticking them on bombs for theoretical delivery by the Squadron. As part of this publicity stunt arrangements had been made to accommodate the Press photographers on 21st June to take publicity pictures before take off. This was a unique occurrence because normally our aircraft were fuelled and bombed-up at dispersal where we joined it before taxiing direct to the runway for take off. On this occasion we were instructed to proceed to the out of use runway on completion of the usual pre-op air test instead of the dispersal and that evening were taken to the aircraft now in line abreast for eventual taxiing in turn from line astern for take off. We were not amused and there was much superstitious muttering about such arrangements, particularly as it in fact kept us hanging about around the aircraft in place of our usual board, checks, taxi, take off, with no nonsense. Who can say we were wrong ? We lost four aeroplanes that night the heaviest loss ever in one go, seventeen men died including the brand new Squadron Commander, I was one of the three survivors".

A 426 Squadron Wellington X, HE916, OW-K made a visit to East Moor ferrying aircrew from Dishforth for conversion training with 1679 HCF.

East Moor received a new Electrical Engineering Officer, Pilot Officer W.Worsnop and a new Station Admin. Officer, Flight Lieutenant W.L Marshall vice Squadron Leader R.G Bradbury who was posted to Marston Moore

Flying Control gained Pilot Officer N.C Robertson from 26 OTU.

17 June 1943

Still no operations called for at East Moor.

Flying training carried out by 1679 HCF and 429 Squadron,

Intelligence Officer, Pilot Officer L.B Scott posted in from Topcliffe.

18 June 1943

Group Captain H.M Carscallen assumed command of RCAF Station East Moor vice Wing Commander A.L Savard the 429 Squadron Commander. The former officer had been the Squadron Commander of 424 Squadron at RCAF Leeming.

19 June 1943

The sixth operation free day at the station.

Flying Officer A.M Crawford arrived from 6 Group for Signals Officer duties.

20 June 1943

And a further respite from operations for the stations personnel.

Flight Lieutenant Summers appointed Officers Mess PMC vice Squadron Leader Ballance-Stewart. Station Warrant Officer W.R Hard was appointed Sergeants Mess Chairman vice Warrant Officer R.G Morgan,

21 June 1943

A seven day break from operations ended with 429 Squadron being called upon to detail crews for a night attack on Krefeld in the industrial Rhur, when a total force of over 700 aircraft carried out a successful attack,

HE865	S/L	A Chipling	HE993	F/S	D OLeary	HF515 F/S	L Kennedy
HZ354	P/O	J Lancaster	HE35O	Sgt	G Clark	HZ312 F/S	T Heyes
HF457	Sgt	R Murray	HF541	Sgt	D Smith	HE992 W/O	W Sneath
HZ519	Sgt	E Star	HZ517	P/O	G De Bussac	HE430 F/L	B Rawson
HE981	F/O	J Lown	HE915	S/L	D French	MS474 P/O	K Johnston
HZ520	Sgt	E Eames					

Of the sixteen crews dispatched, three made early returns to East Moor, while nothing was heard from a further four after take off

Engine troubles forced the crews of Warrant Officer Sneath and Sergeants Smith and OLeary to abort the operation. The German night fighters claimed four Wellingtons from 429 Squadron, Sergeant Eames and crew crashed at Bergeyk killing Flying Officer Mime and Sergeant Holmes. Flying Officer Lapham, Sergeants Eames and Wright became POWs. Sergeant Starr's aircraft crashed between Breda and Roosendaal with the loss of all on board.

The crews of Pilot Officer Lown and De Bussac met the same fate, the formers aircraft is believed to have crashed at Stavenisse and Pilot Officer De Bussacs near Neerkent.

22 June 1943

Two further crews were lost from East Moor making a total of six in a little over 24 hours with the attack on the Steelhead area of Mullheim,

HZ312	W/C	J Savard	HE865	F/O	J Bowen	HE993 Sgt	R Murray
HZ354	F/S	T Heyss	HF457	W/O	W Sneath	HF514 Sgt	D Smith
HF515	Sgt	J Pendleton	HE430	F/L	B Rawson	HE365 F/L	R Brinton
HE915	S/L	D French	HE595	F/S	G Kennedy	HE992 P/O	K Johnston

Wing Commander Savard and crew paid the ultimate price when their aircraft was shot down and crashed in the Nijmegen area.

Only Pilot Officers Clarke and Drummond-Hay survived from Warrant Officer Sneaths crew which crashed near Hasselt, both became POWs.

Sergeant Pendleton aborted with engine trouble and Pilot Officer Johnston with intercom failure and a frost bitten rear gunner.

Earlier in the day an order had been received at East Moor announcing the award of the DFC to Wing Commander Savard.

23 June 1943

An unsuccessful sea search was carried out by four crews from 429 Squadron who took off around 08.56 hours returning just before 13.00,

HE865	F/L	G Pentony	HE915	F/L	P Brinton	HE992 F/S	L OLeary
HF514	Sgt	H Floren					

All returned safely to East Moor.

24 June 1943

429 Squadron dispatched the following fourteen crews to join more than 600 others for an attack on Wuppertal when sadly a further squadron crew was lost,

HE865	F/O	J Bowen	HE993	F/L	G Pentony	HE350	Sgt	D Smith
HE365	P/O	J Lancaster	HF514	Sgt	P Murray	HF541	F/S	T Heyes
JA111	Sgt	E Willey	HZ521	F/S	L OLeary	HE915	Sgt	G Clark
HF495	F/S	G Kennedy	LN281	P/O	K Johnston	HE430	Sgt	J Pendleton
HE992	Sgt	H Floren	MS474	Sgt	L Southwood			

Nothing was heard from Flight Sergeant OLeary and crew after take off and the entire crew was lost when the Wellington crashed in the Heverlee area. Sergeant Willeys crew suffered a hang up and were unable to bomb the target, it was later jettisoned manually.

Sergeant Southwoods aircraft developed engine trouble,turned back, and the crew bombed the runways of Haamsed airfield.

Engine troubles forced the early returns of Pilot Officer Lancaster and Sergeant Clark.

25 June 1943

At 03.54 hours Pilot Officer Johnston and crew crashed on landing at East Moor, their aircraft had suffered a burst tyre on touch down, damaging both props starboard wing and bomb doors, ex Wuppertal, Gelsenkirchen was the target for five 429 Squadron crews in a night attack when take off commenced at 23.35 hours,

HF495	Sgt	D Smith	HE365	Sgt	G Clark	HF514	Sgt	J Pendleton
HE992	Sgt	H Floren	MS474	Sgt	L Southwood			

Sergeant Smith and crew were attacked and set on fire by a Me110 injuring both Flight Sergeant Abbott and Sergeant Nelson. A steep dive resulted in putting the fire out but the aircraft crashed on landing at Hardwick at 04.50 hrs on the 26th.

The crew escaped further injury.The remainder returned safely to East Moor.

26 June 1943

Three of the four 429 Squadron crews sent to lay mines in the Jellyfish fields were successful, the fourth returned without finding the target.

HE865	S/L	A Chipling	HF541	Sgt	S Bruce	HF600	S/L	D French
HF5l4	Sgt	R Murray						

All returned safely, Sergeant Bruce with his mines still on board.

27 June 1943

No operations were carried out from East Moor.

Flying training by 429 Squadron and 1679 HCF continued, the latter engaged in two and three engined flying practice for the crews being converted to the Lancaster II.

28 June 1943

Wing Commander J.A Piddington was posted in to East Moor and assumed command of 429 Squadron.

Twelve Wellingtons from 429 Squadron set out from the station to participate in an attack on Cologne in which more than 600 aircraft were involved. This was another successful raid in the Battle of the Rhur. Take off commenced at 23.10 hours and all were down again by 04.39 on the 29th,

HF541	F/O	J Bowen	HZ992	Sgt	H Floren	HF600	F/O	H Malone
HE430	Sgt	C Jones	HF514	Sgt	F Hingston	HE915	F/S	G Kennedy
MS474	P/O	K Johnston	JA111	Sgt	L Southwood	HE993	F/L	G Pentony
HE350	Sgt	F Turcotte	HE991	Sgt	S Bruce	HE865	Sgt	A Willey

Sergeant Bruce was down again within fifty minutes with a u/s starboard engine, and at 02.00 Sergeant Hingston returned with intercom trouble.

Some flak damage was inflicted on the aircraft of Sergeants Floren and Turcotte.

29 & 30 June 1943

Were both operation free days at East Moor, but local flying was noted with HE572 and HE589.

On the former day, No.4313 A.A Flight of the RAF Regiment was disbanded at East Moor and was replaced by No.2799.

1 July 1943

Information was received at East Moor that Sergeant Burini, Sergeant Kerr and Sergeant Aplin missing from 429 Squadrons operation on 29/30 March were Missing   believed killed in action.   No operations for the third day.

2 July 1943

Pilot Officer T.H Lister a Flying Control Officer from Linton on Ouse, took up duties at East Moor.

The Jellyfish fields were the target for a minelaying operation by four crews from 429 Squadron, all of whom returned safely after a successful mission,

JA114	S/L	A Chipling	HE991	Sgt	S Bruce	HE915	W/O	K Mills
HE992	Sgt	H Floren						

3 July 1943

At 02.45 hours and on returning from the above operation, HE992 suffered a burst starboard tyre, undercarriage collapse and both propellers were broken. Warrant Officer Mills ran short of fuel on the return flight and was forced to land at Lynham.

A Linton on Ouse Intelligence Officer, Flight Lieutenant C.H Brown was posted in to East Moor, and Flight Lieutenant Gurney out to No.4 Group.

Flight Lieutenant F.W Hall took over as Entertainments Officer. Once again more than 600 aircraft visited the Rhur, and East Moor contributed a detail of thirteen, their target Cologne. Of the thirteen 429 Squadron crews dispatched two made early returns and a third one was lost,

HE915	P/O	K Johnston	HF515	Sgt	L Southwood	HE803	Sgt	C Jones
HE802	Sgt	J Pendleton	JA111	Sgt	F Hingston	LN296	F/L	A Brinton
HF600	S/L	D French	HF541	F/O	J Bowen	HE365	Sgt	C Clark
HF514	Sgt	R Murray	HE993	Sgt	A Willey	HE350	P/O	J Lancaster
JA114	Sgt	S Bruce						

Nothing was heard from Flight Lieutenant Brinton and crew after take off and their aircraft crashed at Bergen op Zoom. The bomb aimer Sergeant Rothera died on this operation after two previous escapes by parachute and dinghy. Flight Lieutenant Reynolds the WOP was also lost.

Sergeant Pendleton landed within the hour after fire broke out in the aircraft. Squadron Leader French returned early with intercom trouble, and Sergeant Clark with engine trouble. The remainder were down again by 04.46 hours on the 4th. Sergeant Hingston and crew landed at Pocklington

4 & 5 July 1943

There were no operations scheduled at East Moor.

JAlll returned from Pocklington on the 4th and the Lancasters of 1679 HCF were seen to be very active on both days.

Flying training exercises were carried out by 429 Squadron.

6 July 1943

429 Squadron were in to gardening once again with four crews attempting the planting their vegetables in the Jellyfish fields, before returning safely to East Moor,

HE991	Sgt	G Clark	HE365	Sgt	E Willey	HF600	F/L	B Rawson
HF515	W/O	K Mills			

Accurate flak from a ship found Flight Lieutenant Rawsons Wellington,shooting away the hydraulic jacks and damaging the bomb doors. he was unable to locate the garden and returned his vegetables to station along with Warrant Officer Mills who was similarly frustrated.

7 to 11 July 1943

Five days without any operations from the station,

On the 10th news was received to the effect that Pilot Officer Geale and crew were classified missing - believed killed in action they had failed to return on May 12/13.

On the brighter side,Flight Sergeant G.H Murray missing since 27 March 45 had returned safely to the United Kingdom. He was the bomb aimer in Flying Officer Foxs crew. He had arrived on 28 June after three months abscence.

Flight Lieutenant L R Freeman was attached to RCAF Topcliffe and 1659 HCU.

12 July 1943

And yet another mining operation was carried out from East Moor and again the target was the Jellyfish fields. Six crews from 429 Squadron departed around 23.30   hours and after a successful mission all were safely down again by 06.16,

HE915	F/O	H Malone	HE350	Sgt	L Southwood	HE365	Sgt	G Clark
HF514	Sgt	R Murray	HF541	Sgt	F Turcotte	JA115	Sgt	S Bruce

13 July 1943

Flight Lieutenant W.M Connors assumed Adjutant duties at East Moor on attatchment from Linton on Ouse.

The popular Protestant Padre, Flight Lieutenant H. Lowrey was posted out. Aachen was the target for a bombing raid by twelve crews from 429 Squadron led by their new Commanding Officer who lifted his Wellington off East Moor's runway at 23.55 hours,

JA114	W/C	J Piddington	HE993	F/L	G Pentony	HE350	Sgt	D Smith
HE991	Sgt	G Clark	HF514	Sgt	R Murray	HF541	Sgt	F Turcotte
JA115	F/L	B Rawson	JA111	Sgt	F Hingston	HF515	F/O	H Malone
HE803	Sgt	H Mitchell	JA112	Sgt	J Fendleton	JA113	Sgt	L Southwood

Sergeant Southwood was forced to return early with engine trouble. The remainder attacked and returned safely.

14 July 1943

Two East Moor Flying Control Officers were posted out to No.8 PFF at Wyton, Flying Officers Pitwood and Fenn. A new Senior Flying Control Officer, Flight Lieutenant M.D Louches arrived from RCAF Station Topcliffe, and from Wyton came Flying Officer C.J Lewis.

15 to 23 July 1943

Completed a ten day break from operations at East Moor.

Accounts Officer, Flight Lieutenant Collins left for a post with Headquarters Bomber Command.

Considerable local flying was witnessed during this period and two 429 Squadron

Wellingtons were seen over the bombing range at Strensall.

On the 16th JA119 a Wellington X broke up and crashed approximately one and a half miles west of Malton.

A combination of bad weather and a shortage of Lancaster IIs at East Moor hampered the conversion of 426 Squadron by 1679 HCF, and consequently this was not completed during July as planned.

Information was received via Air Ministry that the American air gunner, Sergeant J. Burns lost on 11/12 June, had been classified Missing - believed killed in action

24 July 1943

429 Squadron took part in a total force of almost 800 aircraft in what was regarded as the first attack in the so called Battle of Hamburg. The following twelve crews left East Moor in a night raid from which all returned safely,

JA114	S/L	A Chipling	HE993	F/L	G Pentony	HE991	Sgt	S Bruce
JA112	W/O	J Piddington	HE365	Sgt	S Kelso	JA111	Sgt	G Clark
HE915	W/O	K Mills	HE803	P/O	K Johnston	JA115	Sgt	L Southwood
HF600	F/O	H Malone	HF515	Sgt	W Tighe	HZ482	Sgt	F Hingston

Sergeant Bruce aborted the mission with engine trouble.

25 July 1943

It was back to the Rhur and an attack on Essen in which the Krupps works was badly damaged. East Moor crews from 429 Squadron commenced take off at 22.30 hours and with one exception all returned safely,

JA114	S/L	A Chipling	JA115	F/L	B Rawson	HF600	F/O	H Malone
HE915	W/O	K Mills	HE803	P/O	K Johnston	HF515	Sgt	L Southwood
HZ482	Sgt	S Bruce	HE993	F/L	C Pentony	JA112	Sgt	C Hall
HE350	Sgt	D Smith	HE365	Sgt	S Kelso			

Sadly Pilot Officer Johnston and crew failed to return from this operation and nothing was heard from them after leaving East Moor. Their aircraft crashed at Tilb erg.

Sergeant Smith returned early with Gee and W/T trouble and overshot on landing at 00,37 hours on the 26th.

26 July 1943

A day without any operational commitment at the station.

27 July 1943

429 Squadron mounted two operations, one bombing and one mining involving fifteen Wellingtons. The bombing raid against hamburg got under way at 22.28 hrs led by the Squadron Commander,

JA114 W/C	J Piddington	HE993 F/L	G Pentony	JA113 Sgt	S Bruce
JA111 F/O	J Bowen	HF600 S/L	D French	HF541 Sgt	W Tighe
HF514 Sgt	F Hingston	JA112 F/O	H Malone	HZ482 Sgt	J Pendleton

Wing Commander Piddington and crew were shot down over Hamburg by a night fighter killing Pilot Officers Farquhar and Renton.

Flight Lieutenant Pentony and Sergeant Tighe aborted the mission with a u/s starboard engine and u/s Gee equipment respectively.

At 22.39 hours, the first of the Gardeners took off bound for the Eglantine fields,

JA115 F/L	B Rawson	HF515 Sgt	L Southwood	HE915 W/O	K Mills
HE350 Sgt	M Smith	HE365 Sgt	S Kelso	HE991 Sgt	C Hall

Sergeant Kelso was unable to locate the target area and brought his mines back, while Sergeant Smith, due to a hang up was only able to release one. All six crews returned safely.

28 July 1943

Was a day free from operational commitment at East Moor.

29July1943

Another trip to Hamburg for 429 Squadron when the following thirteen crews set out on a night raid from which all returned safely,

JA115 F/L	B Rawson	HF600 S/L	D French	HF541 Sgt	W Tighe
HF514 Sgt	F Hingston	HE915 W/O	K Mills	HZ482 Sgt	J Pendleton
HF515 Sgt	L Southwood	HE801 F/O	H Malone	HE993 F/L	C Pentony
JA113 Sgt	D Smith	JA112 Sgt	C Hall	HE991 Sgt	S Kelso
HE365 F/O	J Bowen				

The guns in Sergeant Pendleton's Wellington were found to be u/s forcing his early return.

30 July 1943

Wing Commander J.D Pattison arrived at East Moor. Holder of the DFC,he was to take command of 429 Squadron.

information was received at the station to say that Flying Officer Lapham, Flight Sergeant Eames and Sergeant Wright were POWs and that Flight Sergeant Holmes and Flying Officer Milne were dead, The crew failed to return on 22/6/43.

31 July 1943

No operations were scheduled at the station.

Average aircraft strength on 429 Squadron during July was 19 Wellington Mk X.

1679 HCF were believed to have eight Lancaster Mk II'S on strength.

Numerous concert parties had entertained the station personnel during the month and the station cinema was functioning on a regular basis.

1 August 1943

Information was received at East Moor to the effect that Sergeant MacLachlan, and Pilot Officer Davies, missing since June 11/12 had been classified Missing believed killed in action.

No operations were carried out at East Moor.

2 August 1943

Ten Wellingtons left East Moors runways shortly before midnight on what was 429 Squadrons last bombing operation from the station. The target was again Hamburg and eight crews attacked before returning safely,

HE993	F/L	G Pentony	HE350	Sgt	D Smith	JA113	Sgt	G Clark
HE991	Sgt	S Kelso	HF541	Sgt	W Tighe	HF600	F/O	H Malone
HF514	Sgt	F Hingston	HZ482	Sgt	H Mitchell	HF515	Sgt	L Southwood
JA115	Sgt	R Murray					

The crews experienced severe icing conditions and electrical storms making it difficult to identify the target or to observe their results.

Flying Officer Malones aircraft developed engine trouble and on return he put down at Swanton Morley.

Sergeant Hingstons aircraft received flak damage to fuselage and tailplane. Sergeants Smith and Clark made early returns due to icing and engine trouble respectively, the latter landed at Leconfield.

All declared it an unsatisfactory trip.

3 August 1943

Squadron Leader D.T French and crew left East Moor for RCAF Station Croft and 1664 HCU to convert to the Halifax.

429 Squadrons last operation from East Moor was a mining one when six crews were detailed to target the Beeches fields. Five planted their vegetables as ordered and Sergeant Tighe was unable to locate the target area and brought his mines back,

LN444	S/L	A Chipling	HE993	Sgt	P Murray	HE350	Sgt	D Smith
LN448	Sgt	W Tighe	HE915	Sgt	H Mitchell	HF515	Sgt	L Southwood

5 & 6 August 1943

No operations were scheduled at East Moor.

Information was received at the station that Pilot Officer G.H De Bussac, Flying Officer W.A Follows, Pilot Officer M.B Spence, Flight Sergeant G.D Coe and Sergeant B.E Palmatier had been reclassified Missing - believed killed in action.

7 August 1943

No operations were scheduled at East Moor.

In view of 429 Squadrons impending move to RCAF Station Leeming, a farewell dance was held in the Officers Mess at Sutton Hall. Officers on the strength of East Moor Station also attended.

8 August 1943

No operations were carried out from the station, and it was the Sergeants turn to celebrate their departure. Their Mess was the scene of a farewell party.

9 August 1943

information was received at East Moor to the effect that Flight Sergeant H.V Holmes had been classified as Missing believed killed in action and that Flying Officer E.F Lapham had been reclassified as Prisoner of War.

An all service cast staged a concert in the station cinema and was followed by an airmans dance and the Station Orchestra played.

11 August 1943

429 Squadrons advance party of thirty five men under the command of Flight Lieutenant Dilworth left East Moor by road transport at 10.00 hours. This was the beginning of the squadrons move to RCAF Station Leeming.

12 August 1943

Flight Lieutenaant G Pentony headed the main party of 429 Squadron from East Moor to Leeming by bus departing at 10.00 hours.

13 August 1943

Information was received at East Moor that Sergeants D.I Havard, A.E Atkinson, F.R Windibank and W.J Reid had been classified Missing - believed killed in action.

Flying Officer Lister was posted from East Moor to Flying Control at Tholthorpe.

14 August 1943

Bomb aimer,Flying Officer G. Jarvis was posted out to 432 Squadron at Skipton.

Pilot Officer L.B Scott and Flight Lieutenant Brown, Intelligence Officers were posted out to RCAF Linton on Ouse and RCAF Thoithorpe respectively.

16 August 1943

The first section of 429 Squadrons rear party travelled by road from East Moor to RCAF Leeming.

Eight aircrews from 429 Squadron proceeded to Topcliffe and 1659 HCU for conversion training on the Halifax, the skippers were Squadron Leader A.Chipling., Flight Lieutenant B.F Pawson, Flying Officers H. Malone and J, Bowen, Flight Sergeant G. Hall, Sergeants F.W Hingston, S.R Kelso and H. Mitchell. No.1679 HCF was now the only flying unit left at East Moor.

18 August 1943

Pilot Officer Fitzgerald led the remainder of 429 Squadrons rear party from East Moor to RCAF Leeming thus completing the movement order. Information was received that Flight Sergeant E.A Eames had been reclassified to Prisoner of War.

Two Lancaster II crews each received fifteen minutes fighter affilliation experience in the afternoon. 1679 HCF had secured a Spitfire for their first exercise of that type from the AFNU at RCAF Dalton.

19 August 1943

Air Ministry notified the station that Sergeant J.P OReilly had been classified Missing - believed killed in action

22 August 1943

Flight Lieutenant J.G McNeill was appointed Chief Flying Instructor with 1679 HCF vice Flight Lieutenant A. Avant DFC who took over as Chief Ground Instructor.

The former officer had just completed his tour with 426 Squadron.

General:

After many months of intensive operations, East Moor Station was non operational from 12 August to 18 September 1943, during the transitional period of 429 Sqds departure and the take over by 432 Squadron.

429 Squadron Aircrew at East Moor

Role	Number	Rank	Name	Number	Rank	Name
Pilot	NZ415300	F/O	I.S Johnson	AU5405771	Sgt	L. Rogers
Navigator	1095177	Sgt	C. Rissingham	1235336	Sgt	C. Davies
Bomb Aimer	120887	P/O	I.N.Sturton	1414771	Sgt	D. Lewis
WOP/AG	1290666	Sgt	W.G Dymick	1376825	Sgt	A.G. Allen
Air Gunner	1350310	Sgt	J. Stuart	1314288	Sgt	G. Amos
Pilot	R118059	Sgt	J.L.Black	R55965	F/S	R.F Conroy
Navigator	J15235	F/L	C. Campbell	R79393	F/S	E. Bell
Bomb Aimer	1387043	Sgt	P. Rothera	R104206	Sgt	D.R Densmore
WOP/AG	126387	P/O	F.M Bartlett	R105521	F/S	G.A Nelson
Air Gunner	751750	F/S	W.D Billington	R144158	Sgt	J. Burns
Pilot	1387125	Sgt	K.A Holbeck	123109	F/O	G. Fox
Navigator	1501159	Sgt	R.P Parry	1235043	Sgt	A.A Skelly
Bomb Aimer	124313	P/O	D.J Cartwright	1082668	Sgt	Murray
WOP/AG	1292990	Sgt	J.E Hayden	126739	P/O	P.S Bastian
Air Gunner	117954	Sgt	Tremblay	1108414	Sgt	J.M Murray
Pilot		Sgt	E. Willey	1379057	Sgt	K.A Burini
Navigator		Sgt	P.M Vann	1314645	Sgt	W.G Aplin
Bomb Aimer		Sgt	S.B Tucker	1378669	Sgt	G.W Kerr
WOP/AG	1267261	Sgt	R.A Kettel	1192438	Sgt	W.E Jones
Air Gunner		Sgt	W. Richardson	638615	Sgt	Dolibear
Pilot	1334915	Sgt	H.D Carty	908611	W/O	D.W Jefferies
Navigator	R106671	F/S	D.L Bain	127184	P/O	S.L Knott
Bomb Aimer	111590	F/S	E.K Hart	970018	W/O	Beckett
WOP/AG	1126204	Sgt	R.E Scott	948288	F/S	A.G Lewis
Air Gunner	133644	Sgt	W.F Whitehead		F/S	K.D Franklin
Pilot DFC	124868	F/O	C.W Gray	37015	S/L	A. Holmes
Navigator	129766	P/O	L.A Walker	50436	P/O	J. McMaster
Bomb Aimer	1095055	Sgt	C. Marr	R1044442	Sgt	D. Ritchie
WOP/AG	121958	Sgt	W.J Whittaker	940017	F/S	G. Gill
Air Gunner	R50428	Sgt	R.E Clark	J10875	F/L	G.A Lunn
Pilot	R110847	Sgt	D.W Smalley	R101482	Sgt	S. Hannan
Navigator	R133691	Sgt	G.T Garvey	77881	Sgt	M.P Brown
Bomb Aimer	J21460	Sgt	W.H Leham	R105100	F/S	F.H Purchase
WOP/AG	R114712	Sgt	J.D Montgomerie	776126	Sgt	Litchfield

Air Gunner	R104907	Sgt	W.W Marks	81411	Sgt	Lane
Pilot	42692	S/L	J.C Cairns	131641	F/O	B.A Geale
Navigator	117353	F/O	G.H Larkins		P/O	H.A Tennis
Bomb Aimer	J15639	F/L	C.M Awad	R93441	F/S	J.S Vose
WOP/AG	544898	F/S	R.J Lang	1282904	Sgt	J. Piggott
Air Gunner	15702	F/O	S.M Pozer	R131089	Sgt	R.F Crimmings
Pilot	R103244	Sgt	F.R Windibank	1313054	Sgt	A. Haistead
Navigator	R142433	Sgt	W.J Reid	130271	P/O	P.J Dunger
Bomb Aimer	R134035	Sgt	A.E Atkinson	49765	P/O	S.A Willoughby
WOP/AG	R126252	Sgt	V.P McKinley	1219035	Sgt	C. Taylor
Air Gunner	R139636	Sgt	D.I Havard		Sgt	D. Broughton
Pilot	J21221	F/O	E.A Richmond		Sgt	P. Ellison
Navigator	R135017	Sgt	I.S Levitt	1392374	Sgt	W.G Bailey
Bomb Aimer	R113936	Sgt	E.C Bailey	1187663	Sgt	H.E Horton
WOP/AG	1384547	Sgt	A. Coilman	1378793	Sgt	D.E Nicholson
Air Gunner	R95701	F/S	W. Anglin		Sgt	W Mullaney
Pilot	J29139	P/O	R.P Davies		P/O	G.H Debussac
Navigator	R128774	Sgt	D.E Campbell	R97318	P/O	M.B Spence
Bomb Aimer	R148402	Sgt	P Zeidel	J12302	F/O	W.A Follows
WOP/AG		Sgt	L.P Tailefer	R109811	F/S	G.D Coe
Air Gunner	R128072	Sgt	A.J McLachlan	R116471	Sgt	D.E Palmatier
Pilot	J13992	P/O	F.W Lown	R13174	Sgt	E.A Starr
Navigator	R119786	Sgt	A.J Seiffert	R153169	Sgt	J. Kopchuk
Bomb Aimer	R82786	Sgt	J.K Wood		Sgt	J.P OReilly
WOP/AG	R131818	Sgt	A. Rhodes	P137317	Sgt	C.F Orlinsky
Air Gunner	R116334	Sgt	W.H Calder	P105126	Sgt	W.G Parkinson
Pilot	138021	Sgt	E.A Eames		W/C	J.L Savard DFC
Navigator	130258	P/O	C.F Lapham	J100500	F/O	J.S McIntyre
Bomb Aimer		Sgt	H.B Holmes		F/S	J.C Laberge
WOP/AG	1383566	Sgt	W.H Wright	971456	W/O	J Allen
Air Gunner	J13068	F/O	D Milne		F/S	P. Bonenfant
Pilot	R80220	W/O	W.A Sneath	R90360	F/S	L.F O'Leary
Navigator	J21825	P/O	R.G Clarke	R133222	Sgt	E.B Peart
WOP/AG	1058762	P/O	J.T Hindley	1191334	Sgt	J.M Meech
Air Gunner	R176395	Sgt	J.O Hills	R155751	Sgt	H.S Hicks
Bomb Aimer	J21465	P/O	Drummond-Hay	R15092	Sgt	G W Keay
Pilot	85935	F/L	H. Brinton	J16097	P/O	K.M Johnston
Navigator	R133344	Sgt	J.P Bishop	R130684	Sgt	H.W Clarke
Bomb Aimer	1387043	Sgt	P. Rothera	1320228	Sgt	F.W Frost
WOP/OG	J9657	F/L	F.A Reynolds	R79144	Sgt	J.A Lortie
Air Gunner	921967	Sgt	E.C Blackman	J10014	Lt	J.C Elliott (USA)
Pilot DFM	39562	W/C	J.A Piddington		Sgt	D.N Smith
Navigator	J14805	P/O	P. Farquhar		Sgt	W Pass
Bomb Aimer	136394	P/O	P. Renton	R114313	F/S	D.R Nelson
WOP/OG	1129410	Sgt	L. Reineck		Sgt	Abbott
Air Gunner	591518	Sgt	P. Scarth	147287	Sgt	P.H Davis
Pilot		Sgt	A.M Bruce	104584	F/L	G. Pentony
Navigator		P/O	M.G Lagesse	120566	F/O	J.G Messenger
Bomb Aimer	R114126	P/O	W.J Cathorne	116203	F/O	L.E Thompson
WOP/OG	R117580	F/S	Godden		F/S	K.A Craig
Air Gunner		Sgt	Strachen	R102870	F/O	G₁A Fitzgerald
Pilot	142541	P/O	J.A Lancaster	J10982	F/L	B.F Rawson
Navigator	R96473	P/O	R.W Hale	J11940	F/O	J.W Kerr

Bomb Aimer		Sgt	L.J Boyes	J11962	F/O	I.S McIntosh
WOP/OG		F/S	A.L Thom	953413	F/S	J. Smith
Air Gunner		P/O	M Rabinovitch	R93894	Sgt	J.S Jakeman
Pilot	108178	S/L	A.P Chipling	NZ41411	F/S	G.L Kennedy
Navigator	J97804	F/O	N.W Baker		Sgt	A.C McConnell-Jones
Bomb Aimer	J8811	F/O	R.J Benner	1436510	Sgt	J. Begg
WOP/OG	643239	P/O	F.C Edmonds	1212975	Sgt	D.F Walker
Air Gunner DFM	903458	P/O	W.P Litson	1389199	Sgt	D.H Chard
Pilot	1389771	Sgt	G.A Clarke	655460	F/S	T.S Hayes
Navigator	134380	P/O	H.F Blackman	1139604	Sgt	A. Lewis
Bomb Aimer	658040	Sgt	W.H Smart	1314150	Sgt	T.E.Banks
WaP/OG	1027322	Sgt	W.I Stables	1271666	Sgt	R.A Impney
Air Gunner	1600620	Sgt	A.J Morgan	R112696	Sgt	C.E Monty
Pilot		Sgt	W.A Tighe		Sgt	S.P Kelso
Navigator		F/O	R.A Irwin		Sgt	H.M Schade
Bomb Aimer		Sgt	K.C Sweatman		Sgt	F.P Morro
WOP/OG		Sgt	W.G Wakely		Sgt	C.H Schofield
Air Gunner		Sgt	V Poppa		Sgt	J.L Cabana
Pilot		Sgt	F.W Hingston		F/S	G.E Hall
Navigator		F/O	H0M Brown		F/S	WeJ Bernard
Bomb Aimer		F/S	L.C Lochead		F/S	F.C Brooks
WOP/OG		Sgt	J.R Wiilliams		F/S	E.A Shaul
Air Gunner		Sgt	J. Vilim		F/S	G.P McLaren
Pilot		F/O	H.G Malone		Sgt	H.W Mitchell
Navigator		F/O	J.J Thurmier		Sgt	T.B Fjeldsted
Bomb Aimer		Sgt	G.D Allester		Sgt	L.G Churchill
WOP/OG		Sgt	P. Grieve		Sgt	P. Goatham
Air Gumner		Sgt	G.D Hamilton		P/O	W.W Tucker
Pilot		Sgt	P.E Murray		W/O	K.P Mills
Navigator		Sgt	G.I Phillips		F/S	E. Gwynne
Bomb Aimer		Sgt	P.B Paul		Sgt	J.F Johnson
WOP/OG		F/S	R.E Moden		F/S	N.P Mallen
Air Gunner		Sgt	J.G Stuffco		Sgt	F.P Christenson
Pilot		P/O	B.G Jackson		Sgt	A.S Wick
Navigator		F/O	J.A Padford		Sgt	P.S Clendinneng
Bomb Aimer		P/O	P.H Freiburger		P/O	J.H Warkentin
WOP/OG		Sgt	P.G Redstone		Sgt	S. Boustead
Air Gunner		Sgt	S. Kay		Sgt	L.J Keeley
Pilot		W/C	J.d Pattison DFC		S/L	D.T French
Navigator		P/O	A.C McConnell-Jones		P/O	J.A DePosenroll
Bomb Aimer		P/O	R.V Smyth		P/O	J.P Greco
WaP/OG		F/S	P.A Impney		P/O	A. Miles
Air Gunner		P/O	A.E Clowes DFM		Sgt	D.D Salmon
Pilot		Sgt	A.L Merkley		Sgt	W.A Jamieson
Navigator		F/O	P.O Marrion		Sgt	J. E Hall
Bomb Aimer		P/O	C.W Peasland		Sgt	T.W Atkins
WOP/OG		Sgt	E.N Parker		F/S	W.F Willsher
Air Gunner		Sgt	A.G Innes		Sgt	H.J Holloway
Pilot		F/O	J. Bowen			
Navigator		Sgt	S.W Posner			
Bomb Aimer		Sgt	A.C Forsyth			
WOP/OG		Sgt	T.A Brown			

Air Gunner	Sgt	P. Gilfeather				

Pilot	F/S	K.P Mills	W/O	K.P Mills	Sgt	H.A Floren
Navigator	Sgt	E Gwynne	Sgt	E.R Hart	Sgt	H Gamberg
Bomb Aimer	Sgt	J.F Johnson	Sgt	W Bailey	P/O	J.N Astbury
WOP/OG	F/S	J Bales	F/S	J Bales	Sgt	N Johnson
A/G	Sgt	F.R Christenson	F/S	E Collett	Sgt	N Leone

Pilot	Sgt	G.R Kilburn	Sgt	R.J McIntyre	Sgt	J.E Pendleton
Navigator	P/O	HeA Tennis	Sgt	C.C McMillan	Sgt	D Collins
Bomb Aimer	Sgt	D.R Nelson	Sgt	M.R Hamilton	P/O	G Jarvis
WOP/OG	Sgt	W.J Nicol	Sgt	F.S Dennis	Sgt	R.C White
A/G	Sgt	J.B Quirie	Sgt	G.S Pearce	Sgt	R.B Pierce

Pilot	Sgt	H.M Wilton	Sgt	D.W Smalley	P/O	Elliott
Navigator	Sgt	K.W Moore	Sgt	J.G Garvey	Sgt	K Cairns
Bomb Aimer	Sgt	K.R Welte	P/O	W.H Lehman	P/O	L.K Armitage
WOP/OG	Sgt	W Meyer	Sgt	J Montgomerie	Sgt	S.S McPhadden
A/G	Sgt	W.A Marshall	Sgt	W W Marks	Sgt	D Ovellette

Pilot	F/S	E.C Champion	F/O	J Bowen	P/O	K.M Johnston
Navigator	Sgt	T.J Thomas	Sgt	S.W Posner	Sgt	H.W Clarke
Bomb Aimer	Sgt	G.C Evans	Sgt	A.C Forsythe	Sgt	F.W Frost
WOP/OG	Sgt	R Ranger	Sgt	T.A Brown	Sgt	J.A Lortie
A/G	Sgt	J Perrin	Sgt	H.H Rodgers	Lt.	J.C Elliott

Pilot	Sgt	F.H Turcotte	Sgt	C.R Jones	Sgt	W Trofanenko
Navigator	Sgt	L.E Ford	P/O	W.F Armstrong	P/O	J Kennedy
Bomb Aimer	Sgt	J.S Stokes	Sgt	G.R Evans	P/O	J.F Bittner
WOP/OG	Sgt	M.F Tupper	Sgt	E.J Legault	Sgt	J.E McGrogan
A/G	Sgt	L.S Lafoy	Sgt	Lajeunnesse	Sgt	G Patterson

Pilot	Sgt	L.G Southwood	F/S	G.R Kilburn	Sgt	D.E Crockatt
Navigator	F/S	A.W Puffer	F/O	H.W Burton	Sgt	S.Sleeth
Bomb Aimer	F/S	J.C Grover	Sgt	W.A Nesbitt	Sgt	J.Marriott
WOP/OG	Sgt	J.H Blue	F/S	W.G Pipes	Sgt	W.Davis
A/G	F/S	N.W Chalk	Sgt	J.B Quirie	F/S	OHare

Pilot	Sgt	J.E Pendleton	Sgt	D.O Olsvik	Sgt	D.R Wilson
Navigator	Sgt	D. Collins	Sgt	J.P McKenzie	Sgt	W. Colangelo
Bomb Aimer	P/O	J.G Jarvis	Sgt	P.L Warren		
WOP/OG	Sgt	P.C White	Sgt	D.W Jonnasson	Sgt	G.H Longley
A/G	Sgt	R.F Pearce	Sgt	P. Tobin	Sgt	W.R Hewitt

B/A   Nav.

429 Sqd Wellington III's at East Moor

X3357 AL-	No ops recorded at East Moor, was transferred to OTU	
X3399 AL-U	9 ops recorded at East Moor before transfer to OTU	
X3480 AL-	No ops recorded at East Moor, was transferred to 419 8quadron	
X3704 AL-S	4 ops recorded at East Moor before transfer to OTU	
Z1670AL-A	11 ops recorded at East Moor before crashing at South Kilvington after hitting high tension cable during training exercise	3/ 4/43
Z1696 AL-	5 ops recorded at East Moor before transfer to OTU	
BJ715 AL-K	1 op recorded at East Moor before transfer to OTU	
BJ755 AL-Z	4 ops recorded at East Moor, crashed on t/o there	5/ 3/43
BJ798 AL-E	No ops recorded at East Moor, overshot the landing ground at Henley having mistaken it for White Waitham	24/ 2/43
BJ799 AL-X	2 ops recorded at East Moor before transfer to OTU	
BJ908 AL-W	4 ops recorded at East Moor before transfer to OTU	
BJ920 AL-	FTR from Bochum on its 3rd recorded operation and crashed NE of Duisburg	30/ 3/43
BK146 AL-	No ops recorded at East Moor before transfer to OTU	
BK162 AL-B	FTR from Mannheim on its 16th recorded operation and crashed at Soissons, also recorded as 'F'	17/ 4/43

BK163 AL-	FTR from Lorient on its 1st operation from East Moor, and was lost at sea	27/ 1/43
BK429 AL-	FTR from Mining in the Carrots field, Kiel-Lille Belt area and was lost at sea on its 8th recorded operation	10/ 3/43
BK430 AL-P	No ops recorded at East Moor before transfer to OTU	
BK432 AL-	FTR from Mining in Terschelling area on its 1st recorded op and crashed Papenzy in the Zuider Zee	22/ 1/43
BK499 AL-J	6 ops recorded at East Moor before transfer to OTU	
BK540 AL-C	FTR from Bochum and was lost at sea on its 9th recorded operation	30/ 3/43
DF622 AL-N	6 ops recorded at East Moor	
DF624 AL-	No recorded ops at East Moor and crashed on a training flight at 2½ miles SE of Stokesley	21/12/42
DF625 AL-V	6 ops recorded at East Moor before transfer to OTU	
DF629 AL-	No ops recorded at East Moor	

429 Sqd Wellington Xs at East Moor

HE16O AL-R	9 ops recorded at East Moor	
HE16l AL-	No ops recorded at East Moor before transfer to OTU	
HE162 AL-	No ops recorded at East Moor before transfer to OTU	
HE163 AL-	No ops recorded at East Moor before transfer to OTU	
HE164 AL-	No ops recorded at East Moor before transfer to OTU	
HE165 AL-	No ops recorded at East Moor before transfer to OTU	
IIE166 AL-	No ops recorded at East Moor before transfer to OTU	
HEl67 AL-	No ops recorded at East Moor before transfer to OTU	
HE168 AL-	No ops recorded at East Moor before transfer to 0TU	
HE169 AL-	No ops recorded at East Moor before transfer to OTU	
HE170 AL-	No ops recorded at East Moor before transfer to OTU	
HE171 AL-	No ops recorded at East Moor before transfer to OTU	
HE172 AL-G	13 recorded ops before crashing at Linton on Ouse on return from Bochum at 00.58 hours on 30/3/43, trans to OTU.	
HE350 AL-	10 ops recorded at East Moor and overshot East Moor on return from Essen at 00.57 hrs, 26/7/43, transferred to OTU	
HE365 AL-G	10 ops recorded at East Moor before transfer to OTU	
HE382 AL-	FTR from Duisburg on its 5th recorded operation, cr Borne	27/ 4/43
HE414 AL-	15 ops recorded at East Moor and crashed and burnt at Exeter on return from Brest at 02.55 hrs,	21/ 4/43
HE423 AL-	FTR from Duisburg on its 2nd recorded operation	13/5/43
HE429 AL-J	12 ops recorded at East Moor	
HE430 AL-P	16 ops recorded at East Moor	
HE572 AL-A	7 ops recorded at East Moor with 429 Sqd before transfer to 432 Sqd at Skipton on Swale.	
HE589 AL-	3 ops recorded at East Moor before transfer to OTU	
HE593 AL-M	FTR from Dusseldorf on its 18th recorded operation	12/6/43
HE595 AL-H	7 ops recorded at East Moor before transfer to OTU	
HE635 AL-C	12 recorded ops before overshooting East Moor on return from Eglantine at 01.49 hrs, 28/4/43, transferred to OTU	
HE636 AL-Q	FTR from Frankfurt on its 5th recorded operation	11/4 /43
HE684 AL-T	8 recorded ops at East Moor with 429 Sqd, was transferred to Dalton - 428 Sqd returned to East Moor with 432 Sqd	
HE737 AL-J	FTR from Duisburg and crashed at Bergen op Zoom on its 1st op	27/ 4/43
HE801 AL-	1 op recorded at East Moor before transfer to OTU	
HE802 AL-	1 op recorded at East Moor before transfer to OTU	
HE803 AL-Y	FTR from Essen and crashed at Tilberg, on its 4th recorded op from East Moor, also recorded as W	26/ 7/43
HE820 AL-	No ops recorded with 429 Sqd and transferred to 432 Sqd at Skipton on Swale.	
HE82l AL-	No ops recorded at East Moor before transfer to OTU	
HE823 AL-	No ops recorded at East Moor before transfer to OTU	
HE824 AL-	No ops recorded at East Moor before transfer to OTU	

429 Sqd Wellington X at East Moor

| HE865 AL-A | 14 ops recorded at East Moor before transfer to OTU | |
| HE912 AL- | 2 ops recorded at East Moor before overshooting Wattisham on return from Mannheim at 04.00 hrs, 17/4/45, trans to OTU | |

HE913 AL-	FTR from Duisburg, crashed at Asten on its 4th recorded op	13/ 5/43
HE914 AL-	2 ops at East Moor before transfer to OTU	
HE915 AL-U	24 ops recorded at East Moor, some recorded as 0, trans to OTU	
HE981 AL-T	FTR from Krefeld, believed crashed NW of Bergen op Zoom onits 2nd recorded operation	22/6/43
HE991 AL-	8 ops recorded at East Moor before transfer to OTU	
HE992 AL-S	11 ops recorded at East Moor before u/c collapsed on landing returning from Jellyfish at 02.45 hrs, 5/6/45,trans to OTU	
HE993 AL-B	14 ops recorded at East Moor before transfer to OTU	
HF457 AL-	FTR from Mullhiem, crashed in Heverlee area on its 2nd op	23/ 6/43
HF495 AL-	2 ops recorded at East Moor before crashing at Hardwick on return from Gelsenkirchen at 04.50 hrs,26/6/43,trans to OTU	
HF514 AL-Z	15 ops recorded at East Moor before transfer to OTU	
HF515 AL-Y	15 ops recorded at East Moor before transfer to Gunnery Flight	
HF541 AL-	12 ops recorded at East Moor before transfer to Gunnery Flight	
HF542 AL-	FTR from Dusseldorf and crashed at Wisch on its 4th op	12/ 6/43
HF600 AL-	9 ops recorded at East Moor before transfer to OTU	
HZ260 AL-	FTR from Nectarines, lost at sea on,5th recorded op	2/ 3/43
HZ303 AL-G	2 ops recorded at East Moor before crashing at Huntington during an air test	14/4/43
HZ312 AL-	FTR from Mullheim, crashed at Oudenbosch on its 17th op	23/6/43
HZ354 AL-	14 ops recorded at East Moor before transfer to QTU	
HZ355 AL-G	FTR from Dusseldorf, crashed SW of Ophoven on 10th op	12/ 6/43
HZ363 AL-	13 ops recorded at East Moor before transfer to OTU	
HZ470 AL-W	5 ops recorded at East Moor before transfer to OTU	
HZ471 AL-	FTR from Wuppertal, lost at sea on its 2nd recorded op	30/5/43
HZ473 AL-	No ops recorded at East Moor before transfer to OTU	
HZ482 AL-X	5 ops recorded at East Moor before transfer to OTU	
HZ517 AL-	FTR from Krefeld, crashed NW of Poermond on its 1st op	22/6/43
HZ519 AL-	FTR from Krefeld, crashed Netherlands, Nijmegan ?, 1st op	22/6/43
HZ520 AL-Z	FTR from Krefeld, crashed Bergeyk on its 1st operation	22/6/43
HZ521 AL-	FTR from Wuppertal, crashed Heverlee area on 1st recorded op	25/6/43
JA111 AL-M	7 ops recorded at East Moor before transfer to OTU	
JA112 AL-	5 ops recorded at East Moor before transfer to OTU	
JA113 AL-	4 ops recorded at East Moor before transfer to 0TU	
JA114 AL-A	FTR from Hamburg	28/ 7/43
JA115 AL-B	7 ops recorded at East Moor before transfer to OTU	
JA119 AL-	Broke up and crashed 1 1/2 miles west of Malton.	16/7/43

429 Sqd Wellington X at East Moor

LN281 AL-	Crash landed at East Moor at 05.54 lirs, 25/6/43 on return from Wuppertal,its 1st operation, tyre burst.	25/ 6/43
LN296 AL-	FTR from Cologne, crashed at Bergen op Zoom on its 1st op	4/ 7/43
LN438 AL-	Crasned on take off at East Moor, when undercarriage collapsed 1 op recorded at East Moor	4/ 5/43
LN439 AL~	FTR from Bochum, crashed in the Rhur Valley on its 1st op	14/ 5/43
LN444 AL-	1 op recorded at East Moor before transfer to OTU	
LN447 AL-	No ops recorded at East Moor before transfer to OTU	
LN448 AL-	1 op recorded at East Moor before transfer to OTU	
LN449 AL-	No ops recorded at East Moor before transfer to OTU	
MS474 AL-X	9 ops recorded at East Moor	
MS487 AL-T	FTR from Duisburg, crashed in Utrecht Leiden area on 2nd op	27/ 3/43
MS488 AL-C	No ops recorded at East Moor	
MS489 AL-	No ops recorded at East Moor	

Aircraft of 1679 HCF at East Moor Lancaster II

DS601	ex l657 HCU & later transferred to 408 sqd
DS607	believed to have moved with the Flight to Wombleton
DS615	"" "" ""
DS621	"" "" ""
DS 624	"" "" ""
DS626	suffered a minor accident at East Moor transferred to 408 sqd

DS634   K transferred to 408 sqd
DS635   V swung on landing at East Moor, u/c collapsed, burnt out   2/ 9/43
DS648   crashed on 21/9/43 and repaired
DS649   E crashed at Rose Cottage Farm, Terrington   6/11/43
DS650   transferred to 1660 HCU
DS651   A transferred to 408 sqd
DS657   transferred to 408 sqd
DS688   transferred to 408 sqd
DS730   transferred to 1666 HCU
DS739   transferred to 432 sqd
DS839   crashed at Ridgemont after icing up   25/1 /44

Known 1679 HCF Instructors at East Moor,

Squadron Leader	F. Parker DFC
Squadron Leader	A. Avant DFC
Pilot Officor	McGavock
Pilot Officer	S. Boczar
Flying Officer	Morton
Pilot Officer	Gailbert
Sergeant	Hargreaves (Flight Engineer)
F/Sergeant	S. Legge
F/Sergeant	Cooper

2 September 1943

During the evening, DS635 a Lancaster II of 1679 HCF with Flight Lieutenant McNeill at the controls was completely destroyed by fire when landing at East Moor.

Fortunately all the crew escaped.

Fig 11. Setting out on a Wellington training excersie at East Moor 432 Sqd. September 1943. From L to R. A Logan A/G, Bert Sonley B/A, George Rogers Nav, Ivor Beckwith Pilot, F Kemp WOP. Photo G.Rogers

4 September 1943

Flight Lieutenant D.B Davies, Intelligence Officer was posted out to East Kirkby while Flight Lieutenant W.K Russell a Medical Officer was posted in from RCAF Linton on Ouse.

7 September 1943

Pilot Officer Parry, Meteorological Officer returned to East Moor from detached duty at RCAF Topcliffe.

9 September 1943

Four crews from 432 Squadron at RCAF Skipton on Swale arrived at East Moor for conversion training on Lancaster IIs with 1679 HCF. The skippers were Flight Lieutenant Barrett and Sergeants Meaden, Esdale and Burgess.

10 September 1943

A telephone call was received at RCAF Skipton on Swale instructing 432 Squadron RCAF to move to East Moor on 18 September 1943.

Fig 12 and xx . Top left and right. View of Halifax VII, NP697 432 Sqd. Photo M Pryce.

Fig 13 left. Lancaster II. East Moor Dec 1943. Photo J. Banks.

Fig 14 right. Wally Metcalfe 432 Sqd. With 2,00 pounder. Photo J. Banks.

BOMBER COMMAND MOVEMENT ORDER

R ef:-BC/S 293/11/org   11th
September 1943

MOVE OF 432(RCAF) SQUADRON & RE EQUIPMENT WITH LANCASTER II

1. It has been decided that No.432 (RCAF) Squadron is to move from RCAF
Station, SKIPTON ON SWALE (Satellite of Leeming) to RCAF Station EASTMOOR (In
the Linton on Ouse Base), on the 18th September 1943, and is to commence
re-equipment from Wellington X to Lancaster II aircraft with effect from 25th
October 1943.

2. Arrangements for the move are to be made by Headquarters, No.6(RCAF)
Group.

5. The squadron will then work to Establishment No.WAP/BC/336 with 16 + 4
Lancaster II
The I.R establishment having been increased in accordance with this groups
Headquarters letter BC/S.29587/Org dated 7th April 1943 (To Bomber Grps
only).

4. It is requested that Headquarters No.6(RCAF) Group will inform this HQ
(E.3) when the aircraft can be accepted at EASTMOOP and that HQ No.41 Group
will allot and issue in consultation with Bomber Command.

5. Wellington X airoraft thrown up as a result of this re-equipment will be
absorbed within Bomber Command.

6. It is further requested that the Air Officer i/c Records, in consultation
with HQ No.6(RCAF) Group will effect the necessary adjustment in personnel.
7. The conversion of aircrews and maintenance personnel is to be arranged by
HQ No.6(RCAF) Group. Authority for the increase of the establishment of No.
1679 HCF to 12 + 0 Lancaster IIs is being issued in this HQ letter
BC/S.25546/OPG of even date

8. Copies of Establishment No.WAR/BC/336 will be issued to all concerned in
due course.

Signed....

for Air Vice Marshal
 i/c Administration,
BOMBER COMMAND

---

432 (RCAF) Squadron Movement Order

MOVEMENT ORDER NO. 1

OF

NO. 432 (RCAF) SQD

Authority:-
ADO No.6 (RCAF) Group
Organisation Circular No.32

APPENDIX A - ADVANCE PARTY
APPENDIX B - MAIN PARTY
    APPENDIX C - AIR PARTY
APPENDIX D - REAR PARTY
APPENDIX E - SUPPLEMENTARY

INFORMATION

1.   No. *432* (RCAF) Squadron is being moved from RCAF Skipton on Swale to RCAF Station EASTMOOR, YORKSHIRE, on Saturday the 18th September 1943.

The Squadron aircraft consisting of Wellington X and equipment (including tool kits) will be taken with the squadron from Skipton on Swale to Eastmoor.

INTENTION

2. To move personnel by road with squadron Mechanical Transport. Additional M.T required for the movement will be arranged by HQ No.6 (RCAF) Group for transfer of Main Party only.

EXECUTION

3.   The squadron will move in four parties,

(a) The Advance Party consisting of personnel listed in Appendix A will proceed by road under the command of F/O G.D Mitchell, on Wednesday 15th September 1943, excepting when otherwise stated.

Personnel will parade on the perimeter track outside squadron offices at 08.30 hrs on Wednesday 15th September 1943. All personal kit and equipment will be left at the main picquet post of their respective sites and trsnsport will collect same on Wednesday 15th September 1943 at 08.00 hrs.
They will proceed by Mechanical Transport to RCAF Station EASTMOOR at 09.00 hrs. F/O Mitchell will retain one 5/10 cwt van at EASTMOOR, to be used for duty, purpose.
The Officer i/c of the advance party is to report to the Squadron Leader Administration at EASTMOOR on arrival.

Unconsumed rations will be arranged by the Messing Officer and will be put in one parcel

(b) The MAIN PARTY consisting of personnel listed in Appendix B will proceed by road under command of Squadron Leader C B Hess on Saturday 18th September 1943.

Personnel will parade on the perimeter track outside squadron offices at 08.50
        hrs on Saturday 18th September 1943. All personal kit and equipment will be left at the main piquet post of their respective sites and transport will collect same at 08.00 hrs on Saturday 18th September 1943. Unconsumed rations will be arranged by the Messing Officer and will be put in one parcel.

(c) The AIR PARTY consisting of personnel listed in Annendix C will proceed by air under command of Squadron Leader S.B Sinton on Saturday 18th September 1943.

The party will take off at 10.30 hrs on Saturday 18th September 1943. All personal kit and equipment will be left at the main piquet post of their respective sites and transport will collect same at 08.00 hrs on Saturday 18th September 1943.

(d) The REAR PARTY consisting of personnel listed in Appendix 1) will proceed by road under command of F/O A.L Rorke on Monday 20th September 1943. They will remain at Skinton on Swale to ensure that all buildings at present occupied by *432* Squadron are clean and tidy to the satisfaction of the Station Commander.

Unconsumed rations will be arranged for by the Messing Officer and will be put in one parcel.

Personnel will parade on the perimeter track outside the squadron offices at 08.30 hrs on Monday 20th September 1943. All kit and equipment will be left at the main piquet post of their respective sites and will be collected by transport at 08.00 hrs on Monday 20th September 1943.

(e) The SUPPLEMENTARY PARTY list in Appendix E will proceed from RCAF Station LEEMING on cessation of Non-effectiveness under arrangements to be made by RCAF Station LEEMING.

ADMINISTRATION

4. (a) All station equipment held on personal charge is to be returned to the appropiate Section before departure. This does not include flying clothing. Bicycles are to be returned to the Station Warrant Officer by 17.00 hrs on Thursday 16th September 1943.

(b) BEDDING
All bedding is to be left neatly folded on individual bedsteads.

(c) KEYS FOR FLYING CLOTHING LOCKERS
All aircrew holding such keys are to hand them in to Squadron Discipline Office.

(d) KEYS FOR OFFICE FILING
All keys to be placed in locks for checking by the clerk of works.

(e) KEYS FOR SAFE, OFFICE AND CHESTS STEEL
All keys are to be turned in to Flight Officer W.J Wood the Station Equipment Officer.

(f) SECRET & CONFIDENTIAL DOCUMENTS, FILES & PAPERS
Flight Lieutenant H.G Phillips will be in charge of all secret and confidential papers, files and documents, which are to be securely packed and sealed. This officer is to be armed.

11 September 1943

East Moor Station was advised that the planned formation of No.455 Squadron RCAF would not be taking place on the station, and that instead No.432 Squadron would be moving in from RCAF Station Skipton on Swale on 18th September 1943.

No. 432 Squadron Commander Wing Commander W.A McKay, Squadron Leader C.B Sinton and Flight Lieutenant H.G Phillips arrived at East Moor by road from RCAF Station Skipton on Swale to make the arrangements for the squadrons move on the 18th.

No.1679 HCF commenced converting four of No.432 Squadrons operationally experienced crews from Wellington to Lancaster II bombers with a shortened course, and skippered by Flight Lieutenant O.K Barrett, Flight Sergeant J. Esdale and Sergeants P.C Burgess and W.H Meaden.

13 September 1943

Five airecrews from Nos 429 and 431 Squadrons arrived at East Moor to join No. 432.

Wing Commander W.A McKay again made the road journey to East Moor and was accompanied by Squadron Engineering Officer, Flight Lieutenant Boone to make further arrangements for No.432 Squadrons move.

No.6 Group made arrangements with the M.T Officer at RCAF Station Leeming for that section to provide the necessary road transport for No.432 Squadrons move from RCAF Station Skipton on Swale to RCAF Station East Moor.

14 September 1943

Bomber Command issued a movement order for No.432 Squadron to move from RCAF Station Skipton on Swale to East Moor.

15 September 1943

At 08.45 hours an Advance Party of 432 Squadron left Skipton on Swale by road for East Moor where they arrived in time for lunch.

16 September 1943

At least two of 432 Squadrons Wellington Xs were seen at East Moor, those being HE818 and HF456.

17 September 1943

Equipment was being moved daily from Skipton on Swale to East Moor and further 432 Squadron Wellingtons were seen at the latter station.

18 September 1943

There proved to be a shortage of buses available for the move of 432 Squadrons main party to East Moor, the first of two trips commencing at 09.00 hours was soon concluded and the whole operation was over by 14.00 hours, and was recorded as most successful.

The movement of the squadron was carried out under the command of Wing Commander W.A McKay assisted by Intelligence Officers,Flight Lieutenants E.F Kusch and H.F Lount.

19 September 1943

There was no operational commitments at East Moor.

The Station Commander Group Captain Carscallen DFC, held a meeting with the 432 Squadron Commander and other officers when Station regulations were the topic of conversation. It was said that the movement of 432 Squadron had gone without a hitch and that they were all settling in very well.

20 September 1943

The personnel of 432 Squadron were finding the station quite acceptable,with good food and efficiently run messes.

No.1679 HCF continued to convert crews to the Lancaster II with a further three from 432 Squadron, Flight Lieutenant Strachans and those of Pilot Officers Hatfield and Rae.

At 18.20 hours, Pilot Officer L. Hayes lifted Wellington HF571 off East Moors runway to become the first 432 squadron operational sortie from the station,when eight crews set out on a Gardening mission to the Jellyfish fields off Brest,

HF456 D	P/O	A Atkinson	LN457 G	Sgt	L Tierney
HE825 H	Sgt	H Murray	LN546 L	P/O	P Sullivan
HE818 Q	W/O	A Erickson	LN394 S	F/S	L Southwood
HF571 U	P/O	L Haynes	HE352 V	Sgt	W Pay

Two crews brought their mines back, not being able to pinpoint the target. All returned safely.

21 September 1943

At 00.40 hours, Pilot Officer Atkinson and crew in Wellington HF456, overshot East Moor on their return from Brest.

Operations were called for a further Gardening operation but later scrubbed. Air Commodore McEwan AOC No.6 Group visited the station.

STATEMENT BY SURVIVING MEMBERS OF LN554 DITCHED ON 22/23 SEPTEMBER 1943

Everything went fine on the way to the target which was located and bombed.After leaving the target area the fuel guages were checked and found satisfactory. About halfway to the Dutch coast the fuel was checked again, when the starboard showed nil and the port 40 galls. Then we thought we might run short of petrol. Shortly after the starboard engine cut and the pilot gave orders to open Balance Cock B. This was done and the engine picked up again. Balance Cock B was closed and the nacelles were turned on. We continued for half an hour and then the skipper gave orders to prepare for ditching. This was carried out and the bomb containers jettisoned. The navigator passed the latest data to the wireless operator, who sent it out and a third class fix was sent back. After using the nacelles for three quarters of an hour the navigator gave the WOP the latest position which he sent. The pilot was running as economically as possible, losing height gradually. Another fix was given to the WOP by the navigator one hour after the nacelles had been turned on. Ten minutes later the starboard engine cut and the pilot ordered the crew to take up ditching stations. Then the pilot started to give a running commentary. At 1,500 feet the Floatation bags were opened. The pilots commentary continued until the aircraft hit the water. It was a marvellous landing and the pilots last words were Best of luck boys.

On hitting the water the aircraft started to Fill up immediately. The navigator released the dinghy and we abandoned the aircraft. The dinghy was sighted Floating by the tailpiane, indicating that it was not attached to the aircraft. The plane Filled with water so quickly that it was impossible to get any equipment out. The navigator and the bomb aimer were the first to get to the dinghy and then the air gunner was spotted swimming towards it.

He was assisted into the dinghy by the navigator and by then only the aircraft tail was visible. We shouted and blew our whistles but there was no reply. It was very dark and the sea was rough. After half an hour we gave up hope of seeing the other two members of the crew. We three prepared ourselves for the long cold night ahead. The night was spent bailing out and trying to keap warm. At last morning came and we started arranging the articles in the kit which had been fastened to the dinghy

At 9 am , an Anson at about 2,000 feet was sighted by the navigator. Two cartridges were fired but the Anson continued on its way apparantly missing the dinghy. About 9.45 a Wellington was sighted, again cartridges were shot off and it was evident that the aircraft had spotted us. He circled flashed his downward identification light and continued in ever enlarging circles until we lost sight of him. Our morale picked up considerably and we figured it would only bc a matter of tIme before we were rescued. At 11.15 we sighted a Stirling, cartridges were shot off and the aircraft spotted us. He flew away in the direction he had come, circled and came back again, indicating that he was directing a boat to us. We then spotted two boats coming towards us. The sea was quite rough and choppy. R.M.L 553 came within a hundred yards of us and stopped for a minute. It circled its way into a favourable position approximately 15 yards from the dinghy. The skipper, Lieutenant Pratner, shouted that two ropes were coming, one for the dinghy and one for us. As soon as we got aboard the R.M.L we were given a good rub down and put to bed. The Captain asked if we wanted anything hot to eat or drink, which seemed a splendid idea. Almost immediately hot soup and hot rum was brought to us. For the rest of the trip into port we slept like tops. Just before coming in to dock we were given dry naval clothing. We were able to get up and walk around the boat.

At the dock we awaited the arrival of the MO. Here we met the Captain of the other R.M.L and the Flag Officer of the base. We were taken to the naval hospital by ambulance, where we were given a medical check. After a very good meal we hopped into bed in the naval sick bay and had a restful night. The naval authorities were very good to us, nothing was too much trouble for them to do. The next morning after a recheck by the MO, we were called into the Admirals office. We had a very pleasant chat with him for about half an hour. He made us feel a lot better. That afternoon we were taken to R.M.L 553 by one of the crew. We were to pick up our clothing which was still slightly damp and Lt.Pratner refused to let us have it. He had his second in command show us over the boat which was very interesting. We were entertained in a first class manner until our clothes were dry. After changing we found it had started to rain and the officers insisted that we wear their raincoats in which we returned to the hospital sick bay.

The next morning we were outfitted at the naval stores with the necessities which we did not have. About 9.30 our Air Force car arrived to take us back to our station. Our visit to the Navy was over but not forgotten. The men on the R.M.L's are doing a marvellous job and deserve a great deal of credit. About 10.15 am we started our journey, arriving at our station about 5.pm on September 25th 1943.

R137827   Sgt Buchanan, B   R1459241 Sgt Mayo WJ   R83180 Sgt Haggins,A.

22 September 1943

Fifteen Wellingtons were detailed for 432 Squadrons first bombing operation crews from East Moor, an attack on Hannover in which seven hundred took part.

One aircraft, LN394 and piloted by Flight Sergeant Southwood, crashed on take off and came to rest more than one hundred and fifty yards beyond the runway, fortunately without any injuries to the crew.

LN554 P	Sgt	R Barlow		HE820 J	P/O	P Sullivan	
LN454 B	Sgt	J Cooper		HE818 Q	W/O	A Erickson	
LN546 L	W/O	B Sorge		HE817 K	P/O	S Atkinson	
	F/O	C Whales	2/Plt		Sgt	I Bowden	2/Plt
HE825 H	Sgt	R Murray		HF568 ZI	P/O	L Haynes	
HE352 V	Sgt	W Pay		HE8OO A	F/O	R Mercer	
HZ485 0	P/O	R Davies		LN451 Y	Sgt	T Spink	
HF480 F	Sgt	A Slegg		LN457 G	Sgt	L Tierney	

Sergeant Tierney and crew failed to return from this operation.

Sergeant Barlow ran out of fuel on the return flight and at *00.45* hours on the 23rd, he ditched in the North Sea. After being in the dinghy for more than twelve hours, Sergeants Mayo, Buchan and Haggins were rescued, some sixty miles off Flamborough.

An early return was made by Flying Officer Mercer due to instrument failure.

23 September 1943

Wing Commander Dabb visited East Moor and gave lectures on Air Sea Rescue work.

Operations were called for and subsequently cancelled.

Four crews from 432 Squadron carried out a Sea Search for Sergeant Barlow and crew, but Sergeant Beckwiths aircraft lost its dinghy and touched down within five minutes of take off.

HE918 C	Sgt	I Beckwith	HE483O	P/O	W Fisher
HZ484 N	P/O	L Haynes	LN546 L	F/O	A Mercer

Flying Officer Mercers crew located a dinghy with three occupants and stood by until they were rescued by the Royal Navy. Sadly, Sergeants Barlow and Reeson had been unable to get out of the Wellington after ditching.

24 September 1943

No.1679 HCF suffered a setback when Lancaster II, DS626 with Sergeant Burgess at the controls, crashed at the end of runway No.3. The aircraft was damaged but the crew escaped injury.

Ten Wellington crews from 432 Squadron carried out a Gardening operation in the Nectarine fields of the Frisians and south of Texal,

LN452 Y	F/O	W Fisher	HE352 V	Sgt	W Pay
HF571 U	Sgt	T Spink	HE818 Q	W/O	A Erickson
LN546 L	Sgt	I Bowden	HE817 K	Sgt	A Slegg
HE825 H	Sgt	R Murray	HE820 J	P/O	R Sullivan
HE918 C	F/O	I Beckwith	LN454 B	F/O	A Mercer

25 September 1943

No operations were carried out from the station.

A further four 432 Squadron crews nominated for Lancaster II conversion with 1679 HCF, Flying Officers Mercer and Whales, Sergeant Spink and Flight Sergeant Baker.

Sergeant Buchan, Mayo and Haggins arrived back at East Moor after their ditching ordeal.

26 September 1943

A bombing operation was called for and then scrubbed later in the day.

The Sergeants Mess held a successful guest night.

27 September 1943

Nine Wellington crews from 432 Squadron participated in an attack on Hannover in which almost seven hundred took part.

HE820 J	P/O	R Sullivan	HE825 H	Sgt	R Murray
HE800 A	Sgt	A Slegg	HZ480 Z	Sgt	J Cooper
HE818 Q	W/O	A Erickson	HZ483 0	F/O	W Fisher
HZ484 N	Sgt	D Palmer	HE352 V	Sgt	W Pay
HE817 K	P/O	S Atkinson			

Pilot Officer Atkinson and crew failed to return from this operation. Several aircraft were diverted on their return.

28 September 1943

No operations were scheduled at East Moor.
All the diverted aircraft returned to the station.

Wing Commander McKay and Squadron Leader Hess travelled to RCAF Station Linton on Ouse to confer with the AOC in C No.6 Group, Air Marshal H. Edwards.

30 September 1943

There was no operational commitment at East Moor.

Five new crews were expected to arrive which would bring the strength of 432 Squadron up to thirty three. As of this date the squadron consisted of eleven available for operations, five were non effective, eleven were under-going conversion to the Lancaster II with 1679 HCF,and one was on leave.

General:

Word was received that the town of Leaside in Ontario wished to adopt No.432 RCAF Squadron. The information came via Mr R.Kerby the father of a former Squadron Commander, Wing Commander H Kerby, and had been endorsed by the Air Ministry through the Ottawa Headquarters.

The aircraft strength at East Moor was nineteen Wellington Mk X bombers and eight Lancaster Mk II heavy bombers.

Several Lancaster IIs from 426 Squadron at nearby RCAF Station Linton on Ouse were noted in and out of East Moor around this time, presumably, their visits were connected with that squadrons conversion to the type by 1679 HCF.

Halifax DT675 and DT781 were noted at East Moor during the month, these were Mk IIs and probably from 408 Squadron.

1 October 1943

Operations were not called for at East Moor.

1679 HCF was continuing with its conversion programme on the Lancaster II.

2 October 1943

Twelve crews from 432 Squadron were detailed for a mining operation to the Rosemary fields off Lorient. All took of f, three made early returns, four were unable to pinpoint the target area and five successfully laid their mines. All returned safely to East Moor,

JA451 C	Sgt	P Dennis	HF571 U	F/S	J Poole
LN241 G	Sgt	J Cooper	LN236 P	Sgt	J McIntosh
HE818 O	W/O	A Erickson	LN240 S	Sgt	W Pay
LN454 B	P/O	I Beckwith	LN452 Y	F/O	W Fisher
HE825 H	P/O	R Murray	LN546 L	F/S	H Whaley
LN451 W	F/O	D Von Laufer	HE820 J	Sgt	D Maddock

Seven crews made early returns, Sergeants Dennis, Cooper and McIntosh and Flight Sergeant Poole with u/s rear turrets, while Pilot Officers Beckwith, Murray and Sergeant Maddock were unable to locate the target.

4 October 1943

Lancaster II, DS649 of 1679 HCF ended in the ditch at the Strensall Road end of runway 16 with Flight Lieutenant Strachen at the controls. All crew members escaped unscathed.

Flight Lieutenant Barrett and crew completed their conversion course with 1679 HCF and returned to 432 Squadron.

Group Captain Carscallen DFC, the Station Commander was granted permission to undergo the Lancaster II conversion course with 1679 HCF.

7 October 1943

No.432 Squadron returned to ithe Rosemary fields off Brest, and dispatched the following ten Wellington crews,

LN451 W	F/O	D Von Laufer	LN240 S	P/O	L Legace
LN236 P	Sgt	J McIntosh	HE818 Q	W/O	A Erickson
LN706 R	Sgt	D Maddock	LN546 L	F/S	H Whaley
HE825 H	P/O	R Murray	JA541 C	F/S	P Dennis

| LN452 Y | F/S | D Palmer | LN454 B | P/O | W Beckwith |

Early returns were made by Pilot Officers Legace and Beckwith, Flight Sergeants Palmer and Whaley, all were unable to locate the target.

At 00.24 hours on the 8th, Sergeant Quesnal the rear gunner in JA541 shot down a MellO before a second one attacked inflicting damage to flaps, hydraulics and tanks. He drove the second one off, the Wellington limped home and Sergeant Quesnal had earned the DFM.

Sergeant R. Burgess and crew returned to 432 Squadron after completing their Lancaster conversion course with 1679 HCF.

8 October 1943

Pilot Officer Boczar an instructor with 1679 HCF, ferried in to East Moor from RCAF Station Linton on Ouse the Lancaster X, KB7OO The Rhur Express. He was a member of the crew that had Flown the aircraft across the Atlantic. Following completion of filming and publicity work with KB7OO they returned to duties with 1679 HCF. Many of 432 Squadron crews were undergoing Lancaster II conversion training during the day and operating their Wellingtons at night. Four such crews were those captained by Flying Officers Wales and Mercer, Flight Sergent Baker and Sergeant Spink, all were included in the detail to attack Hannover that night.

Fourteen Wellington crews left East Moor on what proved to be one of the worst attacks that Hannover experienced throughout the war with over five hundred aircraft concentrating their attack on the city centre,

LN241 G	Sgt	A Slegg	LN240 S	F/S	T Spink
LN546 L	P/O	R Sullivan	HF571 U	F/S	J Poole
LN236 P	F/S	P Dennis	HZ483 O	F/L	C Barrett
HE825 H	Sgt	R Murray	HE818 Q	W/O	A Erickson
HE800 A	P/O	H Hatfield	HZ480 F	F/O	A Mercer
HZ484 N	F/O	W Fisher	LN451 W	F/S	D Baker
HE352 V	Sgt	W Pay	LN452 Y	F/S	D Palmer

Pilot Officer Sullivan and Flight Sergeant Spink made early returns with technical failures while Sergeant Poole became ill before turning back.

At 01.35 hours on the 9th, a JU88 attacked HZ484 and was shaken off only to be attacked by another at 04.41 hours. The Wellington received some damage before the enemy was seen to crash with its port engine on fire, the results of return fire from Warrant Officer Saunders.

LN236 was also attacked by a JU88, around 03.05 hours it was shaken off Flight Sergeant Baker and crew failed to return from this the last Bomber Command operation in which Wellingtons participated in the bomber role.

11 October 1943

Informationwas received at East Moor to the effect that the Canadian town of Leaside wished to adopt No.432 Squadron RCAF.

WAAF Section Officer F.M Maxfield assumed duties as the Senior Officer of that Section at East Moor.

12 October 1943

RCAF Station East Moor was advised that the Lancaster II aircraft destined for 432 Squadron had been delivered to RCAF Station Linton on Ouse.

Flying Officer C.J Lewis a Flying Control Officer at East Moor was posted out to RCAF Station Dalton.

Flying Officer F.T Maher arrived on detached duty from Flying Control at Croft.

14 October 1943

No.1679 HCF found it necessary to modify its flying instruction policy so that 432 Squadron crews could be converted in the shortest possible time. This was as a result of a request to do so by No.6 Group and led to the suspension of all cross country and local flying details, air to air firing, bombing and Gee Homings. This enabled the Lancasters to be used in a continuous programme of day and night circuits and landings. The ground school schedule was likewise modified and adapted to meet the same demands.

Flight Sergeant Esdale and crew completed their conversion course with 1679 HCF and returned to 432 Squadron.

15 October 1943

Flight Lieutenant Strachan and crew returned to 432 Squadron after successfully completing their Lancaster conversion with 1679 HCF.

The new shortened conversion course got under way with four of 432 Squadrons crews, Flight Sergeants DeMaria and Slegg, Pilot Officer R.A Davies and Sergeant N.C Pay

17 October 1943

Wing Commander W.A McKay, and Squadron Leaders C.B Hess and Cinton, DFC reported to 1679 HCF for Lancaster II conversion training

Flying Officer Hatfield and Pilot Officer Rae together with their crews had completed the conversion course with 1679 HCF, and returned to 432 Squadron.

A detail of six crews drawn from 432 Squadron took off from East Moor on a Gardening operation to the Jellyfish fields off Biscay, Brest and Den Helder,

HE825 H	Sgt	D Maddock	LN708 K	F/S	J Cooper
LN546 L	P/O	R Sullivan	HE818 Q	W/O	A Erickson
LN240 S	F/S	D Palmer	HF571 U	F/S	J Poole

Sergeant Maddock was unable to identify the target and returned early. Back at East Moor, Flight Lieutenant L.R McPhee was appointed Bar Officer.

18 October 1943

Flying Officer C.V Wales and crew, 432 Squadron, completed their conversion to the Lancaster II with 1679 HCF.

East Moor dispatched six of 432 Squadrons Wellington crews on a Gardening mission
to the Trefoil fields of f Texal,

LN708 K	P/O	R Murray	HE825 H	Sgt	D Maddock
LN546 L	P/O	P Sullivan	LN245 P	F/S	D Palmer
HE818 Q	W/O	A Erickson	HF571 U	F/S	J Poole

All returned to East Moor without incident.

20 October 1943

1679 HCF instructors, Pilot Officer Boczar DFC, Flight Sergeant R.K Burgar, and Sergeants P.S Webb and M. Baczinsky left East Moor for detached duty at the Air Ministry, London. They recorded the sound track for the film being made about KB;700 Rhur Express, the first Canadian built Lancaster which they had flown to Britain. The aircrafts French Poodle mascot Bambi, which had slept all the way across the Atlantic was put into six months quarantine by its owner Flight Sergeant Burgar. The dog was greatly missed by the East Moor personnel to whom it had become a familiar sight.

Squadron Leader Summers, Station Engineering Officer and Officers Mess PMC was posted out to No.5 Group. A popular officer, he was replaced by Squadron Leader Marshall.

Six crews from 432 Squadron took part in a Sea Search, nothing was sighted and all returned without incident,

HF456 D	P/O	P Murray	LN241 G	F/S	J Poole
HE825 H	F/S	D Palmer	LN546 L	P/O	P Sullivan
LN236 P	Sgt	D Maddock	HE818 Q	Sgt	J McIntosh
LN706 R	P/O	L Legace	HF571 U	W/O	H Whaley

22 October 1943

The Station Crash Tender was in collision with a Flight Truck and as a result two 432 Squadron personnel were seriously injured. Admitted to York Military Hospital were groundstaff P57829 Corporal K.R Eckel and P104609 LAC J. Proudette.

No.432 Squadrons last Wellington operation involved a seven crew detail and the following set out on a Gardening mission to the Trefoil fields off Den Helder and Brest,

HF456 D	W/O	H Whaley	LN708 K	F/S	J Cooper
LN546 L	P/O	P Sullivan	LN236 P	Sgt	J McIntosh
LN7Q6 R	F/O	W Fisher	LN240 S	F/S	D Palmer
HF571 U	F/S	J Poole			

All returned to East Moor without incident.

432 Squadron Wellington crews at East Moor

Pilot	P/O Atkinson	S	Sgt Tierney	L	F/O Beckwith	L
Navigator	Sgt Cook	L	Sgt Sewell	J	F/O Rogers	G
Bomb Aimer	Sgt Grant	W	P/O Whitton	L	Sgt Sunley	H
WOP/OG	P/O Chubb	A	Sgt Mercer	J	Sgt Thompson	W
Air Gunner	Sgt Turner	H	F/S Williams	P	Sgt Logan	K
Pilot	W/O Sorge	B	W/O Erickson	A	F/S Southwood	L
Navigator	P/O Gardiner	W	Sgt Hulme	B	F/S Puffer	A
Bomb Aimer	Sgt Hodges	G	Sgt Plaster	E	F/S Grover	J
WOP/OG	P/O Cruickshank	L	Sgt Jenkins	E	F/S BlueJ	
Air Gunner	F/S Brown	O	Sgt Seddon	W	F/S Chalk	N
Pilot	P/O Haynes	L	F/S Poole	J	Sgt Pay	W
Navigator	P/O Garnham	A	Sgt Thomson	W	Sgt Baker	J
Bomb Aimer	P/O Brown	H	Sgt Bailmache	W	Sgt Armstrong	B
WOP/AG	P/O Williams	L	Sgt Myer	M	Sgt Bell	J
Air Gunner	Sgt Robb	A	F/S ODonnell	W	Sgt King	A
Pilot	Sgt Dennis	P	P/O Davies	R	Sgt Murray	R
Navigator	Sgt Atkins	J	Sgt Burns	J	Sgt Phillips	A
Bomb Aimer	P/O OGorman	J	Sgt MacDonald	A	Sgt Paul	R
WOP/AG	Sgt Woolfenden	P	Sgt Hunt	S	F/S McGrew	P
Air Gunner	Sgt Quesnal	H	Sgt Green	P	Sgt Stuffco	J
Pilot	Sgt Bowden	L	P/O Sullivan	P	Sgt Barlow	R
Navigator	Sgt Phillips	G	F/O Tierney	B	Sgt Buchan	A
Bomb Aimer	Sgt Blau	P	F/O Frost	S	Sgt Mayo	W
WOP/OG	Sgt Shaw-Brown	K	Sgt Rowe	F	Sgt Reeson	F
Air Gunner	F/S Weekes	J	Sgt Payne	L	Sgt Haggins	A
Pilot	Sgt Cooper	J	F/O Mercer	P	Sgt Spink	T
Navigator	Sgt Burrill	F	F/O Nicholson	W	P/O Laberge	J
Bomb Aimer	Sgt McClintock	P	P/O Simpson	H	Sgt Naylor	H
WOP/AG	Sgt Short	L	Sgt Pett	S	Sgt McFarlane	J
Air Gunner	Sgt Oseman	W	Sgt Clifford	N	F/S Leadley	W

Pilot	Sgt Slegg	A	P/O Fisher	W	P/O Fisher	W
Navigator	Sgt Lowle	G	Sgt Harmon	D	Sgt Briegkl	J
Bomb Aimer	P/O Baker	S	Sgt Turmeau	P	Sgt Pragnell	T
WOP/AG	Sgt Morgan	A	F/S Brudell	M	F/S Brudell	M
Air Gunner	Sgt Green	P	W/O Saunders	P	W/O Saunders	P
Pilot	Sgt Palmer	D	F/S Whaley	H	F/O Von Laufer	D
Navigator	Sgt Delbridge	K	P/O Burrows	J	P/O Derry	M
Bomb Aimer	Sgt Porter	H	Sgt Doyle	K	Sgt Phimester	M
WOP/AG	P/O Brown	E	F/S MacDonald	D	Sgt Holt	P
Air Gunner	Sgt Mitchell	J	Sgt Drive	P	Sgt MacFadden	J
Pilot	Sgt Maddock	D	P/O Legace	L	F/L Barrett	C
Navigator	P/O Milner	H	P/O Mahoney	J	F/O Bentley	D
Bomb Aimer	Sgt Urquhart	K	Sgt McDonald	D	F/S Goundrey	T
WOP/AG	F/S McNaught	J	P/O Hunter	D	Sgt Coe	E
Air Gumner	Sgt Forrest	C	Sgt Douglas	W	F/S Hamilton	S
Pilot	P/O Hatfield	H	F/S Baker	D		
Navigator	P/O Higgs	J	F/S HurlC			
Bomb Aimer	F/O Hazeldene	B	F/S Thompson	P		
WOP/AG	Sgt Poole	W	Sgt Black	J		
Air Gunner	F/L Rainville	C	Sgt Taylor	J		

Wellington X - 432 Sqd - East Moor

HE352	QO-V	5 Ops	transferred to OTU	
HE800	QO-A	3 Ops		
HE817	QO-K	3 Ops	FTR - Hannover	28/ 9/43
HE818	QO-Q	9 Ops	transferred to OTU	
HE820	QO-J	4 Ops	" "	
HE825	QO-H	10 Ops	ex 429 sqd " "	
HE918	QO-C	2 Ops	" "	
HF456	QO-D	3 Ops	overshot East Moor, ex minelaying, 00.40 hrs	21/ 9143
HF567	QO-X			
HF568	QO-Z	1 Op	transferred to OTU	
HF571	QO-U	8 Ops	" "	
HZ480	QO-F	3 Ops	" "	
HZ483	QO-O	4 Ops	" "	
HZ484	QO-N	3 Ops	" "	
JA128	QO-E		" "	
JA451	QO-C	2 Ops	" 300 sqd	
LN236	QO-P	5 Ops	" OTU	
LN240	QO-S	5 Ops	" "	
LN241	QO-G	3 Ops	" "	
LN245	QO-P	1 Op	crashed on t/o,East Moor, 150 yds into fields 22/9/43 repaired and transferred to OTU	
LN451	QO-W	4 Ops	FTR - Hannover	9/10/43
LN432	QO-Y	4 Ops	transferred to OTU	
LN454	QO-B	4 Ops	" "	
LN457	QO-G	2 Ops	FTR - Hannover	23/ 9/43
LN546	QO-L	11 Ops	transferred to OTU	
LN554	QO-P	1 Op	ditched 50 miles of Scarborough, ex Hannover	23/ 9/43
LN706	QO-R	3 Ops	transferred to OTU	
LN708	QO-K	3 Ops	" "	
MS485	QO-T			

23 October 1943

A signal was received at the station to say that Leading Aircraftman J.G Poudrette had died from the injuries which he sustained in the road accident on 22nd October.

The first of 432 Squadrons Wellington aircraft were flown out of East Moor.

24 October 1943

The remaining Wellingtons of 432 Squadron were flown out of East Moor.

Bad weather conditions in the East Moor area was hampering the conversion of aircrews from Wellingtons to Lancaster IIs.

This date was officially 432 Squadrons last one as a Wellington unit and it was intended that the next day would see it established as a Lancaster II squadron.

Twelve crews had already been converted, four were in the process of being so, and a further nine were awaiting.

25 October 1943

No.432 Squadron were stood down from operations and were advised that they would not be required before 9th November, but that meanwhile the conversion courses would be hastened to ensure that at least one full flight would be operationally ready by that date.

Squadron Leader Parker DFC, Officer Commanding 1679 HCF left East Moor for his repatriation to Canada. His successor was Flight Lieutenant A. Avant DFC who vacated his position as the units Chief Ground Instructor.

A further ten crews from 432 Squadron commenced Lancaster II training courses with 1679 HCF, Flying Officers Fisher and Von Laufer, Flight Sergeants Dennis, Palmer, Cooper, Poole and Whaley, and Sergeants McIntosh, Maddock and Pilot Officer Legace.

Flying Officer Maher, the Flying Control Officer was detached from East Moor to RCAF Station Tholthorpe.

The first Lancaster IIs for 432 Squadron were flown in to East Moor from RCAF Station Linton on Ouse.

26 October 1943

WAAF Squadron Officer N.E Langley, Intelligence Officer returned to East Moor from detached duty at RCAF Station Thoithorpe.

Inclement weather precluded any flying from East Moor.

27 October 1943

East Moor Station soccer team played York City Police on the latters ground losing by 7 goals to 5 in what was the first leg of the Mid-Week Shield.

A further three Lancaster IIs arrived from RCAF Station Linton on Ouse, ferried by crews of 432 Squadron.

28 October 1943

The Station Signals Officer Flight Lieutenant B.V Smith, who was also the Officers Messing Officer was posted out to Liecester East.

Inclement weather continued to prevent any flying at East Moor.

29 October 1943

Pilot Officer Boczar and crew returned to East Moor and resumed instructional duties with 1679 HCF after being detached to the Air Ministry at London, where they had been involved in the making of a publicity film about the first Canadian built Lancaster.

Still no flying training due to adverse weather conditions.

30 October 1943

The RAF Regiment defence force at East Moor were successful in repelling an attack of the Station by Sheriff Hutton Home Guard. The spirited battle which lasted over two hours saw the attacking force from the northern perimeter most severely routed. Station aircrew assisted the RAF Regiment.

Bad weather again precluded any local flying.

31 October 1943

In a Station soccer match, 432 Squadron were outplayed by No.1679 HCF.

The last week of the month was proving to be one of continuing adverse weather in the area around East Moor Station hampering flying training and the conversion of aircrews to the Lancaster II.

An Officer's Mess meeting was held and amongst the changes in appointments made the following were included,

Major W.G Fanning, the East Moor Station Defence Adviser to be Officers Mess PMC
Flight Lieutenant M.D. Louche (C8588) to be Mess Secretary,
Flight Lieutenant E.J. Strathdee (C9292) to be Bar Officer,
Lieutenant P.K. Russell (C12519) to be Messing Officer,
Flight Lieutenant L.R. McPhee (C13681) to be Chairman.

The Station Photographic Section moved into the purpose built new accommodation on the Technical Site.

432 Squadron crews were still being converted to the Lancaster II by 1679 HCF and familiarising themselves with their new squadron aircraft.

No flying was possible because of bad weather.

1 November 1943

Flight Lieutenant F.W. Hall Technical Officer, posted to 61 RCAF Base. He had also carried out the duties of entertainments officer at East Moor.

Civilian Meteorologist Officer Mr. R.H. Murdoch at East Moor posted to the Met branch of the RAF.

No flying was possible because of bad weather.

2 November 1943

East Moor hockey team lost the first game in the YMCA league 8 - 0, to the RCAF Station team at Middleton St.George.

No flying recorded due to bad weather.

3 November 1943

East Moor soccer team lost 8 goals to nil to the village team at Brafferton - Helperby.

Flying Officer L.B. Scott, Intelligence Officer on detached duty to Linton on Ouse. Weather improved, 1679 HFC continued with conversion training.

5 November 1943

The following crew arrived at East Moor from 24 OTU to be converted to the Lancaster II by 1679 HCF, R55051 Sgt. O.D. Lewis (pilot), R161134 Sgt D. McLeoud,(nav), J26299 P/O R.M. Potts (B/A), 1397359 Sgt J. Chadwick (WOP/OG), R205169 Sgt G.A. Turrenne (MU/AG), 1624932 Sgt J. Sowerby (AG).

Squadron Leader C.B. Sinton is to leave East Moor and 432 Squadron to command the newly formed 433 Squadron at Skipton on Swale which is equipped with Halifax bombers.

Squadron Leader Sinton posted out to command 433 (RCAF) Squadron.

6 November 1943

Tragedy struck 1679 HCF when Lancaster II, DS649 crashed at Rose Cottage Farm, Terrington after striking some trees. The following crew members were killed,P/O R.A. Davis, (Pilot), F/S A.H. MacDonald (B/A), Sgt F.W. Hunt (W/OP),Sgt L.W. Lenny (M/U), Sgt R.L. Green (A/G), and Sgt P.C. Mitchell (F/E). Only the Navigator survived. All night flying was cancelled.

At 17.00 hrs, seven crews participated in a Bullseye exercise.

REPORT BY FLYING CONTROL OFFICER EAST MOOR ON CRASH OF DS649

1. I was Duty Flight Controller on the afternoon of November 6th 1943, during which period details of circuits and landings fo 1679 Con. Flight started at 14.18 hrs with three aircraft A, F and E. Runway in use No.4. Magnetic heading 349 degrees, Wind 300 degrees true 20 mph.

2. Lancaster E first take off 14.18 hrs and continued detail making final take off at 16.46 hrs.

3. At 1705 hrs a member of our crash crew sighted smoke NE of Al/drome about ten miles distant. Since we had A 1679 on the ground and F 1679 on Pancake, we immediately tried to contact E 1679 on R/T. About 17.04 we informed the C.F.I of what had transpired, requested permission for him to allow F 1679 to take off and investigate smoke. At the same time we advised the Medical Officer, Engineering Officer and the Acting Station Commander and placed crash tender and ambulance on Stand By also requested R.O.C plots from base.

4. Lancaster F 1679 took off and on reporting that it was an a/c burning the crash tender, ambulance, Medical Officer and Engineering Officer set out immediately. F 1679 continued to circle to assist in locating the crash. At 17.25 Base gave position of crash as HOVINGHAM and as this is within our area of responsibility a guard from the RAF Regiment was arranged.

5. The final position of the crash was established as being near Rose Cottage Farm.

6. Our crash tender succeeded in putting out what fire there was, the a/c was completely smashed, there were no survivors.

The met. report for 1700 hrs was weather fine - wind 300 degrees true 15 mph - cloud 3/10ths at 2,000 feet - visibility 25/30 miles.

        Signed,   A.McCullough

Flying Control Officer.

Fig 15. S/L Strachan and crew, East Moor winter 1943/44.
Photo G. Rogers

Fig 16. Setting out for a spot of leave. Sgt Martin, 432Sqd Navigator, 1943/44

9 November 1943

A soccer match staged between 432 Squadron and the East Moor contingent of the RAF Regiment resulted in a win for the latter by 2 goals to nil.

The station hockey team fared no better losing to Topcliffe 5 - 2.

11 November 1943

Rembembrance day saw the station personnel on parade at 0.730 hrs on an extremely foggy airfield and in the presence of the 62 Base Commander. The latter saw fit to comment upon the headgear of some officers and suggested that the use of ring stiffeners would improve their appearance.

12 November 1943

Sergeants Slegg, De Maria and Pay completed their conversion courses with 1679 HCF and returned to 432 Squadron which was declared a strictly Lancaster one from that date.

13 November 1943

1679 HCF continued with conversion training programmes which were evidenced by the Lancasters carrying out circuits and bumps exercises, and a further two 432 squadron crews, F/S Maddock and Poole completing their courses.

14 November 1943

Was an extremely bad day with contiuous heavy rain prevailing over East Moor.

Intelligence Officers F/Lt's E.F Kusch and H.F.Lount became established at East Moor after being temprorary attached from Skipton on Swale.

15 November 1943

1679 HCF were engaged on circuits and bumps exercises throughout the day, and another two converted 432 Squadron crews were turned out, R149073 Sergeant J.R. Goodwin being one of them.

16 November 1943

1679 HCF were engaged in cross countries and circuits and landing exercises all day.

432 Squadron suffered the loss of Lancaster II, DS847 when Sergeant R.C.Burgess and crew attempted a landing at Ingham, Three engines were on fire and had to be cut before the attempt which resulted in a crash in which Flight Sergeants Burgess and Mayo (BIA) lost their lives along with Sergeant K.F.Simmons (F/E). F/S Mayo had survived the ditching of Wellington LN554 on 23rd September.

17 November 1943

V30203 Squadron Officer M.P.Thompson posted in to East Moor from 3 PRC at Bournemouth.

Runway 17 saw the completion of its Sodium Light Funnel facility and which was declared serviceable.

The station football team defeated RCAF Tholthorpe by 5 goals to 2.

The ENSA concert party staged Sunny Skies on the station and afterwards the cast entertained in the officers mess.

1679 HCF were placed on stand by for a possible Sea Search.

18 November 1943

432 Squadron carried out their first operation since the 22nd October,when four Lancaster crews were dispatched on a Sea Search,

DS851 'D'		DS788 'E'		LL618 'F'		DS792 'U'	
F/O Hatfield	H	F/O Mercer	A	F/S Slegg	A	Sgt Pay	W

Flying Officers Hatfield and Mercer made early returns with Technical failures. No flying training carried out by 1679 HCF who were on stand by.

21 November 1943

Air Ministry Works Department advised that all contractors work force were due to leave the station by 31st December 1943. There were still several small buildings to be completed and some major ones including the Operations Block and the aircrew locker rooms.

The station suffered inclement weather which hampered flying during the day, but 1679 HCF carried out circuits and landings at night.

22 November 1943

Group Captain J.A. Searby (43128) of Path Finder fame visited East Moor along with Air Commodore C.M. McEwan, MC, DFC. The former officer gave PFF lectures to 432 Squadron and 1679 HCF personnel.

23 November 1943

Three of 432 Squadrons Lancaster crews were out on a further Sea Search,

DS829 'A'		DS831 'N'		DS843 'O'	
F/S Poole	J	P/O Meaden	W	P/O Spink	T

24 November 1943

The following four 432 Squadron crews completed a further Sea Search,

DS851 'D'		DS829 'A'		DS852 'C'		DS830 'S'	
F/S Slegg	A	F/S De Maria	C	F/S Dennis	P	F/S Poole	J

25 November 1943

C1940 Squadron Leader H.B. McKibbon attached East Moor from Middleton St.George for supernumerary Admin duties.

C5630 Flight Lieutenant J.O.Doehler attached East Moor from 331 Wing for temporary Engineering duties, pending posting.

26 November 1943

From this date 432 Squadron was known as the Leaside having been adopted by the Ontario town of that name.

Ten 432 Squadron Lancasters left East Moor for an attack on the German capital Berlin in a force of 443 aircraft. This was the first bombing operation carried out from the station involving Lancasters and was led by the 432 Squadron Commander,

DS848 'R'		DS843 '0'		DS830 'S'		LL618 'F'	
W/C McKay	A	Sgt Pay	W	P/O Spink	T	F/S Slegg	A

DS832 'K'		DS844 'H'		DS831 'N'		DS829 'A'	
F/O Hatfield	H	F/O Wales	C	F/L Strachan	W	P/O Esdale	J
F/S DeMaria 2nd Plt				F/S Goodwin 2nd Plt			

DS740 'Z'		LL632 G	
P/O Rae E		F/S Dennis	P

All returned safely from a reasonably successful raid on a clear night, but not without incident.

Flight Sergeant P.W.Dennis and his air gunner Sergeant J.H.Quesnal were awarded DFMs for their conduct and the following is taken from their citation;

Flight Sergeant Dennis has completed numerous sorties and has displayed great skill, determination and devotion to duty. In November 1943 he piloted an aircraft detailed to attack Berlin. Whilst over the target area his aircraft was attacked on three occassions by enemy fighters. Nevertheless he skillfully evaded the enemy aircraft and successfully attacked the target, afterwards flying his badly damaged aircraft to base.

As rear gunner, Sgt Quesnal has taken part in several sorties and proved himself to be a cool and reliable member of aircraft crew. During a sortie one night in October 1943 his aircraft was attacked by enemy fighters. In the engagement Sgt Quesnal fought with great resolution and destroyed one of the attackers. On another occasion in November 1943 his aircraft was attacked three times by enemy fighters. His turret was rendered unserviceable but he cooly directed his pilots combat manouvres and the attackers were evaded.

30 November 1943

Squadron Leader W.W. Strachan appointed A Flight Commander, 432 Squadron.

1 December 1943

143316 Pilot Officer W.Ramage posted to East Moor from Linton on Ouse as Gas & Fire Officer.

The station Hockey team were undergoing a severe physical training period in an effort to ensure their peak fitness for future games.

2 December 1943

432 Squadron dispatched the following ten crews to take part in Bomber Commands fifth raid in the so called Battle of Berlin[1] when their Lancasters formed part of a force of 458 aircraft,

DS850 'M'		DS832 'K'		DS851 'D'		DS843 'O'	
SIL Hess	C	F/O Hatfield	H	F/O Wales	O	Sgt McIntosh	J

DS789 'V'		LL617 'J'		DS829 'A'		DS788 'E'	
P/O Spink	T	F/S Dennis	P	F/L Barrett	C	F/O Mercer	A

DS792 'U'		LL618 'F'	
Sgt Pay	W	F/S Slegg	A

F/O Wales and crew were attacked by an enemy aircraft on the return flight. Sgt Dickinson the rear gunner spotted an unidentified four engine aircraft below and instructed the pilot to corkscrew as cannon and machine gun fire hit the Lancaster rendering the mid upper turret u/s and damaged the pressure lines.

Sgt Dickinson returned fire and the attacker was shaken off. Back at East Moor DS851 overshot the runway and was completely destroyed in the fields beyond.

FlSgt Dennis suffered engine failure and did not take off.

F/L Barrett, F/O Mercer and Sgt Pay made early returns due to Technical failures.

Flight Sergeant Slegg and crew failed to return.

Sgt McIntosh landed at Manston out of fuel.

3 December 1943

With Leipzig as the target, eight crews of 432 Squadron left East Moor, forming part of a force of 527 aircraft which made the most succeeful attack of the war on that city,

LL636 'B'		DS740 'Z'		DS792 'U'		DS829 'A'	
S/L Strachan	W	P/O Rae	D	F/S Pay	W	P/O Esdale	J

DS851 'D'		LL617' J'		DS848 'R'		DS830 'S'	
F/O Mercer	A	F/S Dennis	P	F/O Fisher	W	F/S De Maria	C

Five crews made early returns with u/s guns, P/O Esdale, F/O Mercer, F/S Dennis, F/O Fisher and F/S De Maria.

4 December 1943

Squadron Leader Marshall, A & SD posted to Linton on Ouse.

C1666 Squadron Leader W.D. Flatt posted to East Moor from Linton as S.AD.0

7 December 1943

Despilte the struggle to reach a higher standard of play the station hockey team suffered defeat at the hands of Linton on Ouse. It was said that practice was required but as the nearest rink was at Durham the team was handicapped.

9 December 1943

An organized football game between aircrew and the Armament section of 432 sqd saw the former side win 4 goals to 1.

10 December 1943

1679 HCF having completed the conversion to Lancaster IIs of 408, 426 and 432 squadrons had received instructions to prepare to leave East Moor for nearby Wombleton and the Advance Party moved to the latter station on this date.

13 December 1943

1679 HCF completed their move to Wombleton.

16 December 1943

Ten 432 Squadron crews set out for Berlin, sadly only eight returned to East Moor.

DS832 'K'
F/O Hatfield   C

DS789 'V'
P/O Meaden   W

DS792 'U'
F/S Pay W

DS830 'S'
P/O Spink   T

DS848 'R'
FIS Palmer   D

LL617 'J'
F/S Dennis   P

LL636 'B'
F/L Strachan W

DS851 'D'
F/L Wales   C

DS831 'N'
F/O Fisher   W
FIS Lewis 2nd Plt

DS843 '0'
P/O Legace

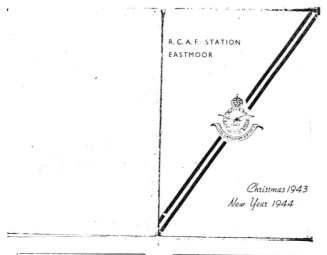

Fig 17.

Christmas menu 1943.

- 97 -

On the return flight F/O Hatfield and crew were diverted to Leeming but short of fuel and unable to locate the airfield in poor visibility it was decided to abandon DS832 over Danby Beacon. The crew survived and the bomber crashed at Castleton, the WOP suffered a broken arm, 1386694 Sgt Poole.

At 20.04 hrs Sergeant Gilliard the rear gunner in LL636 fired a burst at an aircraft astern which broke into 3 pieces and disappeared.

Sadly F/O Fisher and crew failed to return from this operation.

Earlier in the day Flight Lieutenant Keen visited East Moor and gave a lecture to 432 sqd personnel on German methods of Prisoner of War interrogation methods.

20 December 1943

East Moor dispatched ten 432 Squadron Lancaster IIs to form part of an attacking force of 650 aircraft with Frankfurt as the target,

DS829 'A'	DS850 'M'	DS848 'R'	DS830 'S'
P/O Esdale J	S/L Hess C	F/S Palmer D	P/O Spink T

DS740 'Z'	LL6l7 'J'	DS788 'E'	LL647 'D'
F/S Pay W	F/S Dennis P	F/O Mercer A	F/L Wales C

DS794 'W'	DS789 'V'
F/O Von Laufer D	P/O Meaden M

The rear gunner of DS788 hit an unidentified aircraft at 20.20 hrs with tracer fire which was seen to enter the fuselage before the aircraft disappeared.

At 19.46 hrs a JU88 opened fire on F/L Wales aircraft but overshot and was lost to view.

Christmas 1943 came and went in traditional style at East Moor where the Station Commander, Group Captain H.M. Carscallen DFC sent the seasons greetings to all. The Menu in the ranks mess included soup, roast turkey and ham, sausage dressing, roast potatoes, brussels sprouts, creamed spinach and gravy to be followed by Christmas pudding, custard sauce and mince pies all of which was of course served by the officers.

In the evening a station dance was held in the gymnasium.

29 December 1943

And it was business as usual when the station dispatched fourteen Lancasters to Berlin in a 712 strong force, and Lieutenant Hodenfield was a passenger in F/S Denniss aircraft - collecting material for a broadcast - and gaining an impression of a bombing operation,

DS740 'Z'	P/O	D Rae	LL647 'D'	F/L	C Wales
DS852 'C'	F/L	C Barrett	DS829 'A'	P/O	J Esdale
DS830 'S'	P/O	L Legace	DS848 'R'	P/O	J McIntosh
LL618 'F'	F/O	J Seiben	DS788 'K'	F/S	P Dennis
DS792 'U'	F/S	W Pay	DS739 'Y'	P/O	H Whaley
DS843 'O'	F/S	J Poole	DS794 'W'	F/O	D Von Laufer
DS844 'H'	F/S	W Ferneyhough			

Pilot Officer Rae returned with heavy flak damage to DS740.

Flight Sergeant Pay and crew had to take evasive action to avoid colliding with two other aircraft which had collided ahead of theirs, and at 20.15 hrs DS792 received damage to the mid upper turret.

Flying Officer Von Laufer and Flight Sergeant Poole returned early with technical faults, as did Flight Sergeant Ferneyhough who was unfortunate to crash DS844 on landing.

1944

1& 2 January 1944

Nine 432 Squadron crews were dispatched to the German capital Berlin

DS848 'R'	P/O	J McIntosh	DS794 'W'	F/O	D Von Laufer
DS788 'E'	F/O	A Mercer	DS852 'C'	F/L	C Barrett
DS830 'S'	P/O	T Spink	LL686 'F'	F/S	W Ferneyhough
DS739 'Y'	F/L	J Allen	DS850 'M'	F/O	L Legace
DS792 'U'	F/S	W Pay			

Flight Lieutenant Barrett and crew were fired upon by friendly ack ack over Southampton on the return flight and DS852 was damaged as a result.

Flying Officer Legace and crew mistook searchlights over the English coast for enemy intruder activity, and after cicling them were too late for zero hour and jettisoned their load and returned to East Moor.

Johnny Banks was the flight engineer in DS830 which took off at 00.30 hours and was at 18,000 feet by the time that the Dutch coast was reached. The target was found to covered by 10/10 cloud, successfully attacked and a course set for the Lancasters return, crossing the coast just south of Calais. The crew were watching a formation of B17s heading outwards when the skipper discovered that the throttle to the port inner engine was jammed. Difficulties arose when a landing was attempted at East Moor, and the pilot was forced to overshoot. A second attempt was made and after touch down the bomber became unmanageable. It left the runway, careered across the airfield and with the crash tender and the ambulance in hot pursuit, it narrowly missed the Flight Office before coming to rest on a vacant dispersal. DS830 was badly damaged but the crew escaped injury.

After debriefing they crawled into bed by 10.30 hrs to be roused again at 17.00 to be briefed for another trip to Berlin, their fifth to that city.

2& 3 January 1944

Within fifteen hours of the previous operation to Berlin, 432 Squadron crews were dispatched to the German capital again, the following ten being involved,

DS788 'E'	P/O	T Spink	LL647 'D'	F/L	C Wales
LL617 'J'	F/S	P Dennis	LL636 'B'	F/S	C De Maria
DS757 'L'	P/O	H Whaley	DS850 'M'	P/O	L Legace
DS792 'U'	P/O	J McIntosh	DS843' 0'	P/O	W Meadon
DS794 'W'	P/O	D Rae	DS739 'Y'	F/L	J Allen

This proved to be an eventful trip for at least two of the East Moor crews. Sgt Johnny Banks was flight engineer in DS788 and was again involved in a hairy do. Hampered all the way to the target by a severe weather front, they were attacked while in cloud by a four engined FW200 Kondor gun ship. Only the prompt action of the skipper averted a mid air collision, as he threw the Lancaster into a steep dive. After a rapid descent of around 6,000 feet level flight was only regained with some difficulty. It was then realised that the oxygen system had been rendered u/s in the attack. On arrival at the target it was found that the damage to the electrics prevented the release of the bomb load. However, the crew did manage to release their cookie by hand before setting course for England. Throughout the return leg the flight engineer fed his skipper, P/O Spink with oxygen from a portable bottle, and the aircraft was put down at Coleby Grange. Pilot Officer Spink was awarded the DFC. At Coleby Grange it was discovered that the photo flash unit had come adrift and had been rolling around making a hole in in the aircrafts floor. Another lucky escape.

The other East Moor crew referred to was skippered by Pilot Officer J McIntosh and was visiting Berlin for the third time. Despite a delayed take off due to a faulty turret, and the altimeter and air speed indicator becoming u/s en route, the target was reached and bombed almost on time. On leaving the target area DS792 was attacked by a Me110 and cannon shells ripped into the Lancaster. The two gunners got in some return fire just before their skipper found himself wrestling with the controls of a rapidly descending aircraft. A superhuman effort by P/O McIntosh followed and the bomber was brought under control at around 10,000 feet. Course was set for home with many of the instruments shattered, the hydraulics and radio damaged beyond any use and the bomb doors hanging down. By some miracle, the skipper was able to mantain a steady course and height as the crew chopped out equipment to lighten the bomber. Finally Woodbridge was reached where a landing on one wheel preceded a ground loop. The Lancaster had been raked from end to end.

Sadly, Flight Lieutenant J Allen and crew failed to return from this mission. The entire crew paid the ultimate price. F/L Allen was on his second tour.

3 January 1944

Flight Lieutenant H.H Harris assumed duty as Adjutant of 432 Squadron vice Flight Lieutenant H.G Phillips.

Wing Commander Pierce and a photographic team from Air Force Headquarters at Ottawa visited East Moor.

5 & 6 January 1944

Stettin was the target for East Moors crews and 432 Squadron dispatched the following   twelve,

DS843 'O'	LL686 'F'	DS829 'A'	DS850 'M'
F/O Lagce L	F/O Ferneyhough W	P/O Esdale J	P/O Rae D
DS848 'R'	DS797 'W'	LL636 'B'	DS852 'C'
F/S Palmer D	F/O Von Laufer D	F/S Pay W	F/L Barrett C
LL617 'J'	LL647 'D'	DS789 'V'	DS757 'L'
F/S Dennis P	F/L Wales C	P/O Meaden W	P/O Whaley H

LL686 was attacked by an enemy aircraft but a combination of return fire from the rear gunner and corkscrewing by the pilot shook it off.

Pilot Officer Whaley aborted with technical failure.

Fig 18. East Moor Radar Workshop
Rear. Kopperson, Thompson, F/O Budzak, Hayes, Flett
Centre, Atkinson, Hamilton. Front, Pinkey Christoff, Parsons, Hainsworth, Mahaffey.
Photo G Rogers

The Naval yards suffered considerable damage and at least eight ships were sunk there.

6 January 1944

The new Officers Mess for the WAAF compliment was opened on the WAAF Site.

Air Commodore MeKewan was on the station and had been present at the aircrews debriefing.

432 Squadron were stood down

7 January 1944

Station Commander inspected the Intelligence Section.
No operations were carried out from East Moor.

8 January 1944

Group Captain F.L Trethewey visited the station.

Squadron Leader C.B Hess assumed temporary command of 432 Squadron which was still stood down.

9 January 1944

A soccer match was staged on the station between two RAF Regiment teams.

There were numerous visiting officers at East Moor during this period, Wing Commanders H.M Smith (Engineer), and C.O King (Equipment).

10 January 1944

Group Captain P.C Gordon visited the Intelligence Section along with Squadron Leader K.G Greenwood an Intelligence Officer.

Fig 19. 'Tony' Yaunish and colleages outside their favourite York 'Watering Hole'

Photo T. Yaunish.

11 January 1944

In the interests of security, all the civilian workers at East Moor were given a lecture by Flight Lieutenant E.F Kusch in the station gymnasium.

432 Squadron were still stood down.

A team of Medical Officers visited the station and included Wing Commander J.C Whyte, and Flight Lieutenants N. Foster and A. Martin.

A lecture was given at 14.30 hours in the Briefing room by Flying Officer L.B Scott, the subject - The Effect of Allied Bombing on Germany.

12 & 13 January 1944

432 Squadron were still without any operational commitments.
Further visitors to the Intelligence Section included Air Commodore C. Slemon and the Group Signals Officer, Wing Commander Smith.

14 January 1944

Flight Lieutenant E.F Kusch was appointed Station Entertainments Of ficer and in the evening the WAAFs held a most successful dance in the NAAFI to the music of East Moors orchestra.

Lieutenant Colonel Crawford brought a detachment of the York Home Guard to East Moor to take an RAF Regiment course on the latest anti tank gun.

Sixteen crews from 432 Squadron took off for what was the first heavy attack on Brunswick when nearly 500 aircraft were involved and it was said that most of the bombing was scattered,

DS829	'A'	P/O	J Esdale	LL63	'B'	S/L	W Strachan	LL686	'F'	F/S	J Seiben
DS830	'S'	P/O	T Spink	DS852	'C'	F/L	C Barrett	DS843	'0'	F/S	J Poole
LL718	'K'	F/S	P Dennis	DS844	'H'	F/S	C DeMaria	LL647	'D'	F/O	A Mercer
DS850	'M'	F/S	C Wales	DS740	'Z'	P/O	D Rae	LL724	'N'	P/O	W Whaley
DS848	'R'	F/S	D Palmer	DS794	'W'	F/L	D VonLaufer	DS792	'U'	F/S	W Pay
DS789	'V'	F/O	L Lagace								

Two crews failed to return from this mission, Flight Sergeant Wales and that of Pilot Officer Rae.

Flight Lieutenant Cooper was 2nd pilot in B and Flying Officer Smith in 'S'.

Air Vice Marshal Brookes and Air Commodore McKewan were present at take off and and the former was accompanied by Group Captain Bradshaw, Major Stephenson, G/FO and Major Slater at the debriefing.
Two Lancasters from Linton on Ouse landed at East Moor, OW-W of 426 Squadron and DS705 EQ-K of 408 Squadron and the crews were debriefed there.

Squadron Leader W.W Strachan earned the DFC on this operation. On approach to the target LL636 had been attacked by a Me109 and shortly after leaving the target a four engined gun ship inflicted considerable damage. The two air gunners returned the fire which together with the pilots corkscrewing shook the enemy off . However,the upper turret was holed, the rudders damaged and numerous holes appeared in the fuselage. Unkown at that time the Lancasters undercarriage had been damaged and upon landing at East Moor, it swung off the runway at a ninety degree angle. The time down was 22.55 hours.

15 January 1944

It became neccessary to accommodate No. 1666 and 1679 Heavy Conversion Units at East Moor when the runways at Wombleton became unserviceable and the AdvanceParty arrived on this date.

432 Squadron were stood down.

16 January 1944

Group Captain D.E Wray, AEC the Commanding Officer at RCAF Skipton on Swale and Group Captain C.O Lightbourne the Senior Protestant Chaplain visited East Moor where the latter conducted the evening service.

The weather at East Moor prevented the move from Wombleton of the HCU, but the former station received a visit from an ATC party who were given a lecture on security, by Flight Lieutenant L.B Scott.

18 January 1944

432 Squadron were still on stand down.

The Group Intelligence Officer, C.H Ashlin together with the Groups new FLO Major Slater visited the Station Intelligence Section.

Air Commodore McKewan paid another visit to East Moor.

The RCAF East Moor hockey team beat RCAF Station Croft 5 goals to one in a match held at Durham.
The Station basketball team were in winning form too beating No.6 Group H.Q 14 to 11 at York.

19 January 1944

This was the fifth consecutive day without any operational commitments at East Moor.

The Senior Flying Control Officer Flight Lieutenant T.D Brundage and Flight Lieut G.   Munro Intelligence, both of Skipton, visited East Moor Intelligence Section.

20 January 1944

Despite recent losses, East Moor and 432 Squadron managed to put up fifteen crews for an operation against Berlin,

DS825 'A'	P/O	J Esdale		DS852 'C'	F/L	C Barrett
	P/O	C Cooper	2/Plt			
LL647 'D'	F/O	A Mercer		LL686 'F'	F/S	J Seiben
LL723 'H'	F/S	D DeMaria		LL617 'J'	F/S	P Dennis
LL718 'K'	F/O	H Smith		DS757 'L'	P/O	J Whaley
LL724 'N'	P/O	L Legace		DS843 'O'	F/S	J Poole
DS848 'R'	F/S	D Palmer		DS830 'S'	P/O	D Spink
					F/O	Patterson 2/Plt
LL719 'U'	F/S	W Pay		DS789 'V'	P/O	W Meaden
					F/O	Reid 2/Plt
DS794 'W'	F/L	D Von Laufer				

There were two early returns, Pilot Officer Esdale with a navigational breakdown and Flight Sergeant Poole with oxygen failure.

Air Commodore McEwan and Wing Commander M.M Smith (BTO) attended the de-brief.

21 January 1944

The Stations: RAF Regiment.soccer team played their counterparts at RCAF Station Linton on Ouse losing by 4 - 2.

Thirteen Lancasters were dispatched from the station when 432 Squadron contributed to a total force of almost six hundred and fifty aircraft attacking Magdeburg,

LL724 'N'	F/O	L Legace		DS843 'O'	F/S	J Poole
LL719 'U'	F/S	W Pay		LL632 'G'	P/O	W Esdale

					F/L	Cooper 2/Plt
DS757 'L'	P/O	H Whaley		LL718 'K'	F/O	H Smith
DS830 'S'	P/O	T Spink		LL723 'H'	F/S	D DeMaria
	F/O	Patterson	2/Plt			
DS789 'V'	F/S	G Seiben		LL647 'D'	F/O	A Mercer
LL617 'J'	F/S	P Dennis		DS794 'W'	F/L	D Von Laufer
DS852 'C'	F/L	C Barrett				
	F/O	Reid	2/Plt			

Sadly, two further crews were lost on th is operation, those of Flying Officer Legace and Flight Sergeant Poole.

Flight Lieutenant Von Laufer made an early return with u/s guns and had to put down at RCAF Station Linton Ouse at 00.17 hours due to a crashed Halifax, presumably from 1666 HCU, blocking East Moors runway.

Flight Lieutenant Barrett was forced to put down at RAF Station Wratting Common with flak damage while the remainder of East Moors crews were diverted to Mepal, Horham and Methal.

22 January 1944

Flight Lieutenant Barrett and crew had to leave their badly shot up DS852 at Wratting Common and returned to York by train and thence by road to East Moor.
Air gunner, Pilot Officer Logan had been admitted to a local hospital with a foot injury.
432 Squadron were stood down from operations and in the afternoon lectures were given to the aircrew on security measures.

23 January 1944

There was no operational commitments at East Moor.

Two Canadian Army Officers arrived at East Moor to participate in a familiarization exercise with 432 Squadron.

A visiting party of Air Training Corps were given a conducted tour of the Station Intelligence Section and a security lecture. They went on to see the Operations Block and some of the Technical Buildings before being permitted to take some photographs of the Flying Control and the interior of the Airmens Mess.
Lancaster II, DS839 from 1679 HCF was lost in a crash at Ridgemont after icing up over Bedfordshire.

24 January 1944

432 Squadron were on stand down.

Trade Tests for the stations Intelligence Section clerical staff were conducted by Squadron Leader F.H Ballance Stuart.

25 January 1944

Operations were called for but subsequently scrubbed after the briefing had taken place.

Squadron Leaders A.C Tufts, N. Foster and W.D Flatt from 62 Base inspected the Station Intelligence Section and the Aircrew Quarters.

East Moor defeated RCAF Station Leeming in a Ice Hockey game held at Durham, the score 7-2, while the Basketball team defeated RCAF Station Linton on Ouse 34-7.

26 January 1944

Confirmation of the award of the DFC to Squadron Leader Strachan was received. Advice was received at East Moor that 432 Squadron would shortly convert from the Lancaster II to the Halifax III!.

Flight Lieutenant L. Scott took over Chief Flying Control Officer duties from Squadron Leader M.D Loucks posted out to RCAF Station Linton on Ouse.

ENSA Concert Party staged Something New to a full house during the evening.

27 January 1944

Fifteen Lancaster crews from 432 Squadron set out for Berlin,

DS829 'A'	P/O	J Esdale		LL617 'J'	F/S	P Dennis
DS848 'P'	F/S	D Palmer		DS830 'S'	P/O	T Spink
					W/O	Jones 2/Plt
LL725 'O'	P/O	J McIntosh		LL719 'U'	F/S	W Pay
DS757 'L'	F/S	W Ferneyhough		LL686 'F'	F/S	C Seiben
LL632 'G'	F/O	H Smith		LL723 'H'	F/S	D DeMaria
LL637 'Z'	F/O	E Reid		DS794 'W'	F/L	D Von Laufer
LL647 'D'	F/L	J Cooper		DS789 'V'	P/O	W Meaden
LL638 'M'	F/O	D Patterson				

Flying Officer Patterson and crew failed to return from this mission. Three aircraft landed away, D and V at Wratting Common, W at Middle Wallop.

28 January 1944

Berlin was again the target for East Moors crews when 432 Squadron provided thirteen in a total force of over six hundred and seventy,

DS829 'A'	P/O	J Esdale		LL719 'U'	F/S	A Pay
DS757 'L'	S/L	W Strachan		LL617 'J'	F/S	P Dennis
	F/O	Rance	2/Plt		F/S	Vincent 2/Plt
LL686 'F'	F/S	J Seiben		LL723 'H'	F/S	C DeMaria
LL647 'D'	F/O	A Mercer		LL718 'K'	F/S	W Ferneyhough
LL632 'G'	F/O	H Smith		LL725 'O'	P/O	J McIntosh
DS848 'R'	F/S	D Palmer		DS830 'S'	S/L	C Hess
	W/O	Jones	2/Plt			
LL637 'Z'	F/O	E Reid				

Forty six aircraft were lost on this operation but fortunately all the East Moor contingent returned safely. Pilot Officer Esdale suffered some facial cuts when his aircraft was hit by flak.

29 January 1944

There was no operational commitment at East Moor.

30 January 1944

No. 1666 and 1679 HCUs main party and the air party returned to their base at
Womble ton.

For the third time in four days, 432 Squadron crews set out for Berlin on what was a concentrated attack involving more than 550 aircraft. The following twelve took part in what was East Moors last Lancaster bombing operation,

DS829 'A'	P/O T Spink	LL647 'D'	F/L J Cooper	DS788 'E	F/O A Mercer
LL686 'F'	F/S D Ferneyhough	LL632 'G'	F/O W Smith	LL723 'H	F/S 'C' DeMaria
LL617 'J'	F/S P Dennis	DS757 'L'	S/L W Strachan	LL725 'O'	P/O J Mcintosh
DS848 'R'	F/S D Palmer	DS789 'V	P/O W Meaden	LL637 Z'	F/O 'E' Reid

Flying Officer Mercer returned early with a sick navigator.

31 January 1944

The first Halifax III for 432 Squadron arrived at East Moor.

Flight Lieutenant Harris appointed Squadron Adjutant vice Flight Lieutenant Phillips.

A case of Scarlet Fever was reported in the WAAF Site.

1 February 1944

Air Commodore McKewan visited East Moor accompanied by Wing Commander M. Smith Gourdeau, 22nd Royal Montreal Regiment arrived on the station for a weeks detached duty and liasion exercise.

East Moor basketball team beat RCAF THolthorpe at York by 22 - 13.

Flying training continued apace both day and night in the absence of any ops.

2 February 1944

Lancaster II, LL686 failed to recover from a dive and crashed near Ripon with the loss of all on board, F/S J.G Seiben (pilot), F/O D.S. Kerr (nav), F/S W. Wolf (b/a), Sgt R. Pratt-Robinson (wop), F/S P.J. Power (a/g), Sgt G Finch (a/g) and Sgt K. Huggins (f/e).

The rear party of 1666 and 1679 HCU returned to Wombleton.

432 Squadron stood down.

3 February 1944

Authority was received at East Moor for 432 Squadron to re-equip with the Halifax III aircraft.

Fig 20. Dispersal No.33 - and a well earned rest for 432 Squadron ground crew in the summer of 1944. 'A' Flight rigger 'Bob' Day (right), Joe Colleax(left) and and unknown colleague. Photo R.Day

Six 432 Squadron crews carried out 'Bullseye' exercises.

In line with policy, nine crews were on leave with the commencement of the moon period.

Wing Commander W McKay the 432 Squadron Commander and Section Officer P. Thompson announced their engagement and intention to marry during the next long stand down period.

Flight Lieutenant E.F Kusch was promoted to Squadron Leader. (Intelligence)

4 February 1944

Information was received that the Station Commander Group Captain H. Carscallen DFC, was to be posted to Canada.

Flying training continued with 432 Squadron engaged in cross countries, circuits and landings and fighter affilliation exercises.
The WAAF's held a dance in their NAAFI and the band was made up of personnel from East Moor and Tholthorpe stations.

6 February 1944

The Senior Roman Catholic Padre Group Captain McCarthy visited East Moor, and with Squadron Leader LaPlante from Tholthorpe, conducted Mass.

7 February 1944

Two Halifax Mk III aircraft arrived at East Moor heralding the conversion of 432 Squadron to the type.

The funeral of Flight Sergeant Seiben and five of his crew was arranged for the 8th at Harrogate. Sergeant Huggins body had been sent for a family funeral at Bradford.

The old Sergeants Mess at East Moor was the scene for the newly created Corporals club first dance which was said to have been a success.

8 February 1944

Still no operations from East Moor.

A farewell party for Group Captain H. Carscallen DFC was held with an excellent dinner being provided by Flying Officer J.C Thurston and the Catering staff, and the Station Commander was presented with a silver tankard. The guests included Group Captain Gordon, Station Commander RCAF Station Tholthorpe and Squadron Leader W.L Marshall from RCAF Linton on Ouse.

432 Squadron's Lancaster Ii's were flown out of East Moor to nearby Linton on Ouse to be absorbed by the squadrons based there.

The fourth Halifax III arrived at East Moor, and 432 Squadron were converting to the type.

The Station basketball team enjoyed another victory beating No.6 Group H.Q by 19 to 6.

9 February 1944

Ten officers and a party of NCO's from East Moor attended the funeral service for Flight Sergeant Seiben and crew.

Nine Lancaster II's were flown out of the airfield to Linton on Ouse.

A Court Martial party arrived to convene at East Moor led by Squadron Leader Martin and Flight Lieutenant S. Berger from RCAF Overseas Headquarters.

The station enjoyed an ENSA concert featuring 'Marita' and her Gypsy Band.

Section Officer M Langley was posted out to Little Snoring.

10 February 1944

Group Captain J.E Fauquier DSO, DFC assumed command of RCAF Station East Moor.

A roaring north wind brought a heavy snowstorm to the base, the first of the winter, making the Canadians feel at home.

432 Squadron were busy converting to the Halifax and instructions were received that it would not become operational for at least a further ten days.

Four more Halifaxes arrived bringing the strength up to eight aircraft.

11 February 1944

A Valentine dance was held at which Group Captain Carscallen said goodbye to his other ranks in the station gymnasium. Music was provided by Linton on Ouse musicians.

Nursing Officer Sister M.D Arnett arrived for duty at East Moor.

12 February 1944

The new Station Commander G/Cpt Fauquier held a tour of Inspection on the Station.

Bad weather prevented flying training except for some circuits and landings by the Flight C$_0$mmanders.

13 - 15 February 1944

Some flying training was carried out during this period by 432 Squadron, but considerable time was spent in ground training and lectures.

The ATC were hosted once again and Flying. Officer Scott held further lectures on security.

Aircrews were shown an instructional film 'Prepare for Ditching in their briefing rooms, and were given lectures by Wing Commander P.G Powell DSO, DFC from 6 Group headquarters.

The Station Commander also gave talks during this period.

432 Squadron were still 'stood down' and converting to the Halifax III.

432 Sqd Lancaster crews at East Moor

Pilot	F/O Hatfield	H	F/O Mercer	A	F/S Slegg	A
Navigator	F/O Higgs	J	F/O Nicholson	W	F/S Lowle	G
Bomb Aimer	F/S Sunley	H	P/O Simpson	M	P/O Baker	S
WOP	Sgt Poole	W	Sgt Pett	S	F/S Morgan	A
M/Upper	Sgt Hutchinson	R	Sgt Peterson	J	Sgt Stinson	W
R/Gunner	F/S McGregor	A	Sgt McCluskie	A	Sgt Green	W
F/Engineer	Sgt Phillips	A	Sgt Thompson	J	Sgt Wadsworth	J
Pilot	Sgt Pay	W	Sgt Goodwin	J	P/O Rae D	
Navigator	Sgt Baker	J	P/O Doull	H	F/O Holmes	G
Bomb Aimer	Sgt Armstrong	G	P/O Crawford	M	W/O Lyng	D
WOP	Sgt Bell	J	W/O Scott	J	Sgt Howe	E

M/Upper	Sgt Houston	J	Sgt Dupuis	I	Sgt Carr	C
R/Gunner	Sgt King	A	Sgt Cobbett	J	F/S Hoppus	H
F/Engineer	Sgt Carr	S	Sgt Collier	W	Sgt Evans	K

Pilot	F/S Poole	J	P/O Meaden	W	P/O Spink	T
Navigator	F/S Thompson	W	P/O Barker	J	F/S Harmon	D
Bomb Aimer	Sgt Bailache	W	P/O West	W	Sgt Naylor	F
WOP	Sgt Myer	E	Sgt Ward	K	Sgt McFarlane	J
M/Upper	Sgt Keeler	W	Sgt Shaughnessy	G	Sgt Proulx	L
R/Gunner	F/S O'Donnell	W	F/S Alexander	P	F/S Leadley	W
F/Engineer	Sgt Williams	J	Sgt Chamberlain	H	Sgt Banks	J

Pilot	F/S De Maria	C	F/S Dennis	P	F/O Wales	C
Navigator	F/S Pearson	W	F/S Atkins	G	F/S Evans	J
Bomb Aimer	Sgt Quinn	C	P/O O'Gorman	J	Sgt Garvey	W
WOP	F/S Huddleston	A	Sgt Woolfenden	P	Sgt Aplin	J
M/Upper	Sgt Dupuis	I	Sgt Piding	W	F/L Painville	G
R/Gunner	Sgt Cobbett	J	Sgt Quesnel		Sgt Dickinson	J
F/Engineer	Sgt Hamilton	H	Sgt Kent	W	Sgt Thomas	D

Pilot	F/L Strachan	W	W/C McKay	W	P/O Esdale	J
Navigator	P/O Martin	M.	F/o Pogers	G	P/O D'Eye	K
Bomb Aimer	P/O Baron	H	F/O Grimsey	M	P/O Goom	G
WOP	P/O Stuart	P	F/S Thompson	P	F/S Middleton	G
M/Upper	F/O Pourke	K	W/O McEwan	P	Sgt Peterson	J
R/Gunner	F/S Stewart	H	F/S Thompson	W	F/S Pigeon	A
F/Engineer	Sgt Gilliard	A	P/Q Duncanson	P	Sgt Ibbotson	H

432 Sqd Lancaster crews at East Moor

Pilot	S/L Hess	C	Sgt McIntosh	J	F/L Barrett	G
Navigator	F/L Kemley	H	F/O Small	A	F/O Bentley	D
Bomb Aimer	F/S Hayward	G	Sgt Elvin	P	P/O Goom	G
WOP	P/O Hanniford	P	W/O Schell	C	F/S Logan	E
MlUpper	W/O McEwan	P	Sgt De Dauw	A	F/S Hamilton	A
R/Gunner	W/O Burnett	H	Sgt Bandle	L	Sgt Shaw	W
F/Engineer	Sgt Buckley	J	Sgt King	W	Sgt Coe	D

Pilot	F/O Fisher	W	F/S De Maria	C	P/O Meaden	W
Navigator	W/O Briegell	J	P/O Doull	M	P/O Bell J	
Bomb Aimer	F/S Pragnall	T	Sgt Quinn	G	P/O Pedman	A
WOP	F/S Brudell	N	W/O Haddleton	A	Sgt Ward	K
M/Upper	W/O Saunders	P	Sgt Strapps	L	W/O McEwan	P
R/Gunner	F/S Turner	H	F/S McIntyre	P	F/S Alexander	P
F/Engineer	Sgt Hodges	F	Sgt Hamilton	A	Sgt Chamberlain	H

Pilot	F/S Palmer	D	F/S Seiben	J	F/L Allen	J
Navigator	F/S Delbridge	K	F/O Kerr	D	F/O Doull	N
Bomb Aimer	F/S Porter	H	Sgt Wolf	W	F/O Crawford	K
WOP	F/S Calderwood	W	Sgt Pratt-Robinson		W/O Scott	J
M/Upper	F/S Rogers	H	Sgt Finch	D	Sgt Dupuis	I
R/Gunner	Sgt Mitchell	J	F/S Power	P	Sgt Cobbett	J
F/Engineer	Sgt Cakebread	J	Sgt Cakebread	J	Sgt Collier	W

Pilot	F/S Ferneyhough	W	P/O Whaley	H	F/O Smith	H
Navigator	Sgt Musser	J	F/O Burrows	J	F/OPlommer	P
Bomb Aimer	Sgt Kennedy	H	Sgt Doyle	K	F/O Balsden	C
WOP	F/S Lamphier	G	W/O McDonald	D	Sgt Clench	P
M/Upper	Sgt Lagimodiere	A	W/O Lynch	J	Sgt Pingle	P
R/Gunner	Sgt Racher	D	Sgt Driver	P	Sgt Pudland	P
F/Engineer	Sgt Hembry	J	Sgt Phillips	A	Sgt Le Strange	E

Pilot	F/O Reid	E	F/L Cooper	J	F/O Patterson	D
Navigator	P/O Smith	J	P/O Dryden	P	F/O Bell A	
Bomb Aimer	F/S McDonald	V	Sgt Zacharok	A	Sgt Heinen	F
WOP	Sgt McGuire	G	T/S Butkewitz	L	F/S Sherwood	C

M/Upper	Sgt Clarkson	P	Sgt Burton	P	F/S Wilson	P
R/Gunner	Sgt Barr	J	F/S Elliott	L	P/O Gates	A
F/Engineer	Sgt Nay	J	Sgt Oakeby	H	Sgt Greenaway	W

Lancaster II - 432 S/d - East Moor

DS633	QO-			transferred to HCU	
DS739	QO-Y	2 Ops	FTR	- Berlin (ex 1679 HCF)	3/ 1/44
DS740	QO-Z	6 Ops	FTR	- Brunswick 15/ 1/44	
DS757	QO-L	8 Ops		transferred to 408 sqd, Feb 1944	
DS788	QO-E	7 Ops		" " "	
DS789	QO-V	10 Ops		''' 426 "	
DS792	QO-U	8 Ops		crash landed Woodbridge - ex ops to Berlin	3/ 1/44
DS794	QO-W	9 Ops		transferred to 426 sqd, Feb 1944	
DS829	QO-A	13 Ops		" "	
DS830	QO-S	12 Ops		" "	
DS831	QO-N	3 Ops	FTR	- Berlin 6 crashed at Huizm 17/12/43	
DS832	QO-K	3 Ops		abandoned, ex Berlin, crashed at Castleton, no fuel,	17/12/43
DS839	QO-			transferred to 1679 HCF	
DS843	QO-O	10 Ops	FTR	- Magdeburg	21/ 1/44
DS844	QO-H	3 Ops		transferred to 408 sqd, Feb 1944	
DS847	QO-P			crashed 1 mile west of Ingham - engine fire	16/11/43
DS848	QO-R	12 Ops		transferred to 426 sqd, Feb 1944	
DS850	QO-M	6 Ops	FTR	- Brunswick	15/ 1/44
DS851	QO-D	5 Ops		overshot East Moor,ex Berlin, damaged	3/12/43
DS852	QO-C	7 Ops		transferred to 426 sqd, Feb 1944	
LL617	QO-J	11 Ops	"	" "	
LL618	QO-F	5 Ops	FTR	- Berlin	3/12/43
LL632	QO-G	4 Ops		transferred to 408 sqd, Feb 1944	
LL636	QO-B	5 Ops		" " "	
LL637	QO-Z	3 Ops		" " "	
LL638	QO-M	1 Op	FTR	- Berlin	28/1/44
LL647	QO-D	10 Ops		transferred to 426 sqd, Feb 1944	
LL686	QO-F	7 Ops		struck trees - crashed Pipon - night exercise	02/02/44
LL718	QO-K	4 Ops		transferred to 408 sqd, Feb 1944	
LL719	QO-U	4 Ops		" "	
LL723	QO-H	5 Ops		" "	
LL724	QO-N	2 Ops	FTR	- Magdeburg	21/01/44
LL725	QO-O	3 Ops		transferred to 408 sqd, Feb 1944	

A 432 Squadron navigator recalls......

"We arrived at Eastmoor on February 1 1944. 432 had Lancaster II's at the time, and we were assigned DS844. Our last flight was on Feb 8, after which someone took all the Lancasters away, and flew in some Halifax III's. We had flown a couple of Halifax II's at Wombleton, and I don't remember being vastly impressed with them; The III's were quite different, though, and we found them rugged and reliable!"

"A representative from Handley Page spent a whole day in the crew room, giving us a complete description of the new aircraft, all of which I have forgotten except for one sentence: 'You will notice gentlemen,that when you cut the power on a Halifax, it immediately assumes the gliding characteristics of a brick'. He was right too!"

"When the Halifaxes arrived we were assigned LW595, and made our first operation on 1st March 1944. About two weeks later, we were on a 'Bullseye' training flight, where we visited quite a few prohibited areas, to give the ground forces some practice in air defence. Sometime during the flight, our I.F.F began to sqidder. We were on a 180 track over Hull, and we were shot at by the ground defences. The fourth shot was like hitting a bad bump in the road, so we abandoned the rest of the trip and headed for East Moor. The ground crew found a hole about a foot long in the leading edge of the port fin, so LW595 went to Y.AR.D for a new assembly. We got her back about the first week in April, and flew anything handy in the meantime."

During July 1944, 432 Squadron received new Halifax VII's, they were cleaner in outline, with rounded wingtips and fitted with H25. We did eight ops in ours, NP693, before being screened. We did the whole 35 operations without firing our guns in anger: we shot up a few waves in the North Sea on occasion to give the gunners some practice. Not a wave survived !

16 February 1944

At 13.26 hours, Flight Sergeant Pay lifted the first of five 432 Halifaxes from the station's runway to commence a Sea Search,

LK761 'B'	F/S	W Pay	LW584 'Y'	F/O	E Reid
LW614 'S'	F/L	D Von Laufer	LW592 'A'	F/S	W Ferneyhough
LW596 'D'	F/O	W Smith			

Flying Officer Smith made an early return with u/s hydraulics.

In the evening, LK761 piloted by Squadron Leader Strachan, was one of four crews detailed for night cross country exercises. At 19.43 hours, and shortly after take off, the aircraft crashed between Huby and Stillington, was totally destroyed and the entire crew perished.

17 February 1944

The Station Commander, Group Captain J.E Fauquier DSO, DFC gave lectures to 432 Squadron airerews during the afternoon of this and the previous day.

No.432 Squadron were still on 'stand down'.

18 February 1944

The conversion of 432 Squadron to the Halifax III continued apace, with cross-country and fighter affilliation exercises being carried out.

Group Captain Fauquier DSO, DFC, held briefing proceedure and Intelligence briefings assisted by Squadron Leader E.F Kusch.

No.432 Squadron received a new Signals Leader in Flying Officer Sheriff posted in from 425 Squadron.
Wing Commander G.A Saunders visited the station from Bomber Command Headquarters.

The new Officer's Mess Committee included Major W Fanning as PMC, Flight Lieut. H. Lount as Secretary, while the House Committee was composed of Flying Officer J.Kemp, Squadron Leader P.J Doehler, Nursing Sister M.D Arnett and Flying Officer M.F Grimsey.

19 & 20 February 1944

No.432 Squadron was still 'stood down'.

The station hosted a contingent of the Air Training Corps whose itinery included security lectures given by Flying Officer L.B Scott.

21 February 1944

There was still no operational commitment at East Moor.

The Station Defence Officer Major W. Fanning assumed the duties of Base Defence Officer during the absence of Lieutenant Colonel Padfield.

The Corporal's Club invited dancing. partners from the local Land Army hostels and from Rowntrees Chocolate factory to a jig in the Old Sergeant's Mess.

22 February 1944

All Hallows Church at Sutton on Forest was the scene of the funeral service for 432 Squadron's 'A' Flight Commander Squadron Leader W. Strachan DFC, and his crew. Pilot Officer N. Martin (Nav), Flying Officer N. Baron (B/A), Pilot Officer

P. Stewart (WOP), First Lieutenant A. Rorke USAF (A/G), Pilot Officer H.Stuart (A/G) and Sergeant A. Gilliard (F/E). The service took place at 09.00 hours and was preceded by a parade of station and squadron personnel numbering three hundred and twenty five who marched from East Moor to the church. Interrment was at Stonefell Cemetery at 11.00 hours when comrades acted as pall bearers. Squadron Leader C.B Hess led the parade which included a Silver Band from the Fulford Barracks.

With the exception of First Lieutenant A. Rorke USAF, who was interred at the Brookwood Cemetery in Surrey, the crew received full British Military Honours.

24 February 1944

No.432 Squadron's first Halifax operation saw nine crews set off along the run-way for an attack on Schweinfurt and Germany's main ball bearing industry. Only eight became airborne, Flying Officer Reid left the runway and crashed LK754 at 18.25 hours, ending amongst trees near the perimeter. The crew escaped.

LW597 'C'	P/O	H Whaley		LW594 'G'	F/O	W Smith	
	F/S	Clarke	2/Plt				
LW596 'D'	F/L	Cooper		LW617 'J'	F/S	D Maddock	
	F/S	Menzies	2/Plt				
LW615 'U'	P/O	W Pay		LW582 'M'	P/O	J McIntosh	
					F/O	Barker	2/Plt
LK765 'H'	F/S	J Cooper		LK754 'Z'	F/O	E Reid	
	Sgt	Narum	2/Plt		F/S	Clarke	2/Plt
LW592 'A'	F/S	W Ferneyhough					

Pilot Officer McIntosh made an early return with oxygen failure and Flight Sergeant Cooper with a fuel leak in the overload tank.

With the exception of 'U', the remainder landed away, 'C' and 'G' at Little Horwood, 'D' at Ford, 'Y' at Waddington and 'J' at Stanton Harcourt.

25 February1944

Augsburg was the target for six crews from 432 Squadron when the town was devastated by almost six. hundred strong force,

LW593 'O'	F/O	E Reid	LW615 'U'	P/O	W Pay	
	F/S	Clarke 2/Plt		F/O	Barker	2/Plt
LW598 'K'	F/S	D Maddock	LW592 'A'	F/S	J Cooper	
				F/S	Narum	2/Plt
LW616 'R'	W/C	W McKay	LW597 'C'	Lt	A Lubold	

Lieutenant Al Lubold and crew failed to return from this operation.

Flight Sergeant Maddock made an early return with Technical failure.

Aircraft 'A' and 'P' landed at Middle Wallop, short of fuel on return.

The East Moor Station Orchestra provided the music for a WAAF dance in their NAAFI.

26 & 27 February 1944

East Moor crews were not required for operations. Heavy snow fell on the 27th.

28 & 29 February 1944

Air Vice Marshal NcEwan made his first visit to East Moor as AOC No.6 Group.

Operations were called for and scrubbed on the 28th.

432 Squadron was 'stood down' on the 29th. (Leap year). Five of the most experienced crews had reported sick.

1 March 1944

Eleven of 432 Squadron's Halifaxes participated in an attack on Stuttgart when the total force was around five hundred and sixty aircraft.

LW596 'D'	F/L	J Cooper		LW595 'Q'	F/O	J Barker	
LK764 'F'	F/S	D Maddock		LW615 'U'	P/O	W Pay	
					P/O	Hawkins	2/Plt
LK779 'W'	P/O	J McIntosh		LK766 'V'	F/S	W Ferneyhough	
	Sgt	Studnik	2/Plt		F/S	Millar	2/Plt
LW594 'G'	F/O	S Smith		LW582 'M'	F/O	E Reid	
	Sgt	Narum	2/Plt		F/S	Clarke	2/Plt
LW583 'L'	P/O	H Whaley		LW616 'R'	F/L	A Lowe	
LW617 'J'	P/O	P Dennis					

Flight Lieutenant Cooper made an early return with a u/s port inner engine. Ten crews bombed the primary target, six landed away from East Moor on diversion and four returned to base.

Six airc:raft, 'Q', 'U', 'V', 'F' and 'D' included were diverted to Wing returning to East Moor later in the day.

Contractors commenced work at the Strensall Bombing Range to provide additional accommodation and buildings for the Electrical Power Plant.

2 March 1944

432 Squadron were stood down.

WAAF Squadron Officer N. Holland, 'G' Officer from 62 Base (RCAF) visited East Moor and conducted an informal inspection.

At 20.05 hours a 425 Squadron Halifax, KW-A from Tholthorpe crashed north of East Moor station from where crash tender and ambulances were dispatched. Six of the crew died and one was seriously injured in the accident.

3 March 1944

No.6 Group's Senior Admin. Officer, Group Captain G.E Scott visited the station to discuss admin affairs with the Station Commander. The former was accompanied by Squadron Leader A.C Tufts, the Base Admin Officer.

The Kings Royal Rifle Corps Regimental Hand from Strensall provided the music for a most successful station dance held in the gymnasium.

On the eve of their wedding, Wing Commander W.A McKay and Squadron Officer M.P Thompson were presented with an antique silver sugar castor by personnel of the Intelligence Section.

4 March 1944

All Hallows Church at Sutton on Forest was the scene for a very happy occasion when W/C W.A McKay married S/0 M.P Thompson. Amongst the many guests were Air Vice Marshal M. McKewan DFC,the AOC of No.6 Group (RCAF) and the Station Commander Group Captain J.E Fauquier DSO, DFC. The Station Padre Squadron Leader

H.G Lowrey was assisted by Squadron Leader W.P Pleasance and the Rev. Canon Coombs vicar of Sutton and Dean of Easingwold.

The reception was held in the Officers Mess.

At 18.27 hours, Halifax LW617 overshot East Moor's runway in bad visibility and damaged the undercarriage, mamplane, tailplane and port propellers. The crew were uninjured.

5 March 1944

Flying Officer J.A Kemp, RAF Regiment assumed command of No.2799 Squadron of the RAF Regiment during the absence of Squadron Leader Aldrich. This squadron had detachments at RCAF Tholthorpe and at RCAF Linton on Ouse as well as East Moor.

6 March 1944

Group Captain J.E Fauquier DSO,'DFC assumed command of No.62 Base (RCAF) vice

Group Captain A.S Ross during the latters temporary absence.

East Moor's basketball team had yet another victory, this time over Linton at York Railway Institute, the score 25 - 11.

Squadron Leader R.M Trites the Group Armaments Officer visited East Moor to discuss the fitting of .5 Brownings to the Halifaxes.
Fourteen 432 Squadron crews were dispatched to attack railway targets at Trappes a successful operation and all East Moor aircraft returned safely to base
,

LW592 'A'	F/L	A Lowe	LW682 'C'	F/S	C Narum	LW643 'E'	F/O	A Mercer
LK764 'F'	F/S	D Maddock	LW594 'G'	F/O	W Smith	LW583 'L'	P/O	H Whaley
LW582 'M'	F/S	C Millar	LW593 'O'	P/O	J Mcintosh	LW595 'Q'	F/O	O Barker
LW616 'R'	P/O	P Dennis	LW615 'U'	P/O	W Pay	LK766 'V'	F/S	A Clark
LK779 'W'	F/S	E Clark	LW584 'Y'	F/L	J Cooper			

7 March 1944

The following fourteen crews were dispatched by 432 Squadron for the Railway Yard at Le Mans where severe damage was caused to locomotives and rolling stock,

LW592 'A'	F/L	A Lowe	LW682 'C'	F/S	C Narum
LW596 'D'	F/L	J Cooper	LK764 'F'	F/S	D Maddock
LW594 'G'	F/O	W Smith	LK765 'H'	P/O	W Pay
LW583 'L'	P/O	J Mcintosh	LW582 'M'	F/O	A Mercer
LW595 'Q'	F/O	J Barker	LW616 'R'	P/O	P Dennis
LW614 'S'	P/O	S Hawkins	LK766 'V'	F/S	A Clark
LK779 'W'	F/S	E Clark	LW584 'Y'	F/S	W Studnik

Flight Sergeant P Anthony was 2nd pilot with Pilot Officer Dennis.

Six crews brought their bombs back to East Moor as instructed by the Master Bomber.

Two crews aborted the mission, Flight Sergeant Narum with hydraulic failure and Flight Sergeant E Clark after the accidental release of his bombs in open country between four and six miles east of York.

8 March 1944

An M.T accident at Strensall Railway Station resulted in the death of R117405 LAG A.S Blanchard an Electrician 1, who was attached to Station Headquarters East Moor. His body was brought to East Moor and funeral arrangements were made for Saturday 11th March.

A new Senior Admin Officer arrived, Squadron Leader B.J Knight vice Squadron Leader W.D Flatt.

The 62 (RCAF) Base Electrical Engineering Officer, Squadron Leader F. Humphreys, was called in to East Moor to investigate a number of electrical failures on 432 Squadron Halifaxes during the Le Mans operation.

An operation was called for but was subsequently scrubbed.

9 March 1944

No operations for the East Moor crews but flying training continued with air to air firing and bombing exercises on Strensall Bombing Range plus a 'Bullseye'. Rowntrees Chocolate and Cocoa Works at York hosted a party of airmen and WAAF personnel from the East Moor Corporals Club which culminated in tea being served in the factory canteen.

10 March 1944

Flying Officer J.A Kemp assumed duty as LDA of No.2799 Flight, RAF Regiment in the absence of the Army Commander, Major W.G Fanning.

No operations on this wet and foggy day when visibility was reduced to 2,000 yards.

11 March 1944

The Station Padre, Squadron Leader H.G Lowrey conducted the funeral service for LAG. A.S Blanchard who was killed in the MT accident at Strensall. The service at All Hallows, Sutton on Forest was well attended by Officers and airmen from East Moor and followed by internment at Stonefall Cemetary, Harrogate.

There was no operation scheduled at East Moor.

12 March 1944

The fifth consecutive day without any operations at East Moor.

Wing Commander W.A McKay returned from honeymoon and assumed the duties of Station Commander East Moor in the absence of Group Captain J.E Fauquier,DSO, DFC who was presiding over a General Court Martial at Castle Archdale in Northern Ireland.

13 March 1944

Twenty personnel drawn from No.2799 Flight RAF Regiment attended York Public Baths and received swimming instruction from East Moor Physical Training Instructor.

The station's WAAF's were visited by Wing Officer Carby-Hall from 6 Group Head Quarters together with Squadron Officer N.Holland from 62 Base Headquarters.

432 Squadron made another visit to Le Mans and the following eight crews helped to destroy numerous locomotives, rolling stock and damage several factories,

LW596 'D'	F/L J Cooper	LK765 'H'	F/S C Narum	LW614 'S'	F/S A Clarke
LW643 'E'	F/S G Millar	LW582 'N'	P/O E Reid	LW615 'U'	P/O S Hawkins
LK766 'V'	F/S W Studnik	LW687 'Z'	F/S P Anthony		

F/L Gawker and P/O Webb were second pilots in 'J' and 'E' respectively.
All Bomber Command's aircraft returned safely. Johnny Banks was now the flight engineer in a completly new crew. 'Z-Zebra' left East Moor at 22.45 hours and after an outward flight in moonlight, a dummy run was first made across the target. The Marshalling Yards here were certainly a change from Berlin, where it would have been very unwise to attempt such. The crew released their bombs on the second run, and the only opposition was one searchlight and some flak, with some coastal guns opening up on the return leg.

14 March 1944

The East Moor Station WAAF site was nominated to represent No.6 Group in the Sunderland Cup. a competition to determine the best one in Bomber Command.

No operations were called for on the station, 432 Squadron crews were engaged in a 'Bullseye' exercise around midnight, and one crew had what can only be described as an 'experience'. The navigator in LW595, 'Q'- Queen recalls that they took off at 22.50 hrs and wandered all around the defended areas to give the ground defences some practice, and visited quite a few prohibited areas. The Halifax carried infra red film in the cameras with which to record the ground markers, and it passed over London, Southampton, Portsmouth, Plymouth and Liver-pool without the crew realising that the IFF had started to 'squidder'.

Over Hull, and on a 180 degrees track, the ground defences fired four shells at Queenie, the last one striking home. It was said to be like hitting a hole in the road and prompted the pilot to abort the rest of the exercise. Back at dispersal, no damage was noticed, but in daylight the ground crew found a gash 18 inches long in the leading edge of the port fin. LW595 was taken to Y.A.R.D for a new tail assembly.

15 March 1944

A further 'experience' was had by the same crew on the following night. Briefed for an operation to Stuttgart in LW593, 'O-Oboe', they took off at 18.25 hrs with a 230 gallon overload tank in the bomb bay. After an hours flight, the pilot asked the flight engineer to transfer the overload fuel to the main tanks. A strong smell of fuel swept through the aircraft, and an inspection of the bomb bay revealed gallons of fuel sloshing around . The crew members were affected by the fumes, some of them seeing double. Their return to East Moor was inevitable, but the Halifax was too heavy to land so a journey out to sea was made and bombs dumped.

Apparently, the overload tank's delivery pipe was not connected.

The engineering staff at East Moor reckoned that the crew just might have had enough fuel to cross the French coast at around 2,000 feet on their return.

Two hours and thirty five minutes after take off the Halifax was put down on East Moor's runway.
It had been one of fourteen dispatched from East Moor,and 432 Squadron's contribution to a force of 860 aircraft on that operation. All the East Moor crews returned safely, LW754 landing at RAF Station West Malling. Luck must have been with them on what was a clear night with many German night fighters in evidence.

LW687 'Z'	F/S P Anthony	LW594 'G'	F/O W Smith	LW583 'L'	P/O L Whaley
LK766 'V'	F/B G Millar	LW592 'A'	F/S W Fernyhough	LK765 'H'	F/L J Cooper
LW593 'O'	P/O J Barker	LK779 'W'	F/S W Studnik	LW643 'E'	F/O A Mercer
LW582 'M'	F/O E Reid	LW596 'D'	F/S E Clarke	LW616 'R'	F/S C Narum
LW615 'U'	P/O S Hawkins				

F/S Kuleski, Sgt's Buckley and McHeleron were second pilots in 'A','H' and 'L'.

16 March 1944

Bad weather caused a stand down at East Moor, but the station became involved in two flying; accidents.

At 10.12 hours, Halifax DG295, DH-'O' of 1664 HCU Dishforth, crashed on the station Bombing Range at Strensall On arrival at the scene, East Moor's ambulance and crash crews found the aircraft burnt out and all the crew dead.

At 22.26 hours, Wellington BK494 FQ-G,of 12 OTU Chipping Warden, was attempting a one engined landing when it crashed into fields east of the airfield, injuring one crew member.

17 March 1944

A number of 432 Squadron crews rendezvoused over RCAF Station Dalton with that base's Martinet tugs from 1695 Bomber Defence Training Flight before setting out on an air to air firing exercise.

At 22.30 hours, WAAF driver LAGW G Jolliffe knocked down and injured two of the station's personnel when she was blinded by the lights of a civilian vehicle which did not stop, and therefore was not identified. Sergeant G W Hutchinson (RAF) and Corporal P Godfrey (WAAF) were taken to York hospital where the latter was found to be seriously injured.

18 March 1944

Group Captain J E Fauquier, DSO, DFC, resumed command of East Moor Station and Air Commodore Ross the No.62 Base Commander visted, both attended the briefing of 432 Squadron crews for an attack against Frankfurt.

Fourteen set out and after a successful operation in a force of more than 840 aircraft, the East Moor contingent were diverted on their retun,

LW593 'O'	F/L J Cooper	LW615 'U'	F/O J Barker	LW584 'Y'	Sgt W Studnik
LW687 'Z'	F/S P Anthony	LW592 'A'	F/O A Mercer	LK765 'B'	F/S E Clarke
LW682 'C.'	F/S C Narum	LW596 'D'	F/L N Pettit	LK764 'F'	F/S W Ferneyhough
LW617 'J'	P/O P Dennis	LW583 'L'	P/O H Whaley	LK779 'W'	F/S A Clarke
LK8ll 'N'	F/L G Cawker	LW594 'G'	F/O W Smith		

F/S Kuleski and F/O Tindall were second pilots in') 'O' and 'A', respectively.

This was the first operation of Flight Lieutenant Pettit's second tour, having arrived at East Moor on the thirteenth of the month.

Flight Sergeant Anthony returned early with a u/s compass.

19 March 1944

Group Captain Fauquier, DSO, DFC was awarded a bar to the DSO.

East Moor hosted a contingent of local ATC Cadets and were given numerous lectures and demons tuitions

Senior Officers visiting the station included Air Vice Marshal C.V Walsh from RC.AF Headquarters, Ottawa and Group Captain J.G Bryans the RCAF Station Leeming Station Commander.

20 March 1944

A second operation free day at East Moor. Flying training continued, day and night.

East Moor basketball team defeated 6.Group Headquarters 21--11 when Corporal T.M Howard was the station's outstanding player.

More than 400 personnel enjoyed a performance by the RCAF 'Blackouts of 1943' in the station theatre.

21 March 1944

And yet another day without operational commitment but 432 Squadron were engaged in some night cross country exercises.

Senior Admin Officer, Squadron Leader W.D Flatt departed East Moor for Canada.

22 March 1944

The WAAF Corporal P Godfrey's condition was still very critical in York hospital, while Sergeant Hutchinson was said to be recovering from the road accident on 17th. In the evening a large number of WAAF's attended classes in hairdressing held on the station.

Command dispatched more than 800 aircraft on a further attack on Frankfurt and fourteen 432 Squadron crews joined the aerial armada,

LW592 'A'	F/L A Lowe	LK765 'B'	F/S E Clarke	LW686 'H'	W/O J Cooper
LW617 'J'	F/S G Millar	LW598 'K'	F/L M Pettit	LW583 'L'	P/O H Whaley
LW582 'M'	F/O E Reid	LK8II 'N'	F/S D Maddock	LW593 'O'	P/O J Mcintosh
LW616 'R'	F/O W Smith	Mz506 'X'	F/S A Clarke	LW687 'Z'	F/S J McElheren
LK779 'W'	F/L C Cawker	LW584 'Y'	F/S W Studnik		

Sg.Ibbotson & P/O Patterson were second pilots on 'H' and 'R' respectively.

Flight Lieutenant Cawker, Flight Sergeant Studnik and their crews were lost on this operation.

Flight Lieutenant Pettit returned early with a u/s compass.

23 March 1944

Pilot Officer Pay was posted to 1659 HCU on completion of his tour.

No operations and the Station Commander and the S.A.D.0 proceeded to RCAF Linton to attend the first 62 Base Admin Conference.

A variety show was staged in the Station Theatre during the evening by ENSA.

24 March 1944

Berlin, the 'big city' was once again the target for East Moor's crews when 432

Squadron dispatched the following,

LW592 'A'	F/L N Pettit	LK765 'B'	F/S E Clarke	LW686 'H'	F/S C Narum
LW617 'J'	F/S G Millar	LW582 'M'	F/O E Reid	LW614 'S'	F/S A Clarke
MZ506 'X'	F/O W Smith	LW687 'Z'	P/O S Hawkins	LW598 'K'	F/ S J McElheren
LW593 'O'	P/O J McIntosh				

Sadly Pilot Officer McIntosh and crew failed to return from this operation. After take off was completed a Station Dance got under way in the Gymnasium where the music was supplied by 62 (RCAF) Base Orchestra.

25 March 1944

Seven Lancasters were noted at East Moor bearing 103 Squadron codes PM and *576* Sqd UL, having been diverted from Elsham Wolds during the early hours ex Berlin Four of 432 Squadron crews joined a small force of heavies to attack the railway yards at Aulnoye where it was said that the bombs fell wide of the target, the following then returned safely to East Moor,

LW682	'C' F/S C Narum	LK764	'F' P/O G Webb	MZ506 'X'	F/S S Kuleski
LK8II	'N' F/S H Menzies				

26 March 1944

No.2 Flight of 2799 Squadron RAF Regiment moved from East Moor to the South coast, after a farewell party given by East Moor Station to them and their Commanding ofricer Flying Officer J.A Kemp (RAF).

The Station was again host to local ATC Squadrons, Air Commodore Ross the 62 Base Commander visited East Moor and attended the briefing of 432 Squadron crews for an operation to Essen. Fourteen set out,

LW592 'A'	F/L A Howe	LK765 'B'	F/S E Clarke	LW682 'C'	F/L C Barrett
LW643 'E'	P/O H Whaley	LK764 'F'	F/S D Maddock	LW594 'G'	F/O W Smith
LW617 'J'	F/S G Millar	LW582 'M'	P/O G Webb	LW614 'S'	F/S A Clarke

Fig 21. Nose art seen on 432 Squadron Halifax VII, a biblical quote from a tract of St Luke.

Examples of nose art

Photos W. Miller

| LW615 'U' | P/O S Hawkins | MZ506 'X' | F/S H Menzies | LW687 'Z' | W/O J Cooper |
| LW598 'K' | W/C W McKay | LK8ll 'N' | F/S Kuleski | | |

Patterson was second pilot in 'K' which made an early return with loss of power on the port outer engine. Sgt Kuleski aborted with both port engines giving trouble.

27 March 1944

A foggy day with visibility down to 1,000 yards on the airfield.
No operations called for at East Moor.
The contractors handed over to the Station a fully completed small arms range.

28 March 1944

Still foggy and 432 Squadron were stood down. The Station's personnel donated well over 100 pints of blood to a visiting Donor Team.

29 March 1944

Group Captain G.L Wurtele assumed duty as Station Commander RCAF Station East Moor
Vice Group Captain J.E Fauquier DSO ,DFC who was posted to 62 (RCAF) Base Headquarter
The former Officer had been acting Station Commander at RCAF Linton on Ouse.

Operations were called for but subsequently cancelled.

30 March 1944

East Moor contributed fourteen crews to a force of more than 800 which set out to attack the far distant target of Nuremburg on a night when by some quirk the nearby town of Schweinfurt was also marked and bombed. The following 432 Squadron take off commenced at 21.55 hours,

LW592 'A'	F/L A Lowe	LK765 'B'	F/S W Ferneyhough	LK764 'F'	F/S D Maddock
LW616 'P'	W/C A McKay	LW614 'S'	F/L J Cooper	LW615 'U'	P/O S Hawkins
LK766 'V'	P/O G Webb	MZ506 'X'	F/S S Kuleski	LW594 'G'	P/O H Whaley
LW617 'J'	F/L M Pettit	LK8ll 'N'	F/S H Menzies	LW686 'H'	W/O J Cooper
LW687 'Z'	F/O E Reid	MZ504 'C'	F/S C Narum		

Sadly Flying Officer Reid, Flight Sergeant Narum and crews were lost. The former pilot had notched up 12 operations in approximately 8 weeks and the latter 10 in around 5 weeks.

31 March 1944

Many of the 432 Squadron crews had been in the air between eight and nine hours on the Nuremburg raid, so flying activity was restricted to fighter affilliation exercises during the day with a few night cross countries.

LW617 returned from RAF Ford where Flight Lieutenant Pettit had landed owing to a fuel shortage.

General:

East Moor Station strength as at 31 March was as follows:

RCAF	Officers	81	RAF	Officers	20
WD	Officers	2	WAAF	Officers	1
RGAF	Other Ranks	760	RAF	Other Ranks	158
WD	Other Ranks	NIL	WAAF	Other Ranks	156
AUS	Other Ranks	1	USAAF	Officers	2

Fig 22. Intelligence Section party - January 1944.

L to R. S/l Eric Kusch, Eric Janburg, 'Ruby' Rutosk, Jeff Jeffries, Bernie Robertson, F/L Lapchuk. Photo H. Goodrow.

Total: 1,181

During the month contractors were engaged erecting additional accommodation and other buildings to house the electrical power plant at the station's bombing range at Strensall.

432 Squadron had carried out an extensive flying training programme during the month and involved many 'freshman' crews. A total of well over four hundred flying hours were put in on cross countries and other exercises and was thought to be a record for an operational squadron to that date.

The squadron's total flying for March was 1,129 hours.

The Station Commanders report stated that the general health of East Moor personnel was quite good and that the drinking water and sanitary arrangements were quite satisfactory.

AN INSIGHT INTO CATERING AT EAST MOOR APRIL 1944

Messing Officer Helen Goodrow arrived at East Moor in April 1944, not too long before 'D' Day, to find that the catering environment consisted of nissen huts -kitchens, messes and living quarters.

In the RCAF women were referred to as WDs (Women's Division) and the Catering Officers as Messing Officers. Each Messing Officer held a Bachelor Degree in food Science.

The kitchen equipment at East Moor was not very modern to say the least. Large stock pots fired by coal were used for general cooking. The fire would be built up and when the stews and soups etc were cooked the fire was removed to prevent over cooking. Only the dilligence of the cooks prevented many burnt offerings. S/0 Goodrow remembers that potatoes and vegetables were cooked in steam cookers in which the pressure limit was 2lbs, consequently timing was most unpredictable.

The East Moor catering facilities did not rur. to refrigeration so food such as fish had to be used immediately. Frozen food in the form of beef and mutton was received from Australia and was usually quite old, and it is said that returning servicemen did not touch lamb for many years. Apparently onions were always scarce and chicken was rarely on the menu.

Helen recalls, 'We had RAF rations - plus one shilling per day, per man/Woman from the NAAFI stores'.

When 415 Squadron arrived at East Moor, there were twice the number of mouths to feed and the limited amount of space and equipment made for some difficulties. Table service in the Officer's Mess had been manageable with only one squadron to cater for but with two it was decided to go cafeteria style. This must not be thought of as resembling todays cafeteria with shiny steel tables and pans etc, theirs was make do with whatever was available and it did not always make for a good presentation.

S/0 Goodrow cannot recall where they managed to get the food for Christmas Dinner but presumes that a special ration was made available.

Meals for ops came at any hour of the day or night, and for those a special treat of bacon and eggs was usually available. The Canadians thought that English tea was excellent but tried all their combined skills to improve the coffee. The latter was the first thing that the returning crews tasted, and it was greatly improved during the later months at East Moor with the addition of rum. Food for parties created a problem - some was scrounged - some saved from stores - and when funds were available some was bought.

A 'stand down' was usually the signal for a party - occasionally minds were changed and ops were on again - and could well be in the midst of preperations. Catering was a long and arduous task but provided the staff with a large measure of job satisfaction, all feeling that they were making a contribution.

1 April 1944

No operations were scheduled at East Moor. Eight crews of 432 Squadron were engaged in flying training between 13.55 hours and 17.00.

The month saw the introduction of Under Gunners within 432 Squadron,and the Station Armoury received 14 sets of .5 guns to be fitted to the ventral turrets.

Public Relations Branch sent a representative to the station, Pilot Officer J.M Coldwell from No.62 (RCAF) Base.

2 April 1944

432 Squadron were 'stood down' from operations.

The station hosted a large ATG contingent who were given lectures and shown around.

The 62 (RCAF) Base Armaments Officer, Squadron Leader A. Knowles, visited the station and gave a lecture on Chemical Warfare to the Armaments personnel. Also visiting was Flight Lieutenant E.V Grandhais, 62 Base Catering Officer.

3 April 1944

A foggy and rainy day with no operations scheduled at the station.

4 April 1944

No improvement in the weather, and no operational commitments at East Moor.

No.62 (RGAF) Base Commander, Air Commodore A.D Ross visited the station and and held a number of interviews with applicants for commissions. The 6 Group Gunnery Leader, Squadron Leader J.F Clark also visited.

York Railway Gymnasium was the scene of the station's Basketball teams 21 - 20 win over RCAF Station Dalton.

5 April 1944

The weather still precluded any flying from the station, only ground training was pursued, and included a full and wet fire drill.

No.62 (RCAF) Base Engineering Officer, Wing Commander Smith visited the station.

Squadron Leader D.G Carlson, the Protestant Padre held a talk and followed up with a question and answer session on the subject of 'Repatriation' to a very large audience of NCO's and airmen.

6 April 1944

Two aircraft of 432 Squadron were detailed for a bombing mission but that was later scrubbed.

Visual Monica was being installed by the Radar Section to the Halifaxes.

Some difficulties were being experienced with the Halifaxes bomb release mechanism, these were attributed to the electrical switches..Flight Lieutenant W.H Newman the RAF Bomber Command Armament Officer arrived at East Moor to look into the matter.

Air Commodore A.D Ross, 62 (RCAF) Base Commander held an 'East Moor Station Inspection at 14.00 hours, this was followed by an inspection of the parade drawn from all of f duty personnel.

In the evening the Riggers defeated the Fitters at Softball, 14 - 7.

7 April 1944

Immediately after their briefing, four of 432 Squadron's crews were told that the operation was cancelled. A further four participated in cross countries.

The Station Commander, Group Captain G.L Wurtele together with Squadron Leader J.B Knight the SADO, visited 62 (RCAF)Base for the first meeting of the Victory Loan Campaign.

62 (RCAF)Base Catering Officers, Flight Lieutenant E.~ Grandais and Section Officer (WD) O.E Park visited East Moor.

Group Captain H.H Rutledge OBE, was appointed Station Commander at East Moor, vice Group Captain G.L Wurtele.

Night flying training exercises were carried out by 432 Squadron.

8 April 1944

East Moor airfield was completely closed in by bad weather during the morning precluding any flying. During the afternoon and evening it improved and a 'Bullseye' and three cross country exercises were managed by 432 Squadron.

The RCAF Orchestra played for a very successful dance held in the Station Gymn.

9 April 1944

Cloud and rain dispersed during the afternoon leaving visibility at 15 miles. The Marshalling Yards at Villeneuve-St.Georges were successfully attacked by fourteen crews from 432 Squadron, take off commenced at 21.00 hours and after a well concentrated operation all returned safely,

LW592 'A'	F/L A Lowe		LK765 'B'	F/S E Clarke
	Ft/O Lekis	2/Plt		
LW596 'D'	WO D Maddock		LW594 'G'	F/S W Ferneyhough
				P/O Lauzon 2/Plt
LW686 'H'	WO J Cooper		LK807 'J'	F/S G Millar
LW583 'L'	P/O H Whaley		LK8ll 'N'	F/L J Cooper
				F/O Evenson 2/Plt
LW595 'Q'	F/O J Barker		LW616 'R'	P/O J Patterson
LW614 'S'	F/S A Clarke		LW615 'U'	P/O S Hawkins
LW582 'M'	P/O G Webb		MZ506 'X'	F/S S Kuleski
				Sgt Proulx 2/Plt

10 April 1944

A Station Victory Loan Committee held its first meeting with Intelligence Officer, Flight Lieutenant H.F Lount in the chair, and East Moor was set a target of 31,000 Canadian dollars.

The station dispatched fourteen 432 Squadron Halifaxes to attack Rail Yards at Ghent where much damage to buildings was inflicted,

LW592 'A'	F/L A Lowe	LW765 'B'	F/S E Clarke
LW596 'D'	W/O D Maddock	LW643 'E'	F/O L Evenson
LW594 'G'	F/S J McHeleron	LW583 'L'	F/S G Millar
LW582 'N'	P/O G Webb	LK8ll 'N'	F/O J Barker
LW616 'P'	P/O J Patterson	LW614 'S'	F/S A Clarke
LW615 'U'	P/O S Hawkins	LK766 'V'	P/O L Lauzon
MZ506 'X'	F/S S Kuleski	LW686 'H'	Ft/O Lekis W
	F/S Riding U/G		

Warrant Officer Maddock made an early return with
hydraulic trouble.

11 April 1944

No.432 Squadron was stood down from operations, and the 'A' Flight ground crew defeated 'B' Flight at Softball 15 - 13.

The semi final of No.5 District Headquarters Basketball League saw East Moor defeat RCAF Station Skipton on Swale 39-20 at York Pauway Gymnasium.

Squadron Leader A Knowles, Armament Officer from 62 (RCAF)Base visited the station.

12 April 1944

The new Station Commander, Group Captain H.H Rutledge OBE, assumed his duties inspecting the station and 432 Squadron and was shown around by Wing Commander W.A McKay the latter's Commander

The Station Section Commanders held a meeting in the Photographic Section's lecture room at which they bade farewell to the outgoing Station Commander, Group Captain G.L Wurtele (RAF).

At 17.30 hours, a telephone message was received at East Moor to the effect that after an air firing exercise off Scarborough, LW614 had suffered engine failure and had crashed at 16.10 hours at Hackness. Six aircrew and one ground crew fitter, who was a passenger were killed. The rear gunner, Sergeant McNeil survived. Lost were, Flight Sergeant's A Clarke and T. Woodward (pilot and nav) Sergeants F. Cranch (B/A), F. Hindmarsh (WOP), B. Bell (AIG), H. Halliwell (FIE) and LAC D. McKenzie (fitter).

13 April 1944

There was no operational commitments at the station.

Group Photographic Officers, Squadron Leader A.S Archer and Pilot Officer H.C Beaupre visited the station.

East Moor Station soccer team defeated Stillington Village 4 - 0 on the latters home ground.

14 April 1944

A detail of eight 432 Squadron aircraft was called for but subsequently cancelled at 21.00 hours.

Visual Monica had been fitted to the Halifaxes and Squadron Leader L.D Izzard the RAF Group Signals Leader visited in connection with the training of its use by the Air Wirless Operators.

15 April 1944

There was a 'stand down' for the station's crews regarding operational readiness.

The Station's Roman Catholic Padre, Squadron Leader G.J Fitzgerald held a Mass at 17.00 hours for Sergeants J.H Woodward and F.C Hindmarsh.

It was announced that the station had raised 3,750 Canadian dollars in the 16th Victory Loan Campaign.

16 April 1944

Another operation free day at the station.

A joint exercise between East Moor Fire Section and The National Fire Service from Easingwold,included full drills and was most successful.

The 'Riggers' defeated the 'Fitters' 10-5 in a Softball Game.

17 April 1944

432 Squadron was still on operational 'stand down', but eleven aircraft took part in daytime cross country exercises and eleven in night ones.

A very large crowd of visitors from RCAF Station's Thoithorpe and Linton on Ouse attended the No.6 Group Boxing Tournament at East Moor.

The Station Padre, Squadron Leader E.S Lautenschlager, conducted funeral services at All Hallows, Sutton on Forest for Flight Sergeant A.K Clarke and LAG D.V McKenzie.

Halifaxes PT-X and I from 420 Squadron landed at East Moor.

18 April 1944

Two WAAF Officers, Wing Officer E. Carby-Hall and Squadron Officer N Holland visited East Moor Station.

Two Halifax III's, MZ458 QB-G and QB-T of 424 Squadron were diverted in to East Moor from their base at RCAF Station Leeming.
In the final of No.5 District RCAF Basketball Championship, East Moor beat Warrington 27-15 at York, each player receiving a prize.

Fourteen crews from 432 Squadron were dispatched and obtained good results in an attack on the Railway Marshalling Yards at Noisy-Le-Sec near Paris,

LK765 'B'	P/O L Lauzon	LW596 'D'	F/L N Pettit
LW643 'E'	F/O A Mercer	LW592 'A'	F/S W Ferneyhough
LK764 'F'	W/O D Maddock	LK807 'J'	F/S G Millar
LW583 'L'	W/O J Cooper	LW582 'N'	P/O G Webb
LK8ll 'N'	F/S N Nenzies	LW595 'Q'	F/O J Barker
LW615 'U'	P/O J Patterson	MZ506 'x'	F/O W Evenson
LW616 'P'	W/O W McKay	LW594 'G'	F/O W Smith
	F/L Larson 2/Plt		F/O Jack 2/Plt

Sadly, Flying Officer Mercer and crew failed to return, their Halifax had collided with another aircraft. Miraculously, Sergeant Shaughnessy the rear gunner escaped the crash which followed a steep descent from around 15,000 ft. Unable to get out of the aircraft when his parachute unfolded, and with the exit door jammed, he had waited for the inevitable. He was found by troops but he escaped as bombs were falling around them. After receiving first aid and food from firemen he became 432 Squadrons first evader.

19 April 1944

No operations were scheduled at East Moor.

The Station Theatre was the stage for an ENSA Concert 'More Heather Breezes' in the evening and was much enjoyed.

At 23.50 hours an Air Raid message 'Red' was received at East Moor with 'White' Ifollowing without incident at 00.42 Hours on the 20th.

20 April 1944

East Moor soccer team defeated Easingwold Town on the latters ground 9- 2. The Railway Marshalling Yards at Lens were attacked successfully by fourteen crews from 432 Squadron, and all returned safely,

LW592 'A'	S/L A Lowe	LK765 'B'	Ft/0	W Lekis
LW596 'D'	F/S J MoHeleron	LK764 'F'	W/0	G Maddock
LW594 'G'	F/S W Ferneyhough	LW686 'H'	W/O	J Cooper
LK807 'J'	F/S G Millar	LW582 'N'	P/O	G Webb
LW595 'Q'	F/O J Barker	LK8ll 'M'	F/S	H Menzies
LW616 'R'	P/O J Patterson	LK766 'V'	P/O L	Lauzon
LW615 'U'	F/L J Cooper	MZ506 'X'	F/S P	Anthony

21 April 1944

Two new Halifaxes arrived at East Moor for 432 Squadron and were already fitted with .5 ventral guns. These were MZ585 and MZ586.

Two senior Administration Officers visited the station, Group Captain G. Scott and Wing Commander A.C Tufts. The Group Entertainment Officer, Squadron Officer I.M Much (WD) was also on station.

22 April 1944

Wide spread damage was caused at Dusseldorf when fourteen crews from 432 Sqd formed part or a 600~strong attacking force. All of the East Moor aircraft returned safely to the UK, LK8ll and LW615 with flak damage, LW583 put down at Wo odbridge due to fuel shortage.

The following were dispatched from East Moor,

LW583 'L'	F/S J McHeieron	LK765 'B'	F/S E Clarke	
LK807 'J'	F/S G Millar	LW595 'Q'	F/O J Barker	
LK811 'N'	F/S H Menzies	MZ585 O'	F/S P Anthony	
LW615 'U'	P/O W Lauzon	MZ506'X'	F/O L Evenson	
LW596 'D'	F/L N Pettit	LK764 'F'	W/O D Maddock	
	F/O DeLoughty 2/Plt		P/O Webb 2/Plt	
LW594 'G'	F/Q W Smith	LW686 'H'	F/S J Cooper	
	P/O Smith 2/Plt		F/O Lawrenson 2/Plt	
LW616 'R'	W/C W McKay	LW582 'M'	F/L J Cooper	
	F/L Larson 2/Plt		F/O Jack 2/Plt	

23 April 1944

432 Squadron was not called for operations.

A further three Halifax III's were delivered to East Moor already equipped with .5 ventral gun positions.

Night cross country exercises were carried out by eight 432 Squadron crews.

Squadron Leader E.F Kusch, Station Intelligence Officer gave a talk which was followed by a discussion on 'What Bomber Command was doing to Germany', to a large crowd.

Station Softball result was Radar 18, Instrument Section 4.

Four of East Moor's boxers got through to the finals of the competition held at RCAF Station Dishforth.

24 April 1944

East Moor Station was chosen as the best WAAF Site in No.6 Group and was awarded the Bomber Command Trophy in the Sunderland Cup campaign.

The MT Section defeated the Bomb Dump in a Softball game by 26 to 12. Karlesrhue was the target for 432 Squadron who dispatched the following fourteen crews all of whom returned safely,

LK766 'V'	P/O L Lauzon	LW6i5 'U'	P/O S Hawkins	
LW595 'Q'	F/O J Barker	LW582 'N'	F/O L Evenson	
LK807 'J'	F/S G Millar	LW594 'G'	W/O J Cooper	
LK764 'F'	W/O D Maddock	LK765 'B'	F/S E Clarke	
LW592 'A'	P/O H Whaley	MZ585 '0'	F/S P Anthony	
LW596 'D'	F/L N Pettit	LW598 'K'	F/S W Ferneyhough	
	F/O Smith 2/Plt		Sgt Davies U/G	
MZ590 'C'	F/L C Barrett	MZ506 'X'	F/S S Kuleski	
	Sgt Robinson U/G		Sgt Easy U/G	

Flight Sergeant Millar returned early with hydraulic failure, and Flight Lieutenant Barrett put down on his return at RAF Station Manston due to a shortage of fuel.

25 April 1944

Operations were called for but later cancelled just as briefing was over.

LAC T.E Brookes won the Featherweight boxing championship for East Moor while LAC's J.H Cooper, D. Richmond and L. Brilliant put up excellent fights in the finals but lost the decision in the No.5 Group Championship Tournaments held at RCAF Station Dishforth. The Air Officer Commanding No.6 (RCAF) Group, Air Vice Marshal C.M McEwan presented the prizes.

26 April 1944

The following fourteen crews from 432 Squadron participated in a raid on Essen, fifteen had been detailed but LW582 suffered hydraulic failure just before take off,

LW592 'A'	P/O H Whaley	LK765 'B'	F/S E Clarke
LW596 'D'	F/S H Menzies	LK764 'F'	W/O D Maddock
LW594 'G'	F/O H Smith	LW686 'H'	W/O J Cooper
LK807 'J'	F/S G Millar	MZ585 'O'	F/S P Anthony
LW595 'Q'	F/O J Barker	LW616 'R'	P/O L Lauzon
LW615 'U'	P/O S Hawkins	LW598 'K'	F/S W Ferneyhough
			Sgt Wells U/G
LW552 'S'	F/L J Cooper	MZ586 'Y'	F/L A Lowe
	Sgt Ziomko U/G		F/O Martin 2/Plt
			Sgt Paquette U/G

All returned safely to East Moor.

27 April 1944

During the morning a full and 'wet' Fire Drill was carried out on station.

It was announced that the target of 31,000 Canadian dollars had been reached in the East Moor's donation to the 6th Victory Loan.

In the evening the RCAF Overseas Band played for a well tended dance in the Station Gymnasium.

At 23.30 hours the first of fourteen 432 Squadron Halifaxes rose from East Moor's runway for an attack on Montzen

LK764 'F'	W/O D Maddock	LW582 'M'	F/O L Evenson
LW616 'R'	W/O W McKay	LW595 'Q'	F/L G Larson
LW552 'S'	F/S H Menzies	LK766 'V'	P/O L Lauzon
LW594 'G'	F/O H Smith	MZ506 'X'	F/S W Ferneyhough
	F/O Martin 2/Plt		Sgt Mcaartney U/G
MZ586 'Y'	S/L A Lowe	LW615 'U'	F/O P Lawrenson
MZ588 'W'	F/O L Deloughty	LW592 'A'	P/O H Whaley
LK807 'J'	F/S G Millar	MZ585 'O'	P/O J Webb

Flying Officer Deloughty, Pilot Officer Whaley and Flight Sergeant Millar and their crews failed to return from this operation.

Pilot Officer Webb and crew were unable to open the bomb doors due to flak damage received as they crossed the Belgian coast. Whilst the flight engineer struggled to free them, the skipper detoured. Eventually, after using the emergency system they were freed and the Halifax was turned in to attack. During the run up MZ585 was attacked by a MellO and fire from both aircraft was exchanged simultaneously with the 'bombs gone' shout from the bomb aimer, Pilot Officer Webb threw the Halifax into a evasive manouvre as the enemy closed in to around 1,000 yards before falling away to port with its starboard engine damaged.

As they left the target they were intercepted again, and again they corkscrewed and again the gunners scored hits. After a third attack they managed to shake the enemy off.

Twenty three minutes after the first attack, another fighter was encountered and MZ585 was hit, putting the starboard outer engine out of action. The aircraft was was landed at Woodbridge with some difficulty, and at the second attempt, having swung violently to starboard on the first as the starboard inner failed.

Pilot Of fic'er Webb received the DSO on what was his first operation as a skipper, and his two gunners the DFM.

28 April 1944

This was an operation free day at East Moor.

During the afternoon the station held an 'air raid practice', which was responded to in a most satisfactory manner, all the defence guns being manned with dispatch.

At 20.00 hours, the Station Commander, Group Captain H.H Rutledge OBE,addressed a parade of No.9432 Servicing Echelon.

The East Moor soccer team defeated Easingwold Town 4 - 1 on the latters ground.

29 April 1944

And another operational stand down at the station.

It was the first anniversary of the forming of 432 Squadron on the 1st of May, but it was decided to celebrate it on this date. To that end a gala party was held in the Officer's Mess followed by a grand dance when the PMC, Major W.G Fanning was congratulated on the success of both events.

A Station Commanders Parade was held earlier in the day when personnel of Station Headquarters together with those of 432 Squadron were addressed.

30 April 1944

It was announced that East Moor had reached a total of 34,000 Canadian dollars in the 6th Victory Loan Campaign, representing almost 10% more than the target set for it, by the Base.

Senior Engineering Officers visited the station, Wing Commander's B.H Roles and N.M Smith from RAF Headquarters Bomber Command and No.6 (RCAF) Group respectively.

The following ten crews returned safely to East Moor after an attack on Somaine,

LK765 'B'	F/S E Clarke	LW596 'D'	F/O W Lawrenson
LK764 'F'	F/O W Smith	LW594 'G'	F/S S Kuleski
LW686 'H'	F/O L Evenson	LW598 'K'	F/S P Anthony
LW595 'Q'	F/L G Larson	LW616 'R'	F/O J Patterson
LW615 'U'	P/O J Webb	LK766 'V'	P/O L Lauzon
			Sgt Jones U/G

General:

Quarantine regulations were put on certain billets after Diptheria had been diagnosed on the station. An airwoman was admitted to York Military Hospital and a male Nursing Orderly to Harrogate Fever Hospital with the illness. Flying Training amounted to 300 hours during April.

East Moor Station strength as at 30 April 1944 was,

RCAF	Officers	93	RCAF	Other Ranks	678
RAF	Officers	21	RAF	Other Ranks	128
WD	Officers	3	WAAF	Other Ranks	134
WAAF	Officers	1	Aust	Other Ranks	1
USAF	Officers	1	USAF	Other Ranks	1

Grand Total,   1,061

Four East Moor officers were awarded the DFC during April, the 432 Sqd Commander, Wing Commander McKay and Pilot Officers Pay, Phillips and Thompson.

By the month end it was reported that there was a marked shortage of aircraft on the station, 432 Squadron being down to a strength of just sixteen Halifaxes.

An outbreak of Diptheria amongst the WAAF fraternity resulted in at least one billet being quarantined. Subsequently, a male Nursing Orderly was diagnosed with the illness.

April was not a particularly busy month at East Moor (operationally) the resident squadron took part in nine bombing missions. Operational flying hours amounted to 560 involving 122 sorties while a further 300 hours were devoted to flying training.

1 May 1944

The Station MeT Section defeated the Bomb Dump Section at Softball, 18 - 3.
Two Education Officers visited the station, Squadron Leader P.M Winter from RCAF Overseas Headquarters and Flight Lieutenant G. Apperley from No.5 District Headquarters ,York.

Eleven 432 Squadron Halifaxes were dispatched on what proved to be a very accurate and successful attack on the Railway Yards at Ghislain,

LK766 'V'	F/O P Jack	LW616 'R'	W/C W McKay
LW595 'Q'	F/S H Menzies	LK765 'B'	Ft/O Lekis W
LW596 'D'	F/L M Pettit	LW598 'K'	P/O W Ferneyhough
LW486 'H'	Sgt H McHeleron	LW594 'G'	F/O H Smith
LW615 'U'	P/O S Hawkins	MZ586 'Y'	S/L A Lowe
LW552 'S'	F/O P Lawrenson		

Flight Sergeant Menzies returned early with his port engine on fire. (inner) Squadron Leader Lowe was forced to return early with hydraulic failure.

In a 4 minute combat with a JU88, Flight Lieutenant Williams and Sergeant Logimodiere the two gunners in LW598 scored hits and claimed a 'probably destroyed' as the enemy was seen to spiral down.

2 May 1944

With no operations called for, the aircrew spent the afternoon watching combat films in the briefing room.

A new Station Armaments Officer, Flight Lieutenant P.C Nelaon took up his duties replacing F l ight Lieutenant A.N Roth who was posted to become 62 Base A.O.

The Station Warrant Officer, W.H Ard, presided over the Sergeants Mess Meeting when Flight Sergeant F.C Page was elected CMC, and Flight Sergeant G. Segal to Mess Treasurer.

No.62 (RCAF) Base Public Relations Officer, Pilot Officer J.M Coldwell visited East Moor.

More than 350 personnel watched film shows in the Gymnasium and in the Hospital sponsored by ENSA.

3 May 1944

Again a day free of operations at the station, but a successful 'Bullseye' was carried out by eleven of 432 Squadron's crews.
Easingwold Town soccer team finally defeated East Moor, the score 2 - 1, while No.432 Squadron Aircrew beat Headquarters 7 - 5 in a Softball game.

More than 300 people enjoyed a live ENSA Concert 'Happy Thoughts' in the Station Theatre.

Station visitors included Catering Officer, Flight Lieutenant E. Grandois and Flight Officer D. Delius, Code and Cyphering Officer from 62 (RCAF) Base.

4 May 1944

Still no operations called for at East Moor, and eleven crews from 432 Sqd carried out ni~ht cross country exercises without incident.

The No.62 (RCAF) Base Engineering Officer, Wing Commander M.N Smith visited the station.

5 May 1944

The station had no operational commitments and planned 'Bullseye' exercises for late evening were scrubbed. During the day the Station Bomb Stores were visited by 'Works and Bricks' who carried out extensive concreting to the incendiary stores.

Maintenance Section defeated 'B' Flight by a score of 10-6 at Softball. The Station Gymnasium was the scene of a very successful dance for more than 350 people.

6 May 1944

Operations were called for but subsequently scrubbed on a day when visibility around East Moor area was down to less than three miles, and the aircrew spent most of the afternoon watching film and listening to lectures on Photographic Recognition.

Armaments Officers from 6 Group and 62 (RCAF) Base were engaged at East Moor in trying to establish a suitable location for the detonation of bombs in an emergency

A conducted tour of East Moor Station was given to thirty two employees of the Fairey Aviation Company. Lunch and tea was provided in the Sergeant's Mess and it was the first of regular week end visits.

In the evening an informal record dance was held in the 'Y' Lounge.

7 May 1944

At 04.00 hours, fire was discovered in the ante room of the Officer's Mess. The Station Fire Section responded to the alarm in exceptionally good time and soon had the blaze extinguished. This was the first application of fire fighting on the station since an exercise of intensive drill had been carried out, and only minor damage was suffered.

Later in the day, Halifax III, LW615 met with a training accident which ended with the aircraft colliding with one of the old air raid shelters behind the old Airmen's Mess. The bomber was said to be on a familiarisation flight and on landing it overshot the Strensall Road, striking a tree in Goose Wood as it went. Broken in two just behind the cockpit area, and minus its nose section, the Halifax was a complete write off. Fortunately none of the occupants were injured.

Further conducted tours were given to the party from Fairey Aviation and to a local squadron of the Air Training Corps.

The usual Sunday Forum was held, and on this occasion the speaker was one of Station's Padres, Squadron Leader Lauteenschlager whose subject was 'What I Saw in China'.

No.6 Group Navigation Officer, Flight Lieutenant A.G Rowe visited the station. An unsuccessful attack was carried out against the gun batteries at St. Valerie-en-Crux by the following eight crews from 432 Squadron, all returned safely,

LW686 'E'	FtO W Lekis (USAF)	LK764 'F'	F/O V Smith
LW582 'M'	P/O G Webb	LW598 'K'	P/O W Ferneyhough
LW594 'G'	F/O H Smith	LW616 'R'	P/O J Patterson
MZ586 'Y'	F/L G Larson	LW595 'Q'	F/O J Barker

On landing, Flying Officer Barker's Halifax suffered hydraulic failure but unfortunately he was able to maintain control of the bomber.

Fig 23. 'U-Bend-Em, We-Mend-Em' LW615 after crashing through Strensall Road on the South West boundary. 7th May 1944. Photo M Pryce.

8 May 1944

Headquarters No.6 Group (RCAF) defeated East Moor 11 - 9 in a softball game,and in the Station League, the navigators defeated the gunners 11 - 9.

No.432 Squadron achieved better results than on the previous day's operation, but sadly,two crews were lost on this one against the Railway Yards at Haine St.Pierre, Nothing was heard from Flying Officer Martin and crew nor from Pilot Officer Hawkins and his crew after their take off from East Moor.

East Moor dispatched the following crews from 432 Squadron,

LK765 'B'	F/S E Clarke	LW594 'G'	P/O S Hawkins
LW596 'D'	F/S S Kuleski	LW582 'N'	P/O G Webb
LW552 'S'	F/O P Lawrenson	LW595 'Q'	F/O J Barker
LW583 'L'	F/O P Martin	LW686 'H'	P/O J Webb
LK764 'F'	F/S L McHeleron	MZ632 'W'	F/L J Cooper
			F/S Shanks U/G
MZ585 'O'	F/S P Anthony	MZ586 'Y'	S/L A Lowe
	Sgt Robinson U/G		Sgt Easy U/G
MZ603 'E'	Ft/O Lekis W		
	Sgt Irwin U/G		

Fighter activity was intense from leaving the target area all the way to the coast. Flight Sergaent NcHeleron and crew were attacked by an enemy aircraft which damged the undercarriage, starboard mainplane and the starboard inner engine

9 May 1944

No operations were called for at East Moor, but considerable local flying was carried out.

Two Station Softball games were held, Instrument Section defeated Armaments 14-3 and Bomb Dump outplayed MT Section 23-17.

Around 350 people attended film shows in the Gymnasium and in the HosPltal, both of which were sponsored by ENSA.

10 May 1944

Another operation free day at the station. Fourteen crews from 432 Squadron carried out night cross country exercises.

A District Courts Martial was convened at East Moor under the presidency of Squadron Leader J.C Campbell of RCAF Overseas Headquarters.

The Station Commander, Group Captain H.H Rutledge OBE, held a meeting of all Section Commanders at 09.00 hours and decisions werevreached on a range of matters and policies.

The need to empty the static water pool on No.5 Site was incorporated into a full and 'wet' practice fire drill. The tank had sprung a leak.

WAAF Administration Officer, Squadron Officer N Holland from 62 Base, visited.

11 May 1944

Boulogne-sur-Mer and the Marshalling Yards there were the target for East Moor's crews and 432 Squadron dispatched foutreen on what was described as not being a very successful attack,

MZ601 'A'	F/O H Smith	LK765 'B'	F/S E Clarke
LW596 'D'	P/O D Maddock	MZ603 'E'	Ft/O Lekis W
LW686 'H'	P/O J Cooper	LW582 'M'	P/O G Webb
LW595 'Q'	F/O J Barker	LW616 'R'	W/C W McKay
LW552 'S'	F/S H Menzies	LK766 'V'	P/O J Webb
NA500 'G'	S/L C Barrett	MZ585 'O'	F/S P Anthony
	Sgt Thompson U/G		Sgt Robinson U/G
MZ632 'W'	F/L J Cooper	MZ586 'Y'	F/S S Kuleski
	Sgt Irwin U/G		Sgt Crum U/G

Flight Sergeant Anthony and crew lost so much time en route that it was decided to turn back as they would have been 18 minutes late over the target.

Squadron Leader Barrett and crew failed to return from this operation, nothing was heard from them after take off.

12 May 1944

The first shipment of American 500 lb bombs arrived at East Moor, these had a different type of fusing and method of fusing control to the ones normally handled by the Station Armaments Section.

RCAF Station Tholthorpe trounced East Moor at Softball, the score 20-10, but East Moor soccer team had better luck at RCAF Station Dishforth, score 3-2 in favour.

Considerable damage was inflicted on the Rail Yards at Louvain when amongst a small force were fourteen crews from 432 Squadron,

MZ601 'A'	F/S J McHeleron	MZ590 'C'	F/S E Clarke
LW596 'D'	F/L M Pettit	MZ603 'E'	Ft/O Lekis W
LW686 'H'	F/S S Kuleski	Lw582 'M'	P/O G Webb
LK811 'N'	F/O P Jack	MZ585 '0'	F/S P Anthony
LW595 'Q'	F/O J Barker	LW616 'R'	P/O J Patterson
LW552 'S'	F/O P Lawrenson	LK766 'V'	P/O J Webb
MZ632 'W'	F/L J Cooper	LW598 'K'	P/O D Maddock
	Sgt Houston U/G		Sgt Easy U/G

Pilot Officer Maddock and crew were unable to identify the target and so did not bomb.

13 May 1944

A frustrating day for nine crews of 432 Squadron who were briefed for an operation only to have it cancelled immediately afterwards at 18.00 hours.

With continuous rain and clouds down to 3,000 feet, visibility was reduced to 2 miles precluding any flying training at East Moor.

Catering Officers, Flight Officer R.A Bink WD and Flight Lieutenant Grandoise From No.6 Group Headquarters visited the station.

In the evening a dance held in the Station Gymnasium attracted 300 people.

14 May 1944

No operations were called for at the station, but a full programme of Flying Training was carried out including day and night cross countries and fighter affiliation exercises.

East Moor played host to further parties of employees from Fairey Aviation and local Air Training Corps.
Wing Commander's A.C Tufts and C.O King, Administration and Engineering Officers respectively, visited the station from No.62 Base.

'Ganada's Relationship with Britain and America tomorrow', was the weekly forum subject and the speaker, Flying Officer F Maher the Flying Control Officer,

15 May 1944

Another operation free day at the station. Flying Training went ahead apace with fighter affiliation, cross countries (night), air to air firing, air to sea

and bombing practice at Strensall Bombing Range.

RCAF Station Linton on Ouse defeated East Moor 8-2 at Softball.

Visitors to East Moor included the station's ex Armaments Officer, Flight Lieut A.N Roth who was then 62 Base Armaments Officer, and Squadron Officer Holland WAAF also from Baee.

16 May 1944

432 Squadron were not required for operations but carried out eight aircraft cross country exercise.

East Moor Station's Victory Loan target was exceeded by 11,450 Canadian dollars ma king a grand total of 42,450.

A lecture on 'Prisoners of War' was given by Intelligence Officer, Flight Lieut H.F Lount to aircrew from 432 Squadron.
Two Navigation Officers from 6 Group Headquarters visited East Moor, they were Squadron Leader's H.A Forbes and A.M Doilvie, and were accompanied by Pilot Officer C. Massey a Bombing Leader.
The Airmen's NAAFI attracted 350 personnel to watch an ENSA sponsored movie.

17 May 1944

The Station ground crews acting on instructions from Group, stacked sufficient bombs for one operation on each occupied dispersal point,but no operational details were called for.

There were fifteen day and night cross country exercises carried out from the station by 432 Squadron crews.

A Station Commander's Conference was held by Group Captain H.H Rutledge and the Section Commanders, where the latter's problems were discussed.

At Station level, Radar defeated 'B' Flight 12-8 in a Softball game.

In the evening 62 (RGAF) Base String Quartette played before an audience of 53.

18 May 1944

Still no operations and a 'Bullseye' exercise scheduled for the evening was cancelled due to adverse weather conditions at East Moor.
Air Commodore A.D Ross, No.62 (RCAF) Base Commander visited East Moor and spent some time interviewing aircrew applicants for commissions.

19 May 1944

The Station Padre, Squadron Leader E. Lautenschlager gave a talk to aircrew in the Briefing Room at 11.00 hours on 'German Phrases and Pronunciations'.

The Station Softball team avenged themselves by defeating 6 Group Headquarters on the latter's ground, 11-6.

No.62 Base Engineering Officers, Squadron Leader's Carr-Harris and F. Humphries visited East Moor along with Base AdministrationOfficers Wing Commander A Tufts and Squadron Leader B. Kehow.

The Gun Emplacements at Le Clipon were the targets for East Moor's crews when fourteen were detailed and dispatched. It was found that the bombing up operation using the ones stacked at dispersal on the 17th took considerably longer than the normal method carried out from the Station Bomb Dump.

Take off commenced at 23.48 hours and all were down again by 03.33 returning an average landing time of 2 mins 4 secs.

MZ672 'G'	F/O H Smith		LW582 'M'	P/O G Webb	
LW595 'Q'	F/O J Barker		LW616 'R'	P/O J Patterson	
LW552 'S'	F/O P Lawrenson		MZ6O1 'A'	F/S J McHeleron	
				Sgt Lindblom	U/G
LK765 'B'	P/L Lauzon		LW686 'H'	P/O W Ferneyhough	
	F/O Tobias	2/Plt		F/O Friedman	2/Plt
	Sgt McDermott U/G			Sgt Lounsbury	U/G
MZ654 'L'	F/O V Smith		LK811 'N'	F/O P Jack	
	Sgt Laundrum U/G			Sgt Beauchesne	U/G
MZ603 'E'	Ft/O Lekis W		MZ632 'W'	F/O L Evenson	
	Sgt TrottU/G			F/S Shanks	U/G
MZ586 'Y'	S/L A Lowe		MZ585 'O'	P/O R Anthony	
	F/O Best	2/Plt		Sgt Layton	U/G
	Sgt Crum	U/G			

20 May 1944

No operations were called for at East Moor. Local flying took place all day.

It was reported by the Armaments Section that twin adaptors which permitted the carrying of 12 x 500 lb bombs in the fuselage, had been used for the first time and that no snags had resulted.

21 May 1944

A second day without any operational commitment at East Moor, practice bombing was carried out at Strensall Bombing Range, fighter affiliation, air to air firing and day and night cross countries were also pursued.

The subject at the weekly Forum was 'Imperial Tie' and Professor Baines from Leeds University was the speaker.

More than 350 personnel attended YMCA films screened in the Airmen's NAAFI.

22 May 1944

The Station Softball team suffered a setback when RCAF Station Thoithorpe beat them in the Group League, 11-3.

Bomber Command detailed a small force to attack the Railway Yards at Le Mans where considerable damage was inflicted on nearby factories also, it was an early hours take off and the first of fourteen Halifaxes rose from East Moor's runway at 7 minutes past midnight and the last one was down at 05.16 hours,

MZ601 'A'	F/S	J McAeleron	LK765 'B'	F/O V Smith	
MZ672 'G'	Ft/O	Lekis W	MZ660 'J'	F/L J Cooper	
				Sgt Anderson	U/G
LW598 'K'	P/O	W Ferneyhough	LW582 'M'	P/O G Webb	
	F/O	Friedman 2/Plt		Sgt Easy	U/G
	Sgt	Lounsbury U/G			
LK811 'N'	F/S	H Menzies	MZ585 'O'	P/O P Anthony	
	P/O	Card 2/Plt		Sgt Lindblom	U/G
LW595 'Q'	F/O	J Barker	LW552 'S'	P/O J Patterson	
	F/O	Best 2/Plt			
LK766 'V'	F/O	R Jack	MZ632 'W'	F/O W Evenson	
				Sgt Irwin U/G	
MZ506 'X'	F/S	S Kuleski	MZ586 'Y'	S/L A Lowe	
	Sgt	Crum U/G		F/O Vickeman 2/Plt	
				Sgt Beauchesne U/G	

Five of the East Moor crews found it neccessary to orbit the target several times and two brought their bombs back to base unable to identify it.

Flight Sergeant Kuleski and crew failed to return from this operation, nothing was heard from them after take off. In the evening an informal dance was held to records in the Gymnasium and a YMCA film show in the Airmen's NAAFI was watched by 400 people.

At 21.40 hours, Halifax MZ603 sustained damage to its starboard wing when the perimeter track gave way beneath it.

23 May 1944

No operations were scheduled at the station and the aircrews were given ground training until evening. Some night cross countries were carried out.

NCO's and 'Other Ranks' were confined to camp for the evening for the purpose of giving the billets and domestic sites a clean up and for a salvage drive. Much salvage was collected and the living sites were considerably improved.

A Signals Officer, Squadron Leader R.B Hoodspith and Flight Lieutenant Crawford Radar, visited East Moor from 62 Base Headquarters. Another visitor was WAAF Squadron Officer P.R Kelly from RCAF Station Croft.

24 May 1944

The second day without any operations. Twelve crews from 432 Squadron carried out night exercises and the gunners in MZ501 damaged their own tailpiane in practice firing.

The Armaments Officer reported that all the station's Beaverette armoured vehicles had been fitted with .303 machine guns of the Vickers type, and were servicaable for ground to ground or ground to air defence.

The staff at East Moor's isolated Strensall Bombing Range were happy to receive Mr. Jack Mclelland the YMCA representative with his load of comforts. They were located some 10 road miles from the airfield.

The East Moor WAAF's were inspected by Squadron Officer N. Holland from 62 Base.

25 May 1944

Further Airfield Defence measures were announced and numbers of Gerard rifles and Browning machine guns were made ready and available at East Moor.

Adverse weather prevented any flying training at the station and was the cause of cancelling within an hour of briefing, an operation that promised to be 432 Squadron's largest effort to date, and involved eighteen crews.

Members of the Royal Artillery from the Searchlight Battery at Thornton Le Clay were guests of the station and watched a Softball exhibition during their visit.

Fig 24. Halifax III, MZ603 minus undercarriage, another victom of the notorious ditch at the Strensall Road end of East Moor's runway. 26th May 1944. Photo G. Inns.

26 May 1944

Airfield Defence was again to the forefront at East Moor. A quantity of Sten guns were available together with considerable amounts of ammunition, and staff were busily engaged preparing and Filling magazines for the former and for the Browning machine guns and Gerard rifles.

The station now boasted a 'Cycle Club' and sixteen enthusiasts set out on their first venture, a trip to the ruins at Sheriff Hutton Castle.

27 May 1944

During the early hours, seven 432 Squadron crews landed after completing night across country exercises.

Visitors to the station included, WD Catering Officer, Section Officer 0. Park, Flight Lieutenant W.E Killeen an MT Officer and Public Relations Officer, Pilot Officer J.M Coldwell all from No.62 (RCAF) Base.

At 16.20 hours the WAAF Site in Goose Lane participated in a practice Fire Alarm. A response time of 2 mins 20 secs was recorded for the appearance of the apparatus, and all hoses were rolled out and were ready for 'Water On' within 4 mins 10 secs of the alarm being sounded.

The WAAF's took over the Airmen's Mess and held a Social Evening with around eighty people attending. Their own NAAFI building was undergoing re-decoration.

A German Rehabilitation Camp at Bourg Leopold was the target for fifteen crews from 432 Squadron. Take off was completed by 23.59 hours and the last one to touch down did so at O4.34,

MZ6O1 'A'	P/O D Maddock		MZ603 'E'	Ft/O Lekis W	
	F/O Morrow	2/Plt			
	Sgt Sharko	U/G			
MZ672 'G'	P/O W Ferneyhough		LW686 'H'	F/O W Vickeman	
	P/O Johnston	2/Plt		F/S Shanks	U/G
	Sgt Johnston	U/G			
MZ660 'J'	F/O W Tobias		MZ654 'L'	F/O V Smith	
	Sgt McFar1and	U/G			
LW582 'M'	P/O G Webb		MZ633 'O'	P/O J Webb	
	P/O Card	2/Plt		Sgt Irwin	U/G
LW595 'Q'	F/L G Larson		LW616 'R'	P/O J Patterson	
LW552 'S'	P/O L Friedman		MZ586 'Y'	F/O B Best	
MZ586 'U'	F/O L Evenson		MZ632 'W'	F/L D Von Laufer	
				Sgt Anderson	U/G
LK811 'N'	F/S H Menzies				
	Sgt Hall	2/Plt			

During the attack, a huge explosion was seen and presumed to have been a bomb dump going up. It was so big that it saturated the whole target area.

Seventeen aircraft and crews had been detailed but at the last moment, MZ672 and LK766 suffered engine failure and unable to take part in the attack.

All crews reported that the target was very well marked and that the Master-Bombers instructions were very efficient and led to a most concentrated raid.

Thick black smoke rose to over 5,000 feet and many fires were seen. There were no searchlights in the target area and only spasmodic flak but enemy aircraft were active both over the target and on the homeward flight.

On arriving back at East Moor at 03.52 hours MZ603 with the American First Officer W. Lekis at the controls, touched down on runway 17 before crashing through the airfield boundary. The undercarriage came to rest in the no-torious ditch~at the Strensall Road end.

The remaining aircraft were unable to land for some time, orbiting the airfield until it could be ascertained that it was possible to use that runway.

Flight Sergeant H.J Menzies and crew failed to return from this operation, he was on his 13th trip, while Flying Officer Rutherford the navigator, Sergeant McClay air gunner and flight engineer Sergeant Clark had all completed ten. The other air gunner, Warrant Officer H.H Rodgers had completed twenty five missions and second pilot Sergeant Hall was on his first.

The other two crew members had nine operations each under their belts.

Flight Sergeant Menzies together with three of his crew survived when LK811 was lost near the Belgian border with Holland. Navigator Flying Officer Gouinlock,and Bomb Aimer Flying Officer Rutherford,despite some eventful experiences managed to evade capture until liberated by Allied Forces.

28 May 1944

At 03.52 hours, MZ506 was landing on runway 16 when it crashed through the fence at Strensall Road ending with its wheels in the ditch there. Further landings were held up until 04.07 hours.

Twelve 432 Squadron crews were later engaged in fighter affiliation exercises

29 May 1944

A 'Purple' Air Raid Warning was received at the station at 03.15 hours

with the 'White' following ten minutes later.

A two weeks course of Physical Training commenced and involved all staff not engaged on urgent duties. The duration was one hour per day

East Moor Station defeated 6 Group HQ at softball - score 10-9.

30 May 1944

All 432 Squadron Officers attended a Mess Dinner in honour of Wing Commander W.A McKay, DFC, who was being repatriated. The popular squadron C.O was presented with an antique silver mug in happy memories of time spent under his command. The Base Commander Air Commodore A.R Ross also attended.

31 May 1944

Wing Commander J.K MacDonald arrived at East Moor and assumed command of 432 Squadron.

The Station Bicycle Club had its second outing, thirty two members making the trip to Kirkham Abbey and return.

Over 200 personnel attended 'Nordic Lights', a live concert staged by ENSA. Fifteen 432 Squadron crews set out for an attack on on the RDF 'Jamming' station at Mont-Couple, results were good and obtained without too much opposition,

MZ586 'Y'	S/L A Lowe	MZ632 'W'	F/L Von Laufer	LK766 'V'	P/O L Lauzon
MZ686 'U'	F/O P Card	LW552 'S'	F/O E Lawrenson	LW595 'Q'	F/L G Larson
MZ654 'L'	F/O V Smith	MZ633 'O'	P/O J Webb	MZ591 'K'	F/O W Vickerman
MZ660 'J'	F/L J Cooper	MZ603 'E'	Ft/O W Lekis	LW596 'D'	F/O D Best
MZ590 'C'	F/O W Tobias	LK765 'B'	F/O L Friedman	MZ6Ol 'A'	F/O H Smith

'Y' had Sgt Campbell as a 2nd/Plt and Sgt Justason as U/G. Sgt Scarff was U/G in 'W', Sgt McFarland in 'U', P/O Ryan in 'L', Sgt Irwin in '0', Sgt Shanks in 'E', W/0 Rowe in 'C' and Sgt Wilburn in 'A'.

Squadron Leader J.K MacDonald was posted in to East Moor from 431 Squadron to become 432 Squadron's Commanding Officer.

By this date, more than half of 432 Squadron's Halifax III's had been fitted with a mid under gunners position requiring an extra crew member.

That squadron's aircraft strength had risen to 26~Halifaxes and the crew strength to 32.

General:

The monthly total of flying training hours at East Moor was 498 while operations counted for a further 427, and all were accomplished without any serious flying accidents.

The Station Commander, Group Captain H.H Rutledge OBE, carried out an inspection of Station Headquarters on the 17th.

The Strength of RCAF Station East Moor at 31 May 1944 was,

RCAF	Officers	108	RAF Officers	18	
WD	Officers	0	WAAF Officers	1	
RCAF	Other Ranks	735	RAF Other Ranks	115	
USAF	Personnel	I	WAAF Other Ranks	130	

Total   1,208

The Strength of 432 Squadron was,

RCAF	Officer Aircrew 78	RCAF Airmen Aircrew	111
RAF	Officer Aircrew 14	RAF Airmen Airerew	47
RCAF	Groundcrew 265	RAF Groundcrew 20	
RCAF	Officer Groundcrew 2		
Total 537			

Flight Lieutenant Jaques assumed the duties of Squadron Adjutant on the 23rd with the postimg of Flight Lieutenant Harris.

Group Captain E.C Noble and Flight Lieutenant Montgomery, Medical Officers, visited the station on the 27th, and it was reported that the 'Health' of the station as a whole was good.

1 June 1944

Operations were called for but subsequently scrubbed, after sixteen of 432 Squadron's Halifaxes had been prepared. No flying training took place.

The Station Armoury received an allocation of 1,000 lb bombs, the first for some considerable time. Apparantly there was a shortage of the type.
The East Moor WAAF's were inspected by Squadron Officer N.Holland from No.62 Base, and not found wanting.

2 June 1944

The station Softball team suffered a 11-9 loss against RCAF Station Thoithorpe. The station WAAF Section had further visitors, Squadron Officer N. Holland was in attendance again,accompanied by Squadron Officer Loring from No.61 Base.

The Station Gymnasium was the scene for a Station Dance when 400 people attended. At 22.19 hours, the first of fourteen Halifaxes from 432 Squadron took off for their first target for the month, heavy anti aircraft batteries at Neufchatel on the French coast,

MZ60l 'A'	F/S J McHeleron		LK765 'B'	F/O D Johnston	
LW596 'D'	F/L M Pettit		MZ603 'E'	F/O E Morrow	
				Sgt Lee	U/G
MZ591 'K'	P/O W Ferneyhough		MZ660 'J'	P/O D Maddock	
	W/O Rowe	U/G		F/S Shanks	U/G
MZ654 'L'	F/O W Vickeman		LW582 'M'	P/O G Webb	
	Sgt Sharko	U/G		Sgt Campbell	U/G
LW595 'Q'	F/O J Barker		LW616 'R'	P/O J Patterson	
	F/S McKean	2/Plt			
LW552 'S'	S/L J MacDonald		MZ686 'U'	F/O L Evenson	
	P/O Quesnal	U/G		Sgt Lafleche	U/G
LK766 'V'	P/O L Lauzon		MZ632 'W'	F/O P Jack	
				Sgt Rice	U/G

Due to a navigational error, Flight Lieutenant Pettit did not reach the target, and returned his bombs to base.

All aircraft returned safely.

3 June 1944

No operations were called for.

No.3 Domestic Site, located inland from Goose Lane, was handed over to 432 Squadron for occupation by aircrew, Senior NCO's and some Officers. The complex had undergone a complete renovation and re-decoration project.

Twenty six employees from the Fairey Aviation Company were guests at East Moor,
this was the fifth visit to date, and was conducted by Flying Officer N. Doe Technical Adjutant of the Station Servicing Wing.

4 June 1944

Cross country exercises were the order of the day for seven 432 Squadron crews. The Station Manning Services, Police, Flying Control and Fire Section were all involved in a full scale Fire Drill which also involved the National Fire Service. At 11.00 hours, the Station Tannoy announced that a fire had broken out in No.1 Hanger. The Station Fire Section were on the scene within 3 minutes and the National Fire Service from Easingwold arrived 12 minutes later, a very satisfactory outcome.

Canon Harrison of York Minster addressed the weekly Forum and spoke on the 'History of York Minster'.

A further 26 employees of Fairey Aviation were given a conducted tour of the station.

5 June 1944

Seventeen 432 Squadron crews successfully bombed the coastal gun batteries at Houlgate in the early hours, take off commenced at 01.40,

MZ6O1 'A'	F/O H Smith		LK765 'B'	F/S E Clarke
	Sgt Supergis U/G			
MZ603 'E'	Ft/O Lekis W		NA516 'F'	F/O W Smith
	W/O Rowe U/G			Sgt Justason U/G
LW686 'H'	F/O W Tobias		MZ660 'J'	F/L J Cooper
	Sgt McFarland U/G			F/S Smith 2/Plt
				Sgt Wilburn U/G
MZ591 'K'	F/L M Pettit		MZ686 'U'	F/O L Evenson
	Sgt Cornell U/G			Sgt Lee U/G
LW582 'M'	P/O J Webb		NA527 'N'	F/O P Jack
				Sgt Lafleche U/G
LW595 'Q'	F/O J Barker		MZ633 'O'	P/O P Card
	F/S McKean 2/Plt			Sgt Irwin U/G
LW616 'R'	F/O L Friedman		LW552 'S'	F/O P Lawrenson
LK766 'V'	P/O L Lauzon		MZ632 'W'	S/L J MacDonald
				P/O Quesnal U/G
MZ586 'Y'	F/L G Larson			
	P/O H Houston U/G			

Pilot Officer Card returned early with a u/s compass.

More than 1,000 aircraft attacked coastal gun batteries along the French coast of Normandy on this date, when the 5,000 tons of explosives dropped, was believed to be the greatest dropped in one night to date.
In the interests of security, it,was announced at 17.05 hours that all East Moor Station and Squadron personnel were to be 'Confined to Camp' until further notice. Other extra security measures were also taken.

6 June 1944

'D'-Day, The great news of the Allied landings was received with great pleasure as the beginning of the end. All ranks were keyed up, and all the stops were pulled out to get twenty Halifaxes into the air for an attack on the Railway Bridge at Coutances. This was the first occasion that 432 Squadron crews had been asked to bomb at the low level of 1,500 to 2,000 feet. Take off commenced at 21.58 hours, and all returned safely,

MZ601 'A'	F/S J McHeleron	LK765 'B'	F/S E Clarke
LW596 'D'	F/L M Pettit	MZ603 'E'	F/O H Smith
			Sgt McFarland U/G
NA516 'F'	P/O P Maddock	LW686 'H'	F/O W Vickeman
MZ660 'J'	F/O V Johnston	MZ591 'K'	P/O W Ferneyhough
	W/O Rowe U/G		

LW582 'M'	P/O J Webb	NA527 'N'	F/O R Jack
MZ633 'O'	P/O P Anthony	LW595 'Q'	F/O J Barker
LW616 'R'	F/L G Larson	LW552 'S'	Sgt P Campbell
MZ686 'U'	P/O P Card	LK766 'V'	P/O L Lauzon
	Sgt Cornell U/G		
MZ586 'Y'	S/L A Lowe	MZ632 'W'	F/O H Morrow
LL547 'X'	F/O L Friedmen	MZ654 'L'	F/O V Smith

All aircraft except 'E' and 'L' were diverted to RAF Station Wing where 'F' crashed on landing. The former two landed at Horwood.

Flying Officer Morrow and crew aborted on the Master Bomber's instructions. Once again the East Moor crews were part of an attacking force of more than 1,000 aircraft.

Earlier in the day, an 'Inlying Picket' of fifty men and one officer was mounted. The latter was to remain in,and sleep when neccessary in one of the Beaverette armoured vehicles positioned near Flying Control. He would receive any messages and instructions from the Duty Flying Control Officer.

375 personnel attended ENSA films in the Airmen's NAAFI

7 June 1944

Six aircraft from RCAF Station Leeming landed at East Moor.
Visitors to the station included Squadron Officer N. Holland WAAF, from No.62 Base and Public Relations Officer, Pilot Officer J. Coldwell also from Base.

Everyone on the station was keen to get the war over and volunteers came in large numbers to perform additional duties in the Bomb Dump, amongst them were many WAAF's who were used to F/Lt the ammunition belts.

The take off by eleven crews from 432 Squadron was completed by 23.09 hours when they set course for the Marshalling Yards at Ancheres,

MZ60l 'A'	F/S J McHeleron	LK765 'B'	P/O D Maddock	
	P/O Houston U/G		F/S McKean	2/Plt
LW596 'D'	F/O H Morrow	MZ603 'E'	Ft/O Lekis W	
			Sgt Wilburn	U/G
LW686 'H'	F/O W Tobias	MZ660 'J'	F/L J Cooper	
	Sgt Irwin. U/G		F/L Smith	
			2/Plt Sgt Cornell	U/G
MZ633 'O'	P/O R Anthony	LW582 'M'	F/O W Vickeman	
	P/O Quesnal U/G			
LW595 'Q'	F/O P Lawrenson	MZ632 'W'	F/O L Evenson	
			Sgt Scarff	U/G

Sadly, nothing was heard from Flying Officer Vickeman and crew after their departure from East Moor.

First Officer Lekis (USAF), made an early return with technical failure, and Squadron Leader Lowe with the starboard inner engine u/s.

8 June 1944

Squadron Leader Bryson and crew, with twenty one operations already behind them, reported in to East Moor from 425 Squadron. A further two crews arrived and the three formed a third Flight with 432 Squadron which in turn was to form the nucleus of 415 Squadron (RCAF). This squadron was scheduled to take on the role of a bomber unit at East Moor in July 1944.

Pilot Officer J.M Bates from No.3 PRC RAF Station Innsworth visited East Moor. An audience of 350 people attended evening showings of 'Y' films in the Station Hospital, Airmen's NAAFI and Sergeant's Mess.

The Marshalling Yards at Mayenne provided ten East Moor crews with a target when the operation was said to be successful and only medium flak was present and no enemy fighters. All returned safely,

LW596 'D'	F/L M Pettit	LW616 'R'	F/L G Larson
LK766 'V'	P/O L Lauzon	MZ591 'K'	F/O W Ferneyhough
LK765 'B'	F/S E Clarke	LL547 'X'	P/O J Webb
MZ686 'U'	P/O P Card	MZ603 'E'	F/O H Smith
MZ660 'J'	F/O V Smith	MZ586 'Y'	SIL A Lowe

Aircraft 'D' and 'Y' were diverted to RCAF Station Dalton while the remainder landed at RCAF Station Dishforth, all being accounted for by 05.20 hours on the 9th.

9 June 1944

All the diverted aircraft were back on East Moor by 08.58 hours.

The Station Armaments Section had a very busy day, in addition to bombing up and preparing ten Halifaxes for a night operation, they took delivery of twenty four truck and trailer loads of bombs and components. Due to the extra work neccessitated by support for the second Front, the ground crews were unable to fulfill numerous sporting fixtures, and those had to be suspended.

Nevertheless, the Station Cycling Club managed to get twenty five members off on a trip to Byland Abbey under the direction of Pilot Officer M. Nittel the Station Sports Officer.

Three WAAF Equipment and Messing Officers, Flight Officer I.V Gibson and Section Officer's E.E Rising and G.H Torno visited East Moor from RAF Station Innsworth.

An ex 432 Squadron Halifax, LW598 suffered starboard inner engine failure before crashing at Newton on Ouse and burning out, a few days after transfer to 426 Squadron.

News was received at East Moor that Pilot Officer J. Webb had been awarded an immediate DSO for outstanding devotion to duty in spite of tremendous odds on the night of 27 April 1944, during his first mission as a captain.

Two further crews were added to the nucleus of 415 Squadron, in readiness for that squadrons change of role from Coastal to Bomber Command.

Despite what would normally be regarded as impossible weather conditions, the East Moor crews continued to make the most effective and severe attacks on their objectives since 'D' Day.

Le Mans Airfield was singled out as their target on this date when the following ten crews were dispatched, and to use their own words, 'plastered[1] the place,

MZ603 'E'[1]	F/O L Friedman		LW686 'H'	F/O V Johnston	
MZ660 'J'	F/O W Tobias		MZ654 'L'	F/L H Smith	
	Sgt Irwin	U/G		Sgt Justason	U/G
NA527 'N'	F/O R Jack		MZ633 'O'	Sgt P Campbell	
LW595 'Q'	F/O J Barker		MZ632 'W'	S/L M Bryson	
				P/O Quesnal	U/G
LW616 'R'	W/C J MacDonald		LL547 'X'	P/O G McKean	

All returned safely to East Moor.

10 June 1944

This was the fourth consecutive day that 432 Squadron had been asked to provide a ten aircraft detail for operations.

The target was the Railway Centre with its many junctions at Versailles -Matelot near Paris, which served as another link in the German supply system.

Squadron Leader A. Lowe and crew were the first away at 22.15 hours and all ten were airborne by 22.21, leaving only half a minute intervals

Nine aircraft attacked the primary target, Flying Officer Best and crew reached it before it had been marked, as the Master Bomber was late. This crew brought their bombs back to East Moor.

No enemy aircraft were encountered but lots of air tracer was seen in the target area.

All East Moor crews returned safely to base, Flying Officer Best and crew while first over the target,were the last to land at 03.42 hours,

LK765 'B'	F/S E Clarke	MZ603 'E'	F/O D Best
LW686 'H'	P/O D Maddock	MZ660 'J'	F/L J Cooper
			P/O Houston U/G
MZ633 'O'	P/O J Webb	MZ686 'U'	F/O L Evenson
	Sgt Hosier U/G		P/O Quesnal U/G
MZ632 'W'	F/O D Von Laufer	MZ586 'Y'	S/L A Lowe
			P/O Gingrich 2/Plt
			Sgt Justason U/G
LW596 'D'	F/L M Pettit	LW552 'S'	F/O P Lawrenson
	Sgt Kerr 2/Plt		

11 June 1944

No.62 (RCAF) Base Headquarters ordered a complete stand down for all East Moor's operational crews, giving them a much needed rest.

All Flying Training was cancelled owing to indifferent weather in the area, and consequently the 'freshmen' crews got a rest too.

The Editor of the 'Yorkshire Evening Post', Mr. A. Kenyon, addressed the weekly Forum held in the 'Y' Lounge, when sixty personnel attended. His talk was on the subject of 'British Journalism'.

Air Commodore A.D Ross the No.62 (RCAF)Base Commander together with Brigadier

Martin of the Canadian Army visited East Moor. Other visitors included two

Administrative Officers from 6 Group Headquarters, Flight Lieutenant P Kiombies

and Flight Officer K.L Ball, WD.

12 June 1944

The East Moor emergency services responded to a call from the staff at Strensall Bombing Range. At 00.35 hours Halifax JN953, NA-0 of 428 Squadron, Middleton St.George crashed and burnt near Claxton Hall after being abandoned by all except the pilot, Flying Officer Martin. He was taken to York Military Hospital suffering from shock, burns and fractures, the remainder of the crew were taken to East Moor.

The Sergeants Mess held a dance at which Air Commodore Ross, 62 Base Commander and Brigadier Martin of the Canadian Army attended.
Fifteen 432 Squadron crews attacked the railway junction at Cambrai,

LW616 'R'	P/O L Lauzon	MZ601 'A'	F/S J McElheren	LW596 'D'	F/O H Morrow
LK764 'F'	F/O W Tobias	LW686 'H'	F/O D Best	MZ654 'L'	F/O V Smith
NA527 'N'	F/O P Jack	MZ633 'O'	P/O P Anthony	LW412 'P'	S/L M Bryson
LW595 'Q'	F/O J Barker	MZ686 'U'	P/O P Card	MZ591 'K'	P/O Ferneyhough
MZ586 'Y'	F/L G Larson	LK803 'Z'	F/O H Damgaard	MZ632 'W'	FtO W Lekis

Pilot Officer Lauzon, Flight Sergeant McElheren and their crews failed to return, nothing was heard from them after leaving East Moor and both skippers were nearly half way through their tours.

Flying Officer Tobias's crew were attacked by a FW190 but corkscrewing manouvres ~hook it off. A few minutes later Flying Officer V. Smith had a similar experience. First Officer Lekis's crew bombed Amiens in error due to his navigator's watch being ten minutes adrift.

Sgt Irwin was U/G in 'A', Sgt McFarland in 'F', Sgt Justason in 'V' ,P/O Quesnal '0' Sgt Wilson in 'K', Sgt James in 'Y' and W/O Rowe in 'W'.

13 June 1944

The station enjoyed an operational stand down. Nine crews carried out a 'Bullseye' exercise and a further three practiced night bombing at Strenaall.

14 June 1944

Advice was received from 6 Group Headquarters that the additional flight which had been formed to provide a nucleus of personnel for 415 (RCAF) Squadron's new role as a bomber unit, was to be disbanded and the crews to return to their former units.

Seventeen 432 Squadron Halifaxes took off to join more than three hundred other aircraft in an operation against the railway yards at St. Pol and it was said that these were well bombed,

Unable to raise the undercarriage, Flight Sergeant Kicak made an early return, and Flight Lieutenant Smith's crew were unable to release their bombs. After a while two were finally jettisoned and the remaining thirteen were brought back to East Moor. The original order of battle was as follows,

NA516 'A'	F/S J Kicak	LK765 'B'	F/S E Clarke	LW596 'D'	F/O V Johnston
MZ603 'E'	FtO W Lekis	LK764 'F'	F/O H Smith	LW686 'H'	P/O J Cooper
MZ660 'J'	F/L J Cooper	MZ591 'K'	P/O Ferneyhough	NA527 'N'	Sgt R Campbell
MZ633 '0'	P/O J Patterson	LW595 'Q'	P/O G Webb	LW552 'S'	F/O R Lawrenson
MZ686 'U'	P/O J Webb	MZ632 'W'	W/C J MacDonald	LL547 'X'	P/O G McKean
MZ586 'Y'	P/O H Morrow	LK803 'Z'	F/L H Smith		

On the above operation Sgt Kerr was second pilot in 'J' and under gunners Sgt Anderson was carried in 'E', P/O Quesnal in 'F', Sgt Lindblom in 'H', W/0 Rowe in 'K', F/S Shanks in 'J', Sgt Hosier in 'N' and Sgt Justason in 'W".

Flight Lieutenant Smith 'and crew were forced to abort their mission when the bomb doors of LK803 could not be opened.

The first 'Flying Bombs' had been launched against England on 12 June 1944 and for the following ten weeks their launch sites and supply depots were regarded as high priority targets by Bomber Command. Many of the 'V-l' launching sites were situated in the Pas de Calais area and the bombing campaign against them was given the code name 'Operation Crossbow'.

15 June 1944

A concentration of 'E' Boats and Minesweepers in the inner harbour at Boulogne became the next target for East Moor crews and thirteen were dispatched by 432 Squadron, on their first daylight operation when almost three hundred aircraft were in the attacking force escorted by twelve squadrons of Spitfires. All of the stations aircraft returned safely.

NA5l6 'A'		MZ590 'C'		MZ603 'E'		MZ660 'J'	
F/S Kicak	J	F/O Best	D	Ft.O Lekis	W	F/OTobias	W
F/S Shanks	U/G	Sgt Boyce	U/G	Sgt Cook	U/G		
LK764 'F'		NA527 'N'		MZ633 '0'		NA5l7 'R'	
F/O Smith	V	F/O Jack	P	P/O Anthony	P	F/O Lawrenson	R
Sgt Lee U/G		Sgt Burgess	U/G	P/O Quesnal	U/G	W/O McKewan	U/G
Mz686 'U'		MZ632 'W'		LL547 'X'		MZ586 'Y'	
F/O Damgaard	H	F/L Larson	G	F/ORobertson	D	S/L Lowe	A
		Sgt McFarland U/G		Sgt Wilson	U/G	Sgt Justason	U/G
LW686 'H'							
F/L Cooper	J						
W/O Rowe	U/G						

Flight Lieutenant Cooper landed at Manston with a u/s airspeed indicator about an hour and a quarter after take off.

16 June 1944

Nineteen 432 Squadron crews set out for an operation to the Ru hr Valley where the synthetic oil plant at Sterkrade - Holten was the target,

NA516 'A'		LK765 'B'		MZ590 'C'		LW596 'D'	
F/O Morrow	H	W/O Clarke		F/O Smith	H	F/L Pettit	M
				Sgt McFarland U/G			
LK764 'F'		**MZ660 'J'**		**MZ591 'K'**		**_LW576_ 'M'**	
F/O Smith	V	F/O Cooper	J	P/O Ferneyhough W		P/O Webb	G
		F/S Shanks	U/G				
MZ603 'E'		**NA527 'N'**		**MZ633'A'**		**LW412 'P'**	
Ft.O Lekis	W	F/O Jack	P	P/C Anthony	P	Sgt Campbell	P
Sgt Justason	U/G	w/a Rowe	U/G	P/O Quesnal	U/G	Sgt Sharko	U/G
LW595 'Q'		**NA517 'R'**		**MZ686 'U'**		**MZ632 'W'**	
F/O Johnston	V	P/O Patterson	J	P/C McKean	G	W/C MacDonald J	
		Sgt Flick	U/G			Sgt Wilson	U/G
LL547 'X'		**M.Z586 'Y'**		**LK803 'Z'**			
F/O Tobias	W	F/L Larson	G	P/O Webb	J		
W/O Gates	U/G	Sgt James	U/G				

Flying Officer V.Smith made an early return with a u/s rear turret and FlightLieutenant Larson was unable to identify the target and abandoned his task. Flying Officer Morrow and crew failed to return from this operation, nothing was heard from them after take off, it was their fourth operation.

Wing Commander MacDonald's crew came under attack from a JU88 and his gunners were successful in scoring several hits on it.

Pilot Officer Anthony's crew were twice attacked by enemy aircraft. They had taken off at 20.05 hrs and lifted '0--Oscar' into clear night air and set course for the target which was reached before darkness fell. Despite heavy flak rising through the cloud layer they were able to complete a successful bombing run before turning for home. Just as the crew were beginning to think that it had been a relatively easy trip, flight engineer Johnny Banks spotted a JU88 at around 3,000 feet above the Halifax on the starboard side. Keeping his skipper informed as the JU88 passed over to the port side he remembers that the gunners commenced firing as soon it approached. Successful evasive action by the pilot prevented the enemy fr6m scoring any hits on the Halifax during the first attack. The second attack was a beam one and the two gunners combined fire soon had it rolling over on to its back before it was seen to crash with a tremendous explosion.

17 June 1944

Pilotless plane supply bases at Oisemont came under attack from a small force to which 432 Squadron contributed fourteen crews,

LK765 'B'	W/O E Clarke	MZ590 'C'	F/O D Best	LW596 'D'	F/O V Johston
MZ603 'E'	F/O B Smith	LK764 'F'	P/O R Gingrich	MZ672 'G '	S/L A Lowe
	P/O Quesnal U/G				W/O Rowe U/G
MZ660 'J'	F/L J Cooper	MZ591 'K'	P/O J Cooper	MZ633 'O'	Sgt J Kerr
	F/S Shanks U/G		W/O Alexander U/G		
LW595 'Q'	F/O R Lawrenson	NA517 'R'	P/O J Paterson	MZ686 'U'	P/O J Webb
MZ632 'W'	P/O G Webb	LL547 'X'	Sgt R Campbell		

All returned safely to East Moor.

Flying Officer Johnston and crew had the experience of being fired upon by another Halifax crew which was at the time flying approximately fifty yards ahead of LW596.

Between the 17th June and 29th August, the East Moor crews operated against no less than twenty three of the 'Crossbow' targets, without loss to themselves.

'Operation Crossbow' was the name given as a code to the counter measures taken against the German 'V' weapons attacks on Britain during 1944. The bombing accuracy was a tremendous challenge to the crews as many of the sites were so tiny and were placed between well concealed ramps.

18 June 1944

Eighteen 432 Squadron Halifaxes were bombed up for an operation which was subsequently cancelled late in the day. As a result, no flying training was arranged.

Mr.H.P Davies was the speaker on the subject 'What is Communism' at the weekly held Forum.

Sunday evening film shows were held in the Airmen's NAAFI and the Officer's Mess.

19 June 1944

An additional Halifax was bombed up when 432 Squadron were detailed for an attack on Rennescure, briefing took place and the operation was scrubbed. Again, it was not possible to organise any flying training with all the aircraft bombed up.

20 June 1944

The nineteen Halifaxes of 432 Squadron were still bombed up and on stand by but no operation materialised.

East Moor received several aircraft which were unable to land at their own bases due to weather conditions.

No.432 Squadron began to re-equip with the Halifax VII, and the first to arrive was NP687. When it was realized that the new aircraft were fitted with H25, the aircrews were not at all happy at the thought of losing their ventral guns as fitted on the Mk III's.

21 June 1944

The drivers were injured when two M.T vehicles collided on the perimeter track. After the cancellation of one planned operation, 432 Squadron did eventually get off when nineteen crews were dispatched to attack the Flying Bomb Sites and construction factory at St.Martin L'Hortier. The first aircraft lifted off at

17.30 hours and all were away by 17.43

MZ632 'W'	W/C	J MacDonald		LK765 'B'	W/O	E Clarke
	Sgt	Stockdale	U/G		Sgt	Hosier	U/G
MZ590 'C'	F/O	D Best		LW596 'D'	F/O	V Johnston
	Sgt	Boyce	U/G		Sgt	James	U/G
MZ603 'E'	P/O	G Webb		MZ672 'G'	F/L	H Smith
					Sgt	Hoffman	U/G
LW686 'H'	F/O	R Lawrenson		MZ660 'J'	P/O	R Card
	F/S	Shanks U/G			Sgt	Harrington	U/G
MZ591 'K'	F/O	L Friedman		MZ654 'L'	F/O	V Smith
					Sgt	Dickinson	U/G
NA527 'N'	F/O	R Jack		MZ633 'O'	P/O	R Anthony
	Sgt	Asselin U/G			P/O	Quesnal	U/G
LW595 'Q'	F/O	J Barker		NA517 'R'	F/L	D VonLaufer
	Sgt	Rice			Sgt	M McFarland	U/G
MZ686 'U'	F/O	L Evenson		LL547'X'	P/O	G McKean
	Sgt	Justason	U/G		Sgt	Sharko	U/G
MZ586 'Y'	F/L	G Larson		LK803 'Z'	P/O	J Webb
	Sgt	Wilson U/G			F/S	Graham	U/G

Pilot Officer's Webb and Anthony made early returns with a u/s port inner and starboard outer engines respectively.

The Station Armament staff had experienced a difficult few days, the constant on/off of operations and change of targets had led to several debombing and reloading of the Halifaxes.

22 June 1944

No operations were scheduled at East Moor.

More than four hundred personnel attended movies screened in the Airmen's NAAFI and the Sergeant's Mess.

Visitors to the station included, Technical Engineer Squadron Leader F. Humphreys and Squadron Leader F.H Fearnside from 62 Base and 6 Group respectively.

23 June 1944

Air Commodore A.D Ross visited East Moor, the Base Commander attended the briefing of sixteen 432 Squadron crews for an attack on Flying Bomb launching and supply sites at Bentiques,

MZ590 'C'	F/L	G Larson		LW596 'D'	F/L	M Pettit	
	Sgt	Diamond	2/Plt		Sgt	Franko 2/Plt	
	F/S	Graham	U/G		Sgt	Fullerton	U/G
MZ603 'E'	Sgt	J Kerr		LK764 'F'	P/O	R Card	
	Sgt	Hoffman	U/G		Sgt	Harrington	U/G
MZ672 'G'	F/L	H Smith		MZ660 'J'	F/O	V Johnston	
	F/O	Britton	2/Plt		Sgt	Black	U/G
MZ591 'K'	F/O	K Friedman		MZ654 'L'	F/O	V Smith	
	Sgt	Ziomko	U/G		F/S	McFadden	U/G
NA527 'N'	P/O	G Webb		MZ633 'O'	P/O	R Anthony	
	F/S	Peterson	U/G		W/O	Alexander	U/G
MZ686 'U'	F/O	L Evenson		LW595 'Q'	F/O	J Barker	
	Sgt	Ramey	U/G		F/O	Craig	2/Plt
					Sgt	Graham	U/G
NA517 'R'	P/O	J Patterson		MZ632 'W'	F/L	D Von Laufer	
	Sgt	Rice	U/G		Sgt	McFarland	
LL547'X'	P/O	G McKean		LK8O3 'Z'	F/O	R Lawrenson	
	Sgt	Walker	U/G		Sgt	Sharko	U/G

Earlier in the day, the Station Cycling Club made a trip to York Museum and the Softball team defeated RCAF Station Tholthorpe by 31 - 9.

24 June 1944

No.432 Squadron were called to attack the Flying Bomb sites at Biemere where excellent results were achieved. The station was a hive of activity up to and around midnight and the first of sixteen crews were away by 00.10 hours,

MZ590 'C'	F/O	D Best		LW596 'D'	F/L	M Pettit	
	Sgt	Black	U/G		Sgt	Harrington	U/G
MZ603 'E'	Sgt	J Kerr		LK764 'F'	P/O	D Maddock	
LW686 'H'	F/L	J Cooper		MZ660 'J'	F/O	H Smith	
	Sgt	Young	U/G		Sgt	Dickinson	U/G
MZ591 'K'	F/O	L Friedman		LK803 'Z'	P/O	J Webb	
	Sgt	Anderson	U/G		F/S	Graham	U/G
M'Z654'L'	F/O	V Smith		NA527 'N'	F/O	R Jack	
	Sgt	Seaman	U/G		Sgt	Lee	U/G
MZ633 'O'	P/O	R Gingrich		NA517 'R'	P/O	J Patterson	
	Sgt	Justason	U/G		Sgt	Farrell	U/G
MZ686 'U'	F/O	L Evenson		MZ632 'W'	F/L	D Von Laufer	
	Sgt	Walker	U/G		Sgt	McFarland	U/G
LL547 'X'	P/O	a Webb		MZ586 'Y'	Sgt	R Campbell	

Sgt	Diamond	2/Plt
Sgt	Lafleche	U/G

Flying Officer Friedman's crew managed to evade the threatened attack upon them by a FW190, and all returned safely to East Moor.

25 June 1944

There was no operational flying at the station which was required to 'stand by' in readiness for an anticipated daylight mission on the 26th. Extensive training was carried out.

'What is Capitalism' was Dr. Henderson's subject at the weekly Forum, held as usual in the 'Y' Lounge.

26 June 1944

A briefing of 432 Squadron crews took place at 08.30 hours but the operation was later scrubbed. They were asked to be prepared for early the next day.

The WAAF Commandant, Lady R.M Welsh accompanied by Wing Officer E. Carby-Hall inspected the WAAF Sites and Messes. Squadron Officer N. Holland was also present. Signals Officers Squadron Leader L. Izzard and Flying Officer H. Hitchon visited the station from Headquarters No.6 Group.

27 June 1944

The anticipated daylight operation did not materialise, however, 432 Squadron was later briefed for a night mission to the Flying Bomb Sites at Foret-de-Eawy,when more than seven hundred and twenty aircraft attacked six of those locations

LW686 'H'	F/O	Johnston V		MZ660 'J'	F/O Lawrenson R		
	Sgt	Gibson U/G			Sgt	Barrie	U/G
MZ603 'E'	Sgt	R Campbell		LW595 'Q'	F/L	J Barker	
	Sgt	T Graham	U/G		Sgt	Hoffman	U/G
LK766 'V'	P/O	R Card		LK764 'F'	P/O	D Maddock	
	Sgt	Harrington	U/G		Sgt	Wilson U/G	
MZ591 'K'	F/L	H Smith		MZ686 'U'	F/O	L Evenson	
	Sgt	Dickinson	U/G		Sgt	Farrell	U/G
MZ590 'C'	F/O	D Best		MZ632 'W'	W/C	J MacDonald	
	Sgt	Black	U/G		Sgt	Stockdale	U/G
MZ654 'L'	P/O	C McKean		LK765 'B'	W/O	E Clarke	
	Sgt	James	U/G		W/O	Gates	U/G
MZ633 'O'	P/O	R Anthony		NA517 'R'	P/O	R Gingrich	
	Sgt	Justason	U/G		Sgt	Walker	U/G
MZ586 'Y'	F/L	A Larson		NA527 'N'	F/O	R Jack	
	Sgt	Edwards	U/G		W/O	Flick	U/G

G Pilot Officer Maddock's port outer engine failed while over East Moor and he aborted the mission.

No flak or fighters were encountered by the station's crews and all returned safely to East Moor.

28 June 1944

East Moor's Flying Control observed several large flashes followed by flames and a huge explosion from the direction of RCAF Station Thoithorpe. The East Moor Ambulance was dispatched to that station when it was learnt that a landing Halifax had collided with a bombed up one at dispersal. The first flash was noted at 03.07 hours

In the evening the WAAF personnel held a tea party to mark their fifth birthday.

RAF Bomber Group Dance Band played for 350 people at a Station Dance held in the Gymnasium.

The following seventeen crews from 432 Squadron were detailed to bomb the Marshalling Yards at Metz when excellent results were achieved despite much night fighter activity,

LW552 'S'	Sgt	R Diamond		NP687 'A'	P/O	R Card	
	Sgt	Justason	U/G		F/S	Shanks	U/G
LK765 'B'	F/O	L Friedman		MZ590 'C'	F/O	W Tobias	
MZ603 'E'	Ft/a	Lekis W		MZ660 'J'	F/L	J Cooper	
LW686 'H'	P/O	H Britton		MZ654 'L'	F/O	J Johnston	
	W/O	McIntyre	U/G				
NP689 'M'	F/O	R Jack		MZ633 '0'	P/O	R Anthony	
LW595 'Q'	F/O	J Barker		NA517 'R'	P/O	J Patterson	
LK766 'V'	F/O	A Craig		MZ632 'W'	F/L	D VonLaufer	
MZ586 'Y'	P/O	G McKean		MZ591 'K'	P/O	W Ferneyhough	

Pilot Officer Ferneyhough and crew failed to return from this operation, nothing was heard from them after take off.

Flying Officer Craig aborted the mission when his port inner engine failed over East Moor and the Halifax swung off the runway at 22 minutes past midnight.

The crews of Pilot Officer Britton and Flying Officer Johnston each claimed an enemy aircraft damaged.

29 June 1944

Operations were called for but cancelled before the briefing took place. The weather at East Moor consisted of heavy rain and thunderstorms reducing the visibility to less than 3,000 yards.

Squadron Leader F.H Fearnside an RAF Technical Enginaer visited the station.

30 June 1944

Fog during the morning was followed by thunderstorms in the afternoon thus precluding any flying activity at East Moor.

A Softball game was managed, and East Moor defeated 6 Group, the score 3~1. The WAAF's were again visited by Staff Officer E.M Carby-Hall and Squadron Officer N. Holland from 6 group and 62 Base respectively.

General:

Aircraft strength at East Moor was fourteen Halifax Mk.III's and ten Halifax Mk.VII', all being 432 Squadron aircraft.

Two Senior Medical Officers had visited theStation Sick Quarters on the 15th, Wing Commander Stone and Flight Lieutenant Montgomery were from Air Force Headquarters in London. They were later joined by No.6 Group's Senior Medical Officer, Squadron Leader Hutton. Whilst the general Health of the station was said to be good, precautions were taken after a WAAF was diagnosed as having contracted Tuberculosis.

July 1944 was an eventful month at East Moor, when for the first time it became a 'two squadron' base. The reformation of No.415 'RCAF Squadron from the role of a Coastal Command unit to that of one in Bomber Command took place at the station.

The large influx of personnel, equipment and aircraft resulting from that move, made necessary certain changes in Technical and Domestic accomodation as East Moor had not been designed to facilitate two operational squadrons.

A shortage of quarters saw officers located in NC0's accommodation and NCO's in airmen's billets. Many of the quarters were without lighting, running water and proper toilet facilities for some time, and not unnaturally, these problems gave rise to feelings amongst all concerned.

Three hundred new bicycles were received late in the month and issued, priority being given to the groundstaff. Whilst those alleviated the shortage somewhat, many of the aircrew living on dispersed sites were still without.

A staff shortage arose in the Cooks and Waitresses trades on the station due to No.415 Squadron arriving without those essential domestics.

As late as December 1944, the station still had problems with overcrowding and various shortages. The latter included such items as officer's batmen, sheets, hot water and bicycles.

July also saw increasing numbers of Halifax VII heavy bombers joining the East Moor scene as 432 Squadron re-equipped with the type. It will be seen in this diary, that by the end of the first week of July only three or four Mk III's were being used by that squadron. Around this time it was noted that an Airspeed Oxford was busily engaged on the station scene. This was V3604, and used by new crews to familiarise themselves with the countryside around East Moor, to ferry crews to and from other stations and for general communications work.

1 July 1944

The station's first Tailor's Shop was opened,and funded by PSI funds it was able to handle minor repairs and pressing.

The month got off with a series of attacks on the Flying Bomb Sites at Biennais,432 Squadron dispatching the following seventeen crews on a daylight mission under a heavy Spitfire cover, the only flak encountered was over the target area and all returned safely to East Moor,

MZ590 'C'	F/O	D Best		MZ686 'U'	F/O	L Evenson	
					W/O	McIntyre	U/G
MZ585 'Z'	P/O	G Mc.Kean		NP690'G'	F/O	L Friedman	
	Sgt	Metcalf U/G					
MZ632 'W'	F/L	D VonLaufer		NA517 'R'	P/O	J Patterson	
LW595 'Q'	F/O	A Craig		NP687 'A'	F/O	W Tobias	
MZ633 'O'	F/O	R Gingrich		LK764 'F'	P/O	D Frost	
	W/O	Rowe	U/G				
LK766 'V'	F/L	J Cooper		MZ586 'Y'	P/O	R Card	
MZ603 'E'	Ft/O	Lekis W		NP689 'M'	F/O	R Jack	
NP695 'K'	F/O	V Johnston		NP692 'D'	F/L	M Pettit	
LK765 'B'	Sgt	N Franko					

2 July 1944

432 Squadron were stood down from operations at 12.30 hours, having been on 'stand by' all morning.

All personnel were required to carry their gas masks for a planned three day gas drill, but when gas was spread throughout the station preventing many from being able to follow their work duties, it was terminated.

3 July 1944

Operations were planned for 18.00 hours take off, but with everyone ready to go they were cancelled just half an hour before.

Leeds University Professor, Mr Raybold presented a talk entitled 'What is Socialism' at the weekly Forum.

The Station Commander, Group Captain H.H Rutledge OBE and other Senior Officers attended a celebration party given by the WAAF Section in their NAAFI to mark the fifth anniversary of the WAAF formation.

4 July 1944

An afternoon attack on the Flying Bomb Sites at Biennais was called for and No. 432 Squadron put a mixed force of Halifax Mk III's and VII's up, take off commenced at 11.54 hours . All returned safely to East Moor, the last one touched down at 16.01. The following crews were dispatched,

MZ660 'J'	F/L	J Cooper		NP690'G'	F/O	G Friedman	
	F/O	Studen	2/Plt				
	Sgt	Siwak	U/G				
MZ603 'E'	Ft/a	Lekis W		NP689 'M'	F/L	G Larson	
	F/O	Benson	U/G				
NP694 'R'	P/O	R Gingrich		LK765 'B'	Sgt	N Franko	
NP695 'K'	P/O	D Frost		MZ585 'Z'	P/O	R Card	
MZ632 'W'	P/O	H Britton		MZ633 'O'	P/O	R Anthony	
	Sgt	Wilburn	U/G		Sgt	Sc.arff	U/G
NA527 'N'	F/O	W Tobias		MZ590 'C'	F/O	D Best	
					W/O	Rowe	U/G
NA687 'A'	W/C	J MacDonald		NP692 'D'	P/O	D Maddock	
NP688'X'	P/O	G McKean		LW595 'Q'	F/L	J Barker	
					WO	McIntyre	U/G
NP698 'U'	Sgt	R Diamond					

Flight Lieutenant Barker's Gee went u/s on approach to the target and he and his crew had to make a second orbit.

Pilot Officer Britton brought MZ632 home with numerous flak holes in it.

A Station Orchestra was formed and held its first rehearsal, it was hoped that it would soon be capable of providing the music for East Moor parties and Station Dances.

A second Post Office was established to accommodate the anticipated increase in the work load with the arrival of 415 Squadron.

5 July 1944

A third consecutive visit to Bennaise for 432 Squadron, and the first aircraft left East Moor's runway at 00.53 hours. After a successful night attack, (the two previous ones were in daylight) all seventeen crews returned safely but all were diverted to other bases owing to adverse weather conditions at East Moor,

MZ632 'W'	F/L	D VonLaufer		NP698 'U'	F/O L Evenson		
LK765 'B'	Sgt	N Franko		NP692 'D'	F/L J Cooper		
	Sgt	Hughes	U/G				
NP691 'V'	P/O	R Card		NP687 'A'	F/O	W Tobias	
MZ590 'C'	P/O	D Maddock		MZ603 'E'	P/O	H Brotton	
	F/S	Shanks	U/G		Sgt	Pegg	U/G
NP690 'G'	F/O	L Friedman		MZ660 'J'	F/L	J Cooper	
					Sgt	Siwak	U/G
NP695 'K'	F/O	V Johnston		NP689 'M'	F/L	G Larson	
MZ633'O'	P/0	R Anthony		NP694 'R'	P/O	J Patterson	
	F/S	Lagimodiere	U/G				
MZ586 'Y'	S/L	A Lowe		MZ585 'Z'	Sgt	R Diamond	

	P/O	Benson			
NP688 'X'	F/O	A Craig			

Six aircraft landed at RAF Station Woolfox Lodge, Three each at RAF Station's Wittering, Tuddenham, at RAF Station Witchford and one each at RAF Station'sMildenhall and Langer.

Remarkably, three Halifaxes from 434 and 431 Squadron's were diverted in to East Moor from RCAF Station Croft.

Air Vice Marshal C.M MoEwan No.62 (RCAF)Base Commander visited East Moor. Group Security Officer, Flight Lieutenant J.B Lacey was involved at the station with 'spoofing' proceedures and their employment in readiness for a second operational squadron arriving.

Squadron Leader R.H Perry assumed the duties of the Senior Station Admin Officer vice Squadron Leader B.J Knight posted out to 6 Group RCAF.

Wing Commander M.M Smith, Engineering Officer from 6 Group Headquarters visited East Moor together with an RAF GD Officer, Squadron Leader J.P Seaborne.

6 July 1944

The unrelenting attacks on the Pilotless Plane Sites continued, and 432 Sqd crews were again involved in a night attack on those at Coquereaux, when twelve set out. This was their smallest target to date and was well hidden in thick woods where they left nothing except a cloud of dust and smoke,

LK765 'B'	P/O	E Clarke		NP687 'A'	W/C	J MacDonald	
	Sgt	Siwak	U/G				
NP692 'D'	F/O	D Best		MZ603 'E'	Ft/O	Lekis W	
					F/S	Shanks	U/G
NP697 'F'	F/L	J Cooper		MZ654 'L'	F/O	V Smith	
NP689 'M'	P/O	J Webb		MZ633 'O'	F/S	R Campbell	
					W/O	Clarke	U/G
LW595 'Q'	F/L	D VonLaufer		LW552 'S'	F/O	R Lawrenson	
	W/O	Rowe	U/G				
NP698 'U'	F/O	L Evenson		NP691 'V'	Sgt	J Kerr	

No enemy aircraft or flak was encountered by the station's crews and all returned safely to East Moor.

The RC'AF Concert Party 'The Tarmacs' entertained 250 people in the Station Theatre with a most enjoyable performance.

7 July 1944

The station was undergoing improvements schemes in the Armouries and to the runways. Authority was received for 40,000 square yards of additional tarmac surfacing to be applied to the latter.

The RCAF 'Tarmacs' gave another 250 personnel a concert in the Station Theatre.

Sixteen Halifaxes crewed by 432 Squadron took off from East Moor for the Normandy Battle Area and in support of the Allied land forces there. The target was a German strongpoint at Caen which consisted of tanks, guns and armoured units. Before the crews had arrived back at East Moor, the 2nd Army had sent a message of appreciation to all for what was described as an impressive attack.

The following set out, the first one was airborne at 19.46 hours,

NP687 'A'	F/O	W Tobias		LK765 'B'	P/O	E Clarke	
					Sgt	Siwak	U/G
NP692 'D'	P/O	H Britton		NP697 'F'	P/O	D Maddock	
NP690'G'	F/O	L Friedmen		MZ660 'J'	F/L	J Cooper	
					F/S	Shanks	U/G
NP695 'K'	Sgt	N Franko		NP704 'L'	P/O	D Frost	
NP689 'M'	P/O	J Webb		NP694 "R'	P/O	J Patterson	
NP701 'S'	Sgt	R Diamond		NP698 'U'	Sgt	R Campbell	

MZ586 'Y'	S/L	A Lowe		NP691 'V'	P/O	R Card
	F/O	Benson	U/G			
MZ632 'W'	P/O	R Anthony		NP688 'X'	F/O	A Craig
	F/S	Lagimodiere	U/G			

The attack was said to be very concentrated and on the markers, which had been dropped in a very small area. Flak was moderate but no enemy aircraft were encountered by the station's crews.

8 July 1944

East Moor crews returned to the Flying Bomb Sites, this time to the area of Mont-Candon. This was a 'middle of the day' operation which nevertheless saw a change in the local weather during the crews absence resulting in seven of them having to be diverted on return.

Again it was said to have been a well concentrated attack from which they all returned safely, no enemy opposition reported.

All aircraft were airborne by 11.06 hours and by 20.14 all the diverted ones had landed back on East Moor.

This was the last ocassion on which No.432 Squadron used the Halifax Mk III on operations.

During the evening, Professor Dalton from Leeds University was the speaker at the Sunday Forum held in the 'Y' Lounge, his subject was 'What is Fascism'. A fair crowd made up of all ranks attended.

RGAF Station Tholthorp's Orchestra provided the music at the monthly dance held in the Sergeant's Mess.

More than 400 people attended films sponsored by the YMCA and screened in the NAAFI and in the Officer's Mess. The following crews participated in response to the call for fourteen for the Mont-Candon raid,

MZ660 'J'	F/O W Tobias	NP692 'D'	F/L J Cooper	NP693 'Q'	F/O J Barker
NP691 'V'	F/O R Lawrenson	NP701 'S'	P/O R Anthony	MZ603 'E'	Ft/O W Lekis
NP695 'K'	F/O D Best	NP687 'A'	W/C J MacDonald	NP697 'F'	P/O D Maddock
NP698 'U'	F/O L Evenson	NP690 'G"	F/O A Craig	NP689 'N'	Sgt J Kerr
MZ632 'W'	F/L D Von Laufer	NP694 'R'	Sgt R Diamond		

9 July 1944
No operations at East Moor but a full programme of flying training carried out. The Halifax III's were noted being towed to the north eastern side of the station in readiness for the arrival of 415 (RCAF) Squadron. Whilst around fifteen of these aircraft retained their individual letters, the changing of the squadron codes from QO to 6U was a relatively simple matter, as both squadrons used what printers refer to as condensed lettering, carried forward or the roundels on the port side and aft on the starboard.

It is worth mentioning that 432 Squadron aircrews were not at all happy about losing the ventral gun position on the Halifax VII which was fitted with H2S

10 July 1944

The day was without any operational commitment but not without excitement. A long delayed 1,000 lb bomb accidentally fell from an aircraft and resisted the first attempt to detonate it. Buried some eight feet down, it finally left a crater forty feet across and fifteen feet deep.

11 July 1944

At 03.55 hours the East Moor emergency services together with an engineering officer were called to the scene of a crash just north of Rowntree's factory at York. Halifax HX147 of 1666 HCU at Wombleton suffered engine failure and crashed killing all on board. A number of 20 lb fragmentation bombs were removed and taken to East Moor where they were detonated in the crater left by the 1,000 pounder on the 10th

12 July 1944

An Advance Party of 415 (RCAF) Squadron arrived at East Moor effectively reforming it within No.6 Group Bomber Command.

432 Squadron operated against the 'P' Plane site at Thiverney, sixteen crews set out

NP702 'B'	P/O E Clarke	NP690 'G'	F/O L Friedman	NP692 'D'	F/L J Cooper
NP708 'E '	FtO W Lekis	NP697 'F'	Sgt N Franko	NP695 'K'	P/O D Frost
NP706 'J'	F/L H Cooper	NP703 'H'	P/O H Britton	NP689 'M'	P/O J Webb
NP722 'S '	F/O R Lawrenson	NP698 'U'	F/O L Evenson	NP691 'V'	P/O R Card
NP707 'W	F/L D Von Laufer	NP705 'Y'	S/L A Lowe	NP693 'Q'	F/L J Barker
NP7O4'L'	F/O V Smith	NP699 'O'	Sgt R Campbell		

Sergeant Campbell was unable to raise the undercarriage and was sent to jettison the bombs.

Flying Officer Lawrenson was forced to make an early return with a sick navigator. The remainder returned safely to East Moor.

13 July 1944

Sixteen aircraft were prepared for an operation to Nucourt but later scrubbed.

A Leeds Concert Party presented 'Northern Lights' in the station theatre, said to have been a great success.

There was a race against time to accomodate the remainder of 415 Squadron, the living sites being in need of cleaning and decorating.

14 July 1944

The Station cycling club had its most successful outing to date visiting Stamford

Bridge where a picnic was held.

Thoithorpe beat East Moor at softball by 13 - 0. The Nucourt raid was again called for and subsequently scrubbed.

15 July 1944

Wing Commander J.G McNeil, DFC, Squadron Commander of 415 (RCAF) Squadron commenced his duties at East Moor where thirteen Halifax IiI's were on squadron strength.

The next few days saw aircrews from 424, 425, 427, 431, 432, 433, and 434 squadrons posted in to join 415.

The Fairey Aviation Company's Orchestra provided the music for what was reported to be the best Station Dance at East Moor to date, over 400 personnel attended.

Nucourt and its Flying Bomb site was attacked by sixteen crews from 432 Squadron,

NP692 'D'	F/L M Pettit	NP703 'H' F/L J Cooper		NP706 'J'	F/L H Cooper
NP697 'F'	P/O D Maddock	NP702 'B' P/O D Frost		NP704 'L'	F/O V Smith
NP690 'G'	P/O H Britton	NP7O8 'E ' F/O W Tobias		NP693 'Q'	F/L J Barker
NP698 'U'	Sgt R Campbell	NP691 'V' P/O R Card		NP707 'W'	P/O R Gingrich
NP689 'M'	Sgt J Kerr	NP699 'O' F/O A Craig		NP707 'W'	P/O R Diamond
		NP694 'R' P/O G McKean		NP705 'Y'	P/O R Gingrich

The bombing results were described as excellent, numerous fires and explosions were seen in the target area and all returned safely to base, the last one touching down shortly before midnight.

16 July 1944

No.415 (RCAF) Squadron's transfer to East Moor became official, and 90% of its ground equipment had arrived.

Flight Lieutenant B.E Wilmot, DFC was appointed as a Flight Commander Other 415 Squadron appointments included Flying Officer S.B McKillop as Navigation Leader, Flight Lieutenant McNichol Bombing Leader, Flying Officer McNamara DFM, Gunnery Leader and Flying Officer S. Chiles DFC Signals Leader.

Twelve 432 Squadron crews were briefed for an attack on Mont Candon and were lined up when it was scrubbed.

In order to provide indoor recreational facilities at East Moor, courts were marked out for Basketball, Badminton and Volleyball in No.2 Hangar.

The Station Fire Section established a record time of four minutes from receiving the call to turning the water on at the Airmen's Mess.

The subject at the weekly Forum was 'The Future of Democracy' and the speaker Professor Dalton from Leeds University.

17 July 1944

Teams from RCAF Station Linton on Ouse defeated East Moor at Softball and Lacrosse, 22 - 2 and 10 - 0 respectively.

Sixty airmen and twenty five WAAF participated in a parade to mark "Salute the Soldier' week in the village of Huby. Squadron Leader M. Pettit DFC, chaired the Local Concert Party held on the occasion.

Once again, the East Moor crews were called upon to support the Allied Land Forces advance in Europe. Sixteen from 432 Squadron bombed and obliterated a heavy concentration of tanks, vehicles and other materials on the eastern side of the River Orne near Caen in a dawn attack,

NP702 'B'	PO	E Clarke		NP692 'D'	F/L	J Cooper
NP708 'E'	F/O	W Saye		NP690 'G'	F/O	L Friedman
NP703 'H'	P/O	D Best		NP695 'K'	F/O	V Johnston
NP706 'J'	F/L	Cooper JH		NP704 'L'	P/O	D Frost
	Sgt	S Wright	2/Plt			
NP689 'M'	F/L	G Larson		NP699'O'	F/O	L Evenson
NP693 'Q'	Sgt	R Campbell		NP694 'R'	P/O	R Diamond
NP701 'S'	F/O	R Lawrenson		NP691 'V'	P/O	R Card
NP707 'W'	F/O	R Jack		NP705 'Y'	S/L	A Lowe
	G/C	H Rutledge	2/Plt		F/L	Johnson 2/Plt

Sadly, Flight Lieutenant J.H Cooper and crew failed to return, the second pilot was on his first operation.

The Station Commander flew with Flying Officer Jack.

18 July 1944

No.415 (RCAF) Squadron commenced flying training flights and the necessity arose for a second 'call sign' at East Moor. 'Singer' was the one issued.

Visitors to the station included Wing Commander D.T French G.T.I from 6 Group Headquarters accompanied by Squadron Leader J.F Clark G.G.L.

In the evening, films were screened to more than four hundred personnel in the Airmen's NAAFI and in the Station Hospital, both were sponsored by ENSA.

Flight Lieutenant H.E Henault the No.62 Base Intelligence Officer attended a Tactics Conference at East Moor and remained on station for the briefing of 432 Squadron's crews for an attack on synthetic oil plants at Wessling.

About an hour before midnight, the first of fourteen Halifaxes rose from the East Moor runway bound for the Rhur where heavy flak and searchlight activity was encountered. With one exception, Flying Officer Cresswell in NP695, all EastMoor crews returned unscathed, the last one touching down at 03.45 hours on the19th.

It was hoped that this attack would help to increase the oil shortage for Germany. Large explosions and fires were observed in the target area which was cloud free and the markers were said to be concentrated.

NP702 'B'	P/O	E Clarke	NP692 'D'	F/L	M Pettit	
				P/O	Gallagher	2/Plt
NP703 'H'	F/O	W Saye	NP708 'E'	F/O	R Jack	
NP697 'F'	P/O	D Maddock	NP690 'G'	F/O	L Friedman	
NP695 'K'	P/O	H Britton	NP704 'L'	F/O	V Smith	
NP699 'O'	F/O	L Evenson	NP694 'R'	P/O	R Diamond	
NP693 'Q'	F/L	J Barker	NP7O1 'S'	F/O	R Lawrenson	
NP695 'V'	F/L	G Larson	NP705 'Y'	F/O	A Craig	

One hundred and ninety four aircraft took part in the operation which was regarded as being very successful.

A quarter of the oil plants were thought to have been destroyed and production was badly affected as a result.

Some of the town area was hit,though very few people were killed. One aircraft was lost. Flying Officer Friedman made an early return with a u/s airspeed indicator, and on the return flight, Pilot Officer Britton's Halifax was coned and hit by flak injuring bomb aimer Pilot Officer Cresswell in the leg.

19 July 1944

East Moor's emergency services answered two calls which took them away from the base. The first was to RCAF Station Tholthorpe to cover the landing of aircraft returning from operations while that station's crash crews were fully engaged with a crashed one.

At 16.20 hours, the East Moor Fire Section notified Flying Control that an aircraft had crashed at Sheriff Hutton. This was Halifax JB844 from 1658 HCU, Riccall and was found north east of the village and burning rapidly. The crew had escaped. The East Moor crash tender and crew were back on station by 18.30 hours.

20 July 1944

Further compliments of 415 Squadron including the Technical staff arrived at East Moor from RAF Station Bircham Newton. Under the command of Flying Officer R. Scott and Sergeant A.C Ironside, they journeyed to York by train and completed the last leg by road transport.

Meanwhile, the 415 Squadron aircrews were into their third day of flying from East

Moor and were engaged in 'Bullseye' exercises and some pilots were accompanying

432 Squadron crews on operations.

Once again, excellent results were achieved on a 'P' Plane site by 432 Squadron who dispatched eleven crews to attack the one at Fermes Du Bois,

NP702 'B'	P/O	E Clarke	NP692 'D'	F/O	W Tobias
NP708 'E'	P/O	D Maddock	NP704 'L'	F/O	V Smith
NP689 'M'	F/L	G Larson	NP699 'O'	F/S	R Campbell
NP693 'Q'	F/L	J Barker	NP7O1 'S'	F/O	R Lawrenson
NP707 'W'	F/O	A Craig	NP705 'Y'	S/L	A Lowe
NP688 'X'	F/O	L Friedman			

Despite the heavy flak which was encountered, ten aircraft returned undamaged. A number of aircraft from 431 and 419 Squadrons were diverted to East Moor.

21 to 23 July 1944

Three days on which the East Moor crews were not required for operations. A number of aircraft from 431 and 434 Squadrons were received by East Moor on diversion from their base at RCAF Station Croft on the 21st, and the Station Softball team defeated 6 Group Headquarters 11-7.

An RCAF All Girl show the 'W Debs' was staged in East Moor's 'New Theatre' and enjoyed by an audience of 400.

On the 22nd, Air Vice Marshal C.M McEwan MC, DFC, opened a Track and Field Meet at the station and afterwards presented the prizes. All stations in the district participated. The Station Softball team again tasted victory, defeating a team from Newbury Priory 11-10.

On the 23rd, Flying Officer Lawrenson and crew made the return journey from RAF Station Woodbridge by rail and road. Due to flak damage to NP701, they had put down there after the operation to Ferme Du Bois.

After operations had been called for and cancelled, nine aircraft from 432 Sqd and seven from 415 carried out a successful 'Bullseye' exercise.

The Sunday Forum was held and two of the station's personnel, Warrant Officer J.H Flick and Corporal W.S Westcott talked of their 'Front Line Experiences'.

24 July 1944

The 'Rear Party' of No.415 (RCAF) Squadron arrived at East Moor from RAF Station Bircham Newton.

At 04.00 hours, East Moor Flying Control once again dispatched the station's emergency services away from base. This time they went in search of a crashed aircraft reported down in the Coneysthorpe/Bulmer area. It was found burned out at 07.30 hours and six bodies were recovered from the RCAF Station Wombleton based Halifax of 1666 HCU.

'P' Plane sites were again attacked by 432 Squadron's crews. Of the twelve dispatched, only six heard the Master Bombers instructions to abandon the mission,
they were in 'A', 'F', 'K', 'O', 'V' and 'X'. All returned safely to East Moor.

NP719 'N'	F/O	R Jack	NP689 'M'	F/L	G Larson
NP708 'E '	FtO	W Lekis	NP702 'B'	F/O	W Saye
NP704 'L'	F/L	D Von Laufer	NP692 'D'	F/L	M Pettit
NP687 'A'	W/C	J MacDonald	NP697 'F'	P/O	J Gallagher
NP695 'K'	F/O	V Johnston	NP699 'O'	P/O	R Anthony
NP691 'V '	P/O	R Card	NP688 'X'	F/L	D Johnson

Not a good day for the station's Softball and Lacrosse teams, the former were defeated 4-5 by RCAF Station Tholthorpe and the latter 1-4 by RCAF Linton on Ouse.

No.6 Group Bombing Leader, Squadron Leader G.A Sweaney visited East Moor Station.

25 July 1944

No.415 (RCAF) Squadron was declared ready to assume operational commitments.

No.432 Squadron were detailed for a raid on Stuttgart, on what was their first major target in almost four months. Fifteen crews took off commencing at 21.00 hours and some of them arrived over the target before it was marked but were able to identify it visually, and the bombing appeared to be accurate. The target area was free of searchlights, flak or enemy aircraft.

NP702 'B'	P/O	E Clarke	NP692 'D'	F/O	W Tobias
NP708'E'	FtO	W Lekis	NP697 'F'	P/O	D Maddock
NP690'G'	F/O	L Friedman	NP695 'K'	F/O	V Johnson
NP689 'M'	F/O	R Lawrenson	NP699 'O'	F/S	R Campbell
NP693 'Q'	F/L	J Barker	NP694 'R'	P/O	J Patterson
NP691 'V'	F/O	L Evenson	NP707 'W'	F/L	D Von Laufer

NP705 'Y'	S/L	A Lowe		NP688 'X'	F/L	D Johnston
	F/L	Vann	2/Pit			
NP687 'A'	W/C	J MacDonald				

Flight Lieutenant V. Johnston and Wing Commander J.K MacDonald were lost on this operation together with their crews. The latter had been a very popular Squadron Commander during his period at East Moor.

Flight Lieutenant Von Laufer and crew put 'Willie Wolf' down at RAF Station Ford in Sussex, where upon landing it struck a totem pole and suffered minor damage.

Unable to identify the target, Flying Officer Evenson's crew bombed an alternative (believed to have been an airfield).

The returning crews found that the new Sodium flarepath at East Moor was being used for the first time. The pilots were reported to found it a great help in landing, the only criticism being,that if anything it was perhaps too bright.

ENSA and YMCA film shows were now said to have been attracting regular 400 strong audiences.

26 July 1944

The day saw the arrival at East Moor of the last three officers and nineteen other ranks thus completing the movement of 415 (RCAF) Squadron from RAF Station Bircham Newton. It had become the fourteenth bomber squadron in the Royal Canadian Air Force and in No.6 Group.

East Moor station's two squadrons were not required for operations on this day. Wing Commander A. Lowe assumed duties as Squadron Commander of No.432 Squadron vice Wing Commander J.K MacDonald who had failed to return from the operation against Stuttgart.

East Moor Station Softball team defeated No.5 District Headquarters on the formers ground, 26-7.

The Station Theatre was the scene for a successful ENSA Concert.

27 July 1944

No flying was recorded at East Moor probably due to adverse weather conditions as on the previous day.

28 July 1944

East Moor witnessed its largest operational take off to date when thirty three Halifaxes of 415 and 432 Squadrons set off along its runway to join a force of over three hundred aircraft in an attack on Hamburg. Despite the fact that one aircraft crashed on take off, all thirty three had cleared the runway in something like thirty four minutes.

Halifax III, MZ686 was the second aircraft on the take off roll but the first of 415 Squadron. It had reached a speed of 105 mph when the starboard outer engine failed causing it to swing off the runway and crash through the northern perimeter before breaking in two just aft of the mid upper turret and exploding.

Pilot Officer D.R Andrews and crew escaped and with only one minor injury to mid upper gunner,Flight Sergeant Conroy.

432 Squadron			**415 Squadron**		
NP702 'B'	P/O	E Clarke	LL575 'A'	F/O	W Brown
NP701 'A'	Sgt	N Franko	LK765 'B'	F/O	C Gue
NP692 'D'	S/L	M Pettit	MZ590 'C'	F/O	J Meagher
NP708 'E'	Ft.O	Lekis	NA582 'D'	P/O	F Forbes
NP697 'F'	P/O	D Maddock	NA583 'F'	F/O	L Patton
NP690 'G'	F/O	L Friedman	LW595 'Q'	F/O	A Stein
NP695 'K'	F/O	V Johnston	NASI7 'R'	P/O	P Gingrich
NP704 'L'	F/O	V Smith	MZ686 'U'	P/O	D Andrews
NP689 'M'	P/O	J Webb	MZ632 'W'	F/L	J Hovey
NP719 'N'	F/O	R Jack	MZ690 'X'	P/O	J Little

NP699 'O'	P/O	P Anthony	LW680 'H'	F/O	W Sherman
NP693 'Q'	F/L	J Barker	MZ660 'J'	P/O	J McKean
INP694 'R'	P/O	J Patterson	LK755 'K'	F/O	E LeGrice
NP701 'A'	F/O	P Lawrenson	MZ654 'L'	Sgt	J Kerr
NP691 'V'	P/O	P Card	LL576 'N'	W/C	J McNeill DFC
NP688 'X'	F/S	P Campbell	LK766 'V'	P/O	O Lindquist
NP705 'Y'	F/O	L Evenson			

Two crews failed to return from this operation, Flying Officer Stein's and Pilot Officer Clarke's. The latter was on the last trip of his tour. A sad start to the two squadron operations but undeterred at the outset the remaining crews took off over the dense smoke and flames being emitted by MZ686.

Squadron Leader Pettit's aircraft was attacked by a JU88 and his gunners returned fire and claimed it as destroyed.

29 July 1944

There was a complete stand down at East Moor which was greatly appreciated by all and the opportunity was taken to hold the first Officers Mess dance in months.

30 July 1944

A second day without any operational commitments, but a full flying training programme was carried out.

31 July 1944

Operations were called for a night raid but subsequently cancelled together with all flying training due to adverse weather conditions.

Flight Lieutenant Jaques, 432 Squadron Adjutant departed on a Senior Admin. course and Flight Lieutenant L. Kennedy deputised in his absence.

It was said that despite the months setbacks, the health and espirit de corps of the East Moor personnel was excellent.

GENERAL:

When 415 Squadron left Bircham Newton for East Moor many of the air crews were transferred to other Coastal Command squadrons in order to complete their tours. The reformed squadron at East Moor was made up of crews from each of the other twelve in 6 Group including the following from 432 squadron,
P/o G.T McKean, Sgt. J.I Kerr, P/O F.M Forbes, F/O J.A Meagher and P/O R.W Gingrich.

It was noted at the time that most of the aircraft transferred from 432 Sqd retained the same individual code letters within 415 Squadron. The latter had on strength some twenty two Halifax III's by the end of July and 432 Squadron had nineteen Halifax VII's.

The two air gunners in Squadron Leader Pettit's crew, Pilot Officer Bullivant and Flight Sergeant Penny were awarded the DSO and DFM respectively for their action in destroying the JU88 on the night of 28/29th July 1944.

It was learnt that Flight Lieutenant J.H Cooper, Warrant Officer K.E Elliott and Sergeant S.D Wright lost on the night of 17/18th July, had become POW's.

Squadron Leader J.K MacDonald and crew, missing on the 25/26th July all managed to evade capture by the enemy, but the popular Squadron Commander was the only one to return to East Moor.

On 415 Squadron's first Bomber Command operation, the first crew to arrive over the target was that of Flying Officer Sherman in LW680, 6U-H.

During the explosions that followed the crash of MZ686, Air Commodore J Fauquier DSO DFC, taxied LL593 to safety and assisted in fighting the fire engulfing 'Tarslag's' building until it was extinguished.

It would perhaps, be appropriate at this point in the diary, to make some reference to the nose art seen on the aircraft at East Moor.

With few exceptions, very little by way of decorative enhancement was to be seen on the station's aircraft prior to mid 1943. The one or two examples sported by 158 Squadron's Halifax II's in 1942, were by comparison of a much less flamboyant style than the ones that were to become so familiar as the war progressed.

It was said that in Bomber Command, any form of artwork applied to the aircraft other than national insignia and unit codes, was unofficial. Presumably, officialdom must have turned a blind eye to the efforts of the East Moor artists as very few of the station's forty or fifty Halifaxes were anadorned by late 1944.

Any motif served to embellish the otherwise drab and sober green, brown and matt black camouflage schemes of the bombers and to personalize them for air and ground crews alike. A common style was for the motif to be based on the aircraft's individual letter ie: 'L' sported ' Leaside Lulu', 'J' - 'Jane', 'M' - 'Moonlight Mermaid' and 'P' with Pistol Packing Peggy'. Probably some were influenced by the air and ground crews who flew and supported them on a regular basis, but all reflected the skill of the artists.

Those not displaying shapely maidens or Disney characters wre seen adorned with animals, birds, nick names and in some cases the motifs reflected the personnel's place of origin. Included amongst the ones which readily spring to mind are 'Willie the Wolf', 'Utopia', 'Queen of thenm All', 'Oscar the Outlaw', 'Block Buzzter', 'eddies Nightmare', 'The Hussey', 'Old Joe Vagabond', 'Fi Fi', 'Jumpin Jimminie', and 'Archie the archer'.

Operational scoreboards and tallies were usually indicated by minature bombs, (red donated night and yellow daylight operations) beer mugs, parachutes (for mining ops) swastikas and crosses. The prowess of the air gunners was reflected in the latter.

Some of the artists were undougtedly extemely talented and are believed to have catered for the needs of those outside their own flights and squadrons. LAC Thomas Dunn and LAC Dean Holditsch members of 432 Squadron ground staff are said to have been responsible for much of the artwork on East Moor's Lancasters and Halifaxes.

1 August 1944

Twenty nine aircraft left East Moor's runway with the intention of bombing 'Flying Bomb' **sites** at Ferme Du Forestel in daylight. On arrival it was found that 10/10's cloud was obscuring the target and the Master Bomber ordered a return to base with all bombs, where not surprisingly a few 'hairy' landings were witnessed.

432 Squadron			415 Squadron		
NP7O8 'E'	P/0	H Britton	LL575 'X'	F/O	J Weir
NP697 'F'	Sgt	N Franko	LK765 'B'	F/O	H Knobovitch
NP690 'G'	F/O	J Gault	MZ590 'C'	F/O	P Chapman
NP703 'H'	S/L	M Pettit	MZ603 'E'	F/O	W Sherman
NP720 'A'	F/O	G Stunden	NA583 'F'	F/L	H Barnes
NP704 'L'	P/O	J Gallagher	MZ660 'J'	F/O	C Gue
NP689 'M'	P/O	J Webb	NA582 'D'	W/O	P Stevens
NP7I9 'N'	F/O	P Jack	LL576 'N'	F/O	J Meagher
NP699 'O'	P/O	P Anthony	NA517 'P'	F/O	P Gingrich
NP694 'R'	F/L	G Vann	LW552 'S'	F/O	A Tinnouth DFM
NP721 'X'	F/L	D Von Laufer	LK766 'V'	F/O	B Roberts
NP691 'V'	F/O	A Craig	MZ632 'W'	P/O	Lindquist
NP595 'K'	F/O	V Johnston	MZ586 'Y'	Sgt	J Kerr
NP722 'S'	F/O	P Lawrenson	LW595 'Q'	F/O	P Sierolawski
NP705 'Y'	P/O	D Frost			

2 August 1944

No operational flying and the East Moor personnel took advantage of the sunny weather and many were seen stripped to the waist.

Requests were received for the supply of personnel to attend an important parade at Linton on Ouse within a few days and 415 Squadron's compliment to consist of five aircrew NCO's, one Flight Sergeant and two Sergeants ground crew plus twenty other ranks.

3 August 1944

Another bright and sunny day when operations were prepared for and the aircraft were marshalled for take off only to be scrubbed.

It was learned that the special parade referred to by Station Headquarters on the 2 August was to be held in the prescence of King George VI, and other members of the Royal Family.

Later in the day further operational details were called for and 432 Squadron dispatched eighteen Halifaxes while 415 Squadron dispatched nineteen when the target was again 'Flying Bomb' sites, this time at Foret De Nieppe

432 Squadron			415 Squadron		
NP708 'E'	P/O	H Britton	LL575 'A'	F/O	W Brown
NP705 'Y'	S/L	A Lowe	LK765 'B'	F/O	W Sherman
NP703 'H'	P/O	D Frost	MZ590 'C'	F/O	P Chapman
NP721 'X'	F/L	D Von Laufer	NA582 'D'	P/O	C Gue
NP694 'R'	F/O	J Patterson	MZ603 'E'	F/O	H Knobovitch
NP691 'V'	F/O	A Craig	NA583 'F'	F/O	L Patton
NP689 'M'	P/O	J Webb	LW680 'H'	F/L	H Barnes
NP697 'F'	Sgt	N Franko	MZ660 'J'	F/O	G McKean
NP720 'A'	F/O	G Stunden	LK755 'K'	W/O	P Stevens
NP722 'S'	P/O	P Diamond	MZ654 'L'	F/O	J Weir
NP690 'G'	F/O	D Best	LL576 'N'	F/O	J Meagher
MZ585 'Z'	F/O	J Gault **	NA587 'Q'	P/O	F Forbes
NP719 'N'	F/L	G Vann	NA517 'R'	P/O	P Gingrich
NP699 'O'	P/O	P Anthony	LW552 'S'	P/O	A Tinmouth DFM
MZ633 'O'	P/O	J Gallagher **	NA600 'U'	F/L	J Hovey
NP704 'L'	F/O	V Smith	LK766 'V'	F/O	B Roberts
NP695 'K'	F/O	V Johnston	MZ632 'W'	P/O	O Lindquist
NP693 'Q'	Sgt	P Campbell	MZ690 'X'	F/O	P Sierolawski
			MZ586 'Y'	F/S	J Kerr

The above thirty seven aircraft constituted the largest total dispatched from East Moor to that date.

** The two Mk III's were 415 Squadron Halifaxes and flown by 432 Sqd crews.

All returned safely.

4 August 1944

With the arrival of 415 Squadron there was an acute shortage of cycles and an order for a further three hundred was placed.

The two resident squadrons each dispatched fifteen aircraft to attack a repair and supply dump at Bois De Cassen and all returned safely,

432 Squadron			415 Squadron		
NP720 'A'	F/O	G Stunden	LL575 'A'	F/O	W Brown
NP723 'D'	S/L	M Pettit	NA582 'D'	F/O	C Gue
NP708 'E'	P/O	H Britton	MZ603 'E'	F/O	H Knobovitch
NP697 'F'	F/S	N Franko	NA583 'F'	F/O	L Patton
NP690 'G'	F/O	L Friedman	MZ660 'J'	F/O	G McKean
NP703 'H'	P/O	D Frost	LK755 'K'	Sgt	J Kerr
NP704 'L'	F/O	V Smith	MZ654 'L'	F/O	J Weir
NP695 'K'	F/O	D Best	LL576 'N'	F/O	J Meagher
NP689 'M'	F/L	D Von Laufer	NA587 'Q'	P/O	F Forbes
NP719 'N'	F/O	P Jack	NA517 'R'	P/O	P Gingrich
NP693 'Q'	F/S	P Campbell	LW552 'S'	F/O	P Sierolawski
NP694 'R'	P/O	J Patterson	NA600 'U'	F/O	P Chapman
NP722 'S'	F/O	P Lawrenson	LK766 'V'	F/O	B Roberts

NP705 'Y'	P/O	P Diamond		MZ632 'W'	P/O	O Lindquist
NP699 'O'	F/L	G Vann		MZ585 'Z'	F/O	W Sherman

Several aircraft returned from this daylight operation with slight damage and Squadron Leader Pettit's was 'well plastered'.

5 August 1944

The following crews were dispatched from East Moor to attack further 'buzz bomb' sites in another daylight operation, target St.Leu D' Esserant. All returnedsafely and the results were described as satisfactory.

432 Squadron				**415 Squadron**		
NP72O 'A'	F/O	G Stunden		MZ660 'J'	F/O	G MeKean
NP736 'B'	P/O	D Frost		LK755 'K'	W/O	P Stevens
NP723 'D'	S/L	M Pettit		MZ654 'L'	F/O	J Weir
NP708 'E'	P/O	H Britton		LL756 'N'	F/O	J Meagher
NP690 'G'	F/O	L Friedman		NA587 'Q'	P/O	F Forbes
NP703 'H'	F/O	D Best		NA517 'P'	P/O	P Gingrich
NP695 'K'	F/O	V Johnston		LL575 'A'	F/O	W Brown
NP704 'L'	F/O	V Smith		LK765 'B'	F/L	H Barnes
NP689 'M'	P/O	J Webb		MZ590 'C'	F/O	P Chapman
NP719 'N'	F/O	A Craig		NA582 'D'	F/O	C Gue
NP699 'O'	P/O	P Anthony		MZ603 'E'	F/O	H Knobovitch
				NA583 'F'	F/O	L Patton
				LW552 'S'	P/O	A Tinmouth DFM
				NA600 'U'	F/L	J Hovey
				LK766 'V'	F/O	B Roberts
				MZ632 'W'	P/O	O Lindquist
				MZ690 'X'	F/O	P Sierolawski
				MZ586 'Y'	Sgt	J Kerr
				MZ585 'Z'	F/O	W Sherman

This trip completed Squadron Leader Pettit's second tour.

6 August 1944

East Moor personnel were engaged in polishing up their 'drill' both on station and at Linton on Ouse in readiness for the forthcoming V.I.P parade. Halifax V11, NP721 overshot East Moor at 16.31 hours and the undercarriage collapsed when it struck the ditch at Strensall Road.

No operational flying recorded.

7 August 1944

The East Moor crews were dispatched to two targets. The 432 Squadron crews found that their target was unmarked, and consequently La Hague escaped and all bombs were returned to base. 415 Squadron fared little better at Caen where the Master Bomber ordered the mission to be abandoned.Their attack was to have been in support of Canadian ground forces around Falaise and was code named 'Totalize' The 432 Squadron crews were diverted to High Ercall on return.

432 Squadron				**415 Squadron**		
NP699 'O'	P/O	P Anthony		LL575 'A'	WO	P Stevens
NP693 'Q'	F/S	P Campbell		MZ633 'B'	F/O	C Gue
NP694 'R'	P/O	J Patterson		NA582 'D'	P/O	F Forbes
NP722 'S'	F/O	P Lawrenson		LW686 'H'	F/L	H Barnes
NP7O4 'L'	F/O	V Smith		MZ660 'J'	F/O	G McKean
NP698 'U'	F/O	A Craig		MZ654 'L'	F/O	J Weir
NP691 'V'	P/O	P Diamond		NA583 'F'	F/O	L Patton
NP708 'E'	F/O	F Jeffrey		LL576 'N'	F/O	P Chapman
NP738 'J'	F/O	J Gault		NA587 'Q'	F/O	W Sharman
NP697 'F'	F/S	N Franko		NA517 'R'	P/O	P Gingrich

NP720 'A'	F/O	G Stunden		LW552 'S'	P/O	A Tinmouth
NP7O3 'H'	P/O	H Britton		NA6OO 'U'	F/L	J Hovey
NP695 'K'	F/O	V Johnston		LK766 'V'	F/O	B Roberts
NP736 'B'	P/O	D Frost		MZ632 'W'	P/O	O Lindquist
NP723 'D'	P/O	J Gallagher		MZ690 'X'	F/O	P Sierolawski
NP690 'G'	F/O	D Best		MZ586 'Y'	Sgt	J Kerr
				MZ585 'Z'	F/O	J Meagher

8 August 1944

On returning from Caen, at 01.05 hrs, LW686 overshot East Moor and one minute later NA517 did likewise, both aircraft ending across Strensall Poad with collapsed undercarriages. Halifax NP713, a 408 Sqd aircraft returned from ops with a u/s radio, mistook East Moor for Linton on Ouse and ended between the two aforementioned. All three aircaft were fully laden and the crews escaped injury.

Later in the day, the following crews set out for Foret De Chantilly, and a third 415 Sqd Halifax crashed through the airfield boundary, this time across the Sutton Poad. Pilot Officer Tinmouth and crew escaped and the bomber crossed two fields, but was repairable on station.

In the evening, 432 Squadron and Station MT personnel held a most successful party in Wigginton Village Hall until sadly, the beer ran out.

432 Squadron				415 Squadron		
NP738 'J'	F/O	F Jeffrey		NA582 'D'	P/O	F Forbes
NP708 'E'	FtO	W Lekis		MZ633 'B'	F/O	C Gue
NP705'Y'	F/L	G Vann		LL575 'A'	W/O	P Stevens
NP694 'R'	P/O	J Patterson		MZ585 'Z'	F/O	J Meagher
NP693 'Q'	F/L	J Barker		MZ690 'X'	F/O	P Sierolawski
NP699 'O'	P/O	P Anthony		LK766 'V'	F/O	B Roberts
NP704 'L'	F/O	V Smith		NA587 'Q'	F/O	W Sharman
NP695 'K'	F/O	V Johnston		LL593 'M'	F/O	L Patton
				MZ654 'L'	F/O	J Weir
				LK755 'K'	F/O	W Brown
				MZ660 'J'	P/O	G McKean
				NA583 'F'	F/L	H Barnes
				MZ603 'E'	F/O	P Knobovitch

All returned safely, the operation regarded as successful against an oil storage dump

9 August 1944

Wing Commander P.G Powell DSO; DFC the Group Navigation Officer visited East Moor and held discussions with squadron Navigation Officers.

The slackening of leave regulations led to a flood of applications on compassionate grounds.

'Buzz Bomb' sites came in for further attention by the East Moor crews when the following were dispatched to Foret De Nieppe and once again all returned safely from a successful operation,

432 Squadron				415 Squadron		
NP704 'L'	F/O	V Smith		NA582 'D'	P/O	F Forbes
NP695 'K'	F/O	V Johnston		LL593 'M'	F/O	L Patton
NP708 'E'	FtO	W Lekis		NA58-3 'F'	F/L	H Barnes
NP736 'B'	P/O	D Frost		LK766 'V'	F/O	B Roberts
NP693 'Q'	F/L	J Barker		MZ690 'X'	P/O	J Little
NP691 'V'	P/O	P Card		NA600 'U'	P/O	D Andrews
NP705'Y'	P/O	P Diamond		MZ660 'J'	P/O	G McKean
NP699 'O'	F/O	P Anthony		MZ585 'Z'	F/O	J Meagher
NP689 'M'	P/O	J Webb		MZ654 'L'	P/O	J Britt
NP738 'J'	P/O	H Britton		MZ632 'W'	P/O	O Lindquist
NP722 'S'	F/S	P Campbell		NA587 'Q'	Sgt	W Lane
NP703 'H'	F/O	F Jeffrey		LL575 'A'	P/O	A Tinmouth
NP723 'D'	F/O	G Stunden		MZ633 'B'	F/O	C Gue
NP697 'F'	P/O	G Sherlock		LK755 'K'	W/O	P Stevens
NP694 'R'	P/O	J Patterson				

NP720 'A'	F/O	D Best
NP698 'U'	F/O	L Evenson
NP719 'N'	F/O	A Craig

Fig 25. The scene at Strensall Road end of runway 9th August 1944 and more lost undercarriages.
Photo R.Day.

10 August 1944

La Pallice, a port in northern France was the target for the crews of 432 and 415 Squadrons where successful attacks on oil storage depots were carried out, without any losses,

432 Squadron			**415 Squadron**		
NP720 'A'	F/O	F Jeffrey	LL575 'A'	F/O	P Chapman
NP719 'N'	F/O	A Craig	NA583 'F'	F/O	L Patton
NP736 'B'	P/O	D Frost	MZ660 'J'	P/O	G McKean
NP723 'D'	F/L	G Larson	LK755 'K'	W/O	P Stevens
NP708 'E'	FtO	W Lekis	MZ654 'L'	F/L	H Barnes
NP697 'F'	F/S	N Franko	LL593 'M'	F/O	W Sherman
NP703 'H'	P/O	G Sherlock	NA587 'Q'	Sgt	W Lane
NP698 'U'	F/O	L Evenson	NA600 'U'	P/O	D Andrews
NP695 'K'	F/O	G Stunden	LK766 'V'	F/O	B Roberts
NP699 'O'	P/O	R Anthony	MZ632 'W'	P/O	A Lindquist
NP693 'Q'	F/S	P Campbell	MZ690 'X'	P/O	J Little
NP722 'S'	P/O	H Britton	MZ586 'Y'	P/O	F Forbes
NP705'Y'	P/O	P Diamond	MZ585 'Z'	P/O	J Britt
NP689 'M'	P/O	P Card	MZ633 'B'	F/O	C Gue

The port outer engine of MZ633 caught fire and as a result it was landed at Exeter on three.

11 August 1944

Several hundred East Moor personnel travelled to Linton on Ouse where His Majesty King George VI held an open air investiture and was accompanied by Queen Elizabeth and Princess Elizabeth. Station personnel were amongst the medal recipients and included, Flying Officer J Webb DSO, Flight Sergeant D.H Wright DFM, Flight Sergeant W.K Ziomko DFM, Wing Commander J McNeil DFC, Squadron Leader B. Wilmot DFC, Pilot Officer **H.J** Powell DFM, Flying Officer P McNamara DFM, and Pilot Officer A. Tinmouth DFM.

While the 'special' personnel journeyed to Linton by transport, every available East Moor cycle made the trip and the station was almost deserted.

Six crews were detailed for Command Bullseye exercises which were later stood down because of inclement weather.

12 August I944

In accordance with a new policy, East Moor squadron's groundcrews were posted to 62 Base Headquarters, a decision which gave rise to feelings. Although it was only a transaction on paper most of the affected personnel felt that whatever glamour they had was now taken away from them, and consequently morale fell. The station experienced an extremely busy day with both squadrons carrying out operations against no less than three targets as follows,

Ammunition dumps at Mont Richard - a mid morning take off....

432 Squadron			415 Squadron		
NP697 'F'	F/S	N Franko	LK755 'K'	W/O	R Stevens
NP695 'K'	F/O	F Jeffrey	NA582 'D'	F/L	J Hovey
NP736 'B'	F/O	W Saye	LW686 'H'	F/L	H Barnes
NP693 'Q'	F/S	P Campbell	MZ654 'L'	P/O	J Britt
NP708 'E'	FtO	W Lekis	NA587 'Q'	Sgt	W Lane
NP738 'J'	P/O	H Britton	LL593 'M'	F/O	W Sherman
NP705 'Y'	F/O	A Craig	MZ632 'W'	F/O	B Roberts
NP703 'H'	P/O	G Sherlock	MZ660 'J'	P/O	G McKean
NP694 'R'	P/O	J Patterson	MZ586 'Y'	P/O	A Tinmouth
NP719 'N'	F/O	P Jack	NA517 'R'	P/O	P Chapman
NP699 '0'	P/O	P Anthony	NA600 'U'	P/O	D Andrews
NP690 'G'	F/O	V Smith	MZ603 'E'	F/O	L Patton
NP689 'M'	P/O	J Webb	MZ585 'Z'	F/O	J Meagher
NP722 'S'	F/L	D Von Laufer	MZ690 'X'	P/O	J Little
NP698 'U'	P/O	P Card			

Four crews set out for Brunswick in the late evening,

NP689 'M'	F/L	G Larson	NP720 'A'	S/L	B Wilmot
NP7O3 'H'	F/O	D Best	NA6OO 'U'	F/O	C Gue

The third effort was against Falaise and commenced a few minutes past midnight and so technically speaking it was 13 August, and involved six crews,

NP704 'L'	F/O	F Jeffrey	LL725 'A'	P/O	J Tims
NP723 'D'	FO	W Lekis	MZ603 'E'	F/O	J McAllister
NP705 'Y'	P/O	J Patterson			
NP691 'V'	P/O	P Card			

Pilot Officer Anthony returned early with a u/s starboard engine.

Flying Officer Jeffrey made an early return from his second mission of the day with NP704's undercarriage u/s.

Warrant Officer Stevens was forced to land at Wing, short of fuel.

The operation to Brunswick was an experiment in blind bombing while troop concentrations were the target at Falaise.

S/L Wilmot's aircraft was badly shot up, but all returned.

13 August 1944

No operations but Flying training took place at East Moor Operations had been called for and finally cancelled.

14 August 1944

Twenty eight Halifaxes left East Moor's runway and contributed to a force of over eight hundred aircraft attacking targets in support of the Allied ground forces,
Bons Tassilly was 432 and 415's target,

432 Squadron				415 Squadron			
NP719 'N'	F/L	Von Laufer		LL593 'M'	F/O	W Sherman
NP689 'M'	P/O	J Webb		NA607 'R'	P/O	A Tinmouth
NP695 'K'	F/O	V Johnston		NA6ll 'T'	Sgt	W Lane
NP738 'J'	P/O	H Britton		MZ632 'W'	P/O	O Lindquist
NP7O3 'H'	F/O	F Jeffrey		NA600 'U'	P/O	D Andrews
NP690 'G'	F/O	G Stunden		LK766 'P'	P/O	D McNeil
NP697 'F'	F/S	N Franko		NA608 'H'	F/L	H Barnes
NP736 'B'	P/O	D Frost		MZ660 'J'	P/O	G McKean
NP694 'R'	P/O	P Anthony		MZ585 'Z'	F/O	J Meagher
NP705 'Y'	F/O	A Craig		MZ654 'L'	F/O	J Weir
NP7O4 'L'	F/O	W Says		MZ690 'X'	P/O	J Little
NP722 'S'	P/O	P Diamond		LL575 'A'	P/O	J Tims
NP698 'U'	F/O	L Evenson		NA582 'D'	P/O	F Forbes
NP693 'Q'	F/S	P Campbell		MZ590 'C'	F/O	P Chapman
				LK755 'K'	P/O	J Britt

All returned safely. Rutledge was second pilot to P/O Evenson.Captain T. Riechen of the Royal Canadian Army Service Corps visited East Moor to study Bomber Command operations, remaining on station for a week. Squadron Leader G Sweaney, Group Bombing Leader, visited the station for talks, and to discuss bombing problems.

15 August 1944

The airfield at Brussells was the target for the following thirty crews when over one thousand attacked enemy Night Fighter bases,

432 Squadron				415 Squadron			
NP691 'V'	F/O	P Card		MZ632 'W'	P/O	a Lindquist
NP693 'Q'	P/O	P Diamond		MZ690 'X'	P/O	J Little
NP699 'O'	P/O	P Anthony		NA582 'D'	P/O	A Tinmouth
NP694 'R'	P/O	J Patterson		NA583 'F'	F/O	L Patton
NP736 'B'	P/O	D Frost		MZ603 'E'	F/O	J Weir
NP723 'D'	F/O	V Smith		NA607 'R'	P/O	J Tims
NP708 'E'	FtO	W Lekis		LL575 'A'	F/O	C Gue
NP690 'G'	F/O	D Best		MZ586 'Y'	P/O	D McNeil
NP689 'M'	P/O	J Webb		MZ654 'L'	P/O	J Britt
NP705 'Y'	F/O	A Craig		NA6ll 'T'	F/L	J Hovey
NP695 'K'	F/O	V Johnston		LK766 'V'	P/O	G McKean
NP738 'J'	F/O	G Stunden		NA587 'Q'	Sgt	W Lane
NP703 'H'	F/O	W Saye		NA612 'P'	F/O	B Roberts
NP698 'U'	F/O	L Evenson		LL593 'M'	F/O	W Sherman
NP719 'L'	F/L	Von Laufer		NA608 'H'	F/L	H Barnes

All returned safely, and the bombing was well concentrated.
An allocation of clothing coupons arrived for the officers.
Another Canadian Army Officer arrived to study Bomber operations, Lieutenant J. Gauthier of the Armoured Recce Corps.
Heavy Flak was encountered by some of the above crews and NA583 suffered some damage as did NA6O7 which became desperately short of fuel.

16 August 1944

The following crews were dispatched from East Moor in the late evening to attack Kiel where serious damage was done to docks and shipbuilding plants,

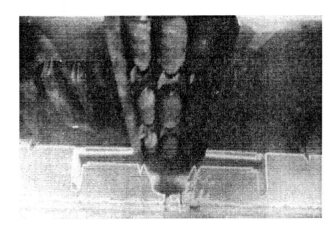

Fig 26. Scenes from around the dispersal of Halifax NP705, QO-Y and depicting members of 432 Squadron groundstaff. This aircraft completed 82 operations, survived the war, and was disposed of in 1947.
Photos M.Pryce.

Fig 27. P/O R Anthony & crew prepare to set out from East Moor in LW687.

Standing: Bill Perry, B/A, John Banks F/E, Wally Metcalf M/U, Hap Segus WOP, Danny Libbert Nav.

Kneeling: Bill Dennis R/G, and skipper Ray Anthony (432 Squadron). Photo J. Banks.

432 Squadron			415 Squadron		
NP736 'B	P/O	D Frost	LL575 'A'	P/O	P Stevens
NP723 'D"	F/O	D Best	MZ590 'C'	S/L	B Wilmot
NP697 'F'	F/S	N Franko	NA582 'D'	P/O	F Forbes
NP703 'H'	F/L	W Tobias	MZ603 'E'	F/O	J Weir
NP738 'J'	F/O	W Saye	NA608 'H'	F/L	H Barnes
NP695 'K'	F/O	V Johnston	MZ660 'K'	P/O	G McKean
NP704 'L'	F/O	G Stunden	LL593 'M'	F/O	W Sherman
NP7l9 'N'	FtO	W Lekis	NA61O 'O'	P/O	J Little
NP693 'Q'	F/L	G Vann	NA612 'P'	F/O	D Roberts
NP694 'R'	P/O	J Patterson	NA587 'Q'	Sgt	W Lane
NP722 'S'	F/O	P Lawrenson	NA61l 'T'	P/O	A Tinmouth
NP698 'U'	P/O	P Diamond	NA600 'U'	P/O	D Andrews
NP691 'V'	P/O	P Card	LK766 'V'	P/O	O Lindquist
NP705 'Y'	W/C	A Lowe	MZ586 'Y'	F/O	C Gue
			MZ585 'Z'	F/O	J Meagher

Flying Officer Saye returned early with starboard inner engine u/s. All aircraft returned safely.

17 August 1944

Operations were on - off all day. Local pubs were well frequented in the evening.

18 August 1944

Thirty two Halifaxes sst off along East Moor's runway for an operation against Bremen.

432 Squadron			415 Squadron		
NP736 'B'	F/O	D Best	NA600 'U'	P/O	D Andrews
NP723 'D'	F/O	W Saye	NA609 'G'	F/O	J Weir
NP708 'E'	FtO	W Lekis (USAF)	MZ632 'W'	F/O	B Roberts
NP697 'F'	F/S	D Franko	LL575 'A'	F/O	W Brown
NP690 'G'	F/O	J Gault	MZ603 'E'	F/O	H Knobovitch
NP738 'J'	P/O	H Britton	LL593 'M'	P/O	J Britt
NP695 'K'	F/O	V Johnston	NA610'O'	P/O	A Tinmouth
NP704 'L¹.	F/O	GStunden	NA6ll 'T'	P/O	P Gingrich
NP689 'M'	F/L	D Von Laufer	MZ586 'Y'	F/S	J Kerr
NP719 'N'	F/O	P Jack	NA587 'Q'	P/O	J Timms
NP693 'Q'	P/O	J Gallagher	NA582 'D'	F/O	L Patton

NP694 'R'	F/O	W Tobias		NA608 'H'	F/L	H Barnes
NP722 'S'	F/O	P Lawrsnson		LW552 'S'	F/O	P Sierolawski
NP698 'U'	P/O	P Diamond		MZ585 'Z'	P/O	D McNeil
NP691 'V'	F/O	P Card		MZ660 'J'	P/O	P Stevens
NP705 'Y'	F/L	G Vann		MZ590 'C'	F/O	T Chapman

Flying Officer Sierolawski and Flight Lieutenant Barnes made early returns with hydraulic failures and had to be diverted to RCAF Station Linton on Ouse due to an aircraft crash on East Moor.

The duty runway was No.16 and a few aircraft had taken off when Halifax, NP690 with Flying Officer J Gault at the controls, swung and caught fire. The crew made a hasty exit and all managed to safely scatter accross the airfield. The Halifax completely blocked the runway. Staff from the control van rushed around to warn the remaining aircraft to use runway 20, which took some time. There were many anxious moments during the urgency to get the stations aircraft off in a reasonable time, and after each one took off, a hurried scan of the area was made to ascertain the state of the burning NP690. The crash site was just beyond the intersection of the two runways, and as the last aircraft cleared the runway, NP690 blew up, With the initial swing the Halifax was headed for the control tower which was hastily evacuated before a huge fireworks display ensued and numerous fires were started around the south east dispersals. The only injury to a crew member was to the neck of rear gunner, Sergeant P.G Walters.

Fortunately, the 2,000 pounder did not explode in the usual way, but rather burned half way through, nevertheless shrapnel and engine parts were scattered more than 700 yards from the scene.

The station's personnel spent many hours sweeping the runways and picking up the debris.
Sergeant 'Bert' Dennis was an air gunner in Pilot Officer P.N Stevens crew and recalls the Bremen operation. Over the North Sea, the starboard outer engine of 6U-J was lost but undeterred the skipper flew on to bomb the target from 10,000 feet. On the return flight the huge bomber became extremely short f fuel and had to be put down at the emergency field at Carnaby. For his efforts Pilot Officer Stevens was awarded the DFC.

The whole of the centre and many outlying parts of Bremen were devastated on this operation . The docks were particularly hard hit and many ships were sunk.
At 02.49 hours, Pilot Officer A.W Tinmouth DFM, overshot RAF Fiskerton's runway in NA6lO, fortunately it was repairable and all escaped.

19 August 1944

News was received at East Moor that Flying Officer Grimsey, Sergeant Justason and Flight Lieutenant Kemley of Wing Commander McDonald's crew had evaded capture and were safe.

Pilot Officer Bullivant and Flight Sergeant Penny received the immediate award of the DFC and the DFM respectively for their joint action in destroying a JU88 on the homeward flight from Hamburg on 415 Squadron's first bomber Command operation on 28 July 1944.

Many of East Moor's personnel were extremely tired after spending the night clearing the runway of wreckage from NP690. Parties commenced at each end and walked at arms length from each other and hand picked all shrapnel and pieces of debris.

The weather had closed in during the early hours and consequently all East Moor's aircraft were scattered to diversionary fields, and there wasn't any flying from the station.

20 August 1944

Another day without any flying from East Moor due to the weather which had prevented the return of the diverted crews after the Bremen operation. 432 Squadron were experiencing considerable difficulty in carrying out a satisfactory training programme due to so many aircraft being unserviceable. Weather conditions drastically curtailed the social activities normally enjoyed by the stations groundstaff, and for a few days the messes were well patronised

21 August 1944

Some flying training was effected and the station's diverted crews began to return, almost all of 432 Squadrons were down by evening.

Tragedy struck the station and 415 Squadron in particular, when two crews and thirteen groundstaff were killed in a mid air collission near Selby. Wing Commander J.G McNeill, DFC the Squadron Commander and Squadron Leader B. Wilmot DFC, had proceeded with their crews in NA609 to collect MZ633 from Exeter. The latter Halifax had undergone an engine change there after the three engined landing on the 10th of the month. The groundstaff were presumably members of the East Moor 'Servicing Wing' whose duties included proceeding on temporary attached duty to work on the stations diverted aircraft. Eyewitnesses at RAF Station Burn said that the Halifaxes were in pieces and burning when they broke through the cloud base. Wreckage fell between Birkin and West Haddlesy. In the transit flight from Exeter to East Moor, 415 Squadron lost not only their C.O but also their Bombing Leader and Navigation Leader.

Aircrew killed in the accident were; W/C J.G McNeill DFC, pilot - F/Lieutenant G.E Steel-Davis, navigator - F/Officer A.H. Bain, bombadier,- Sgt W.H Fox, WOP. -Sgt A.W Mitchell gunner - Sgt T.C Guthrie, engineer.

MZ633 was being flown by S/L B Wilmot DFC together with F/Officer J.A Hudson, navigator - P/Officer T.E Wiltse, bombadier - F/Lieutenant W.R Eagleston, WOP -Sgt P.C Morrison, gunner and Sgt M.L Mallpasse, engineer.

22 August 1944

Wing Commander J.H Lecomte became 415 Squadron Commander, vice W/C McNeill DFC, the former was at the time C.O of 425 Squadron, at RCAF Station Tholthorpe.
There wasn't any flying at East Moor during the day which was overcast, but some night cross countries were carried out. Ground training took place. 415 Squadron's Adjutant visited the previous days crash scene and RAF Station Burn to discuss the accident.

23 August 1944

The weather improved later in the day when flying training resumed with numerous Gross countries being carried out. The East Moor Squadron Adjutants attended a conference at 6 Group Headquarters and voiced their disapproval of the decision to take the ground crews from under the squadron's aegis to that of the HQ's. It was argued that if a unit moved it would place an unreasonable burden on the adjutant if deprived of his staff, and would cause administration difficulties.

24 August 1944

432 Squadron was engaged in local flying and in fighter affilliation exercises during the day, as were 415 Squadron. Both had to cancel planned evening and night cross countries when the weather again deteriorated.
Wing Commander G.A Saunders of 6 Group Accident Branch visited the station re,the accident on 21st of the month.
Fig 29. Wing Commander F. Gaffney from 62 Base HQ held talks at East Moor regarding the proceedures connected with honours awards.

25 August 1944

East Moor resumed operations with thirty three crews joining forces with a further three hundred in an attack on coastal gun batteries at Brest, when the take off commenced at 21.12 hours,

432 Squadron			415 Squadron		
NP698 'U'	F/O	L Evenson	LL575 'A'	F/O	W Brown
NP705 'Y'	P/O	P Diamond	MZ590 'C'	F/O	P Stevens
NP691 'V'	F/O	P Card	NA582 'D'	P/O	F Forbes
NP722 'S'	F/O	P Lawrenson	NA608 'H'	P/O	G McKean
NP694 'R'	P/O	J Patterson	MZ654 'L'	P/O	P Gingrich
NP693 'Q'	F/S	P Campbell	LL593 M'	P/O	J McAllister
NP708 'E'	FtO	W Lekis	NA612 'P'	F/O	B Roberts
NP736 'B'	F/O	F Jeffrey	NA587 'Q'	F/S	W Lane
NP699 'O'	F/L	G Vann	LW552 'S'	P/O	A Tinmouth
NP689 'M'	P/O	J Webb	NA600 'U'	P/O	D Andrews
NP704 'L'	F/O	V Smith	LK766 'V'	P/O	J Britt
NP719 'N'	F/L	P Jack	NA583 'F'	F/O	C Gue

Fig 28. Pictured on dispersal No.32. East Moor Summer 1944. Halifax VII, NP697 of 432 Squadron and below pilot Flight Sergeant N.D Franko who completed 23 operations as its skipper. QO-F'Freddie' was better known as 'Ferdinand II' and went on to complete 79 operations, and survived the war to be sold for scrap in 1949. Photos M.Pryce.

432 Squadron	cont		415 Squadron	cont	
NP738 'J'	F/L	W Tobias.	NA6ll 'T'	F/O	D McTaggert
NP697 'F'	F/S	N Franko	MZ632 'W'	F/O	Sierolawski
NP695 'K'	P/O	G Sherlock	MZ585 'Z'	F/O	J Meagher
NP723 'D'	F/O	D Best			
NP759 'C'	F/O	G Stunden			
NP720 'A'	F/O	W Saye			

Flight Sergeant McGuire flew as 2nd pilot to Flight Lieutenant Jack.

A sudden and most noticeable change of wind direction when approximately half of the aircraft had taken off, resulted in the remainder having to taxy from the south end of the airfield to the north.

All returned safely but due to the weather closing down East Moor all were again scattered to diversionary fields.

Squadron Leader S.P Frankling the new 'A' Flight Commander in 415 Squadron arrived on station and Flight Lieutenant J.A Morris assumed duty as 'B' Flight Commander.

26 August 1944

Most of the diverted aircraft and crews returned to East Moor during the after noon period, and both were hurriedly prepared for a further operation which was subsequently scrubbed.

Flying Officer W. Vickerman, missing in LW582 on 7/8 June visited the station. Shot down by an enemy fighter the 432 Squadron pilot had endured numerous harrowing experiences before being picked up by the 2nd Army.

27 August 1944

The station once again put up thirty two aircraft and the' following crews set out for the 'Flying Bomb' sites at Mimoyecques in the early evening,

432 Squadron			415 Squadron		
NP705 'Y'	W/C	A Lowe	LL575 'A'	P/O	F Forbes
NP721 'X'	P/O	J Gallagher	MZ590 'C'	P/O	P Stevens
NP736 'B'	F/S	N Franko	MZ603 'E'	F/O	H Knobovitch
NP699 '0'	F/L	G Vann	NA583 'F'	F/O	C Gue
NP759 'C'	F/O	D Best	NA608 'H'	P/O	D McNeill
NP694 'R'	P/O	J Patterson	MZ632 'W'	P/O	G McKean
NP689 'N'	F/O	P Lawrenson	LK755 'K'	F/O	J McAllister
NP708 'E'	P/O	G Sherlock	NA612 'P'	P/O	J Tims
NP720 'A'	F/O	W Says	NA587 'Q'	F/S	W Lane
NP689 'M'	F/O	J Webb	LW552 'S'	P/O	A Tinmouth
NP723 'D'	F/O	F Jeffrey	NA600 'U'	P/O	D Andrews
NP698 'U'	P/O	H Britton	LK766 'V'	F/O	P Sierolawski
NP704 'L'	F/O	V Smith	MZ690 'X'	P/O	J Little
NP691 'V'	F/O	P Card	MZ586 'Y'	F/S	J Kerr
NP707 'W'	F/O	J Gault	LL593 'M'	F/O	J Weir
NP693 'Q'	F/S	P Campbell	NA582 'D'	F/L	J Hovey

All returned safely to bass except Pilot Officer Thompson the mid upper gunner in LL593 who sustained some flak injuries. The first aircraft was up at 18.10 and the last one down at 22.20 hours.

28 August 1944

The station's spirits were raised with the return of 432 Squadron's C.O. Wing Commander J.K MacDonald who had been shot down over France on 25 July and had exciting experiences to relate.

East Moor crews attacked three seperate targets as follows - two to Anderbelek construction works,

432 Squadron			415 Squadron		
NP698 'U'	P/O	H Britton	NA608 'H'	F/O	J Weir

a further ten were dispatched to attack German Batteries at Oeuf En Ternois,

NP693 'Q'	F/S	R Campbell	LL575' 'A'	P/O	P Stevens
NP723 'D'	F/O	G Stunden	LK755 'K'	P/O	J Britt
NP759 'C'	F/O	D Best	NA583 'F'	P/O	J Tims
NP699 '0'	F/L	G Vann	LW552 'S'	P/O	D McTaggart
NP736 'B'	P/O	D Frost	LK766 'V'	P/O	G McKean

while thirteen others attacked shipping at Brest,

NP705 'Y'	F/L	P Jack	NA611 'T'	P/O	D McNeill
NP719 'N'	F/O	F Jeffrey	MZ603 'E'	F/O	H Knobovitch
NP708 'E'	F/L	W Tobias	LL593 'M'	F/O	P Sierolawski
NP707 'W'	F/O	J Webb	NA612 'P'	F/O	B Roberts
NP722 'S'	F/O	P Lawrenson	NA587 'Q'	F/S	W Lane
NP695 'K'	F/O	J Patterson	MZ654 'L'	P/O	J Kerr
NP701 'G'	F/O	J Gault			

Flight Sergeant D. Williams the Wireless Operator in NP736 was injured by flak, which was reported to be heavy over the second target.

All aircraft returned safely, NP759 with minor flak damage.

29 August 1944

Flying Training continued apace at East Moor in overcast but clear weather with cross countries, fighter affiliation exercises and circuits and landings.

Operations were prepared for but subsequently scrubbed.

30 August 1944

Flying Training continued on a busy but routine day. Preparations and a Battle Order was into effect for an early operation on the 31st.

31 August 1944

The first of thirty Halifaxes was lifted from East Moor's runway at 10.01 hours when the target was Ile de Cezembre and the coastal gun batteries which were described as 'completely plastered'. No opposition was encountered and all safely returned,

432 Squadron			415 Squadron		
NP694 'R'	F/O	J Patterson	LL575 'A'	F/O	J Meagher
NP693 'Q'	F/S	P Campbell	LK765 'B'	F/O	C Gue
NP723 'D'	P/O	D Frost	MZ590 'C'	P/O	P Stevens
NP695 'K'	P/O	H Britton	NA582 'D'	P/O	F Forbes
NP699 'O'	F/O	J Gault	MZ603 'E'	F/O	H Knobovitch
NP704 'L'	F/O	V Smith	LK755 'K'	P/O	G McKean
NP705 'Y'	P/O	P Diamond	MZ654 'L'	FlO	J Weir
NP698 'U'	F/O	P Card	LL593 'M'	F/O	J Britt
NP708 'E'	F/O	F Jeffrey	NA587 'Q'	P/O	D McNeill
NP722 'S'	F/O	P Lawrenson	LW552 'S'	P/O	D Gingrich
NP701 'G'	P/O	G Sherlock	NA600 'U'	P/O	D Andrews
NP689 'M'	F/O	J Webb	NA611 'T'	P/O	D McTaggert
NP697 'F'	F/S	N Franko	LK766 'V'	F/O	P Sierolawski
NP719 'N'	F/L	P Jack	MZ632 'W'	F/O	B Roberts
NP755 'A'	F/O	W Saye	MZ586 'Y'	P/O	J Tims

The last of the station's aircraft touched down at 15.32 hours and the crews were informed that they were not required again that day, so taking advantage of the 'stand down', many patronized Betty's Bar and the public houses in Strensall, Haxby and other local villages.

General:

Flight Lieutenant R.L Orpen assumed duties as East Moor Station Adjutant on the 7th of the month, vice Flight lieutenant E.J Strathdee who was posted out to No.62 (RCAF) Base.

The station had formed its own orchestra which was providing music for parties and dances.

Fig 30. Pictured under Halifax III, LW616 in the summer of 1944.
L to R: unknown,Bob Duncanson F/E, W/c W.A McKay, DFC, 432 Sqd Commander, M Grimsey, B/A,
Bob Kennerdy WOP, and Buck Rogers, NAV. Photo I. Mulley.

The East Moor contingent participating in the parade for Their Majesties King George VI and Queen Elizabeth's open air investiture on the 11th, totalled seventy five men and fifteen WAAF.

On the 12th, the Station Crash Tender and crew were hastily dispatched first to RCAF Station Tholthorpe and then re-directed to the scene of a crashed Stirling bomber at Alne.

A consignment of cigarettes was received and distributed at the Pay Parade on the 16th.

On the 17th, a General Court Martial was convened at East Moor. Under the Presidency of Group Captain J.G Kerr were, Administration and Service Disciplinary Officers Squadron Leaders E.A Jamieson and W.G Harrison from RCAF Station's Dishforth and Dalton, with Flight Lieutenants A.F Malone and J.E Freil from RCAF Headquarters Overseas.

The Stores and Workshops of the Station Radar Section were damaged by the explosions created by NP690 on the 18th, and more than one hundred personnel spent the following day getting the airfield serviceable again. The Armament Section demolished the incendiaries from the wreckage.

The Armament Section conducted a controlled explosion of a 500 lb bomb on the 29th on their special site.

Two Senior Medical Officers, Lieutenant Commander Gosnell,RNVR and Wing Comm. D.V Hutton from 62 Base visited East Moor.

The month saw all living sites except No.4 provided with hot water facilities, allowing the Officers and NCO's to shave on site instead of in the Messes.

Electric Lighting was installed at the MT Section's Marsden Shed and surrounding roadways.

1 September 1944

The morale on the station was said to be extremely high, many of the aircrew believed that the month would see the collapse of Germany and probably Japan too, before they were able to complete their full 'tours'.

Operations were called for but later cancelled. The station's squadrons were advised to be prepared for an early hours take off on the 2nd.

The ex Station Adjutant, Flight Lieutenant Strathdee and WAAF Squadron Officer N.   Holland visited East Moor from No.62 (RCAF) Base.

ENSA staged a live concert in the Station's Little Theatre before an audience of 250 people.

2 September 1944

On an overcast day which was dominated by high winds and heavy rain, the station's crews were called for operations. It was planned that fifteen from each squadron would attack the airfields at St.Trond and Le Culot in Belgium, but at 14.00 hrs came news of their cancellation.

One of the station's MT drivers, LAC J.M Coupal was admitted to the York Military Hospital with injuries sustained when the vehicle he was driving, was involved in an accident on the York to Easingwold stretch of the A19. The vehicle, RAF1OOOO0 was towing a trailer when it was in collision with a civilian one, BWT 800.

Free Bingo took place in the evening in the 'Y' Lounge,while 150 personnel watched movies sponsored by the YMCA and screened in the Sergeant's Mess.

3 September 1944

The fifth anniversary of the outbreak of World War II and an 09.00 hours briefing took place at East Moor. Thirty aircraft were called for and the target was revealed to be the airfield at Volkel in Holland.

At 14.15 hours, and during the preparations, a practice bomb exploded on the dispersal area of NP721 a 432 Squadron Halifax, injuring several members of Flying Officer Card's crew. Pilot Officer Todd the bomb aimer's injuries proved to be fatal, wireless operator Flight Sergeant Drake had to have his left hand amputated, while Flight Sergeant Anderson was badly burned.

Wing Commander Lowe and crew substituted for the unfortunate crew regardless of the fact that he and his navigator were the only ones knowing the details of the briefing.

A Court of Inquiry was set up to investigate the accident.

The following aircraft and crews were dispatched,

432 Squadron			415 Squadron		
NP705 'Y'	F/L	W Tobias	LL575 'A'	F/L	D Thompson
NP694 'R'	Sgt	L McGuire	NA582 'D'	P/O	F Forbes
NP708 'E'	F/O	F Jeffrey	MZ590 'C'	F/O	J Britt
NP738 'J'	F/O	J Mills	MZ603 'E'	F/O	H Knobovitch
NP699 'O'	P/O	R Diamond	NA583 'F'	P/O	C Chartier
NP697 'F'	F/O	J Gault	NA608 'H'	P/O	W McNeill
NP693 'Q'	W/C	A Lowe	MZ660 'J'	P/O	R Stevens
NP719'N'	F/O	P Lawrenson	LK755 'K'	F/S	W Lane
NP689 'M'	F/O	J Webb	MZ654 'L'	F/O	J Weir
NP695 'K'	F/O	V Johnston	NP612 'P'	F/O	J Meagher
NP707 'W'	P/O	A Potter	LW552 'S'	P/O	P Gingrich
NP704 'L'	F/O	V Smith	NA611 'T'	F/O	C Gue
NP691 'V'	F/O	M Krakowsky	NA600 'U'	P/O	D Andrews
Np723 'D'	F/L	G Larson	LK766 'V'	F/O	P Sierolawski
NP755 'A'	F/O	W Saye	MZ632 'W'	P/O	J Little

Flight Lieutenant Woodward flew as second pilot to Flight Lieutenant Larson. The weather had closed in at East Moor and consequently all aircraft were diverted on return. All except 'A' of 432's contingent landed at Tempsford, the former was put down at Stanstead. Of 415's crews 'A' and 'H' put down at Stradishall, 'F' at Chedburgh and the remainder at Shepherds Grove.

Pilot Officer McNeill lost the use of one engine but was able to effect a safe landing. NP704 and MZ590 received some flak damage.

Flight Sergeant Lane had returned early with faulty undercarriage and bomb doors.

Fig 31. 432 Sqdn, August 1944. **F/O Stunden (P) F/O M Carson (B) Sgt L Pegg (R/G) Sgt S Siwak (M/U) W/O G. Pritchard (WOP) F/O T Roden (N) Sgt W Murray (F/E)**. Photo M. Carson

4 September 1944

No operations were called for at East Moor but a flying training programme was in full swing and included fighter affilliation, air to air, and bombing exercises. The diverted aircraft began to arrive back on station around mid day. The twenty inpatients at the station hospital were shown YMCA movies and each received some comforts.

5 September 1944

The station was without any operational commitments and struggled to maintain a flying training programme due to the extremely heavy rain and overcast.

415 Squadron's Halifax$_3$ Mz603 was returning from its diversion to Shepherds Grove when a heavy landing broke off the tailwheel and after bouncing it was brought under control without further damage or casualties.

6 September 1944

East Moor experienced another of those 'on - off' days where operations were concerned. The first call was at 01.00 hours and was scrubbed before the briefing took placee The crews crawled back into bed around 05.00 hours and a re-scheduled operation was again scrubbed at 10.30 hours. Finally at 16.24 hours, the firstof fifteen 432 Squadron aircraf took off   for an attack on Emden.

NP755 'A'	F/O	W Saye	NP736 'B'	P/O	D Frost
NP723 'D'	F/O	D Best	NP708 'E'	F/O	J Jeffrey
NP697 'F'	Sgt	L McGuire	NP703 'H'	F/O	M Krakowsky

NP738 'J'	P/O	H Britton	NP695 'K'	F/O	J Mills
NP689 'M'	F/O	J Webb	NP699 'O'	P/O	J Gallagher
NP593 'Q'	P/O	P Campbell	NP698 'U'	F/L	L Evenson
NP691 'V'	P/O	A Potter	NP707 'W'	F/O	J Gault
NP721 'X'	P/O	P Diamond			

All returned safely by 20.49 hours.

415 Squadron was without any operational commitment, and the 'stood by' crews Iwere shown YMCA movies.

7 September 1944

An operation to Le Havre had been scheduled but scrubbed with the crews in their aircraft.

Flight Lieutenant Doucet, the 415 Squadron Adjutant was posted to Italy.

8 September 1944

The new 415 Squadron Adjutant, Flight Lieutenant A.B Carveth arrived at East Moor.

Flying Officer J Webb and crew were screened, their tour completed.

Operations were called for and once again they were scrubbed.

Flying training included two and three engined flying.

One of the station's vehicles, RAF110895 a 3 cwt tender driven by LAC Brown and accompanied by Flight Sergeant Page, collided with the shop front of Burton Bos. Ltd in Coney Street, York.

9 September 1944

Amongst a force of almost three hundred aircraft dispatched by Bomber Command to attack Le Havre, the following were from East Moor. All bombs were dropped into the sea en route when the Master Bomber ordered them to abandon the mission, and all returned safely from this early morning take of f.

432 Squadron			415 Squadron		
NP708 'E'	F/O	D Best	NA583 'F'	F/O	L Patton
NP736 'B'	P/O	D Frost	MZ949 'G'	W/C	L LeComte
NP755 'A'	F/O	W Saye	MZ660 'J'	P/O	G McKean
NP70l 'G'	F/O	J Mills	LL593 'M'	F/O	W Sherman
NP703 'H'	F/L	W Tobias	LL576 'N'	F/L	T Chapman
NP738 'J'	F/O	J Gault	NA612 'P'	P/O	W McNeill
NP689 'M'	F/O	J Webb	LL575 'A'	F/O	H Knobovitch
NP719 'N'	P/O	A Potter	MZ947 'C'	P/O	C Chartier
NP699 'O'	P/O	J Gallagher	NA582 'D'	P/O	F Forbes
NP693 'Q'	P/O	P Campbell	NA587 'Q'	F/O	C Gue
NP694 'R'	Sgt	A Stedman	NA607 'R'	P/O	D McNeill
NP698 'U'	F/O	P Card	NA6ll 'T'	F/L	H Barnes
NP691 'V'	F/O	M Krakowsky	NA600 'U'	P/O	D Andrews
NP707 'W'	Sgt	L McGuire	MZ654 'L'	F/O	J Meagher
NP705 'Y'	P/O	P Diamond	MZ690 'X'	P/O	P Stevems

10 September 1944

Le Havre was the target again chosen and this time it did not get of f so lightly when just under one thousand aircraft accurately bombed, and East Moor provided thirty eight crews who all returned safely,

432 Squadron			415 Squadron		
NP694 'R'	P/O	P Diamond	LL575 'A'	F/O	C Gue

NP755 'A'	F/O	W Saye		MZ947 'C'	P/O	P Stevens
NP699 'O'	F/O	M Krakowsky		NA582 'D'	P/O	F Forbes
NP774 'Z'	Sgt	A Stedman		NA583 'F'	F/O	L Patton
NP698 'U'	F/L	L Evenson		MZ949 'G'	W/C	L Lecomte
NP736 'B'	F/O	J Mills		MZ660 'J'	P/O	G McKean
NP689 'M'	F/O	A Craig		LK755 'K'	F/L	H Barnes
NP722 'S'	F/O	J Gault		MZ654 'L'	P/O	C Chartier
NP723 'D'	F/L	G Larson		LL593 'M'	F/O	W Sherman
NP738 'J'	P/O	J Gallagher		LL576 'N'	F/L	T Chapman
NP70l 'G'	F/O	G Stunden		MZ946 'O'	F/O	H Knobovitch
NP691 'V'	F/O	P Card		NA612 'P'	P/O	a Lindquist
NP697 'F'	F/S	N Franko		NA587 'Q'	P/O	J Kerr
NP707 'W'	P/O	A Potter		NA607 'R'	P/O	D McNeill
NP693 'Q'	P/O	P Campbell		LW552 'S'	P/O	P Gingrich
NP705 'Y'	Sgt	L McGuire		NA6ll 'T'	P/O	A Tinmouth
NP729 'N'	F/L	P Jack		NA600 'U'	P/O	D Andrews
NP721 'X'	F/L	J Thompson		LK766 'V'	F/O	P Sierolawski
				MZ632 'W'	F/O	J Meagher
				MZ690 'X'	P/O	J Little

Pilot Officer Dean flew as second pilot to Flight Lieutenant Evenson and Sergeant Hamilton with Flying Officer Card.

11 September 1944

The East Moor 'grapevine' was suggesting that *432* Squadron was to cease operations on the 16th of the month and proceed to the East. Leo Kennedy the squadron adjutant was promoted to Flight Lieutenant and went on leave.

Satisfactory results were obtained by the station's crews in an attack on the industrial plants at Castrop Rauxel. Covered by a heavy fighter escort all made a safe recovery to East Moor.

Fig 32. P/O Martin (NAV), Lt Rourke (A/G) USAF. Photo G Rogers.

Fig 33. Sgt Walters (WOP), F/L Rogers (NAV). Photo G Rogers.

At 18.30 hours a large column of smoke was observed from the direction of Linton on Ouse and found to be from one of that station's aircraft which had crashed on buildings near the MT Section. East Moor's stand by crash tender and crew were dispatched to cover the operational return of Linton's aircraft as their standby vehicle and crew were already engaged, along with ones from Tholthorpe station.

432 Squadron			415 Squadron		
NP736 'B'	F/O	J Mills	LL575 'A'	F/O	W Brown
NP698 'U'	P/O	J Gallagher	LK765 'B'	F/O	C Gue
NP774 'Z'	Sgt	A Stedman	MZ947 'C'	F/O	H Knobovitch
NP701 'G'	F/O	G Stunden	NA582 'D'	P/O	F Forbes
NP691 'V'	F/O	P Card	NA583 'F'	F/O	L Patton
NP721 'X'	F/L	J Thompson	MZ660 'J'	P/O	G McKean
NP707 'W'	P/O	A Potter	LK755 'K'	F/O	J Weir
NP689 'M'	F/O	A Craig	LL593 'M'	F/O	W Sherman
NP699 'O'	F/O	M Krakowsky	LL576 'N'	F/O	P Sierolaweki
NP697 'F'	F/S	N Franko	NA612 'P'	F/O	J Meagher
NP705 'Y'	W/C	A Lowe	NA607 'R'	P/O	J Kerr
NP722 'S'	F/O	J Gault	LW552 'S'	P/O	D McNeill
NP755 'A'	F/O	W Saye	NA587 'Q'	F/S	W Lane
NP693 'Q'	P/O	P Campbell	NA600 'U'	P/O	D Andrews
NP703 'H'	F/L	W Tobias	MZ632 'W'	P/O	O Lindquist

All aircraft attacked the primary target and the crews were able to identify it quite easily due to the absence of cloud in the area.

Flak varied from moderate to intense.

All aircraft and crews were safely down at East Moor by 21.34 hours.

Take off had commenced at 15.50 hours on a fine afternoon and passed without incident.
The East Moor crash crew and tender returned to station in time for the return of the two squadrons.

The starboard outer engine of LL593 became u/s just before landing, NA6OO and LL576 received flak damage as did NP693.

12 September 1944

Another busy day for the station' personnel as Flying Training continued with fighter affilliation, cross country and air to air firing exercises plus almost daily visits to the bombing range at Strensall.

The synthetic oil plants at Wanne Eickel also came in for some attention by the East Moor crews from where the following made safe returns,

432 Squadron			415 Squadron		
NP755 'A'	F/O	W Saye	LL575 'A'	P/O	J Kerr
N P736 'B'	F/O	J Mills	LK765 'B'	P/O	C Chartier
NP723 'D'	F/L	G Larson	MZ947 'C'	F/O	H Knobovitch
NP708 'E'	F/O	G Stunden	NA583 'F'	F/O	D Patton
NP701 'G'	F/S	N Franko	MZ949 'G'	S/L	S Frankling
NP703 'H'	F/L	W Tobias	NA608 'H'	F/L	H Barnes
NP738 'J'	Sgt	A Stedman	MZ660 'J'	P/O	G McKean
NP695 'K'	F/O	V Johnston	LK755 'K'	F/O	P Sierolawski
NP719 'N'	P/O	J Gallagher	MZ946 'O'	F/O	W Sharman
NP689 'M'	F/O	A Craig	NA612 'P'	F/O	J Meagher
NP694 'R'	F/L	J Thompson	NA587 'Q'	F/S	W Lane
NP722 'S'	F/O	J Gault	NA607 'R'	P/O	D McNeill
NP691 'V'	F/O	P Card	NA6ll 'T'	F/O	J Weir
NP707 'W'	P/O	A Potter	MZ632 'W'	P/O	O Lindquist
NP705 'Y'	F/O	M Krakowsky	MZ690 'X'	P/O	J Little
			MZ585 'Z'	F/L	T Chapman

Flak was intense and many aircraft returned with damage from a target left with many large fires, explosions and shrouded in dense black smoke.

13 September 1944

Plans to raise a new Flight within 432 Squadron were made. It was intended to be made up of mainly freshman crews, for the purpose of an efficient training programme.

Pilot Officer S.B McKillop and Pilot Officer J.N Thompson 415 Squadron navigator and gunner respectively received the DFC.

The marshalling yards at Osnabruck were only lightly defended and the following East Moor crews returned safely,

432 Squadron			415 Squadron		
NP755 'A'	F/O	W Saye	LL575 'A'	P/O	C Gue
NP703 'H'	F/L	W Tobias	MZ947 'C'	F/O	J McAllister
NP692 'K'	F/O	V Johnston	NA582 'D'	P/O	W McNeill
NP689 'M'	F/O	A Craig	NA583 'F'	F/O	B Roberts
NP699 'O'	F/O	A Potter	NA608 'H'	P/O	O Lindquist
NP694 'R'	F/L	J Thompson	MZ654 'L'	P/O	D McTaggart
NP722 'S'	F/O	M Krakowsky	NA607 'R'	P/O	P Gingrich
NP736 'B'	F/O	G Stunden	NA6ll 'T'	F/L	J Hovey
NP691 'V'	F/Q	P Card	NA6OO 'U'	P/O	D Andrews
NP721 'X'	F/O	G Barron	MZ690 'X'	F/O	J Little
NP705 'Y	P/O	P Campbell	MZ585 'Z'	F/O	J Meagher
NP698 'U'	F/O	J Mills			
NP723 'D'	F/O	J Gault			
NP708 'E'	Sgt	A Stedman			
NP697 'F'	F/S	N Franko			

Flight Lieutenant Hovey and Flying Officer McAllister's aircraft received some flak damage.

Two of Flying Officer Saye's 500 pounders suffered a 'hang up' and had to be returned to base.

14 September 1944

Bad weather curtailed all flying at East Moor during the day. Nine crews from 432 Squadron and a similar number from 415 were detailed for a Bomber Command 'Bullseye' exercise at night which was subsequently scrubbed.

An open air concert given by the RCAF Bomber Group Orchestra was attended by a large audience and preceded a Dance in the Station Gymnasium.

15 September 1944

Much of Kiel was devastated in a raid carried out by almost five hundred aircraft. The following thirty seven aircraft and crews formed East Moor's contribution,

432 Squadron			415 Squadron		
NP719 'N'	P/O	J Gallagher	LL575 'A'	F/O	L Patton
NP755 'A'	F/O	W Saye	LK765 'B'	F/O	C Gue
NP736 'B'	F/O	J Gault	MZ947 'C'	F/O	H Knobovitch
NP759 'C'	Sgt	A Stedman	NR156 'K'	F/O	J McAllister
NP723 'D'	F/O	J Mills	NA582 'D'	P/O	F Forbes
NP701 'G'	F/O	G Stunden	MZ949 'G'	W/C	J Lecomte
NP703 'H'	F/L	W Tobias	NA608 'H'	F/L	H Barnes
NP692 'K'	F/O	V Johnston	MZ660 'J'	P/O	W McNeill
NP689 'M'	F/O	A Craig	LL576 'N'	F/L	T Chapman
NP699 'O'	F/O	M Krakowsky	NA612 'P'	F/O	B Roberts
NP693 'Q'	P/O	P Campbell	NA587 'Q'	P/O	D McTaggart

NP722 'S'	F/O	G Barron		NA607 'R'	P/O	P Gingrich
NP694 'R'	F/L	J Thompson		NA600 'U'	P/O	D Andrews
NP698 'U'	F/L	L Evenson		LK766 'V'	F/O	P Sierolawski
NP691 'V'	F/O	P Card		MZ632 'W'	P/O	OLindquist
NP705 'Y'	W/C	A Lowe		MZ690 'X'	P/O	J Kerr
NP774 'Z'	F/S	N Franko		MZ585 'Z'	P/O	J Timms

Pilot Officer J Gallagher and crew failed to return from this operation, their Halifax was in collision with another aircraft.

Flying Officer McAllister made an early return after being unable to raise the undercarriage of NP156.

Pilot Officer McNeill's aircraft suffered the loss of both starboard engines forcing an early return toRAF Station Carnaby where he landed on the two port ones.

Pilot Officer Lindquist and crew attacked Flensburg as an alternative target.

Flying Officer Barron's Halifax was damaged (Catagory.B) due to the return landing being too fast.

In the evening a capacity crowd attended the YMCA sponsored film show in East Moor's 'Little Theatre' and 'Record Sessions' were held in the 'Y' lounge.

The East Moor Station Cinema was equipped with first class facilities by ENSA who normally provided entertainment on five nights per week. The YMCA organisation usually operated on the other two, and also provided'Fire Side' shows in the Station Sick quarters, Sergeant's and Officer's Messes.

East Moor Station Orchestra became very popular and was always in much demand at dance functions.

16 September 1944

On returning from Kiel, NP722 with Flying Officer Barron at the controls, met with a too high speed landing accident at 04.31 hrs.(Cat.B)

No operational flying was carried out at East Moor but flying training went ahead with 432 Squadron engaged in fighter affilliation exercises and 415 Sqd in air to air firing and bombing practice.

A detail of East Moor personnel was drawn up to attend a Battle of Britain Memorial Church Service on the 17th, and included around 120 aircrew drawn from each squadron providing that operations were not called for.

17 September 1944

The Church Parade was cancelled when an operation to Boulogne called for details from both squadrons to support a force of over 760 aircraft in an attack on enemy troop positions. This was a successful daylight attack from between 2,000 feet and 4,000, and resulted in the Allied ground forces receiving the surrender of large numbers of the enemy. The following were dispatched from East Moor,

432 Squadron				**415 Squadron**		
NP721 'X'	F/L	J Thompson		LL575 'A'	F/O	W Brown
NP699 'O'	F/O	M Krakowsky		MZ947 'C'	F/O	W Sherman
NP708 'E'	F/L	W Tobias		NA582 'D'	P/O	F Forbes
NP723 'D'	F/L	G Larson		NA583 'F'	F/O	L Patton
NP689 'M'	F/O	A Craig		MZ949 'G'	S/L	S Frankling
NP691 'V'	F/O	A Bews		NA608 'H'	F/L	H Barnes
NP755 'A'	F/O	W Says		NR156 'K'	F/O	J McAllister
NP736 'B'	F/O	J Gault		MZ654 'L'	P/O	W McNeill
NP759 'C'	F/O	V Johnston		NA612 'P'	F/O	B Roberts
NP697 'F'	F/S	N Franko		NA587 'Q'	P/O	D McTaggart
NP738 'J'	Sgt	A Stedman		NA607 'R'	F/O	P Gingrich
NP693 'Q'	P/O	P Campbell		NA600 'U'	P/O	J Tims
NP694 'R'	F/O	S Dean		LK766 'V'	F/O	P Sierolawski
NP698 'U'	F/O	G Barron		MZ690 'X'	F/O	D Stewart

NP774 'Z'	Sgt	J Hamilton	MZ585 'Z"	F/O	J McQuiston
NP70l 'G'	F/O	G Stunden			

All returned safely.

18 September 1944

No operations from East Moor. Lectures were given to the aircrews during the morning and. organised sports took place in the afternoon.

A 'flap' was caused when two bombs fell from a truck near the main gates, and a large explosion was heard when a defective 1,000 pounder was discharged on the airfield.

NP689, QO-M suffered a landing accident but was repairable on station.

19 September 1944

The East Moor crews were not required for operations on a day which was very cloudy with visibility reduced to less than two miles.

The members of 419 Squadron who were still on the station from their diversion during the early hours, were briefed for an operation but it was subsequently cancelled, and they later took off for their base at RCAF Station Middldton St. George. Leaving behind Lancaster KB735 which had crashed on East Moor at 03:15 hours.

In the evening,a very good.crowd enjoyed a 'Popular Record' session in the 'Y' Lounge

Squadron Officer Groundwater a WD Cypher Officer and Squadron Leader Hoodspith Signals, visited the station from No.62 Base.

20 September 1944

No operations were scheduled for the East Moor crews.

A heavy programme of flying training continued with air to air firing, cross-country, bombing and fighter affilliation exercises.

21 September 1944

Still no operations from the station.

No.432 Squadron pilots took advantage of the opportunity to to refurbish and decorate their crew room using the money raised by themselves and suplemented by the YMCA.

Flying training continued, and the Station Lecture Rooms were put to full use. A number of new crews arrived on station to replace those who were nearing the end of their 'tours

In the daytime, a number of visitors arrived at East Moor and included,Squadron Leader F.J Humphreys, Electrical Engineering Officer, the ex Station Adjutant Flight Lieutenant E.J Strathdee from No.62 (RCAF) Base, a Postal Officer, Flying Officer Pattison and Wing Commander W.C King Equipment Officer from No.6 Group Headquarters with Flight Lieutenant G.L Apperley, Education Officer.

In the evening, an audience of three hundred personnel enjoyed a stage play, 'Ropes End', performed by the 'Skipton Players' in East Moor's Little Theatre. The cast remained on station afterwards and were entertained in the NAAFI and shown films.

22 September 1944

And yet another operation free day at East Moor, and the aircrews were 'stood-down' whilst many of the aircraft remained bombed up and ready to go. Some of the groundcrews were also able to enjoy a well earned rest.

At a meeting of the Station Fire Committee it was found necessary to discuss ways of protecting the fire appliances and extinguishers from misuse by some irresponsible personnel.

Some time past, it had been decided to utilise certain areas of suitable ground on the station for the purpose of growing crops. And on this date the harvesting of the current potato crop commenced. Enough potatoes to keep all three of the Station's Messes supplied for around a fortnight were harvested. Amounting to around two hundred bags, it was regarded as a bumper crop.

Posted out was Squadron Officer F.M Schofield, WAAF who had opened their Section at East Moor Station. The WAAF's NAAFI was the scene of a rather sad farewell and representatives of all WAAF Sections gathered to wish her luck.

23 September 1944

Operations to the Calaise Area were called for and later scrubbed. No.432 Sqd carried out some flying training. No.415 Squadron had received a large consignment of cigarettes which had been donated by a Calgary Brewery Company, the town had adopted the squadron earlier. In the evening the squadron's personnel patronized the village dance hall at Sheriff Hutton.

After receiving the operational 'stand down' at 16.40 hours, film shows and Bingo sessions were organised on the station.

Engineering Officer, Wing Commander Carr-Harris visited the station from 62 Base.

24 September 1944

This was the seventh consecutive day without any operational committment at East Moor. It was a wet and foggy Sunday, the Station's Church Services were very well attended and flying was completely out of the question in the area.

The two squadrons were advised to be ready for a operation to Calaise Area on the morning of the 25th.

The Sunday evening Forum was held and a good size crowd listened to a debate on 'Emmigration to Canada'.

The Officers had a film show in their Mess.

25 September 1944

The East Moor crews had a successful operation when their target was Calais, and despite cloudy conditions over the target most were able to bomb, and all returned safely from this daylight attack.

432 Squadron			415 Squadron		
NP708 'E'	Sgt	A Stedman	LL575 'A'	F/O	C Chartier
NP705 'Y'	F/O	P Diamond	LK765 'B'	F/O	C Gue
NP721 'X'	F/O	M Krakowsky	MZ947 'C'	F/O	W Sherman
NP759 'C'	F/O	D Best	NA582 'D'	F/O	F Forbes
NP703 'H'	F/L	W Tobias	MZ603 'E'	F/L	J Hovey
NP698 'U'	F/O	G Barron	NA583 'F'	F/O	L Patton
NP694 'R'	Sgt	L MeGuire	MZ949 'G'	F/L	J McAllister
NP801 'N'	SIL	P Jack	NA608 'H'	F/L	H Barnes
NP755 'A'	F/L	J Woodward	MZ660 'J'	P/O	G MeKean
NP691 'V'	F/O	A Bews	MZ654 'L'	F/O	W McNeill
NP704 'L'	F/O	J Gault	NA612 'P'	F/O	B Roberts

NP774 'Z'	Sgt	J Hamilton	NA587 'Q'	F/S	W Lane
NP697 'F'	F/S	N Franko	NA607 'R'	P/O	D McNeill
NP723 'D'	F/O	J Mills	LW552 'S'	F/L	T Chapman
NP701 'G'	F/O	G Stunden	NA600 'U'	F/O	J Tims
NP692 'K'	F/O	V Johnston	LK766 'V'	F/O	D McTaggart
NP693 'Q'	P/O	P Campbell	MZ690 'X'	F/O	D Stewart
NP722 'S'	F/O	S Dean	MZ586 'Y'	F/O	J McQuiston
			MZ585 'Z'	F/O	J Meagher

This: was Pilot Of ficer Campbell and crew's last op, their tour completed.

26 September 1944

Wing Commander A Lowe and his crew were screened.

A further visit to Calais was made by the following East Moor crews and take

off commenced at 08.49 hrs,

432 Squadron			415 Squadron		
NP70l 'G'	F/O	G Stunden	LL575 'A'	F/O	C Chartier
NP704 'L'	F/O	J Gault	LK765 'B'	F/O	C Gue
NP697 'F'	F/S	N Franko	MZ947 'C'	F/O	J Sherman
NP698 'U'	F/O	G Barron	NA582 'D'	F/O	F Forbes
NP694 'R'	Sgt	L McGuire	MZ603 'E'	F/L	J Hovey
NP759 'C'	F/O	V Johnston	NA583 'F'	F/L	T Chapman
NP691 'V'	F/O	A Bews	MZ949 'G'	F/L	J McAllister
NP801 'N'	F/O	P Diamond	NA608 'H'	F/L	H. Barnes
NP755 'A'	F/L	J Woodward	MZ660 'J'	P/O	G McKean
NP708 'E'	Sgt	A Stedman	MZ654 'L'	F/O	W McNeill
NP736 'B'	F/L	W Tobias	LL576 'N'	F/O	B Roberts
NP723 'D'	F/O	J Mills	NA587 Q'	F/S	W Lane
NP721 'X'	F/O	S Dean	NA607 'R'	P/O	D McNeill
NP699 'O'	F/O	M Krakowsky	NA600 'U'	F/O	J Tims
NP693 'Q'	F/O	F Eilertson	LK766 'V'	P/O	D McTaggart
NP774 'Z'	Sgt	J Hamilton	MZ690 'X'	F/O	D Stewart
			MZ586'Y'	F/O	D McQuiston
			MZ585 'Z'	F/O	J Meagher

Sergeant Hamilton had to put flak damaged NP774 down at Manston with the elevator control and hydraulics u/s.

27 September 1944

Synthetic: oil plants at Botttrop were the morning target and the first East Moor crew lifted off at 07.01 hrs,

432 Squadron			415 Squadron		
NP755 'A'	F/O	W Saye	LL575 'A'	F/L	W Brown
NP759 'C'	F/O	D Best	LK765 'B'	F/O	C Gue
NP723 'D'	F/L	G Larson	MZ947 'C'	F/O	W Sherman
NP697 'F'	F/S	N Franko	NA582 'D'	F/O	F Forbes
NP701 'G'	F/O	G Stunden	MZ603 'E'	P/O	W MeNeill
NP703 'H'	Sgt	A Stedman	NA583 'F'	F/O	L Darychere
NP738 'J'	P/O	H Britton	MZ949 'G'	F/L	J McAllister
NP704 'L'	F/O	F Jeffrey	NA608 'H'	F/L	H Barnes
NP801 'N'	F/O	F Eilertson	MZ654 'L'	F/O	J Weir
NP699 'O'	F/O	J Mills	MZ660 'J'	F/O	C Chartier
NP694 'R'	Sgt	L McGuire	LL576 'N'	F/L	T Chapman
NP722 'S'	F/O	M Krakowsky	NA612 'P'	F/O	B Roberts
NP698 'U'	F/O	G Barron	NA587 'Q'	F/S	W Lane
NP691 'V'	F/O	A Craig	LW552 'S'	F/L	J Hovey
NP721 'X'	F/O	S Dean	NA600 'U'	F/O	J Tims
NP705 'Y'	F/O	P Diamond	LK766 'V'	F/O	D McTaggart
NP692 'K'	F/L	J Woodward	MZ632 'W'	P/O	D McNeill

MZ690 'X'	F/O	D Stewart	
MZ586 'Y'	F/O	J Mcquiston	
MZ585 'Z'	F/O	J Meagher	

Tragedy struck at 432 Squadron when NP692 was struck by flak and Flight Lieut Woodward was badly wounded, and Flying Officer C. Hay the navigator took the controls. The pilots instruments were shattered on the run up to the target and despite being in severe pain and badly shocked, F/L Woodward completed the bombing run with showers of bombs from aircraft above narrowly missing NP692.

With very little experience (a few minutes straight and level flying) Flying Officer Hay pointed the Halifax towards England and eventually reached the emergency field at Woodbridge. Here a Halifax II, HR756 was sent up to formate with NP692 and to assist Flying Officer Hay with instructions on how to land. The gravely wounded skipper assisted with throttle settings etc and the Halifax touched down too fast collapsing the undercarriage before catching fire. All the crew escaped but sadly Flight Lieutenant Woodward died the following day. Flying Officer Hay received an immediate DSO, the second for 432 Squadron.

The remainder of the crew arrived back at East Moor around mid-day.

28 September 1944

This was the fourth day in a row that East Moor's crews were detailed for 'ops'. 432 Squadron made recommendations for F/L Woodward to be awarded the DFC and the remainder of his crew to be mentioned indispatches. Late afternoon saw the following crews take off for Cap Gris Nez and the coastal batteries there,

432 Squadron			**415 Squadron**		
NP755 'A'	F/O	W Saye	LL575 'A'	F/L	W Brown
NP759 'C'	F/O	D Best	LK765 'B'	F/O	C Gue
NP723 'D'	F/O	J Mills	MZ947 'C'	F/O	W Sherman
NP708 'E'	Sgt	J Hamilton	NA582 'D'	F/O	F Forbes
NP697 'F'	F/S	N Franko	MZ603 'E'	F/O	W Regimbal
NP701 'G'	F/O	G Stunden	MZ949 'G'	F/L	J McAllister
NP738 'J'	Sgt	A Stedman	NA608 'H'	F/L	H Barnes
NP704 'L'	F/O	F Eilertson	MZ660 'J'	F/O	L Derychere
NP801 'N'	S/L	P Jack	MZ654 'L'	F/O	D Stewart
NP699 'O'	F/O	M Krakowsky	LL576 'N'	F/L	T Chapman
NP693 'Q'	F/O	F Baxter	MZ946 'O'	P/O	W McNeill
NP694 'R'	Sgt	L McGuire	NA612 'P'	F/O	B Roberts
NP722 'S'	F/O	J Patterson	NA587 'Q'	F/S	W Lane
NP698 'U'	F/O	G Barron	NA607 'R'	P/O	D McNeill
NP691 'V'	F/O	A Craig	LW552 'S'	F/O	C Chartier
NP721 'X'	F/O	S Dean	NA600 'U'	F/O	J Tims
NP705 'Y'	F/O	R Diamond	LK766 'V'	P/O	D McTaggart
			MZ586 'Y'	F/O	J Mcquiston
			MZ585 'Z'	F/O	J Meagher

All returned safely.

Sergeant McGuire returned on three engines and Flying Officer Chartier ran off the end of the runway in LW552, neither aircraft suffered any damage.

At mid day a cow was found wandering around the airfield and some of the more enterprising personnel soon put it to work as a lawn mower around the Flying Control building. Numerous unsuccessful attempts were made to extract milk from the animal before the Service Police took it into custody.

29 September 1944

432 Squadron celebrated the return of its popular Commanding Officer, Wing Commander J.K MacDonald who replaced Wing Commander A. Lowe

Squadron Leader Frankling took command of 415 Squadron in the absence of Wing Commander Lecomte who was on leave.

No operations were called for and many personnel spent the day in the lecture rooms

Thirty six crews set out for Sterkrade during mid morning and all returned safely to base, the last one touching down at 15.21 hours,

432 Squadron			415 Squadron		
NP708 'E'	F/O	F Jeffrey	LL575 'A'	P/O	C Chartier
NP759 'C'	Sgt	A Stedman	LK765 'B'	F/O	C Gue
NP723 'D'	F/O	J Mills	MZ947 'C'	F/O	W Sherman
NP704 'L'	F/O	F Baxter	NA582 'D'	F/O	F Forbes
NP801 'N'	F/O	A Craig	MZ949 'G'	F/L	J McAllister
NP693 'Q'	F/O	J Patterson	NA608 'H'	F/L	H Barnes
NP698 'U'	F/O	L Evenson	MZ660 'L'	F/O	J Weir
NP691 'V'	F/O	G Barron	LL576 'N'	F/L	T Chapman
NP721 'X'	F/O	S Dean	MZ946 'O'	P/O	W Mc'Neill
NP705 'Y'	F/O	P Diamond	NA612 'P'	F/O	B Roberts
NP701 'G'	F/O	G Stunden	NA587 'Q'	F/S	W Lane
NP738 'J'	F/O	H Britton	NA607 'R'	P/O	D McNeill
NP697 'F'	F/S	N Franko	LW552 'S'	F/O	L Deryckere
NP703 'H'	F/O	F Eilertson	NA600 'U'	F/O	J Tims
NP699 'O'	F/O	M Krakowsky	LK766 'V'	P/O	D McTaggart
NP694 'R'	Sgt	L McGuire	MZ690 'X'	F/O	D Stewart
NP722 'S'	Sgt	J Hamilton	MZ586 'Y'	F/O	J Mequiston
NP755 'A'	F/O	W Saye	MZ585 'Z'	F/O	J Meagher

An ENSA show was staged in the 'Little Theatre' and was enjoyed by the station's music lovers during the evening.

General:

All round morale was said to be high despite the optimism of the first day having dwindled with the realisation that victory was still away off.

Each squadron lost only one crew to operational activity in a month which saw them heavily committed. 432 Squadron lost an additional aircraft when NP692 burnt at Woodbridge.

Corporal N.W Cant died as a result of injuries received when he was knocked down by an MT vehicle in York.

Additional help with the heavy work in the Bomb Dump was obtained when the services of a detachment of Army personnel moved in to East Moor.

Misappropiation of bicycles was always a problem and reached serious proportions during September when the Service Police carried out spot checks which resulted in any culprits spending an uncomfortable period in the Guard Room.

Life on the dispersed living sites still left much to be desired, roads and paths turning to mud when it rained. Sheets became unobtainable and regarded as a luxury when the civilian laundry closed down.

Fortnightly dances had become a regular feature as the Station Orchestra under Mr.J. McClelland of the YMCA was much in demand.

A new recreation appeared on the station in the form of roller skating and more than 80 pairs of skates were made available. The pastime was received with much unexpected interest

Sandra Lights were used on the station for the first time on the 26th of the month and were a great help to the Armament personnel during bombing up of the aircraft.

Station Headquarters staff held a party at Stillington which was so well attended and successful that it was decided to make it a regular event.

On the 25th Air Vice Marshal J.A Sully (A.M.P, RCAF) arrived on the station and witnessed the return of the two squadrons from operations before giving a talk on 'Personnel Counselling' and the difficulties associated with that task.

The station received a new tanker from Coningsby and a Morris type 422 from Linton on Ouse. In exchange for the latter, East Moor provided Linton on Ouse with vehicles to replace ones lost when the Halifax crashed on that station's MT Section.

The Station Cinema was by this time operating on five evenings each week with YMCA films and ENSA concerts.

Staff at Station Headquarters purcnased ten small ducklings and these were kept and jealously guarded on a pond nearby, as numerous members of other sections had visions of them on a tastily decorated platter.

1 October 1944

The usual Sunday Church Parades took place on the station and were followed by flying training exercises which included H25, fighter affilliation and air to air firing.

Domestic problems on the station were again highlighted when once again the sheet shortage was queried, together with the lack of batmen and further complaints were raised regarding the standard of the food in the Officers Mess, and the PMC, Squadron Leader A.M. Stockdale DFC, had to exercise a high degree of skill and diplomacy in handling the problems raised.

Meanwhile, the Sergeants celebrated the opening of their new bar with a most successful party and the Mess guests included ATS personnel from Queen Elizabeth Barracks at Strensall, the Land Army from Crayke together with the Station Commander, the SADO and Squadron Commanders. The music was of course provided by the increasingly popular East Moor Orchestra.

The Ministry of Information provided a speaker for a Forum which was held in the 'Y' Lounge. Mr.S.H. Sung's subject was 'China the Land and the people'. The event proved most interesting and resulted in a lengthy question and answer session.

No operations were called for at East Moor.

2 October 1944

No operations were scheduled at the station.

Flight Lieutenant Woodward's crew were bearers at his funeral service which was held at Woodbridge at 10.30 hours. The pilot was afforded full military honours.

A full programme of flying training was carried out at East Moor and at 23.00 hours a lost aircraft was noted circling the airfield. The airfield lights were switched on but the crew elected not to land and were given directions on their request for a QDM for RAF Station Ruf forth.

Errol Flynn starred in 'Desperate Journey' showing in the Station Cinema, and was attended by more than 300 personnel.

3 October 1944

And another day free of operations at East Moor.

More than thirty of the station's aircraft were engaged in a flying training programme which included a night 'Bullseye' exercise.

East Moor WAAF's were the guests of the ATS at Fulford Barracks, York, and found to their dismay that they were required to pay for the evening which included a dance. Not the most enjoyable of evenings it would seem.

4 October 1944

Another full programme of flying training was carried out in the absence of any operational commitment, and was concluded by 23.34 hours.

415 Squadron were informed that they had won the 62 (RCAF) Base Efficiency Award. The Station Commander held a meeting with Section and Squadron Commanders to discuss a variety of topics including kit inspections, morale on the station and the Canadian Victory Loan Campaign.

The Airmen's Mess on the Old Communal Site was the scene for a most successful Roller Skating Party and it was decided to make this a regular Wednesday feature.

A call went out for volunteers from the station WAAF's to embark upon service in Western Europe.

5 October 1944

A further lull in operational commitment for the station resulted in the usual heavy programme of flying training, and presented an opportunity for many to engage in 'bull' sessions around the gardens and driveways.

Preparations were made to receive a number of RCAF Skipton on Swale's aircraft when the weather closed in on that base but they did not arrive. By midnight the weather was just as bad at East Moor and local training exercises were concluded.

Earlier in the evening many of the station's personnel had departed for RCAF Station Linton on Ouse where they attended a station dance.

6 October 1944

A party was given in the NAAFI for the personnel of the Bomb Dump and included the Army contingent who were temporarily employed there. The event was attended by the Station Commander, the SADO and the Armament Officer, who each complimented the efforts of those present.

A rather sudden notification of impending operational requirements resulted in the recruitment of many 'screened' aircrew to assist with the bombing up of the station's Halifaxes, forty three of which were prepared for an attack on Dortmund. This proved to be No.6 Group's biggest raid and involved 293 aircraft. During the operation East Moor's weather deteriorated making the airfield difficult to recover to and consequently only four were able to land there, the remainder being diverted to bases in the south.

The following crews set out in mid afternoon and all returned safely,

432 Squadron			415 Squadron		
NP759 'C'	F/O	D Best	LL575 'A'	F/O	W Regimbal
INP70l 'G'	F/O	G Stunden	LK765 'B'	F/O	C Chartier
NP708 'E'	F/L	W Tobias	MZ947 'C'	F/O	W Sherman
INP697 'F'	F/S	N Franko	NA582 'D'	F/O	S McFaddon
NP803 'I'	F/O	J Mills	MZ603 'E'	F/O	H Knobovitch
NP738 'J'	P/O	H Britton	NA583 'F'	F/O	D McTaggart
NP704 'L'	F/O	J Gault	NA608 'H'	F/L	H Barnes
NP80l 'N'	F/O	A Craig	NP935 'I'	F/L	J McAllister
NP699 'O'	F/O	M Krakowsky	MZ660 'J'	F/O	J Kerr
NP694 'R'	P/O	L McGuire	MZ654 'L'	F/O	J Weir
NP722 'S'	F/O	J Hamilton	NA607 'R'	F/O	P Gingrich
N P812 'T'	F/O	G McNicholl	NA600 'U'	P/O	D Andrews
NP691 'V'	F/O	A Bews	LK766 'V'	F/O	P Sierolawski
NP721 'X'	F/O	S Dean	MZ632 'W'	F/O	a Lindquist
NP705 'Y'	F/O	P Diamond	MZ690 'X'	F/O	J Little
NP693 'Q'	F/O	C Hemming	LL593 'M'	F/O	D Stewart
NP755 'A'	W/C	J MacDonald	LL576 'N'	F/L	T Chapman
NP707 'W'	F/O	A Potter	MZ946 'O'	P/O	W McNeill
NP736 'B'	F/O	W Saye	NA612 'P'	F/O	B Roberts
NP807 'P'	F/L	F Horan	NA587 'Q'	F/S	W Lane
NP723 'D'	S/L	G Larson	MZ585 'Z'	P/O	D McNeill
NP698 'U'	F/O	G Barron			

Diverted aircraft:
432 Sqd -   C,G,,E,F,l,J,L,O,R,X,Y and D   to Sudbury

	S an	to Bury St.Edmunds
	V and W	to Methwold
	A	to Wratting Common
	B	to Tuddenham
	N	to Lavenham
	T	to Woodbridge
415 Sqd -	W and I	to Wratting Common
	B,D,F,N,O,P,R,and X	to Knettishall
	C,V,H,J	to Stradishall
	E	to Coltishall
	L	to Pattlesden
	N	to Snetterton Heath
	A	to Mendlesham (tyre burst on landing)
	Z	to Deepham Green

The crews which landed at American bases reported their treatment as par -excellent.

The results of the operation were good, much of Dortmund's industry was severely damaged.

7 October 1944

Saturday, and no operations, the planned ones being cancellede East Moor staff saw the diverted aircraft return to the station before embarking on a round of parties. Sutton Hall was the scene of oneof the noisiest where it was said that some of the old timers refought the Battle of Newfoundland. The groundcrews of 415 Squadron took over the squadron crewroom where five kegs of beer were soon consumed along with sandwiches and coffee.

8 October 1944

The sabbath was a misty and rainy day at East Moor and was again operation free. Flying Training continued with fighter affilliation and air to air firing exercise. It was decideed that the station's Service Police staff should make closer checks on who was on which bicycle, as there was much 'borrowing without permission' leading to frustration and inconvenience.

9 October 1944

Late afternoon saw the following crews dispatched from East Moor to attack Bochum,

432 Squadron			415 Squadron		
NP704 'L'	F/O	J Gault	LK765 'B'	P/O	D McNeill
NP722 'S'	F/O	W Saye	MZ947 'C'	F/O	J Britt
NP759 'C¹'	F/O	J Mills	NA582 'D'	F/O	H Knobovitch
NP708 'E'	F/O	C Hemming	NA608 'H'	F/L	H Barnes
NP697 'F'	F/S	N Franko	MZ660 'J'	F/O	S McFadden
NP703 'H'	P/O	J Hamilton	LL593 'M'	F/O	J Weir
NP803 'I'	F/L	F Horan	LL576 'N'	P/O	S Moers
NP738 'J'	P/O	H Britton	MZ946 '0'	F/O	D McNeill
NP689 'M'	F/O	A Craig	NA587 'Q'	F/L	J Northrup
NP694 'R'	P/O	L McGuire	NA607 'R'	F/O	P Gingrich
NP812 'T'	F/O	A Potter	LK766 'V'	F/O	P Sierolawski
NP80l 'N'	F/O	P Diamond	MZ690 'X'	F/O	D Stewart
NP698 'U'	F/O	G Barron	MZ586 'Y'	F/O	J Kerr
NP691 'V'	F/O	A Bews	NA612 'P'	F/O	B Roberts
NP721 'X'	F/O	S Dean	NA600 'U'	F/O	J Tims

Tragedy struck 432 Squadron when falling bombs from an aircraft above forced Flying Officer Diamond and crew to bale out of the damaged NP80l. F/O Diamond was on his last trip but one, and had with him Flight Lieutenant Nicholson the Navigation Leader, his usual navigator had been screened.

Pilot Officer McGuire made an early return with starboard outer engine u/s. Flying Officer J. Weir's Halifax was struck by flak preventing it from gaining any further altitude and a loss of power to the port outer engine. A shortage of petrol forced a landing at Manston where the engine stopped on touch down.

10 October 1944

No operations were called for and morale on the station was said to be high despite a number of minor discomforts having to be endured. The Officer's laundry facilities left much to be desired and their batmen were in short supply. Nevertheless, 'A' Flight of 432 Squadron held a party which was a roaring success despite one keg of beer being made off with.The Station Commander and other senior officers attended, and a good time was had by one and all.

Ten cross country exercises were carried out during the night by 415 Squadron.

11 October 1944

Another day free from operational commitment at East Moor. Fog and rain in the morning prevented any kind of flying and most aircrews were at lectures.

Later in the day gale force winds broke the power lines between East Moor and York, and consequently the station was without a main power supply from 16.37 hrs. Pay Parade was conducted with the aid of 'Glim'lights making it a long drawn out business and 'Sandra' lights were used by the bomb dump personnel to assist in bombing up for an operation expected on the 12th.

12 October 1944

Wanne Eickel and the Oil Plants there,became the target for East Moor crews when the first Halifax of thirty called for, lifted from the runway at 07.26 hours,

432 Squadron			415 Squadron		
NP803 'I'	F/L	F Horan	LL575 'A'	F/O	C Chartier
NP721 'X'	F/O	S Dean	MZ947 'C'	F/O	J Britt
NP707 'W'	F/O	A Potter	MZ603 'E'	F/O	H Knobovitch
NP708 'E'	F/O	J Gault	MZ946 'O'	F/O	D McNeill
NP759 'C'	F/O	J Mills	NA582 'D'	F/L	J Northrup
NP736 'B'	F/O	W Saye	NA607 'R'	F/O	D Gingrich
NP697 'F'	F/O	G Stunden	MZ632 'W'	F/O	P Sierolawski
NP689 'M'	F/O	A Craig	MZ690 'X'	F/O	D Stewart
NP699 '0'	F/O	M Krakowsky	LL576 'M'	F/O	J Kerr
NP807 'P'	F/O	G Barron	NA612 'P'	F/O	B Roberts
NP693 'Q'	F/O	C Hemming	MZ660 'J'	F/O	J Tims
NP722 'S'	P/O	J Hamilton	NA583 'F'	P/O	T Donnelly
NP694 'R'	P/O	L McGuire	MZ654 'L'	F/O	D McTaggart
NP812 'T'	F/O	A Bews	NA587 'Q'	F/S	W Lane
NP738 'J'	P/O	H Britton	NP935 'I'	F/L	J McAllister

Flight Lieutenant McAllister's Halifax was hit by flak on the way to the target, damaging the mid upper turret and wounding Flying Officer Prawizik severely. On return they landed at Woodbridge where the starboard tyre blew off injuring Flying Officer Smith in the process. NP935 was a complete write off.

Flying Officer Britt's aircraft was damaged on both mainplanes, both inner engine nacelles and the starboard fuselage.

Sergeant M.Washook, upper gunner in F/O Stewarts crew, received injuries and was landed first at West Raynham and subsequently at Witchford.
The port wing and landing light was damaged on Flying Officer Robert's Halifax.

Flying Officer D.McTaggart landed MZ654 at Woodbridge with flak damage to the nose and fuselage.

Pilot Officer Britton, with second pilot Flight Lieutenant Speller on board, crash landed at Woodbridge after NP738 was struck by heavy flak which killed the bomb aimer and and severely injured flight engineer, Sergeant E.

Knight.The latter hero lost his hand as a result of his injuries and for his bravery during the return flight, was awarded the CGM. It was the crews last trip of their 'tour'

Flying Officer M.Krakowsky returned with flak damage to the starboard outer mainplane,. aileron, petrol tanks and rear fuselage.

Flying Officer Hemming's Halifax had a catergory AC damage rating resulting from hits from flak to the starboard outer mainplane, tailplane and rear fuselage.

A damaged astro dome and rear turret were the results of flak hitting the mount of Flight Sergeant W. Lane.

The heavy flak had been encountered over the target area.

The station's aircraft were all accounted for by early afternoon, but in the meantime, a further operation calling for seven aircraft from each squadron, was called off at 16.50 hours.

The seventh Canadian Victory Loan was opened and East Moor Station was set a target of 72,000 Canadian dollars. It was anticipated that the pressure of campaigning within No.6 (RCAF) Group would be tremendous.

Late in the afternoon, some concern arose when two unidentified 'black objects' were noticed around Station Head-quarters. An investigation by the Station Administrative Officer soon revealed them to be chimney sweeps looking for a place to clean up after a mammoth 'kill' of twenty chimneys, fifty boiler flues and no less than two hundred and eighty four stove pipes.

13 October 1944

'Friday the 13th', definately an unlucky day for 415 Squadron with the sad announcement of the death of two of its members. Flying Officer C.J Prawdzik and Sergeant N.R Washook died from their injuries received from flak on the raid on Wanne Eickel. They were the squadron's first loss of personnel since its initial operation from East Moor.

No.6 Group detailed sixteen aircraft from 432 squadron and seventeen from 415 for an attack on Duisburg on the 14th, and preparations were got under way at 11.00   hours.

Squadron Leader J.A Head an Equipment Officer from No.62 Base visited East Moor in connection with the Seventh Canadian Victory Loan, and was amongst three hundred personnel who saw a Victory Loan film screened in the Of-ficer's and Sergeant's Messes and later in the YMCA.

Friday the 13th did bring a little brightness to the East Moor scene. Without any undue ceremony, from the dining room ovens came a special treat, roast chicken for all. A day to remember indeed.

14 October 1944

In the evening, a farewell party was held for the outgoing. and popular Station Commander, Group Captain H.H Rut-ledge, OBE, in the WAAF Officer's Mess where he was presented with a silver mug, on the eve of his departure. His successor was the ex 408 Squadron Commander, Group Captain R.A McLernon, DFC.

Earlier in the day the East Moor squadrons had commenced a mammoth task, a'doubleheader' against Duisburg. This master effort by the station's personnel got under way soon after first light with thirty three crews lifting their Halifaxes from the station's runway for the first operation. All returned safely, and just before midnight, the last of thirty five crews set out once more.

In the two attacks, Bomber Command dispatched over two thousand aircraft, twenty one of which were lost, East Moor was lucky, all returned on that date.

The first aircraft was airborne at 06.10 hours and the last one at 23.06. The last one down was at 06.17 hours on the i5th a little over twenty four hours later.

The station's personnel were said to be tired but happy in the knowledge that they were beating the enemy.

On the first attack only half of East Moor's crews bombed the primary, others bombed targets of opportunity, rail-ways factories etc, but on the second attack a concentrated pattern was achieved. The order of battle for the attacks was as follows,

Early morning,

432 Squadron			415 Squadron		
NP698 'U'	F/O	F Baxter	LL575 'A'	F/O	C Chartier
NP803 'I'	F/O	F Eilertson	LK765 'B'	F/O	C Gue
NP704 'L'	F/O	J Gault	NA582 'D'	F/O	F Forbes
NP705 'Y'	F/O	A Bews	MZ603 'E'	F/O	H Knobovitch
NP723 'D'	F/O	W Saye	NA583 'F'	F/O	J Britt
NP701 'G'	F/O	G Stunden	MZ949 'G'	S/L	S Frankling
NP689 'M'	F/O	G Spiers	MZ660 'J'	F/O	S McFaddon
NP722 'S'	P/O	J Hamilton	MZ654 'L'	F/O	D McNeill
NP697 'F'	F/S	A Stedman	MZ946 'O'	P/O	W McNeill
NP707 'W'	F/O	A Potter	NA612 'P'	F/O	B Roberts
NP721 'X'	S/L	P Jack	NA607 'R'	F/O	P Gingrich
NP708 'E'	F/O	F Jeffrey	NA611 'T'	F/O	D McTaggart
NP703 'H'	F/L	F Horan	NA600 'U'	F/O	J Tims
NP807 'P'	F/O	J Patterson	MZ586 'Y'	F/O	J Kerr
NP694 'R'	P/O	L McGuire	MZ632 'W'	F/O	R Sierolawski
NP812 'T'	F/O	G McNicholl	MZ585 'Z'	P/O	J Meagher
			NA608 'H'	F/L	J Northrup

Night operation,

432 Squadron			415 Squadron		
NP759 'C'	F/O	F Eilertson	LL575 'A'	F/O	C Chartier
NP697 'F'	Sgt	A Stedman	LK765 'B'	F/O	C Gue
NP698 'U'	F/O	A Potter	NA582 'D'	Sgt	Krocker
NP707 'W'	F/L	J Thompson	MZ603 'E'	F/O	H Knobovitch
NP722 'S'	P/O	J Hamilton	NA583 'F'	F/O	S McFaddon
NP723 'D'	F/L	W Tobias	MZ949 'G'	F/L	T Mears
NP705 'Y'	F/O	A Bews	NA608 'H'	F/L	J Northrup
NP694 'R'	F/O	J Patterson	MZ654 'L'	F/O	J Weir
NP807 'P'	F/O	J Gault	LL576 'N'	F/O	L Deryckere
NP803 'I'	F/L	F Horan	NA587 'Q'	F/O	D Stewart
NP812 'T'	F/O	G Spiers	NA612 'P'	F/O	B Roberts
NP704 'L'	F/O	F Jeffrey	MZ946' O'	F/O	D McNeill
NP701 'G'	F/O	G Stunden	NA607 'R'	F/O	R Gingrich
NP755 'A'	W/C	J MacDonald	LW552 'S'	P/O	T Donnelly
NP736 'B'	F/L	D Speller	NA611 'T'	F/O	D McTaggart
NP689 'M'	F/O	G McNicholl	NA600 'U'	FlO	J Tims
			MZ632 'W'	F/O	P Sierolawski
			MZ586 'Y'	F/O	J Kerr
			MZ585 'Z'	F/O	J Meagher

NP721 received flak damage on the first operation, damaging two port petrol tanks and an oil tank.
NP703 had the port outer mainplane damaged beyond repair.
MZ949 returned with the starboard wing holed.
NA612 had its port wing, aileron and flaps holed by flak.

On the second operation NP755 was attacked by an enemy aircraft, the gunners It returned fire. and claimed a probably damaged.

NA582 was attacked by an enemy aircraft and crashed on approach to East Moor at 04.33 hours near Stillington, the crew survived.

Flying Officer Knobovitch attacked on three engines, not being able to feather the port inner airscrew and some bombs were jettisoned as MZ603 rapidly lost height.

The bomb doors of NA583 were found to have been holed just before bombing believed to have resulted from a 1,000 pounder passing through it.

F lying Officer Deryckere returned early with a u/s port inner engine. Flying Officer Stewart's crew found a hole measuring 7' x 2' in the bomb doors of NA587, beleived to have been caused by a 1,000 pounder coming adrift during evasive action. Short of fuel they put down at Woodbridge.

Flying Of ficer Tims and crew were chased all the way to the English coast by enemy fighters.

15 October 1944

Wilhelmshaven was the target and the following crews were dispatched

432 Squadron			415 Squadron		
NP807 'P'	F/O	A Craig	LL575 'A'	F/O	C Chartier
NP698 'U'	F/O	A Potter	NA610 'B'	F/O	F Forbes
NP705 'Y'	F/L	J Thompson	NA124 'I'	F/L	J Northrup
NP704 'L'	S/L	P Jack	MZ946 'O'	F/O	D McNeill
NP723 'D'	F/L	D Speller	NA612 'P'	F/O	B Roberts
NP759 'C'	F/O	D Frost	NA607 'R'	F/O	P Gingrich
NP755 'A'	F/O	W Saye	LW552 'S'	F/O	H Knobovitch
NP722 'S'	P/O	L McGuire	NA6ll 'T'	F/O	D MeTaggart
			NA600 'U'	F/O	J Tims
			MZ586 'Y'	F/O	J Kerr
			MZ585 'Z'	F/O	L Deryckere

Sadly, Flight Lieutenant D. Speller and crew failed to return from this operation.

Flying Officer Craig landed at Old Buckenham, Flying Officer Chartier at Temps.ford, Flying Officer Forbes at Downham Market, Flight Lieutenant Northrup at Attlebridge, Flying Officer Gingrich at Rackheath, Flying Officer McTaggart at Horsham and Flying Officer Kerr at Carnaby.

16 October 1944

A day without operations provided a breathing space for the station's personnel,many of the aircrews having mounted three in thirty six hours.

Wing Commander LeH Lecomte was awarded a Non-Immediate DFC.

Rumour was rife, suggesting that on completion of their operational tours, all Canadian aircrew would be returning to their native land.

17 October 1944

Funeral services were held for Flying Officer C.J Prawdsik and Sergeant M.R Washooke

Two 432 Squadron crews took off just after mid day and carried out a Sea Search without result, returning approximately four hours later,

NP694 'R' F/O F Baxter and NP736 'B' F/O F Eilertson.

18 October 1944

Operations were called for but subsequently scrubbed, flying training consisted mainly of cross countries.

19 October 1944

With the daylight hours being reduced the aircrews practiced more night take offs and landings on another day without operations at East Moor.

432 Squadron party at the Hop Grove was a great success in the evening.

20 October 1944

There wasn't any flying recorded at East Moor on an extremely wet and dull day.

The Station band provided the music for a most successful dance in the WAAF's NAAFI, and this was followed by traditional parties in the various messes.

21 October 1944

In the late afternoon the following 432 Squadron crews set out for Hannover but were recalled after being in the air for two and a half hours, the last one touching down at 19.49 hours,

NP755 'A'	F/O	W Saye	NP759 'C'	F/O	J Mills
NP708 'E'	F/O	F Jeffrey	NP697 'F'	Sgt	A Stedman
NP803 'I'	F/O	J Patterson	NP704 'L'	F/O	J Gault
NP689 'M'	F/O	A Craig	NP808 'N'	F/O	C Hemming
NP807 'P'	F/O	G Spiers	NP694 'R'	P/O	L McGuire
NP722 'S'	F/O	M Krakowsky	NP812 'T'	F/O	F Baxter
NP698 'U'	F/O	G Barron	NP691 'V'	F/O	A Bews
NP707 'W'	F/O	A Potter	NP705 'Y'	F/O	Dean

The marriage between Corporal Eunice Robinson and Squadron Leader W.E Boone both of East Moor Station, took place in York. Better known as 'Danny' he was a very popular and efficient Chief Technical Officer who had joined the RCAF in January 1942. A Flight Lieutenant when he arrived at East Moor from Skipton on Swale, he was soon promoted and held in high esteem.

22 October 1944

The only flying recorded at East Moor was of the training variety, fighter affilliation exercises with a Spitfire from RCAF Dalton, circuits and landings, bombing practice and Cross countries.

A 432 Halifax struck a lorry on take off before coming to rest in the fields behind Sutton Hall.

A successful Airmens Mess dance was held in the evening when the music was provided by No.6 Group band.

23 October 1944

East Moor was honoured with a visit by His Eminence the Bishop of quebec, Cardinal Villeneve accompanied by Air Commodore Charest, the Chief Roman Catholic Padre. The guests watched the operational take off of aircraft detailed to attack Essen and were greatly impressed and noticeably moved. A dinner followed at which the Cardinal declared that the people of Canada would be told in detail of the efficiency with which an RCAF operational station works and of the heavy responsibility that lies with those in charge as well as the spirit and determination that is evident among all ranks in the execution of their duty.

East Moor provided forty aircraft in a total force of 1,055 in the operation against Essen and happily the station's crews made a safe return,

432 Squadron			415 Squadron		
NP694 'R'	P/O	L McGuire	LL575 'A'	F/O	W Brown
NP812 'T'	F/O	F Baxter	NA610 'B'	F/O	C Gue
NP759 'C'	F/O	J Mills	MZ603 'E'	F/O	H Knobovitch
NP817 'D'	S/L	G Larson	NA583 'F'	F/O	W Regimbald
NP722 'S'	F/O	C Hemming	MZ949 'G'	F/L	T Mears
NP755 'A'	F/O	W Saye	NA608 'H'	F/L	H Barnes
NP736 'B'	F/O	D Frost	NA124 'I'	F/L	J Northrup
NP708 'E'	F/O	F Jeffrey	MZ660 'J'	F/O	S McFaddon
NP697 'F'	Sgt	A Stedman	NP156 'K'	F/O	F Forbes
NP701 'G'	F/O	S Dean	LK765 'M'	F/O	J Britt
INP815 'H'	F/O	F Eilertson	LL576 'N'	F/O	T Chapman
NP803 'I'	F/O	J Patterson	MZ946 'O'	F/O	D McNeill
NP704 'L'	F/O	J Gault	NA612 'P'	F/O	B Roberts
NP689 'M'	F/O	A Craig	NA587 'Q'	F/S	W Lane
NP807 'P'	F/O	G Spiers	NA607 'R'	F/O	R Gingrich

NP802 'S'	F/O	M Krakowsky	LW552 'S'	F/O	L Deryckere
NP698 'U'	F/O	G Barron	NA611 'T'	F/O	C Chartier
NP691 'V'	F/O	A Bews	NA600 'U'	F/O	D Mcquiston
NP705 'Y'	F/O	A Potter	MZ632 'W'	F/O	S Mooers
			MZ586 'Y'	F/L	J Little
			MZ861 'Z'	F/O	J Meagher

Pilot Officer McGuire's aircraft suffered severe icing conditions necessitating an early return to Woodbridge short of fuel.

Flying Officer Hemming made a crash landing at Manston due to icing up. Flying Officer Bews returned early to Tempsford with starboard outer engine u/s and short of fuel.

Flying Officer Brown's Halifax was attacked by a FW190 but evasive action shook it off.

Flying Officer Regimbald diverted to Manston, short of fuel.

Flight Sergeant Lane and crew prepared to abandon NA587 when severe icing caused a loss of control which was only regained at 2,000 feet, bombs brought back. Flying Officer Chartier landed at Levenham, short of fuel and with a u/s ASI. Sergeant Ivan Mulley the Flight Engineer in Flying Officer Dean's crew relates,

'As soon as we had taken off in Halifax VII 'G', the skipper an I realised that the blind flying panel was not working. Panic stations!! A quick check by Walter the bomb aimer to ensure that the pitot head cover had been removed - OK. The pitot head heater was switched on but had no effect ! I remembered that two static vents were situated on either side of the fuselage quite near to the mid upper turret. Each had a seal, the first one I opened was clear but the second was blocked by fine grit and dust. After clearing it and remaking the connection the blind flying panel came to life. Probably the engines of an aircraft on the next dispersal had been run up and dust and grit had been blown over our aircraft. We had lost some flying time near East Moor and Des Pitts, thenavigator quickly revised the course that had been given at briefing, instead of passing over Reading we flew to the east of London and cut several corners on the given route when we reached the continent. I cannot recall that we saw another aircraft. Eventually we reached where the navigator and the bomb aimer said we were over Essen. Below us was a complete sheet of cloud. We could see nothing through it and nothing came up at us. Our bomb load was dropped and we returned safely to base. The next morning when we studied the situation report of the previous nights activities we realised that instead of being in the first wave of an 800 airplane attack, the delay in arriving over the target had placed us in the middle of it. Where had the other aircraft got to ? We did not see any'.

The records for 432 Squadron show two aircraft on this operation carrying the letter 'S'.

24 October 1944

Operations were called for but subsequently scrubbed, the aircraft were bombed up and the crews stood by for many hours on what turned out to be a quiet day except for several loud explosions caused by defective bombs being touched of f.

25 October 1944

East Moor contributed forty aircraft and crews in an attack on the oil plants at Homberg (Meerbeck) and with the exception of Flying Officer Bews who made an early return with a u/s starboard outer engine, all attacked and returned safely,

432 Squadron			415 Squadron		
NP691 'V'	F/O	A Bews	LL575 'A'	F/L	W Brown
NP815 'H'	F/O	F Eilertson	NA610 'B'	F/L	C Thompson
NP707 'W'	F/O	A Potter	MZ882 'C'	F/O	J Britt
NP812 'T'	F/O	C Hemming	LK755 'D'	F/O	F Forbes
NP755 'A'	F/O	W Say	MZ603 'E'	F/O	H Knobovitch
NP736 'B'	F/O	D Frost	NA583 'F'	F/O	W Pegimbald
NP759 'C'	F/O	J Mills	MZ949 'G'	F/L	T Mears
NP817 'D'	S/L	G Larson	NA124 'I'	F/L	J Northrup
NP708 'E'	F/O	F Jeffrey	MZ654 'L'	F/O	C Chartier
NP697 'F'	Sgt	A Stedman	LK765 'M'	F/O	J Meagher

NP70l 'G'	F/O	S Dean		LL576 'N'	F/L	T Chapman
NP803 'I'	F/O	J Patterson		MZ946 'O'	F/O	D McNeill
NP704 'L'	F/O	J Gault		NA612 'P'	F/O	L Deryckere
NP807 'P'	F/O	G Spiers		NA587 'Q'	F/S	W Lane
NP802 'S'	F/O	M Krakowsky		NA607 'R'	F/O	P Gingrich
NP698 'U'	F/O	G Barron		LW552 'S'	P/O	S Mooers
NP705 'Y'	F/L	J Thompson		NA6ll 'T'	S/L	J Hovey
				NA600 'U'	F/O	J Mcquiston
				NR172 'V'	F/O	P Sierolaweki
				MZ632 'W'	F/O	O Lindquist
				NR122 'X'	F/L	J Little
				MZ586 'Y'	F/O	J Kerr
				MZ861 'Z'	W/C	F Ball

26 October 1944

Pilot Officer R.M Stevens was awarded an immediate DFC,the ex 415 Squadron pilot had been posted to 16 OTU.

Operations planned for were scrubbed later in the day. No flying was carried out at East Moor.

27 October 1944

Once again operations were called for and later cancelled. Some traing flights in the form of bombing practice were carried out.

28 October 1944

Thirty seven crews left East Moor commencing at 13.07 hours to join more than six hundred and ninety others for an attack on Cologne when once again all returned safely,

432 Squadron				**415 Squadron**		
NP755 'A'	F/O	W Saye		LL575 'A'	W/C	F Ball
NP736 'B'	F/O	G Stunden		NA6l0 'B'	F/O	H Knobovitch
NP759 'C'	F/O	J Mills		MZ882 'C'	F/O	J Britt
NP817 'D'	F/O	J Patterson		LK755 'D'	F/L	C Thompson
NP708 'E'	F/O	F Jeffrey		NA124 'I'	F/L	J Northrup
NP697 'F'	Sgt	A Stedman		NR156 'K'	F/O	C Chartier
NP815 'H'	F/O	E Eilertson		MZ946 'O'	F/O	D McNeill
NP803 'I'	F/L	F Horan		NA612 'P'	F/O	L Deryckere
NP704 'L'	F/O	J Gault		NA600 'U'	F/O	J Mcquiston
NP689 'M'	P/O	J Hamilton		NR172 'V'	F/O	R Sierolawski
NP807 'P'	F/O	G McNicholl		NA583 'F'	P/O	S Mooers
NP804 'Q'	F/O	S Dean		MZ949 'G'	F/L	T Mears
NP802 'S'	F/O	M Krakowsky		NA608 'H'	F/L	H Barnes
NP691 'V'	F/O	A Bews		MZ654 'L'	F/O	W Regimbald
NP707 'W'	F/O	A Potter		LL576 'N'	F/L	T Chapman
NP705 'Y'	F/O	G Barron		MZ632 'W'	F/O	O Lindquist
NP812 'T'	F/O	F Baxter		NR122 'X'	F/O	F Forbes
				MZ586 'Y'	F/O	J Kerr
				MZ861 'Z'	F/O	J Meagher

Flying Officer Baxter landed at Elvington.

Flight Lieutenant Mears returned with flak damage to port wing, tailplane, rudder and with a three feet long hole in the bomb doors.

Flight Lieutenant Chapman's starboard inner engine became uncontrollable and he landed at Manston.

Flight Engineer Ivan Mulley again recalls,
'We were allocated a new Halifax VII - 'Q' which we kept for the remainder of our time with 432 Squadron. The target was Cologne and our operation involved more than 700 aircraft and was the start of a sharp attack on that city. That night Mosquitos of the Light Night Striking Force returned and added to the destruction. The following day Co-

logne was visited by the might of the 8th USAF On the night of the 30/31 October our target was again Cologne and more than 900 aircraft were involved. When we got there smoke was rising in a column far above our bombing height of 21,000 feet. As we turned across the North Sea it was quite usual for all the navigation lights to be switched on.

No orders were or had been given but when the first plane lit up all of the others followed suit! That night when the illuminations began Bud and I looked round - something was not quite right! Then we realised we were showing red wing tip to starboard and green to port instead of the other way around! We were diverted to Syerston due to bad weather in Yorkshire, and at the interrogation the Engineer Officer expressed some disbelief when we reported the fault but it had been corrected without comment when we took the plane out to return to base on the 31st Octobere We did not fly that night but the attack on Cologne continued with a raid by almost 500 planes'.

At 19.00 hours East Moor Flying Control dispatched the station's crash crew and tenders to investigate an aircraft crash to the west of the airfield. This was located on the A19 York - Thirsk road and the wreckage was widely scattered and mostly burnt out. When a 500lb bomb was found in the wreckage the Fire Officer decided to return the tender and crew to East Moor. Apparently the crew had all bailed out and were safe.

Earlier in the day the wedding of Squadron Leader W.E. Boone, East Moor's CTO and Corporal E. Robinson WAAF, had taken place at Clifton Parish Church, York. The event created considerable local interest and numerous officers and other ranks attended the ceremony.

'Footlight Serenade' starring Betty Grable was going the rounds and was shown in the Sergeants Mess and in the Station Hospital.

29 October 1944

No operational commitment but flying training took place with bombing practice on the Strensall Range, plus an unusual amount of air to air firing.

The Hop Grove was the scene for a continued party which had started at East Moor in celebration of the promotion to Group Captain of 415 Squadron's Commanding Officer, L.H. Lecomte. It ran on well into the 30th October.

A meeting was held on the station and a talk was given by Horticulturist Adviser on the relative merit of raising potatoes, ducks and pigs at East Moor.

30 October 1944

A night raid on Cologne was the order and the following forty crews set out from
East Moor with take off commencing at 17.19 hours, all returned safely but todiversionary bases,

432 Squadron			415 Squadron		
NP755 'A'	F/O	W Saye	NA610 'B'	F/L	C Thompson
NP697 'F'	P/O	A Stedman	MZ882 'C'	P/O	S Mooers
NP736 'B'[1]	F/O	J Patterson	LK755 '[1]D'	F/O	W Mitchell
NP759 'C'	F/O	J Mills	MZ603 'E'	F/O	J Britt
NP817 'D'	F/O	C Hemming	NA583 'F'	F/O	W Regimbald
NP708 'E'	F/O	F Jeffrey	MZ949 'G'	F/L	T Mears
NP701 'G'	F/O	D McKinnon	NA608 'H'	F/L	H Barnes
NP803 'I'	F/L	F Horan	NA124 'I'	F/L	J Northrup
NP695 'K'	F/L	C Fyfe	MZ654 'L'	F/O	R Sierolawski
NP704 'L'	F/O	A Gault	LK765 'M'	F/O	H Knobovitch
NP689 'M'	P/O	J Hamilton	LL576 'N'	F/O	S McFadden
NP804 'Q'	F/O	S Dean	MZ946 'O'	F/O	J Kerr
NP802 'S'	F/L	L Kropf	NA607 'R'	F/O	G Gingrich
NP698 'U'	F/O	G Barron	MZ690 'S'	F/O	J Meagher
NP691 'V'	F/O	A Bews	NA6ll 'T'	F/O	J Mcquiston
NP705 'Y'	F/L	J Thompson	NR172 'V'	S/L	J Hovey
NP807 'P'	F/O	G McNicholl	MZ632 'W'	F/O	a Lindquist
NP812 'T'	F/L	W Miller	NR122 'X'	F/L	J Little
NP815 'H'	F/O	F Eilertson	MZ476 'Y'	F/O	D McNeill
			MZ861 'Z'	W/C	F Ball
			NA587 'Q'	F/O	L Deryckere

All 432 Squadron aircraft were diverted to Syerston,

Thirteen of 415 Squadron were diverted to Metheringham and one each to Balderton, Woodbridge, Conningsby and Bradwell Bay while a further two landed at Martlesham Heath.

Flight Lieutenant Mears made an early return with a burst hydraulic line which prevented the raising of the undercarriage.

31 October 1944

The diverted aircraft returned to Tholthorpe as East Moor was closed in.

Group Captain L.H Lecomte was posted on promotion to become Station Commander at RCAF Station Tholthorpe.

Wing Commander F. Ball assumed command of 415 Squadron. No operations were scheduled at East Moor.

General:

The ditch at the Strensall Road end of runway 16 was filled in just in time to save further loss or damage to two aircraft during the month. This was apparently unauthorized but considered to be so essential that a blind eye was turned to the venture.

Other unauthorised work was carried out during October when several brick walls were removed in a Squadron nissen hut to allow more space for the swelling numbers of aircrew.

One of the monthly gas drills went wrong when the wind suddenly changed direction and the Control Tower and staff were threatened.
Sporting activities had reached a new peak during the month and consequently the general morale was good.

Four 500lb bombs were demolished on station and these created 'one hell of a noise'.

The extra three hundred RCAF groundstaff promised and expected during October did not arrive and so the station was still short of cooks, clerks and GD's.

No.4 Living Site was said to be still without running water and other amenities.

Efforts were being made to generally clean up and decorate some of the stations buildings and money from PSI funds was used to pay some airmen to redecorate the NAAFI and the Corporals Club rooms. The Officers are believed to have paid a number of airmen 2/6d per hour to operate a paint spraying machine on the redecoration of their anterooms and gamesrooms.

1 November 1944

The start of the month saw thirty six crews dispatched from the station for a late afternoon flight to Oberhausen,

432 Squadron			415 Squadron		
NP755 'A'	F/O	A Clarke	MZ586 'A'	F/O	J Meagher
NP736 'B'	F/O	D McKinnon	NA610 'B'	F/L	C Thompson
NP759 'C'	F/O	J Mills	MZ882 'C'	F/O	F Forbes
NP817 'D'	F/O	C Hemming	MZ603 'E'	F/O	H Knobovitch
NP708 'E'	F/O	F Jeffrey	NA608 'H'	F/L	H Barnes
NP697 'F'	P/O	A Stedman	NA124 'I'	F/O	P Gingrich
NP701 'G'	F/O	J Patterson	NR156 'K'	F/O	J Mcquiston
NP803 'I'	F/L	F Horan	LL576 'N'	F/L	T Chapman
NP695 'K'	F/L	C Fyfe	MZ946 'O'	P/O	T Donnelly
NP704 'L'	F/O	J Gault	NA612 'P'	F/O	L Deryckere
NP689 'M'	F/O	J Hamilton	MZ690 'S'	P/O	S Mooers
NP797 'O'	F/O	M Krakowski	NA611 'T'	F/O	D McTaggart
NP804 'Q'	F/O	S Dean	NA600 'U'	F/O	J Tims
NP802 'S'	F/L	L Kropf	NR172 'V'	F/O	P Sierolawski
NP698 'U'	F/O	G Barron	MZ632 'W'	F/O	O Lindquist
NP691 'V'	F/O	A Bews	NR122 'X'	F/L	J Little
NP707 'W'	F/O	A Potter	MZ476 'Y'	F/O	J Kerr

| NP705 'Y' | F/L | J Thompson | NA583 'F' | F/O | W Regimbald |

The target was obscured by cloud of the stratus cumulus type but the crews were able to identify it but had arrived ahead of schedule, nevertheless the bombing results appeared to be good.

All returned safely, with Pilot Officer Donnelly being diverted to Woodbridge with a u/s starboard outer engineer The port rudder and elevator of Flying Officer Gingrich's Halifax was damaged over East Moor when the escape hatch was jettisoned. Flying Officer McKinnon returned early with a u/s intercom.

Said to be a successful operation.

2 November 1944

Severe damage was caused when almost 1,000 aircraft attacked Dusseldorf and sadly two of the East Moor contingent failed to return,

432 Squadron			415 Squadron		
NP707 'W'	F/O	A Potter	MZ586 'A'	F/O	J Tims
NP736 'B'	F/L	F Horan	NA6l0 'B'	F/L	C Thompson.
NP759 'C'	F/O	J Mills	MZ882 'C'	F/O	F Forbes
NP708 'E'	F/O	F Jeffrey	LK755 'D'	F/O	W Mitchell
NP697 'F'	P/O	A Stedman	MZ603 'E'	F/O	H Knobovitch
NP70l 'G'	F/O	C Hemming	NA583 'F'	F/O	W Regimbald
NP695 'K'	F/L	C Fyfe	NA608 'H'	F/L	H Barnes
NP704 'L'	F/O	J Gault	NR156 'K'	F/O	J McQuiston
NP807 'P'	F/O	G McNicholl	LL576 'N'	F/L	J Little
NP689 'M'	F/O	J Hamilton	NA612 'P'	F/O	L Deryckere
NP797 'O'	F/O	M Krakowsky	NA607 'R'	F/O	J Kerr
NP804 'Q'	F/O	S Dean	LW552 'S'	P/O	S Mooers
NP802 'S'	F/L	L Kropf	NA6ll 'T'	F/O	D MeTaggart
NP698 'U'	F/O	G Barron	NA600 'U'	F/L	T Mears
NP691 'V'	F/O	A Bews	NR172 'V'	F/O	R Sierolawski
NP705 'Y'	F/O	J Patterson	MZ632 'W'	F/O	O Lindquist
			NR122 'X'	F/L	T Chapman

Flying Officers Knobovitch and Regimbald were lost with their crews. Attacks by German Fighters and heavy flak resulted in many damaged aircraft on this 'op' One such casualty was MZ882, a JU88 inflicted damage to the rear fuselage and turret, fire broke out, the R/T was blown up, and the elevators were u/s. Flying Officer Forbes made the journey home with 20 degrees flap and with the bomb doors open. Sergeant Afford sustained a back injury. Gunner Sergeant Robertson scored some hits on the enemy aircraft. With a flat tailwheel tyre and two crew members holding on to the elevators control a safe landing was made at Woodbridge. Of the missing aircrew, Sergeant Huskilson air gunner in MZ603 was on the last trip of his tour.

415 Squadron were given notice that the regulations in force did not allow them to change its name to 'Bronco' as had been requested.

3 November 1944

Seems to have been quiet day at East Moor. A large number of screened personnel were posted out to the 'R' depot and proceedures for a forthcoming Courts Martial on the station were being considered.

Several skippers from the Dusseldorf operation complained that searchlights had been extremely troublesome over France and Belgium.

4 November 1944

The Station Commander continued to work his way through a back log of aircrew

Commissioning interviews at the rate of six per day.

A successful attack was carried out on Bochum by almost seven hundred and fifty aircraft and the following formed the East Moor contribution to it,

432 Squadron				415 Squadron		
NP755 'A'	F/O	A Clarke		NA610 'B'	F/L	C Thompson
NP759 'C'	F/O	F Eilertson		LK755 'D'	F/O	W Mitchell
NP817 'D'	F/L	E Hayes		MZ907 'F'	F/L	T Chapman
NP697 'F'	P/O	A Stedman		MZ949 'G'	F/L	T Mears
NP802 'S'	F/L	L Kropf		NA608 'H'	F/O	D Stewart
NP804 'Q'	F/O	S Dean		NA124 'I'	F/O	J McQuiston
NP807 'P'	F/O	G McNicholl		MZ947 'K'	F/L	W Brown
NP701 'G'	F/O	J Hamilton		LL576 'N'	P/O	T Donnelly
NP695 'K'	F/L	C Fyfe		NA612 'P'	F/O	L Deryckere
NP797 'O'	F/O	M Krakowsky		NA607 'R'	F/L	J Little
NP705 'Y'	F/O	C Hemming		NA611 'T'	F/O	D McTaggart
NP707 'W'	F/O	A Potter		NA600 'U'	F/O	J Tims
NP698 'U'	F/O	G Barron		NR172 'V'	F/O	R Sierolawski
NP691 'V'	F/L	W Miller		MZ632 'W'	F/O	O Lindquist
NP708 'E'	F/O	J Gault		MZ476 'Y'	F/O	J Kerr
NP736 'B'	F/L	J Sales		MZ861 'Z'	P/O	S Mooers

Sergeant W. Border the flight engineer in Flying Officer Gault's crew was killed by flak and the aircraft landed at Woodbridge.

A fuel shortage led to Flight Lieutenant Sales being diverted to RCAF Station Dalton. The remaining crews were all safely down by 23.20 hours

5 November 1944

No operations were scheduled at East Moor on a day of high winds and heavy rain.

415 Squadron again won the No.62 Base Pennant for efficiency.

6 November 1944

Around mid day thirty six crews left East Moor for the 'Rhur' where the target was Gelsenkirchen and all but one returned safely,

432 Squadron				415 Squadron		
NP755 'A'	W/C	J MacDonald		NA610 'B'	F/L	C Thompson
NP736 'B'	F/O	D Frost		MZ922 'C'	F/O	J Tims
NP759 'C'	F/O	J Mills		MZ416 'E'	F/L	J Little
NP817 'D'	S/L	G Larson		MZ907 'F'	F/L	A Winmill
NP697 'F'	P/O	A Stedman		MZ949 'G'	F/L	T Mears
NP701 'G'	F/O	G Stunden		NA608 'H'	F/L	H Barnes
NP803 'I'	F/L	J Sales		NA124 'I'	F/L	J McAllister
NP695 'K'	F/L	C Fyfe		MZ947 'K'	F/L	W Brown
NP815 'H'	F/O	F Eilertson		LL576 'N'	F/O	T Donnelly
NP704 'L'	F/L	E Hayes		NA607 'R'	F/O	W Mitchell
NP689 'M'	F/O	A Craig		NA611 'T'	F/O	D McTaggart
NP797 'O'	F/O	M Krakowsky		NR172 'V'	F/O	R Sierolawski
NP807 'P'	F/O	G McNicholl		MZ632 'W'	F/O	O Lindquist
NP804 'Q'	F/O	S Dean		NR122 'X'	F/O	L Deryckere
NP694 'R'	F/O	C Hemming		MZ476 'Y'	F/O	J McQuiston
NP802 'S'	F/L	L Kropf		MZ861 'Z'	P/O	S Mooers
NP812 'T'	F/O	J Hamilton				
NP698 'U'	F/O	G Barron				
NP691 'V'	F/O	A Bews				
NP707 'W'	F/O	A Potter				

Flying Officer Eilertson and crew failed to return, the air gunners Flight Sergeants N. Stuttle and T. McAron were killed and the remainder became POW's. Flying Officer Hamilton returned early with the starboard inner engine u/s, and Flight Lieutenant's Sales and Hayes with a u/s port inner and starboard inner respectively. Flying Officer Stunden's mount received flak damage to ailerons, port inner engine, bomb doors and tyres.

Flying Officer McNicholl put down at Syerston short of fuel.

7 November 1944

No operational duties were carried out at East Moor.Due to staff shortages both resident squadrons were experiencing some difficulty in keeping up with the administration duties and the masses of paperwork continued to pile up.

8 November 1944

Operation called for but subsequently scrubbed. Flying Training carried out and a successful party was held in 432 Sqd Intelligence Section.

9 November 1944

No operations were carried out. The weather at East Moor during this period was wet and high winds prevailed. The station had so many 'screened' personnel that for discipline and adminstration purposes it was decided to form a special section with its own Commanding Officer.

10 November 1944

Another operation' free day on the station. Newly arrived crews were engaged in lectures and link trainer exercises. Information was received at East Moor that Flying Officer Lauzon, lost on the June operation to Cambrai, was now a POW and that he had taken a great personal risk in saving the life of one of his gunners when the aircraft was hit by flak. The CO recommended him for an immediate awarde

11 November 1944

The station's WAAF's collected £38 in their Armistice Day poppy sales.

In the evening a large number of visitors were included in a successful but overcrowded dance held in the Officers Mess.

12 November 1944

Still no operations from East Moor. Guests from Strensall, Crayke and York joined station WAAF's in a Sergeants Mess dance which was described as a violent social enterprise and a roaring success.

13 November 1944

The seventh consecutive day without any operational commitments at East Moor. Both squadrons were engaged in heavy training programmes throughout this period. The pilot of 415 Squadron Halifax 6U-Q was heard on 'Darky' and said he was alone in the aircraft as the crew had bailed out. The airfield lights were turned on but to no avail and at 20.40 hours he telephoned from RAF Station Burn where he had safely landed, An hour later it was learned that the bomb aimer, WOP and flight -engineer were safe at Hebden.

14 November 1944

Air Vice Marshal McKewan, Air Officer Commanding No.6 Group presented the Handley Page Trophy to 432 Squadron at an East Moor ceremony. It was for the month of October and reflected the lowest accident rate held by any unit for each month.

The AOC went on to praise the ground staff for their part in maintaining the high state of aircraft serviceability.

Around mid-day a message was received to say that the the the air gunners from 415 Squadron's NA587 were safe at Grassington and the navigator was likewise at Pately Bridge all had bailed out and were suffering from exposure.

16 November 1944

Excellent results were obtained when the town of Julich was virtually destroyed in support of the Allied armies. The following East Moor crews all returned safely from an early afternoon attack,

432 Squadron			415 Squadron		
NP736 'B'	F/O	D Frost	MZ586 'A'	F/L	A Winmill
NP759 'C'	F/O	'J Mills	MZ922 'C'	F/O	J Britt
NP817 'D'	F/O	G Stunden	MZ416 'E'	F/L	C Thompson
NP708 'E'	F/O	F Jeffrey	MZ949 'G'	F/O	S McFadden
NP697 'F'	P/O	A Stedman	NA124 'I'	F/L	J Northrup
NP803 'I'	F/O	A Craig	MZ947 'K'	F/L	J McAllister
NP695 'K'	F/O	M Krakowsky	MZ483 'M'	F/O	D McTaggart
NP797 'N'	P/O	G Sherlock	NA607 'R'	P/O	T Donnelly
NP804 'Q'	F/O	J Hamilton	NA612 'P'	F/O	L Deryckere
NP694 'R'	P/O	L McGuire	LW552 'S'	S/L	J Hovey
NP802 'S'	F/O	J Patterson	NR172 'V'	P/O	W Lane
NP698 'U'	F/O	G Barron	MZ632 'W'	F/L	H Barnes
NP691 'V'	F/O	C Hemming	NR122 'X'	F/L	J Little
NP707 'W'	W/C	J MacDonald	MZ861 'Z'	P/O	S Mooers
NP721 'X'	F/O	G Spiers			

Pilot Officer Sherlock made an early return with hydraulic failure.

Flight Lieutenant Little's starboard inner engine failed and with it the Gee and consequently was unable to bomb.

Several aircraft returned with flak damage.

17 November 1944

A planned operation was cancelled during the briefing. The crews went back to bed. A rainy day was spent by many in the lecture rooms and link trainer etc.

Wing Commander J.G Stevenson was posted in to join 432 Squadron. The station Fire crew extinguished a fire in Goose Lane and became bogged down.

18 November 1944

Twenty eight crews were dispatched from East Moor just after mid day in clear weather after a rainy morning. All returned safely but were diverted as the weather closed in on the station . The target was Munster and the operation was regarded as satisfactory,

432 Squadron			415 Squadron		
NP694 'R'	F/O	L McGuire	MZ-586 'A'	F/L	C Thompson
NP736 'B'	F/O	D Frost	MZ922 'C'	F/O	J Britt
NP803 'I'	F/L	F Horan	MZ907 'F'	F/L	A Winmill
NP755 'A'	F/O	A Clarke	MZ949 'G'	F/O	S McFadden
NP759 'C'	F/O	J Mills	NA124 'I'	F/L	J Northrup
NP708 'E'	F/O	F Jeffrey	MZ947 'K'	F/L	J McAllister
NP697 'F'	P/O	A Stedman	MZ483 'M'	S/L	J Hovey

NP805 'J'	P/O	G Sherlock	NA612 'P'	F/O	L Deryckere
NP807 'P'	P/O	J Hamilton	NA607 'R'	F/O	T Donnelly
NP804 'Q'	F/O	S Dean	NA611 'T'	F/O	D McTaggart
NP707 'W'	S/L	R Jack	NR172 'V'	P/O	W Lane
NP802 'S'	F/O	C Hemming -	MZ632 'W'	F/L	H Barnes
NP721 'X'	F/O	F Baxter	MZ476 'Y'	F/O	J McQuiston
NP698 'U'	F/O	G Barron	MZ861 'Z'	P/O	S Mooers

Flying Officer Dean returned early with u/s hydraulics and landed at East Moor, just five minutes behind Flight Lieutenant McFadden who had the same problem. Aircraft 'U', 'B', 'I', 'R','A', 'E', 'P', 'W', 'S' and 'X' of *432* Squadron were diverted to RCAF Station Croft, and 'C', 'F' an'J' to RCAF Leeming.

Of the 415 Squadron aircraft, 'I','K','T','W' and 'Z' landed at RCAF Dishforth, 'A','C','M' and 'P' at Crosby, 'F' at Leeming, 'R' at Great Horton, 'V' at Croft and 'Y' at Boreham.

NP736 and NP755 collided at Croft at approximately 18.30 hours resulting in the former being scrapped.

19 November 1944

Most of the diverted aircraft returned to East Moor on what was a rainy day with the emhasis on ground training at East Moor.

432 Squadron commenced briefing eight crews for an operation which was suddenly cancelled.

20 November 1944

No operations at East Moor where it rained all day. A programme of ground training was followed emphasising the latest 'gen' on the H25 equipment. Wing Commander A. Lowe visited East Moor arriving by Airspeed Oxford.

21 November 1944

The oil refineries at Castrop Rauxel were the target for the following East Moor crews. Take off for the Rhur commenced at 15.22 hours and all were down again by -23.00 hours landing at Wombleton with the exception of Flying Officer Clarke -who landed at East Moor(as did the early returns) along- with Flying Officer Dean and Pilot Officer Sherlock.

432 Squadron			415 Squadron		
NP817 'D'	F/O	J Mills	MZ586 'A'	F/O	J Britt
NP708 'E'	F/O	D Frost	NA610 'B'	F/O	W Mitchell
NP70l 'G	F/O	A Clarke	MZ416 'E'	F/O	E Falconer
NP703 'H'	F/L	E Hayes	MZ907 'F'	F/L	A Winmill
NP803 'I'	F/L	F Horan	MZ949 'G'	F/L	T Mears
NP805 'J'	P/O	G Sherlock	NA124 'I'	F/L	J Northrup
NP695 'R'	F/L	C Fyfe	MZ947 'K'	F/L	J McAllister
NP689 'M'	F/L	W Miller	MZ483 'M'	W/C	F Ball
NP797 'N'	F/O	M Krakowsky	NA202 'N'	F/O	S McFadden
NP807 'P'	F/O	G MeNicholl	MZ946 '0'	F/O	D McNeill
NP804 'Q'	F/O	S Dean	LK766 'Q'	P/O	W Lane
NP694 'R'	P/O	L McGuire	LW552 'S'	F/O	J Tims
NP705 'Y'	F/L	J Thompson	NA611 'T'	F/O	D McTaggart
NP774 'Z'	F/O	C Hemming	NA600 'U'	F/O	R Sierolawski
			MZ632 'W'	F/O	O Lindquist
			NR122 'X'	F/O	D Stewart

The two early returns were Flight Lieutenant Horan and Flying Officer McNicholl with a u/s starboard inner engine and blind flying panel respectively. MelO9's attacked Flying Officer Britt's and Sierolaweki's aircraft, both mid upper gunners scored hits on the enemy and the former claimed a probable. Pilot Officer Lane's crew were attacked by an FW190 and return fire from his mid upper gunner scored hits.

22 to 26 November 1944

These five days were free from- operational commitments for the East Moor crews but there was very little let up in their training programmes with fighter affiliation, bombing practice, air to air firing and H25 F/Ouring prominantly. The diverted aircraft began arriving back at East Moor in the afternoon on the 22nd. Operations were called for on that day but were later scrubbed. Flight Lieutenant Kennedy, adjutant of 432 Squadron was admitted to hospital,and 415 Squadron forwarded a dozen applications for non immediate awards of the DFC and the DFM for consideration by the powers that were.On the 26th a sudden change in the weather forced East Moor crews to land at Middleton St.George.

27 November 1944

Flight Lieutenant Duncanson the Flight Engineer Leader on 432 Squadron was posted to RCAF Station Wombleton. A popular and capable Leader and usually flew in the Squadron Commander's crew had completed his tour.

Neuss-, an industrial town on the edge of the Rhur was the target for the East Moor crews all of whom returned safely and regarded the operation as a success.

432 Squadron			415 Squadron		
NP759 'C'	F/O	J Mills	NA6l0 'B'	F/O	J Britt
NP817 'D'	S/L	G Larson	NA181 'D'	F/O	W Mitchell
NP701 'G'	F/O	E McGuire	MZ416 'E'	F/O	E Falconer
NP703 'H'	F/O	D Frost	MZ907 'F'	W/C	F Ball
NP803 'I'	F/L	J Wallace	MZ949 'G'	F/L	T Mears
NP805 'J'	F/L	L Kropf	NR156 'H'	F/O	A Cruickshank
NP695 'K'	F/L	C Fyfe	NA124 'I'	F/O	C Chartier
NP704 'L'	F/O	A Clarke	MZ947 'K'	F/O	J McGuire
NP807 'P'	F/O	G McNicholl	MZ456 'L'	F/O	S McFadden
NP804 'Q'	F/O	C Hemming	LL576 'N'	F/O	J Tims
NP694 'R'	P/O	L McGuire	MZ946 '0'	F/O	D McNeill
NP812 'T'	F/O	M Krakowsky	NA612 'P'	F/O	D Stewart
NP698 'U'	F/O	G Barron	LK766 'Q'	P/O	W Lane
NP705 'Y'	F/L	J Thompson	NA607 'R'	F/O	T Donnelly
NP797 'N'	F/L	W Miller	LW552 'S'	F/O	O Lindquist
NP689 'M'	F/L	E Hayes	NA611 'T'	F/O	D McTaggart
NP774 'Z'	F/O	F Baxter	NR172 'V'	F/O	L Beicher

During their absence the weather closed in on East Moor and consequently all but one were diverted as follows, air-craft 'C','Q' and 'R' of 432 Squadron landed at Bourn, 'H' at Attlebridge and the remainder at Horsham ST. Faith. Flying Officer Peaker flew as second pilot to Flying Officer Jeffrey. Aircraft 'B', 'D' , 'F', 'I', 'O', 'P', 'R' , 'T' and 'V' of 415 Squadron landed at Attlebridge, 'E','H' and 'L' at Horsham St.Faith, 'K' and 'N' at Rackheath 'Q' to to Downham Market, 'S' to Wenleng and 'G' not hearing of the diversion made it into East Moor.

28 November 1944

Squadron Leader Larson the 'A' Flight Commander with 432 Squadron was screened along with his crew.

The diverted aircraft began arriving back on station in heavy rain.

The East Moor Station's newspaper ran a contest to find an original name, and several humourous ones were entered, ie; 'Bull Sheet' and 'Eat More Weekly', but the winning entry came from the Dental Officer, Captain 'Doc' Bigelow who had submitted 'Plane Facts'. Hundreds of suggestions were put forward.

The Station Cinema was usually showing a twice nightly film at 18.00 and 19.45hours where the current prices of admission were

Erks	threepence.	These prices were fixed by the Air Ministry
NCO's	sixpence	and were not subject to entertainment tax.
Officers	one shilling	

29 November 1944

And a drama over the airfield at East Moor. 432 Squadron were engaged in a programme of flying training exercises when Flying Officer F. Clarke's Halifax was discovered to have a defective aileron. While flying back and forth across the airfied at 2,000 feet he ordered four members of his crew to bail out. A large audience gathered to watch what was for- all of them, a new experience. First out was, Flight Sergeant W. Bullock WOP, followed by Flying Officer Hendrick bomb aimer, and the two gunners Flight Sergeants D. Hopkins and A₀ De Salvo. The pilot settled the aircraft down so well that the navigator didn't realize that they had landed.

The remaining aircraft diverted from the Neuss operation arrived back at East Moor.

30 November 1944

Thirty six Halifaxes left East Moor's runway commencing at 16.33 hours for an attack by more than 570 aircraft on Duisburg. The East Moor crews returned safely with the last one down a few minutes before midnight,

432 Squadron			415 Squadron		
NP755 'A'	W/C	J MacDonald	MZ586 'A'	F/O	C Chartier
NP812 'T' -	F/O	F Baxter	MZ922 'C'	F/O	T Donnelly
NP759 'C'	F/O	D Frost	NA610 'B'	F/O	J Britt
NP817 'D'	W/C	J Stephenson	NA181 'D'	F/O	W Mitchell
NP697 'F'	F/L	C Fyfe	MZ949 'G'	F/L	T Mears
NP701 'G'	F/O	E McGuire	NR156 'H'	P/O	A Cruickshanks
NP703 'H'	F/L	J Sales	NA124 'I'	F/L	J Northrup
NP803 'I'	F/L	F Horan	NR249 'J'	F/O	G Grier
NP805 'J'	F/O	J Hamilton	MZ483 'M'	F/L	A Winmill
NP689 'M'	F/O	F Jeffrey	MZ946 'O'	F/O	J McGuire
NP699 'O'	F/L	L Kropf	LW552 'S'	F/O	D Stewart
NP807 'P'	F/O	G Spiers	NA611 'T'	F/O	D McTaggart
NP802 'S'	F/O	G McNicholl	NA600 'U'	F/O	J Tims
NP698 'U'	F/O	A Potter	NR172 'V'	F/O	R Sierolawski
NP691 'V'	F/O	A Bews	MZ632 'W'	F/O	O Lindquist
NP721 'X'	P/O	L McGuire	NR122 'X'	F/O	E Milibank
NP705 'Y'	F/L	W Miller	MZ476 'Y'	F/O	L Beicher
NP774 'Z'	F/L	J Wallace	MZ861 'Z'	F/O	S Mooers

Flying Officer Potter made an early return with a u/s starboard inner engine. While still over East Moor, Pilot Officer Chartier's starboard inner engine throttle linkage became u/s followed shortly by failure of both port engine generators. As he continued with the flight the DR Compass failed along with the ASI, H2S and both gun turrets. Nevertheless the target was reached and attacked.

Pilot Officer Cruickshanks and crew had a lucky escape just after releasing their bombs when another Halifax flew across their course and at right angles to it.A swerve and steep climb followed.

The general morale was said to be high and both squadrons felt that they were getting on with the job and providing higher authority with satisfaction in the process

1 December 1944

Squadron Leader S. Minhinnick arrived from 408 Squadron at Linton on Ouse to assume duties of 'A' Flight Commander, 432 Squadron.

It was learnt at East Moor that,Flying Officer McCoy who had bailed out of LW592 over enemy territory on 27/28 April 1944, and who had safely returned to this country was to be recommended for the award of the Military Cross for his gallant action against the Germans.

There was no operational or flying training carried out from East Moor, but a full programme of ground lectures and H2S procedures were held.

2 December 1944

East Moor chalked up their first win in the Inter Station Basket Ball League when they defeated No.6 Group by 19 to 12 in the York Railway Institute Gym. The newly decorated Airmen's Mess was by this time complete with many outstanding murals expertly done by LAC Bill Creelman, an American from Boston. Previously in the American Army he switched to the RCAF in June 1943 hoping to become aircrew. Just failing to make the grade he was posted to East Moor as a GD. When it was discovered that he was a former artist he was given the task of painting the numbers on the station's cycles and MT vehicles. Finally came the need for some one to paint the murals, each of which took Bill around fifteen hours to complete, and were said to be a credit to him and to the station.

The station was still bemoaning a shortage of bicycles but were told quite firmly that it had enough and many more than some other stations. It was sad to relate that two were stolen from the station Padres premises.

A collection on the station realised £10 sterling towards the Christmas fund for the RAF Hospital at Northallerton and was gratefully received. Christmas parties were being planned for two groups of youngsters and to this end collection points were set up on th& station for toys, chocolate and chewing gum etc. The station staff made many of the toys.

It was announced that the RCAF No.1 show 'The Blackouts' would be making a second visit to East Moor this week, and would remain for four days.

Extensive damage was caused at Hagen when over 500 aircraft attacked, and the following East Moor crews formed a part of it, before returning safely with the exception of one diverted to an airfield near Antwerp,

432 Squadron			415 Squadron		
NP701 'G'	F/O	G Sherlock	NA185 'A'	F/O	C Chartier
NP697 'F'	F/O	G Spiers	NA610 'B'	F/O	J McGuire
NP759 'C'	F/O	E McGuire	NA181 'D'	F/O	W Mitchall
NP705 'Y'	F/O	F Baxter	MZ907 'F'	W/C	F Ball
NP708 'E'	F/O	F Jeffrey	MZ940 'G'	F/O	G Grier
NP817 'D'	F/O	D Frost	NR156 'H'	F/O	A Cruickshank
NP797 'N'	F/O	J Patterson	NR249 'J'	F/O	E Milibank
NP704 'L'	F/L	E Hayes	NR253 'L'	F/O	S McFadden
NP695 'K'	F/O	L Loppe	MZ632 'W'	F/O	D McNeill
NP804 'Q'	F/L	W Miller	LK766 'Q'	F/O	D Stewart
NP689 'U'	F/O	G McNicholl	NA611 'T'	Flo	D McTaggart
NP691 'V'	F/O	A Bews	MZ946 'O'	F/O	J Tims
NP707 'W'	F/L	J Wallace	NR172 'V'	F/O	R Sierolawski
NP703 'H'	F/L	J Sales	NR122 'X'	F/L	J McAllister
NP694 'R'	F/O	L McGuire	MZ861 'Z'	F/O	L Beicher
NP803 'I'	F/L	F Horan	LW552 'S'	F/O	T Donnelly

Flying Officer K. Lunny the navigator in NP803 was injured by flak.
Flying Officer J. McGuire landed NA61O at Downham Market, with engine failure and fuel shortage.
Flying Officer McTaggart came home on three engines, starboard outer feathered.
It was found necessary to land NP803 at Antwerp after jettisoning the bombs over Germany with the injured crewman, flak damage and fuel shortage.

3 December 1944

Operations scheduled but later scrubbed, on an otherwise quiet but cold day.

4 December 1944

A satisfactory night raid on Karlsrhue was made by the following East Moor crews, when happily all returned safely once again,

432 Squadron			415 Squadron		
NP755 'A'	F/O	F Baxter	NA185 'A'	F/O	C Chartier
NP759 'C'	F/O	E McGuire	NA181 'D'	F/O	w Mitchell
NP708 'E	F/O	F Jeffrey	MZ907 'F'	F/O	L Belcher

Fig 34. During an operational take off, Halifax NP721 swung off the runway, struck 432 Squadron's 'B' Flight shack (top) before crashing into trees and burning. The two Hercules engines were hurled several hundred yards when part of the bomb load exploded. Fortunately the crew escaped. Photos R.Day.
5Th December 1944.

NP697 'F'	F/O	G Peaker		MZ949 'G'	F/O	J Britt
	F/L	J Sales		NR156 'H'	F/O	A Cruickshank
NP695 'K'	F/O	L Loppe		NA124 'I'	F/L	J Northrup
NP704 'L'	F/L	E Hayes		NR249 'J'	F/O	E Milibank
NP689 'M'	F/O	J Pattarson		MZ947 'K'	F/O	D McNeill
NP797 'N'	F/L	J Wallace		NR253 'L'	F/O	S McFadden
NP699 'O'	PlO	G Sherlock		MZ483 'M'	F/L	J McAllister
NP807 'P	F/O	G McNicholl		MZ456 'P'	F/O	J McQuiston
NP804 'Q'	F/L	W Miller		LW552 'S'	F/O	T Donnelly
NP802 'S'	F/O	J Hamilton		NA186 'U'	F/O	J Tims
NP698 'U'	PlO	E Patzer		NR122 'X'	F/O	D Stewart
NP691 'V'	F/L	L Kropf		MZ861 'Z'	F/L	C Thompson
NP705 'Y'	F/L	J Thompson				

Flying Officer Stewart landed at Woodbridge with hydraulic failure, as did Flying Officer Cruickshank.

5 December 1944

Soest was the chosen target for the East Moor crews. NP721 of 432 Squadron swung on take of f, before catching fire and exploding thus rendering the airfield unserviceable and five aircraft were unable to take off.   Happily the crew escaped as the tannoy warned all and sundry to get at least one mile away from the scene, which they did just before the huge explosion which showered parts of the Halifax all over the field. Those that did get away were:

432 Squadron				415 Squadron		
NP759 'C'	F/O	G Peaker		NA181 'D'	F/O	W Mitchell
NP755 'A'	F/O	W Clarke		MZ907 'F'	F/L	C Thompson
NP817 'D'	W/C	J Stephenson		MZ949 'G'	F/L	T Mears
NP697 'F'	F/O	L Loppe		NA124 'I'	F/L	G Northrup
NP805 'J'	F/L	J Sales		NA249 'J'	F/O	E Milibank
NP695 'K'	F/O	D Frost		MZ947 'K'	F/O	D McNeill
NP704 'L'	F/L	F Horan		NR253 'L'	F/O	S McFadden
NP691 'V'	F/L	L Kropf		MZ483 'M'	F/L	W Brown
NP707 'W'	F/O	G Spiers		NA612 'P'	F/O	L Beicher
				LK766 'Q'	P/O	W Lane
				PN174 'R'	F/O	T Donnelly
				NA186 'U'	F/O	J Tims
				LW552 'S'	F/O	J McGuire
				MZ476 'Y'	F/O	J McQuiston
				NA185 'A'	F/O	C Chartier

The above were 'up' before 18.06 hours when the unfortunate Flying Officer Baxter crashed.
Flying Officer Peaker returned early with hydraulic failure.
'G',-'S', 'M', 'E' and 'Z' of 432 Squadron were unable to take off.
Flying Officer Chartier and crew experienced a 'hairy do' when they collided with another Halifax, tearing away the top section of the fuselage and the astro dome and shattering the instrument panel.
Pilot Officer Lane returned after being airborne around three and a half hours with an uncontrolable port outer engine and a defective port inner having endeavoured to reach the target. Short of fuel he landed at Hardwick after he had ordered the jettisoning of the bombs.

The following Christmas message was received from the Base Commander, Air Commodore J.L Hurley,

'As we come to the close of another year, and particularly during the Christmas season, many of you are thinking of your families and friends at home. We can look forward, I believe, to the coming year in the knowledge that we have travelled a long way during 1944 and are definately out of the trees and coming- down the home stretch.

This has been possible by the splendid co-operation of all arms, and you men and women of East Moor may well be proud of your contribution to this effort.

Keep up the drive you have shown in 1944 and I am sure that the sincere greetings and wishes for the future that I extend to you at this time will be realized in the coming year'.

The East Moor Station Commander, Group Captain R.A McLernon DFC issued the the following message,
'Merry Christmas to all personnel of East Moor! Although the vast majority of you are far away from your loved

ones and your homes, I do hope that your Christmas here at East Moor will be a really happy one! An especially Merry Christmas to the WAAF's on our station. Some of us are too apt to forget, and take all together too casually, the splendid work our girls are doing on this station. They have undertaken cheerfully the most arduous tasks and have been subjected to hardships and living conditions the like of which, prior to this war, have been unknown to the gentler sex. May I therefore, express the gratitude and admiration of the whole station for their gallant efforts. So have a good time, everyone, and may each one of you spend next Christmas at your homes'.

432 Squadron Commander Wing Commander J.K MacDonald DFC, 415 Squadron Commander Wing Commander F.W Ball and East Moor's Chief Technical Officer Squadron Leader W.E.R Boone issued appropiate Christmas messages to their respective sections. Station East Moor was assured of a bang on Christmas with lots of fun and well organised parties, dances and other entertainments.

Flight Sergeant Fran Dowie of Vancouver headed the list of 30 performers that would make up the show by 'The Blackouts', the first entertainment group to be formed within the RCAF.

6 December 1944

Twenty nine crews lifted their Halifaxes from East Moor's runway on a night raid to Osnabruck. The first one was 'up' at 16.06 and they were all down again by 22.53 hours except for one 432 Squadron crew,

432 Squadron			415 Squadron		
NP755 'A'	F/O	L Loppe	MZ922 'C'	P/O	D McTaggart
NP708 'E'	F/O	F Jeffrey	NA181 'D'	F/O	W Mitchell
NP707 'w'	F/O	G McNicholl	MZ416 'E'	F/L	T Mears
NP691 'V'	F/O	D Frost	MZ907 'F'	F/L	C Thompson
NP812 'T'	F/L	J Wallace	NR156 'H'	F/O	A Cruickshank
NP802 'S'	F/O	J Hamilton	NR249 'J'	F/O	E Milibank
NP797 'N'	F/O	A Bews	MZ947 'K'	F/L	J Northrup
NP689 'M'	F/O	J Patterson	NR253 'L'	F/O	S McFadden
NP704 'L'	F/O	L McGuire	MZ483 'M'	F/L	J McAllister
NP695 'K'	F/O	G Spiers	MZ946 'O'	F/O	D McNeill
NP805 'J'	P/O	G Sherlock	MZ456 'P'	F/O	T Donnelly
N P697 'F'	F/O	E Mc.Guire	PN174 'R'	F/O	L Beicher
NP774 'Z'	F/O	E Patzer	LW552 'S'	F/O	J McGuire
NP804 'Q'	F/L	W Miller	NA186 'U'	F/O	D Stewart
			MZ476 'Y'	F/O	J Mc-Quiston

Flying Officer Spiers and crew failed to return. Their Halifax was abandoned after the port outer prop came off, damaging the port inner engine and making a huge hole in the fuselage. All the navigational equipment was rendered u/s and height could not be maintained. The skipper and his mid upper gunner paid the ultimate price, the remainder of the crew became POW's.

Flight lieutenant Northrup landed without any brakes at Carnaby, Flying Officer Patzer at Woodbridge and Flight Lieutenant Miller at North Creake Flying Officer Jeffrey's Halifax sustained flak damage to port tailpiane and rear turret. Early returns were made by NR253 and MZ483 with hydraulic failures and NR249 was too late away to be able to make up the time.

7 December 1944

On a day of poor weather conditions there was no flying recorded at East Moor, and the Orderly Rooms were getting further bogged down with the paperwork due to postings 'out' without any replacements.

8 December 1944

An improvement in the weather during the early part of the day saw a number of cross country and air to air firing exercises carried out.

A station dance was held in the usual Eastmoor spirit in the evening.

9 December 1944

Wing Commander MacDonald was awarded an immediate DF'C. No flying was recorded due to inclement weather but indoor training continued.

A large shipment of cigarettes was received from the Agent General of British Columbia and were shared by all sections of the station.

The station cinema was showing 'Happy Landing' with Don Ameche and Frances Dee. The new bar in the Officers Mess was well patronized in the evening.

10 December 1944

Sunday,and a further day of atrocious weather prevented any flying at East Moor.

Lectures on 'Rehabilitation' were given and well received by all, the speaker was Flight Lieutenant R.W Scott 415 Squadron Education Officer.

At 19.00 hours the 'WAAF Night' in the gymnasium commenced and included inter hut Net Ball and Roller Skating competitions.

11 December 1944

No operations were scheduled at East Moor but a full programme of air and ground training proceeded.

The Station Commander was having a busy period interviewing personnel for Commissions.

A changeof programme at the station cinema with John Wayne and Jean Arthur in 'Lady takes a Chance'. Flying Officer P.M McLintock (432 Sqd) died at the RAF Hospital - Rauceby the results of an illness.

12 December 1944

Still no operational commitments for the station. 432 Squadron put up ten aircraft for a Command formation flight which was said to be very satisfactory.

Aircrews were still confined to camp as operations were expected.

A lost Halifax was recovered by East Moor control at 17.42 after an SOS was heard.

13 December 1944

Operations were called for but then cancelled at the last moment, when crews were already in the aircraft.It was decided that with such a large number of screened personnel on the station a daily parade at 09.30 hours would be followed by useful activities in an effort to keep them occupied during the daytime. Site duties and lectures were included.

14 December 1944

No flying . It was decided that a joint effort between 432 and 415 Squadron's would be made to stage a three childrens parties for Orphans in York Institutes, and the stations groundstaff would manufacture toys in the various station sections. A Christmas party committee was set up for the purpose and included the Station Admin Officer Squadron Leader R.H Perry, YMCA manager Mr. J McLelland, Flight Lieut. R.W Scott Education Officer and Flight Lieutwnant A.B Carveth the 415 Sqd Adjutant. The latter officer was appointed Father Christmas.

Flying Officer P.M McLintock the 432 Squadron bomb aimer was interred at the Stonefall Cemetery, Harrogate at 10.00 hours.

15 December 1944

Wing Commander Davenport was posted in to 432 Squadron, bringing the total of flying 'Winco's' to three. The RCAF roadshow 'The Blackouts' commenced a four day visit to East Moor appearing at the station's 'Little Theatre'.

Heavy rain and high winds precluded the flying training programme.

16 December 1944

Another day without any operational commitment but some flying training was carried out. Screened personnel were busily employed cleaning windows and buildings, repairing stoves etc.

Bob Hope and Shirley Ross appeared in 'Thanks For The Memory' at the station cinema.

At 21.00 hours a West Raynham based Mosquito became lost in the area and was safely landed at East Moor.

17 December 1944

The eleventh consecutive day without any operational call for East Moor's crews. The station still left much to be desired by way of facilities, with overcrowding in the accommodation blocks and a shortage of water for baths and ablutions, all of which gave rise to feelings which were brought to the attention of the Station Commander on his inspection.

18 December 1944

At 02.14 hours, the first of thirty nine Halifaxes left East Moor's runway and joined a total force of more than five hundred aircraft in an operation against Duisburg. The crew skippered by Flight Lieut J Northrup experienced a 'very close call'. Having left the airfield at 02.26 hours, they were at a height of around 19,000 feet when the skipper blacked out. He came to after a rapid descent to find the Halifax in a spin and was down to around 1,000 feet before control was regained With the crew struggling to stay awake at debriefing the MO was called to find that they were suffering from anoxia. It was revealed that their oxygen bottles had been filled with compressed air.

432 Squadron			415 Squadron		
NP755 'A'	F/O	A Clarke	MZ922 'C'	F/L	T Thompson
NP759 'C'	F/O	J Mills	NA181 'D'	F/O	W Mitchell
NP817 'D'	F/O	L Loppe	MZ416 'E'	F/O	D Falconer
NP708 'E'	F/O	F Jeffrey	MZ907 'F'	F/L	A Winmill
NP697 'F'	P/O	A Stedman	NR156 'H'	F/O	A Cruickehank
NP803 'I'	F/O	G Peaker	NA124 'I'	F/L	J Northrup
NP805 'J'	F/O	G Sherlock	NR249 'J'	F/O	C Chartier
NP693 'K'	F/O	J Hamilton	MZ947 'K'	F/O	G Grier
NP689 'M'	F/O	J Patterson	NR253 'L'	F/O	S McFadden
NP797 'N'	F/O	C Hemming	MZ483 'M'	F/L	T Mears
NP807 'P'	F/O	G McNicholl	MZ946 'O'	W/O	J McKenzie
NP804 'Q'	F/L	W Miller	MZ456 'P'	F/O	W Goodwin
NP694 'R'	F/L	L Kropf	PN174 'R'	P/O	W Lane
NP812 'T'	F/O	F Baxter	NA611 'T'	F/O	J Britt
NP698 'U'	F/O	G Barron	NA186 'U'	F/O	J Tims
NP691 'V'	F/O	A Bews	NR172 'V'	F/O	J McQuiston
NP707 'W'	F/O	A Potter	MZ632 'W'	F/O	O Lindquist
NP705 'Y'	F/L	E Hayes	MZ861 'Z'	F/O	S Mooers
NP774 'Z'	F/O	E Patzer			

| NP699 'O' | F/O | N Krakowsky |
| NP70l 'G' | F/O | D McKinnon |

Flying Officer Krakowsky was the only survivor from his crew and managed to evade capture returning to East Moor in January 1945.

Flying Officer McKinnon and WOP Flight Sergeant E. Harvey were the only survivors of his crew.

Aircraft 'A','C', 'D', 'F', 'M' ,'N','Q'?'U'?'V' and 'W' of *432* Squadron were diverted to Skellingthorpe, 'I' to Fulbeck, 'T' to Manston.

415 Squadron aircraft 'C', 'J' , 'L' 'N', 'T' , 'U' and 'V' to Waddington, 'K' to Bottesford, 'O' to Litchfield, 'P' to Gamston and 'Z' to Skellingthorpe.Several aircraft received flak damage and Flying Officer Thompson returned on three engines.

Squadron Leader J.C Hovey and Flight Lieutenant J McAllister did the honours in the mess to celebrate their awards of the DFC.

Awards of non immediate DFC's to former 415 Squadron members were announced, F/O L Patten and W/O W Steel and DFM's to F/S F Bogle F/S A.J Dennis.

19 December 1944

Operations called for and cancelled and no flying recorded at the station.

Air Gunner, Flying Officer W.S Patterson awarded a non immediate DFC. Squadron Leader R.H. Perry the SADO was posted back to Canada.

Fig 35.

F/L Bill Miller and crew about to take off for Duisburg, 17 dec 1944 (432 Squadron). Photo Bill Chubb.

20 December 1944

The station was fog bound, and the called for operation was cancelled, but ground training went ahead. There were many aircrew members being screened and new names began to appear on the operations board in the following few weeks.

The station WAAF's held a Christmas party for the local children and the Station Commander Group Captain R.A McLernon DFC, played Santa.

21 December 1944

The fog still persistod precluding any flying at East Moor. A Christmas party was held on the station for York's orphans when over 200 toys made by the the personnel were distributed. Father Christmas was played by FlightLieut A.B Carveth. Candies and sandwiches were provided by S/0 H. Goodrow, and both St.Hilda's and St.Stephen's orphanages were the visitors.

22 December 1944

There was still no sign of operation being scheduled but with the fog lifting flying training continued. A musical evening was held in the NAAFI and a choir from Groves Methodist Chapel led the party in carol singing.

23 December 1944

The seventh consecutive day without 'ops' was a 'fair' one allowing flying training to proceed. Further Christmas parties were held for York's orphans who were thrilled to receive toys, sweets and other presents. In the evening the station WAAF's held a dance.

24 December 1944

The day started with clear weather at the station but by afternoon the fog began to close in on the airfield and the last of thirty three Halifaxes just managed to get airborne in time at 12.02 hours. Naturally this meant diversions for the returning crews during the late afternoon which was damned bad luck, considering that it was Xmas Eve, and as a result the station messes were rather quiet.

During the early hours of the day the Air Raid Sirens were sounded when enemy aircraft were reported in the area.

At 16.00 hours a so called 'Christmas Primer' party was held on the station for the groundstaff. The 432 Squadron crew room was used for the occasion which was extremely successful with plenty of refreshment available. A bottle of Irish Whiskey was raffled and the lucky winner passed it around.

The following crews were dispatched to attack Dusseldorf's Lohausen airfield,

432 Squadron			415 Squadron		
NP755 'A'	S/L	S Minhinmick	NA610 'B'	F/O	J Britt
NP759 'C'	F/O	J Mills	MZ416 'E'	F/O	D Falconer
NP817'D'	W/C	J Stephenson	MZ907 'F'	F/L	A Winmill
NP708 'E'	F/O	F Jeffrey	NA124 'I'	F/L	J Northrup
NP697 'F'	F/O	E McGuire	NR249 'J'	F/L	C Thompson
NP703 'H'	F/L	J Wallace	MZ947 'K'	F/O	G Grier
NP805 'J'	F/L	F Horan	NR253 'L'	F/O	W Mitchell
KP689 'M'	F/O	G Peaker	MZ483 'M'	S/L	W Brown
NP797 'N'	F/O	C Hemming	MZ456 'P'	F/O	O Lindquist
NP807 'P'	F/O	G McNicholl	PN174 'R'	F/O	T Donnelly
MP804 'Q'	F/L	L Kropf	NA611 'T'	F/O	D McTaggart
N P694 'R'	F/O	L McGuire	NA186 'U'	F/O	J Tims
NP802 'S'	P/O	R Proud	NR172 'V'	F/O	L Beicher
NP812 'T'	F/O	F Baxter	NR122'X'	F/O	J McGuire
NP698 'U'	F/O	A Barron	MZ476 'Y'	F/L	T Mears
NP705 'Y'	F/O	A Bews	MZ861 'Z'	F/O	S Mooers

NP774 'Z'   F/O   A Potter

No less than seventeen aircraft were damaged by flak but all returned to the following bases, with the exception of 'S' all *432* Squadron landed at Coltishall.

The former was put down at Linton on Ouse, where at 17.00 hours it swung off the runway and collided with another aircraft.

All 415 Squadron aircraft landed at Foulsham.

The station cimema was showing Anne Baxter in 'The Sullivans' and the Sergeants Mess held a successful dance.

25 December 1944

Christmas Day saw East Moor shrouded in fog and no flying was recorded. The diverted aircraft were unable to return and consequently the crews had to spend Christmas amongst strangers.

The meals in all East Moor messes were reported to be par-excellent and in time honoured way the Officers and Senior NCO's served Christmas Dinner to the other ranks.

Special Church Services were held and well planned entertainment was thoroughly enjoyed by all. The station dance was held in the cinema.

26 December 1944

Boxing Day fog precluded a five aircraft detail setting out from East Moor whilst all of the diverted aircraft were still away.

'Johnny Vagabond' starring James Cagney was showing at the station cinema and a clanger was dropped when the station transport bus picked up the wrong. batch of extra ladies from York to attend the Officers Mess dance. Much embarrassment was caused when a number of the younger officers became too high spirited.

27 December 1944

With the lifting of the fog at East Moor the diverted aircraft were able to return, and the crews held several most successful, if delayed, Christmas parties.

28 December 1944

At 02.28 hours Flight Lieutenant Winmill lifted his Halifax off the East Moor runway followed by twenty seven others for an attack on the railway repair sheds at Opladem, from which all returned safely,

432 Squadron			415 Squadron		
NP817 'D'	W/C	J Stephenson	NA185 'A'	F/O	GGrier
NP755 'A'	F/O	J Hamilton	NA610 'B'	F/O	S Mooere
NP697 'F'	P/O	A Stedman	NAI81 'D'	F/O	W Mitchell
NP703 'H'	F/L	J Sales	MZ416 'E'	F/O	J McGuire
KP805 'J'	P/O	R Proud	MZ907 'F'	F/L	A Winmill
NP693 'K'	F/O	L Loppe	MZ949 'G'	F/L	T Mears
NP704 'L'	F/O	E McGuire	NR156 'H'	S/L	W Brown
NP689 'M'	F/O	J Patterson	NA124 'I'	F/L	J Northrup
NP797 'N'	F/O	C Hemming	NR249 'J'	F/L	C Thompson
NP694 'R'	F/O	L McGuire	MZ946 '0'	F/O	J Tims
NP812 'T'	F/O	F Baxter	MZ456 'P'	F/O	L Belcher
NP691 'V'	F/O	A Bews	PN174 'R'	F/O	T Donnelly
NP698 'U'	F/L	J Wallace	NR172 'V'	S/L	J Hovey
NP705 'Y'	F/O	G Peaker	NR122 'X'	F/O	D McTaggart

Pilot Officer Proud landed at North Creake.

Flight Lieutenant Mears aircraft was attacked twice by Mel09's and later by an unidentified twin engined aircraft, his gunners returning fire on each occasion.

29 December 1944

The Marshalling yards at Troisdorf were the target for the station's crews in a late afternoon take off, all made a safe return

432 Squadron were unable to see the results of their attack because of dense clouds, but 13 crews reported a satisfactory result.

432 Squadron				**415 Squadron**			
NP817	'D'	W/C	R Davenport	NA600	'A'	F/S	A McDiamid'
NP708	'E'	F/O	L Loppe	NA610"B' '		P/O	J Hechter
NP697	'F'	P/O	A Stedman	NA181	'D'	F/L	W Mitchell
NP803	'I'	P/O	R Proud	MZ907	'F'	F/L	A Winmill
NP805	'J'	F/O	G Peaker	NR156	'H'	S/L	J Hovey
NP693	'K'	F/O	J Hamilton	NR249	'J'	F/L	C Thompson
NP704	'L'	F/O	E McGuire	MZ456	'P'	F/O	L Beicher
NP689	'M'	F/O	J Patterson	PN174	'R'	F/O	T Donnelly
NP797	'N'	F/O	C Hemming	LW552	'S'	F/O	W Goodwin
NP807	'P'	F/L	F Horan	NA611	'T	F/O	D McTaggart
NP694	'R'	F/O	L McGuire	MZ861	'Z'	F/O	S Mooers
NP698	'U'	F/O	G Barron	MZ416	'E'	F/O	D Falconer
NP691	'V'	F/O	A Bews	MZ949	'G'	F/O	G Grier
NP707	'W'	F/O	A Potter	NA124	'I'	F/L	J Northrup
NP705	'Y'	F/L	J Wallace	MZ483	'M'	F/L	J McAllister
NP774	'Z'	F/L	J Sales	MZ946	'O'	F/O	J McGuire
NP812	'T"	F/O	F Baxter	NR122	'X'	F/O	D Stewart
				MZ476	'Y'	F/O	J McQuiston

Aircraft 'D','E','J' and 'P' of 432 Squadron landed at Dishforth along with I'X','O','M','I','G','E','S','J' and 'H' of 415 Squadron.

Flying Officer McQuiston made an early return after being airborne around three hours with hydraulic failure and was diverted to RCAF Station Croft. Flying Officer Baxter's aircraft was badly shot up and the fuel tanks holed and the two outer engines stopped. Despite his serious leg wounds, Flying Officer Hancox managed to navigate the Halifax to an emergency field at Woodbridge, both officers were awarded the DFC. Sadly the bomb aimer misunderstood the skippers instructions and had baled out.

30 December 1944

Was bright and the station cinema was showing 'The Desert Song' with Irene Manning and Dennis Morgan. The cinema was under new management with Mr.Donald Tiplady replacing Mr.C Gallagher.

The last operation of 1944 for the East Moor crews was as part of a force dispatched to attack Cologne and its railyards where considerable damage was done before all the station's aircraft returned around midnight.

The following thirty three crews began taking off at 17.14 hours, and all were away by 17.43 hours,

432 Squadron				**415 Squadron**			
NP755	'A'	W/C	J MacDonald	NA181	'D'	F/L	W Mitchell
NP759	'C'	F/O	L MeGuire	MZ416	'E'	F/O	D Falconer
NP817	'D'	W/C	J Stephenson	MZ907	'F'	F/L	A Winmill
NP697	'F'	P/O	A Stedman	MZ949	'G'	F/O	G Grier
NP703	'H'	F/L	J Sales	NR156	'H'	F/L	J McAllister
NP803	'I'	P/O	R Proud	NA124	'I'	F/L	J Northrup
NP693	'K'	F/O	L Loppe	NR249	'J'	F/L	C Thompson
NP805	'J'	F/O	G Peaker	NR253	'L'	F/O	T Donnelly
NP707	'W'	W/C	P Davenport	MZ483	'M'	S/L	J Hovey
NP704	'L'	F/O	E McGuire	MZ946	'O'	F/O	J McGuire
NP691	'V'	F/L	J Wallace	LK766	'Q'	F/O	L Goodwin
NP705	'Y'	F/O	J Mills	MZ456	'P'	F/O	L Belcher

NP698 'U'	F/O	G Barron		NA611 'T'	F/O	J McQuiston
NP807 'P'	F/O	J Hamilton		NR172 'V'	P/O	J Hechter
NP797 'N'	F/O	C Hemming		NR122 'X'	F/O	D Stewart
NP689 'M'	F/O	J Patterson		MZ632 'W'	F/O	C Piper
				MZ861 'Z'	F/O	S Mooers

31 December 1944

After three operations on consecutive nights the East Moor crews welcomed a breather. A full flying training programme was carried out during the day,when mostly freshmen participated. New Year parties and dances were held and said to have been a great success, and that in general the morale was high.

General:

The morale of all personnel on the station was said to be high. Food was said to be plentiful but very limited in variety.

The station WAAF.'s held a Christmas party for more than fifty children from nearby Sutton on Forest. Staged in the NAAFI, it was catered for by S/O H. Goodrow and included a special iced cake. Flight Lieutenant Carveth was again in the role of Santa Claus and gave each child a present and sweets.

THE HEROISM GF FLYING OFFICER E HANCOX

Flying Officer F Baxter and crew lifted NP812 from East Moor's runway at 15.14 hours bound for Trois Dorf and the railway yards there on the afternoon of 29th December.

After bombing the target a heavy burst of flak struck QO-T knocking out two engines and wounded the bomb aimer Pilot Officer Barnett who bailed out. The navigator Flying Officer Hancox was severely wounded. He had both legs smashed, lost a lot of blood and was in excruciating pain and fainted frequently. Somehow he managed to plot a course for Woodbridge between bouts of unconciousness The skipper, Flying Officer Baxter pulled off a safe landing on the two inner engines. He and the brave navigator were awarded the DFC. The bomb aimer had apparently misunderstood the captain's orders and left the aircraft.

In a desperate attempt to stem the rise in cycle thefts at East Moor, it was announced that a courts martial would be requested for any culprits that were discovered.

This petty crime had risen to alarming proportions, as many as twenty being reported in one day. A cycle was the most valued possession for the majority of the station's personnel and to have it stolen was both inconvenient and very frustrating, and it was hoped that the new order would put an end to the practice.

During the month it was learned that Flying Officer Max Krakowsky was safe. He was the only survivor when he and his crew were in collision with another Halifax. They were flying NP699 of 432 Squadron when at 05.45 hours on the 18th December it was in collision with LV818, ZA-F of No. 10 Squadron (Melbourne) over the French/Belgian border.

The 432 Squadron skipper found himself tumbling through space and luckily he had his parachute on, and was able to pull the rip-cord and land safely in friendly territory. He arrived back at East Moor in January 1945.
Lost in the tragedy were six crew members in NP699, QO-G who were on their 26th operation,

Flying Officer	R Cann	Navigator
Flying Officer	G G Wilson	Bomb Aimer
Pilot Officer	A Blayney	Wireless Operator
Flight Sergeant	S Zadorozny	Mid-Upper
Flight Sergeant	J Green	Rear Gunner
Pilot Officer	M Boylan	Flight Engineer

Lost in LV818, ZA-F, G Boddy (Pilot), N Tatham (2nd Pilot), G Waldren (Nav),
W Leese RCAF (Bomb Aimer), D Mole (Wireless Operator), K Matthews (Mid-Upper),
W Mawson (Rear Gunner) and E Nicholson (Flight Engineer).
During the month Squadron Leader J.C Hovey and Flight Lieutenant McAllister of 415 (Swordfish) Squadron received the DFC.

A 415 Squadron skipper recalls 14 January 1945

" I had an interesting take off on runway 0900 at dusk one day. We were taking off on our north/south runway into the north on this operation. I was the last aircraft in line and the fellow in front of me ran off the runway, heading straight for the bomb dump. Fortunately the undercarriage collapsed and the aircraft caught fire, the crew baling out and running like hell. Then the bloody thing blew up scattering pieces all over the runway. My aircraft was lifted into the air and blown about six feet sideways. A funny thing was that there was no noise at all in our aircraft and I could not hear my engines. I then had to get turned off around on the taxi strip and get to the west end of runway 090 (one of the short runways). I got a green light as soon as I turned on to the runway. We were now twenty minutes late, as we were thumping down the runway I asked my navigator for our first course. I held her on the runway right to the end of the last foot of black-top, eased her into the air and immediately banked her 60 degrees to head south. The control officer really tore a strip off me when we returned, saying I had damn near given him a heart attack as he thought we were going down. We were good friends so I told him not to worry, I had time to make up and besides he had just seen an expert at work. Nice to be young and confident (or stupid) ".

1945

1 January 1945

Only ground training was carried out during a day which was spent by many in recuperating from the New Year festivities held in the respective messes.

However, things livened up at 22.15 hours when thirteen Lancasters of 195 Sqd from Wratting Common were diverted in to East Moor.

2 January 1945

Operations were called for and the station supplied thirty two aircraft and crews for an attack on Ludwigshafen, all returned safely after a successful mission,

432 Squadron				415 Squadron		
NP755 'A'	W/C	J MacDonald		NA600 'A'	F/O	C Chartier
NP817 'D'	W/C	J Stephenson		NA610 'B'	F/O	C Piper
NP697 'F'	P/O	E Patzer		NA181 'D'	F/O	W Goodwin
NP703 'H'	F/L	J Sales		MZ416 'E'	F/L	A Winmill
NP803 'I'	F/O	A Clarke		NR156 'H'	F/L	A Cruickshank
NP805 'J'	P/O	G Sherlock		NA124 'I'	F/L	C Thompson
NP693 'K'	F/O	L Loppe		NR253 'L'	F/O	S McFadden
NP704 'L'	P/O	P Proud		MZ483 'M'	F/O	D Stewart
NP689 'M'	F/O	J Patterson		MZ946 'O'	F/O	J McGuire
NP797 'N'[1]	F/O	C Hemming		LK766 'Q'	P/O	W Lane
NP807 'P'	F/O	G McNicholl		PN174 'R'	F/O	D Donnelly
NP804 'Q'	F/O	E McGuire		LW552 'S'	P/O	L Belcher
NP694 'R'	F/O	L McGuire		NA611 'T'	F/S	A McDiarmid
NP698 'U'	F/O	G Barron		MZ632 'W'	P/O	J Hechter
NP707 'W'	W/C	R Davenport		MZ476 'Y'	F/L	J McAllister
NP705 'Y'	F/L	J Wallace		MZ861 'Z'	F/O	S Mooers

3 January 1945

A considerable amount of overnight flying training was concluded in the early hours.

A proposed operation requiring thirty of the station's aircraft to attack Marshalling Yards was later scrubbed.
At the evening Pay Parade a record amount of £33 was raised from the sale of National Savings Stamps.

A shipment of pyjamas was received from the sponsors of 432 Squadron and these were issued to the ground staff.

East Moor defeated Linton on Ouse at Basketball by 23 - 15.

4 January 1945

No operations and wintery showers prevailed. The station's runways were treated with salt and sand as further snow warnings were received.

Wing Commander F. Ball's car was reported stolen from outside the Station Commander's house.

WAAF's S/O P. Seccombe and S/O C. Flinn together with Flight Lieutenant Carveth were invited to York Institute's childrens party and thoroughly enjoyed themselves in the company of the children and the Lord and Lady Mayoress.

5 January 1945

Snow showers again prevailed and the station's runways had to be sanded and salted before twenty nine Halifaxes set out for an attack on Hanover,

432 Squadron				415 Squadron		
NP708 'E'	F/L	J Wallace		NA610 'B'	F/O	C Piper
NP697 'F'	P/O	G Sherlock		NA181 'D'	F/O	W Goodwin
NP803 'I'	P/O	R Proud		MZ907 'F'	F/L	A Winmill
NP693 'K'	F/O	L Loppe		MZ949 'G'	P/O	W Lane
NP689 'M'	F/O	J Patterson		NA124 'I'	F/L	C Thompson
NP694 'R'	F/O	L McGuire		NR249 'J'	F/O	C Chartier
NP804 'Q'	P/O	E Patzer		MZ483 'M'	F/L	A Cruickshank
NP807 'P'	F/O	E Mc.Guire		MZ946 'O'	F/O	J McGuire
NP797 'N'	F/O	C Hemming		MZ456 'P'	F/O	L Belcher
NP707 'W'	W/C	R Davenport		PN174 'R'	F/S	A McDiarmid
NP755 'A'	F/O	A Clarke		LW552 'S'	P/O	J Hechter
NP759 'C'	F/L	J Sales		NR172 'V'	F/O	D Falconer
NP817 'D'	W/C	J Stephenson		NR122 'X'	F/O	D Stewart
				MZ476 'Y'	F/O	S McFadden
				MZ861 'Z'	P/O	S Mooers

Sadly three crews failed to return. Wing Commander Stephenson's aircraft caught caught fire and all bailed out to become POW's. The skippers chute had opened inside the bomber and he was held suspended for some time. Flying Officer Fleming, Pickthorne and Bond evaded for a time.

Flight Lieutenant Sales and crew were shot down on their way to the target and he and Flight Sergeant McInnes were killed and the remainder taken prisoner. Nothing was heard from Flying Officer McFadden and crew after take off and Flying Officer Rhind was killed along with Flight Sergeant's Rinder and Clark who were unable to get out of the blazing Halifax. The skipper, Flying Officer Connor, Sgt's Burton and Graves became POW's but believed murdered by the Gestapo. F/O Connor lost his legs in a propeller during his exit from the aircraft and was repatriated in a POW exchange.

6 January 1945

An extremely busy day at East Moor when in addition to a heavy flying training programme being carried out, twenty nine Halifaxes were prepared for an afternoon take of f for Hanau and thirty four Lancasters were diverted in to the station.
The latter comprised eleven from 50 Squadron at Skellingthorpe, twelve from 61 Squadron and eleven from 195 Squadron at Wratting Common.

The German railway system was the target for the following East Moor crews,

432 Squadron				415 Squadron		
NP755 'A'	W/C	J MacDonald		NA610 'B'	F/L	W Barrett
NP697 'F'	P/O	A Stedman		MZ922 'C'	F/L	G Thompson
NP703 'H'	F/O	A Clarke		NA181 'D'	F/O	W Goodwin
NP803 'I'	P/O	R'Proud		MZ416 'E'	F/O	D Falconer
NP693 'K'	F/O	L Loppe		MZ907 'F'	F/O	C Piper
NP689 'M'	P/O	E Patzer		MZ949 'G'	F/L	A Cruickshank
NP797 'N'	F/O	C Hemming		NR249 'J'	F/O	C Chartier
NP807 'P'	F/O	E McGuire		NR253 'L'	F/O	E Wilkinson
NP804 'Q'	F/L	W Miller		MZ483 'M'	S/L	W Brown
NP694 'R'	F/O	L McGuire		MZ456 'P'	F/O	L Belcher
NP691 'V'	F/L	J Wallace		LW552 'S'	F/O	J McGuire
NP707 'W'	W/C	R Davenport		NA611 'T'	P/O	W Lane
NP705 'Y'	F/O	G Barron		NR172 'V'	F/S	A McDiarmid
NP708 'E'	P/O	G Sherlock		NR122 'X'	F/O	D Stewart
				MZ861 'Z'	F/O	S Mooers

Nothing was heard from Flying Officer Belcher and crew after leaving East Moor, the remainder returned safely to base.

7 January 1945

No operational requirements but flying training continued.

Snow was again forecast for the area but did not materialize until after midnight.

The weekly Forum was again well attended when the subject 'Prospects in India' was discussed with Graham Spry a Canadian Rhodes Scholarand personal assistant to Sir Stafford Cripps.

8 January 1945

Another day without any operational flying. Numerous ground training programmes were conducted by the Section Leaders.

Two inches of snow had fallen overnight reminding the Canadians of home,and the Station snow plough was brought into operation clearing the runways

The 'Little Theatre' featured Ralph Richardson in 'Silver Fleet'

9 January 1945

Wing Commander Ball's car was found abandoned and wrecked in a ditch not too far from the station. The culprit was never found.

No operational commitments on a snow covered East Moor. Ground training held.

10 January 1945

No operations as the snow continued to fall on the station, precluding any flying training. The airfield was declared unserviceable as snow ploughing continued. The Station Basketball team defeated No.6 Group (RCAF) by a score of 19 - 17.

11 January 1945

Still no operations at East Moor on what was an extremely windy day, and snow clearing went on throughout.

A performance by the RAF 'Gang Show' was enjoyed by more than 250 personnel and was staged in the 'Little Theatre', and was followed by a supper in the Airmen's Mess.

12 January 1945

The airfield was declared serviceable after all runways were cleared of snow.

Operations were called for and later scrubbed.

A dance for Corporals and ranks below was held in the Station Gymnasium where the music was provided by the RCAF Bomber Group Dance Band and was described as being most successful with 350 personnel attending.

The RAF Regiment contingent were visited by Squadron Leader D Creig (RAF Regt) from No. 62 (RCAF) Base.

13 January 1945

The station's two squadrons were back in business when thirty one aircraft were dispatched to attack the rail way yards at Saarbrucken and all returned safely,

432 Squadron				415 Squadron		
NP755 'A'	F/O	A Clarke		MZ922 'C'	P/O	J Hechter
NP708 'E'	F/L	J Wallace		NAl8l 'D'	F/L	W Mitchell
NP703 'H'	F/O	E McGuire		MZ416 'E'	F/O	D Falconer
NP803 'I'	F/L	F Horan		MZ949 'G'	F/L	T Mears
NP805 'J'	P/O	G Sherlock		NR249 'J¹'	F/L	C Chartier
NP704 'L'	F/O	G Peaker		NR253 'L'	F/O	J McQuiston
NP689 'M'	F/O	L Loppe		MZ483 'M'	F/O	J MoGuire
NP797 'N'	F/O	C Hemming		NA202 'N'	F/O	A Galley
NP961 'O'	P/O	E Patzer		MZ946 'O'	W/O	A McDiarmid
NP807 'P'	F/O	J Hamilton		PN174 'R'	F/L	W Borrett
NP804 'Q'	F/L	W Miller		NA6ll 'T'	F/O	E Wilkinson
NP694 'R'	F/O	L McGuire		NR172 'V'	W/O	L Russell
NP698 'U'	F/L	W Mennie		NR122 'X'	F/O	D Stewart
NP691 'V'	F/O	A Bews		MZ476 'Y'	W/O	J McKenzie
NP707 'W'	F/O	A Potter		MZ861 'Z'	F/O	S Mooers
NP705 'Y'	S/L	Thompson				

Flying Officer Falconer completed the mission despite being unable to raise the undercarriage, but put down at Manston on return almost out of fuel. Warrant Officer McKenzie completed the operation with a u/s port inner engine.

The escape hatch blew out of Flight Lieutenant Mennie's aircraft within an hour of take off damaging the fuselage and leading edge of the port wing, and the Halifax was struck by flak on the run up to the target.

14 January 1945

It was decided by the powers that were, that future operations over Germany would only accrue three points as opposed to four.

415 Squadron Halifax, NA6ll crashed and burnt on take off for operations, happily Flight Sergeant Sirtonski and crew survived but received burns and abrasions.

The remaining detail of thirty three aircraft took off for an attack on the rail yards at Grevonbroich and without loss,

432 Squadron				415 Squadron		
NP755 'A'	W/C	J MacDonald		NA600 'A'	F/L	C Chartier
NP736 'B'	F/O	G Peaker		NA6l0 'B'	W/G	J McKenzie
NP145 'C'	S/L	S Minhinnick		NAl8l 'D'	F/L	W Mitchell
NP708 'E'	F/O	G McGuire		MZ907 'F'	F/O	A Galley
NP697 'F'	F/O	L McGuire		MZ949 'G'	F/L	T Mears
NP703 'H'	F/O	A Clarke		NR156 'H'	F/O	G Hyland
NP797 'N'	F/O	C Hemming		NA124 'I'	F/L	J Northrup
NP803 'I'	F/L	F Horan		MZ483 'M'	F/O	E Wilkinson
NP805 'J'	P/O	E Sherlock		NA202 'N'	W/G	L Russell
NP704 'L'	F/L	W Mennie		MZ946 'O'	F/O	J McGuire
NP689 'M'	F/L	G Thompson		PN174 'R'	F/L	W Borrett
NP699 'O'	F/O	L Loppe		NA6ll 'T'	F/S	E Sirtonski
NP804 'Q'	F/L	W Miller		NR172 'V'	F/O	S Mooers
NP691 'V'	F/L	A Bews		MZ632 'W'	P/O	J Hechter
NP707 'W'	F/L	J Wallace		NR122 'X'	F/O	D Stewart
NP705 'Y'	F/L	E: Hayes				
NP774 'Z'	P/O	E Patzer				

Flight Lieutenant Bews and crew were attacked by an enemy aircraft which scored hits on the fuselage and shot off the tailwheel tyre. Pilot Officer McInnes earned himself the DFC by talking his skipper out of trouble during the attack. The aircraft was damaged beyond repair.

Flight Lieutenant Wallace completed the operation despite being without a port inner engine which failed over East Moor, he too, earned the DFC.

15 January 1945

At 02.22 hours thirteen Lancasters of 467 Squadron from Waddington were diverted in to East Moor and amongst them was the famous 'S' Sugar, R5868.

No operations were scheduled on the station, and in the evening the cinema was showing 'Lifeboat' featuring Talllulah Bankhead.

16 January 1945

The target was Magdeburg for the station's crews and thirty four of them set off along' its runway but sadly NP807 swung off it and became bogged down, the remainder took off and returned safely, some with flak damage,

432 Squadron			415 Squadron		
NP755 'A'	W/O	J MacDonald	NA6l0 'B'	W/O	L Russell
NP145 'C'	F/O	A Clarke	MZ922 'C'	W/O	J McKenzie
NP708 'E'	F/O	J Patterson	NAl8l 'D'	F/L	W Mitchell
NP697 'F'	P/O	A Stedman	MZ416 'E'	F/O	D Falconer
NP703 'H'	P/O	E Patzer	MZ907 'F'	F/L	A Winmill
NP803 'I'	F/O	A Potter	MZ949 'G'	F/L	T Mears
NP805 'J'	P/O	G Sherlock	NR156 'H'	F/L	A Cruickshank
NP693 'K'	F/O	E McGuire	NA124 'T'	W/O	A McDiarmid
NP704 'L'	F/L	W Mennie	NR249 'J'	F/O	E Wilkinson
NP797 'N'	F/O	G Peaker	NR253 'L'	F/L	W Borrett
NP699 'O'	F/L	J Wallace	MZ483 'M'	F/L	J McQuiston
NP807 'P'	F/L	A Bews	NA202 'N'	F/O	G Hyland
NP804 'Q'	F/L	W Miller	MZ946 '0'	F/O	J McGuire
NP694 'R'	F/O	L McGuire	NA186 'U'	P/O	J Hechter
NP705 'Y'	S/L	J Thompson	NR172 'V'	F/L	J McAllister
NP774 'Z'	F/L	E Hayes	NR122 'X'	F/O	D Stewart
			MZ586 'Y'	F/O	E Galley
			MZ861 'Z'	F/O	S Mooers

Wing Commander MacDonald returned on three engines and Flight Lieutenant Mennie with a u/s compass after attacking the target.

Flight Lieutenant Borrett and crew failed to return from this operation and Flight Lieutenant McQuiston made an early return with a u/s starboard outer.

17 January 1945

No operations from East Moor.
Pilot Officer Ballentyne a screened 415 officer created something of a 'rank-record' when he became Liasion Officer at the Aircrew Refresher School at Sheffield with the rank of Flight Lieutenant. He had risen from Flight Sergeant in just over one month.

East Moor Hockey team were defeated by RCAF Station Croft at Durham, 10 - 3.

18 January 1945

Another operation free day and no flying training scheduled.

An armed guard was placed around the airfield when it was learnt that a number of German prisoners of war had escaped from a camp near Ripon. These patrols were maintained until the following day when the escapees were recaptured at Skipton.

Errol Flynn starred in 'Gentleman Jim' at the 'Little Theatre' and was watched by more than 300 station personnel.

19 January 1945

Operations were called for but later scrubbed.

A crate of eggs was reported stolen from the Officers Mess which kept the Station Police busy.

RCAF Skipton on Swale Dance Band supplied the music for a dance held in the cinema.

20 January 1945

The area was hit during the night by winds described as cyclonic and some damage to station buildings was sustained.

No operations but ground training included Link trainer, Air Sea Rescue, H2S and Aircraft Recognition.

The runways were again under snow and ploughing went on throughout the day. The WAAF's at the RDF Station at Stillington were cut off by the deep snow and were without lighting or heating. Assistance was given by a team from East Moor.

21 January 1945

Still no operations and the nights heavy snowfall was regarded as a beautiful sight by the Canadians, reminding them of home

The severe weather led to many difficulties for the station's personnel as the water supplies on many sites became frozen.

22 January 1945

Operations were called for but subsequently scrubbed. A small amount of flying training was pursued.

The severe weather continued and the station's personnel experienced great difficulty in keeping warm. Almost all sites were frozen up and desperate methods of improvisation were introduced in an effort to thaw out water pipes in ablution and shower blocks. To this end home made braziers were made from oil tins.

A call had been made for volunteers from 'screened' aircrew to take up posts in the station Admin, MT and Bomb Dump Sections, but it met with very little response. Many Canadians said that they would be interested if they could have Isome home leave to Canada first.

23 January 1945

There was no flying at East Moor on what was an extremely foggy day. Ground training went ahead.

Three non immediate DFC's were awarded to 415 Squadron members namely, Bombing Leader Flight Lieutenant E.C Atkins, Flight Lieutenant S Chiles the Signals Leader and navigator Flight Lieutenant W.H Boyd.

24 January 1945

With the temperature down to zero there wasn't any flying at the station on a fine but sometimes foggy day.

While the whole area had taken on a Christmas card look with fresh snow in abundance, there was no coal available except for the kitchens and airmen had to use melted snow for washing and shaving. Frost had completely disrupted the station's water system.

Nevertheless, 415 Squadron ground and aircrew managed to stage a most successful 'Beer and Sandwich' party in the evening but sadly the squadron funds were left at a very low 'altitude'.

25 January 1945

Still no operations at East Moor.

Personnel kept themselves warm during the day with snow clearing, especially on the runways, and with thawing out the frozen pipes.

The 'Blackouts' Concert party left the station after a successful visit.

26 January 1945

Snow showers were prevalent on what was another day without any operations at the station.

With more disruption to the water supplies on the sites personnel found it necessary to wash in their respective messes.

432 Squadron engaged in some flying training.

In the evening' the Bomber Group Dance Band played at a very successful dance held in the station cinema for the 'erks'.

27 January 1945

Operations were called for but later scrubbed.

415 Squadron were engaged on circuits and landings and a bus service for officers was started between their mess at Sutton Hall and the airfield.

Ten 'screened' crews from 432 Squadron left East Moor for Warrington. The day being a Saturday, many of the station's personnel attended the dance in Sutton on Forest Village Hall which had become a regular weekly event.

28 January 1945

Regular church services were held in chapel, church and squadron crew rooms and were said to be well attended.

A concert party was formed between YMCA and 415 Squadron and it was planned to be performing within a couple of weeks.
Operations were resumed by East Moor squadrons with an attack on Stuttgart involving the following thirty crews,

432 Squadron			415 Squadron		
NP699 'O'	F/L	L Kropf	NA610 'B'	F/O	B Cowieson
NP755 'A'	F/O	A Clarke	MZ922 'C'	F/O	G Hyland
NP736 'B'	P/O	J Kinniburgh	NA181 'D'	F/L	W Mitchell
NP145 'C'	S/L	S Minhinnick	MZ416 'E'	F/L	A Cruickshank
NP703 'H'	P/O	R Proud	MZ949 'G'	F/L	T Mears
NP803 'I'	F/L	F Horan	NA124 'I'	F/L	J Northrup
NP689 'M'	F/O	J Patterson	NR249 'J'	F/L	C Chartier
NP804 'Q'	P/O	E Patzer	MZ483 'M'	W/C	F Ball
NP694 'R'	F/O	L McGuire	LL593 'N'	F/O	A Galley
NP707 'W'	F/O	A Potter	MZ946 'O'	W/O	I Russell
NP691 'V'	F/L	A Bews	PN174 'R'	F/O	G Grier
NP705 'Y'	F/O	J Hamilton	NA186 'U'	F/L	W Goodwin
NP704 'L'	F/L	W Mennie	NR172 'V'	S/L	W Brown
NP697 'F'	P/O	G Sherlock	MZ586 'Y'	F/O	L Minkler
NP693 'K'	F/O	L Loppe	MZ861'Z'	F/O	D Stewart

Flying Officer Minkler returned early with a u/s oxygen supply.

Due to the weather conditions at East Moor all aircraft were diverted on return, 432 Squadron 'I', 'M', 'Q','R', 'W', 'V', 'L', 'F' and 'K' to Polebrook,along with 'A' and 'B'. 'C' to Tangmere and '0' to Grafton Underwood.
415 Squadron 'B', 'C', 'D','E', 'G', 'I', 'J', 'N', 'V' and 'Z' to Grafton Underwood, while 'M' put down at Dunsfold, 'O' at Deenethorpe, 'R' to Wing and 'U' to Stradishall.

Wing Commander Ball's aircraft was hit by flak setting it on fire which was extinguished after an hour and five minutes.

Squadron Leader Brown's aircraft was attacked by a Me 410 which was shot down by rear gunner Flying Officer Griffiths who had held his fire while guiding his skipper through evasive manouvres earning him the DFC.

29 January 1945

The weather moderated and brought water in abundance to East Moor,floods were everywhere even in many buildings where thawing pipes had burst.

Seventeen of the diverted aircraft returned to the station.

Wing Commander J MacDonald of 432 Squadron was screened and Wing Commander S Minnhinick assumed command of the squadron.

There was no flying training was carried out and no further operations were called for.
Edward G Robinson starred in 'The Destroyer' at the little theatre.

30 January 1945

After a further heavy fall of snow in the area the weather again moderated and allowed more of the crews diverted from the Stuttgart operation to return to East Moor.

415 Squadron carried out some flying training despite the weather.

Flight Lieutenant A.B Carveth awaiting to join the Canadian Army by request.

No operations were called for at the station.

31 January 1945

Another operation free day at East Moor.

Due to unfavourable weather at their base a number of U.S.A.A.F aircraft were diverted to East Moor. An initial 28 were expected but when the weather at East Moor also deteriorated the remainder were re diverted to RCAF Station Dalton.

General:

January proved to be most unusual and severe weatherwise, even for Yorkshire and much discomfort was experienced by the station's uncomplaining staff, during the period that was referred to as 'The Big Freeze'.

Operationwise it was not one of East Moor's busiest months but on the whole it was regarded as satisfactory.
Film shows and other entertaimments were well supported as were the few sporting fixtures.

1 February 1945

A rainy day was brightened for members of 415 Squadron who received a donation of 12,000 gigarettes with the compliments of the Agent General of British Columbia in London.

Squadron Leader B.M Grieg RCAF Base Defence Officer suspended all weapon training at East Moor until an up to date list of all untrained personnel was was drawn up.

In the evening the 'Maple Leaf Concert Party' entertained a large audience with comedy, singing and juggling, and were particularly well received.

A small amount of flying training preceded an operation to Mainz by eighteen of the station's crews with take off commencing at 15. 57 hours, and was without loss,

432 Squadron				415 Squadron		
NP805 'J'	F/O	A Patzer		MZ949 'G'	F/L	T Mears
NP755 'A'	F/L	E McGuire		NR156 'H'	F/L	A Cruickshank
NP704 'L'	F/O	L Loppe		NR249 'J'	F/L	C Chartier
NP961 'O'	F/L	J Wallace		MZ947 'K'	P/O	L Minkler
NP694 'R'	F/L	L Kroppf		NA610 'B'	F/O	E Wilkinson
NP774 'Z'	F/L	A Bews		MZ946 'O'	P/O	G Hyland
NP707 'W'	F/O	A Potter		LL593 'N'	F/O	B Cowieson
NP689 'M'	P/O	J Patterson		NA186 'U'	F/L	W Goodwin
NP691 'V'	F/O	C Hemming		MZ586 'Y'	F/L	J McQuiston

A faulty engine on the return flight caused Flight Lieutenant Goodwin to land at Stradishall.

2 February 1945

The Station Entertainment Committee decided that from hereon it was intended to hold two Station Dances, one WAAF Dance and an Airmen's Dance each week.
The rail facilities at Wanne Eickel was the target for twenty seven East Moor crews, take off commenced at 20.08 hours and all were aiborne by 20.53,

432 Squadron				415 Squadron		
RG455 'X'	F/O	A Patter		NA610 'B'	W/O	J McKenzie
NP736 'B'	F/L	E McGuire		MZ949 'G'	F/L	T Mears
NP703 'H'	P/O	P Proud		NR156 'H'	F/L	A Cruickshank
NP805 'J'	F/O	J Hamilton		NA124 'I'	F/L	J Northrup
NP693 'K'	F/O	L Loppe		NR249 'J'	F/L	A Winmill
NP689 'M'	F/O	J Patterson		MZ947 'K'	F/O	G Grier
NP961 'O'	F/L	J Wallace		LW552 'S'	W/O	A McDiarmid
NP694 'R'	F/L	L Kropf		MZ946 'O'	F/O	G Hyland
RG448 'V'	F/L	A Bews		LK766 'Q'	F/L	W Mitchell
NP707 'W'	F/O	A Potter		PN174 'R'	W/C	F Ball
NP705 'Y'	F/O	C Hemming		LL593 'M'	W/O	D Cowieson
NP774 'Z'	F/L	E Hayes		NR172 'V'	F/O	S Mooers
NP704 'L'	F/L	G Thompson		MZ632 'W'	F/L	L Minkler
				MZ861 'Z'	F/O	E Wilkinson

Pilot Officer Proud's aircraft was hit by flak on the run up to the target. Flight Lieutenant G Thompson and crew failed to return from this operation. Warrant Officer McKenzie and crew had a 'hairy' experience, hit by flak, the mid upper gunner Flying Officer W Broad was wounded. Then followed no less then five attacks by enemy aircraft, a FW190, a Me2lO, two JU88's and another unidentified twin engined aircraft. Fortunately the Halifax did not receive any further damage but Flying Officer Broad was admitted to hospital at Ipswich when the aircraft was landed at Woodbridge.

3 February 1945

Operations were scheduled at East Moor.

As a result of the cold weather, many of the station's sites were left without any running water.

Halifax NA6l0 was flown in to East Moor from Woodbridge bearing flak damage, and with the news that Flying Officer Broad was comfortable in hospital and with an eye injury.

Two Canadian Army Officers, Major S.W Gordon and Lieutenant H Rushaway, arrived at the station to spend a week with 415 Squadron.

The 'Maple Leaf - Macordials' staged further concerts in the Little Theatre on the old communal site.

4 February 1945

The Old George Hotel, Easingwold was the scene for an outstandingly successful send off party for Wing Commander J.K MacDonald, the 432 Sqaudron Commander. Leaving East Moor to take up an appointment with No.63 Base,the popular leader had completed two operational tours and was presented with an inscribed silver mug by his successor, Squadron Leader Minhinick.

Forty two members of the Royal Observer Corps attended aircraft recognition films and lectures before being given a conducted tour of the station.

Bing Crosby and Madge Evans were appearing at the Station Cinema in ' Pennies from Heaven'
The stations crews carried out attacks on two targets, take off commencing at 17.22 hours on that Sunday afternoon, the Benzol plant at Osterfeld was the target for the following crews,

432 Squadron			415 Squadron		
NP755 'A'	F/L	E McGuire	MZ922 'C'	F/O	S Mooers
NP703 'H'	P/O	R Proud	NAl8l 'D'	F/L	W Mitchell
NP693 'K'	F/O	L Loppe	MZ949 'G'	F/L	T Mears
NP689 'M'	F/O	J Patterson	NA124 'I'	F/L	O Piper
RG450 'Q'	P/O	J Bain	NR249 'J'	F/O	E Milibank
NP694 'R'	F/L	L Kropf	MZ947 'K'	F/O	G Grier
RG.448 'V'	F/L	A Bew s	LL593 'N'	F/O	B Cowieson
RG455 'X'	F/L	F Horan	MZ946 'O'	F/O	L Minkler
NP705 'Y'	F/O	C Hemming	NA600 'A'	F/L	A Winmill
NP774'Z'	F/O	A Patzer	NA186 'U'	F/L	W Goodwin
			NR172 'V'	F/L	J McQuiston
			MZ632 'W'	F/O	J Hechter
			NR122 'X'	F/O	E Wilkinson
			MZ586 'Y'	F/O	P Evans

The rail facilities at Bonn were attacked at approximately the same hour by,

NP736 'B'	F/O	G Sherlock	NR146 'E'	W/O	J McKenzie
RG451 'D'	F/L	F Hayes	NR156 'H'	F/L	A Cruickshank
NP961 'O'	F/L	J Wallace	LK766 'Q'	W/O	L Russell
RG449 'S'	P/O	J Daley	MZ861 'Z'	W/O	A McDiarmid
NP707 'W'	F/O	A Potter			

Flight Lieutenant Bews and Pilot Officere Piper made early returns with starboard inner constant speed unit and hydraulics u/s respectively.

Warrant Officer Russell landed on three engines on his return.

5 February 1945

Operations were called for and later scrubbed

New regulations came into force requiring thirty six operations to be completed for a full 'tour'. Sad news for those who had almost completed theirs under the existing system.

A senior NCO air gunner arrived to join 415 Squadron and within a few hours found himself under close arrest charged with stealing the Orderley Officer's car.

An Appreciation Dinner was given by St. Hilda's Orphanage in York for Officers, airmen and airwomen from East Moor for their efforts in providing toys, other gifts and entertainment for the children at Christmas.

The station personnel were reminded that in the interests of security, at no time must East Moor be mentioned in conjunction with squadron numbers in the addresses or in the main body of letters, regardless of where they might be sent.

Greer Garson and Walter Pigeon were starring in 'Madame Currie' at the Station Cinema, and a record session was enjoyed by many in the 'Y' lounge.

6 February 1945

Another operation free day at the station.

7 February 1945

A power failure rendered the Teleprinter Section and the Telephone Exchange ineffective for some time until rectified by the station's electricians.

East Moor Ice Hockey team gained a place in the semi finals when they held RCAF Station Dalton to a draw in a match played at Durham's Ice Rink, the score was 4 - 4, while the station Basketball team defeated RCAF Station Tholthorpe to become league leaders, in the inter station league.

The old communal site was again the scene for the ever popular roller skating sessions.

Operations were called for in the support of the ground forces and the target for the East Moor squadrons was Goch which was described as an important tactical target. Several crews abandoned the mission on advice from the 'Master Bomber' and those included all but one of 415 Squadron. All of the station's crews returned safely despite several combats being reported on the return flight.

The following took part in the operation,

432 Squadron			415 Squadron		
NP755 'A'	F/O	L Loppe	NR156 'H'	F/L	A Cruickshank
NP736 'B'	P/O	J Bain	NA124 'I'	F/O	G Grier
NP708 'E'	P/O	J Daley	NR249 'J'	F/O	E Millbank
NP697 'F'	F/L	E McGuire	NP940 'L'	F/O	E Wilkinson
NP703 'H'	P/O	R Proud	MZ418 'M'	F/L	J McQuiston
NP803 'I'	F/L	F Horan	MZ946 'O'	W/O	L Russell
NP805 'J'	F/O	G Sherlock	MZ922 'C'	P/O	J McKenzie
NP689 'M'	F/O	J Patterson	NA181 'D'	F/L	W Mitchell
NP961 'O'	F/L	J Wallace	NR146 'E'	F/O	L Minkler
NP694 'R'	F/L	L Kropf	NR206 'F'	F/L	O Piper
RG449 'S'	P/O	J Durand	NP936 'P'	F/O	R Evams
RG448 'V'	F/B	P Bradley	MZ356 'Q'	F/O	J Hechter
NP707 'W'	P/O	S Allen	PN174 'R'	W/C	F Ball
NP705 'Y'	F/O	C Hemming	NA186 'U'	F/L	W Goodwin
NP774 'Z'	F/L	E Hayes	NR172 'V'	W/O	A McDiarmid
			NR122 'X'	F/O	B Cowieson
			MZ632 'W'	F/O	S Mooers

The 415 Squadron aircraft which attacked was 'H' ,and from 432 Squadron four crews abandoned and were in the following aircraft, 'F','I', 'S' and 'Y'.

Flight Lieutenant W Goodwin and crew were attacked six times by enemy aircraft, FW190's and JU88's, but remained unscathed.

All crews returned their bombs to base.

8 February 1945

Another attack on Goch was called for but was later cancelled.

The GOC in C of the 1st Canadian Army sent message of appreciation for the support of those crews which did attack the target of the previous night, adding that it was of super quality.

Flying training was called off due to adverse weather conditions but a full programme of ground training continued.

9 February 1945

An early start was made when at 02.33 hours the first of thirty three Halifaxes was lifted from East Moor's runway for an attack on Wanne Eickel.

It is said that NP682 a 426 Squadron Halifax had occassion to take off from East Moor at 02.50 hours and that skipper Flying Officer J.D Wadleigh was unable to maintain height as he continued west- ward with engine failure
The fully laden bomber finally crashed on land belonging to East Ridding Farm, Cowthorpe where it exploded killing all on board.

The East Moor based participants were as follows

432 Squadron			415 Squadron		
NP693 'K'	P/O	J Daley	MZ922 'C'	F/L	T Mears
NP755 'A'	F/S	P Bradley	NA181 'D'	F/L	W Mitchell
NP708 'E'	P/O	J Allen	NR146 'E'	W/O	A McDiarmid
NP703 'H'	P/O	R Proud	NR206 'F'	F/L	O Piper
NP805 'J'	F/O	G Sherlock	NR156 'H'	F/L	A Cruickshenk
NP689 'M'	F/O	J Patterson	NA124 'I'	F/L	J Northrup
NP803 'I'	F/L	F Horan	NR249 'J'	F/O	G Grier
NP961 'O'	F/L	J Wallace	NP940 'L'	F/O	E Wilkinson
RG450 'Q'	P/O	J Bain	MZ418 'M'	F/L	J MeQuiston
NP694 'R'	F/L	L Kropf	MZ946 'O'	F/O	L Minkler
RG449 'S'	F/L	W Miller	NP936 'P'	F/O	R Evans
RG448 'V'	F/L	A Bews	MZ356 'Q'	F/O	J Hechter
NP705 'Y'	F/O	C Hemming	PN174 'R'	S/L	W Brown
NP774 'Z'	F/L	E Hayes	NA186 'U'	F/L	W Goodwin
NP697 'F'	F/L	E McGuire	NR172 'V'	F/L	A Winmill
			MZ632 'W'	W/O	L Russell
			NR127 'X'	F/O	B Cowieson
			NR228 'Z'	F/O	S Moers

Flying Officer Grier and crew were shot down by flak at 07.50 hours and crashed in no mans land near Dunkirk. All bailed out but the skipper was believed killed during his descent, the Flight Engineer to have dropped into safe army hands and the remainder to be POW's.

Warrant Officer Russell made an early return with a u/s port outer engine, which had caught fire after the airscrew broke loose.

Flight Lieutenant McGuire put down at Manston on his return with a uls starboard inner engine.

In the evening the Bomber Group Dance Band played for the Station Hockey Club's event held in the gymnasium.

10 February 1945

Operations were called for and subsequently cancelled.

More than 200 senior NCO's watched the film 'Money for Jam' in the Sergeants Mess, while the YMCA staged a Bingo session.

Flying training was in the form of cross country exercises.

11 February 1945

Strensall Bombing Range was rendered unserviceable when the generator which supplied electricity to the establishment suffered engine failuree The staff at that remote outpost had the task of carrying paraffin flares over half a mile through bog and marsh to illuminate the target area.

Squadron Leader Minnhinick and crew began a tour of Operational Training Units to show off 432 Squadron's veterau battle waggon QO-E 'Eddie, Halifax VII NP708 which had around 59 operations to its credite LAC's Woodward and Watkins flew with them to cater for any servicing requirments.

After the usual Sunday Church services a full programme of ground training was pursued, in the absence of any flying at the station.

12 February 1945

An extremely wet and foggy day at East Moor and another without any operations called for, and the flying training programme was scrubbed.

Wing Commander Frank Ball, CO of 415 Squadron was elected President of the Gfficers Mess, and the newly formed Station Concert Party commenced rehearsals.

Ground training went ahead full swing.

13 February 1945

Weapon training was resumed at East Moor with more than fifty airmen under instuction in an exercise which ran well on into the night.

The station YMCA staff visited the station's outpost at Strensall Bombing Range and distributed comforts amongst the personnel there.

Wing Commander's E.T Duggan and D Fortune, No.62 Base Administration Officers visited the station and held discussions with the East Moor Admin staff.

Plans to introduce 'Mothercraft' practice to the station's WAAF personnel were looked into when representatives from East Moor visited 'Wartime Day Nurseries' in York at the invitation of the resident Matron. It was hoped to be able to release six WAAF's to attend one day per week for six weeks.
The station Basketball team defeated RCAF Station Linton on Ouse 26 - 19 in a match held at York Railway Institute's gymnasium.

15 Squadron's 'B' Flight Commander, J.E McAllister DFC, was promoted to Squadron Leader.

Operations got under way in the late afternoon when twenty nine Halifaxes rose from the station's runway and set out for Bohlen and its synthetic oil plants,

432 Squadron				415 Squadron		
NP755 'A'	F/L	F Horan		NR145 'A'	W/O	A McDiarmid
NP736 'B'	P/O	J Bradley		MZ922 'C'	F/O	A Galley
RG451 'D'	F/O	A Clarke		NA181 'D'	F/O	L Minkler
NP708 'E'	P/O	J Kinniburgh		NR206 'F'	F/L	O Piper
NP803 'I'	P/O	R Proud		NR156 'H'	F/L	T Mears
NP805 'J'	F/L	W Menmie		NP940 'L'	F/O	E Mulbank
NP689 'M'	F/O	J Patterson		MZ418 'M'	F/L	A Winmill
NP694 'R'	F/L	L Kropf		NP961 'O'	F/L	J McQuiston
RG449 'S'	P/O	J Allen		NP936 'P'	Plo	P Evans
RG448 'V'	F/O	C Hemming		MZ356 'Q'	F/O	J Hechter
RG455 'X'	F/L	W Miller		PN174 'R'	F/L	J Northrup
NP705 'Y'	F/O	A Potter		NA186 'U'	F/L	W Goodwin
NP774 'Z'	P/O	J Daley		NR172 'V'	S/L	J McAllister
NP697 'F'	F/L	E McGuire		NPl27 'X'	F/O	D Stewart
				NR228 'Z'	F/O	S Mooers

Pilot Officer Daley returned early with starboard inner engine u/s. Pilot Officer Kinniburgh put down at Brussels short of fuel, whilst 432 Sqd aircraft 'B' and 'J' were diverted to Tibenham and Flying Officer McGuire also short of fuel, landed at Expincy. 415 Squadron aircraft 'C','D','F','H','0', 'P', 'P', 'U', 'V', 'X' and 'Z' were diverted to Framlingham, 'Q' was put down at Woodbridge and 'L' at Nivells, France.

Earlier in the day a Courts Martial had been convened at East Moor for the purpose of trying a senior NCO with 415 Squadron.

14 February 1945

Operations were called for an operation against Chemnitz and the first of twenty three Halifaxes took off at 16.51 hours, despite the difficulties which resulted from the diversion of crews from the previous operation,

432 Squadron				415 Squadron			
RG.450 'Q'	F/L	W Miller		NA185 'B'	P/O	J McKenzie
NP755 'A'	P/O	J Durand		NR146 'E'	F/O	D Falconer
RG451 'D'	F/O	A Clarke		NA202 'I'	F/L	J Northrup
NP208 'G'	F/L	W Mennie		NA204 'J'	F/O	P Evams
NP703 'H'	P/O	P Proud		NR199 'N'	F/O	A Galley
NP803 'I'	F/O	C Hemming		NR124 'S'	F/L	O Piper
NP693 'K'	F/O	A Potter		NP938 'Y'	F/O	L Minkler
NP689 'M'	F/O	J Patterson		NR127 'X'	F/O	D Stewart
NP694 'R'	F/L	F Horan		NR228 'Z'	F/O	S Mooers
RG449 'S'	S/L	J Thompson				
RG448 'V'	F/O	J Paul				
RG455 'X'	P/O	J Allen				
NP736 'B'	P/O	J Bradley				
NP805 'J'	P/O	J Daley				

Sadly, Squadron Leader Thompson and crew failed to return from this operatione

Flight Lieutenant Miller and Pilot Officer Daley landed at Hardwick, Pilot Officer Bradley at Bungay and Pilot Officer Durand at Halesworth. Pilot Officer McKenzie returned early and landed at Carnaby when unable to raise the undercarriage. Flying Officer Evans and Flight Lieutenant Piper of 415 Squadron landed at Hardwick.

The North East Regional Mobile Transfusion Service with Dr, W.S Stanbury (Leeds) visited East Moor and the donated blood was being used on the 'front line' within 24 hours.

In the evening a Valentines Dance was held by the WAAF in their NAAFI where the music was supplied by RCAF Station Skipton's band. The 'Little Theatre' was the setting for RCAF Station Tholthorpe's variety show 'Nissen Huts'.

15 February 1945

No operations were scheduled at the station, but some flying training went ahead.

It was learnt that the 432 Squadron's 'B' Flight Commander, S/L Thompson and crew had been shot down by a JU88. The Flight Engineer was missing and the remainder had become Prisoners of War.

16 February 1945

Breathing space was gained with another operation free day at East Moor.

A specialist party arrived from No.26 Group and commenced fitting the latest VHF radio equipment to all the station's aircraft.

The station was alerted to the possibility of receiving a very large number of diverted American aircraft, but they did not arrive. Later in the day the station was again advised of the probable arrival of a number of NO. 3 Group air craft but once again the diversion was cancelled.

In the first semi-final, RCAF Station East Moor defeated RCAF Station Croft in the hockey game 4 - 2, but the Basketball team suffered a defeat from No.115 American Hospital at Harrogate, 47 - 40.

Major Talbot gave a well attended lecture in the Station Cinema when the subject Iwas the 'Capture of Caen' and the 'Falaise Gap'.

17 February 1945

Between 11.33 hours and 12.00, twenty four Halifaxes were lifted from East Moor's runway and set course for Wesel flying all the way in dense cloud. Such was the cloud density over the target that the 'Master Bomber' gave instructions for the mission to be abandoned. In the meantime the weather had closed in at East Moor and the station's crews were diverted with their bomb loads intact, 415 Squadron to RAF Station Thornaby and 432 Squadron to East Fortune.

432 Squadron				415 Squadron		
NP707 'W'	F/O	A Potter		NR145 'A'	W/O	A McDiarmid
NP694 'P'	F/O	C Hemming		NA181 'D'	F/O	L Minkler
PN208 'G'	F/L	W Mennie		NR206 'F'	F/L	O Piper
NP703 'H'	P/O	R Proud		NR156 'H'	F/O	A Galley
NP803 'I'	P/O	J Kinniburgh		NA202 'I'	F/L	J Northrup
NP693 'K'	P/O	J Allen		NA204 'J'	F/O	P Evans
RG475 'L'	F/O	J Paul		NP938 'Y'	F/L	J MeQuiston
NP689 'M'	F/O	J Patterson		NR199 'N'	F/L	T Mears
RG454 'P'	F/L	J Wallace		NP961 'O'	F/O	D Falconer
NP705 'Y'	F/L	A Bews		NP936 'P'	F/O	J Hechter
				PN174 'R'	S/L	W Brown
				NA186 'U'	F/L	W Goodwin
				NR172 'V'	F/O	S Mooers
				NP127 'X'	F/O	D Stewart

18 February 1945

No operations were called for at East Moor on what was a foggy Sunday.

The Liberal candidate for Southern Manitoba, Flying Officer R.H Jutras, was the speaker at the weekly Forum,and his subject, 'National Unity'.

The film 'Broadway', featuring George Raft was showing in the Officer's Mess.

19 February 1945

No operations were scheduled at the station.

Efforts were being made to improve on the speed and efficiency of the return of documents of posted personnel from the stations and on the general reorganisation of maintenance of records. To this end the station was visited by Wing Commander D Fortune, the Base Adinistration Officer and his assistants.

Sherlock Holmes in Washington' was the film showing at the Little Theatre.

20 February 1945

The RAF Regiment Commander visited East Moor to further a programme of airfield defence involving sten guns and other common weapons.

A night operation to Monheim saw the following East Moor crews dispatched,

432 Squadron				415 Squadron		
NP755 'A'	P/O	R Bradley		NR145 'A'	F/O	R Evans
RG451 'D'	F/L	E McGuire		NA181 'D'	P/O	J McKenzie
NP708 'E'	P/O	J Kinniburgh		NR146 'E'	F/O	D Falconer
PN208 'G'	F/L	W Mennie		NR206 'F'	F/L	O Piper
NP803 'I'	P/O	J Durand		NA156 'H'	F/L	A Cruickshank

NP805 'J'	F/O	G Sherlock	NA202 'I'	F/O	A Galley
RG475 'L'	P/O	J Bain	MZ418 'M'	F/O	J McGuire
NP689 'M'	F/O	J Patterson	NR199 'N'	F/O	J Hechter
RG454 'P'	F/O	J Paul	NP936 'P'	W/O	A McDiarmid
RG450 'Q'	F/L	W Miller	PN174 'R'	S/L	W Brown
NP694 'R'	F/O	C Hemming	NA186 'U'	W/O	L Russell
NP707 'W'	P/O	J Daley	NR172 'V'	S/L	J McAllister
RG455 'X'	F/O	A Patzer	NP961 'O'	F/O	D Stewart
NP705 'Y	F/L	A Bews	NP938 'Y'	F/O	S Mooers

Flying Officer Patzer and crew were shot down by flak, he was killed along with Flight Sergeant W.G Mendenhall and Sergeant C.I Grant, air gunner and flight engineer respectively. The remainder became Prisoners of War.

F light Lieutenant E McGuires crew were in combat with an enemy aircraft on the return flight and submitted a claim 'damaged'.

21 February 1945

This was a black day for the station and for 432 Squadron in particular when three crews failed to return from an early night raid against Worms which was said to be a very accurate attack destroying most of the towns industry The following twenty eight crews set out from the station,

432 Squadron			415 Squadron		
NP755 'A'	P/O	J Durand	MZ922 'C'	F/O	G Hyland
RG451 'D'	F/L	E McGuire	NR146 'E'	F/O	D Falconer
NP708 'E'	P/O	J Kinniburgh	NR206 'F'	F/L	O Piper
PN208 'G'	F/L	W Mennie	NR156 'H'	F/L	A Cruickshank
NP803 'I'	P/O	P Bradley	NA202 'I'	F/O	A Galley
NP805 'J'	F/O	G Sherlock	NA204 'J'	F/O	E Wilkinson
RG475 'L'	P/O	J Bain	NA181 'D'	F/O	J McGuire
NP689 'M'	F/L	J Wallace	NP961 'O'	F/O	B Cowieson
RG454 'P'	F/O	J Paul	NP936 'P'	W/O	A McDiarmid
RG450 'Q'	F/L	W Miller	MZ356 'Q'	F/O	J Hechter
NP694 'R'	F/O	C Hemming	PN174 'R'	W/C	F Ball
RG476 'T'	F/O	F Baxter	NA186 'U'	W/O	L Russell
NP707 'W'	P/O	J Daley	NPl72 'V'	S/L	W Brown
NP705 'Y'	F/L	A Bews	NR127 'X'	F/O	D Stewart

Flight Lieutenant E McGuire and crew were shot down by a JU88 as were Pilot Officer Bradley and crew, the latter became Prisoners of War. An unidentified aircraft shot down Flying Officer Baxter's Halifax killing Flying Officer .A Bleich (Nav), Flying Officer G Cresswell (B/A), Flight Sergeant A Hunter (A/G) and Sergeant A Hogg (F/E). The remainder of this crew became POW's.

The station's Ice Hockey team were finally defeated and were consequently out of the tournament, score was RCAF Station Croft 8 East Moor 5.

In the evening the YMCA organised a Bridge, Cribbage and Chess session in their establishment which roused great interest and was enjoyed by more than 80 personnel.

22 February 1945

An operation free day at the station but flying training was carried out and included air to air firing and fighter affilliation exercises.

News was received at East Moor that Flight Lieutenant W.F Borrett, missing on 16 January, was believed to be dead and that the remainder of his crew were Prisoners of War.

In the evening the WAAF and WD Officers entertained RCAF Officers at a social which was held in the formers mess.

23 February 1945

A daylight operation against Essen when the giant Krupps works suffered great damage, got under way at East Moor before mid-day and all twenty eight crews were airborne by 12.16 hours,

432 Squadron				415 Squadron		
NP708 'E'	P/O	J Kinniburgh		NR145 'A'	F/O	R Evans
NP697 'F'	P/O	J Durand		NA185 'B'	P/O	J McKenzie
PN208 'G'	F/L	W Mennie		MZ922 'C'	F/O	G Hyland
NP805 'J'	F/O	G Sherlock		NA181 'D'	F/O	A Galley
RG475 'L'	P/O	J Bain		NR146 'E'	F/O	D Falconer
RG450 'Q'	F/L	W Miller		NR206 'F'	F/L	O Piper
NP694 'R'	F/L	W Wallace		NR156 'H'	F/L	A Cruickshank
NP707 'W'	P/O	J Daly		NA202 'I'	S/L	W Brown
NP705 'Y'	F/L	A Bews		NA204 'J'	F/L	A Winmill
NP774 'Z'	F/O	J Paul		MZ418 'M'	P/O	J McGuire
				NR228 'Z'	W/O	A McDiarmid
				NP961 'O'	F/O	B Cowieson
				NP936 'P'	W/O	L Russell
				MZ356 'Q'	F/O	J Hechter
				NA186 'U'	F/O	E Wilkinson
				NR172 'V'	S/L	J McAllister
				NR127 'X'	F/O	D Stewart
				NP938 'Y'	F/O	S Mooers

Several aircraft returned with minor flak damage.
415 Squadron were adopted by the town of Bissett in Manitoba with the promise of a supply of comforts to follow.

A 'spot inspection' of the station's WAAF sites was carried out by Wing Officer S.S Dowson from 6 Group Head-quarters accompanied by Squadron Officer H Collett from 62 Base. The general cleanliness, tidiness and environment was not found wanting

The Bomber Group Dance Band again officiated at the airmen's monthly dance.

24 February 1945

A District Court Martial was convened at East Moor to try a senior NCO. The President was Wing Commander W.J Burdy, the Judge Advocate Squadron Leader M.E Richard who was assisted by Flight Lieutenant B.J Gorby.

Shortly after mid-day the station's two squadrons mounted an operation against Kamen and the synthetic oil plants there. The following twenty seven crews were dispatched,

432 Squadron				415 Squadron		
NP755 'A'	P/O	J Durand		NR145 'A'	F/O	R Evans
NP708 'E'	P/O	J Kinniburgh		NA185 'B'	P/O	J McKenzie
NP703 'H'	F/L	J Wallace		NR146 'E'	F/O	D Falconer
NP805 'J'	F/O	G Sherlock		NR206 'F'	F/L	O Piper
RG473 'L'	P/O	J Bain		NR156 'H'	F/L	A Cruickshank
RG454 'P'	F/O	J Paul		NA202 'I'	F/O	G Hyland
RG450 'Q'	F/L	W Miller		NA204 'J'	F/O	B Cowieson
NP694 'R'	F/L	F Horan		MZ418 'M'	F/O	J McGuire
RG448 'V'	F/L	A Bews		NR199 'N'	W/O	A McDiarmid
NP707 'W'	P/O	J Daly		NP936 'P'	W/O	L Russell
PN208 'G'	F/L	W Mennie		PN174 'R'	W/C	F Ball
				NA186 'U'	F/O	E Wilkinson
				NR172 'V'	F/O	A Galley
				NR127 'X'	F/O	D Stewart
				NP938 'Y'	F/O	J Hechter
				NR228 'Z'	F/O	S Mooers

Warrant Officer Russell and crew failed to return from the operation and sadly, all had paid the ultimate pricee No word was heard from them after take off.

Aircraft 'H' and 'Q' of 432 Squadron received some flak damage over the target area.

25 February 1945

415 Squadron played hosts to the Air Training Corps who were given a conducted tour of East Moor airfield and flights in squadron aircraft.

The usual Sunday church services were held and in the evening the weekly Forum's subject was 'Denmark and the Nazis', presented by Helmer Morche the Chaplain to the Danish Forces.

There was no operational commitments at the station.

26 February 1945

The East Moor squadrons were not required for operations, but flying training continued apace with 415 Squadron on bombing practice.

The station learnt that Flying Officer Regimald's crew were known to be dead after failing to return from operations on November 2nd 1944.

27 February 1945

Another popular 432 Squadron Commander departed the station for the 'R' depot, Squadron Leader Minnhinick was succeeded by Wing Commander K.A France.

The Lord Mayor of York, the Lady Mayoress together with the Sheriff and his lady hosted a group of East Moor Officers at the Mansion House. After tea, they enjoyed a conducted tour and shown everything of interest in the house.

Squadron Officer H.E Collette from 62 Base visited East Moor's WAAF's and after speaking about discipline and morale issues, urged all to begin thinking about their future careers in civilian life.

The No.6 Group String Quintette entertained the station's WAAF's, airmen and officers in their respective messes.

Ten aircraft of 432 Squadron and sixteen of 415 were detailed for an attack on Mainz, in what was proved to be the town's worst blitz of the war,

432 Squadron			415 Squadron		
NP755 'A'	F/L	A Bews	NA185 'B'	P/O	J McKenzie
NP697 'F'	F/L	W Miller	MZ922 'C'	F/O	G Hyland
NP703 'H'	P/O	P Proud	NR146 'E'	F/O	D Falconer
NP805 'J'	F/O	G Sherlock	NR206 'F'	F/L	O Piper
RG475 'L'	F/L	E Hayes	NR156 'H'	F/L	A Cruickshank
NP961 'O'	F/S	W Gelineau	NA202 'I'	F/O	P Evans
RG454 'P'	P/O	J Kinniburgh	NA204 'J'	F/O	E Millbank
NP694 'P'	F/O	D Wylie	NR199 'N'	F/O	J Hechter
NP774 'Z'	F/O	J Paul	NP961 'O'	F/O	B Cowieson
NP689 'M'	F/O	A Potter	PN174 'R'	F/O	J McGuire
			NR124 'S'	W/O	A MoDiarmid
			NA186 'U'	F/O	E Wilkinson
			NR172 'V'	S/L	J McAllister
			NR127 'X'	F/O	D Stewart
			NP938 'Y'	F/O	A Galley
			NR228 'Z'	F/O	S Mooers

Aircraft 'A' and 'Z' of 432 Squadron were damaged by flak over the target. Flying Officer Evans and crew were the first to bomb when more than 200 had overshot the target. These then executed a 'U' turn and caused hundreds of bombs and incendiaries to rain down on NA202 knocking off one of the ailerons in the process.

Flying Officer Hyland made an early return when he was unable to raise the undercarriage.

An operation free day at East Moor. Flying training was carried out and included Fighter affilliation and circuits and landings.

Wing Commander K.A France the ex 408 Squadron pilot assumed command of 432 Squadron.

A very popular figure at East Moor, C of E Padre, Squadron Leader E.S Lautenslager departed to Warrington. It was hoped that his successor Flight Lieutenant J.A Payton, would carry on all the good work that the former had introduced to improve station life.

Squadron Leader R.M Matthews assumed Senior Medical Officer duties.

General:

During the month all the Halifax III's of 415 Squadron were converted from carrying mid under gunners to having H2S equipment.

The station took on charge three new Dodge trucks and these were issued to the Instrument Section. It was reported that tyres for the David Brown tractors were in very short supply and that there was a general shortage of service transport serviceability.

East Moor station was well to the fore in the 'National Savings' promotion with the WAAF's taking the lead from all other stations in the base with the sum of £125/5/6.

1 March 1945

The Canadian element rejoiced with the arrival of the first Canadian milk on the station. This had been made possible with a 'Mechanical Cow' having been aquired at Base to process it, and had been affectionately named Mrs. Ferdinand'.

Flight Lieutenant A.J Doran was posted in from RCAF Station Wombleton to assume duties of Station Armaments Officer.

415 Squadron Adjutant, Flight Lieutenant A. Carveth learnt that he was three years too old to transfer to the Canadian Army as requested.

It was found necessary to recruit a number of the fairer sex from York to supplement the shortage for a station dance. Transport was provided and the event was said to have been a great success.

A daylight operation was mounted by the station's two squadrons who provided Ithe following crews to attack Mannheim. Take off commenced at 11.33 hours and all twenty five were airborne by 11.59

432 Squadron			415 Squadron		
NP755 'A'	F/O	L Loppe	MZ922 'C'	P/O	J McKenzie
PN229 'C'	W/C	France	NR146 'E'	F/O	D Falconer
NP708 'E'	P/O	J Kinniburgh	NR206 'F'	F/L	O Piper
PN208 'G'	P/O	R Proud	NR156 'H'	F/L	A Cruickshank
NP703 'H'	F/O	D Wylie	NA202 'I'	F/O	R Evans
NP693 'K'	F/G	A Clarke	NA204 'J'	F/O	E Millbank
NP689 'M'	F/L	E Hayes	MZ418 'M'	F/O	J McGuire
RG454 'P'	P/O	J Allen	NP940 'L'	F/L	E Wilkinson
RG478 'U'	F/O	W Gregory	NA185 'B'	F/O	J Hechter
NP707 'W'	F/O	A Potter	PN174 'R'	S/L	W Brown
NP705 'Y'	F/O	G Sherlock	NR124 'S'	W/O	A McDiarmid
			NR172 'V'	F/L	A Winmill
			NR127 'X'	F/O	A Galley
			NP938 'Y'	F/O	B Cowieson

2 March 1945

The first of the station's Halifaxes was airborne again at 06.50 hours when twenty five crews were detailed to attack Cologne in daylight,

432 Squadron				415 Squadron		
NP736 'B'	F/O	L Loppe		NR172 'V'	W/C	F Ball
NP708 'E'	P/O	J Kinniburgh		NA202 'I'	F/L	J Northrup
NP805 'J'	F/O	G Sherlock		NR199 'N'	F/L	T Mears
NP693 'K'	P/O	R Proud		NA145 'A'	F/L	W Mitchell
RG475 'L'	F/L	W Miller		NR146 'E'	F/O	D Falconer
NP689 'M'	F/L	F Horan		MZ418 'M'	F/O	J McGuire
PN224 'O'	F/S	W Gelineau		MZ922 'C'	P/O	J McKenzie
RG454 'P'	P/O	J Allen		NR124 'S'	W/O	A McDiarmid
NP707 'W'	F/O	D Wylie		NR228 'Z'.	F/O	J Hechter
NP705 'Y'	F/O	W Gregory		NA186 'U'	F/O	A Galley
RG479 'N'	F/O	A Clarke		NR206 'F'	F/O	B Cowieson
				NA204 'J'	F/O	L Minkler
				NP938 'Y'	F/L	J Mcquiston
				NP940 'L'	F/O	E Wilkinson

Aircraft 'E','J','W' and 'Y' of 432 Squadron were damaged by flak over the target, and 'V' and 'Z' of 415 Squadron returned damaged.

Appointments made within 432 Squadron included Flight Lieutenant E. Hayes to be 'A' Flight Commander, Flight Lieutenant F Horan to be 'B' Flight Commander and Flight Lieutenant Foy Signals Leader.

The station was the scene of a minor 'flap' when the tannoy announced that a mass break out of German Prisoners of War had occurred in the locality. The message should have read 1 or two and not 102.

Flying training was carried out from the station during the day.

The airmens mess was the scene for a party given to the staffs of all three East Moor messes.. The YMCA provided the music, Officers and Sergeants the beer and the three bar tenders were Station Catering Officer,Section Officer Helen Goodrow, 415 Sqd Adjutant, Flight Lieutenant A. Carveth and the SADO, Squadron Leader G.H MeMahon.

3 March 1945

Flying at East Moor was restricted to training with the best day for months being accomplished, with fifteen 432 Squadron aircraft and twelve from 415 being involved.

During the night enemy raiders were active but no damage was inflicted on the station. The Master switch was thrown imposing a total blackout and many of the personnel took to the slit trenches which were found to contain a lot of water.

The sounding of the station's air raid siren was the first for a long time and was effected just after midnight of the 3rd. One raider was close to the station and those brave eneough to watch were treated to a small display of tracer and flak.

4 March 1945

Operations were called for but were later scrubbed. Poor weather prevented any flying training being carried out at the station.

Sunday Church Services were very well attended and in the evening the Forum's guest speaker was Dr. C.G Schweitzer and his subject 'The Churches Struggle Against Nazism' was listened to by more than 200 personnel. The speaker was himself a refugee from a Nazi Internment Camp.

5 March 1945

Flying training during the day included air to air firing and fighter affilliation exercises which were resumed after a two day lull.

NP755 of 432 Squadron blew a tyre at midday whilst on training,

Chemnitz was the target chosen for East Moor crews and the following set out on a night raid which started badly for No.6 Group when no fewer than nine bombers crashed shortly after take off in freak icing conditions,

432 Squadron				415 Squadron		
PN229 'C'	PlO	J Kinniburgh		NR145 'A'	F/O	L Minkler
PN233 'D'	F/L	A Clarke		NA185 'B'	P/O	J McKenzie
NP736 'B'	F/O	G Sherlock		MZ922 'C'	F/O	D Falconer
PN208 'G'	P/O	R Proud		NR156 'H'	F/L	A Cruickshank
RG475 'L'	S/L	E Hayes		NR228 'Z'	F/L	A Winmill
NP689 'M'	F/S	W Gelineau		NA204 'J'	F/L	W Mitchell
PN224 'O'	F/L	J Wallace		NP940 'L'	F/O	E Wilkinson
RG454 'P'	P/O	J Daly		MZ418 'M'	F/O	J McGuire
RG450 'Q'	P/O	J Bain		NR199 'N'	F/L	T Mears
NP707 'W'	F/O	D Wylie		NP961 'O'	F/O	B Cowieson
NP705 'Y'	F/O	J Paul		LW122 'Q'	F/O	J Hechter
				PN174 'R'	S/L	J McAllister
				NR127 'X'	F/O	A Galley
				NP938 'Y'	F/L	J McQuiston
				NR172 'V'	F/O	T Donnelly

The station lost two aircraft and crews on this operation. Flight Lieutenant

W.R Mitchell evaded capture but the remainder of his crew became prisoners of war. The navigator, Flying Officer R.C Barteaux was on his first operation

Tragically the other crew paid the ultimate price when returning over England Squadron Leader Hayes mount, RG475 was shot down by so called 'friendly' anti aircraft fire. The Halifax crashed between Earles Colne and Walton on Naze in Essex.

Pilot Officer Bain's gunners returned fire when twice attacked by enemy aircraft and put down at Manston where it was then badly damaged by another aircraft on that station.

Aircraft 'B','G','W' and 'Y' of 432 Squadron put down at Mildenhall and 'P' at Tuddenham. 'B','C','H','Z','Q' and 'Y' of 415 Squadron landed at Tangmere, 'N','O','R' and 'X' at Thorney Island, 'V' at Ford, 'A' and 'M' in France at Juvincourt and Lielle.

6 March 1945

Flying Officer's S.W Mooers and D.J Stewart having completed their tours were departing East Moor to participate in the making of a film at 62 Base.

The station's squadrons were without any operational commitments but routine training flights were carried out.

A new Station Intelligence Officer, Flight Lieutenant W. Pilkington was posted in from RCAF Station Linton on Ouse.

A number of Canadian personnel took advantage of the visit of Flying Officer Sales Engineer and representative of Sarco Heating and Ventilation Company from Torontoe After a lecture on the opportunities in that field, several airmen signed up for further studies with the Station Education Officer.

Three 432 Squadron ground crew members, LAC's Waterhouse, Forbes and Christiansen were said to be sporting motorcycles provided by their grateful aircrews whose aircraft they looked after.

7 March 1945

The Officers Mess at Sutton Hall (a mansion) was sold to Mr.Galliers-Pratt who intended living in it when the war was over and it was derequistioned.

Operational commitments precluded any flying training at East Moor and thirty one aircraft were detailed for an operation to Hemmingstedt when several crews reported hearing a 'spoof' Master Bomber at work.

The take off commenced at 18.10 hours and the last one lifted off the runway at 18.42, and involved the following,

432 Squadron			415 Squadron		
NP736 'B'	F/O	H Kearle	NR145 'A'	F/O	T Donnelly
PN229'C'	P/O	J Bain	NA185 'B'	P/O	J McKenzie
PN233 'D'	F/L	A Clarke	NR146 'E'	F/O	D Falconer
NP708 'E'	P/O	J Kinniburgh	NR206 'F'	F/L	J McQuiston
PN208 'G'	P/O	R Proud	NR156 'H'	F/L	A Cruickshank
NP703 'H'	F/O	A Smith	NA202 'I'	F/L	J Northrup
NP805 'J'	F/O	G Sherlock	PN236 'J'	F/L	A Winmill
RG479 'N'	F/O	J Paul	NP940 'L'	F/O	E Wilkinson
PN224 'O'	F/S	P Neville	MZ418 'M'	F/O	J McGuire
PN235 'S'	P/O	J Durand	NR199 'N'	F/L	T Mears
RG478 'U'	F/S	G Jamer	NP961 'O'	F/O	B Cowieson
RG448 'V'	F/O	J Patterson	LW122 'Q'	F/O	L Minkler
NP707 'W'	F/L	D Wylie	PN174 'R'	S/L	J McAllister
NP705 'Y'	F/S	W Gelineau	NA186 'U'	W/O	A McDiarmid
NP774 'Z'	P/O	J Daly	NR127 'X'	F/O	A Galley
			NR228 'Z'	P/O	C Emsom

All returned safely.

8 March 1945

A small amount of flying training was carried out and the station's Airspeed Oxford was busily engaged in ferrying crews to and from RCAF Station Linton.

Station Intelligence Officer, Squadron Leader E.F Kusch was posted out to RCAF Overseas Headquarters.

Again, thirty one aircraft and crews were detailed and the target was Hamburg.

432 Squadron			415 Squadron		
PN229 'C'	W/C	K France	NA185 'B'	P/O	J McKenzie
NP703 'H'	P/O	J Bain	MZ922 'C'	F/O	D Falconer
NP774 'Z'	P/O	J Kinniburgh	NR206 'F'	F/O	A Galley
NP707 'W'	F/O	E Martindale	NR156 'H'	F/L	A Cruickehank
RG448 'V'	P/O	J Daly	NA202 'I'	F/L	J Northrup
RG478 'U'	F/O	A Smith	PN236 'J'	F/L	A Winmill
PN224 'O'	F/S	D Jamer	NP940 'L'	F/O	E Wilkinson
RG479 'N'	F/O	J Paul	MZ418 'M'	F/O	J McGuire
NP697 'F'	F/S	W Gelineau	NR199 'N'	F/L	T Mears
NP689 'M'	F/O	J Patterson	NP961 'O'	F/O	B Cowieson
NP805 'J'	F/O	G Sherlock	LW122 'Q'	S/L	J McAllister
PN208 'G'	P/O	R Proud	PN174 'R'	F/O	T Donnelly
PN233 'D'	F/L	A Clarke	PN237 'T'	F/O	L Minkler
NP736 'B'	F/S	P Neville	NA186 'U'	W/O	A McDiarmid
NP755 'A'	P/O	H Kearle	NP938 'Y'	F/L	J McQuiston
			MZ907 'P'	P/O	C Emsom

Sadly, Warrant Officer McDiarmid and crew were missing from this operation and nothing was heard from them after take off.

Wing Commander France's aircraft was damaged by flak and he landed at Carnaby. Pilot Officer Bain's port outer engine failed just after take off followed by the starboard inner, as he was unable to maintain height the bomb load was jettisoned into the North Sea and he put the aircraft down at Carnaby.

Flight Sergeant Gelineau returned from the target on three engines, the port outer having failed after two hours flying.

Pilot Officer McKenzie abondoned the mission while still over East Moor when he was unable to raise flaps or undercarriage but continued to jettisoning area in the North Sea.

9 March 1945

Operations were called for and subsequently cancelled. Day and night flying training was carried out from the station, most of which was cross country exercises.

Another 'first' for the station when a bus load of personnel travelled to the town of Ripon and swam in the public baths there. It was expected to become a regular event.

No.62 Base Equipment Officer, Wing Commander J.Head and Administration Officer Wing Commander D. Fortune visited East Moor Station.

10 March 1945

There was no operational commitment at the station but a heavy programme of day training was pursued.

Steps were taken to form squadron teams to compete in various sports in order to provide an outlet for surplus energy and to encourage a spirit of friendly co-operation between squadrons. The Station Sports Officer was successful in providing new equipment for basketball and football.

Mr.F Fitton, a representative of the Bristol Aeroplane Company at East Moor together with Chief Technical Officer, Squadron Leader W.E Boone travelled to RAF Station Carnaby near Bridlington to look over Halifax NP703 which had landed there on two engines.

A Court Martial was held at East Moor and amongst the officiating officers were Wing Commander H.M Sinclair (RCAF Overseas HQ), Flight Lieutenant Sullivan (No.6 Group), Wing Commander P.D Turner (RCAF Overseas HQ), and Squadron Leader S.Berger and Flight Lieutenant J. Royan of 420 Squadron.

11 March 1945

Sunday, and a very busy one too with the resumption of operations by the two squadrons, considerable flying training and a visit by the Air Training Corps. The latter witnessed the operational take off before enjoying some familiarisation flying.

At 11.29 hours Flying Officer Nears lifted the first of twenty seven Halifaxe~ from East Moor's runway to join over a thousand other aircraft to attack Essen on what proved to be the last operation against that city,

432 Squadron			415 Squadron		
PN229 'C'	P/O	J Turner	NR145 'A'	P/O	J McKenzie
PN233 'D'	F/L	A Clarke	MZ814 'D'	P/O	R Pallin
PN208 'G'	P/O	H Kearle	NR146 'E'	F/O	D Falconer
NP805 'J'	P/O	J Kinniburgh	NR206 'F'	P/O	C Ensom
NP693 'K'	F/O	S Bonter	NR156 'H'	F/O	J Patterson
NP689 'M'	F/O	J Patterson	NA202 'I'	F/O	E Wilkinson
RG479 'N'	F/O	J Paul	PN236 'J'	P/O	V Clouthier
PN224 'O'	F/O	A Smith	NR199 'N'	F/L	T Mears
RG454 'P'	P/O	J Bain	PNl74 'R'	F/O	G Hyland
RG478 'U'	P/O	J Bigland	RG447 'S'	S/L	W Brown
RG448 'V'	P/O	J Daly	PN237 'T'	F/O	L Minkler
NP707 'W'	F/S	D Jamer	NP754 'U'	F/O	A Galley
NP774 'Z'	F/O	E Martindale	PN239 'V'	F/O	J McGuire
			NP938 'Y'	F/L	J McQuiston

All returned safely to East Moor where many crews described the operation as 'a piece of cake'.

12 March 1945

The pressure was being kept up as another daylight operation involving twenty seven of the station's crews was scheduled for a raid on Dortmund and from which all returned safely,

432 Squadron				415 Squadron		
NP755 'A'	P/O	J Bain		PN174 'R'	F/O	R Evans
NP736 'B'	P/O	H Kearle		MZ814 'D'	P/O	R Pallin
PN229 'C'	P/O	J Turner		NR146 'E'	F/O	E Millbank
PN233 'D'	P/O	R Proud		NR206 'F'	F/L	O Piper
PN208 'G'	W/O	W Gelineau		MZ922 'C'	F/O	G Hyland
NP805 'J'	F/S	P Neville		NR156 'H'	F/L	A Cruickshank
NP693 'K'	F/O	S Bonter		NA202 'I'	F/O	E Wilkinson
NP689 'M'	F/O	J Patterson		NR199 'N'	F/L	T Mears
RG479 'N'	F/O	J Paul		RG447 'S'	S/L	W Brown
RG478 'U'	P/O	J Bigland		PN237 'T'	F/O	L Minkler
RG448 'V'	P/O	J Daly		PN239 'V'	F/O	J McGuire
NP707 'W'	F/S	W Jamer		NR127 'X'	F/O	A Galley
NP774 'Z'	F/O	E Martindale		NP754 'U'	F/L	J NcQuiston
				NR228 'Z'	F/O	B Cowieson

The RAF Gang Show attracted a full house at the Little Theatre having recently toured the Far Easte It was said to have been one of the best shows seen at East Moor to that date.

13 March 1945

For the first time at East Moor a Halifax VII was weighed. Squadron Leader Boone together with the Base Engineering Officer confirmed the gross weight as 59,560 lbs~ This included 2,190 gallons of fuel, the bomb carriers and seven fully kitted aircrew members.

Catering Officers, Squadron Officer H.A Bulk from 6 Group and Flight Officer E.O Little from 62 Base, visited East Moor.

Twenty nine crews were dispatched from the station for another daylight raid, this time the target was Wuppertal, all returned safely,

432 Squadron				415 Squadron		
NP736 'B'	P/O	J Bain		NR145 'A'	F/O	R Evans
PN233 'D'	F/L	A Clarke		NA185 'B'	F/O	J Patterson
NP697 'F'	P/O	J Durand		MZ814 'D'	F/O	R Pallin
PN208 'G'	F/O	R Proud		NR206 'F'	F/L	O Piper
NP693 'K'	F/O	S Raymond		NR156 'H'	F/L	A Cruickshank
NP689 'M'	PlO	J Turner		NA202 'I'	F/O	E Wilkinson
PN224 'O'	F/S	D Jamer		PN236 'J'	F/O	W Milbank
RG454 'P'	P/O	J Bigland		MZ907 'P'	P/O	V Clouthier
PN235 'S'	F/O	E Martindale		PN174 'R'	F/L	T Mears
RG478 'U'	F/O	W Gregory		RG447 'S'	S/L	W Brown
RG448 'V'	PlO	J Daly		PN237 'T'	F/O	L Minkler
NP707 'W'	F/L	D Wylie		PN239 'V'	F/O	J McGuire
NP698 'X'	F/S	P Neville		NR127 'X'	F/O	A Galley
RG479 'N'	P/O	J Kinniburgh		NP938 'Y'	F/O	B Cowieson
				NP754 'U'	P/O	C Ensom

Flight Lieutenant A.A Tiplin, Intelligence Officer was posted in from RCAF Station Linton on Ouse.
Flying Officer C.H Cotton, Education Section was posted out to Warrington.

14 March 1945

415 Squadron received over 10.000 cigarettes and more than one and a half thousand packets of chewing gum and gifts from the Agent General of Canada. The gum was strictly for aircrew only everything else was shared by all.

Considerable flying training was carried out from the station, and the Airspeed Oxford was kept busy, being flown by 'skippers' of new crews to RCAF Station Linton on Ouse and RAF Station Carnaby ferrying passengers and familiarising themselves with the surrounding countryside.

The East Moor Basketball team defeated RCAF Station Linton 41   26 in the first of a two game final, putting them in a very strong position for the Group championship.

Two of the twenty eight crews that took off for attack on Zwiebrucken made early returns, Pilot Officer Kinniburgh with a u/s starboard outer engine and Flight Lieutenant Cruickshank with u/s W/T equipment and upper turret firing circuit. The remainder returned safely,

432 Squadron			415 Squadron		
NP755 'A'	F/O	L Loppe	MZ814 'D'	P/O	R Pallin
NP736 'B'	P/O	S Allen	NR206 'F'	F/L	O Piper
PN233 'D'	F/L	A Clarke	NR156 'H'	F/L	A Cruickshank
NP697 'F'	P/O	J Durand	NA202 'I'	F/O	E Wilkinson
PN208 'G'	P/O	P Proud	PN236 'J'	F/O	E Milibank
NP805 'J'	F/S	P Neville	MZ907 'P'	F/O	G Hyland
NP689 'N'	F/O	S Bonter	RG447 'S'	F/O	J McGuire
PN224 'O'	F/O	S Raymond	PN237 'T'	F/O	L Minkler
RG454 'P'	F/S	D Jamer	NA185 'B'	F/O	P Evans
PN235 'S'	F/O	E Martindale	PN239 'V'	S/L	J McAllister
RG478 'U'	F/O	W Gregory	PN240 'W'	F/L	T Mears
RG448 'V'	P/O	J Daly	NR127 'X'	F/O	A Galley
NP707 'W'	S/L	F Horan	NP938 'Y'	F/O	B Cowieson
NP708 'E'	P/O	J Kinniburgh	NR228 'Z'	P/O	C Ensom

15 March 1945

The Commanding Officer accompanied by the Adjutant carried out an inspection of 432 Squadron quarters on No.3 Site where it was said the standard was satisfactory considering that the occupants had been operating on five consecutive days.

415 Squadron once again were awarded the Base Pennant for efficiency during the month of February.

A very busy day for the stations two squadrons, ten from each took off for a daylight operation to Castrop Rauxel just after midday and shortly before their return to East Moor a further seven from each took off for Hagen.

The following was the 'Battle Order' for Castrop Rauxel,

432 Squadron			415 Squadron		
PN229 'C'	P/O	J Turner	NR206 'F'	F/L	O Piper
NP697 'F'	P/IO	J Durand	NA185 'B'	F/L	A Cruickshank
PN241 'I'	P/O	J Bigland	MZ814 'D'	F/O	E Wilkinson
NP693 'K'	F/O	S Raymond	PN236 'J'	F/O	E Millbank
RG479 'N'	P/O	S Allen	NR145 'A'	F/O	R Evans
RG454 'P'	F/S	D Jamer	RG447 'S'	F/O	A Galley
PN235 'S'	P/O	J Bain	PN239 'V'	F/O	T Donnelly
RG478 'U'	F/O	W Gregory	PN174 'R'	W/C	F Ball
RG448 'V'	F/S	P Neville	PN237 'T'	F/L	W Goodwin
NP774 'Z'	F/O	L Loppe	PN240 'W'	F/L	T Mears

All returned safely but several with flak damage, aircraft 'A' and 'S' of 415 Squadron and 'F' and 'P' of 432 Squadron.

The Hagen operation involved,

NP755 'A'	F/O	E Martindale	NR146 'E'	P/O	C Ensom
PN233 'D'	F/L	A Clarke	NR156 'H'	F/O	J Patterson
PN208 'G'	P/O	R Proud	NP940 'L'	F/O	G Hyland
NP805 'J'	P/O	J Kinniburgh	NR199 'N'	F/O	B Cowieson
NP689 'M'	F/O	S Bonter	NR127 'X'	F/O	J McGuire
PN224 'O'	P/O	J Daly	NP938 'Y'	F/O	L Minkler

NP707 'W'	S/L	F Horan	NR228 'Z'	P/O	R Pallin

Pilot Officer Bonter and crew failed to return from this operation, the remainder returned safely.

16 March 1945

Both of the station's squadrons carried out routine training programmes in the absence of any operational commitments. Much of the flying training consisted of cross countries.

East Moor WAAF's defeated their counterparts from RCAF Station Tholthorpe 24 - 4 in a netball match, and the now weekly bus left for the Ripon baths.

In the evening a St.Patrick's Day Dance was held in the airmen's NAAFI which had been suitably decorated for the occasion with plants and flowers. The Station Commander, Group Captain R. A McLernon, DFC attended as did the Station Adjutant, Flight Lieutenant G.W Jaques and the music was provided by the band from RCAF Station Skipton on Swale.

17 March 1945

The station was once again without any operational commitment though a full training programme was carried out and involved both squadrons.

It was the Officers turn to celebrate St.Patrick's Day which they did with a party and a dance when the music was supplied by No.62 Base Band. The festivities were carried out in true Irish fashion in a mess decorated with daffodils,tulips and cedars enhanced with coloured lights.

At 21.00 hours the air raid warning was sounded but enemy aircraft passed over the station without attacking and the all clear was given at 22.30 hours.

18 March 1945

It was noticeably quiet around the squadron offices as many of the party revellers slept in as long as possible.

The Air Training Corps again visited the station but due to operational activity were unable to enjoy further familiarisation flights.

A snap inspection at the isolated Strensall Bombing Range was carried out by the Armaments Officer who found everything satisfactory there.

The Sunday Forum's guest speaker was Palle Bistrup a Danish saboteur, and his subject 'Denmark and the Nazis' kept a large audience hanging on to every word of his most graphic account of his experiences.

After a 21.45 hours briefing the station dispatched twenty eight crews for an attack on Witten and from which all returned safely, take off commenced midnight,

432 Squadron			415 Squadron		
NP697 'F'	P/O	J Durand	NA185 'B'	F/O	D Clark
PN235 'S'	F/O	E Martindale	MZ922 'C'	F/O	a Hyland
NP755 'A'	F/O	L Loppe	MZ814 'D'	P/O	R Pallin
PN229 'C'	P/O	J Turner	NR206 'F'	F/L	O Piper
PN233 'D'	F/L	A Clarke	NA202 'I'	P/O	C Ensom
PN208 'G'	P/O	R Proud	PN236 'J'	F/O	E Mulbank
NP805 'J'	P/O	J Bain	NR156 'H'	F/O	A Galley
NP693 'K'	P/O	J Kinniburgh	NR199 'N'	F/O	J Patterson
RG479 'N'	P/O	S Allen	NR127 'X'	F/O	R Evans
RG454 'P'	P/O	J Bigland	PN174 'R'	F/O	T Donally
RG478 'U'	P/O	O Brown	RG447 'S'	S/L	W Brown
RG448 'V'	F/O	A King	PN237 'T'	F/O	L Minkler
NP698 'X'	F/S	D Jamer	PN240 'W'	F/L	W Goodwin
NP774 'Z'	F/O	S Raymond	NP938 'Y'	F/O	J McGuire

Engine trouble forced Flying Officer McGuire to put down at Cambria Epinoy. Leaving NP938 they took a Dakota to Swindon later in the day and returned to East Moor by Anson on the 20th.

Four crews were unable to recover to East Moor before the weather closed in, aircraft 'C' and 'I' of 415 Squadron landed at RCAF Station Tholthorpe while 'F' and 'S' of 432 landed at RCAF Station Linton on Ouse.

19 March 1945

The crews from the operation to Witten did not arrive back until almost 08.00 hours so there was no further commitment on this day, and no flying training was carried out.

A new Station Signals Officer, Flight Lieutenant G.F Harfield was posted in from RCAF Station Dishforth.

20 March 1945

Operations were called for at the station but later scrubbed. Only one aircraft was engaged in flying training, a three hour cross country exercise. Ground training was carried out by both squadrons.

East Moor WAAF Netball team were defeated by RCAF Station Leeming 17 - 5, in a game played at that station. At 22.00 hours the air raid warning was given, no attack on the station occurred and the all clear was given at 22.30.

21 March 1954

At 10.00 hours thirty of the station's aircraft were detailed for an attack on Rheine and take off commenced at 14.33 hours,

432 Squadron			415 Squadron		
NP755 'A'	F/O	L Loppe	MZ922 'C'	F/O	G Hyland
PN229 'C'	P/O	J Turner	MZ814 'D'	P/O	R Pallin
PN233 'D'	P/O	R Proud	NR146 'E'	F/O	D Falconer
NP708 'E'	P/lO	J Allen	NR206 'F'	P/O	J McKenzie
NP703 'H'	F/O	A Smith	PN236 'J'	F/O	F Mulbank
PN241 'I'	F/O	S Raymond	NP940 'L'	F/L	A Cruickshank
NP805 'J'	P/O	J Bain	NR199 'N'	P/O	J Patterson
NP693 'K'	P/O	H Kearle	NR256 'Q'	F/O	B Cowieson
RG479'N'	F/O	J Paul	PN174 'R'	W/C	F Ball
RG454 'P'	F/O	E Martindale	RG447 'S'	P/O	C Ensom
NP802 'Q'	W/O	W Gelineau	PN237 'T'	F/O	L Minkler
NP694 'R'	P/O	J Bigland	NP754 'U'	F/O	R Evans
RG478 'U'	F/O	W Gregory	PN239 'V'	F/O	V Clark
RG448 'V'	P/O	J Daly	PN240 'W'	F/O	J Hechter
NP774 'Z'	F/O	A King	NR127 'X'	F/L	F Cahill

Aircraft 'J' of 432 Squadron bombed Ahaus in error, and 'P' attacked Heek. Flying Officer Hechter had trouble with the undercarriage while still over East Moor but continued with it down. After bombing, the bomb doors would not close and with insufficient fuel it was decided to land at Eindhoven.

The remainder returned safely to East Moor.

22 March 1945

An exceptionally warm and sunny day at East Moor. A small number of aircraft were engaged in flying training exercises.

Flying Officer Hechter and crew returned to East Moor with the undercarriage still not retracted. Apparantly they had been escorted from the target area to Eindhoven by two Typhoons and said to be most appreciative of the support.

The station put thirty four Halifaxes into the air for an operation against Dorsten, a rail and canal centre. Take off commenced at 11.31 hours and all
were airborne by 12.04

432 Squadron				**415 Squadron**			
NP755 'A'	F/L	L Loppe		NR145 'A'	F/O	P Evans
NP736 'B'	P/O	J Allen		NA185 'B'	P/O	J McKenzie
PN229 'C'	P/O	J Turner		MZ922 'C'	F/O	G Hyland
PN233 'D'	F/O	A Smith		MZ814 'D'	P/O	P Pallin
NP708 'E'	P/O	P Ritchie		NR146 'E'	F/O	D Falconer
PN208 'G'	P/O	P Proud		NR206 'F'	F/L	O Piper
NP703 'H'	F/O	A King		NA202 'I'	F/L	F Cahill
PN241 'I'	P/O	H Kearle		PN236 'J'	F/O	F Mulbank
NP693 'K'	P/O	J Bain		NR199 'N'	F/O	J Patterson
RG479 'N'	F/O	J Paul		MZ907 'P'	F/O	J McCollum
PN224 'O'	W/O	W Gelineau		PN174 'R'	F/O	B Cowieson
RG454 'P'	P/O	J Bigland		RG447 'S'	F/L	A Cruickshank
NP694 'R'	S/L	F Horan		PN237 'T'	F/O	L Minkler
PN235 'S'	F/O	E Martindale		NP754 'U'	F/L	W Goodwin
RG478 'U'	F/O	W Gregory		PN239 'V'	F/O	V Clark
RG448 'V'	P/O	J Daly		NR127 'X'	F/L	E Wilkinson
NP774 'Z'	P/O	D Brown		NR228 'Z'	P/O	C Ensom

Flying Officer Ritchie and crew suffered a total hang up over the target and later managed to jettison part of the load.

Pilot Officer Kearle's Halifax received several flak holes in the rear fuselage tail unit and starboard wing.

All aircraft returned safely to East Moor.

23 March 1945

Considerable flying training was carried out at the station but no operations were called for.

46 personnel took advantage of the weekly bus trip to Ripon Baths.

The stations squadrons competed with each other at Softball and the score was 432 Squadron 14, 415 Squadron
The first 'Station' dance for some time was held in the gymnasium and music was provided by the dance band from RCAF Station Linton on Ouse.

No.6 Group Quintette played lunch time music in the officer's mess, and was followed by the Film 'In Society'.

24 March 1945

East Moor Basketball team defeated RCAF Station Skipton on Swale 32 - 24.

Squadron Leader N.T Chappel No.6 Group Chaplain and Group Captain G.O Lightbourn the Protestant Chaplain from RCAF Overseas Headquarters visited East Moor and witnessed the daylight take off of the station's aircraft for a mission to Gladbeck.

A Canadian Rally was held at RCAF Station Dishforth and a number of East Moor personnel attended what was said to be an outstanding event. Excellent talks were given by Dr.Cyril James President of McGill University and the head of RCAF Education Group Captain Lowe.

Eighteen aircraft of 432 Squadron and seventeen of 415 were made ready for the Gladbeck raid and all took off between 08.56 hours and 09.30. Early returns were made by aircraft 'B', Pilot Officer Allen of 432 Squadron with a u/s starboard outer engine, and 'B', Pilot Officer NcKenzie of 415 Squadron who had hydraulic failure on take off and overheating inner engines. The former was down again by 12.53 hours and the latter at 11.27. Four of the aircraft received flak damage but the target was said to be 'plastered'.

The order of battle was as follows,

432 Squadron				415 Squadron		
NP736 'B'	P/O	J Allen		NR145 'A'	F/O	R Evans
RG448 'V'	P/O	J Daly		NA185 'B'	P/O	J McKenzie
PN233 'D'	F/O	A Smith		MZ922 'C'	F/O	G Hyland
PN241 'I'	F/O	R Proud		MZ814 'D'	PlO	V Clouthier
NP708 'E'	P/O	J Turner		NR146 'E'	F/O	D Falconer
NP755 'A'	F/O	L Loppe		NR206 'F'	F/L	O Piper
PN224 'O'	W/O	W Gelineau		LV941 'G'	F/O	E Wilkinson
NP707 'W'	F/L	D Wylie		NP940 'L'	F/L	F Cahill
RG479 'N'	F/O	J Paul		NR199 'N'	F/O	J Patterson
NP802 'Q'	F/O	A King		NR256 'Q'	F/O	J McCollum
NP693 'K'	P/O	J Bain		PN174 'R'	F/O	B Cowieson
RG478 'U'	F/O	W Gregory		RG447 'S'	F/L	A Cruickshank
PN229 'C'	W/C	K France		PN237 'T'	F/O	L Minkler
NP703 'H'	F/O	S Raymond		NP754 'U'	F/L	W Goodwin
RG454 'P'	P/O	J Bigland		PN239 'V'	F/O	V Clark
NP694 'R'	P/O	D Brown		PN240 'W'	F/O	J Hechter
PN235 'S'	F/O	E Martindale		NR228 'Z'	P/O	C Ensom
NP774 'Z'	F/O	R Ritchie				

Pilot Officer McKenzie's aircraft suffered hydraulic failure on take off and overheating inner engines, after jettisoning the bomb load into the North Sea he returned to East Moor and landed on three engines at 11.27 hours.

Flying Officer's Patterson and Martindale together with Pilot Officer Ensom returned with considerable flak damage to their Halifaxes.

25 March 1945

06.45 hours and the first of thirty six of the stations crews were airborne for a further operation, this time to Munster,

432 Squadron				415 Squadron		
NP755 'A'	F/O	L Loppe		NR145 'A'	F/O	R Evans
PN229 'C'	P/O	J Turner		NA185 'B'	F/O	J McKenzie
PN233 'D'	F/O	A Smith		MZ922 'C'	F/O	G Hyland
PN208 'G'	F/O	R Proud		MZ814 'D'	P/O	R Pallin
NP703 'H'	F/O	S Raymond		NR146 'E'	F/O	D Falconer
PN241 'I'	P/O	J Allen		NR206 'F'	F/L	W Goodwin
NP693 'K'	P/O	J Bain		LV941 'G'	F/O	J Patterson
RG479 'N'	F/O	J Paul		NR156 'H'	F/L	A Cruickshank
PN224 'O'	W/O	W Gelineau		NA202 'I'	F/L	F Cahill
NP802 'Q'	F/O	A King		PN236 'J'	F/O	F Millbank
RG454 'P'	F/O	J Bigland		NP940 'L'	F/L	E Wilkinson
PN235 'S'	F/O	E Martindale		MZ907 'P'	F/O	J McCollum
RG478 'U'	W/C	K France		NR256 'Q'	F/O	J Addison
RG448 'V'	P/O	J Daly		PNl74 'R'	F/O	B Cowieson
NP707 'W'	P/O	H Kearle		PN237 'T'	F/O	L Minkler
NP774 'Z'	F/O	P Ritchie		NP754 'U'	F/O	V Clouthier
NP694 'R'	P/O	D Brown		PN239 'V'	F/O	V Clark
				PN240 'W'	F/O	J Hechter
				NR127 'X'	P/O	C Ensom

Flying Officer McCollum and crew failed to return from this operation, and nothing was heard from them after leaving East Moor.
Pilot Officer Brown made an early return with a u/s starboard outer engine. Heavy flak was encountered in the target area and the aircraft of Wing CommFrance, Flying Officer Ritchie and Pilot Officer's Allen, Bigland and Daly were damaged.

Due to unfavourable weather, only one aircraft returned to East Moor the remainder were diverted, aircraft 'C','G','K', of 432 Squadron to RCAF S Station Croft, and 'D','H', 'I','N', 'O', 'Q','P', 'S','U', 'V','W' and 'Z' at RCAF Station Wombleton. Aircraft 'A','E' and'R' of 415 managed to get to East Moor while 'B' ,'C' ,'F' ,'G' ,'H' ,'I' ,'J' ,'L',' Q' ,'T', 'U' ,'W' and 'X' landed at RCAF Station Wombleton, 'D' at RCAF Station Croft and 'V' at RAF Station Carnaby.

A party from the station attended York Minster for the performance of Bach's 'St.Matthew Passion' and were said to have left greatly inspired.

A very sobering address was given by the Sunday evening Forum speaker, Hugo Kuranda a Vienna journalist whose subject was 'The Continent looks to the Empire', pointing to ones responsibilities after the war.

The station's WAAF Section held an 'Exhibition of Handicrafts' on their site and amongst the guests were Wing Officer S.S Dowson and the WD Staff Officer Squadron Officer K.L Ball from No.6 Group.

26 March 1945

No operations were scheduled at the station but both squadrons were heavily engaged in flying training.

27 March 1945

Another operation free day and flying training continued apace.
The news from the Rhine area was Very good and morale was running very high at East Moor as it was learned that General Eisenhower and his staff had led the troops into a situation of complete mastery on the ground. The station's personnel were sure that the end was in sight.

It is worth mentioning that one of the station's crews, that of Pilot Officer Ensom, had completed no fewer than twelve operations between the 7th and the 25th of March.

Five DFC's and one DFM were announced for members of 415 Squadron, including Flying Officer G.F McGlone who was an 'old man' in the aircrew world, being 38 years of age.

The Station's Airmens Mess played and defeated a team of 415 Squadron ground staff 10 - 9 at Softball.

28 March 1945

The station's crews were not required for operations, but flying and ground training programmes were pursued. Aircrew were given a 'stand down'.

News was received at East Moor that Flying Officer's D.N Sloan, J.K Daniel, and Flight Sergeant's R.A Collins and G.A Binne were prisoners of war. They were members of Flight Lieutenant Borrett's crew missing on 17th January 1945.

415 Squadron's Gunnery Leader, Flying Officer W.F Griffiths was credited with a Me2lO and screened at the end of his 2nd 'tour'.

Wing Commander R.D Blagrave arrived at East Moor with his crew and joined 415 Squadron.

F light Lieutenant S.F Harfield Station Signals Officer was posted in from RCAF Station Dishforth.

East Moor Basketball team retained their Championship standing by defeating RCAF Station Dalton at York while the Station soccer team defeated the village team at Stillington 4 - 3.

29 March 1945

Still no operational calling for the station's crews. Many of the personnel attended lectures on Rehabilitation, Administration and Personal Hygene.

RCAF Station Tholthorpe sent over a WAAF Netball team who were beaten 18 - 3 by the East Moor girls.

Visitors to the station included 62 Base Accounts Officer, Flight Lieutenant T.D Berry, Code and Cypher Officer Flight Officer K. Smith and Air Bomber Flight Lieutenant J.F Neilens also from 62 Base.

30 March 1945

Good Friday, and with no operations scheduled at East Moor the station's Church Services were well attended.

The Roman Catholic Chief Chaplain visited the station. Group Captain W.V McArthy as always cheered everyone up.

Twelve of 415 Squadron's aircraft and several 432 Squadron were engaged in flying training exercises in the afternoon.

The RCAF party 'The Airscrews' gave two well attended shows in the Corporal's NAAFI and followed by supper.

31 March 1945

The early hours saw thirty three Halifaxes lifted from East Moor's runway for a mission to Hamburg, the first was airborne at 05.57 hours and the last one at 06.46,

432 Squadron			415 Squadron		
NP707 'W'	S/L	F Horan	NR145 'A'	F/O	R Evans
PN233 'D'	F/L	A Clarke	NA185 'B'	F/O	J McKenzie
PN229 'C'	P/O	H Kearle	MZ922 'C'	F/O	G Hyland
PN208 'G'	P/O	R Proud	MZ814 'D'	P/O	R Pallin
NP708 'E'	F/O	J Kinniburgh	NR146 'E'	F/O	D Falconer
NP693 'K'	P/O	J Allen	NR206 'F'	F/L	O Piper
PN241 'I'	F/O	A Smith	LV941 'G'	F/O	F Millbank
PN224 'O'	F/L	J Wallace	NR156 'H'	F/O	J Addison
PN235 'S'	F/O	W Gregory	NA202 'I'	F/L	F Cahill
RG448 'V'	P/O	J Daly	MZ474 'K'	P/O	V Clouthier
RG479 'N'	F/O	J Paul	NR199 'N'	F/O	J Patterson
NP774 'Z'	F/S	D Jamer	NR256 'Q'	F/O	E Wilkinson
NP802 'Q'	F/O	A King	PN174 'R'	F/O	B Cowieson
NP694 'R'	P/O	D Brown	RG447 'S'	P/O	C Ensom
NP736 'B'	W/O	W Gelineau	PN237 'T'	F/O	L Minkler
NP755 'A'	F/O	L Loppe	PN240 'W'	F/O	J Hechter
			PN236 'J'	F/O	V Clark

Sadly, Flying Officer G.A Hyland and crew failed to return from this operation.

Flying Officer Loppe made an early return with a u/s port outer engine.

Heavy flak over the target found the Halifaxes of skippers J. Clouthier and V.Clark of 415 Squadron.

The aircraft of No.6 Group are said to have been late over the target area and consequently their fighter escort had been withdrawn leaving them to become the unexpected victims of the Luftwaffe's elite Jagdverbande 44.

No less than thirty Me262 jet fighters tore into the bombers and had shot down five Lancasters and three Halifaxes within twelve minutes. One of the latter was MZ922 of 415 Squadron in which Flying Officer Hyland and crew paid the ultimate price.

General:

It was generally thought that the month had seen the 'beginning of the end' and at a conference held with the Station Commander Group Captain R.A NcLernon DFC, the senior officers discussed the possible participation in the Pacific theatre. A request for volunteers for that area met with a good response at East Moor.

Due to the heavy programme of operations and flying training, all sections of the station had been extremely hard worked. Many 'flaps' were created when very short notice was given to prepare for operations. The station mounted seventeen during March and the two squadrons dropped more than 1,236 tons of bombs.

Plans were made to refit all the station's Halifaxes with new mid upper gun turrets. The 'C' types were to be peplaced with Mk VIII which were fitted with a Gyro gun sight installation.

A new catering innovation was introduced at the station, 'post op meals' for aircrew who had completed their last mission were welcomed by all and included steaks and chops etc. Messing was said to have improved considerably during March in all the station's messes.

By the end of the month all ground staff had received weapon training and had become familiar with the use of sten gun, rifle and hand grenade.

415 Squadron were again the winners of the 62 Base Pennant for efficiency.

SUMMARY OF ACTIVITIES
EAST MOOR

	June 18th 1944	March 31st 1945	
Squadron	415	432	Totals
No of Nights	51	130	-
No of Days	46	55	-
No of aircraft Detailed	1,523	2,639	4,162
No attacking Primary	1,460	2,401	3,861
% attacking Primary	95.86	90.98	-
No Missing	12	49	61

OPERATIONAL ACTIVITY FOR MARCH 1945

Squadron	415	432	Totals
No of Nights	6	6	-
No of Days	11	11	-
No of aircraft Detailed	248	231	479
Non Starters	-	-	-
No Took Off	248	231	479
No of Early Return	3	5	8
No attacking Primary	242	221	463
No of Missing	4	1	5
% Non Starters	-	-	-
% Early Returns	01.21	02.16	-
% Missing.	01.63	00.44	-
% attacking Primary	95.35	95.67	-

1 April 1945

Easter Sunday, and all the Church services were well attended and the Padres were said to be very happy. Group Captain R.A McLernon, the Station Commander read the lesson to a very large congregation in the Station Cinema.

It was the 21st Anniversary of the forming of the Royal Canadian Air Force, and while no operations were called for at East Moor, flying training went on as usual with Fighter affilliation, air to air firing, SBA and H25 exercises.

A very large audience gave a rousing response to the speaker at the Sunday Forum, Squadron Leader C.K Sansbury spoke on 'The Ideology of Japan'.

Tom Conway featured in the film 'Falcon in Hollywood' in the 'Y' Lounge.

2 April 1945

Operations were called for but later cancelled, flying training proceeded. News was received at East Moor that Warrant Officer W.F McDiarmid and crew missing on 8th March, had become prisoners of war, and so too had Flight Lieut W.R Mitchell and crew missing on the 5th.

The station WAAF Section said goodbye to a popular Staff Officer from 62 Base, Squadron Officer H.E Collett who paid a final visit to East Moor before taking up an appointment at Headquarters Bomber Command.

3 April 1945

After being briefed no less than three times, the station's aircrews were on 'stand by' all day which precluded any flying training.

In anticipation of a visit from the Bomber Command Engineering Officer, the Servicing Wing had a 'splurge of bull' and a general clean up was effected.

The station was visited by the District Provost Marshal Flight Lieutenant W.G Chisnell.

The Music Club was the setting for an excellent performance by the No.6 Group Quintette who entertained a large audience.

All the WAAF night workers received a visit during the night from Wing Officer S.S Dowson from No.6 Group.

4 April 1945

An inspection of the station's Servicing Wing was carried out by Bomber Command's Engineering Officer, Air Commodore H.J Roach accompanied by No.6 Group Engineer

Officer Wing Commander N.M Smith. The wing was able to show a 100% serviceability record.
The station was also visited by No.6 Group's Air Sea Rescue Officer, Squadron Leader R.H Strouts.

The East Moor Netball team defeated RCAF Station Linton on Ouse 19 - 0. and the Basketball team won at Warrington 33 - 29.

The first operation of the month got underway at 19.24 hours when the first of thirty Halifaxes rose from East Moor's runway and set out for an attack on Harburg - Rhenhanian and its oil plants,

432 Squadron			415 Squadron		
NP755 'A'	F/O	L Loppe	MZ814 'D'	F/O	R Evans
NP736 'B'	P/O	J Allen	NR146 'E'	F/O	D Falconer
PN229 'C'	S/L	W Miller	NR206 'F'	F/L	O Piper
PN233 'D'	F/L	A Clarke	LV941 'G'	F/O	V Clarke
NP708 'E'	P/O	J Kinmiburgh	NA202 'I'	F/L	F Cahill
NP697 'F'	F/O	J Paul	MZ474 'K'	P/O	J Clouthier
PN208 'G'	F/L	D Wylie	NR199 'N'	F/O	J Patterson
NP805 'J'	F/O	R Ritchie	PN174 'R'	F/O	T Donnelly
NP693 'K'	P/O	H Kearle	NP940 'L'	F/L	W Goodwin
RG454 'P'	F/O	A King	RG447 'S'	F/O	F Milibank
PN241 'I'	F/O	A Smith	PN237 'T'	F/O	L Minkler
PN235 'S'	F/S	P Neville	PN239 'V'	F/L	A Winmill
NP694 'R'	P/O	D Brown	PN240 'W'	F/O	J Hechter
RG448 'V'	P/O	J Daly	NR127 'X'	F/O	A Galley
NP774 'Z'	F/S	D Jamer	NR228 'Z'	F/O	J McKenzie

2nd Pilots were carried as follows,

'A'	W/O	Brewer	'D'	W/C	Blagrave
'C'	F/O	Collins	'F'	F/O	Jupp
'D'	F/O	Nicholson	'R'	F/O	Addison

'G'	P/O	MeTaggart	'L'	F/O	McLatchie
			'V'	F/O	Molter
			'W'	F/O	Huffman

Flying Officer Ritchie's Halifax was attacked by a Me163 which was seen to explode when his gunners returned fire.

Flying Officer Smith made an early return with u/s hydraulics.

5 April 1945

An operation free day at the station but both squadrons participated in a considerable programme of flying training which included cross country and bombing practice exercises.

Victory 'fever' must have been in the air. The Station Commander Group Captain R.A McLernon DFC, held a meeting of senior officers when discussions were held on the subject of victory celebrations and precautions.

432 Squadron held a party for all who had any connection with that squadron.

6 April 1945

A second day without any operational commitment at East Moor. Considerable local flying took place checking out new crews.

The WAAF NAAFI was the scene for the formers Easter Dance when music was provided by RCAF Station Skipton on Swale's Dance Band.

7 April 1945

And yet another day free of operations for the station although an attack on Kiel had been called for but cancelled during the afternoon.

Fig 36. RCAF East Moor 1945. L to R. Sgt Harpin FE, F/O McKenzie B/A, F/L Cahill Pilot. Outside Officers hut. (415 Squadron).

The station's Basketball team competed at Bournemouth in the RCAF Overseas Championship losing 37-17 to London and winning 30 - 20 against Honeybourne, with further games to be played next day.

The station grape vine was buzzing non stop with rumours, suggestions that the war was already over, that the squadrons would be in Canada within a month, or that they were destined for the Pacific theatre. With all the excitement morale was extremely high.

8 April 1945

The last Basketball game was played at Bournemouth where East Moor were finally knocked out of the championship.

The evening Forum was an outstanding Canadian speaker, Major Jones who was Liasion Officer between Marshal Tito and the British Forces in Yugoslavia.

St.Stephen's Orphanage in York conveyed special thanks to staff at East Moor and 415 Squadron in particular for donations of chocolate and gifts to that institution's children at Easter time.

Although it was a fine clear day at East Moor it was anticipated that the station's crews detailed for operations would have to be diverted on their Ireturn in the early hours of the 9th. The same Battle Order as detailed on the 7th was to attack Hamburg and involved the following,

432 Squadron			415 Squadron		
PN229 'C'	W/C	K France	MZ814 'D'	F/O	J McKenzie
PN235 'S'	S/L	W Miller	NR146 'E'	F/O	D Falconer
PN233 'D'	F/L	A Clarke	LV941 'G'	F/O	R Jupp
PN224 'O'	F/O	L Loppe	NR156 'H'	F/O	J Addison
NP697 'F'	P/O	J Kinniburgh	NA202 'I'	F/L	F Cahill
PN208 'G'	P/O	H Kearle	PN236 'J'	F/O	F Millbank
NP736 'B'	P/O	J Allen	MZ474 'K'	P/O	J Clouthier
NP805 'J'	P/O	J Bain	NP940 'L'	P/IO	L Harker
NP705 'Y'	F/O	A Smith	NR199 'N'	F/O	J Patterson
NP693 'K'	W/O	D Brewer	NR256 'Q'	F/O	V Clark
RG457 'P'	P/O	J Daly	RG447 'S'	F/O	C Holter
RG479 'N'	F/O	J Paul	PN237 'T'	F/O	L Minkler
NP812 'T'	F/S	D Jamer	PN239 'V'	F/L	A Winmill
NP707 'W'	F/O	A Nicholson	PN240 'W'	F/O	J Hechter
NP694 'R'	F/S	P Neville	NR127 'X'	F/O	A Galley

Squadron Leader Miller returned early with a u/s starboard outer engine and bombsight, Pilot Officer Bain with u/s starboard outer engine and Warrant Officer Brewer with the same problem.

All 415 Squadron were diverted to Chipping Warden and 432 to Market Harborough.

Flight Lieutenant Clarke's Halifax was hit by flak over the target knocking out his starboard inner engine and the prop fell off.

The crew of Flight Sergeant Neville were attacked by a FW190 on the homeward track and fire was returned by the rear gunner who claimed it as damaged.

9 April 1945

The diverted crews returned during the day and some flying training was carried out at the station.

PN233 was at RAF Station Little Staughton where it had landed on three engines. The station's WAAF Section had picked a drill team to represent them in the Sunderland Cup Group Heat, and commenced their daily drill practice in the afternoon.

The 8th Canadian Victory Loan Campaign Overseas opened on this date and East Moor Station had been set a target of 90,000 Canadian dollars. This figure was soon raised and there were high hopes that it would be doubled bdfore the campaign closed.

10 April 1945

The station witnessed a very smart parade and inspection of the WAAF Section, all personnel of the fairer sex were involved and put on 'a very good show' There followed a WAAF General Meeting and the Catering Officer, Squadron Officer N.H Goodrow was on hand to discuss messing.

At lunch time the No.6 Group Quintette played to the officers in their mess, and in the evening the Music Club provided a programme of recorded music in the NAAFI on the WMF site.

The station's newly formed camera club had acquired premises and a dark room on the Old Communal Site, received a good response from interested personnel and were being encouraged by the Station Photographic Section.

Flying training was carried out in the form of cross country and local flying and at 13.27 hours take off commenced for the following crews who set out to attack Leipzig,

432 Squadron				415 Squadron		
NP802 'Q'	S/L	W Miller		NA185 'B'	F/O	R Evans
RG448 'V'	P/O	J Daly		NR146 'E'	F/O	D Falconer
PN224 'O'	F/O	J Paul		LV941 'G'	F/O	L Harker
NP774 'Z'	F/S	D Jamer		NR156 'H'	F/O	J Addison
NP698 'X'	F/S	P Neville		NA202 'I'	F/L	F Cahill
PN235 'S'	F/O	E Martindale		PN236 'J'	F/O	E Millbank
NP705 'Y'	P/O	D McTaggart		NR256 'Q'	F/O	C Holter
NP707 'W'	F/O	A Nicholson		RG447 'S'	F/O	R Jupp
NP755 'A'	F/O	L Loppe		PN237 'T'	F/O	J Hultman
PN208 'G'	P/O	H Kearle		PN239 'V'	F/O	T Donnelly
NP703 'H'	P/O	J Kinniburgh		PN240 'W'	F/O	J Hechter
NP736 'B'	P/O	J Allen		NR228 'Z'	P/O	R McClatchie
NP805 'J'	P/O	J Bain		PN174 'R'	F/O	J Huffman
NP694 'R'	P/O	J Turner				
IPN229 'C'	F/O	A Smith				
NP693 'K'	W/O	D Brewer				
RG478 'U'	F/O	S Pepler				
NP697 'F'	F/O	J Collins				

Flying Officer Evans and crew failed to return from this operation and were 415 Squadron's last operational losses from East Moor. NA185 was on its 42nd mission while Sergeant Andrews the flight engineer, had been shot down on the 9th February and returned to East Moor.

Aircraft 'H','0' and 'S' of 432 Squadron received flak damage along with 'J' of 415 Squadron.

Pilot Officer Turner and Warrant Officer Brewer made early returns with u/s starboard outer engines.

11 April 1945

East Moor squadrons were not required for operations but both carried out routine training flights.

Group Captain R.A McLernon DFC, the Station Commander carried out an inspection of squadron 'Working and Living' sites and found all to his satisfaction.

National Savings Stamps to the sum of £28/11/11- were sold at the Pay Parade, and the YMCA provided music and refreshments for the ever popular roller skating party.

12 April 1945

And another operation free day at the station. No flying was recorded but a heavy ground training programme was carried out and included Link Trainer Flying, H25, Turret Manipulation, Engine Handling, and Navigation lectures.

The station Netball team defeated RCAF Station Topcliffe 22 - 0 at East Moor. The Station Cinema was showing 'One Body Too Many'.

Fig 37. 'Hang Up'. We opened the doors and out fell the 1,000 pounder, and we lived to photograph it !.
Photo R. King.

13 April 1945

415 Squadron received their official 'Adoption' letter from San Antonio Gold Mines at Bisset in Manitoba, and were looking forward to receiving some comforts.

RCAF Station Linton on Ouse provided the dance band for the Airmen's jig held in the NAAFI and the bus for Ripon Baths was well filled once again.

It was announced that East Moor personnel had subscribed 140,650 Canadian dollars to the 8th Canadian Victory Loan Campaign, this was more than 56% above the station's original quota.

A night operation to Kiel was mounted by the East Moor crews from which all returned safely, but due to the weather were diverted,

432 Squadron				**415 Squadron**		
NP703 'H'	S/L	W Miller		PN174 'R'	F/O	J McKenzie
NP697 'F'	F/O	J Kinniburgh		MZ814 'D'	P/O	R McClatchie
NP736 'B'	P/O	J Allen		NR146 'E'	F/O	J Addison
NP805 'J'	P/O	J Bain		NR206 'F'	F/L	O Piper
PN208 'G'	P/O	H Kearle		LV941 'G'	F/O	L Harker
PN229 'C'	F/O	A Smith		NR156 'H'	F/O	J Hultman
NP755 'A'	W/O	D Brewer		NA202 'I'	F/L	F Cahill
RG448 'V'	P/O	J Daly		PN236 'J'	F/O	E Milibank
PN224 'O'	F/O	J Paul		MZ474 'K'	P/O	J Clouthier
NP774 'Z'	F/S	D Jamer		NP940 'L'	F/L	C Wilkinson
RG478 'U'	F/S	P Neville		NR199 'N'	F/O	A Huffman
PN235 'S'	F/O	E Martindale		NR256 'Q'	F/O	C Holter
NP707 'W'	F/O	A Nicholson		RG447 'S'	F/O	E Jupp
NP705 'Y'	P/O	D McTaggart		PN237 'T'	F/O	T Donnelly
PN241 'I'	F/O	J Collins		PN299 'V'	W/C	K Blagrave
				PN240 'W'	F/O	J Hechter
				MZ483 'M'	F/O	A Galley
				NP938 'Y'	P/O	C Ensom
				NR228 'Z'	F/O	B Cowieson

Pilot Officer Kearle made an early return with a u/s starboard inner engine, and Flying Officer Galley with u/s Gee and H25.

Pilot Officer McClatchie's port outer engine became u/s on approach to target.

432 Squadron aircraft 'H' landed at Honeybourne, 'I' at Tarrant Rushton, 'B' and 'A' at Morton in the Marsh and the remainder at Long Marston. Two of 415 Squadron's aircraft made it into East Moor, 'E' and'V', while 'D' went to Langham and the remainder to Wellsbourne.

14 April 1945

Seventeen of the diverted aircraft returned to East Moor during the day, and no further operations were called for.

15 April 1945

Flying Training was the only flying carried out at the station and included bombing practice at Strensall and fighter affilliation with aircraft from RCAF Station Dalton.

Promotion to Flight Lieutenant for Flying Officer R.S Evans was authorized, sadly he had gone missing on the 10th April.

Weekly Forum and film shows were well supported as usual.

16 April 1945

No operational Commitment for the station's crews but a warning to be on stand by for a daylight attack on the 17th was received.

Both squadrons were engaged on flying training exercises including bombing practice at Strensall range, fighter af-filliation, air to air firing, air to sea firing and cross countries.

At 12.10 hours, Halifax NP805 was taking off on a training flight when it swung off the runway and crashed into the woods. It completely demolished a picket post on the old communal site killing the occupants, LAC's R.F Charbon-neau and J.D Bedard. The pilot, Flying Officer W.H Porritt died in the ensuing fire but the remainder of the crew escaped.

At 14.25 hours, Halifax PN235 also swung on take off and crashed but fortunately did not burn and there were no in-juries involved.

17 April 1945

There was no flying recorded at East Moor. Operations had been called for early afternoon but cancelled just prior to take of f, leaving the crews very frustrated.

Word was received that a 'tour' would from hereon, consist of 30 operations for pilots and 28 for other aircrew.

The East Moor WAAF Section came under scrutiny when they were judged for the Group Heat of the Sunderland Cup. The Inspection included the entire WAAF Sites and messes and was carried out by Wing Officer S.S Dowson and Squadron Officer K L Ball from 6 Group Headquarters. The 'Judges' watched other WAAF features a netball game between M.T Section and the remainder of the station's WAAF, a drill display, P.T display together with First Aid, Hairdressing and Dressmaking classes.

18 April 1945

East Moor contributed thirty nine Halifaxes to a mixed force of almost one thousand aircraft on an operation to Heli-goland. 415 Squadron's Commander, Wing Commander F. Ball was appointed 'Gaggle Leader' for this attack, and the squadron's personnel were keeping their fingers crossed for all to go well.

Fig 38. The scene at Goose Wood, East Moor on 16th April 1945 when this 432 Squadron Halifax swung on take off for a training exercise. After striking a building, the aircraft crashed into the trees killing the skipper, Flying Officer Porritt. The remainder of the crew escaped. Photo R.Day.

After being airborne for around one and a half hours, Flying Officer Holter had to return with a u/s port inner engine.

Som.e confusion arose and .was reflected in the squadron's records after Flying Officer Sadler of 415 Squadron flew his crew in a 432 Squadron Halifax, NP812.

The Order of Battle was as follows and all returned safely,

432 Squadron				415 Squadron		
PN224 'O'	F/L	Wallace		NRl45 'A'	F/O	J McKenzie
RG479 'N'	F/L	J Paul		MZ814 'D'	P/O	P McClatchie
RG448 'V'	W/O	W Gelineau		NR146 'E'	F/O	J Addison
NP698 'X'	F/S	P Neville		NR206 'F'	F/O	T Donnelly
NP705 'Y'	F/L	E Martindale		LV941 'G'	F/O	L Harker
RG454 'P'	F/L	J Bigland		NR156 'H'	F/O	J Hultuan
NP802 'Q'	F/O	A King		NA202 'I'	F/O	A Huffman
NP694 'R'	P/O	D Brown		P11236 'J'	F/O	E Milibank
NP693 'K'	F/O	P Ritchie		MZ474 'K'	P/O	J Clouthier
NP755 'A'	F/O	S Pepler		NP940 'L'	F/L	E Wilkinson
NP707 'W'	F/L	V Bugslag		MZ483 'M'	W/O	P Blagrave
PN229 'C'	F/O	A Smith		NR256 'Q'	F/O	C Holter
PN208 'G'	P/O	H Kearle		RG447 'S'	F/O	P Jupp
NP697 'F'	P/O	J Kinniburgh		PN237 'T'	F/L	W Goodwin
NP736 'B'	F/L	J Allen		**NP812 'T'	F/O	J Sadler
NP703 'H'	F/L	J Bain		PN174 'R'	W/C	F Ball
PN241 'I'	F/O	S Raymond		PN240 'W'	F/O	J Hechter
RG478 'V'	F/S	D Jamer		NR127 'X'	F/O	A Galley
				NP938 'Y'	P/O	C Ensom
				NR228 'Z'	F/O	B Cowieson
				PN239 'V'	F/L	A Winmill

Flying Officer Pepler's aircraft was damaged by an exploding aircraft in the target area.

This was a very successful daylight operation.
** 432 Sqd aircraft

19 April 1945

Flying Officer Porritt's funeral service was held followed by interrment at the Harrogate War Cemetery. His bomb aimer and flight engineer were absent and in hospital, the remaining crew members attended together with a bearer and supporting party.

In the absence of any operational calling at East Moor, the two squadrons engaged in a heavy flying training programme of cross country, fighter affilliation and bombing excercises.

In the evening the Station Cinema was packed to capacity for the 'Victory Loan Dance:the music being supplied by No.2 RCAF (Overseas) Band. More than 6,00 Canadian dollars worth of 'Victory Bonds' was raised by raffles.

The 6 Group Air Sea Rescue Officer, Squadron Leader P.H Strouts again visited the station

20 April 1945

No operations were scheduled at East Moor, but once again a heavy programme of flying training was pursued with around thirty aircraft involved.

The station Netball team defeated RCAF Station Topcliffe 26 - 6 and the weekly swimming party went off to Ripon Baths.

A snap inspection of various sites by the 6 Group's Sanitation and Hygene NCO revealed nothing to complain about.

21 April 1945

No operations at the station but many aircraft and crews engaged in flying training determined not to be found wanting when targets could be found for them.

At noon the Station Commander, Group Captain R.A McLernon DFC, drew the the winning ticket out of the hat for Flying Officer K.U Lunney of 432 Squadron's Navigation Section. The lucky man received 1,000 Canadian dollars worth of bonds.

Fig 39. Flight Lieut F Cahill, under Halifax NA202, 6U-'I' early April 1945.

Photo J. Harpin.

The award of an immediate DFC was made to 415 Squadron's Flying Officer W.F Griffiths in recognition of shooting down a Me2O9 during his second tour.

22 April 1945

Thirty four crews were dispatched from East Moor for an attack in support of Allied Ground Forces at Bremen. The take off commenced at 16.04 hours and all were down again by 22.13 after the Master Bomber had given instructions to abandon the mission,

432 Squadron			415 Squadron		
PN233 'D'	F/O	A Smith	NR145 'A'	F/O	J McKenzie
PN208 'G'	P/O	H Kearle	MZ814 'D'	F/O	W Abram
NP697 'F'[1]	F/O	J Kinniburgh	NR146 'E'	F/O	J Addison
NP736 'B'	F/L	J Allen	NR206 'F'	F/O	L Harker
NP755 'A'	F/L	J Bain	NR156 'H'	F/O	J Hultman
PN241 'I'	F/O	R Raymond	PN236 'J'	F/S	H Ward
NP812 'T'	F/O	N Breeze	MZ474 'K'	P/O	R McClatchie
PN229 'C'	F/L	V Bugslag	NP940 'L'	F/L	B Cowieson
PN224 'O'	F/L	D Wallace	NR228 'Z'	W/O	R Blagrave
NP698 'X'	F/L	J Paul	NR199 'N'	F/O	J Patterson
RG448 'V'	W/O	W Gelineau	NR256 'Q'	F/O	J Sadler
NP694 'R'	F/S	D Jamer	PN174 'R'	F/L	T Donnelly
NP707 'W'	F/S	P Neville	RG447 'S'	F/O	R Jupp
NP705 'Y'	F/L	E Martindale	PN237 'T'	F/O	L Minkler
RG454 'P'	F/L	J Bigland	PN239 'V'	F/L	A Winmill
NP802 'Q'	F/O	A King	PN240 'W'	P/O	V Clark
			NR127 'X'	F/L	A Galley
			NP938 'Y'	P/O	C Ensom

Four second pilots were carried on the operation, Flying Officer Kirkbride in NP697, Pilot Officer Shott in NP755, Flying Officer Finnan in NP940 and Flying Officer Fornssler in PN174.

Flight Lieutenant Paul made an early return with a u/s starboard outer engine.

After completing the operation, Flight Lieutenants Martindale and Donnelly landed at the emergency strip at RAF Station Carnaby with mechanical problems.

The weekly Forum attracted a very large audience who listened to Flying Officer J; McLean a Personnel Counsellor, discuss the future prospects for Canadians on their return. He gave a talk entitled 'Will Canada Back Our Jobs'.

Flying Officer N. Connor; the navigator missing with Flying Officer McFadden on the operation to Hanover on 5th January 1945, made a return to East Moor. When relating his experiences it transpired that on leaving the damaged MZ476, he was struck by a propeller which severed his left leg.

Realizing the extent of his injuries, he had presence of mind during his parachute descent to stuff his clothing into the wound and thus stem the flow of blood. Fortunately, he landed in a forest clearing without further injury. He then utilised the silk threads and bamboo riggings and fashioned a tourniquet.

After lying in the clearing for 22.1/2 hours Flying Officer Connor was at last discovered by a German farmer, taken to hospital and underwent an operation on his leg. Following his hospitalisation he was released in a prisoner 'exchange' and returned to the United Kingdom.

415 Squadron recommended him for a non immediate DFC.

He and his crew had been due to join 405 (RCAF) Pathfinder squadron on the day following their ill fated flight from East Moor.

23 April 1945

The station's squadrons were not required for operations and only routine flying was carried out.

The 8th Canadian Victory Loan Campaign ended with RCAF Station East Moor having attained 203% of their quota which meant that the personnel had subscribed to more than 182,000 Canadian dollars worth of Bonds. 415 Squadron finished in second place from all squadrons in No.6 Group, with 67,000 dollars donated.

Recognition of the bravery of one 415 Squadron member was received at East Moor from the Lancashire Chief Constables Office. Pilot Officer John Haley was on leave when he watched a Wellington Bomber crash into the sea off Fleetwood.

The aircraft broke up and the crew including Sergeant Edwin Bedell were thrown into the tidal current. Sergeant Bedell suffering from serious facial injuries was being carried towards the' mouth of the River Wyre and his cries for help were answered by Pilot Officer John Haley and Joseph Scott. After swimming more than 250 yards the two men supported Sergeant Bedell until the arrival of a fishing boat.
The Chief Constable recommended that the two rescuers be considered for a Royal Humane Society Award for their gallant action.

East Moor Netball team defeated RCAF Station Thoithorpe 18 - 3.

24 April 1945

Another frustrating experience for the East Moor crews when operations were called for only to be cancelled. Several of them only needed one more operation to complete their 'tours'.

Flying training got under way With some cross. country and bombing exercises some of which were carried out at night, including a 'Bullseye' on London.

Squadron Leader H.L Saunders DFC, arrived from 408 Squadron to take up duties as 'A' Flight Commander with 415 Squadron. He was on his second tour.

No.62 (RCAF) Base Linton on Ouse was the scene for a Royal Visit by HRH the Princess Royal. Amongst the East Moor personnel presented at the Review of WAAF and WD were Section Officer P.E Seccombe, Flight Officer G.D Findlay from Intelligence Section, Section Officer H.M Goodrow Catering Officer and Flight Officer M.W Peacock Nursing Sister. After a Parade and March Past all attended a luncheon party given in the Princess Royal's honour.

25 April 1945

The last raid of the war from East Moor Station was carried out when thirty eight crews were detailed to attack gun batteries on the island of Wangerooge.

All detailed Halifaxes were bombed up but at the last minute aircraft 'Z', NR228 of 415 Squadron was found to have a cracked sleeve in its port inner engine and was unable to participate..

Take off commenced at 14.36 hours and at 15.12 Flying Officer R. Raymond and crew lifted NP698 off to become the last sortie to leave East Moor's runway in anger.

All the station's aircraft returned safely, the last one to touch down being PN224 with Flying Officer N.Breeze at the controls.

432 Squadron			**4'15 Squadron**		
PN229 'O'	W/O	K France	NR145 'A'	F/O	J McKenzie
PN233 'D'	F/O	A Smith	MZ814 'D'	P/O	R Pallin
NP697 'F'	F/O	J Collins	NR146 'E'	F/O	J Addison
NP736 'B'	F/L	J Kinniburgh	NR206 'F'	F/O	A Huffman
PN208 'G'	F/L	J Bain	NR156 'H'	F/O	J Huitman
NP693 'K'	P/O	J Turner	NA202 'I'	F/L	F Cahill
NP698 'X'	F/O	R Raymond	PN236 'J'	F/O	L Harker
PN224 'O'	F/O	N Breeze	MZ474 'K'	W/C	R Blagrave
RG448 'V'	F/L	J Daly	NP940 'L'	F/L	B Cowieson
RG479 'N'	F/L	J Paul	NR199 'N'	F/O	J Patterson
NP774 'Z'	F/S	D Jamer	NR256 'Q'	F/O	R McClatchie
RG478 'U'	F/S	P Neville	PN174 'R'	F/S	H Ward
RG454 'P'	F/L	J Bigland	RG447 'S'	F/O	R Jupp

Fig 40. Wangerooge imminent 25th April 1945.
F/S Middleton WOP, P/O Clyde A/G, F/O Mackenzie B/A, F/L Cahill Pilot, F/S Campbell NAV,
Sgt Harpin F/E   P/O Goring A/G.

Photo J.Harpin.

NP802 'Q'	F/O	A King	PN237 'T'	F/O	L Minkler
NP694 'R'	P/O	D Brown	PN239 'V'	F/L	A Winmill
NP812 'T'	F/L	V Bugslag	PN240 'W'	P/O	V Clark
NP755 'A'	W/O	W Gelinean	NR127 'X'	F/L	A Galley
NP705 'Y'	P/O	D McTaggart	NP938 'Y'	P/O	C Ensom
NP707 'W'	F/O	A Nicholson			

Flight Sergeant Jamer's Halifax suffered some flak damage.

26 April 1945

Operations were called for and subsequently cancelled. Despite the cloudy and rainy weather, many crews found their way to York and their favourite watering holes.

An exhibition soccer match between East Moor and Stillington Village resulted in the station team winning by an unbelievable score of 32 - 6.

27 April 1945

No operations were scheduled at East Moor but local flying training and bombing exercises were carried out after a two day lull in training.

The weekly bus left for Ripon Baths and in the evening an Airmen's Dance was held in the NAAFI with music from the Base Band at RCAF Station Linton.

28 April 1945

Fig 41. Sgt Harpin F/E, F/S Campbell NAV, F/S Middleton WOP, F/O Aikenhead NAV, F/L Cahill Plot, F/L Winmill Pilot.
Photo J. Harpin.

No operations were called for at the station, and it seemed that there weren't any more targets for the station's squadrons. Nevertheless, flying went ahead full swing in anticipation of the 'Second Phase'.

East Moor station was honoured by a visit from the Canadian High Commissioner, the Honourable Vincent Massey and Mrs. Massey. The pride and joy of the Officer's Mess, the Palm Room, was the scene for a pre luncheon cocktail. Section Officer H.M Goodrow provided an excellent lunch after which Mr.Massey spoke in appreciation of the part that Canadians had played in the war and of the difficulties with which they might be faced with after.

More than 450 personnel enjoyed a show in the Station Theatre staged by the RCAF party 'The Tarmacs'.

The station WAAF and WD Officers held a party in the WAAF Officer's Mess.

29 April 1945

There was no flying recorded at the station. Ground training took up most of what was a showery and cloudy day.

Another capacity crowd gave a great response to a second show by 'The Tarmacs'

30 April 1945

There was no operational commitments for the station's squadrons.

Fig 42. F/O Mackenzie, Air Bomber, 25th April 1945 before setting out on the Wangerooge op. Photo J.Harpin.

08.00 hours saw a Station Parade assemble on the aerodrome, with all personnel not on essential duties present. At 09.00 hours the Station Commander, Group Captain R.A McLernon DFC inspected the parade and took the salute as it Marched Past. It was a long time since East Moor had seen a parade on that scale.

Flying training commenced at 19.00 hours with no less than ten aircraft engaged on local flying.

General:

The general war situation led to speculation that the end of hostilities in Europe must be close at hand and prepera-tions for Victory Thanksgiving Services were being made at East Moor. Further parties and celebrations were also anticipated. The Station Commander, not sure just how the personnel might respond to the expected news of victory, made a 'Tannoy' appeal for everyone to maintain a semblance of order and made a promise that everything would be done to plan and stage suitable celebrations.

One of the pastures at Gaping Goose Farm was named 'The McLernon Stadium' and two Fast Ball Diamonds were in operation there.

Small Arms training had continued and by the end of April no less than 1,053 airmen had been trained. Rifle compe-titions were now held for airmen not used to firing the .303 and excellent results were obtained.

RCAF East Moor Station strength as at 30th April 1945,

RCAF	Officers	324	RAF Officers	17
IWD	Officers	2	WAAF Officers	1
RCAF	Other Ranks	1353	RAF Other Ranks	72
Aust	Other Ranks	4	WAAF Other Ranks	144
NZ	Other Ranks	1	Army Officers	2

Total 1,920

Aircraft on charge,

42 Halifaxes   1 Oxford

415 Squadron strength (aircrew)

RCAF	Officers	148		RCAF Other Ranks	118
RAF	Officers	7		RAF Other Ranks	30
RAAF	Airmen	1		NZ Airmen	1

432 Squadron strength, (aircrew)

RCAF	Officers	127		RAF	Officers6	
RCAF	Airmen	128		RAF	Airmen	26
RCAF	Ground crew Officer.					

The station received two new Padres, Squadron Leader Davignon a Roman Catholic and Squadron Leader J.A Payton, Protestant, who succeeded Squadron Leader Lautenslager.

It was learnt that Squadron Leader J.Thompson and crew missing on the 14th February, were prisoners of war. Safe too, was Warrant Of ficer McDiarmid and crew, missing on the 8th March.

A 432 Squadron rear gunner recalls the 16th April 1945

" I recall we were on our way to the officer's mess for either a late breakfast or lunch when we heard the first aircraft explode or crash. So I believe we were the next one to have the same problem. The first aircraft had a new crew on circuits and bumps exercise, as I heard it. There was an extreme cross wind on the runway. Don't know why they (control) used that runway. What happened was the crosswind - or due to the crosswind the plane's right wheel ran off the runway on to the grass, the pilot tried to take off with disastrous results. We were then eating while this was taken care of by the fire waggons etc. My skipper was a keen type and urged us to get cracking so we could get to our own aircraft, take off and have practice bombing and gunnery. So we were the next aircraft to take off on that same runway. One of the groundcrew wanted to fly with us but our skipper wisely said no. We were now lined up, ready for take off, me in the rear turret. On the intercom I heard the skipper tell the Flight Engineer, that if we have trouble like the other fellow, we will close the gate, meaning cut off all power. So away we go, then my end, the tail starts to swing off the course. I guess we were pretty close to take off speed when one wheel went off the concrete runway. I heard 'Jesus Christ' from our skipper who swung his hand and knocked the power controls to the off position. He decided not to attempt a take off. The end result, our right wheel dragged and the Halifax swung around pivoting on the right wheel. The undercarriage buckled, the wing touched the ground and the plane was now facing the way from where we started. Fearing an explosion I immediately turned my turret so that the doors opened to the side. I don't remember how I got out but I was running when I realized that I could run faster if I got rid of my parachute on which I sat. It required a simple turn and punch and then fell away. I had turned the turret doors back into position so that others could have an exit if they needed one. I recall lots of airmen on the grass yelling to our skipper to 'CUT THE IGNITION' but good old skip was giving it a proper shut down. Fortunately the whole crew escaped injury, however I injured my thumb on returning to the aircraft to retrieve my cap. A dose of rum and a band-aid soon put things right".

A 432 Squadron skipper recalls

" We had returned from a raid on Heligoland on April 18 1945. After I parked, I heard one of the groundcrew say 'OPEN THE BOMB DOORS'. What he had said was 'DON'T OPEN THE BOMB DOORS'. We were not to open the doors on return, but I thought that he was trying to avoid climbing up into the aircraft to do it himself - and I figured I wouldn't be sticky on routine, because the bomb bay had been checked after leaving the target area and reported clear".

The skipper opened the doors and out dropped a 1,000 pounder on to the East Moor dispersal. The crew are glad to be able to tell the tale.

THE FOLLOWING OBSERVATIONS WERE MADE BY BASE H.Q.

APRIL 1945

CAPTAIN'S CORNER

During the past month we had a case of one of our aircraft being brought down by our own defences resulting in the loss of one crew and aircraft. Captains, as apart from taxi drivers, are responsible for the safety of their crews, and the excuse of ignorance or forgetfuilness is a very poor substitute for unneccesary loss of life. Skippers are reminded that they should be thoroughly familiar with all proceedures, so that when the occasion arises, they are in a position to cope. Make sure you know the proper procedure for identifying your self when coming home early or off track or you might just as well have.gone on!

Every month we run into cases of aircraft flying into the ground either breaking cloud or in poor visibility. Know your 6 Group cloud breaking procedure, consult your navigator and don't take chances.

Do not bail out when your air intakes freeze over and restrict the flow of air into your carburettor. Consult your Flight Commanders and your ground crew first. (This must be done before take off).

Captains are reminded that their duties are not finished after they grease their aircraft on to the runway for the fourth time returning. from an operation. To improve crew co-operation and to keep the "pencil pushers union" on their toes, at the same time improving their own navigation, they are to go over the trip in detail studying any mistakes and failures which may have occurred. This habit definately improves both crew co-operation and navigational efficiency, at the same time greatly increasing the crews chances of wearing the operational wing.

PILOTS GENERAL

The attention of all pilots is drawn to the fact that since the installation of V H.F, numerous dangerous breaches of security have occuurred due to the transmitter inadvertantly turned on. Breaches consist mostly of informing the Hun as to target, course, air speeds, turning points, height. In other words practically all the gen on the operation. Naturally this information is of great value to the enemy, enabling him to successfully complete interceptions, lay on flak etc, and it is interesting to note that the American 8th Air Force recognised that V.H.F natter seriously. attributed to their losses and hampered the success of operation.

SECURITY

For many months past, it has been an accepted fact that secret operational information is freely discussed in Betty's Bar. The advisability of staffing local. pubs with civilian Service Police is being reviewed - so heed this warning and remember "Buttoned lips make no slips".

THE FLOWER SHOP

Bouquets are extended to 415 Squadron for the lowest accident rate in the Base over the past three months - a tribute to the efficiency of the ground and air crews.

Congratulations to 415 Squadron for winning the Base Efficiency Pennant. They were the only squadron to show up favourably in Navigation in the Base, and won a well earned victory with the 100 points bonus for being the best. The squadron was the winner for the second consecutive month with a grand total of 1,192 points.

1 May 1945

There was very little let up in the station's flying training programme, but it was still without any operational commitment.

East Moor Station and Squadron Adjutants together with senior Administration Officers attended a conference at RCAF Station Linton on Ouse which was presided over by Wing Commander D. Fortune the Senior Base Admin Officer. The major item discussed was V.E Celebrations and a personnel programme for the period immediately after. It was hoped to include in the latter, organised sport, tours of Yorkshire, lectures and other pastimes.

A Station Sports Day was planned to take place at East Moor on the 24th May, and to this end the WAAF Section held a General Meeting.
Squadron Leader B.S Braiden a new Senior Medical Officer was posted in to East Moor from RCAF Overseas Headquarters.

Films and the weekly Music Club were held as usual.

2 May 1945

A comprehensive programme of flying training saw the station's crews engaged in gaggle practice, fighter affilliation, air to air firing, bombing etc.

The Station Commander conducted the official opening of East Moor's playing field.

In a squadron Softball game, 415 Air Gunners defeated the Pilots 5 - 3. A Games night held in the 'Y' Lounge saw more than seventy personnel enjoying Bridge, Cribbage, Checkers and Chess.

3 May 1945

Flying training continued and involved both squadrons. 432 Squadron practiced a 'Victory Formation' when the lead aircraft was noted as NP229 'C'.

Rumours were running rife as to what the future might hold for the station and its personnel, conversion to other aircraft types and service in the Pacific Theatre after flying back to Canada, being just a few.

In the evening 432 Squadron held a party for the pilots at the 'Hazel Bush' Cafe on Malton Road. After supper the party was continued at the 'Hop Grove Hotel' where amongst the guests was 415 Squadron Commander, Wing Commander F. Ball.

Results of the Group Heat in the Sunderland Cup showed East Moor WAAF's were runners up to RCAF Station Middleton St. George, only three marks in it.

Fig 43. Target Token for Heligoland, 18th April 1945.

Mickey Rooney was featured in 'Andy Hardy's Blonde Trouble' at the Station Cinema.

4 May 1945

On a cloudy but fair day, the station was again engaged in a heavy programme of flying training, with no less than fourteen crews involved mainly with cross country exercises.

An air of expectancy was experienced around the station as newspaper reports on the war situation pointed to the capitulation of Germany at any moment.

At 19.15 hours operations were called for the following day and thirty five aircraft and crews were involved, but at 21.30 hours the thing was cancelled. The target would have been Wangerooge again.

Two bus parties left for the weekly trip to Ripon Baths which was becoming more popular each week.

5 May 1945

Only 432 Squadron were engaged in flying training whilst 415 personnel attended ground lectures with their Section Leaders.

The station's hospital patients were treated to a film show in the afternoon.

415 Squadron were advised that if the squadron was to be converted to a new aircraft with which to fly to Canada, the proceedures for the venture would be given to pilots and navigators commencing on the 17th of the month.

6 May 1945

Sunday, and all the Church Services were well attended.

Wing Commander F. Ball the 415 Squadron Commander introduced a new training policy whereby 'A' and 'B' Flights began flying training on an alternative day and night basis, as opposed to the previous afternoon periods being fully taken up. Ground training could then be followed during the evening period. 'B' Flight commenced operating the new policy with ten aircraft involved during the afternoon and 'A' Flight commenced the night training with the first of four aircraft becoming airborne at 23.00 hours.

A 'Release and Resettlement' lecture was given to the station's WAAF Section by Flight Officer Percy from Air Ministry.

The Sunday night Forum was held and Dr. Leonard Marsh a leading Canadian Economist drew a very large audience which included visiting groups from other RCAF Stations.

The film 'Patrick the Great' was currently showing in the Station NAAFI.

7 May 1945

Excitement abounded at East Moor. The morning saw the station a real hive of activity with plans for the expected 'Victory' announcement being rushed to 432 Squadron continued training with seven aircraft engaged on various exercises but no flying was recorded by sister squadron 415. Lieutenant S.A Tims of the Canadian Army arrived at the station to spend a week on familiarisation experience with 432 Squadron.

The Code and Cypher Officer from 62 Base, Squadron Officer A.M Groundwater, visited East Moor.

In the late afternoon came the advice that the 8th May 1945 was to be recorded as Victory in Europe Day, and that an official declaration would be made at 15.00 hours on that date by the Prime Minister of Great Britain.

The station's firearms were stored away.

At 19.00 hours the station heard an announcement by the BBC that the next day would be VE Day, and strangely instead of the expected unrestrained celebrations the feeling of relief was such,that everyone fell into a mood of silent reflection and meditation.

8 May 1945

After six years of war, many of which saw East Moor's personnel seperated from their families and loved ones, it was at last 'Victory in Europe' Day.

Open air Church services were held and conducted by the station's Padres and said to have been most impressive. At the Protestant thanksgiving, Wing Comm F.Ball read the lesson and laid a wreath at the alter in memory of those who had died.

Only essential services were maintained

At 15.00 hours Winston Churchill's booming tones came over the East Moor 'Tannoy' system relating how the Armed Forces of the Allied Nations had achieved victory in Europe.

At 18.00 hours no fewer than three parties sprang up simultaneously in the 432 Squadron crew rooms and briefing premises. 415 Squadron celebrations got underway after the Prime Ministers speech, and by evening Section and Squadron festivities were in full swing. Everyone had an enjoyable time. Officers and NCO's contributed to kegs of beer for the 'erks'. After listening to His Majesty King George VI brodcast to the world at 21.00 hours, a Station Dance ended a perfect day.

9 May 1945

All East Moor aircraft had been marshalled and were guarded on instructions from No.62 Base Headquarters, and extra Service Police patrolled the station. The first two days of celebrations proved to be free of any untoward incidents.

The morning was very quiet, the only interuptions to the tranquility of the place was the occasional complaints from those who had over indulged during the previous days festivities.

An evening Pay Parade realised a further £21/11/6 in National Savings Stamps. Following the station film shows, a Station Dance was held and music was supplied by RCAF Station Linton on Ouse's 'The Lintonaires' band. Many of that station's WD's were invited and thoroughly enjoyed themselves.

10 May 1945

After VE Day came 'R' for rumour day at East Moor, with everyone contemplating the return to the land of the Maple Leaf. During the morning selections were made of crews to fly Lancaster aircraft to that continent, and ground training of those chosen was started.

In the afternoon RCAF Station Tholthorpe's netball team arrived on station for a friendly game.

In the evening the usual film show was screened.

11 May 1945

Flight Lieutenant G.W Jaques, East Moor Station Adjutant was posted out to London Headquarters and was succeeded by Flight Lieutenant R. Bennet the former assistant Adjutant.

The 'Flying Ban' was lifted at East Moor Station but none was authorised. The two weekly buses to Ripon Baths were again well patronised.

415 Squadron learnt that they were to be disbanded on the 15th of the month,and 50% of them went on eleven days leave.

A Baseball game between pilots and navigators of 415 Squadron saw the latter win 23 - 19.

A lunchtime Band Concert was given in the NAAFI by 6 Group Quintette.

12 May 1945

The flying was resumed at East Moor with five of 432 Squadron's crews taking part in local flying and cross countries.

432 Squadron Commander announced that it would not be flying home to Canada, whilst 415 were eagerly awaiting further news as to their future. The latter were sure that they were 'Canada Bound' and a brisk business had sprung up in the sale of used cars and motor cycles on the station.

The station's personnel enjoyed their first 'Yorkshire Tour' when points of interest within a thirty mile radius of York were visited.

13 May 1945

Thundery showers during the day restricted the flying at the station.

Sixteen of 432 Squadron's crews went on leave and as many of the 415 members were still away, the messes became rather quiet.

A lack of flying and operational commitments was having its effect on the station's personnel, and in an effort to prevent boredom, liberty buses were organised to nearby towns.

The Sunday Forum was held when Flying Officer Max Cobber's subject was 'Back to Canada' and drew a large gathering.

14 May 1945

The thunder storms prevailing around the area grounded the East Moor crews in the early part of the day, but 432 Squadron did get three airborne later who carried out some air to sea firing details and some local flying.

415 Squadron were busy planning a Golf Tournament to be played at Strensall Golf Club later in the week.

Buses were laid on in the evening for supporters of the station's Softball team to travel to Allerton Park where they defeated No.6 Group.

15 May 1945

415 Squadron disbanded at East Moor.
Wing Commander F.W Ball was appointed Station Commander vice Group Captain R.A McLernon DFC.

RCAF Station East Moor was reduced to a 'Non Operational' status and assumed the role of a 'Holding Unit - cum-Transit Camp'.

It was 'Business as Usual' for 432 Squadron with five crews on flying training exercises that included H2S, air to sea firing and bombing practice.

The 432 Squadron Offices were broken into and 50,000 cigarettes and ten bottles of Gin were stolen. The Station Police called in the Darlington Branch of the SIB in an effort to apprehend those responsible.

Music and Camera Club meetings were held in the YMCA and said to be proving most popular interests on the station.

16 May 1945

The only flying at East Moor was an air test carried out by a 432 Squadron crew, whilst others were involved in ground training.

The Strensall Firing Ranges were the scene for a shoot out between a large number of 415 and 432 Squadron members when the latter defeated the former by 72.1- 66.6.

Flight Lieutenant W.J Wilson of the RCAF Medical Branch visited the station to prepare Medical Records for the Historical Records section of No.6 Group.

This was the last date on which any 432 Squadron records are noted, and in a letter from RCAF Station East Moor to 6 Group Headquarters it is stated that, disbandment instructions were received some time after the 15th May 1945.

17 May 1945

The station cinema wasfilled to capacity to welcome 'The Northern Lights' a Leeds based variety show. The Canadians were said to have fully appreciated the different type of humour and entertained the party afterwards in the Officer's Mess.

18 May 1945

Squadron Leader F.N Neilson, 62 Base Accounts Officer visited the station along with Flying Officer G.R Gambles.

East Moor Station Band played for an Airmen's Dance, and everyone enjoyed an excellent debut by them.

19 & 20 May 1945

Seemingly very little of note occurred at East Moor. The latter date being a Sunday, the usual Church Services were held and the evening Forum. The guest speaker was Colonel G.W Beecroft,and a large audience including personnel from RC.AF Station's Thoithorpe and Linton, listened to his subject 'Engineering Opportunities in Canada'. with great interest.

A further 200 personnel watched a film at the Station Cinema.

21 & 22 May 1945

Routine days, WAAF Section held a dance in the NAAFI on the former day, and the weekly Music Club meeting was held on the latter. The two 62 Base Accounts Officer's, S/L Neilson and F/L Gambles again visited the station.

23 May 1945

Several East Moor personnel moved out and included, Intelligence Officer Squadron Leader W. Pilkington,to 6 Group Headquarters and Engineering Officers F light Lieutenants N.J Thompson and II. Hagen to 64 Base.

The Lieutenant Governor of British Columbia, Colonel W. Woodward, arrived at East Moor in the early afternoon and met all the station personnel from that area. After discussing with them at length their prospects on returning home he was entertained to tea by the Officers in their mess . At 17.00 hours he left for RCAF Station Tholthorpe.

24 May 1945

Sports Day. And a very outstanding day it proved to be, when after a cloudy start it became fine and warm and a picnic lunch was served between straight races, three legged ones, high, broad and long jumps, bicycle races, and Softball games. in the evening boxing and wrestling events were staged. The day was rounded off with an Officer's Mess Dance and one for the 'Other Ranks' held in the Station Cinema. The day was proclaimed a 'Red Letter' one for East Moor Station.

25 May 1945

The Base Administration Officer Wing Commander C.C.W Marshall visited the station

In the evening a three act mystery play 'Murder Without Crime' was staged at the station by the 33 ASD players. The story was written by an RAF Air Gunner and the set and performance said to be excellent.

27 May 1945

Sunday, started with light rain but brightened later enabling members of the Station Camera Club to enjoy an organised tour of places of special interest.

Several rolls of film were shot off around Fountains Abbey and underground in the Goyden Caves.

The evening film showing in the NAAFI was 'Murder My Sweet'.

One of Reuter's News Correspondents, Mr Hugo Kuranda a Viennese, was the guest speaker at the Forum. His talk 'From Capital to Capital in Europe' was well appreciated.

At 19.00 a boxing and wrestling show was put on for the station's personnel.

28 May 1945

East Moor Softball team lost 8 - 4 to RCAF Station Tholthorpe.
No.5 District Headquarters Engineering Officer, Flight Lieutenant S.G Snell visited East Moor.

'Gentle Annie' was the film being shown in the Officer's Mess.

29 May 1945

The 'Hopgrove Hotel' on the York-Malton Road, was the scene for an appreciation party for RCAF Officers at East Moor given by a number of York business men. If the number of headaches experienced next morning were anything to go by, it must have been 'one hell of a party'.

30 & 31 May 1945

The station received a new Equipment Officer, Squadron Leader J R Arthur was posted in from No.6 Group.

Good crowds were attending the regular Games Nights and the Station Cinema was pulling in audiences 400 strong.

General:

East Moor Station Strength - 31 May 1945

RCAF	Officers	277	RAF	Officers	13
WD	Officers	3	WAAF	Officers	1
RCAF	Other Ranks	1158	RAF	Other Ranks	65
Aust.	Officers	1	WAAF	Other Ranks	142
NZ	Other Ranks	1	Army	Officers	2

Grand Total 1,662

432 Sqd Halifax III's at East Moor

LK754 QO-Z	Swung on t/o for Schweinfurt at 18.23 hrs on 24/2/44 was rebuilt at Y.A.R.D. and issued to 76 Sqd.	
LK755 QO-K	No ops recorded with 432 at East Moor, transferred to 426 Sqd and later returned to East Moor with 415 Sqd.	
LK761 QO-B	No ops recorded at East Moor, crashed during a night exercise between and Stillington at 19.43 hrs, 16/12/44.	
LK764 QO-F	25 ops recorded before transfer to 434 Sqd.	
LK765 QO-H	4 ops recorded as 'H' and a further 38 as 'B' before transfer to 415 Sqd.	
LK766 QO-V	22 ops, swung on a 3 engined landing **ex** Metz, 00.22 hrs, 29/6/44 repaired and transferred to 415 Sqd.	
LK779 QO-W	FTR from Frankfurt on its 5th recorded operation.	23/ 3/44
LK803 QO-Z	6 ops recorded at East Moor before transfer to 420 Sqd.	
LK807 QO-J	FTR from Montzen on its 13th recorded operation	28/ 4/44
LK8ll QO-N	FTR from Bourg Leopold, 14th op, crashed Beverloo	28/ 5/44
LK868 QO	No ops recorded at East Moor, transferred to 431 Sqd.	
LL547 QO-X	10 ops recorded before transfer to 429 Sqd.	
LW412 QO-P	2 ops recorded at East Moor before transfer to a HCU.	
LW437 QO-	No ops recorded at East Moor before transfer to 434 Sqd.	
LW552 QO-S	15 ops recorded before transfer to 415 5qd.	
LW576 QO-L	No ops recorded at East Moor before transfer to 431 Sqd.	
LW582 QO-M	FTR from Aucheres on its 25th recorded operation.	8/ 6/44
LW583 QO-L	FTR from Haine St. Pierre on its 11th recorded operation	9/ 5/44
LW584 QO-Y	FTR from Frankfurt on its 14th recorded operation.	23/ 3/44
LW592 QO-A	FTR from Montzen on its 17th recorded operation.	28/ 4/44
LW593 QO-O	FTR from Berlin on its 6th recorded operation.	25/ 3/44
LW594 QO-G	FTR from Haine St. Pierre on its 19th recorded operation.	9/ 5/44
LW595 QO-Q	34 ops recorded before trnsfer to 415 Sqd.	
LW596 QO-D	31 ops recorded before transfer to 434 Sqd.	
LW597 QO-C	FTR from Augsburg on its 1st recorded operation.	26/ 2/44
LW598 QO-K	9 ops recorded before crashing at Newton on Ouse due to the starboard inner engine having failed, aircraft burnt out.	9/ 6/44
LW614 QO-S	9 ops recorded before crashing at Hackness due to engine failure during air to air firing exercise off Scarborough.	12/ 4/44
LW615 QO-U	17 ops recorded before crashing into buildings after overshoot at East Moor during training and familiarization flight.	7/ 5/44
LW616 QO-R	FTR from Cambrai on its 22nd recorded operation.	13/ 6/44
LW617 QO-J	7 ops recorded before transfer to 158 Sqd. Had suffered an u/c collapse after skidding on ice during a landing at East Moor at 18.27 hrs,	4/3/44.
LW643 QO-E	FTR from Noisy le Sec on its 6th recorded operation.	19/ 4/44
LW682 QO-C	6 ops recorded as 'C' and a further 5 as 'W' before transfer to 426 Sqd.	
LW686 QO-H	28 ops recorded before transfer to 415 Sqd.	
LW687 QO-Z	FTR from Nurnberg on its 7th recorded operation, shot down by nightfighter and crashed Friedburg.	31/ 3/44
* MZ504 QO-C	FTR from Nuremburg on what is believed to be its 1st op from East Moor, shot down by a night F/Ohter and crashed at Grossmaishe, Koblenz.	31/ 3/44
MZ506 QO-X	FTR from Le Mans on its 12th recorded operation.	23/ 5/44
MZ536 QO-	No ops recorded at East Moor before transfer to 431 Sqd.	
MZ585 QO-O	9 ops as 'O' and a further 3 as 'Z' before transfer to 415 Sqd.	
MZ586 QO-Y	23 ops recorded before transfer to 415 Sqd.	
*MZ588 QO-E	FTR from Montzen on what is believed to be its 1st operation.	28/ 4/44
MZ590 QO-C	13 ops recorded before transfer to 415 Sqd.	
MZ591 QO-K	FTR from Metz on its 14th recorded operation.	29/ 6/44
MZ6O1 QO-A	FTR from Cambrai on its 11th recorded operation.	13/ 6/44
MZ603 QO-E	27 ops recorded before transfer to 415 Sqd.	
MZ632 QO-W	25 ops recorded before transfer to 415 Sqd.	
MZ633 QO-O	21 ops recorded before transfer to 415 Sqd.	
MZ653 QO-	No ops recorded at East Moor.	
MZ654 QO-L	13 ops recorded before transfer to 415 Sqd.	

MZ656 QO-   No ops recorded before transfer to 431 Sqd.
MZ660 QO-J   23 ops recorded before transfer to 415 Sqd.
MZ672 QO-G 5 ops recorded before transfer to 429 Sqd.
MZ674 QO-   No ops recorded before transfer to 425 Sqd.
MZ686 QO-U 17 ops recorded before transfer to 415 Sqd.
NA500 QO-G   FTR from Bologne sur Mcr on its 1st recorded operation.   12/ 5/44
NA516 QO-F   2 ops as 'F', transferred to 434 Sqd, returned to 432 Sqd where
                 a further 3 ops are recorded as 'A' before
                 FTR from Sterkrade-Holten on its 5th East Moor operation.   17/ 6/44
NA517 QO-R   9 ops recorded before transfer to 415 Sqd.
NA527 QO-N   12 ops recorded before transfer to a HCU.
NA550 QO-   No ops recorded at East Moor before transfer to 434 Sqd.
NA552 QO   No ops recorded at East Moor before transfer to 434 Sqd.

*   Unfortunately, the available information relating to MZ504 and MZ588 is not conclusive.

432 Squadron Halifaxes at East Moor

Halifax VII

NP687 QO-A	10 Ops FTR Stuttgart	26/7/44
NP688 QO-X	7 Ops FTR Stuttg&rt	26.07/44
NP689 QO-M	85 Ops FTR Hagen	15/03/45
NP690 QO-G	20 Ops Crashed on take ofr, East Moor and burnt	18/08/44
NP691 QO-V	62Ops DBR by night F/Ohter, ex Grevenbroich	15/01/45
NP69:2 QO-D&K	21 Ops Crash landed Woodbridge, burnt, ex Bottrop	27/9/44
NP693 QO-Q&K	71 Op.	
NP694 QO-R	85 Op.	
NP695 QO-K	39 Op. FTR Osnabruck	6/12/44
NP697 QO-F	80 Op.	
NP698 QO-X&U	61 Op.	
NP699 QO-O	42 Op. FTR Duisburg, collided with a/c over Belgium	18/12/44
NP7O1 QO-S&G	36 Op. FTR Duisburg	18/12/44
NP702 QO-B	8 Op. FTR Hamburg	29/ 7/44
NP703 Q0-H	58 Op.	
NP704 QO-L	56 Op. FTR Wanne Eickel	3/2/45
NP705 QO-Y	82 Op.	
NP706 QO-J	3 Op. FTR Caen	18/7/44
NP707 QO-W	67 Op. Overshot Ford, 05.06 hr., 26/7/44, repaired	
NP708 QO-E	73 Op.	
NP7l0 QO-	No ops recorded at East Moor before transfer to 408 Sqd.	
NP712 QO-	No ops recorded at East Moor before transfer to 408 Sqd	
NP716 QO-	No ops recorded at East Moor before transfer to 408 Sqd	
NP718 QO-	No op. recorded at East Moor before transfer to 408 Sqd	
NP719 QO-N	21 Ops FTR Kiel, collided with a/c over target	16./9/44
NP720 QO-A	9 Op. transferred to 426 Sqd.	
NP721 QO-X	22 Op. Overshot East Moor, 16.31 hrs 6/8/44, repaired	
	Crashed and burnt on take off East Moor, 18.06 hrs	5/12/44
NP722 QO-S	30 Ops Crash landed Manston at 21.03 hrs, ex Essen	23/10/44
	previously Cat.B at East Moor 04.31 hrs ex Kiel	
		16/9/44
NP723 QO-D	28 Ops FTR Wilhelmshaven	15/10/44
NP736 QO-B	59 Ops Damaged by NP755 which was landing at Croft,ex Munster	
	18.30 hrs, 18/11/44, repaired	
NP738 QO-J	21 Ops Crashed into trees, Woodbridge ex Wanne Eickel	12/10/44
NP755 QO-A	69 Op. Landing Accident with NP736 as above, repaired.	
NP759 QO-C&O	35 Ops FTR Hannover	5/10/45
NP774 QO-Z	38 Op.	
NP778 QO-	No operations recorded at East Moor before transfer to 426 Sqd	
NP779 QO-	No operations recorded at East Moor before transfer to 426 Sqd	
NP797 QO-N&C	21 Ops recorded before transfer to 426 Sqd	
NP801 QO-N	7 Ops FTR Bochum	9/10/44
NP802 QO-S&O	21 Ops Collided with a/c while landing at Linton on Ouse	
	17.15 hrs, 24/12/44 ex Dusseldorf, repaired	

NP803 QO-E		35 Ops FTR Worms	22/.2/45
NP804 QO-Q		22 Ops transferred to 408 Sqd	
NP805 QO-J	40 Ops	Crashed om take off,East Moor, 12.10 hrs	16/04/45
NP807 Q0-P	27 Ops	Swung on t/o became bogged down	
		16/1/45, transferred to 408 Sqd	
11P808 QO-N	1 Op	transferred to 426 Sqd	
11P812 QO-T	21 Ops		
NP813 QO-		No ops recorded at East Moor, transferred to 426 Sqd	
NP815 QO-H	8 Ops	FTR Gelsenkirchen	6/11/44
NP817 QO-D	20 Ops	FTR Hannover 5.1.45	
NP961 QO-O	7 Ops	transferred to 415 Sqd	
NP968 QO-		No ops recorded at East Moor before transfer to 466 Sqd	
NP971 QO-		No ops recorded at East Moor before transfer to 466 Sqd	
PN208 QO-G	27 Ops		
PN224 QO-O	18 Ops		
PN229 QO-C	20 Ops		
PN233 QO-D	18 Ops		
PN235 QO-S	13 Ops	Crashed East Moor, on take off	16/4/45
PN236 QO-		No ops recorded before transfer to 415 Sqd	
PN237 QO-		No ops recorded before it swung on to East Moor at 14.59 hrs	
		16/4/45, repaired and transferred to 415 Sqd	
PN241 QO-I	10 Ops	transferred to 1665 HCU	
RG448 QO-V	26 Ops		
RG449 QO-S	5 Ops	FTR Chemnitz	15/.2/45
RG450 QO-Q	8 Ops		
RG451 QO-D	5 Ops	FTR Worms	22/2/45
RG454 QO-P	22 Ops		
RG455 QO-X	5 Ops	FTR Monheim	21/2/45
RG475 QO-L	8 Ops	Shot down by 'friendly' ex Chemnitz	6/3/45
RG476 QO-T	1 Op	FTR Worms	22/2/45
RG478 QO-U	18 Ops		
RG479 QO-N	16 Ops		
NR145 QO-C	3 Ops	transferred to 415 Sqd	

432 Squadron crews at East Moor

(Halifax)

Pilot	F/O	Reid	E	F/S	Pay	W	F/L	Von Laufer	D
Navigator	F/O	Smith	J	Sgt	Baker	J	P/O	Derry	M
Bomb Aimer	F/S	McDonald	V	F/S	Armstrong	G	F/S	Phimester	A
WOP	Sgt	McGuire	G	Sgt	Bell	J	Sgt	Holt	P
A/G	Sgt	Clarkson	R	Sgt	Houston	J	Sgt	Ramey	N
A/G	Sgt	Barr	J	Sgt	King	A	Sgt	McFadden	J
F/Engineer	Sgt	May	J	Sgt	Ibbotson	H	Sgt	Kinch	S
Pilot	F/S	Ferneyhough	W	F/O	Smith	W	P/O	Whaley	H
Navigator	F/S	Musser	J	F/O	Plommer	R	F/O	Burrows	J
Bomb Aimer	Sgt	Kennedy	H	F/O	Balsdon	J	F/S	Doyle	H
WOP	W/O	Lamphier	G	Sgt	Clench	P	W/O	McDonald	D
A/G	Sgt	Lagimodiere	A	Sgt	Pingle	R	P/O	McCoy	D
A/G	Sgt	Racher	D	Sgt	Rudland	J	Sgt	Driver	P
F/Engineer	Sgt	Hembrey	J	Sgt	Lestrange	E	Sgt	Phillips	A
Pilot	F/L	Cooper	J	F/S	Maddock	D	Pl0	McIntosh	J
Navigator	F/O	Dryden	R	W/O	Buchan	A	F/O	Small	A
Bomb Aimer	Sgt	Zacharuk	A	F/S	Urquart	K	P/O	Elvin	R
WOP	T/S	Butewitz	L	W/O	McNaught	J	P/O	Calderwood	W
A/G	Sgt	Burton	R	Sgt	Peterson	J	Sgt	Bandle	L
A/G	F/S	Elliott	K	Sgt	Forest	C	Sgt	Dedaw	A
F/Engineer	Sgt	Oakbey	H	Sgt	Newsome	A	Sgt	King	W
Pilot	F/S	Cooper	J	W/C	McKay	W	Lt	Lubold	A
Navigator	F/S	Burrill	H	F/L	Rogers	G	F/O	Turton	J
Bomb Aimer	F/S	McClintock	P	F/O	Grimsey	M	F/O	Richards	R
WOP	Sgt	Short	L	P/O	Kemp	R	Sgt	Cannon	J
A/G	Sgt	Waddington	G	P/O	Logan	E	Sgt	Robineau	G
A/G	Sgt	Oseman	W	P/O	Thompson	W	Sgt	Thompson	W
F/Engineer	Sgt	Haining	C	F/L	Duncanson	R	Sgt	Bean	D
Pilot	Sgt	Anthony	R	F/O	Barker	J	F/L	Barrett	C
Navigator	F/O	Lybbert	D	F/S	Cooper	E	F/O	Bentley	D
BombAimer	Sgt	Perry	W	F/O	McDonald	H	P/O	Goundrey	T
WOP	F/O	Seguss	A	F/O	Thompson	C	F/S	Coe	G
A/G	Sgt	Dennis	W	Sgt	McCullom	C	P/O	Logan	E
A/G	Sgt	Metcalf	W	Sgt	Cosgrove	J	F/S	Hamilton	A
F/Engineer	Sgt	Brown	A	Sgt	Jarvis	H	P/O	Shaw	W
Pilot	F/L	Cawker	G	F/S	Clarke	A	F/S	Clarke	E
Navigator	F/O	Storen	F	Sgt	Woodward	T	Sgt	Bishop	E
Bomb Aimer	Sgt	McNeil	E	Sgt	Cranch	F	Sgt	Brown	W
WOP	Sgt	Beaumont	A	Sgt	Hindmarsh	F	Sgt	Lewis	H
A/G	Sgt	Frizzell	H	Sgt	McNeil	D	Sgt	Cook	J
A/G	Sgt	Campbell	J	Sgt	Bell	D	Sgt	Burgess	G
F/Engineer	Sgt	Thorne	H	Sgt	Halliwell	H	Sgt	Bradshaw	G
Pilot	F/S	Kuleski	J	P/O	Dennis	P	P/O	Hawkins	S
Navigator	F/O	Matthews	W	P/O	Atkins	G	P/O	Raetzan A	
Bomb Aimer	Sgt	Richmond	B	F/O	O'Gorman	J	Sgt	O'Leary	M
WOP	F/s	Desmarian	J	Sgt	Woolfendon	P	P/O	Parkinson	W
A/G	Sgt	Wiwsisnakie	M	Sgt	Riding	W	Sgt	Banks	R
A/G	Sgt	Tumbull	A	P/O	Quesnal	H	Sgt	Hand	G
F/Engineer	Sgt	Horton	E	Sgt	Kent	W	Sgt	McCart	J
Pilot	F/L	Lowe	A	F/S	McElheron	J	Sgt	Menzies	N
Navigator	F/S	McLeod	D	F/S	Botsford	R	P/O	Goumlock	J
Bomb Aimer	F/O	Potts	R	F/S	Blanchard	W	P/O	Rutherford	D

Role	Rank	Name	Initial	Rank	Name	Initial	Rank	Name	Initial
WOP	Sgt	Chadwick	J	F/S	Disno	G	Sgt	Rowan	W
A/G	Sgt	Sowerby	J	F/L	Williams	G	Sgt	McClay	T
A/G	Sgt	Purreno	G	Sgt	Easy	S	Sgt	Boutilier	R
F/Engineer	Sgt	Darnell	D	Sgt	Mellor	A	Sgt	Clarke	J
Pilot	F/O	Mercer	A	Sgt	Millar	G	FIS	Narum	C
Navigator	P/O	Bell	J	P/O	Holmes	A	F/s	Geeson	R
Bomb Aimer	P/O	Redman	A	Sgt	McAuley	D	Sgt	Pigeon	L
WOP	Sgt	Pett	S	Sgt	McPherson	W	Sgt	Narini	J
A/G	Sgt	McCluskie	A	Sgt	Harmsworth	R	Sgt	Saprunoff	S
A/G	P/C	McGregor	A	Sgt	Flather	G	Sgt	Rathwell	R
F/Engineer	Sgt	Thompson	J	Sgt	Musgrove	S	Sgt	Thompson	R
Pilot	F/L	Pettit	M	F/S	Studnik	W	F/L	Larson	G
Navigator	W/O	Buchan	K	P/C	Bailey	D	Sgt	Cole	M
Bomb Aimer	F/C	Gray	M	Sgt	Laird	D	F/C	Mills	R
WOP	W/C	Keogh	G	W/C	O'Brien	D	F/C	Forman	G
A/G	W/O	Bullivant	P	Sgt	Bertony	J	Sgt	Robinson	A
A/G	Sgt	Penny	D	Sgt	Murdoch	D	Sgt	Vienneau	F
F/Engineer	Sgt	Plummer	A	Sgt	Denning	L	Sgt	Edward	C
Pilot	F/O	Evenson		F/O	Lawrenson	R	P/O	Webb	G
Navigator	F/O	Miller	C	F/O	McKay	W	F/O	Painter	V
Air Bomber	F/O	Sewell	E	F/O	Donohoe	D	F/S	Young	C
WOP	Sgt	Burton	S	F/S	Earle	A	Sgt	Bova	G
A/G	Sgt	Waddell	J	Sgt	Paquette	A	P/O	Ryan	D
M/Upper	Sgt	Coghill	A	Sgt	Ison	E	Sgt	Scarffe	C
F/Engineer	Sgt	Driscoll	T	Sgt	Barrie	J	Sgt	Whitehouse	J
Pilot	P/O	Lauzon	L	P/O	Patterson	J	P/O	Webb	J
Navigator	W/O	Hodder	W	F/O	Sled	J	Sgt	Murdoch	A
Bomb Aimer	W/O	Wallis	G	F/O	Jannsen	J	Sgt	Warring	H
WOP	F/S	Olivier	J	F/S	James	M	Sgt	Rawle	R
M/Upper	Sgt	Christoff	C	Sgt	Stockdale	W	Sgt	Ziomko	W
R/G	Sgt	Beattie	J	Sgt	Asselin	W	Sgt	Wright	D
F/Engineer	Sgt	Miles	R	Sgt	Millar	L	Sgt	Addy	F
Pilot	F/O	Deloughry	L	FtO	Lekis	W	F/O	Jack	R
Navigator	F/O	McLay	J	Sgt	Beaupre	P	F/O	Derry	M
Bomb Aimer	F/O	Parker	G	Sgt	Ellis	R	F/S	Phimester	A
WOP	F/S	Small	R	Sgt	Ede	W	Sgt	Holt	P
M/Upper	Sgt	Davis	H	Sgt	Jones	F	Sgt	Ramey	M
R/G	P/O	Kerr	J	Sgt	MacDougall	J	Sgt	MacFadden	J
F/Engineer	Sgt	Shearer	J	Sgt	Collins	R	Sgt	Kinch	S
Pilot	W/C	MacDonald	J	P/O	Card	R	P/O	McKean	G
Navigator	F/O	Andrews	C	F/O	Myers	C	F/O	Wakelin	D
Bomb Aimer	F/O	Hieland	E	F/O	Todd	F	F/S	Moffat	J
WOP	F/O	Touchie	W	Sgt	Drake	P	Sgt	Higgins	O
M/Upper	W/O	Johnson	A	Sgt	Seaman	H	Sgt	LaFleche	J
RIG	W/O	Alexander	R	Sgt	Anderson	H	Sgt	Lee	H
F/Engineer	F/S	Looney	H	Sgt	Dewar	W	Sgt	Gage	H
Pilot	F/S	Campbell	R	F/O	Friedman	L	F/O	Best	D
Navigator	Sgt	Cassels	S	F/O	Robertson	J	F/O	Barlow	J
Bomb Aimer	Sgt	Fenton	D	Sgt	Smith	S	F/O	Hopkins	D
WOP	Sgt	Telford	T	Sgt	Benton	I	Sgt	Malham	R
M/Upper	Sgt	Rice	H	Sgt	McDermott	B	Sgt	Laudrum	F
R/G	Sgt	Sharks	M	Sgt	Loundsbury	B	Sgt	Lindblom	F
F/Engineer	Sgt	Wilkie	D	Sgt	Preece	P	Sgt	Tarleton	E
Pilot	F/O	Tobias	W	F/O	Johnston	V	P/O	Gingrich	R
Navigator	W/O	Craig	J	F/O	Buckley	J	F/a	Vaughan	G
Bomb Aimer	F/S	Larmon	R	F/O	Smith	P	F/a	Gosling	D
WOP	F/O	Jessup	J	W/O	Titus	J	F/O	Winch	J

M/Upper	Sgt	Trott	E	Sgt	Wilburn	G	Sgt	Boyce	H
R/G	Sgt	Easey	S	F/s	Scarffe	B	Sgt	Hosier	M
F/Engineer	Sgt	Yarham	A	Sgt	Gibson	P	Sgt	Tait	E
Pilot	Sgt	Kerr	J	F/O	Smith	V	P/O	Britton	H
Navigator	Sgt	Bolhartz	H	F/O	Given	S	Sgt	Hyatt	P
Bomb Aimer	F/O	Hayes	R	F/O	Ferguson	A	P/O	Cromwell	G
WOP	W/O	Veryard	G	F/S	McFadden	W	F/O	Walker	S
M/Upper	Sgt	Wilison	D	Sgt	Wells	J	Sgt	Dickinson	P
R/G	Sgt	James	P	Sgt	Easton	N	Sgt	Hoffman	W
F/Engineer	Sgt	Atkin	D	Sgt	Hollingsworth	G	Sgt	Knight	E
Pilot	Sgt	Diamond	R	Sgt	Franko	N	P/O	Frost	D
Navigator	P/O	Harmon	D	Sgt	Pryce	M	F/O	Shearer	P
Bomb Aimer	F/O	Stohlberg	W	F/O	Locke	P	F/S	Harmon	E
WOP	F/S	Sharpe	A	F/O	Hunt	L	Sgt	Williams	D
M/Upper	F/S	Graham	H	Sgt	Fullerton	P	Sgt	Farrell	L
R/G	Sgt	Harrington	N	Sgt	Black	H	Sgt	Young	P
F/Engineer	Sgt	Hutchinson	K	Sgt	Hughes	P	Sgt	Haley	J
Pilot	F/O	Craig	A	F/O	Stunden	G	Flo	Jeffrey	F
Navigator	F/O	Howard	W	F/O	Poden	T	P/O	Henderson	W
Bomb Aimer	F/O	Semple	J	F/O	Krakowsky	N	F/O	Underhill	K
WOP	Sgt	Forbes	R	W/O	Pritchard	G	F/S	Chartrand	P
M/Upper	Sgt	Walker	G	Sgt	Siwak	S	Sgt	Tanner	F
R/G	Sgt	Graham	T	Sgt	Pegg	L	Sgt	Henderson	P
F/Engineer	Sgt	Stock	F	Sgt	Murray	W	Sgt	Barnes	P
Pilot	F/O	Dean	S	F/O	Eilertson	F	F/L	Miller	W
Navigator	F/O	Pitts	D	F/O	Morrissey	F	F/O	Hall	B
Bomb Aimer	F/O	Hayden	W	F/O	Hossie	L	Sgt	Righetti	P
WOP	F/O	Beaton	N	Sgt	MacDonald	C	Sgt	Dupuis	F
N/Upper	Sgt	Shaw	N	Sgt	Suttle	N	Sgt	Armstrong	G
R/G	W/O	Cloutier	J	Sgt	McAron	T	Sgt	Petaske	A
F/Engineer	Sgt	Mulley	I	Sgt	Vaughan	C	Sgt	Chubb	W
Pilot	F/O	Martin	T	F/O	Vickeman	W	*S/L	Bryson	M
Navigator	F/O	Panzer	L	F/O	Watson	E	P/O	Thompson	P
Bomb Aimer	F/O	D'Andrea	D	F/O	Hoffman	H	F/S	Verry	P
WOP	Sgt	Kannings	K	P/O	O'Grady	L	P/O	Tupper	M
A/G	Sgt	Cantlon	W	Sgt	Beauchesne	N	P/O	Yeoman	P
A/G	Sgt	McKartney	K	Sgt	Layton	F	F/S	Elliott	S
F/Engineer	Sgt	Mellor	P	Sgt	Dobson	E	Sgt	Marshall	P
Pilot	*F/O	Damgaard	H	F/O	Morrow	H	F/S	Kicak	J
Navigator	F/S	Diamond	B	PlO	Slimon	J	F/O	Stewart	H
Bomb Aimer	F/O	O'Gorman	J	Sgt	Gelfand	P	F/O	Wray	W
WOP	W/O	Regan	J	W/O	McElroy	P	F/S	Aune	A
A/G	Sgt	Wright	J	Sgt	Johnston	J	Sgt	Burton	J
A/G	Sgt	Wearing	L	Sgt	Shanks	J	Sgt	Boyce	H
F/Engineer	Sgt	Nelson	L	Sgt	Herrick	V	Sgt	Mead	P
Pilot	*F/O	Robertson	D	*F/L	Smith	H	P/O	Gallagher	J
Navigator	P/O	Murdock	G	F/O	Sisman	J	F/O	LeBlanc	J
Bomb Aimer	F/O	Freberg	M	F/O	White	W	Sgt	LaFreniere	J
WOP	P/O	Cole	E	F/S	Dorrell	M	Sgt	LaBelle	J
A/G	P/O	McGovern	F	Sgt	Cornell	W	Sgt	Crowe	C
A/G	F/S	Brown	J	Sgt	Supergia	G	Sgt	McCarthy	D
F/Engineer	F/s	Doig	T	Sgt	Embree	L	Sgt	Gill	C
Pilot	F/L	Johnson	D	P/O	Patterson	J	F/O	Saye	W
Navigator	F/O	Ellis	G	F/O	Sled	J	F/O	Tinevez	F
Bomb Aimer	F/O	Moss	K	F/O	Janssen	J	Sgt	Flanagen	J
WOP	F/O	Wittmack	F	W/O	James	M	Sgt	Thomas	G
A/G	Sgt	Giles	J	F/S	Stockdale	W	W/O	Clarke	A

Role	Rank	Name	I	Rank	Name	I	Rank	Name	I
A/G	Sgt	Martin	G	F/S	Asselin	W	P/O	Benson	L
F/Engineer	Sgt	Crawford	F	Sgt	Millar	J	Sgt	Spivey	P
Pilot	F/O	Gault	J	P/O	Sherlock	G	Sgt	McGuire	L
Navigator	F/O	Howard	P	Sgt	Yard	W	F/O	Steele	W
Bomb Aimer	F/C	Handkamer	G	Sgt	Marsh	H	F/O	Drynan	J
WOP	Sgt	Lawson	A	W/O	Head	D	Sgt	Soderlund	L
A/G	Sgt	Carman	W	Sgt	Augustine	A	Sgt	Davies	J
A/G	Sgt	Walters	P	Sgt	Jeffreys	H	Sgt	Bowen	M
F/Engineer	Sgt	Border	W	Sgt	Moss	C	Sgt	Smart	P

*   Crews posted in to form a 3rd Flight as nucleus for 415 Squadron and later returned to their original units.

Role	Rank	Name	I	Rank	Name	I	Rank	Name	I
Pilot	F/L	Vann	G	F/O	Mills	J	F/O	Krakowsky	M
Navigator	F/O	Spencer	R	F/O	Muldowney	W	F/O	Cann	P
Bomb Aimer	F/O	Gouchey	H	Sgt	Caron	L	F/O	Wilson	C
WOP	W/O	White	E	Sgt	Burke	B	F/S	Blayney	A
A/G	Sgt	Marceau	L	Sgt	Anton	G	Sgt	Zadorozny	S
A/G	Sgt	Robinson	C	Sgt	Beaulieu	W	Sgt	Green	J
F/Engineer	Sgt	Church	J	Sgt	Rimmer	K	Sgt	Boylan	M
Pilot	Sgt	Stedman	A	F/L	Thompson	J	F/O	Potter	A
Navigator	F/O	Gapes	L	F/O	Serne	J	F/O	Rutherford	O
Bomb Amer	F/O	Fox	E	F/O	Borland	A	F/O	Mjolsness	J
WOP	W/O	Hartley	J	F/O	Harrison	F	F/O	Reid	G
A/G	Sgt	Campbell	P	Sgt	Worthington	W	Sgt	Taylor	L
A/G	Sgt	Busby	G	Sgt	Thompson	P	Sgt	Tuer	W
F/Engineer	Sgt	Young	J	Sgt	Sorrell	G	Sgt	Searle	P
Pilot	F/O	Baxter	F	F/L	Woodward	J	F/O	Hemming	C
Navigator	F/O	Hancox	E	F/O	Hay	C	F/O	Bishop	J
Bomb Aimer	W/O	Barnett	G	F/O	Fox	G	F/O	Holmes	H
WOP	Sgt	Armstrong	G	F/O	McLennan	D	P/O	Bruzone	J
A/G	F/S	Hunter	A	Sgt	Palmer	E	F/S	Gallant	J
A/G	Sgt	MacDonald	H	Sgt	Duffy	O	F/S	Brown	P
F/Engineer	Sgt	Hogg	A	Sgt	Bentley	W	Sgt	Hemeley	E
Pilot	F/L	Horan	F	F/O	Hamilton	J	F/O	Barron	G
Navigator	F/O	Lunny	K	F/S	Stokx	G	F/O	Rees	E
Bomb Aimer	F/O	MacKerrow	P	W/O	Panson	F	F/O	McGill	H
WOP	F/O	Traynor	C	F/S	Marcus	N	W/O	Scrafton	J
A/G	F/S	Fraser	J	F/S	Wyers	J	F/S	Robinson	A
A/G	F/S	Nicholson	D	F/S	Walker	C	F/S	Wemp	A
F/Engineer	Sgt	Davison	G	Sgt	Slaughter	E	Sgt	Allen	G
Pilot	F/O	Spiers	G	F/L	Kropf	L	F/L	Fyffe	C
Navigator	F/S	Gallaghan	P	F/O	Sangster	A	F/O	Thompson	H
Bomb Aimer	F/O	Wilkinson	C	Sgt	Hurley	J	Sgt	La France	C
WOP	P/O	Soles	G	F/S	Hodgert	A	Sgt	Campbell	J
A/G	F/S	Quinn	H	F/S	Alwood	J	F/S	Robb	J
A/G	F/S	Waterbury	S	F/S	Machin	D	F/S	Zelenitsky	G
F/Engineer	Sgt	Jonas	J	Sgt	Mortimore	J	Sgt	Clark	C
Pilot	F/L	Hayes	E	F/O	Clarke	A	F/O	Bews	A
Navigator	F/O	Hemming	J	F/O	Smith	L	F/O	Faulkener	P
Bomb Aimer	F/S	Ringrose	J	F/O	Hendrick	P	Sgt	Foley	P
WOP	F/O	Harris	G	F/S	Bullock	W	W/O	McInnes	A
A/G	Sgt	Orser	G	Sgt	Hopkins	D	F/S	Beaton	M
A/G	Sgt	Neilson	M	Sgt	DeSalvo	A	Sgt	Lacroix	J
F/Engineer	Sgt	Cooke	D	Sgt	Bloy	C	Sgt	Burnside	E
Pilot	F/L	Wallace	J	F/O	Loppe	L	W/C	MacDonald	J
Nayigator	F/O	Wilson	C	F/O	Ewing	G	F/O	Hay	C
Bomb Aimer	F/O	Casey	J	Sgt	Sturton	C	F/O	Fox	G
WOP	F/O	Hunter	E	P/O	Malloch	M	F/O	McLennon	D

A/G	Sgt	Croulx	E	F/S	Hardie	J	Sgt	Palmer	E
A/G	Sgt	Choquette	J	F/S	McGill	J	Sgt	Duffy	O
F/Engineer	Sgt	Davies	J	Sgt	Woodley	J	F/L	Duncanson	R
Pilot	F/O	McGuire	E	W/C	Davenport	R	F/O	McKinnon	D
Navigator	F/O	McGuire	J	F/O	Hechter	D	F/O	Hitchcock	D
Bomb Aimer	F/O	McMillan	C	F/O	Rink	W	F/O	March	G
WOP	F/O	Moir	C.	Sgt	Fraser	C	Sgt	Harvey	E
A/G	Sgt	McLachlan	F	Sgt	Pettifor	A	Sgt	Harvey;	J
A/G	Sgt	McClarty	E	Sgt	Lacky	R	Sgt	Farrell	D
F/Engineer	Sgt	McDonald	A	F/S	Gray	B	F/S	Eccleston	A
Pilot	F/L	Sales	J	S/L	Minhinnick	S	F/O	McNicholl	G
Navigator	F/O	Marcille	J	F/O	Bleich	J	F/O	Fleming	W
Bomb Aimer	F/S	Aikens	S	F/O	Harriman	J	F/O	Gray	L
WOP	F/S	Young	R	P/O	Staples	D	P/O	Burgoyne	E
A/G	Sgt	McInnes	C	P/O	Bulbeck	A	Sgt	Bath	E
AG	Sgt	Charles	J	F/O	Bowser	C	Sgt	McLean	A
F/Engineer	Sgt	Dalton	J	Sgt	Partridge	K	Sgt	Baker	G
Pilot	W/C	Stephenson	J	P/O	Patzer	E	F/L	Speller	D
Navigator	Sgt	Bailey	M	F/O	Henson	C	F/O	Fisher	T
Bomb Aimer	F/O	Donaldson	R	F/O	Hay	G	F/O	Gilbert	G
WOP	F/O	Pickthorpe	E	F/S	Daley	F	Sgt	Hogg	J
A/G	W/O	McMahon	W	F/S	Hendenhall	W	Sgt	Cook	G
A/G	F/O	Bond	T	F/S	Mcintosh	W	Sgt	Odobas	K
F/Engineer	Sgt	Hodges	L	Sgt	Grant	C	Sgt	Scott	R
Pilot	F/O	Peaker	G	P/O	Proud	R	P/O	Kinniburgh	J
Navigator	F/O	Hayes	E	P/O	Pauliuk	M	P/O	Smillie	G
Bomb Aimer	F/O	Butterworth	R	F/O	McManus	C	P/O	Schafer	G
WOP	F/S	Baker	R	W/O	Bastine	J	Sgt	London L	
A/G	F/S	Adam	J	Sgt	Franklin	W	Sgt	Powell	T
A/G	F/S	Perrault	E	Sgt	Howes	C	Sgt	Byron	R
F/Engineer	Sgt	Kilkaldy	A	Sgt	Bigger	H	Sgt	Jones	W
Pilot	F/L	Mennie	W	S/L	Thompson	J	F/L	Thomson	G
Navigator	F/O	Gurevich	S	F/O	Serne	J	F/O	Bloch	H
Bomb Aimer	F/O	Sherritt	S	F/O	Borland	A	F/O	Robinson	J
WOP	F/S	Whitworth	T	F/O	Harrison	S	F/S	Jones	A
A/G.	F/S	Jones	F	P/O	Worthington	W	Sgt	Valuer	P
A/G	F/S	Cowell	J	P/O	Thompson	P	Sgt	Haryett	W
F/Engineer	Sgt	Haigh	D	Sgt	Sorrell	G	Sgt	Silver	P
Pilot	P/O	Allen	S	P/O	Bain	J	P/O	Bradley	P
Navigator	Sgt	Wood	C	Sgt	Cohen	S	F/O	Fraser	J
Bomb Aimer	F/O	Kolstead	W	Sgt	Maxwell	J	F/O	Mueller	P
WOP	Sgt	Hennan	A	Sgt	Jone8	P	P/O	Stephen	J
A/G	Sgt	Owen	J	F/S	Prince	B	Sgt	Smith	V
A/G	Sgt	Taschuk		F/S	Sullivan	S	Sgt	Duffy	D
F/Engineer	Sgt	Stiles	C	Sgt	Brolly	P	Sgt	Reid	J
Pilot	P/O	Daly	J	P/O	Durand	J	F/S	Gelineau	W
Navigator	F/O	Friedman	W	F/S	Anderson	N	F/S	Paul	J
Bomb Amer	F/O	Nunn	P	F/S	McLaren	P	Sgt	Hutchens	J
WOP	F/O	Newson	L	Sgt	Pyke	L	Sgt	Steffler	C
A/G	Sgt	Mann	K	Sgt	Crane	J	F/S	Blair	P
A/G	Sgt	Lee	M	Sgt	Alexander	J	Sgt	Bulley	B
F/Engineer	Sgt	Nosworthy	P	Sgt	Lowes	G	Sgt	Shufelt	H
Pilot	F/L	Hayes	E	F/O	Paul	J	F/O	Wyllie	D
Navigator	F/O	Hay	V	F/O	Anderson	H	F/O	Sangster	A
Bomb Aimer	F/S	Ringrose	J	F/O	Servage	W	P/O	Hurley	J
WOP	F/O	McLennan	D	F/O	Petrow	S	F/S	Hodgert	A

Position	Rank	Name	Init	Rank	Name	Init	Rank	Name	Init
A/G	F/S	Orser	G	F/O	Wagetaff	D	F/S	Alwood	J
A/G	F/S	Neilson	M	F/O	Yaunish	A	F/S	Machin	B
F/Engineer	F/S	Cook	D	P/O	Baryluk	M	Sgt	Mortimore	J
Pilot	P/O	Bigland	J	F/O	Bonter	S	P/O	Brown	D
Navigator	F/O	Hood	J	F/O	Vachon	M	F/O	Martin	A
Bomb Aimer	F/O	Ashton	W	F/O	Hinchcliffe	A	F/O	Lawrence	K
WOP	Sgt	Stewart	J	W/O	Anderson	E	Sgt	Brooks	D
A/G	Sgt	Kuffner	F	Sgt	Lawton	D	Sgt	Crawford	G
A/G	Sgt	Bean	P	Sgt	Scott	T	Sgt	Barker	G
F/Engineer	F/S	Chisholm	P	Sgt	Colquhoun		Sgt	Pearce	G
Pilot	W/C	France	K	F/O	Gregory	W	F/S	Jamer	D
Navigator	W/O	Marsh	H	F/S	Jamieson	P	F/O	Franklin	W
Bomb. Aimer	F/O	Dunn	F	Sgt	Ellis	J	F/O	Muzyka	E
WOP	F/O	Graham	P	F/S	Morgan	M	F/S	Rudolph	E
A/G	F/S	Schmuck	H	Sgt	Sideen	E	Sgt	Poe	P
A/G	F/S	Lee	J	Sgt	McLeod	L	Sgt	Kinch	J
F/Engineer	Sgt	Long	M	Sgt	Morphy	C	Sgt	Burnett	W
Pilot	P/O	Kearle	H	F/O	King	A	F/O	Martindale	E
Navigator	Sgt	Olsen	E	F/O	Wallace	F	F/O	Dunlop	B
Bomb Aimer	F/O	Rogers	L	F/O	Waldron	T	F/O	Steele	W
WOP	Sgt	McNamee	E	Sgt	Dickson	A	F/O	McKay	W
A/G	Sgt	Conduit	G	Sgt	Stiddolph	F	Sgt	Gurica	M
A/G	Sgt	Smith	A	Sgt	Wright	J	Sgt	Miller	J
F/Engineer	Sgt	Oliver	J	Sgt	Stone	D	Sgt	Wagstaff	J
Pilot	F/S	Neville	P	F/O	Raymond	S	F/O	Ritchie	P
Navigator	F/O	Matthews	F	Sgt	Cooke	S	F/O	Henderson	M
Bomb Aimer	P/O	Phillips		F/O	Bialogrecki	H	F/O	Liznick	G
WOP	P/O	Demers	E	Sgt	Turner	A	F/O	Howie	A
A/G	Sgt	Blomley	W	Sgt	Clark	W	Sgt	Brooks	J
A/G	Sgt	Naherne	P	Sgt	Carruthers	O	Sgt	Billard	W
F/Engineer	Sgt	Pynn	H	Sgt	Germaney	F	Sgt	Jackson	W
Pilot	F/O	Smith	A	P/O	Turner	J	F/O	Breeze	N
Navigator	F/O	Noble	J	P/O	Millican	J	F/O	Beam	A
Bomb Aimer	F/O	Campbell	G	F/S	Lalonde	J	F/O	Trickett	G
WOP	Sgt	Miller	D	Sgt	Hunter	J	W/O	Kreontel	H
A/G	Sgt	Delano	M	Sgt	Rose	T	Sgt	Pickron	P
A/G	Sgt	Baker	E	Sgt	Matheson	J	P/O	Miller	A
F/Engineer	Sgt	McPeake	E	Sgt	Fuller	A	Sgt	Sheen	J
Pilot	W/O	Brewer	D	F/L	Bugslag	V	F/O	Collins	J
Navigator	F/S	Martyn	I	F/O	Barrett	H	F/O	Cote	J
Bomb Aimer	F/O	Ferguson	C	Sgt	Bloy	P	P/O	Eskins	G
WOP	Sgt	Burford	A	Sgt	Lord	P	W/O	Sparks	E
A/G	F/S	McKay	J	Sgt	Boles	K	Sgt	Farrell	F
A/G	F/S	McLaughlin	E	F/S	Golench	P	W/O	Murray	P
F/Engineer	Sgt	Jones	G	P/O	Fisher	G	Sgt	Roveley	T
Pilot	P/O	McTaggart	D	F/O	Nicholson	A	F/O	Pepler	S
Navigator	F/S	Hawkins	S	Sgt	Root	C	F/O	Dempsey	F
Bomb Aimer	F/O	Maeers	S	F/O	Horton	A	F/O	Cameron	C
WOP	W/O	Cartmell	J	Sgt	Gallant	P	W/O	Greer	G
A/G	F/S	Seymour	C	Sgt	Trayling	J	F/O	Stacy	J
A/G	F/S	Jensen	W	Sgt	Conroy	J	F/O	Mullin	W
F/Engineer	Sgt	Wheelhouse	W	Sgt	Murray	N	P/O	Robertson	J
Pilot	F/O	Patterson	J						
Navigator	F/O	Hans	G						
Bomb Aimer	F/O	Doherty	J						
WOP	F/O	Duncan	P						
A/G	P/O	Kerry	I						

A/G	P/O	Seehuber	P
F/Engineer	Sgt	Burgess	P

415 Squadron aircraft at East Moor

Halifax III

LK755 6U-K,D	21 Ops	ex 432 sqd	transferred to	HCU	
LK765 6U-B	**20** Ops	ex 432 sqd	"	HCU	
LK766 6U-V, Q	34 Ops	ex 432 sqd	"	187 sqd	
LL575 6U-A	41 Ops		"	HCU	
LL576 6U-N	28 Ops		"	HCU	
LL593 6U-M	22 Ops				
LV860		No ops recorded at East Moor before transfer to		429 sqd	
LV941 6U-G	8 Ops	SOC	after ops to Heligoland		18/ 4/45
LW122 6U-Q	3 Ops		transferred to 420 Sqd		
LW552 6U-S	35 Ops	ex 432 sqd	crashed on take off at East Moor		8/ 8/44
			repaired and transferred to HCU		
LW595 6U-Q	2 Ops	ex 432 sqd	FTR - Hamburg		29/ 7/44
LW680 6U-H	4 Ops				
LW686		ex 432 sqd	overshot East Moor u/c collapsed		8/ 8/44
MZ356 6U-Q	5 Ops		transferred to	158 sqd	
MZ416 6U-E	15 Ops		"	187 sqd	
MZ418 6U-M	12 Ops				
MZ456 6U-P	10 Ops		FTR - Hanau		6/ 1/45
MZ474 6U-K	7 Ops				
MZ476 6U-Y	14 Ops		FTR - Hannover		5/ 1/45
MZ483 6U-M	20 Ops				
MZ585 6U-Z	25 Ops	ex 432 sqd	transferred to	HCU	
MZ586 6U-Y,A	30 Ops	ex 432 sqd	"	187 sqd	
MZ590 6U-C	11 Ops	ex 432 sqd	"	HCU	
MZ603 6U-E	28 Ops		FTR - Dusseldorf		2/11/44
MZ632 6U-W	46 Ops	ex 432 sqd	transferred to	HCU	
MZ633 6U-B	4 Ops	ex 432 sqd	collided with	NA609 and crashed	
			near Selby at	18.12 hours	21/8/44
MZ654 6U-L	30 Ops	ex 432 sqd	transferred to	HCU	
MZ660 6U-J	29 Ops	ex 432 sqd	"	HCU	
MZ686 6U-U		ex 432 sqd	crashed on t/o	- East Moor -22.l8hrs	28/7/44
MZ690 6U-S,X	25 Ops		transferred to	HCU	
MZ814 6U-D	17 Ops				
MZ861 6U-Z	23 Ops	transferred to 187 sqd			
MZ882 6U-C	5 Ops	SOC after ops to Dusseldorf			2/11/44
MZ907 6U-P	23 Ops	FTR - Munster			25/3/44
MZ922 6U-C	28 Ops	FTR - Hamburg - shot down by Me262			31/3/45
MZ946 6U-O	35 Ops	transferred to	187 sqd		
MZ947 6U-C	29 Ops	"	HCU		
MZ949 6U-G	38 Ops	"	187 sqd		

NA124 6U-I	26 Ops	transferred to	HCU		
NA181 6U-D	25 Ops				
NA185 6U-A,B	21 Ops	FTR - Leipzig			11/ 4/45
NA186 6U-U	22 Ops	FTR - Hamburg			9/ 3/45
NA20l		transferred to 425 sqd and later returned to 415			
NA202 6U-N,I	30 Ops	"	426 sqd	" 415	
NA204 6U-J	9 Ops		FTR - Chemnitz		6/ 3/45
NA517 6U-R	7 Ops	ex 432 sqd overshot East Moor whilst fully laden			
		after ops to Gaen, 0l.6;hrs 6/8/44-trans to 190 sqd			
NA582 6U-D	33 Ops	crashed 2 miles NE of Stillington while recovering to			

			East Moor ex Duisburg at 04.33 hrs	15/10/44
NA583	6U-F	32 Ops	FTR - Dusseldorf	2/11/44
NA587	6U-Q	33 Ops	transferred to HCU	
NA600	6U-U,A	43 Ops	" 187 sqd	
NA607	6U-R	29 Ops	" HCU	
NA608	6U-H	29 Ops	" HCU	
NA609	6U-G	1 Op	collided with MZ633 and crashed near Selby	21/ 8/44
NA610	6U-B	26 Ops	crash landed at Fiskerton 02.49 hrs on	19/8/44
			repaired	
NA6ll	6U-T	35 Ops	crashed on take off at East Moor at 15.33 hours	14/ 1/45
NA612	6U-P	32 Ops	transferred to HCU	
NR122	6U-X	22 Ops		
NR124	6U-S	7 Ops	transferred to 420 sqd	
NR127	6U-X	25 Ops	" HCU	
NR140		No ops	recorded at East Moor	
NR145	6U-A	18 Ops	ex 432 sqd	
NR146	6U-E	27 Ops		
NR156	6U-H	48 Ops		
NR172	6U-V	36 Ops	transferred to 420 sqd	
NR199	6U-N	23 Ops	recorded at East Moor	
NR206	6U-F	30 Ops		
NR228	6U-Z.	21 Ops	transferred to 427 sqd	
NR249	6U-J	20 Ops	FTR - Wanne Eickel - shot down	
			by flak over Dunkirk	9/ 2/45
NR253	6U-L	11 Ops	FTR - Magdeburg	16/ 1/45
NR256	6U-Q	10 Ops		
NR288		No ops	recorded at East Moor before transfer to 427 sqd	
PN174	6U-R	41 Ops		
PN236	6U-J	17 Ops	ex 432 sqd	
PN237	6U-T	20 Ops	ex 432 sqd	
PN239	6U-V	17 Ops		
PN240	6U-W	14 Ops	transferred to HCU	
PN367		No ops	recorded at East Moor	

Halifax VII

NP754	6U-U	8 Ops		
NP935	6U-I	2 Ops	crash landed at Woodbridge ex Wanne Eickel	12/10/44
NP936	6U-P	9 Ops	FTR - Kamen	25/2/45
NP938	6U-Y	19 Ops	Force landed at Cambrai Epinoy after engine failure	
			ex Witten. 05.50 hours	19/ 3/45
NP961	6U-0	9 Ops	ex 432 sqd transferred to 420 sqd	
NP940	6U-L	18 Ops		
RG447	6U-S	17 Ops	transferred to HCU	

415 Squadron crews at East Moor

Pilot	P/O	McKean	J	F/O	Stein	A	F/O	Brown	W
Navigator	F/O	Wakelin	D	F/O	Penaud	G	F/L	Thompson	D
Bomb Aimer	F/S	Moffatt	G	Sgt	Harvey	P	Sgt	Baptiste	F
WOP	Sgt	Higgins	O	Sgt	Reeson	G	F/O	McGill	P
M/Upper	Sgt	Morris	J	Sgt	Profosky	A	Sgt	Labercane	C
P/Gunner	Sgt	Lee	H	Sgt	Robertson	W	F/O	Huskilson	W
F/Engineer	Sgt	Gage	H	Sgt	MacIver	A	Sgt	Larke	P
M/AG	Sgt	McPhee	W	Sgt	McElroy	L	Sgt	Vine	J

Pilot	P/O	Gingrich	P	F/O	Patten	L	Sgt	Kerr	J
Navigator	F/O	Vaughan	E	F/O	Provias	P	Sgt	Beilhartz	H
Bomb Aimer	F/O	Gosling	D	Sgt	Hill	P	P/O	Hayes	P
WOP	F/O	Winch	J	Sgt	Ford	J	W/O	Veryard	G
N/Upper	Sgt	Boyce	N	Sgt	Kell	A	Sgt	Wilson	E
R/Gunner	Sgt	Hosier	M	Sgt	Turner	E	Sgt	James	P
F/Engineer	Sgt	Tait	E	Sgt	Watson	P	Sgt	Atkin	D
M/AG	F/S	Bridle	W	Sgt	Moulden	W	Sgt	Bayerle	S

Pilot	F/O	Sherman	W	P/O	Andrews	D	Sgt	Lane	W
Navigator	F/O	Aubrey	G	F/O	Willis	J	F/O	LeGrice	E
Bomb Aimer	F/O	Dworkin	D	W/O	Pelletier	J	Sgt	Graham	W
WOP	F/a	Quinlan	W	W/O	Evans	P	W/o	Roberts	P
M/Upper	P/a	McGlashan	L	Sgt	McDonald	J	Sgt	Smallbridge	W
P/Gunner	P/O	Sears	E	F/S	Conroy	J	Sgt	Bannister	F
F/Engineer	Sgt	Park	L	Sgt	Grant	G	Sgt	Eltherington	S
M/AG	Sgt	Mitchell	J	Sgt	Valde	V	Sgt	Fox	H

Pilot	P/O	Lindquist	O	P/O	Forbes	F	P/O	Little	J
Navigator	Sgt	Mahoney	E	P/O	Fernie	J	Sgt	Hancock	C
Bomb Aimer	F/O	McQuado	J	Sgt	Morris	S	Bgt	Bouvier	W
WOP	W/O	Lomieux	A	F/S	Vitarell	D	Sgt	Smith	H
M/Upper	Sgt	Main	J	Sgt	Lovie	C	Sgt	Brynjoisfen	D
R/Gunner	Sgt	Honuset	A	Sgt	Scarf	J	P/O	Thompson	J
F/Engineer	Sgt	Gilboy	C	Sgt	Afford	P	Sgt	Cottoy	P
M/AG	Sgt	Lowe	P	Sgt	Morrison	P	Sgt	Ballantyne	L

Pilot	W/C	McNeill DFC	.J	F/O	Meagher	J	F/a	Gue	C
Navigator	P/O	McKillop	S	F/O	Belkin	D	F/O	Sinclair	S
Bomb Aimer	F/L	McNicholl	W	F/O	Foster	D	F/O	Horie	A
WOP	Flo	Rowsell	C	W/O	Kelly	J	W/O	McQueen	A
M/Upper	F/S	Glaisher	L	Sgt	Lording	E	F/S	Scott	J
P/Gunner	P/O	Graham	N	F/O	Timmermans	W	F/S	Bell	P
F/Engineer	P/O	Hargreaves	J	Sgt	Wood	A	F/S	Simpson	A
M/AG	F/O	Powell	H	W/O	Fry	F	Sgt	Webb	W

Pilot	F/L	Hovey	J	F/O	Weir	J	F/O	Knobovitch	H
Navigator	F/O	Connel	C	F/O	Fleming	P	P/O	Orchard	A
Bomb Aimer	F/O	Wittingham	A	F/O	Bowen	P	F/O	Anderson	B
WOP	Sgt	Currie	J	F/O	Lyons	H	Sgt	Harper	J
M/Upper	Sgt	Gordon	J	Sgt	Parkes	G	Sgt	Seeley	C
P/Gunner	Sgt	Maxham	A	F/S	Warner	H	Sgt	Valde	V
F/Engineer	Sgt	Coulter	S	Sgt	Potter	J	Sgt	Kirkpatrick	S
M/AG	Sgt	Barrett	D	Sgt	Labercane	C	F/S	Tisdalle J	

Pilot	F/O	Chapman	P	F/L	Barnes	H	W/O	Stevens	P
Navigator	F/O	Barron	G	F/O	Moulden	J	W/O	Murray	G
Bomb Aimer	F/O	Edwards	A	Sgt	McLeod	W	F/S	Nunziate	H
WOP	Sgt	Fox	H	W/O	Dubois	J	W/O	Steele	W
M/Upper	Sgt	Mitchell	A	Sgt	Ballantyne	L	Sgt	Dennis	A
P/Gunner	Sgt	Morrison	P	Sgt	Bayerle	S	F/S	Bogle	F
F/Engineer	Sgt	Guthrie	T	Sgt	Rome	J	P/O	Mount	J

Position	Rank	Name	I	Rank	Name	I	Rank	Name	I
Pilot	P/O	Tinmouth	A	F/O	Poberts	B	F/O	Sierolawaki	P
Navigator	P/O	Richardson	A	F/O	Kelly	E	P/O	Page	J
Bomb Aimer	F/S	Todere	L	Sgt	Switzer	P	Sgt	Webb	W
WOP	P/O	Nelson	P	Sgt	Mihell	P	F/O	Joyce	A
M/Upper	F/S	Parr	E	Sgt	McConnel	J	Sgt	Vine	J
R/Gunner	F/S	Webber	G	Sgt	McPhee	W	Sgt	Molden	W
F/Engineer	Sgt	Warren	E	Sgt	Natheson	D	Sgt	Wood	J
M/AG	P/O	Graham	M	Sgt	Gordon	J	F/O	Huskilson	W
Pilot	P/O	Britt	J	S/L	Wilmot	B DFC	P/O	Tims	J
Navigator	F/S	Pape	J	P/O	McKillop	S	F/L	Davies	P
Bomb Aimer	F/O	Gray	A	F/L	McBain	A	Sgt	Deschambeault	J
WOP	F/S	Blau	P	F/O	Eaglestone	W	F/O	Scanlon	P
M/Upper	Sgt	Barrett	D	W/O	Fry	W	Sgt	Cunningham	S
R/Gunner	F/S	Bridle	W	P/O	Thompson	J	Sgt	Stewart	P
F/Engineer	Sgt	Ramsbottom	C	Sgt	Malpass	N	Sgt	Bell	N
M/AG	Sgt	Roy	C				Sgt	Shubrook	D
Pilot	F/O	McAllister	J	F/O	McTaggart	D	P/O	Chartier	C
Navigator	F/O	Prawdsik	C	F/O	Pritchard	E	Sgt	H₁arrison	J
Bomb Aimer	Sgt	Rhodes	J	F/O	Stack	J	Sgt	Veales	J
WOP	Sgt	Moynes	E	Sgt	Taylor	F	W/O	Morrison	F
M/upper	Sgt	Smith	G	Sgt	Boyle	J	Sgt	Hunt	D
R/Gunner	P/O	Smith	A	Sgt	Allah		Sgt	Beharriell	J
F/Engineer	Sgt	Geneva/Watling		Sgt	Thompson	W	Sgt	Antrobus	P
M/AG	Sgt	Sample	D	Sgt	Smallbridge	W	Sgt	Sample	D
Pilot	F/O	Chapman	P	F/L	Thompson	C	W/C	Ball	F
Navigator	F/O	Barrow	C	F/O	Gladding	P	F/L	McDonald	L
BombAimer	F/O	Edwards	K	F/O	Mallard	J	P/O	Johnson	G
WOP	F/S	Hollman	S	Sgt	Gallery	N	P/O	Blackburn	B
M/Upper	Sgt	Sample	D	Sgt	Garner	H	P/O	Patterson	W
P/O	Sgt	Shubrook	B	Sgt	Stringer	P	F/O	Samwald	J
F/Engineer	Sgt	McLeod	J	Sgt	Bancroft	G	Sgt	Goodenough	P
M/AG	F/S	Glaisher	L	Sgt	Geadron	J	Sgt	McPhee	W
Pilot	F/O	Mitchell	W	F/L	Winmill	A	F/O	Falconer	E
Navigator	F/O	Loveridge	P	F/O	Donley	W	F/S	Ferris	F
Bomb Aimer	F/S	Noble	D	F/O	Carreau	P	F/S	Perkins	N
WOP	Sgt	Mosey	W	Sgt	Jenner	W	W/O	Chowon	W
M/Upper	Sgt	Gill	W	Sgt	Kilgore	A	Sgt	McNeil	J
P/O	Sgt	Gendron	J	P/O	Pegg	F	Sgt	Skidmore	W
F/Engineer	Sgt	Wridley	A	Sgt	Fox	W	Sgt	Coleman	A
M/AG	W/O	Walker	B				F/O	Murray	L
Pilot	F/O	McGuire	J	F/O	Belcher	L	P/O	Cruickshank	A
Navigator	F/O	Vaizial	N	P/O	Brier	H	F/O	Wynne	J
Bomb Aimer	W/O	Barnet	T	F/O	Strosberg	N	F/O	Brush	G
WOP	F/O	Donlan	P	F/O	Irving	H	F/S	Barr	W
M/Upper	F/S	Penaud	J	F/O	Murray	L	Sgt	Lesage	
P/O	F/S	Begin	A	F/S	Butler	N	Sgt	Valliere	C
F/Engineer	Sgt	Howard	D	Sgt	Mawson	L	Sgt	Wosley	J
M/AG									
Pilot	P/O	Grier	G	F/O	Milibank	E	W/O	McKenzie	J
Navigator	F/O	Mikalchuk	P	F/S	Absom	J	F/S	Herring	P
Bomb Aimer	Sgt	Marshall	J	F/O	Bucko	H	F/O	Fuller	L
WOP	F/S	Harrigan	J	W/O	Andrew	W	Sgt	Bailey	E
M/Upper	Sgt	Aickon	J	F/S	Zator	J	Sgt	Hogg	J
P/O	Sgt	Johnston	G	F/S	Morris	J	F/a	Broad	W
F/Engineer	Sgt	Andrews	J	Sgt	Swan	M	Sgt	Charlebois	J
M/AG							Sgt	Graham	J
Pilot	F/S	McDiarmid	A	P/O	Hechtor	J	F/O	Goodwin	W

Navigator	Sgt	Mracek	W	F/O	Kirkland	J	F/O	Frew	H
Bomb Aimer	F/O	Hibbon	A	F/O	Webster	H	F/S	Ross	O
WOP	Sgt	Adams	F	W/O	Vaughan	E	F/S	Clitheros	H
N/UpperS	gt	Tonello	N	Sgt	Jaques	J	F/S	Stewart	A
P/O	Sgt	Roberts	G	Sgt	Harrison	G	F/S	Woytowich	W
F/Engineer	Sgt	Gale	W	Sgt	Hunter	J	Sgt	Gault	P
M/AG	Sgt	Flett	G	Sgt	Richardson	J	Sgt	Bradley	K

<u>415Sqd crews continued</u>

Pilot	P/O	MacNeil	W	P/O	McNeil	D	W/C	LeComte	L
Navigator	F/o	Roy	P	F/O	Fletcher	C	F/O	Boyd	W
Bomb Aimer	F/S	Sante	D	F/O	Underhill	W	P/O	Cox	J
WOP	F/S	Salchenberger		F/S	Davies	F	P/O	Bright	E
M/Upper	Sgt	Rafferty	A	F/S	White	W	F/B	Glaisher	L
P/O	Sgt	Main	J	F/S	Ward	P	F/L	McNamara	P
F/Engineer	Sgt	Parker	C	Sgt	Owens	D	Sgt	Swarbrigk	A
M/AG	Sgt	Labercane		P/O	Stephens	P	P/O	Stephens	T
Pilot	S/L	Frankling	S	F/O	Stewart	E	F/O	McQuiston	J
Navigator	F/O	Ringwall	T	F/O	Huddar t	J	F/O	McGlone	G
Bomb Aimer	P/O	Cox	J	P/O	Somers	P	F/O	Egan	J
WOP	F/S	Brown	P	F/S	Greaves	A	Sgt	Walker	A
N/Upper	F/S	Grondin	J	Sgt	Fleming	P	Sgt	Cavanagh	J
P/O	F/S	Lennard	P	Sgt	McVean	W	P/O	Stephens	T
F/Engineer	Sgt	Duff	P	Sgt	Munford	A	Sgt	Stogryn	J
M/AG	F/O	Huskilson	W	Sgt	Harringan	J	Sgt	Sidon	A
Pilot	F/O	Darychere	L	F/O	Regimbal	W	F/O	McFadden	B
Navigator	F/O	Dean	P	F/O	Rose	P	F/O	Connor	M
Bomb Aimer	F/O	Switzer	K	F/O	Rabkin	H	F/O	Rhind	E
WOP	F/S	Moorhouse	D	P/O	Zubra	G	Sgt	Rinder	J
M/Upper	P/O	Hanna	W	Sgt	Nelson	V	Sgt	Clarke	J
P/O	Sgt	Harrigan	J	Sgt	Morton	K	Sgt	Graves	F
F/Engineer	Sgt	Harrison	A	Sgt	Spence	S	Sgt	Burton	J
M/AG				Sgt	Lechance	J	Sgt	O'Connor	P
Pilot	P/O	Mooers	S	F/L	Northrup	J	F/O	Britt	J
Navigator	F/a	Wright	P	F/a	Thanvette	P	F/S	Pape	J
Bomb Aimer	Sgt	Fuller	P	Sgt	Paradis	J	F/S	Blau	P
WOP	F/S	Gillard	J	W/O	Amboise	J	F/O	Gray	A
M/Upper	Sgt	Grant	J	Sgt	Sullivan	J	Sgt	Barrett	D
P/O	Sgt	Everett	E	Sgt	Lechance	J	F/S	Bridle	W
F/Engineer	Sgt	Hewitt	E	Sgt	Bryden	A	Sgt	Ramsbottom	C
M/AG	W/O	Rowe	C	Sgt	Clarke	J			
Pilot	P/O	Donnelly	T	Sgt	Krocker	C	F/L	Nears	T
Navigator	P/O	Kufta	A	Sgt	Nicolls	P	Sgt	Warren	F
Bomb Aimer	F/O	Dunston	I	Sgt	Chatfield	P	Sgt	Gerrie	C
WOP	F/S	Keddie	L	F/S	Doyle	G	W/O	Vaughan	E
M/Upper	Sgt	Porter	P	F/S	Walker	B	Sgt	Russell	J
P/O	F/S	Wiseman	N	Sgt	Orbach	N	Sgt	Taylor	J
F/Engineer	Sgt	Boyack	P	Sgt	Tongue	L	Sgt	Weston	V
M/AG	Sgt	Taylor	J	W/O	Rowe	C	Sgt	Snell	D
Pilot	F/O	Piper	C	F/L	Barrett	W	F/O	Galley	A
Navigator	F/O	Summerville	D	F/O	Sloan	D	F/O	Warren	J
Bomb Aimer	F/O	Robinson	A	F/O	Daniel	T	F/O	Gingras	F
WOP	Sgt	Gonik	H	Sgt	Collins	P	Sgt	Bartholomew	H
M/Upper	Sgt	Richardson	J	Sgt	Mogridge	P	Sgt	Warrington	P
R/G	Sgt	Flott	G	Sgt	Bradley	K	Sgt	Smith	L
F/Engineer	Bgt	Kerr	J	Sgt	Binnie	D	Sgt	Kuchma	P
M/AG	F/O	Baltzer	P	F/S	Roy	C	Sgt	Gaton	E
Pilot	W/O	Russell	L	F/O	Wilkinson	E	F/O	Hyland	G
Navigator	F/S	Gallagher	J	F/O	Thomson	A	F/O	Lewis	T

Role	Rank	Name	I.	Rank	Name	I.	Rank	Name	I.
Bomb Aimer	W/O	Poyryeka	P	F/O	Standing	W	F/O	Suttak	J
WOP	F/S	Craigie	C	F/S	Schultz	G	F/S	Anderson	a
M/Upper	F/B	Brown	P	F/O	Baltzer	P	Sgt	Pedon	G
P/O	F/S	Jones	W	Sgt	Ashton	J	Sgt	Rude	G
F/Engineer	Sgt	Trowsdale	L	Sgt	Fyfe	W	P/O	Boles	L
M/AG									
Pilot	F/S	Sirtonski	E	F/O	Cowieson	B	F/O	Minkler	L
Navigator	F/S	Campbell	I	F/O	Stewart	G	F/S	Wilson	J
Bomb Aimer	F/O	Abel	G	F/O	Mealing	N	F/O	Milibank	D
WOP	F/S	Fasang	F	W/O	Dewan	L	F/B	JohnsonG	G
M/Upper	F/S	Engman	E	F/S	Dekur	W	Sgt	Sheppard	P
P/O	F/S	Gates	E	F/S	Harvey	W	Sgt	McKenzie	N
F/Engineer	Sgt	Broughton	L	Sgt	Law	A	Sgt	Abram	G
M/AG	Sgt	Dekur	W						
Pilot	F/O	Evans	P	P/O	Emsom	C	F/O	Pallin	P
Navigator	F/O	Spry	L	F/O	Sargent	E	F/O	John6on	E
Bomb Aimer	F/O	Veitch	L	F/O	House	J	F/O	Mooney	N
WOP	F/O	Kelly	J	F/S	Rampton	D	F/S	Bird	P
M/Upper	F/S	Lorenz	D	W/O	Lamphier	J	Sgt	Shelley	T
P/G	F/S	Teevin	D	W/O	Brewsrer	C	P/O	McLean	G
F/Engineer	Sgt	Wylie	B	Sgt	Walby	J	P/O	Haley	J
M/AG									
Pilot	F/O	Patterson	J	P/O	Clouthier	V	S/L	McAllister	J
Navi gator	F/O	Kingston	G	F/S	Laimon	N	F/L	Montgornery	A
Bomb Aimer	F/O	Harding	J	F/O	Murray	L	P/O	Moynes	E
WOP	Sgt	Jackson	H	Sgt	Derricott	D	P/O	Rhodes	J
M/Upper	F/O	Bowman	A	Sgt	Bevans	W	F/S	McNeil	J
R/G	F/O	Maitland	K	Sgt	Carmicheal	H	F/O	Smith	G
F/Engineer	Sgt	Bell	B	Sgt	Holman	G	P/O	Taylor	C
Pilot	F/O	Clarke	D	F/O	Cahill	F	F/O	McCollum	J
Navigator	F/O	Kirk	W	F/O	Aikenhead	D	F/O	Aylesworth	P
Bomb Aimer	Sgt	Page	A	F/O	McKenzie	J	Sgt	Paul	P.
WOP	Sgt	Belanger	J	Sgt	Middleton	P	F/S	Knight	A
M/Upper	Sgt	Fortin	N	P/O	Clyde	P	Sgt	Brennan	L
R/G	F/O	Oates	C	P/O	Goring	P	W/O	Jones	J
F/Engineer	Sgt	Minnikin	E	Sgt	Harpin	J	Sgt	Lowe	S
Pilot	F/O	Addison	J	F/O	Jupp	E	F/O	Harker	L
Navigator	F/O	Mahalek	A	F/O	Telford	A	F/O	NcKenna	K
BombAimer	Sgt	Edgar	J	F/O	Riel	S	P/O	Goranson	D
WOP	F/O	Rackley	F	F/O	Mitchell	D	Sgt	Sterling	H
M/Upper	F/O	Burroughs	J	F/O	Johnston	L	P/O	Wilson	W
P/O	F/O	Handson	A	F/O	Knight	T	P/O	McAllum	E
F/Engineer	Sgt	Stoker	L	Sgt	Swetman	H	Sgt	Dickson	W
Pilot	F/O	Holter	C	F/O	Huitman	J	P/O	McLatchie	P
Navigator	F/O	Smith	A	F/O	Harris	P	F/S	Kitchin	T
Bomb Aimer	F/O	Burke	W	F/O	Thompson	D	F/O	Savage	J
WOP	F/O	Bateman	H	W/O	Hood	J	Sgt	Langford	W
M/Upper	Sgt	Paifsky	H	F/S	Martin	D	Sgt	Fletcher	G
P/O	Sgt	Miller	H	Sgt	NcKellar	P	Sgt	Delaney	J
F/Engineer	Sgt	Jones	J	Sgt	Stones	T	Sgt	Gibb	J
Pilot	F/O	Huffman	D	W/C	Blagrave	P			
Navigator	F/O	Meadus	H	F/O	Paul	G			
Bomb Aimer	F/O	Hale	F	F/O	Lod	B			
WOP	F/O	Blenkhorn	A	F/O	McCall	P			
M/Upper	Sgt	French	S	W/O	Gaust	P			
R/G	F/S	Clayton	K	F/S	Vandwater	V			
F/Engineer	Sgt	Lavers	N	Sgt	Adair	G			

Pilot	F/S	Ward	H	F/O	Sadler	J
Navigator	F/B	Robinson	S	F/O	Hannah	H
Bomb Aimer	Sgt	Heaverman	A	F/O	Crawley	K
WOP	F/S	Cameron	L	F/S	Casey	D
M/Upper	Sgt	Slaney	N	F/S	Wood	T
R/G	Sgt	McPhee	F	F/S	Weeks	W
F/Engineer	Sgt	Fawcett	J	Sgt	Brown	W

June and July 1945

Following the cessation of hostilities in the European Theatre of war, East Moor's two operational squadrons were disbanded at the station, and over the next few weeks the aircraft were flown out to Maintenance Units and scrapyards at High Ercall, Bracklea and to the York Aircraft Repair Depot at nearby Rawcliffe

Noted at the latter airfield while awaiting the breakers hammer were, NP755 (Avenging Angel) with thirty missions recorded, NP693 with seventy one, NP707 (Willie the Wolf) sporting sixty seven, NP708 seventy three, LK766 fifty six, and fitted with a .5 ventral gun, MZ586 ('Y Worry') thirty missions, also with ventral gun, and NR228.

Meanwhile the station at East Moor was undergoing the transition from being an 'Operational' one to that of a 'Holding Unit cum - Transit Camp, and was experiencing a general tidy up.The M.T Section claimed that they were busier than before VE Day, with cleaning up and disposing of the many vehicles.

1 June 1945

News was received at East Moor that Squadron Leader J.A Thompson and crew,who failed to return from the Chemnitz operation on 14th February, had become prisoners of ware It was also believed that Warrant Officer NcDiarmid and his crew were safe, missing from the operation to Hamburg on 8th March 1945.

This date saw the beginning of large scale movements of personnel into and out of East Moor with one hundred and twenty aircrew being posted to RCAF Station Middleton St.George.

4 June 1945

Monday morning saw the staff of the Station Armoury busy clearing up and getting rid of explosives and incendiaries. The latter were loaded on to Lancasters of 424 Squadron from RCAF Station Skipton on Swale and ferried to a dumping ground in the North Sea.

9 June 1945

One hundred and ten of the station's groundcrew were posted out to the RCAF Stations at Topcliffe and Wombleton.

20 - 22 June 1945

During this period six hundred and seventy groundcrew left East Moor for the Repatriation Depot, and from then on the station saw a continuous flow of both air and groundcrew in and out.
Life became considerably easier for the station's personnel who were no longer required to maintain a state of wartime readiness. The change over to peacetime routine did not bring as much 'bull' as had been feared by many, and was introduced gradually allowing everyone to become relaxed and very bored during the first few months.

By July, the two obligatory daily parades had been reduced to just one. That was held in the morning, leaving the ever increasing numbers of transistory personnel with even more time on their hands, and adding to the problems of maintaining discipline. With everyone in such high spirits, and thousands of service personnel of varying cultures frequenting York, one or two 'skirmishes' did occur, resulting in the city being 'Out of Bounds' to the station's personnel during. the last week in the month.

On the station, ever increasing sports and entertainment programmes helped to pass what were for many, long,boring and frustrating days as they stamped their feet awaiting repatriation.

Education facilities were in bigger demand than ever, and at full stretch with courses in Business Management, Languages, Mathematics and numerous other subjects.

The Station Library together with Hobby and Handicraft Shops were at that time being used to full capacity. Many new books had become available and amateur craftsmen were producing a wide selection of gifts, handbags, wallets, cigarette lighters, brooches and other jewelry.

Due to the constant movement of personnel, it became difficult to maintain the small arms training programme, nevertheless, a number of rifle shoots were arranged at Strensall Firing Ranges.

28 July 1945

Wing Commander W.F McKinnon assumed duties as Station Commander at East Moor, vice Wing Commander F.W Ball who became due for repatriation to Canada.

Throughout the month, the regular events took place and included, organised sports, roller skating, games nights, dances, film and variety shows. Add to those the Church Services and access to Padres, Music and Camera Clubs.

Although East Moor Station was never officially designated as a Holding Unit, it did, during the next few months settle down in its non-operational status and into the routine of such a unit.

1 August 1945

43 airerew officers and NCO's were posted in from RCAF Station Wombleton.

Commencing at 19.00 hours, the Old Communal site was the stage for the 160 roller skating enthusiasts that attended, indicating that the pastime was still very much in favour at East Moor. Music and refreshments were provided.

RCAF Station Dalton invited the East Moor WAAF's to their farewell dance.

A good attendance was registered at the Games Night, cribbage and bridge etc were enjoyed.

2 August 1945

61 aircrew officers and NCO's were posted out to the repatriation depot at Torquay.

The film being shown at the Station Cinema was 'The Suspect'.

3 August 1945

The City of York was again opened to Canadians after being placed 'out of bounds' for one week. At 15.00 hours a muster parade was held at which the station's personnel were warned of the disadvantages of mixing with any provocative characters, and were advised to be on their best behaviour.

[1]Youth and Swing', a Maple Leaf show was staged in the station cinema at 20.15 hours before an appreciative audience of more than 380 people.

RCAF Station Topcliffe Lacrosse team visited East Moor and gave an exhibition with the final score being a 2 - 2 draw.

4 August 1945

A small batch of aircrew departed on posting to the Holding Unit at RAF Station Rufforth.

Many talented performers were brought to the fore when East Moor Officers Mess staff held a party in Sutton on Forest, for married waitresses on release. The WAAF's were said to have had a most enjoyable time.

Being a Saturday, 12.00 hours saw a week end 'stand down' granted to all personnel not on essential duties.

The film 'Dancing in Manhatten' was shown to the hospital patients at 14.30 hours and to the Senior NCO's at 19.00 hours in their mess.

6 August 1945

Was August Bank Holiday and an extension of the week end 'stand down' was enjoyed by the station's non-essential staff.

More than fifty people attended a dance in the WAAF's NAAFI which commenced at 20.00 hours, the music being provided by records.

The Officer's Mess film was 'Hangover Square'.

7 August 1945

RCAF Station Dishforth hosted the No.5 District Volleyball tournament and a team from East Moor made a very good showing but failed to reach the finals which were won by RCAF Station Leeming.

The music enthusiasts gathered for their club meeting in the evening which was held in the 'Y' lounge at 20.00 hours.

8 August 1945

Two educational films were shown in the Station Cinema commencing at 13.00 hrs 'Canada Commmunique' together with a film on farming. Following those a new programme 'Information Please' was introduced, when airmen were invited to ask questions pertaining to the Air Force, repatriation, demobilisation and post-war employment etc. In attendance to try to answer the questions were the Station Administrative Officer, Personnel Counsellor and the Station Padres.

The WVS ladies from the neighbourhood were on the station to attend to the airmens sewing, darning and mending. As there was a shortage of customers it was thought that the airmen were either becoming proficient themselves, or that they were well in with the WAAF's.

Roller Skating at the Old Communal Site again proved popular with around 125 people attending. Cribbage and Bridge were again enjoyed at the Games Night.

9 August 1945

And the first of the married WAAF's due for release were posted to 105 PDC, and included women from various trades.
Groundcrew drafts departed for several other stations, RCAF Station Topcliffe, No.3 PRO Bournemouth, No.4422 SE, 4426 SE and No.6 RCAF Operations HQ.

Mr. Neil Morrison of the BBC Current Affairs was the guest speaker in a talk and discussion held at 19.00 hours in the NAAFI, the subject was 'Canadian Trends' Mr Morrison rated very highly as a speaker and proved to be very well informed on his subject and created quite an impression on his audience.

RCAF Station Skipton on Swale provided the band for an 'All Ranks' dance held in the Station Cinema at 20.30 hours. Unfortunately there was a noticeable shortage of female dancers in the large gathering.

10 August 1945

Heavy bombers were to be seen at East Moor once again when the Lancaster X's of 424 Squadron, RCAF Station Skipton on Swale were engaged in ferrying the station's surplus incendiaries to a dumping ground in the North Sea.

A further number of WAAF's were posted out to 105 PDC for release.

Station Intelligence Officer Flight Lieutenant C.N Pennie, was posted out to No.62 (RCAF) Base at Linton on Ouse.

The East Moor Officer's Mess was showing the film 'Man in Half Moon Street'.

11 August 1945

The Lancaster crews of 424 Squadron were still busy helping to clear the Station Armoury and Bomb Stores.

The station's Saturday 'stand down' took effect from 12.00 hours and included all non-essential staff.

The Station Hospital screened the film 'Man in Half Moon Street' to the patients at 14.30 hours, and it was later shown in the Sergeant's Mess.

12 August 1945

An All Ranks' dance was held in the Station Cinema at 20.30 hours with music provided by the 'Streamliners', an RCAF band whose excellent music helped to ensure that a memorable night was enjoyed by all.

13 August 1945

The Station Bomb Dump was finally cleared up. The 424 Squadron Lancaster crews ferried out the last of 140 loads of incendiaries, clusters and ammunition and jettisoned the lot into the North Sea.

A small batch of groundstaff of various trades were posted out to the Torquay repatriation depot.

The film being shown in the Officer's Mess was 'Tahiti Nights'.

14 August 1945

Around 250 Officers and NCO aircrew were posted out to the Holding Unit at RAF Station Ruf forth.

It was the Sergeant's Messes turn to show the film 'Tahiti Nights' while a crowd of music lovers attended the Music Club evening in the 'Y' Lounge and listened to records.

15 August 1945

At long last, the day for which everyone had been waiting for had arrived, and it was declared V-J Day. The Japanese had surrendered and victory was a reality.

The Station Church held a Thanksgiving Service which was attended by 150 people. The station's personnel had heard so many rumours about the likiehood of Japan collapsing, that the news that it had done so, caught them unawares. What was even worse, was that many were broke as Pay Parade was not due until Friday the 17th.

No plans had been made to celebrate that most historic of occasions. However, a programme was soon put together and a festive spirit was assumed. A film 'Since You Went Away' was shown in the Station Cinema during early afternoon to followed by a dance in the evening.

Those with money spent two days in York, but the celebrations never reached the peak of those held to welcome V-E Day. There were several reasons for this,apart from lack of finances, the station liquor stocks were at an all time low and the East Moor Station strength had fallen considerably since that time.

16 August 1945

A further draft of WAAF personnel left for 105 PDC and release,bringing the monthly total to 26 of various trades.

17 August 1945

A draft of groundstaff of various trades were posted out of East Moor to 426 Squadron and to 4426 SE at RAF Station Tempsford, while others went to No.4423 SE and to No.4422 SE both at Bassingbourn.

A new Station Equipment Officer arrived from RCAF Station Dalton and took up his duties.

No.62 (RCAF) Base Linton on Ouse provided the band for an 'All Ranks' dance held at 20.30 hours in East Moor's Station Cinema. The band attracted a large crowd.

18 & 19 August 1945

Non essential staff were given a week end stand down at 12:00 hours, on the Saturday, and at 19.00 hours the film 'Lets Go Steady' was screened in the Sergeants Mess,and on Sunday in the NAAFI.

20 August 1945

A draft of 88 ground crew of various trades was posted out to RCAF Station Leeming and to No.1659 Heavy Conversion Unit at RCAF Station Dishforth.

A small band of enthusiasts attended a dance to records in the WAAF NAAFI at 20.00 hours.

The film 'Enter Arsene Lupin' started its rounds of East Moor Station in the Officer's Mess at 19.30 hours.

21 August 1945

A draft consisting of 31 groundcrew of various trades was posted out to the Torquay Repatriation Unit.

Code and Cypher Officer Flight Lieutenant P.K Peach was posted from the station to RCAF Station Leeming.

Due to the many postings out, attendances at the Station Cinema, where the film 'Delightfully Dangerous' was shown, and at the Music Club were rather smaller than usual.

22 August 1945

All aircrew with more than 105 priority points were granted leave until the usual 23.59 hours on the 31st August.

A further small batch of personnel in groundcrew trades was posted out to the 6412,6416 and 6443 SE's.

The ladies of the WVS were on the station once again, offering their mending and darning services from 10.00 to 15.00 hours.

Games night at 19.00 and Roller Skating at 19.30 hours were still proving to be popular pastimes but with smaller attendances due to the many postings out of the station.

23 August 1945

Station Education Officer Flight Lieutenant J.C Jensen was detached to No.9 Instructors School at RAF Station Bourn to conduct a Job Instructor's Training Course.

The East Moor Station Cinema was packed to capacity at 20.00 hours when a performance by the RCAF 'Swingtime' Unit was appreciated.

A further batch of groundcrew left the station, not for release but for service overseas. They too, were of various trades.

24 August 1945

Aircrew were again on the move from East Moor and destined for Torquay and eventual repatriation. The group consisted of both Officers and NCO's.

No.6 Group Dance Band provided the music for an 'All Ranks' dance held in the Station Cinema at 21.00 hours and attended by a good crowd. Earlier in the afternoon they had given a fine programme in the NAAFI.

25 & 26 August 1945

The usual weekend 'stand down' commenced at 12.00 hours on the Saturday and was granted to all personnel not on essential duties.

'Molly and Me' was the weekend film and was screened in the Sergeants Mess on Saturday evening and in the NAAFI on Sunday.

27 August 1945

Wing Commander T.N O'Brien an Administrative Officer from No.6 Group Headquarters was posted in to East Moor to assume Station Commander duties pending the posting of Wing Commander W.F McKinnon.

The Station Signals Section was the scene of a combined Signals and Orderly Room party. The old operations room was utilised as a dance floor, and the Intelligence Library as a bar room. It was a most successful event with plenty of refreshments and dancing was to records.

28 August 1945

A total of 44 aircrew Officers and NCO's were posted out to RAF Station Rufforth.

There was a most noticeable fall off in the attendance at the Music Club's weekly meeting held in the 'Y' Lounge at 20.00 hours.

The films that were going the station rounds were 'Half Way House' and 'Phantom Lady'.

29 August 1945

Another of the station's regular events, the Games Night, showed a marked decrease in attendance due to the many postings away from East Moor.

30 August 1945

A large draft of 170 aircrew Officers and NCO's were posted in to East Moor from RCAF Station Thoithorpe, while a small number were posted out to the Repatriation Unit at Torquay.

At 20.30 hours the WAAF Section held an 'Invitation Dance' in their NAAFI when the ever popular RCAF Linton Base Band provided the music and quite a large crowd had an enjoyable evening.

The Station Cinema was showing a film 'Princess and the Pirate' at 19.00 hrs.

31 August 1945

A small group of aircrew were posted in from RCAF Station Linton on Ouse. Physical Training Officer Flying Officer C.W Cutrass was posted in to assume duties at East Moor from RCAF Station Dalton.

The Friday evening film screened in the Station Cinema was 'Lost in a Harem'.

East Moor Station Strength was,

RCAF Officers	94	Other Ranks	518
RAF Officers	2	Other Ranks	20
WD Officers	3		
WAAF Officers	1	Other Ranks	134
Grand Total	772		

General:

Regular organised classes and events at the station were getting more and more difficult to maintain due to postings and repatriations of personnel.

The main diversion from work or otherwise, was sports, roller skating, tennis, squash and badminton. East Moor Station did not have a tennis court and the enthusiasts used the facilities at Rowntrees of York.

The Station Padres reported a very quiet month with falling church attendance and response to Padres Hour at an all time low.

Happily the Station Hospital admissions and sick parade attendance had also dwindled.

1 September 1945

Leave was granted to 168 aircrew Officers and NCO's to 23.59 hours on the 9th, thus relieving the congestion in the two messes which had filled to capacity.

Nursing Sister E.S Lubeque returned to East Moor from detached duty at the RAF Hospital at Northallerton.

Preparations were being made to provide a sports layout in No.1 Hanger to be used in the event of bad weather.

'Charles Laughton' was the star in 'Mutiny on the Bounty', the film being screened to a fair audience in the Sergeants Mess from 19.00 hours. Only the essential staff remained on camp after the 12.00 hours weekend 'stand down'.

2 September 1945

Sunday, and a congregation of 25 attended the Protestant Church Service at 11.00 hours. 'Mutiny on the Bounty' did somewhat better at 19.00 hours when 110 personnel attended its showing in the NAAFI.

3 September 1945

Wing Commander J.F Clark, DFC was posted in from RCAF Station Dalton to become Station Commander East Moor and took over from Wing Commander W.F McKinnon who was due for repatriation to Canada.

Flight Lieutenant N.R O'Dell an Intelligence Officer from No.6 RCAF Rear Headquarters was posted in to East Moor Station.

20.00 hours saw the commencement of a pleasant evenings dancing to records in the WAAF's NAAFI, when 40 enthusiasts attended.

4 September 1945

Only 15 people attended the weekly meeting of the Music Club as many of its most enthusiastic supporters had been posted out of the station.

The Sergeants Mess audience of 150 people watched the movie 'Mr Emanuel' at 11:00 hours.

It was 'bull' night for the WAAF Section followed by the RC Padre's Hour.

5 September 1945

Wednesday, and the famous St.Leger race meeting was held at York Knavesmire, so with a 'stand down' being granted and transport laid on in both directions, many of the East Moor personnel attended.

The weekly Games Night was held in the Corporal's Club with the usual bridge and cribbage being enjoyed.

The local WVS ladies were again on hand at the station between 10.30 hours and 15.00 to carry out the airmen's mending and darning requirements.

6 September 1945

A successful record dance held in the Station Cinema at 21.00 hours attracted more than 170 dancers.

The audience at the Station Cinema earlier in the evening totalled more than 300 to see 'High Powered' a 'Y' film.

7 September 1945

An Autumn Softball League was formed and the first game took place between East Moor Station teams, 'the Dead End Kids' and the 'Coastal Command NCO's'.

The popular Chief Technical Officer on the station, Squadron Leader W.E.R Boone was posted out to the RAF Station at Tempsford.

70 aircrew officers and NCO's were posted in from RAF Station Bircham Newton. At 20.00 hours the Maple Leaf Show 'Hip Hooray' saw th. Station Cinema filled to capacity and an excellent performance was enjoyed, while 80 Officers watched the film 'Winged Victory' in their mess.

8 September 1945

Saturday again, and the week end 'stand down' was granted as usual to those not required on station.

Section Officer G.I Hunt, Catering Offiber arrived at East Moor on detached duty from No.6 Group Rear Headquarters.

175 Senior NCO's watched the film 'Destiny' in their mess at 19.00 hours.

9 September 1945

Wing Commander W.F McKinnon the former Station Commander East Moor, started on his long journey back to Canada with the first leg to Torquay 'P' Depot, together with the Station Armament Officer Flight Lieutenant A.J Doran and Nursing Sister M.W Peacock.

Sunday Church Services were held and the congregation at the Protestant. one was again 25.

In the Station Softball League, the 'Coastal Command Officers' defeated the 'Dead End Kids' 13 - 6.

The Sunday night film shown in the NAAFI was 'Destiny' when 75 attended.

10 & 11 September 1945

These two days saw the tempo of personnel movements in and out of East Moor stepped up considerably with numerous postings out to the repatriation depot at Torquay,and to various other stations in the United Kingdom, while the arrivals were from Merryfield and Snaith.

Pilot Officer R.M Davies an MT/Equipment Officer was posted in to East Moor Station from No.3 PRC and assumed MT Officer duties.

Film shows on the station were only averaging 70 people daily, the Music Club was down to 15 and a records dance drew 35.

12 September 1945

The Station Dental Officer Major D.L McLean of the Canadian Dental Corps, and and his assistant Sergeant B.C Mason were posted out to RCAF Overseas Headquarters.

The Station's depleted staff of Cooks and Waitresses received reinforcements when 7 WAAF members were posted in from RCAF Station Tholthorpe.

A Radar Officer from 18AHC'U, Flight Lieutenant V.F Bruce and a WD Catering Office:

Flight Officer E.J Campbell from RCAF Station Dalton were added to the strength of East Moor Station.

Games Night, Roller Skating and the film 'Harrigan's Kid' attracted 48, 50 and **75** persons respectively. All slightly up on previous Wednesday.

13 September 1945

Pay Parade got around again, and the WAAF Section donated the sum of £15/13/0 in National Savings Stamps.
A further 27 aircrew Officers and 12 NCO's left the station bound for the repatriation unit at Torquay.

250 people attended the 14.00 hours screening or 'National Velvet' in the Station Cinema, and at 21.00 more than 300 turned out for an 'All Ranks' dance at the same venue. Music for the latter function was provided by the band of No.6 Group RCAF.
A sign that Strensall Bombing Range was obselete came with the removal of its telephones by the General Post Office, who had earlier in the day collected the surplus from Station Signals Section.

14 September 1945

Air and ground crew members continued to flow in and out of East Moor Holding IUnit.
Flight Lieutenant G.W Hyslop, Flying Control Officer was posted out to RAF Station Aldermaston.

The Station Softball game between 'Linton Champs' and the 'Coastal Command Officers' was washed out.

The Station Cinema was the venue for a performance given by the 'RCAF Topcliffe Show' at 20.00hours, and was greatly appreciated by more than 300 persons. The cast were entertained later in the Sergeant's Mess.

15 & 16 September 1945

And another weekend which saw the usual Saturday 'stand down' at 12.00 hours, and the Sunday Protestant Church Service at 11.00.

There was only 11 postings in and no outgoing movements during the two days. The weekend film. at East Moor was 'Keep Your Powder Dry' watched by a total of 180 persons.

17 & 18 September 1945

Transient postings amounted to 12 in and 7 out during these two days.

40 enthusiasts attended a WAAF dance in the NAAFI at 20.00 hours on the former date and 15 met at the Music Club at the same time on the latter.

'Royal Scandal' and 'Double Exposure' were the films being screened in the Officer's and Sergeant's Messes respectively.

There was only 4 personnel movements on this date.

The WVS ladies from nearby Sutton on Forest and Huby villages were again in attendance from 10.00 hours and accomplished a large amount of sewing and mending for the station's personnel.

Being Wednesday, there was an afternoon film showing, 'Double Exposure' attracted more than 100 personnel at 14.00 hours.

Roller Skating and Games Night attendances fell off considerably.

20 September 1945

Transient movements of personnel amounted to a mere 10 in and 4 out.

Attendances at the Cinema rose to 200 for the film 'Girl in Overalls' in the afternoon, while more than 300 returned at 21.00 hours for an 'All Ranks' Dance. The Station band from RCAF Leeming had been booked but had to be replaced at the eleventh hour by the one from RCAF Skipton on Swale.

21 September 1945

22 postings in and 2 out were the days transient movement totals.

A new RCAF Show 'The Re - Pats' were very well received in the Station Cinema at 20.00 hours, with a mixture of music and comedy.

Hospital patients saw the movie 'The Brighton Stranger' at 14.00 hours and the Officers Mess screened it at 19.30.

22 & 23 September 1945

The weekend saw only 3 postings in and 1 out at East Moor. The usual 'stand down' was granted, films were shown in the NAAFI and in the Sergeant's Mess, and 35 attended Church Service on Sunday.

24 - 26 September 1945

Transient movements of personnel totalled 29 out and 4 in during the three days.

Movies shown were 'Bowery to Broadway', and 'Tonight and Everynight' and attracted a total of 220 persons.

The WAAF Section held their usual record dance in the NAAFI on Monday, 10 enthusiasts met at the Music Club on Tuesday and 24 at Wednesdays Games Night.

27 September 1945

Morale received a boost at East Moor when a draft of 35 personnel was posted out to the Torquay Repatriation Unit.

'Hi Beautiful', a 'Y' movie attracted 250 people for an afternoon showing in the Station Cinema.

The Maple Leaf Show Party put 'It's a Pleasure' at 20.00 hours in the Station Cinema. The show contained much typical 'RAF Humour' and performed before a packed house of 350 persons.

28 September 1945

The days transient movements amounted to only 10 airmen of various trades and all were outgoing.

A 'Y' film, 'The Clock', was screened twice, to a mixed audience in the Station Cinema during the afternoon and in the Officer's Mess in the evening.

The RCAF Band 'The Westernaires', played for 300 dancers at an 'All Ranks' dance in the Station Cinema at 21.00 hours.

29 & 30 September 1945

The usual weekend 'stand down' took effect at 12.00 hours on the Saturday for all non-essential staff on the station.

A Protestant Church Service attracted 30 personnel at 11.00 hours on Sunday. There was only 6 postings in, and 1 out during the weekend.

General:

Not a very eventful month at East Moor Station. The activities were not particularly interesting, and only small groups of personnel came and went. It was a most difficult job providing entertainment for the transient airmen and women, as the station was for a time without a Sports Officer, short of Physical Training Staff and had the additional problem of adverse weather conditions. A number of films shown by the Personnel Counsellor were followed by question and answer periods and proved very popular with such topics as Portage, Man and his Home, Home on the Land, Goods and Prices and the Niagara Frontier.

There were two Padres on the station at that time, and they delivered talks on sex, marriage and parenthood.

The Transient Movements at East Moor for September 1945,

Aircrew	Officers in,	149	Aircrew	Officers out,	69
Aircrew	NCO's in,	296	Aircrew	NCO's out,	19
Groundcrew	Officers in,	7	Groundcrew	Officers out	12
Groundcrew	O Ranks in,	9	Groundcrew	O Ranks out,	91
Total		461	Total		191

East Moor Station Strength at 30 September 1945,

RCAF	Officers	199	RCAF	Other Ranks	735
RAF	Officers	0	RAF	Other Ranks	13
WD	Officers	3	WAAF	Other Ranks	124
Army	Officers	1	Army	Other Ranks	2
WAAF	Officers	1			

Grand Total (Station)	1,078

October 1945

The month started very quietly at East Moor, the only transient postings up to the 15th were 22 aircrew out and 3 in, with 17 groundcrew out. The regular Station activities continued, film shows, dances, sports and games etc.

11 October 1945

The 'Modernaires' band provided the music for 300 dancers at an 'All Ranks' event held in the Station Cinema at 21.00 hours.

12 October 1945

The Maple Leaf Concert Party staged the show 'Ankles Away' in the Station Cinema at 20.00 hours to an appreciative 250 people, and were later entertained in the YMCA.

14 October 1945

It was 'Open House' at the Station Sergeant's Mess where bingo and dancing was included in the programme.

15 October 1945

The 9th Canadian Victory Loan Campaign got underway and East Moor was set a most ambitious target of 90,000 Canadian dollars.

A dramatic change in the station's tempo resulted when news was received that it was to be handed over to RAF No.12 Group Fighter Command on the 1st November 1945.

With more than 700 personnel on the station that instruction was to send everyone into a flurry of activity.

17 October 1945

This was the last time that the ladies of the WVS visited RCAF Station East Moor. They had been regular visitors for a considerable time, and earned much gratitude for their sewing, mending and darning services to the airmen.

18 October 1945

More than 400 aircrew personnel left the station on postings to RCAF Stations Topcliffe and Thoithorpe.

19 October 1945

More than 200 aircrew NCO's were posted out to RCAF Station Skipton on Swale.

22 October 1945

A further 38 personnel departed East Moor to RCAF Stations Tholthorpe and Skipton on Swale. This left No.5 as the only occupied living site at East Moor, enabling the remainder to be cleaned up in preparation for the impending hand-over to the RAF.

23 October 1945

East Moor's Motor Transport Section held a farewell party at Farlington Village where a Grand Dinner had both chicken and duck on the menu. Afterwards all adjourned to the village 'pub' for further refreshment.

24 October 1945

The Station Medical staff threw a party for the Station Headquarters staff with a steak dinner washed down with plenty of liquid refreshment. A most memorable evening was rounded off with a dance.

Green Hammerton was the scene of the Equipment Section's farewell party and it was said to have been another success.

26 October 1945

East Moor Station was turned over to the 'erks' and to the WAAF's for the night, and a gala event it turned out to be. Commencing with a chicken dinner served by the Officers and NCO's, a Station Dance followed with music provided by the 'Westernaires' band. Free beer was provided to all 'Other Ranks'and the NAAFI provided the refreshments.

27 & 28 October 1945

The usual weekend stand down was given to all personnel not engaged on essential duties, and took effect at 12.00 hours on Saturday.

The Station Chapel was the venue for the last Protestant Church Service at RCAF Station East Moor on the Sunday at 11.00 hours.

29 October 1945

An 'Advance Party' comprising 14 Officers and 18 'Other Ranks' from No.54 Operational Training Unit arrived at East Moor from RAF Station Charterhall in Berwickshire, and proceeded with an Inventory check and 'Marching In' inspecti on.

30 October 1945

With No 54 Operational Training Unit's advance party ready to take over, there was a final flurry of activity to dispose of files and publications pertaining to RCAF Station East Moor.

Three further parties of No.54 Operational Training Unit arrived at East Moor by road and rail and some of their aircraft were flown in.

31 October 1945

This was the last day that East Moor Station served as a Royal Canadian Air Force establishment, thus ending two years and eight months in that role under the aegis of No.6 (RCAF) Group Bomber Command.

The changeover was effected very smoothly as the last of the Canadians moved out to RCAF Station Tholt.horpe, leaving East Moor once more in the hands of the Royal Air Force.

The Canadians did not leave East Moor without some regrets. They took with them many happy memories of station activities and entertainments and said that they would miss the many 'watering holes' around the local villages and in York. The English public house had become part of their existence, and a place where they could both let off steam and spend a relaxed few hours.

1 November 1945

RCAF Station East Moor transferred from NO.6 Group Bomber Command and became RAF Station East Moor under NO. 12 Group, Fighter Command.

Station Commander Group Captain F.B Bristow.

Three trains were chartered to carry the Main Party of N0.54 Operational Training

Unit from Marchmont in Berwickshire to Yorkshire and hence by road to East Moor. The only hitch was when the train carrying the WAAF contingent broke down en route and consequently their arrival at East Moor was not until 06.30 hours on the 2nd. They had departed Marchmont at 20.47 hours on the 1st of the month.

2 November 1945

Personnel of 54 OTU commenced 'shaking down' in their new quarters and preparations for the arrival of pupils was under way.

The unit had flown no less than 80 aircraft in to East Moor during the previous few days, 47 Mosquitos of various marks, 10 Wellington XVIII's, 9 Martinet's, 6 Hurricane 11C's, 5 Ansons, 2 Masters and an Oxford.

3 to 10 November 1945

These days were taken up with unpacking and general organisation throughout the station.

11 November 1945

Armistice Day and runway '22 - 04' was the parade ground for a 100% turn out when the salute was taken by the Station Commander, Group Captain F.B Bristow.

The parade march past was led by No.1 Squadron Commander Wing Commander L.W Gill followed by Wing Commander Arthur at the head of No.2 Squadron and Flight Officer Ainslie (WAAF) leading No.3 Squadron.

13 November 1945

The station was honoured by the visit of Air Vice Marshal J.W Baker, CB, NC, DFC.

14 to 22 November 1945

The task of organising the various sections continued with emphasis on the Flying Training Wing.

23 November 1945

Flying Training commenced with two of the four scheduled courses participatinge 4 hours and 2 3/4 hours of daylight flying was carried out by No's 59 and 60 courses respectively.

27 to 29 November 1945

Two pilot and two navigator /radar courses were in full swing and flying training was being carried out during both day and night time.

31 November 1945

The strength of No.54 OTU was as follows,

Total number of	Officers	53	Total number of	airmen pilots	20
Total number of	airmen	803	Total number of	aircrew	22
Total number of	WAAF Officers	6	Total number of	Officer pilots	43
Total number of	aircrew	57	Total number of	WAAF airwomen	299

General:

No.54 OTU was a Commonwealth unit with personnel drawn from all over the world and its major role was the training of night fighter crews, pilots and navigator /radar operators.

The Mosquito NF3O's were equipped with Airborne Interception radar which enabled them to seek out and attack enemy aircraft. The trainee navigator /radar operators familiarised themselves with this equipment during lessons in the Wellington flying classrooms, while the Hurricanes and Martinets served as target aircraft. The two latter types were referred to as 'playmates' by the Wellington crews. The Ansons were used for 'Gee' training and the Oxford to check out pilots on twin engine aircraft, and for communication work.

The Mosquitos carried the code letters LX and YX and other types the letters ST.

After successfully completing their training at East Moor, the pilots and navigators were then posted to an Operational Conversion unit and many were destined for the night fighter squadrons that were based in Germany.

The Hurricanes were phased out soon after their arrival at East Moor while the Wellington and Martinet strength rose to eleven of each type.

During 54 OTU's stay at East Moor RAF Station Croft was used as a satellite field.

1 December 1945

No flying recorded

2 December 1945

No flying recorded

3 December 1945

40 hours of flying training carried out.

4 December 1945

No flying recorded

An intake of 6 trainees arrived on the station.

5 December 1945

54 hours flying training was carried out.

6 December 1945

43 hours and 30 minutes flying training recorded.

7 December 1945

No flying recorded

8 December 1945

22 hours and 45 minutes flying training recorded.

9 December 1945

No flying recorded

10 December 1945

19 hours and 35 minutes flying training was carried out.

The SOA of No.12 Group Fighter Command, Group Captain J. Warfield and Squadron Leader Mitchell visited East Moor.

11 December 1945

34 hours and 45 minutes flying training was carried out.

12 December 1945

12 hours and 10 minutes flying training was carried out.

13 December 1945

38 hours and 25 minutes flying training was carried out.

14 December 1945

19 hours and 40 minutes flying training carried out.

15 - 17 December 1945

No flying was recorded on these days.

18 December 1945

19 hours and 20 minutes flying training was carried out.

19 December 1945

Only one hours flying training was carried out.

20 December 1945

No flying was recorded.

21 December 1945

10 hours and 20 minutes flying training was carried out.

No further flying was recorded during the month of December 1945.

General:

Unit strength as at 31 December 1945,

Total number of	Officers	47	Total number of	airmen pilots	21
Total number of	airmen	788	Total numbur of	aircrew	22
Total number of	Officer pilots	41	Total number of	airwomen	266
Total number of	aircrew	54	Total number of	WAAF Officers	5

1946

January 1946

During the first two weeks of the month the crews from No.59 course were posted out and numerous pilots and navigators in for refresher courses and nav/radar courses 62 and 65.

1 January 1946

37 hours and 35 minutes flying training recorded.

2 January 1946

40 hours of flying training was carried out.

3 January 1946

16 hours and 20 minutes of flying training was carried out.

4 January 1946

No flying was recorded.

5 January 1946

14 hours and 25 minutes of flying training was carried out.

6 January 1946

No flying was recorded.

7 January 1946

No flying was recorded.

The Air Officer Commanding No.12 Group Fighter Command, Air Vice Marshal Baker, CB, MC, DFC, visited East Moor.

8 January 1946

26 hours and 30 minutes of flying training was carried out.

9 January 1946

No flying was recorded.

10 January 1946

31 hours and 25 minutes of flying training was carried out.

Sadly the pupil crew were killed when Mosquito XXX, NT544 crashed into high ground near Aygill during a night training flight. Category E.

11 January 1946

No flying was recorded.

12 January 1946

10 hours and 25 minutes of flying training was carried out.

13 January 1946

No flying was recorded.

14 January 1946

14 hours and 10 minutes flying training was carried out.

15 January 1946

4 hours and 30 minutes of flying training was carried out.

16 January 1946

No flying was recorded.

17 January 1946

37 hours and 30 minutes of flying training was carried out.

18 to 28 January 1946

No flying training was carried out at East Moor.

29 January 1946

18 hours and 15 minutes of flying training was carried out.

Instructor pilot Flying Officer Turner and Instructor navigator Flight Lieut. Thornton were involved when Mosquito XXX, NT241 overshot East Moor ending in the fields during an emergency single engined landing. Sadly, Flight Lieut Thornton was killed in the category 'E' accident.

30 January 1946

17 hours of flying training was carried out.

31 January 1946

12 hours of flying training was carried out.

General:

The aircraft strength of No.54 OTU as at 31 January 1946 was,

Type		Strength
Mosquito	111	6
Mosquito	V1	4
Mosquito	XXX	30
Martinet		11
Master	11	2
Oxford		1
Anson		4
Hurricane	11C	2
Wellington		10

Personnel strength

Total number of	officers	50
Total number of	airmen	754
Total number of	officer pilots	70
Total number of	aircrew	70
Total number of	airmen pilots	21
Total number of	airrnen aircrew	18
Total number of	WAAF officers	4
Total number of	airwomen	238

1 February 1946

No.54 OTU carried out 26 hours and 25 minutes of flying training.

A category AC accident occurred at East Moor and involved Mosquito XXX, NT459 piloted by Flying Officer Loveland. Fortunately he was uninjured when the undercarriage was retracted during a daytime landing.

2 & 3 February 1946

No flying was recorded at East Moor on those days.

4 February 1946

No 54 OTU carried out 18 hours and 50 minutes of flying training.

5 February 1946

No.54 OTU carried out 25 hours and 45 minutes of flying training.

Mosquito NT268 of 54 OTU suffered engine failure during single engined flying and made a forced landing at map reference MR226736. The instructor pilot Squadron Leader Primaveis was uninjured in the category 'E' accident which occurred during daylight.

6 February 1946

No.54 OTU carried out 16 hours and 45 minutes of flying training.

7 February 1946

32 hours and 5 minutes of flying training was carried out by 54 0TU.

8 & 9 February 1946

No 54 OTU carried out 12 hours and 55 minutes of flying training and 19 hours and 20 minutes respectively.

10 February 1946

There was no flying recorded by 54 OTU.

11 & 12 February 1946

Flying training time amounted to 38 hours and 30 minutes on the first day and 14 hours and 30 minutes on the latter.

13 February 1946

No flying recorded by 54 **OTU.** Flight Sergeant Prescott-Decie was posted in to assume duties as a NaviRadar instructor.

14 & 15 & 16 February 1946

No.54 OTU carried out 19 hours and 30 minutes, 27 hours and 1hour and 55 mins of flying training from East Moor on these days.

17 February 1946

No flying was recorded by 54 OTU.

18 February 1946

hours and 40 minutes of flying training was carried out by 54 OTU.

19 February 1946

36 hours and 25 minutes of flying training was carried out by 54 OTU. During daylight hours, Mosquito XXX, NT558 was on a cross country exercise when after breaking and reentering cloud it spun and crashed near Pitsford Church in Northants. The pupil crew Sergeant Aird (pilot) and Sergeant Graves (nav) were killed. The aircraft fell from approximately 2,000 feet.

East Moor and 54 OTU suffered a further setback during darkness when Mosqito XXX NT511 swung off the runway whilst landing in a strong cross wind. The pupil pilot, Flight Lieutenant Thomas was uninjured in the category 'A' accident.

20 - 23 February 1946

Total amounts of flying training time carried out by 54 OTU was 6 hours and 25 minutes, 45 hours and 20 minutes, 44 hours and 4 hours and 35 minutes respectively.

24 February 1946

No flying was recorded.

25 - 28 February 1946

Flying training periods for these days amounted to 19 hours and 15 minutes, 24 hours and 10 minutes, 15 hours and 20 minutes and 19 hours respectively and recorded by No.54 OTU.

February aircraft strength return at East Moor was,

Mosqito	111	6	Oxford		1
Mosquito	V1	4	Anson		4
Mosquito	XXX	24	Hurricane	11C	1
Martinet		14	Wellington		10
Master	11	2			

Personnel strenth.		
(54 OTU)	Total nimber of Officers	104
	Total number of airmen	688
	Total number of officer pilots	37
	Total number of aircrew	39
	Total number of airmen pilots	21
	Total number of airmen aircrew	16
	Total number of airwomen	229
	Total number of WAAF Officers	5

1 March 1946

No.54 OTU carried out 15 hours and 55 minutes of flying training. Anson EG369, with Warrant Officer Lane the instructor pilot at the controls suffered starboard engine failure and a forced landing was effected at RAF Station Marston Moor. No injuries occurred in what was a category 'AC' accident during daylight hours.

2 March 1946

Only 2 hours and 20 minutes of flying traing was recorded at the station.

3 March 1946

There was no flying training recorded at East Moor.

4 - 9 March 1946

Flying training was carried out at East Moor by 54 OTU and amounted to 3 hours and 40 minutes, 3 hours and 25 minutes, 45 hours and 55 minutes, 48 hours and 45 minutes, 13 hours and 55 minutes and 13 hours and 5 minutes respectively.

10 March 1946

No flying training was recorded by 54 OTU.

11 March 1946

54 OTU carried out 22 hours and 20 minutes of flying training.

12 March 1946

No flying training was recorded by 54 OTU.

Intakes of pilots and navigatorlradar personnel arrived for training from 21 PAFU and from 7 PRC.

13 - 16 March 1946

Flying training continued at the station and amounted to 5 hours 25 minutes, 33 hours and 75 minutes, 29 hours and 5 minutes and 26 hours 55 minutes respectively on these days.

17 March 1946

No flying training was recorded by 54 OTU.

18 - 23 March 1946

NO.54 OTU's programme of flying training continued with a record * 67 hours and 45 minutes carried out on the 21st. The other days saw 17 hours and 45 minutes, 34 hours and 55 minutes, 26 hours and 25 minutes, 8 hours and 15 minutes and 10 hours 45 minutes respectively. *(54 OTU at East Moor)

On the latter date the station was visited by the Air Officer Commanding No.12 Group Fighter Gommand, Air Vice Marshal J.H Baker, CB, MC, DFC.

24 March 1946

No flying training was recorded by 54 OTUe

25 - 30 March 1946

Flying training from East Moor amounted to 59 hours and 5 minutes, 40 hours and 10 minutes, 23 hours and 5 minutes, 17 hours and 35 minutes, 7 hours and 5 mins and 15 hours and 40 minutes on these respective days.

31 March 1946

No flying training was recorded.

Aircraft strength at the station was

Mosquito	111	6	Wellington	XV111	10
Mosquito	V1	3	Anson		3
Mosquito	XXX	24	Hurricane	11C	1
Martinet		13	Oxford		1
Master	11	2			

54 OTU Personnel strength,

Total number of	officers	93
Total number of	airmen	742
Total number of	officer pilots	25
Total number of	aircrew	20
Total number of	airmen pilots	15
Total number of	airmen aircrew	6
Total number of	airwomen	227
Total number of	WAAF officers	5

Group Captain E.N Donaldson, DSO,AFC had assumed command of RAF Station East Moor on the 28th of the month vice Group Captain F.B Bristow.

1 April 1946

The month opened with five courses under flying training and a sixth commenced towards the end.

There was no flying training recorded by No.54 OTU on the 7th, 14th, 19th, 20th, 21st, 22nd, 25th and 28th of the month.

The following table shows the dates upon which flying training did take place at East Moor and the number of training hours recorded on each,

1st	26 hours 20 mins		16th	37 hours 5 mins		
2nd	13 "	50 "	17th	21 "	5 "	
3rd	27 "	30 "	18th	44 "		
4th	39 "	35 "	23rd	4 "	50 "	
5th	62 "	10 "	24th	29 "		
6th	14 "	15 "	26th	38 "	20 "	
8th	35 "	30 "	27th	28 "	5 "	
9th	47 "	25 "	29th	1 "	55 "	
10th	59 "	5 "	30th	1 "	15 "	
11th	40 "					
12th	38 "	40 "				
13th	8 "	10 "				
15th	26 "	40 "				

Aircraft strength at East Moor as at 30 April 1946,

Mosquito	111	7	Wellington	XVIII	10
Mosquito	VI	3	Anson		3
Mosquito	XXX	23	Oxford		1
Martinet		13			
Master	11	2			

No.54 OTU Personnel strength

Total number of	Officers	80
Total number of	airmen	832
Total number of	Officer pilots	19
Total number of	aircrew	18
Total number of	airmen pilots	13
Total number of	airmen aircrew	10
Total number of	airwomen	228
Total number of	WAAF Officers	5

May1946

NO.54 OTU's flying training programme at East Moor continued throughout the month on all but three days viz, 5th, 19th and 26th.

The unit recorded in excess of 650 hours of flying training from the airfield, involving no fewer than five courses for pilots and navigator /radar operators.

16 May 1946

Mosquito III, TW102 crashed on take off at East Moor when the undercarriage was raised before it became airborne.

24 May 1946

East Moor Station's ranks were swelled with the arrival from nearby Hutton Cranswick of No.288 (Anti Aircraft) Squadron, bringing with them several versions of the Supermarine Spitfire and Vultee Vengeance Mk IV.
With the exception of some solo aerobatic flying by Spitfire pilots, very little flying by 288 Squadron was witnessed during the month.

29 May 1946

A new Station Commander Group Captain P.S Ryan, succeeded Group Captain E.M Donaldson, DSO, DFC.

Around this time Airspeed Oxford, HN595 was seen in and out of East Moor and was probably on the strength of 288 Squadron.

31 May 1946

A variety of aircraft could be seen at East Moor including the Mosquitos, Martinets, Masters, Wellingtons, Ansons and Oxford of 54 OTU together with Spitfires and Vengeances of 288 Squadron.

It was around this time that the station was to experience a shortage of personnel in many trades, cooks, fitters, clerks and GD's and senior NCO's were said to be disappearing at an alarming rate. The latter were possibly the ones with the longest service and all were anxious to get back to their families and to continue with their civilian lives.

1 June 1946

With the introduction of a temporary training policy, No.54 OTU was engaged in twin engine conversion but was expected to resume the full operational training of night fighter crews.

A shortage of crews on the front line squadrons necessitated the change of programme for the East Moor OTU.

Wing Commander H.E Arthur, OBE the Chief Technical Officer was posted out and was succeeded by Squadron Leader Chapman. The former officer had been at East Moor since the arrival of 54 OTU.

The aircraft of 288 Squadron were rarely seen in the air probably due to the fact that there was not much call for their speciality of Anti Aircraft and Searchlight Co-operation.

6 June 1946

The ex No.64 Course crews were posted out on completion of their training.

Warrant Officer O'Connor was posted in from 1 PSC to assume duties as a Test Pilot with 54 OTU.

12 June 1946

Wing Commander P.T Philpott, OBE presided over a District Court Martial at East Moor when the accused was an NCO with 54 OTU.

15 June 1946

A Movement Order No. 1146 was received at East Moor ordering. No.54 Operational Training Unit to move to RAF Station Leeming.

No.288 Squadron disbanded at East Moor.

17 June 1946

A Court of Inquiry was held on the station to investigate the 'Absence without Leave' of LAC Backman.

18 June 1946

An Advance Party of 54 OTU moved from East Moor to RAF Station Leeming.

21 June 1946

No.54 OTU commenced flying their aircraft out of East Moor for their new base at RAF Station Leeming, and continued to do so over the next few days as each one became due for inspection.

A change in command of the WAAF was effected when Flight Officer Wilson took over from Flight Officer Williams.

24 June 1946

Formal Investigations were held on the station to look into the disappearance of a Parachute Pack No.92061 and a typewriter from Station Headquarters.

28 June 1946

The Main Party of No.54 OTU departed from East Moor by road and by air to RAF Station Leeming.

The personnel who travelled by road were conveyed in transport supplied by 'Northern Command Movement Control'. Stores and Equipment was moved by the 'Ministry of Road Transport'.

30 June 1946

RAF Station East Moor was reduced to 'Care and Maintainance' status and became a satellite of RAF Station Leeming.

The Camp Commandant was Flight Lieutenant R.S Wilson.

At the time of departure from East Moor, No.54 OTU had on strength some 62 aircraft comprising, 6 Mosquito Mk 111, 7 Mosquito Mk VI, 22 Mosquito XXX. 12 Martinet, 2 Master Mk 11, 10 Wellington Mk XVlII, 2 Anson and 1 Oxford.

Total flying training hours for June recorded by 54 OTU amounted to 242 hours for pilots and 187 for navigator/radar operators.

Strength of 54 OTU personnel was

101	Officers	14	airmen aircrew
720	airmen	191	airwomen
35	Officer pilots	5	WAAF Officers
31	aircrew		
19	airmen pilots		

After the departure of No.54 OTU, a contingent of German Prisoners of War were engaged in cleaning up operations at East Moor and upon completion of that task, they too moved to RAF' Station Leeming where they were employed in similar work.

When the RAF finally relinquished all interest in East Moor, the station was selected for amost unusual role and became 'home' to a large number of people who were described as 'Displaced Persons'.

Amongst those poor unfortunates were people of several nationalities, many of whom had fled to Britain in the face of the Nazi occupation of Europe and from Communism. The majority were of Polish extraction.

The quarters which were previously occupied by the WAAF in Goose Lane together with the gymnasium and cinema sites became a temporary home to the refugees.

During their stay at East Moor they were often treated to a 'beat up' of their quarters by a Polish compatriot and pilot who was at the time based at RAF' Station Topcliffe. These visits were said to have been a great morale raiser to those on the ground and were presumably, unofficial.

Probably the last aircraft to use East Moor was a Gloster Meteor whose pilot put down in an emergency in the mid 1950's. After walking to Low Carr Farm to summon assistance he made the long trek back to find his aircraft had attracted a number of spectators.

There followed a visit by an RAF Mobile unit (probably from nearby Linton on Ouse) after which the pilot was seen to make a spectacular take off from a runway which by that time was in a state of disrepair with large areas covered in moss and tall grass.

The whole area was soon returned to agriculture, the hangers demolished and other buildings fell into dereliction. At the time of writing (1980), there is very little to remind one of the very important part that the station and its personnel played in World War II.

Several modern dwellings have been erected within the airfield perimeter, some of the dispersed sites contain light industrial buildings and deep litter poultry units stand on the intersection of the three runways. Gone is High Carr House and on the bomb stores site stands a game rearing construction.

Halifax II, 158 Squadron, June to Nov 1942

Wellington III, 429 Squadron, Nov 42 to Aug 43

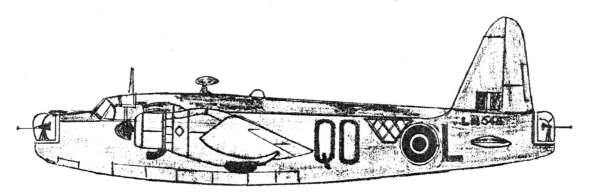

Wellington X, 432 Squadron , Sept 43 to Nov 43

Lancaster II, 432 Squadron, Nov 43 to Feb 44

Halifax III, 415 Squadron, July 44 to May 45   **Fig 44. Squadron aircraft.**

54. OTU November 1945 - June 1946

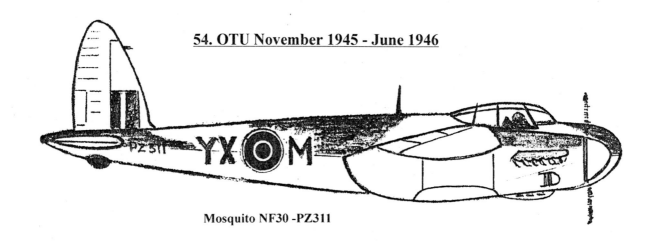

Mosquito NF30 -PZ311

Anson Mk 1, MG866

Wellington T18 - ND115

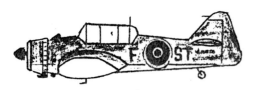

Martinet

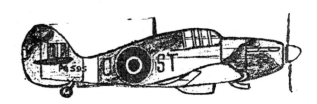

Hurricane IIc - PG595

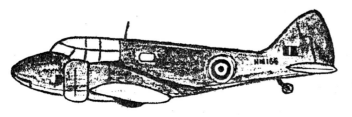

Oxford, HN166